Applying Ethics

A Text with Readings

Eighth Edition

JEFFREY OLEN

Regis University
Colorado Springs

VINCENT BARRY

Bakersfield College

JULIE C. VAN CAMP

California State University
Long Beach

THOMSON
━━━★━━━
WADSWORTH

Australia • Canada • Mexico • Singapore • Spain
United Kingdom • United States

To Jane Cullen
—J.O.

To My Students
—J.C.V.C

To Jim Wilson
—V.B.

Publisher: Holly J. Allen
Philosophy Editor: Steve Wainwright
Assistant Editors: Lee McCracken, Anna Lustig
Editorial Assistant: Barbara Hillaker
Marketing Manager: Worth Hawes
Marketing Assistant: Annabelle Yang
Advertising Project Managers: Bryan Vann, Vicky Wan
Print/Media Buyer: Kristine Waller
Permissions Editor: Joohee Lee

Production Service: Matrix Productions
Interior Designer: Lois Stanfield
Copy Editor: Cheryl Smith
Cover Designer: Yvo Riezebos
Cover Image: "Park Restaurant" by Auguste Macke
© Bettmann/CORBIS
Compositor: International Typesetting and Composition
Cover and Text Printer: Banta–Harrisonburg

For more information about our products, contact us at:
Thomson Learning Academic Resource Center
1-800-423-0563
For permission to use material from this text or product, submit a request online at
http://www.thomsonrights.com
Any additional requests about permissions can be submitted by email to thomsonrights@thomson.com

Library of Congress Control Number: 2004100348

ISBN: 0-534-62658-0

Wadsworth/Thomson Learning
10 Davis Drive
Belmont, CA 94002-3098
USA

Asia
Thomson Learning
5 Shenton Way #01-01
UIC Building
Singapore 068808

Australia/New Zealand
Thomson Learning
102 Dodds Street
Southbank, Victoria 3006
Australia

Canada
Nelson
1120 Birchmount Road
Toronto, Ontario M1K 5G4
Canada

Europe/Middle East/Africa
Thomson Learning
High Holborn House
50/51 Bedford Row
London WC1R 4LR
United Kingdom

Latin America
Thomson Learning
Seneca, 53
Colonia Polanco
11560 Mexico D.F.
Mexico

Spain/Portugal
Paraninfo
Calle/Magallanes, 25
28015 Madrid, Spain

Contents

Preface

For most students taking applied ethics, it will be their first—and maybe only—philosophy course. They may have thought and argued about such topics as abortion and the death penalty, welfare and affirmative action, but they enter the classroom with little experience in moral philosophy or critical thinking. Nor do they always have a firm handle on the legal, scientific, and other information relevant to the issues they'll be discussing. Throughout the eight editions of *Applying Ethics,* the book's goal has been to meet these students' needs. *Applying Ethics* is, as the subtitle says, a text with readings, providing a variety of features to help students and their instructors approach the most significant moral controversies of the day.

The book contains two distinct parts. Part 1, "Moral Reasoning," provides the philosophical background that many users will find helpful. The first chapter deals with moral reasons and principles, drawing on the views of such philosophers as Aristotle, Kant, Mill, and Rawls. It also includes discussions of ethical relativism and what it means to think morally. The second chaper is an introduction to critical thinking, with particular emphasis on the evaluation of moral arguments.

The chapters in Part 2, "Issues," begin with introductory essays by the book's authors. Each lays out the relevant moral issues and background material. Next come pro and con arguments on the chapter's central dispute, written in colloquial "point–counterpoint" style. After that comes four readings, each preceded by head notes summarizing the main points and followed by questions for analysis. And then, to provoke further class discussion, each chapter ends with four Case Presentations.

NEW FEATURES

1. Chapter 8, "Terrorism and Civil Liberties."

2. Updates of Case Presentations: "*Lawrence v. Texas:* Private Rights and Public Morality," in Chapter 3; "Marriage and Civil Unions," in Chapter 3; "Recommendations of the President's Council on Bioethics on Human Cloning and Human Dignity," in Chapter 6; "*Grutter v. Bollinger:* Taking Race into Account," in Chapter 10.

3. Updates of Chapter 3, including discussions of the significance of the U.S. Supreme Court decision, *Lawrence v. Texas,* and recent developments on same-sex marriage and civil unions.

4. Updates of Chapter 7, including discussions of the execution of people with mental retardation and minors, the significance of DNA testing on moral reasoning, and J. S. Mill's pro-death penalty arguments.

5. Updates of Chapter 10, including discussions of discrimination in education and employment, the latest Supreme Court decisions on affirmative action, and the rights of people with disabilities.

6. Updates of Chapter 11, including the treatment and protection of animals today.

7. Updates of Chapter 12, including current environmental conditions.

8. An expanded Glossary.

9. New appendixes on "How to Write a Philosophy Paper," "Plagiarism: What It Is, Why It's Wrong, and How to Avoid It," and "How to Do Research and Citation on the Web."

10. "Selections for Further Reading" and "Web Sites" have been updated and moved to the Wadsworth Web site, where other supplementary information can be found.

ACKNOWLEDGMENTS

As a teacher who has used this book for many years, I have long been grateful for the work of Vincent Barry, who produced the first two editions alone, and Jeffrey Olen, who joined him as co-author. Ken King was the Wadsworth philosophy editor for the first four editions, followed by Tammy Goldfield, Peter Adams, and now Steve Wainwright and his assistant Lee McCracken. Along with the many helpful suggestions from teachers over the years on successive editions, the following provided special help for this one: Nancy Stanlick, University of Central Florida; Sean Millard, The Florida State University; and Matt Eklund, University of Colorado.

I am honored to join such an exceptional team for this latest edition and hope it lives up to the expectations of our most important readers, our students.

Julie C. Van Camp

PART 1

MORAL REASONING

1

MORAL REASONS

When we act, we act for reasons. We eat breakfast because we are hungry or because it gives us the energy we need to get through the morning. We read a book because we want to be entertained or because we want to learn something. We buy a car because it's reliable, fun to drive, or affordable.

At any one time, we might—and usually do—have many reasons to do all sorts of things. Most of what we do we do for more than one reason. We buy a car because it's reliable *and* fun to drive and affordable, and we read a book because it's entertaining *and* informative.

But not all of our relevant reasons support the same course of action when we choose to do something. Often, we find ourselves faced with conflicting reasons, reasons both to do and not to do something. In addition to our reasons *for* eating breakfast, we might have reasons for *not* eating it. We might be in a hurry, or we might be trying to lose weight.

When our reasons lead us in different directions like that, we must decide which direction to take. Although we can make our decision in a purely arbitrary way—by flipping a coin, perhaps—the rational way to proceed is to weigh the conflicting reasons and ask ourselves which of the conflicting reasons are the best reasons. If we are lucky, we will answer the question correctly. That is, we will choose the best thing to do, the right course of action. We will do what we ought to do under the circumstances. If we are unlucky, we will choose the wrong course of action. We will do what we ought not do.

Of course, whether we choose correctly is not merely a matter of luck. If it were, rational deliberation would be no more trustworthy than the flip of a coin. Whether we choose correctly is also a matter of how well informed we are, how carefully we reason, how accurately we gauge the pros and cons of the alternatives, how exhaustive our deliberations are. Thus, we can minimize the element of luck when buying a car by test-driving various models, by reading reports in *Car and Driver* and *Consumer Reports,* and by giving careful attention to our own needs and preferences. Do we really need a car with this much power? Does appearance matter that much to us? Can we afford all of these options?

We can also minimize the element of luck by making sure that we reason in a reliable way. In the next chapter, we will take a careful look at what makes reasoning reliable. For the rest of this chapter, though, we concentrate on a particular kind of reasoning—moral reasoning.

MORAL REASONING

To reason morally is not to reason in a certain way. Rather, it is to consider certain kinds of reasons—moral reasons. It is to try to arrive at the best moral reasons for acting, to choose the morally right course of action, to do what we morally ought to do.

There are, after all, many different ways in which an action can be right or wrong. An artist who puts the right finishing touches on a painting does what is aesthetically right. An investor who buys and sells stock at the right times does what is financially right. Someone who gives up smoking cigarettes does what is right for her health. And someone who returns a found wallet does what is morally right. In the first case, we have an action supported by the best aesthetic reasons. In the second, one supported by the best financial reasons. In the third, one supported by the best health-related reasons. In the fourth, one supported by the best moral reasons.

Sometimes an action will be right in one way but wrong in another. That is, the best reasons of one kind will support it, while the best reasons of another kind will support something else. Reasons of self-interest, for example, might lead us to conclude that we ought to keep a found wallet. Moral reasons, on the other hand, lead us to conclude that we ought to return it. In cases like that, we must decide which kind of reason is best. We must decide what we ought to do, all things considered.

When we make these all-things-considered judgments, we generally do so based on what matters to us most. Some people are willing to risk their health because they enjoy smoking; others are not. Some people are willing to forego a higher paying job for a more pleasant one; others are not. Some people are willing to set aside their self-interest to do what is morally right; others are not.

Although we generally give people a lot of leeway in determining what most matters to them, we do expect them to give moral reasons high priority. And when the moral stakes are very high, we expect people to give moral reasons top priority. We expect them to realize that the morally right course of action is the best course of action—what they ought to do, all things considered.

These are not unreasonable expectations. If we are to live together in society, we must cooperate with one another. And if we are to cooperate with one another, we must trust one another. And we cannot trust people who treat honesty, good faith, and loyalty lightly.

INDIVIDUAL MORALITY AND SOCIAL MORALITY

Honesty, good faith, and loyalty are important considerations of *individual* morality. When each of us, as individuals, must decide what to do, we must, if we are to decide morally, consider whether we are being honest or dishonest, faithful to our commitments to others or unfaithful to them, loyal to those who deserve our loyalty or disloyal to them. The roles that such considerations play in our lives are crucial to our understanding of ourselves as moral people. And the roles that they play in the lives of others are crucial to our moral judgments of both them and their actions.

Because the topics discussed in Part 2 of this book concern the morality of various kinds of actions, considerations of individual morality will play an important role in those discussions. But so will moral considerations of another kind—*social* morality. In discussing issues such as abortion, we will be concerned not only with whether it is moral for an individual woman to have an abortion in various kinds of circumstances, but also with how society as a whole should deal with abortion.

The two concerns are related, of course, but as we shall see, answering the first does not necessarily settle the second. Rape and armed robbery are obviously immoral, and even rational rapists and armed robbers, we can safely suppose, understand why we require laws forbidding such behavior and why we are perfectly justified in locking up people who disobey them. But no rational person believes that every immoral act should be punishable by imprisonment or even made illegal. Who would want to prosecute everyone who cheats in a "friendly" game of tennis?

Also, we might have good reason to want society to regulate various kinds of behavior that do not violate any considerations of individual morality. Many people feel, for instance, that a mature, psychologically sound adult does nothing immoral by enjoying pornography in the privacy of his or her home, but these same people might also feel that pornography presents serious social dangers and should be curbed or outlawed.

Obviously, what we need are some general principles of social morality to guide us when we ask ourselves how society ought to deal with morally important social issues. And just as obviously, we need some general principles of individual morality to guide us when we ask ourselves how individuals ought to act in particular situations.

But before we take a look at various principles of individual and social morality, we should take a look at another issue, the issue of ethical relativism.

ETHICAL RELATIVISM

Ethical relativism is the view that moral truths are not absolutely true but true relative to a particular society or individual. According to an ethical relativist, whether an action is right or wrong depends on the moral norms of society or the moral commitments of the individual, and no absolute standard exists by which differing rules or commitments can be judged. So what's morally right in one society may be morally wrong in another, and what's morally right for Mary might be morally wrong for John.

As this description suggests, there are two forms of relativism—**cultural relativism** and **individual relativism**. According to the cultural relativist, the rightness or wrongness of an action depends on society's norms. According to the individual relativist, the rightness or wrongness of an action depends on the individual's own commitments.

The appeal of ethical relativism rests on two points. First, different societies often do have different moral norms, and individuals often do have different moral commitments. Second, there seems to be no decisive way to settle moral disputes as there are decisive ways to settle many other kinds of disputes. If two individuals or societies differ radically about right and wrong, there seem to be no tests or experiments we can run to confirm the views of one or the other.

Both kinds of relativism exist in varying degrees. Someone can be a relativist about some matters—sexual morality, for instance—but a nonrelativist about others—slavery, for instance. Someone can also be a cultural relativist about some matters and an individual relativist about others or both a cultural and individual relativist about all moral matters. Relativism can also come in more or less sophisticated versions. In the least sophisticated versions, arguing about abortion, affirmative action, or any other issue we address in Part 2 is like arguing about whether chocolate tastes better than vanilla. In other words, morality is merely a matter of taste or custom; and one taste or custom is as good as another, whether the taste is for slavery or brightly colored clothes, for theft or science fiction. In the more sophisticated versions of relativism, morality is much more complicated; and arguments about the issues in Part 2 concern much more than individual taste or social custom, leading to the conclusion that some tastes or customs are decidedly worse than others.

Relativism is, of course, a controversial view. Opponents argue that variation in moral commitments does not prove that moral truth is relative any more than variation in scientific belief proves that scientific truth is relative. They also argue that the difficulty of deciding moral disputes can be dispelled by a deeper understanding of morality. Although we cannot go through all the arguments for and against the many forms of relativism here, we should note a few points that pertain to the rest of the book.

First of all, even if it turns out that some form of relativism is true, that does not mean we cannot criticize the norms of our society or the moral commitments of others. Morality is not, as the least sophisticated forms of relativism would have it, merely an arbitrary matter of taste, like the preference for vanilla over chocolate, nor is it merely a matter of custom, like Fourth of July fireworks. As will be stressed throughout this book, we have the norms and commitments we do for *reasons,* and because they govern the most important areas of our lives, it is important that we examine these reasons carefully. Perhaps some of our moral commitments rest on false beliefs. Perhaps some rest on outmoded assumptions about what makes for a harmonious or desirable society. Perhaps some are inconsistent with other more deeply held moral commitments, such as fairness. Perhaps we neglected important considerations when we first arrived at some of our moral commitments.

The discovery of such flaws in our moral reasoning has led us to abandon a variety of practices, from racial segregation to involuntary medical treatment. As we shall see, many people feel that similar flaws undercut our justification of other practices—abortion, for instance, or treatment of animals, or capital punishment. And whether we feel that our conceptions of fairness and a desirable society are absolutely valid or only relatively valid, we can—and must, if we are to consider our society a good one—test our practices against them.

PRINCIPLES OF INDIVIDUAL MORALITY

It is easy to think of morality as a system of rules—some telling us not to do certain things, like cheat, lie, break promises, steal, rape, and kill, and others telling us to do certain things, like help others in need, pay our debts, and be loyal to friends and family. But why do we have these rules and not others?

The quick answer is that these are the rules we were taught. And there is no arguing with that answer. Moral rules are the rules accepted by the members of a given society, the rules we agree to follow and expect others to follow, in large part because we were taught to do so. But if we look at morality in only that way, we do both morality and ourselves a disservice. We do morality a disservice by making it look arbitrary. We are in effect saying that we have the moral rules we do because we have the moral rules we do. And we do ourselves a disservice by making ourselves look like mindless followers of arbitrary rules.

But moral rules are not arbitrary. We have the rules we do for good reason. And we are not mindless followers of them. We accept them because we understand that we have them for good reason. And when we feel that reason requires us to change them, we do just that.

Consider one timely example of moral change. Not too long ago, women were expected to live their lives within narrowly defined roles. It was considered their duty to stay home with their children, their obligation to see to various household tasks, and while men might be praised for helping out every now and then, they were not morally required to do so. They were morally required to be the family breadwinner, and women were morally required not to take jobs from other family breadwinners.

All that has changed, of course—or is at least in the process of changing. Many women and an increasing number of men have come to doubt the acceptability of such rules. And what makes them unacceptable is that they are now seen as violating some general moral *principles*—the principle of fairness, most notably. Women do not believe it fair that their lives are so restricted, and many men have come to agree.

What this example shows is that morality is not merely a matter of rules but also of principles—general standards for evaluating conduct, standards that we apply to all behavior and rules.

This point can be made in another way. No moral rule is exceptionless. Sometimes we are morally justified in breaking a promise. Sometimes we are morally justified in failing to help someone in need. Consider how easy it is to find yourself in a situation in which you must break a promise to Mary to help John or must fail to help John to keep your promise to Mary. Unless we allow that the two rules have exceptions and one of them applies here, we are left with a morally immovable object and a morally irresistible force—that is, a morally impossible situation. To resolve the dilemma, we must recognize that one of the rules takes prece dence in this particular case and that we are dealing with a legitimate exception to the other. How do we decide which takes precedence? By appealing to some general moral principle.

There is also one more thing that shows the importance of moral principles. The debates of Part 2 of this book are, in part, about what moral rules we should adopt. Should we adopt a rule that forbids us to give terminally ill patients in great pain a lethal injection if they request it? Should we adopt a rule that permits us to do so? Or should we adopt a rule that requires us to do so? Should we adopt a rule forbidding all abortions, some abortions, or no abortions? If suitable answers are to be found, we must appeal to moral principles.

The Principle of Utility

One of the best known general moral principles is closely associated with a number of moral philosophers, most notably the British philosopher John Stuart Mill (1806–1873). It is known as both the **principle of utility** and the **greatest happiness principle**. It tells us to produce the greatest balance of happiness over unhappiness, making sure that we give equal consideration to the happiness and unhappiness of everyone who stands to be affected by our actions.

The principle of utility can be applied in two different ways. The first is to apply it to individual *acts*. How are we to do that? Well, we might ask ourselves every time we act which of the options open to us will maximize happiness, but Mill did not recommend that procedure because it would be much too time consuming. Since we know that lying and stealing and cheating will rarely maximize happiness when everyone is taken equally into account, the sensible thing to do is avoid such behavior without worrying about the principle of utility.

But we sometimes have reason to believe that what usually maximizes happiness might not. Remember the example in which you cannot both keep your promise to Mary and help John. Although keeping promises usually maximizes happiness and helping others usually maximizes happiness, in this case, one will not. That's when Mill tells us to appeal to the principle of utility before we act.

The second way is to apply the principle to *rules* rather than to acts. Following this method, we appeal to the principle of utility only when we are considering which moral rules we should adopt. We ask ourselves which of the alternatives will maximize happiness if generally followed by the members of our society. Would a moral rule permitting mercy killing maximize happiness, or would one forbidding it? Whichever one would, that's the rule we ought to adopt.

The principle of utility is certainly a reasonable moral principle, whether applied to acts or rules. How our behavior affects others should be of moral concern to us. Moreover, we want our moral rules to make our society a good society, and it is hard to argue against the claim that a happy society is better than an unhappy society. So it is not surprising that utilitarian considerations play an important role in the moral reasoning of many individuals. Nor is it surprising that they play an important role in many of the arguments of Part 2.

Still, most people believe that it would be a mistake to make the principle of utility the final arbiter of *all* moral decisions. Suppose Bill borrows $10 from

Carol on the condition that he pay her back tomorrow. Doesn't that create an obligation to her? And since it does, does Bill have the moral right to neglect that obligation merely because he can maximize happiness by doing something else with the money?

That's one reason for recognizing limits to the principle. Another is that it is a very demanding principle. Very rarely, after all, do most of us take into equal account everybody's happiness before we act. Often, we think that our own happiness and the happiness of people who most matter to us should take precedence. That's why we sometimes splurge on presents for our families, even though we might create greater happiness by spending our money on the poor instead. Although we might agree that it would be commendable to do otherwise, it hardly seems *wrong* to splurge on the people we love.

Even when applied to rules rather than acts, the principle of utility seems to have its limitations. Although we want our moral rules to create happiness and avoid unhappiness, we don't want them to do only that. We also want them to be fair. And we sometimes find that the principle of utility justifies unfair rules. For example, we can easily imagine rules allowing researchers to experiment on selectively chosen human beings. Such rules might very well create the greatest balance of happiness over unhappiness but still be morally unacceptable—because the chosen few would be involuntary subjects or because they would have to be "sacrificed" during the experiments. Although the medical knowledge gained might benefit the rest of us so enormously that it outweighs the harm to the subjects, it is unfair of us to benefit at their expense in that way.

So the principle of utility cannot be, as Mill thought, the one fundamental moral principle that underlies all of morality. But the effect of our actions and moral rules on the happiness and unhappiness of people remains an important moral consideration all the same.

Fairness

Fairness, we just saw, often plays a crucial role in moral reasoning. But as we shall see in Part 2, it's not always easy to know what the fairest thing to do is. The problem will be especially acute when we discuss affirmative action, an issue in which different but equally important notions of fairness lead to different resolutions. We can't look at all the conceptions of fairness that come into play in moral reasoning here—some are better considered in Part 2 and some in connection with principles of social morality—but we can look at some.

The Golden Rule. Many people take the golden rule to be the best standard of fairness. Certainly, it is a principle that most of us learned very early in our moral education and one that plays a very large role in our moral lives. But applying it is not as simple a matter as most people think.

For most of us, to do unto others as we would have them do unto us is to do much more than we are inclined to do. Even more important, it is to do much more than we think we ought to do. Most of us would be very pleased if utter strangers walked up to us and gave us wads of $100 bills, for example. Yet we do not think that we ought to do the same for others.

The reason we rarely think of such things when we think of the golden rule is that we usually apply it in the context of other moral rules and principles. That is, we don't necessarily think that we ought to act toward others as we would *like* them to act toward us so much as we think that we ought to act toward others as they *ought* to act toward us. If we are to act morally, we must follow the same moral rules in our dealings with others that we expect them to follow in their dealings with us.

When we look at the golden rule that way, we recognize that none of us is a special case. The same moral standards apply to all of us. That is indeed an important thing to recognize if we are to reason morally, but it doesn't always tell us what those standards are.

The negative version of the golden rule gives us more help here. The negative version tells us *not* to treat others as we would *not* have them treat us. That is certainly one reason we find a moral rule allowing experimentation on unwilling subjects morally unacceptable. We would not have somebody experiment on us against our will.

But even the negative version requires a context of other rules and principles for its application because not all of us find the same treatment unacceptable. Consider one common example. Some people prefer to be lied to rather than face unpleasant truths, while others insist on the truth come what may (a fact that physicians are probably most aware of). But that does not mean that the people who don't want to hear the truth should withhold it from those who do.

Respect for Persons.   Why shouldn't people who want the truth withheld from them withhold it from others who don't? The answer is simple. In such cases, they should respect the wishes of others. How the other person feels about being lied to matters more than how the would-be liar feels.

More generally, we should always treat other people with respect, and many moral philosophers take **respect for persons** to be *the* fundamental moral principle. The kind of respect they have in mind should not be confused with the kind of respect exemplified by calling people by their appropriate titles. It is a special kind of respect, often called Kantian respect, after the German philosopher Immanuel Kant (1724–1804). Kantian respect is captured by this moral principle: Never use other people merely as a means to your own ends. The reading "Respect for Persons," included here, discusses this in more detail.

Be sure to notice the word "merely" in the principle. It makes a crucial difference, telling us when it is moral to use another person for our own ends and when it is not. It tells us that it is moral to use a bank teller to cash our checks, a waiter to bring our food, a mechanic to fix our cars, and an accountant to prepare our tax forms. Why are they and other like examples moral? Because the people involved are not *merely* serving our own ends. They are serving their own ends as well. They are, among other things, earning their food and rent money.

For an example of using others merely as a means to our own ends, we can return to an earlier one. To experiment on unwilling subjects is a perfect illustration. To do that is to give no consideration to the subjects' ends. It is to treat them as mere things that exist for our own ends, not as persons who have their own ends in life.

Put another way, respect for persons is intimately connected to the recognition that persons are *autonomous* beings. Our behavior is the product of our choices, and our choices are the product of what we take to be the best reasons for acting. And that is what makes us autonomous. We have our own goals and aspirations, we are capable of evaluating and weighing them against one another, we can reject or change them as we see fit, and we can determine how best to achieve those goals and then act accordingly.

To respect persons, then, is to recognize them as autonomous beings and treat them accordingly. It is to recognize that they have their own reasons for acting and to give those reasons the same respect we feel our own reasons warrant from others. And forcing someone to be a subject in a medical experiment is an obvious case of failing to respect his or her autonomy. So is any kind of coercion—from extortion and armed robbery to slavery and murder.

Many other cases are less obvious. Lying is one. When John lies to Maria, he is trying to manipulate her. His goal is to get her to act as he wants her to act, not as she would act if she knew the truth. Withholding information is another. If Maria wants to borrow John's car for purposes he doesn't approve of, she violates Kantian respect by not telling him. She is manipulating him. And the same is true of making commitments we have no intention of honoring.

Does that mean we should never lie, withhold information, or break a promise? Kant thought we should never lie, but we needn't agree with him. Not only do we find white lies permissible, but we also think it right to lie in some cases if there is no other way to prevent someone from doing serious harm. Respect for persons certainly justifies the moral rule "Don't lie," but it needn't lead to the conclusion that lying to save an innocent life isn't a legitimate exception. The important thing about respect for persons is that it cannot justify lying merely for our own convenience or merely to maximize happiness.

If we want to know what does count as a legitimate exception, probably the best thing to do is apply the following test. Imagine that a group of reasonable people is trying to decide what rules they ought to follow and that the rules they pick will include a list of all the exceptions. If it seems likely that they would freely agree to the proposed exception, then we may consider it legitimate.

Many moral philosophers like that test because it manifests Kantian respect. To apply it is to treat others as they would agree to be treated if it were up to them to participate in the making of our moral rules. And to treat them that way is to recognize them as autonomous beings.

Kantian respect is a very powerful notion. It can explain why various kinds of behavior are wrong and why others are right. Also, it is a very reasonable thing to accept as a general moral principle. But many people believe that it's not powerful enough. Since animals are not autonomous beings, it provides no guidelines for our treatment of them. The same can be said about fetuses. Also, Kantian respect seems to permit a variety of practices that many people consider immoral, like homosexuality among consenting adults or giving lethal injections to terminally ill patients who ask for them.

Whether these practices are immoral is, of course, a matter of great controversy, which is why we will look at them in Part 2. Still, the fact that they are controversial shows that many people adhere to other moral principles. Respect for persons may give us an excellent handle on fairness, but like the principle of utility, it may not be our only fundamental moral principle.

Proper Human Excellences

The moral principles we have looked at so far focus on an individual's obligations to others. They provide general guidelines for how we ought to act toward one another. But ethical thought has also paid close attention to another aspect of human life—the human good. Philosophers who pursue this line of thought do not focus on obligations but on character traits and activities that are distinctively human and, when taken together, constitute the good life for human beings. According to this approach to ethics, there are certain excellences uniquely proper to human life, and the full moral life involves the development of these excellences.

Before considering what these excellences might be, let's look at why this line of thought is so appealing. A good place to start is with the ancient Greek philosopher Aristotle (384–322 B.C.E.), included in the readings here. As Aristotle pointed out, human artifacts have distinctive purposes. The purpose of a pen is to write; of a lamp, to give light; of a knife, to cut. And knowing the purpose of any artifact, we also know how to tell whether it is a good or bad one. A knife with a strong blade is better than one with a weak blade. So is a knife with a handle that gives us a sure, comfortable grip better than one with a handle that does not. Thus, a strong blade and a sure, comfortable grip can be called excellences proper to a knife.

Similar remarks hold for human activities—from performing surgery to playing basketball. Each has its own purpose (or purposes), and there are corresponding excellences appropriate to engaging in each of them. Good basketball players are able to shoot, pass, rebound, and make it difficult for opponents to shoot, pass, and rebound; various physical and mental skills, plus proper conditioning, will help them do just those things.

Of course, not all of us are basketball players—or surgeons, welders, attorneys, or lifeguards, for that matter. So the distinctive excellences proper to those roles need not concern us. But some excellences are proper to all of these roles, and those that are, such as concentration and pride in our work, should concern us. Even more important, we are sons or daughters, friends, neighbors, co-workers, and citizens, and we are—or are likely to be—lovers, spouses, parents, and grandparents. And the excellences proper to these roles—loyalty, generosity, honesty, kindness, and the like—are proper to us all. They are, that is, proper human excellences, which are often called **virtues**.

Are there proper human excellences apart from our social roles? Aristotle thought so. He believed that there are natural purposes as well as social purposes. To him, everything in nature has a natural purpose or goal—from the acorn, whose natural purpose is to become an oak tree, to the human being. The human being's natural purpose is *eudaimonia*, a Greek word usually translated as "happiness" but better understood as total well-being. It is what all of us naturally strive for.

Aristotle believed that a good part of *eudaimonia* is fulfilling our social roles, but far from all of it. We are not, after all, just social animals (or as he put it, political animals). We are also rational animals. Indeed, our ability to reason as we do is, he thought, the trait that best defines us. So an essential part of *eudaimonia* must consist in the proper use of reason. And that means that we must live well-ordered lives, lives not given to extremes. We should not let courage turn to foolhardiness or generosity turn to extravagance. Nor should we let our emotions run away with us.

We should display them only when appropriate, and then only to the appropriate degree.

To avoid extremes is the key to what Aristotle called practical wisdom, which is one of the two kinds of wisdom that humans are capable of. The other is the wisdom that comes from contemplating the world in which we live. It is a deep understanding of the world, and like practical wisdom, it too is a proper human excellence. We cannot achieve total well-being without it.

Aristotle's concern with contemplation takes us far from the issues of Part 2, but his other points do have relevance for us. For one thing, many of the issues we'll be discussing relate directly to various social roles and the excellences proper to them. Is it the proper role of healthcare professionals actively and intentionally to bring about the death of a terminally ill patient? To treat a baby born three months premature one way and a fetus of six months another?

These issues also touch on the more general human excellences. Thus, we will consider compassion for the dying, respect for nature, mercy for those convicted of capital crimes, understanding toward pregnant women, and concern for fetuses.

Moreover, virtue and the notion of a well-ordered life play a large role in the discussion of sexual morality. The Catholic thinker Thomas Aquinas (1225–1274) is most important here. Taking his cue from Aristotle's view on purpose in nature, he argued that our sexual organs have as their natural purpose procreation, and any sexual activity that is not open to that end is disordered and immoral. Catholic thinking since Aquinas has continued to emphasize that purpose, but it has also emphasized another proper purpose of human sexuality—the expression of fully human love and dignity. According to this line of thought, sex that is not such an expression, including all sex outside of marriage, is disordered and immoral.

The Catholic position is, of course, highly controversial. So, for that matter, is Aristotle's view that there are natural purposes in addition to social ones. But those controversies are matters for Part 2. For now, the important point is this: Ethical thinking includes consideration of human virtues as well as of obligations to others. And in asking what moral rules to adopt, we must ask ourselves what kind of people we should be and how we should live our lives.

The Will of God

To many people, religious belief provides the final word on moral questions. And because the issues we'll be looking at later have been addressed by religious traditions of all kinds, many people rely on their religious belief for guidance. It is not surprising, then, that much of the popular debate that we find in such places as the letter-to-the-editor sections of local newspapers is filled with appeals to the will of God.

Why give God the final word in these matters? Two possibilities come readily to mind. The first is that God is the ultimate source of morality. God made the universe and put human beings in it for some purpose, and whether we act rightly or wrongly depends on how well we pursue that purpose. In other words, there are both moral laws and physical laws, and God is the author of both.

That was the view of Thomas Aquinas, who referred to the system of divine moral laws as **natural law**. Unlike the conventional laws enacted by legislatures, the natural law, according to Aquinas, is embedded in nature, just as natural purposes are embedded in nature. It is also embedded in human reason. So the natural law is not only the law of God but the law of reason as well. And by turning our reason to moral matters, Aquinas said, we can know such basic moral truths as "Thou shalt not kill" as surely as we know that two plus two equals four.

According to the other possibility, God is not so much the source of morality as the best authority on morality. What makes God the best authority depends on how we think of morality. Some people think of morality as a collection of moral facts, much as they think of science as a collection of scientific facts. And God, being all knowing, knows both kinds of facts. Others think of morality in a different way. To them, the right thing to do is what an ideal observer would consider the best thing to do—an ideal observer being someone who is fully informed about the case at hand and totally impartial. And God alone is in that position.

Reliance on God does raise some problems, though. Can we really be certain what God wants us to do? Different religious traditions do give conflicting answers to various moral questions, and even within any given religious tradition, we can often find conflicting answers. Moreover, we should not forget agnostics and atheists, nor should we forget religious individuals who, for one reason or another, sincerely believe that they must look to their own consciences for the ultimate answers to moral questions.

Such considerations needn't lead to disrespect for religious belief, of course, any more than they need lead to the conclusion that religious people should disregard religious belief when making moral decisions. But they do show the limitations of religious belief for purposes of moral argument.

As we shall see in the next chapter, a good argument goes from statements accepted as true to a conclusion well supported by those statements. If the initial statements are not accepted by our opponents, our arguments will have no force. Also, the better our justification for accepting those initial statements as true, the better the argument. And given the role that faith plays in religious belief, statements about God can have less independent justification than the conclusions they are asked to support.

It is for those reasons, more than antipathy toward religious belief, that moral philosophers addressing a varied audience concentrate on arguments that do not rely on statements about God's will. And it is for the same reasons that this book will do the same.

References to natural law, on the other hand, will appear in Part 2, since philosophers from the time of Aristotle to the present have argued that human behavior can be divided into the natural and unnatural without reliance on the will of God. In Chapter 3, for example, Roger Scruton bases his position on sexual morality on his views on human nature, and J. Gay-Williams argues in Chapter 5 that "mercy" killing violates human nature.

PRINCIPLES OF SOCIAL MORALITY

So far, we have been concerned with how individuals ought to act. Our focus has been on the moral principles that guide individuals when they must determine what they, and others, ought to do.

But we act collectively as well as individually. Most important for our purposes, we act as a municipality, as a state, as a nation. We enact laws, we imprison, fine, and execute people, we enter into treaties and wage war. And collective action, like individual action, can be moral or immoral. Whether it is one or the other, like individual action, depends on how well it is supported by moral principles.

As we shall see, the relevant principles are often the same. Individually and collectively, we should be concerned with human happiness, so the principle of utility is an important principle of social morality. Individually and collectively, we should be concerned with fairness, so respect for persons too is an important principle of social morality. And when we act collectively, we care about what kind of society we should be as much as we care about what kind of individuals we should be when we act individually.

But collective action does pose one special difficulty. When Congress acts, the United States acts, but many U.S. citizens will invariably disagree with how Congress acts, including some members of Congress itself. Their disagreement notwithstanding, they are bound by the acts of Congress. They must pay taxes for purposes they find abhorrent, they must submit to regulations they find offensive, and they must give up freedoms they hold dear—that, or face fine or imprisonment. Governments, even democratic governments like our own, are inherently coercive. That is the special difficulty, and it is why we need additional principles of social morality.

Social Justice

If we ask ourselves what kind of society we should be, the natural answer is this: a just society. Candidates on the campaign trail may disagree on all sorts of issues, but none will speak out in favor of injustice. Many will speak out in favor of positions that others consider unjust, but they will argue in turn that our own positions are the unjust ones. We disagree about what justice requires, but not that we are morally required to be just.

In other words, the issue of social justice—what makes a society a just one—is a very controversial matter. People of good will who share the same principles of individual morality—people who are fair, loyal, honest, faithful, and kind—have great difficulty agreeing on principles of social justice.

That difficulty is due largely to the difficulty noted just before. Government action is coercive action. All of us are in principle against coercion, but we also recognize the occasional need for it. Unfortunately, we don't always recognize it on the same occasions. A look at some important principles of social justice will explain why.

Individual Rights

The Bill of Rights explicitly guarantees us a number of individual freedoms—freedoms of speech, press, religion, and assembly, for example. As part of our Constitution, these guarantees are part of the fundamental law of the land, as are the Bill of Rights' guarantees of a fair trial and its protection against unreasonable search and seizure.

Although these guarantees are set forth in plain enough English, many people of good will disagree about how they should be interpreted. That our guarantee of a free press allows us to criticize government policies is not a matter of controversy.

That it allows us to print and sell hard-core pornography is. When such controversies arise, they are settled by the courts, which are the ultimate legal arbiters of how these guarantees are to be understood.

The courts also serve as the ultimate legal arbiters in controversies about implicit constitutional guarantees. The right to privacy, to pick an example that will concern us in Part 2, is not explicitly mentioned in the Bill of Rights or anywhere else in the Constitution. Still, the courts have held that it is a constitutionally protected one.

If enough of us disagree with the courts, we can amend the Constitution. But barring such amendments, the decisions of the courts remain the law of the land. They set the legal limits on what kinds of individual behavior the various levels of government can regulate and on the ways it can regulate them. Even if we doubt that a woman has a moral right to abort a fetus in the early months of her pregnancy, we cannot doubt, as matters now stand, that she has the legal right to do so.

But ought she have that legal right? Ought consenting adults have the legal right to engage in private homosexual acts? Ought we grant pornography the same protections as weekly newsmagazines? What legal rights should we grant? And why?

Natural Rights.   One historically important answer to these questions is this: We ought to have the legal right to do whatever we have the natural right to do because no government can justly violate our natural rights. That answer was powerfully advanced by the English philosopher John Locke (1632–1704) and echoed by Thomas Jefferson in the Declaration of Independence. Among its most recent champions was the American philosopher Robert Nozick (1938–2002).

Natural rights are rights that all of us are born with. They belong to us by virtue of the fact that we are human beings, and no one has the right to interfere with our exercise of them. Locke and Nozick list them as life, liberty, and property; Jefferson as life, liberty, and the pursuit of happiness. Because no one can interfere with the exercise of our natural rights, we cannot interfere with anyone else's. And that places the only legitimate limits on our exercise of those rights. Our right to swing our arms, the popular saying has it, stops at someone else's nose. But as long as no one's nose (or property, for that matter) is in the way, we are free to swing.

Even the government, according to natural rights theorists, has no right to interfere. The reason is simple. The government derives its rightful powers from the governed, and the governed cannot transfer to the government any rights they do not have by nature. Since all of us have the right to protect our natural rights, we can transfer the right to protect our lives, liberty, and property to the government. Since none of us has the right to interfere with anyone else's natural rights, we cannot transfer any such right to the government. A just society can have police forces, then, but it cannot tell us what we can and cannot read. It can imprison thieves and rapists, but it cannot imprison its peaceful critics.

These restrictions on government action are more severe than they might at first seem. They leave much behavior—even immoral behavior—free of government interference. The 1964 Civil Rights Act forbidding racial discrimination in privately owned places of public accommodation like theaters and restaurants is, on this view, an unjust law. Since no one has a natural right to enter anyone's property against the owner's wishes, racial exclusion is an exercise of natural property rights that the government cannot interfere with. It goes without saying, then, that this view would not endorse government-mandated affirmative-action programs, one of the topics to be considered in Part 2. Nor would it endorse government payments to the poor, another topic we will consider. Since no one has the natural right to force others to give to the poor, we cannot transfer that right to the government.

Mutual Agreement behind the Veil of Ignorance.

Many philosophers are suspicious of natural rights. Where do they come from? How do we get them? Locke and Jefferson thought them God given, but few philosophers today are willing to argue that way. And that leaves the origin of natural rights mysterious at best.

John Rawls (1921–2002), another American philosopher, takes a different approach to individual rights. Instead of saying that a just society is one that protects but does not interfere with natural rights, he says that the individual rights we ought to have are those that a just society would give us.

What is a just society, according to Rawls? A society in which no one has an unfair advantage over others. And how do we ensure that no one has an unfair advantage over others? By adopting fundamental principles of social justice that pass the following test: They must be principles that we would rationally agree upon behind the **veil of ignorance**. And what, finally, is it to be behind the veil of ignorance? It is to know how the principles would shape society but not to know what particular positions each of us would have in that society.

The reason that test would work, Rawls says, is that rational people would not agree to live in any unjust society if they did not know whether they would be the ones who would be unfairly taken advantage of. They would not, for example, be willing to institute slavery if they didn't know whether they'd be slave or master. Anything they would agree to behind the veil of ignorance, therefore, must be just.

What they would agree to are the following two principles:

The equality principle: Every person has a right to the greatest basic freedom compatible with equal freedom for all. That is, there must be equal freedom for all, and if freedom can be increased without violating that requirement, it must be.

The difference principle: All social and economic inequalities must meet two requirements. First, they must be to everyone's advantage, including the people at the bottom. It is, for example, to the advantage of everyone that surgeons make more money than unskilled workers. Everyone, including unskilled workers, benefits by having enough surgeons, and financial rewards help guarantee that enough people will pay the cost in time and money of going through medical school. Second, the inequalities must be attached to positions open to all. If surgeons are to be paid more than unskilled workers, then no one can be excluded from becoming a surgeon because of, say, race or sex.

The first principle gives us many freedoms covered by Locke's and Nozick's natural rights, including speech, press, religion, assembly, and more generally, the freedom to do as we please as long as we do not interfere with the rights of others.

The second principle, on the other hand, gives us many individual rights that are not among Locke's and Nozick's natural rights. In doing so, it places some important restrictions on Locke's and Nozick's natural rights—most important, on property rights. For example, the difference principle gives people at the bottom of the social-economic ladder the right to a minimum level of income. If their income falls below that level, the government has the obligation to supplement it with money collected through taxes. And that, from the viewpoint of natural rights advocates, is an unjust restriction on other people's property rights. The government is taking money that they earned so it can help the poor rather than letting them spend it as they see fit.

Equality

Another central principle of social justice is equality. A society in which all citizens are not treated equally can hardly be considered a just one. On that we all agree, just as we all agree that we ought to be a just society. But we do not all agree on what equal treatment requires of us any more than we all agree on what justice requires of us.

Consider equal treatment under the law, for example. To many people, equal treatment under the law is merely a procedural matter. As long as each of us is treated according to the same legal procedures, we are granted equal treatment under the law. Thus, what matters in criminal trials, say, is that all defendants are allowed full exercise of their rights, including their rights to counsel, to subpoena witnesses, to cross-examination, and to a jury of their peers. To others, equal treatment under the law means much more. If, for example, juries are more likely to apply the death penalty in cases where the victim is white than in cases where the victim is black, then equal treatment under the law is denied in capital cases, regardless of procedural guarantees.

Similar difficulties muddle the issue of equal opportunity. To some people, equal opportunity means lack of discrimination: As long as employers and universities choose employees and students on the basis of merit, not on the basis of sex or race, equal opportunity is secured. To others, equal opportunity requires affirmative action. Given the history of oppression against blacks, they argue, mere lack of discrimination cannot secure equal opportunity. Others go even further. Can we really believe, they ask, that the son of a millionaire and the daughter of a welfare recipient begin life with equal advantages? How many of you have enjoyed the same opportunities in life as George W. Bush? Can we really believe that differences in natural endowment make no difference to opportunity? How many of you have enjoyed the same opportunities as Michael Jordan or Julia Roberts?

People who argue that way generally conclude that equal treatment requires equality of results. Given that we cannot start out equally, there can be no real equal opportunity. The just thing to do, then, is see that society's wealth is distributed equally. Or they might reach a variation of that conclusion, arguing instead that the just thing to do is see that society's wealth is distributed according to need. Rawls, as we saw, argues in favor of equal distribution, except when it is in everyone's interest that some people have more. The German philosopher Karl Marx (1818–1883) famously advanced another principle: From each according to his abilities, to each according to his needs.

The General Welfare

The doctrine of natural rights greatly influenced the American Founding Fathers. Its influence appears not only in the Declaration of Independence but also in the Bill of Rights. The preamble to the Constitution shows another concern of the

Founding Fathers—the general welfare—which brings us to another important principle of social morality: The different levels of government should promote the general welfare, or as it is often put, the common good, or the public interest.

Thus, we have come to expect our governments to do much in the promotion of the general welfare. We expect public schools and libraries, public funding of highways and medical research, zoning ordinances that guarantee us livable neighborhoods, laws protecting our rivers and air, and much else that is no longer controversial.

Much else that governments do to promote the general welfare is controversial. So is much else that various people propose that our governments do to promote it. Sometimes the controversy is merely over practical considerations, as when we debate whether one policy or another will better increase worker productivity. Often, though, the controversy is over profoundly moral considerations, as when we debate the issues of Part 2 of this book.

One particularly profound moral consideration concerns the general welfare itself. Many people of good will differ over what constitutes the general welfare. Another concerns how far the government can rightly go in promoting it. Many people of good will also differ about the proper limits of government action.

Public Decency and Morality.   To most people, the general welfare includes a healthy moral environment. Part of a healthy moral environment is public decency. Some things—like sex between married people—are obviously moral in private but generally considered indecent in public thoroughfares. Other things—like drinking a few Scotches too many—are less obviously moral in private (here reasonable people will differ) and also considered indecent in public thoroughfares. Thus, we have laws against indecent exposure and drunk and disorderly conduct, laws that most people agree promote the general welfare.

More controversially, some people feel that the general welfare requires more and that a healthy moral environment includes more than public decency. They feel that it includes various restrictions on private behavior too. Homosexual acts between consenting adults constitute one area of private behavior that is illegal in many jurisdictions. Another involves pornography. In some jurisdictions, certain films cannot be shown in theaters even if minors are kept out and billboards visible to the passing public are not themselves pornographic.

What principles do proponents of these restrictions appeal to? The following three are most important.

The principle of **paternalism**:   John Stuart Mill distinguished what he called self-regarding virtues and vices from other-regarding virtues and vices. Gluttony is an example of a self-regarding vice. Although overeating might cause direct harm to ourselves, it does not cause direct harm to others. A propensity to settle disagreements by beating up those who disagree with us, on the other hand, is an other-regarding vice. It does cause direct harm to others.

The legitimacy of laws forbidding assault and battery is not to be disputed. And the same goes for many similar laws involving other-regarding vices. But when we turn to self-regarding vices, the legitimacy of laws involving them is often disputed. People who steal from us, extort money from us, or rape us violate our most cherished rights, and it is the job of government to protect those rights. Gluttons do not violate our rights. Nor do homosexuals or pornography watchers.

If homosexuality and pornography viewing are vices (and reasonable people disagree), they do not on the face of it seem to be other-regarding vices.

Some people justify restrictions on such behavior by appealing to a principle of paternalism: Just as parents are justified in preventing their children from harming themselves, so are governments justified in preventing their citizens from harming themselves. And if homosexuality and pornography cause us moral harm, governments should outlaw them. Otherwise, they do not promote the general welfare.

Protecting the public morality: Mill's distinction between self-regarding and other-regarding vices rests on the presence or absence of direct harm to others. Many self-regarding vices, though, can and do cause *indirect* harm to others. A glutton can eat himself into a fatal heart attack, for example, and then his wife and children will suffer.

The courts have made similar claims about the indirect harm that can result from homosexuality and pornography. Sometimes, the harm they refer to is moral harm. If society tolerates behavior it considers immoral, that behavior may spread. And that means that people who engage in that behavior may be causing indirect moral harm to others.

Moreover, the indirect moral harm may come to minors as well as adults. Even if pornography is limited by law to adults only, minors will always find a way to view it. Just as legal drinking ages don't prevent minors from drinking their parents' liquor or getting adults to buy it for them, so do laws prohibiting sales of pornography to minors fail to prevent minors from looking at their parents' pornography or getting adults to buy it for them.

Whether or not the behavior does spread to minors, courts have repeatedly held that governments do have a legitimate interest in protecting the public morality, and that their legitimate interest in doing so does justify prohibiting behavior that many of us would consider self-regarding.

Preventing indirect social costs: The glutton who eats himself into a fatal heart attack may end up harming more than just his wife and children. His death may have social costs as well, especially if his family is forced to go on welfare. Indeed, many self-regarding vices have social costs. Smoking-related illnesses exact enormous costs in lost work hours, medical care, and insurance premiums. So do injuries resulting from failure to use automobile seat belts.

Much debate over the issues of Part 2 also involves the social costs of private behavior. Many people have expressed concern about the long-term effects of legal tolerance of homosexuality. How will it affect society's family structure? And what changes will that lead to in other areas of society? Will legal recognition of "**civil unions**" among people of the same gender lead to a deterioration of the sanctity of traditional marriage among heterosexuals?

Many other people reject the claim that such considerations can justify restrictions on private behavior. Many more reject the principle of paternalism and the principle of protecting the public morality. To them, such principles of collective action lead to unacceptable limits on individual freedom. Some worry that these principles, carried to their extremes, would lead to the outlawing of everything bad for us, including ice cream and other foods high in cholesterol. Others have even stronger objections. Their concern is that such considerations are in principle unacceptable.

People like Nozick would rule them out on the grounds of natural right. If our natural right to liberty is to count for anything, it must include the right to decide for ourselves what is morally harmful to us. Others would rule them out on different grounds. To them, the basic issue is that we live in a free society. In a free society, the general welfare is not to be advanced at the cost of individual freedoms that cause direct harm to nobody else. The government has an obligation to prevent violence toward women, but in a free society, it should fulfill that obligation by educating its citizens and punishing offenders—not by restricting the legitimate freedoms of nonoffenders.

Pluralism and Freedom

In the previous section, we looked at reasons in favor of government action. It's now time to look at reasons against government action. All can be seen as arguments in favor of individual freedom. They can also be seen as arguments in favor of **pluralism**.

A pluralistic society is a society with many independent centers of power, a society in which no one institution has unlimited power over the others. The more independent and varied the institutions of society are, the more pluralistic the society; the more limits that are placed on the most powerful institution of society, the more pluralistic the society.

In our society, of course, the federal government is the most powerful institution. Among the independent centers of power are the family, the press, religions, business and labor organizations, private (and perhaps even public) universities, and the like. And to the extent that the government allows these other institutions to pursue their own ends in their own ways, the more pluralistic our own society.

Although pluralism is not highly valued in all societies (the People's Republic of China and Iran, for example), it is highly valued in our own. The Founding Fathers, in placing limits on the powers of the federal government, sought to protect pluralism. And the frequent calls we hear to limit governmental interference in matters best left to the family, or the medical professions, or any other institutions are calls to protect or advance pluralism.

Individual Freedom.   One reason for valuing pluralism is its close connection to individual freedom. The connection is twofold.

First, to allow institutions to pursue their own ends in their own ways is, more often than not, to allow individuals to pursue their own ends in their own ways. If the government leaves certain areas of concern to the family, it leaves them to individual family members. If it allows research decisions to be made by the scientific community, it allows them to be made by individual scientists. And the less it interferes with media organizations, the less it interferes with individual journalists.

Second, the more independent centers of power there are and the more independent they are permitted to be, the more bulwarks there are against government restrictions on individual freedom. A free press protects the freedoms of all of us, not just of journalists. Independent universities, hospitals, and businesses protect the freedom to choose among varied alternatives of all of us, not just the freedoms of professors, physicians, and managers.

To be sure, independent institutions can also threaten our freedoms. Businesses with monopoly powers, for instance, can greatly restrict our freedom of choice in the marketplace. They can also threaten vital public goods such as clean air and water. So we cannot allow them to be unbridled centers of power, any more than we can allow the government to be one. Nor can we give parents unbridled power over their children or hospitals unbridled power over their patients.

How and where to set these limits fuel many of the controversies of Part 2. Is the joint decision to withhold treatment from defective newborns within the proper bounds of parents and physicians? Should private businesses be free to pursue affirmative action, should they be forced to pursue it, or should they be barred from doing so?

How we answer such questions depends on a number of factors, some specific to each issue and others relating to the general principles we've been examining. Fairness, of course, is an important factor. So is the matter of individual rights. But where fairness should lead us and what rights are at stake are not always clear. What is fair to the minority woman might not be fair to the white male. And the question of what rights we ought to extend to a newborn child or fetus is far from settled.

The general welfare is also an important factor. It can, after all, be harmed by government action as well as advanced by government action. So far, we have looked only at ways in which government action can advance it. But pluralists are equally concerned about the ways government action can harm it.

The Social Utility of Pluralism.

For Locke, Jefferson, and Nozick, the individual freedoms that rightfully belong to us are matters of natural right, and they need no further justification than that. For Rawls, the individual freedoms that rightfully belong to us are the ones we would agree to under ideal conditions of fairness. For Mill, the individual freedoms that rightfully belong to us are the ones that will maximize human happiness.

Mill felt very strongly that the only freedom that will not maximize human happiness is the freedom to harm others. He felt that other-regarding vices fall under the legitimate control of governments, but not self-regarding ones. Many of his arguments for this claim center on specific individual freedoms, and it would take us far beyond our purposes here to look at all of them. But two general arguments are very important for us.

The first is one we often hear in political debates: Individuals are in a better position to know what makes them happy than paternalistic governments are. Individuals will make mistakes from time to time, but so will governments. The important point is that individuals will make them less frequently. For one thing, we know ourselves better than our governments know us. For another, each of us is different, and it is extremely unlikely that one judgment about self-regarding behavior made for all individuals in society will promote individual happiness as efficiently as individual judgments made by each of us.

The second deals directly with the link between public morality and the general welfare. According to Mill, the best way to live our lives must always remain an open question. Nobody can now know for certain that particular ways of life are the best ways of life. If we outlaw certain kinds of self-regarding behavior, Mill said, we cut off moral experimentation that might help us discover better ways of life. And even if we can be fairly certain that some ways of life are not good ones, we will not maximize happiness by outlawing them. Bad ways of life may still have some good in them. Also, the rest of us can always learn from bad examples, even if what we learn is only to have greater confidence in the goodness of our own ways of life. A docile citizenry, one that does what it is told rather than what it thinks best, is not a citizenry likely to maximize happiness. Nor, those who agree with Mill might add, are docile hospitals, universities, or media organizations likely to maximize happiness.

SUMMARY AND CONCLUSIONS

We have looked at a variety of general moral principles in this chapter, some primarily concerned with individual morality and others with social morality. In doing so, we have also looked at the most important considerations we can bring to bear when deciding how we should act, whether individually or collectively. Among them are human happiness, fairness, justice, individual rights, equality, individual freedom, and the general welfare.

What conclusions can we draw from our discussions? Perhaps the most obvious conclusion is that moral questions can be very difficult questions. One moral principle can lead us to one answer, while another equally important moral principle can lead us to another answer. Thus, we may very well be stuck with some very hard choices—between respecting individual freedoms and promoting the general welfare, for example. Also, we may very well find that the same moral principle leads us to different answers. In cases like that, we will find ourselves stuck with hard choices of another kind—between being fair to one group or another, for example, or between protecting one individual's rights or another's.

The existence of such moral dilemmas often leads to a kind of moral skepticism, the view that our answers to moral questions are opinions, not knowledge. Whether that view is correct is a much too complicated matter to deal with here. But even if it is correct, it does not mean that we should give up trying to answer moral questions. They remain very important questions. The answers we eventually decide on will have great impact on the kind of society we are and on the lives of all of us who live in it. We have a responsibility to deal with these questions as best we can, even if we cannot be sure that our answers represent knowledge.

And even if our answers are opinions, not all opinions are equal. At the beginning of a baseball season, nobody can know who will win the World Series, but that doesn't mean that we can't distinguish good picks from bad picks. Few of you can know which career choice will work out best for you, but that doesn't mean that any opinion on the matter is as good as any other. Similarly, perhaps none of us can know whether a woman really has a moral right to an abortion or whether justice really requires affirmative action, but that doesn't mean that we can't distinguish better and worse ways of dealing with those issues.

Basing our judgments on moral principle is one thing we must do if we are to deal with these issues well. But we must also do something else. We must make sure that our debates on these issues are thoughtful, careful, and well reasoned. The combination of good moral principles and faulty reasoning guarantees very little. In this chapter, we look at the principles; in the next, we will look at reasoning.

Moral Virtue

Aristotle

The following selection is from Book II of Aristotle's *Nichomachean Ethics.* In Book I, Aristotle argues that the highest human good is *eudaimonia* (total well-being, or happiness). It is, he says, our only self-sufficient goal and the ultimate goal of all human action. He then argues that human happiness is determined by the proper function of humans, which he defines as "an activity of the soul or a course of action in accordance with reason." Thus, a happy individual is one who lives in accordance with reason, and each individual should develop virtues (character traits or dispositions) that lead to this goal. Because human reason is both practical and intellectual, human virtues come in two kinds, moral and intellectual.

In Book II, Aristotle turns to a discussion of the moral virtues. After stressing the importance of childhood training and self-discipline in the development of moral virtues, he proceeds to define the nature of moral virtue. Moral virtue is, he concludes, a "mean" between the vices of deficiency and excess; that is, virtue is a form of moderation, a midpoint between two extremes. Courage, for example, is a midpoint between cowardice and foolhardiness. Friendliness is a midpoint between flattery and surliness.

CHAPTER I

Virtue, then, is of two kinds, intellectual and moral. Of these the intellectual is in the main indebted to teaching for its production and growth, and this calls for time and experience. Moral goodness, on the other hand, is the child of habit, from which it has got its very name, ethics being derived from *ethos,* "habit," by a slight alteration in the quantity of the *e.* This is an indication that none of the moral virtues is implanted in us by nature, since nothing that nature creates can be taught by habit to change the direction of its development. For instance a stone, the natural tendency of which is to fall down, could never, however often you threw it up in the air, be trained to go in that direction. No more can you train fire to burn downwards. Nothing in fact, if the law of its being is to behave in one way, can be habituated to behave in another. The moral virtues, then, are produced in us neither *by* Nature nor *against* Nature. Nature, indeed, prepares in us the ground for their reception, but their complete formation is the product of habit.

Consider again these powers or faculties with which Nature endows us. We acquire the ability to use them before we do use them. The senses provide us with a good illustration of this truth.

We have not acquired the sense of sight from repeated acts of seeing, or the sense of hearing from repeated acts of hearing. It is the other way round. We had these senses before we used them; we did not acquire them as a result of using them. But the moral virtues we do acquire by first exercising them. The same is true of the arts and crafts in general. The craftsman has to learn how to make things, but he learns in the process of making them. So men become builders by building, harp players by playing the harp. By a similar process we become just by performing just actions, temperate by performing temperate actions, brave by performing brave actions. Look at what happens in political societies—it confirms our view. We find legislators seeking to make good men of their fellows by making good behaviour habitual with them. That is the aim of every lawgiver, and when he is unable to carry it out effectively, he is a failure; nay, success or failure in this is what makes the difference between a good constitution and a bad.

Again, the creation and the destruction of any virtue are effected by identical causes and identical means; and this may be said, too, of every art. It is as a result of playing the harp that harpers become good or bad in their art. The same is true of builders and all other craftsmen. Men will become good builders as a result of building well, and bad builders as a result of building badly. Otherwise what would be the use of having anyone to teach a trade?

From *The Ethics of Aristotle,* translated by A. K. Thomson, George Allen & Unwin Ltd. Reprinted by permission.

Craftsmen would all be born either good or bad. Now this holds also of the virtues. It is in the course of our dealings with our fellow-men that we become just or unjust. It is our behaviour in a crisis and our habitual reactions to danger that make us brave or cowardly, as it may be. So with our desires and passions. Some men are made temperate and gentle, others profligate and passionate, the former by conducting themselves in one way, the latter by conducting themselves in another, in situations in which their feelings are involved. We may sum it all up in the generalization, "Like activities produce like dispositions." This makes it our duty to see that our activities have the right character, since the differences of quality in them are repeated in the dispositions that follow in their train. So it is a matter of real importance whether our early education confirms us in one set of habits or another. It would be nearer the truth to say that it makes a very great difference indeed, in fact all the difference in the world.

CHAPTER II

Since the branch of philosophy on which we are at present engaged differs from the others in not being a subject of merely intellectual interest—I mean we are not concerned to know what goodness essentially is, but how we are to become good men, for this alone gives the study its practical value—we must apply our minds to the solution of the problems of conduct. For, as I remarked, it is our actions that determine our dispositions.

Now that when we act we should do so according to the right principle, is common ground and I propose to take it as a basis of discussion.[1] But we must begin with the admission that any theory of conduct must be content with an outline without much precision in details. We noted this when I said at the beginning of our discussion of this part of our subject that the measure of exactness of statement in any field of study must be determined by the nature of the matter studied. Now matters of conduct and considerations of what is to our advantage have no fixity about them any more than matters affecting our health. And if this be true of moral philosophy as a whole, it is still more true that the discussion of particular problems in ethics admits of no exactitude. For they do not

fall under any science or professional tradition, but those who are following some line of conduct are forced in every collocation of circumstances to think out for themselves what is suited to these circumstances, just as doctors and navigators have to do in their different *métiers*. We can do no more than give our arguments, inexact as they necessarily are, such support as is available.

Let us begin with the following observation. It is in the nature of moral qualities that they can be destroyed by deficiency on the one hand and excess on the other. We can see this in the instances of bodily health and strength.[2] Physical strength is destroyed by too much and also by too little exercise. Similarly health is ruined by eating and drinking either too much or too little, while it is produced, increased and preserved by taking the right quantity of drink and victuals. Well, it is the same with temperance, courage, and the other virtues. The man who shuns and fears everything and can stand up to nothing becomes a coward. The man who is afraid of nothing at all, but marches up to every danger, becomes foolhardy. In the same way the man who indulges in every pleasure without refraining from a single one becomes incontinent. If, on the other hand, a man behaves like the Boor in comedy and turns his back on every pleasure, he will find his sensibilities becoming blunted. So also temperance and courage are destroyed both by excess and deficiency, and they are kept alive by observance of the mean.

Let us go back to our statement that the virtues are produced and fostered as a result, and by the agency, of actions of the same quality as effect their destruction. It is also true that after the virtues have been formed they find expression in actions of that kind. We may see this in a concrete instance—bodily strength. It results from taking plenty of nourishment and going in for hard training, and it is the strong man who is best fitted to cope with such conditions. So with the virtues. It is by refraining from pleasures that we become temperate, and it is when we have become temperate that we are most able to abstain from pleasures. Or take courage. It is by habituating ourselves to make light of alarming situations and to confront them that we become brave, and it is when we have become brave that we shall be most able to face an alarming situation.

CHAPTER III

We may use the pleasure (or pain) that accompanies the exercise of our dispositions as an index of how far they have established themselves. A man is temperate who abstaining from bodily pleasures finds this abstinence pleasant; if he finds it irksome, he is intemperate. Again, it is the man who encounters danger gladly, or at least without painful sensations, who is brave; the man who has these sensations is a coward. In a word, moral virtue has to do with pains and pleasures. There are a number of reasons for believing this. (1) Pleasure has a way of making us do what is disgraceful; pain deters us from doing what is right and fine. Hence the importance—I quote Plato—of having been brought up to find pleasure and pain in the right things. True education is just such a training. (2) The virtues operate with actions and emotions, each of which is accompanied by pleasure or pain. This is only another way of saying that virtue has to do with pleasures and pains. (3) Pain is used as an instrument of punishment. For in her remedies Nature works by opposites, and pain can be remedial. (4) When any disposition finds its complete expression it is, as we noted, in dealing with just those things by which it is its nature to be made better or worse, and which constitute the sphere of its operations. (5) Now when men become bad it is under the influence of pleasures and pains when they seek the wrong ones among them, or seek them at the wrong time, or in the wrong manner, or in any of the wrong forms which such offenses may take; and in seeking the wrong pleasures and pains they shun the right. This has led some thinkers to identify the moral virtues with conditions of the soul in which passion is eliminated or reduced to a minimum. But this is to make too absolute a statement—it needs to be qualified by adding that such a condition must be attained "in the right manner and at the right time" together with the other modifying circumstances.

So far, then, we have got this result. Moral goodness is a quality disposing us to act in the best way when we are dealing with pleasures and pains, while vice is one which leads us to act in the worst way when we deal with them.

The point may be brought out more clearly by some other considerations. There are three kinds of things that determine our choice in all our actions—the morally fine, the expedient, the pleasant; the three that we shun—the base, the harmful, the painful. Now in his dealings with all of these it is the good man who is most likely to go right, and the bad man who tends to go wrong, and that most notably in the matter of pleasure. The sensation of pleasure is felt by us in common with all animals, accompanying everything we choose, for even the fine and the expedient have a pleasurable effect upon us. (6) The capacity for experiencing pleasure has grown in us from infancy as part of our general development, and human life, being dyed in grain with it, receives therefrom a colour hard to scrape off. (7) Pleasure and pain are also the standards by which with greater or less strictness we regulate our considered actions. Since to feel pleasure and pain rightly or wrongly is an important factor in human behaviour, it follows that we are primarily concerned with these sensations. (8) Heraclitus says it is hard to fight against anger, but it is harder still to fight against pleasure. Yet to grapple with the harder has always been the business, as of art, so of goodness, success in a task being proportionate to its difficulty. This gives us another reason for believing that morality and statesmanship must concentrate on pleasures and pains, seeing it is the man who deals rightly with them who will be good, and the man who deals with them wrongly who will be bad.

Here, then, are our conclusions. (a) Virtue is concerned with pains and pleasures. (b) The actions which produce virtue are identical in character with those which increase it. (c) These actions differently performed destroy it. (d) The actions which produced it are identical with those in which it finds expression.

CHAPTER IV

A difficulty, however, may be raised as to what we mean when we say that we must perform just actions if we are to become just, and temperate actions if we are to be temperate. It may be argued that, if I do what is just and temperate, I am just and temperate already, exactly as, if I spell words or play music correctly, I must already be literate or musical. This I take to be a false analogy, even in the arts. It is possible to spell a word right by accident or because somebody tips you the answer. But you will be a scholar only if your spelling is done as a scholar does it, that is thanks to the scholarship in your own mind. Nor will the suggested analogy with the arts bear scrutiny. A work of art is good or bad in itself—let it possess a certain quality, and that is all we ask of it. But virtuous actions are not done in a virtuous—a just or temperate—way merely because *they* have the appropriate quality. The *doer* must be in a certain frame of mind when he does them. Three conditions are involved. (1) The agent must act in full consciousness of what he is doing. (2) He must "will" his action, and will it for its own sake. (3) The act must proceed from a fixed and unchangeable disposition. Now these requirements, if we except mere knowledge, are not counted among the necessary qualifications of an artist. For the acquisition of virtue, on the other hand, knowledge is of little or no value, but the other requirements are of immense, of sovran, importance, since it is the repeated performance of just and temperate actions that produces virtue. Actions, to be sure, are *called* just and temperate when they are such as a just or temperate man would do. But the doer is just or temperate not because he does such things but when he does them in the way of just and temperate persons. It is therefore quite fair to say that a man becomes just by the performance of just, and temperate by the performance of temperate, actions; nor is there the smallest likelihood of a man's becoming good by any other course of conduct. It is not, however, a popular line to take, most men preferring theory to practice under the impression that arguing about morals proves them to be philosophers, and that in this way they will turn out to be fine characters. Herein they resemble invalids, who listen carefully to all the doctor says but do not carry out a single one of his orders. The bodies of such people will never respond to treatment—nor will the souls of such "philosophers."

CHAPTER V

We now come to the formal definition of virtue. Note first, however, that the human soul is conditioned in three ways. It may have (1) feelings, (2) capacities, (3) dispositions; so virtue must be one of these three. By "feelings" I mean desire, anger, fear, daring, envy, gratification, friendliness, hatred, longing, jealousy, pity and in general all states of mind that are attended by pleasure or pain. By "capacities" I mean those faculties in virtue of which we may be described as capable of the feelings in question—anger, for instance, or pain, or pity. By "dispositions" I mean states of mind in virtue of which we are well or ill disposed in respect of the feelings concerned. We have, for instance, a bad disposition where angry feelings are concerned if we are disposed to become excessively or insufficiently angry, and a good disposition in this respect if we consistently feel the due amount of anger, which comes between these extremes. So with the other feelings.

Now, neither the virtues nor the vices are feelings. We are not spoken of as good or bad in respect of our feelings but of our virtues and vices. Neither are we praised or blamed for the way we feel. A man is not praised for being frightened or angry, nor is he blamed just for being angry; it is for being angry in a particular way. But we *are* praised and blamed for our virtues and vices. Again, feeling angry or frightened is something we can't help, but our virtues are in a manner expressions of our will; at any rate there is an element of will in their formation. Finally, we are said to be "moved" when our feelings are affected, but when it is a question of moral goodness or badness we are not said to be "moved" but to be "disposed" in a particular way. A similar line of reasoning will prove that the virtues and vices are not capacities either. We are not spoken of as good or bad, nor are we praised or blamed, merely because we are *capable* of feeling. Again, what capacities we have, we have by nature; but it is not nature that makes us good or bad.... So, if the virtues are neither feelings nor capacities, it remains that they must be dispositions....

CHAPTER VI

It is not, however, enough to give this account of the *genus* of virtue—that it is a disposition; we must describe its *species*. Let us begin, then, with this proposition. Excellence of whatever kind affects that of which it is the excellence in two ways. (1) It produces a good state in it. (2) It enables it to perform its function well. Take eyesight. The goodness of your eye is not only that which makes your eye good, it is also that which makes it function well. Or take the case of a horse. The goodness of a horse makes him a good horse, but it also makes him good at running, carrying a rider and facing the enemy. Our proposition, then, seems to be true, and it enables us to say that virtue in a man will be the disposition which (a) makes him a good man, (b) enables him to perform his function well. We have already touched on this point, but more light will be thrown upon it if we consider what is the specific nature of virtue.

In anything continuous and divisible it is possible to take the half, or more than the half, or less than the half. Now these parts may be larger, smaller and equal either in relation to the thing divided or in relation to us. The equal part may be described as a mean between too much and too little. By the mean of the thing I understand a point equidistant from the extremes; and this is one and the same for everybody. Let me give an illustration. Ten, let us say, is "many" and two is "few" of something. We get the mean of the thing if we take six;[3] that is, six exceeds and is exceeded by an equal number. This is the rule which gives us the arithmetical mean. But such a method will not give us the mean in relation to ourselves. Let ten pounds of food be a large, and two pounds a small, allowance for an athlete. It does not follow that the trainer will prescribe six pounds. That might be a large or it might be a small allowance for the particular athlete who is to get it. It would be little for Milo but a lot for a man who has just begun his training.[4] It is the same in all walks of life. The man who knows his business avoids both too much and too little. It is the mean he seeks and adopts—not the mean of the thing but the relative mean.

Every form, then, of applied knowledge, when it performs its function well, looks to the mean and works to the standard set by that. It is because people feel this that they apply the *cliché*, "You couldn't add anything to it or take anything from it" to an artistic masterpiece, the implication being that too much and too little alike destroy perfection, while the mean preserves it. Now if this be so, and if it be true, as we say, that good craftsmen work to the standard of the mean, then, since goodness like nature is more exact and of a higher character than any art, it follows that goodness is the quality that hits the mean. By "goodness" I mean goodness of

moral character, since it is moral goodness that deals with feelings and actions, and it is in them that we find excess, deficiency and a mean. It is possible, for example, to experience fear, boldness, desire, anger, pity, and pleasures and pains generally, too much or too little or to the right amount. If we feel them too much or too little, we are wrong. But to have these feelings at the right times on the right occasions toward the right people for the right motive and in the right way is to have them in the right measure, that is somewhere between the extremes; and this is what characterizes goodness. The same may be said of the mean and extremes in actions. Now it is in the field of actions and feelings that goodness operates; in them we find excess, deficiency and, between them, the mean, the first two being wrong, the mean right and praised as such.[5] Goodness, then, is a mean condition in the sense that it aims at and hits the mean.

Consider, too, that it is possible to go wrong in more ways than one. (In Pythagorean terminology evil is a form of the Unlimited, good of the Limited.) But there is only one way of being right. That is why going wrong is easy, and going right difficult; it is easy to miss the bull's eye and difficult to hit it. Here, then, is another explanation of why the too much and the too little are connected with evil and the mean with good. As the poet says,

Goodness is one, evil is multiform.

We may now define virtue as a disposition of the soul in which, when it has to choose among actions and feelings, it observes the mean relative to us, this being determined by such a rule or principle as would take shape in the mind of a man of sense or practical wisdom. We call it a mean condition as lying between two forms of badness, one being excess and the other deficiency; and also for this reason, that, whereas badness either falls short of or exceeds the right measure in feelings and actions, virtue discovers the mean and deliberately chooses it. Thus, looked at from the point of view of its essence as embodied in its definition, virtue no doubt is a mean; judged by the standard of what is right and best, it is an extreme.

But choice of a mean is not possible in every action or every feeling. The very names of some have an immediate connotation of evil. Such are malice, shamelessness, envy among feelings, and among actions adultery, theft, murder. All these and more like them have a bad name as being evil in themselves; it is not merely the excess or deficiency of them that we censure. In their case, then it is impossible to act rightly; whatever we do is wrong. Nor do circumstances make any difference in the rightness or wrongness of them. When a man commits adultery there is no point in asking whether it is with the right woman or at the right time or in the right way, for to do anything like that is simply wrong. It would amount to claiming that there is a mean and excess and defect in unjust or cowardly or intemperate actions. If such a thing were possible, we should find ourselves with a mean quantity of excess, a mean of deficiency, an excess of excess and a deficiency of deficiency. But just as in temperance and justice there can be no mean or excess or deficiency, because the mean in a sense *is* an extreme, so there can be no mean or excess or deficiency in those vicious actions—however done, they are wrong. Putting the matter into general language, we may say that there is no mean in the extremes, and no extreme in the mean, to be observed by anybody.

CHAPTER VII

But a generalization of this kind is not enough; we must show that our definition fits particular cases. When we are discussing actions particular statements come nearer the heart of the matter, though general statements cover a wider field. The reason is that human behaviour consists in the performance of particular acts, and our theories must be brought into harmony with them.

You see here a diagram of the virtues. Let us take our particular instances from that.

In the section confined to the feelings inspired by danger you will observe that the mean state is "courage." Of those who go to extremes in one direction or the other the man who shows an excess of fearlessness has no name to describe him,[6] the man who exceeds in confidence or daring is called "rash" or "foolhardy," the man who shows an excess of fear and a deficiency of confidence is called a "coward." In the pleasures and pains—though not all pleasures and pains, especially pains—the virtue which observes the mean is "temperance," the excess is the vice of "intemperance." Persons defective in

the power to enjoy pleasures are a somewhat rare class, and so have not had a name assigned to them: suppose we call them "unimpressionable." Coming to the giving and acquiring of money, we find that the mean is "liberality," the excess "prodigality," the deficiency "meanness." But here we meet a complication. The prodigal man and the mean man exceed and fall short in opposite ways. The prodigal exceeds in giving and falls short in getting money, whereas the mean man exceeds in getting and falls short in giving it away. Of course this is but a summary account of the matter—a bare outline. But it meets our immediate requirements. Later on these types of character will be more accurately delineated.

But there are other dispositions which declare themselves in the way they deal with money. One is "lordliness" or "magnificence," which differs from liberality in that the lordly man deals in large sums, the liberal man in small. Magnificence is the mean state here, the excess is "bad taste" or "vulgarity," the defect is "shabbiness." These are not the same as the excess and defect on either side of liberality. How they differ is a point which will be discussed later. In the matter of honour the mean is "proper pride," the excess "vanity," the defect "poor-spiritedness." And just as liberality differs, as I said, from magnificence in being concerned with small sums of money, so there is a state related to proper pride in the same way, being concerned with small honours, while pride is concerned with great. For it is possible to aspire to small honours in the right way, or to a greater or less extent than is right. The man who has this aspiration to excess is called "ambitious"; if he does not cherish it enough, he is "unambitious"; but the man who has it to the right extent—that is, strikes the mean—has no special designation. This is true also of the corresponding dispositions with one exception, that of the ambitious man, which is called "ambitiousness." This will explain why each of the extreme characters stakes out a claim in the middle region. Indeed we ourselves call the character between the extremes sometimes "ambitious" and sometimes "unambitious." That is proved by our sometimes praising a man for being ambitious and sometimes for being unambitious. The reason will appear later. In the meantime let us continue our discussion of the remaining virtues and vices, following the method already laid down.

Let us next take anger. Here too we find excess, deficiency and the mean. Hardly one of the states of mind involved has a special name; but, since we call the man who attains the mean in this sphere "gentle," we may call his disposition "gentleness." Of the extremes the man who is angry overmuch may be called "irascible," and his vice "irascibility" while the man who reacts too feebly to anger may be called "poor-spirited" and his disposition "poor-spiritedness."

There are, in addition to those we have named, three other modes of observing the mean which in some ways resemble and in other ways differ from one another. They are all concerned with what we do and say in social intercourse, but they differ in this respect, that one is concerned with truthfulness in such intercourse, the other two with the agreeable, one of these two with the agreeable in amusement, the other with the agreeable element in every relation of life. About these two, then, we must say a word, in order that we may more fully convince ourselves that in all things the mean is to be commended, while the extremes are neither commendable nor right but reprehensible. I am afraid most of these too are nameless; but, as in the other cases, we must try to coin names for them in the interests of clearness and to make it easy to follow the argument. Well then, as regards veracity, the character who aims at the mean may be called "truthful" and what he aims at "truthfulness." Pretending, when it goes too far, is "boastfulness" and the man who shows it is a "boaster" or "braggart." If it takes the form of understatement, the pretense is called "irony" and the man who shows it "ironical." In agreeableness in social amusement the man who hits the mean is "witty" and what characterizes him is "wittiness." The excess is "buffoonery" and the man who exhibits that is a "buffoon." The opposite of the buffoon is the "boor" and his characteristic is "boorishness." In the other sphere of the agreeable—the general business of life—the person who is agreeable in the right way is "friendly" and his disposition "friendliness." The man who makes himself too agreeable, supposing him to have no ulterior object, is "obsequious"; if he has such an object, he is a "flatterer." The man who is deficient in this quality and takes every opportunity of making himself disagreeable may be called "peevish" or "sulky" or "surly."

Even when feelings and emotional states are involved one notes that mean conditions exist. And here also, it would be agreed, we may find one man observing the mean and another going beyond it, for instance the "shamefaced" man, who is put out of countenance by anything. Or a man may fall short here of the due mean. Thus anyone who is deficient in a sense of shame, or has none at all, is called "shameless." The man who avoids both extremes is "modest," and him we praise. For, while modesty is not a form of goodness, it is praised; it and the modest man. Then there is "righteous indignation." This is felt by anyone who strikes the mean between "envy" and "malice," by which last word I mean a pleased feeling at the misfortunes of other people. These are emotions concerned with the pains and pleasures we feel at the fortunes of our neighbours. The man who feels righteous indignation is pained by undeserved good fortune; but the envious man goes beyond that and is pained at anybody's success. The malicious man, on the other hand, is so far from being pained by the misfortunes of another that he is actually tickled by them. . . .

CHAPTER IX

I have said enough to show that moral excellence is a mean, and I have shown in what sense it is so. It is, namely, a mean between two forms of badness, one of excess and the other of defect, and is so described because it aims at hitting the mean point in feelings and in actions. This makes virtue hard of achievement, because finding the middle point is never easy. It is not everybody, for instance, who can find the center of a circle—that calls for a geometrician. Thus, too, it is easy to fly into a passion—anybody can do that—but to be angry with the right person and to the right extent and at the right time and with the right object and in the right way—that is not easy, and it is not everyone who can do it. This is equally true of giving or spending money. Hence we infer that to do these things properly is rare, laudable and fine. . . .

NOTES

1. There will be an opportunity later of considering what is meant by this formula, in particular what is meant by "the

right principle" and how, in its ethical aspect, it is related to the moral virtues.

2. If we are to illustrate the material, it must be by concrete images.

3. $6 - 2 = 10 - 6$

4. What applies to gymnastics applies also to running and wrestling.

5. Being right or successful and being praised are both indicative of excellence.

6. We shall often have to make similar admissions.

Questions for Analysis

1. According to Aristotle, moral qualities can be destroyed by both excess and deficiency. What examples does he give? What other examples might he have used?

2. What connections does Aristotle make between virtue and pleasure? What roles do pleasure and pain play in moral education?

3. Whether an action is virtuous, Aristotle says, depends on both the action and the doer's frame of mind. Why? What must the frame of mind be?

4. Why does Aristotle call goodness a mean? In what sense does goodness aim at and hit the mean? Can you think of virtues that are not aptly described as means?

Respect for Persons

Immanuel Kant

In this selection from *Foundations of the Metaphysics of Morals,* Immanuel Kant develops his principle of respect for persons. In earlier sections of the book, he explains his concept of the **categorical imperative**, which he contrasts with hypothetical imperatives. Hypothetical imperatives are conditional commands. They are commands we have reason to follow if they serve some desire of ours. According to Kant, all imperatives except the supreme principle of morality are hypothetical. For example, "Be at the theater at eight" is conditional on our desire to see the movie from the beginning. A categorical imperative, on the other hand, is a command that applies to all rational beings *independent* of their desires. It is a command that reason tells us to follow no matter what. Because its authority does not depend on subjective factors, Kant considers it an objective law of reason. Because it applies to all of us, he calls it a universal practical law for all rational beings. And because this universal law has its source in our own capacity to reason, he calls us *legislators* of the universal law.

Though Kant says there is only one categorical imperative, he offers three formulations. The first, which Kant gives earlier in the book, is "[N]ever act in such a way that I could not also will that my maxim should be a universal law." By **maxim**, he means the principle on which a person's decision to act is made. To use one of Kant's own examples, someone who borrows money with no intention of repaying it would be acting on the maxim, "Whenever I need money I'll borrow it and promise to repay it though I know I never will." That maxim could never be a universal law, he says, because under those conditions, no one would believe promises any more and the institution of promising would self-destruct.

The third formulation is similar to the first, though Kant does not state it in the form of an imperative. It is "the idea of the will of every rational being as making universal law."

In the sections of the book included here, Kant gives the second formulation: "Act so that you treat humanity, whether in your own person or in that of another, as an end and

From *Foundations of the Metaphysics of Morals,* 2nd ed., translated by Lewis White Beck, Copyright © 1990. Reprinted by permission of Pearson Education, Inc., Upper Saddle River, NJ.

never as a means only." Human beings, he says, have unconditional worth; that is, we do not consider our own existence to be a means to some further end but we consider it to be an end in itself. Therefore, we should not treat one another merely as a means to some further end. He then discusses the inherent worth and dignity of persons. Because we are subject only to the laws of our own reason, he says, we are autonomous beings. And our autonomy gives us a dignity and worth beyond all price. Because of our priceless dignity and worth, all persons are worthy of respect.

[G. THE ULTIMATE WORTH OF PERSONS]

. . . Suppose that there were something the existence of which in itself had absolute worth, something which, as an end in itself, could be a ground of definite laws. In it and only in it could lie the ground of a possible categorical imperative, i.e., of a practical law.

Now, I say, man and, in general, every rational being exists as an end in himself and not merely as a means to be arbitrarily used by this or that will. In all his actions, whether they are directed to himself or to other rational beings, he must always be regarded at the same time as an end. All objects of inclinations have only a conditional worth, for if the inclinations and the needs founded on them did not exist, their object would be without worth. The inclinations themselves as the sources of needs, however, are so lacking in absolute worth that the universal wish of every rational being must be indeed to free himself completely from them. Therefore, the worth of any objects to be obtained by our actions is at all times conditional. Beings whose existence does not depend on our will but on nature, if they are not rational beings, have only a relative worth as means and are therefore called "things"; on the other hand, rational beings are designated "persons" because their nature indicates that they are ends in themselves, i.e., things which may not be used merely as means. Such a being is thus an object of respect and, so far, restricts all [arbitrary] choice. Such beings are not merely subjective ends whose existence as a result of our action has a worth for us, but are objective ends, i.e., beings whose existence in itself is an end. Such an end is one for which no other end can be substituted, to which these beings should serve merely as means. For, without them, nothing of absolute worth could be found, and if all worth is conditional and thus contingent, no supreme practical principle for reason could be found anywhere.

Thus if there is to be a supreme practical principle and a categorical imperative for the human will, it must be one that forms an objective principle of the will from the conception of that which is necessarily an end for everyone because it is an end in itself. Hence this objective principle can serve as a universal practical law. The ground of this principle is: rational nature exists as an end in itself. Man necessarily thinks of his own existence in this way; thus far it is a subjective principle of human actions. Also every other rational being thinks of his existence by means of the same rational ground which holds also for myself; thus it is at the same time an objective principle from which, as a supreme practical ground, it must be possible to derive all laws of the will. The practical imperative, therefore, is the following: Act so that you treat humanity, whether in your own person or in that of another, always as an end and never as a means only. . . .

[H. MORAL AGENTS AS LAW-GIVERS TO THEMSELVES]

If we now look back upon all previous attempts which have ever been undertaken to discover the principle of morality, it is not to be wondered at that they all had to fail. Man was seen to be bound to laws by his duty, but it was not seen that he is subject only to his own, yet universal, legislation, and that he is only bound to act in accordance with his own will, which is, however, designed by nature to be a will giving universal laws. For if one thought of him as subject only to a law (whatever it may be), this necessarily implied some interest as a stimulus or compulsion to obedience because the law did not arise from his will. Rather, his will was constrained by something else according to a law to act in a certain way. By this strictly necessary consequence, however, all the labor of finding a supreme ground for duty was irrevocably lost, and one never arrived at duty but only at the necessity of action from a certain interest. This might be his own interest or that of another, but in either case the imperative always had to be conditional and could not at all serve as a moral command. This principle I will call the principle of *autonomy* of the will in contrast to all other principles which I accordingly count under heteronomy.

The concept of each rational being as a being that must regard itself as giving universal law through all the maxims of its will, so that it may judge itself and its actions from this standpoint, leads to a very fruitful concept, namely, that of a *realm of ends.*

By "realm" I understand the systematic union of different rational beings through common laws. Because laws determine ends with regard to their universal validity, if we abstract from the personal difference of rational beings and thus from all content of their private ends, we can think of a whole of all ends in systematic connection, a whole of rational beings as ends in themselves as well as of the particular ends which each may set for himself. This is a realm of ends, which is possible on the aforesaid principles. For all rational beings stand under the law that each of them should treat himself and all others never merely as means but in every case also as an end in himself. Thus there arises a systematic union of rational beings through common objective laws. This is a realm which may be called a realm of ends (certainly only an ideal), because what these laws have in view is just the relation of these beings to each other as ends and means.

A rational being belongs to the realm of ends as a member when he gives universal laws in it while also himself subject to these laws. He belongs to it as sovereign when he, as legislating, is subject to the will of no other. The rational being must regard himself always as legislative in a realm of ends possible through the freedom of the will, whether he belongs to it as member or as sovereign. He cannot maintain the latter position merely through the maxims of his will but only when he is a completely independent being without need and with power adequate to his will.

Morality, therefore, consists in the relation of every action to that legislation through which alone a realm of ends is possible. This legislation, however, must be found in every rational being. It must be able to arise from his will, whose principle then is to take no action according to any maxim which would be inconsistent with its being a universal law and thus to act only so that the will through its maxims could regard itself at the same time as universally lawgiving. If now the maxims do not by their nature already necessarily conform to this objective principle of rational beings as universally lawgiving, the necessity of acting according to that principle is called practical constraint, i.e., duty. Duty pertains not to the sovereign in the realm of ends, but rather to each member, and to each in the same degree.

The practical necessity of acting according to this principle, i.e., duty, does not rest at all on feelings, impulses, and inclinations; it rests merely on the relation of rational beings to one another, in which the will of a rational being must always be regarded as legislative, for otherwise it could not be thought of as an end in itself. Reason, therefore, relates every maxim of the will as giving universal laws to every other will and also to every action toward itself; it does so not for the sake of any other practical motive or future advantage but rather from the idea of the dignity of a rational being who obeys no law except that which he himself also gives.

In the realm of ends everything has either a *price* or a *dignity.* Whatever has a price can be replaced by something else as its equivalent; on the other hand, whatever is above all price, and therefore admits of no equivalent, has a dignity.

That which is related to general human inclinations and needs has a *market price.* That which, without presupposing any need, accords with a certain taste, i.e., with pleasure in the mere purposeless play of our faculties, has an *affective price.* But that which constituted the condition under which alone something can be an end in itself does not have mere relative worth, i.e., a price, but an intrinsic worth, i.e., *dignity.*

Now morality is the condition under which alone a rational being can be an end in itself, because only through it is it possible to be a legislative member in the realm of ends. Thus morality and humanity, so far as it is capable of morality, alone have dignity. Skill and diligence in work have a market value; wit, lively imagination, and humor have an affective price; but fidelity in promises and benevolence on principle (not from instinct) have intrinsic worth. Nature and likewise art contain nothing which could replace their lack, for their worth consists not in effects which flow from them, nor in advantage and utility which they procure; it consists only in intentions, i.e., maxims of the will which are ready to reveal themselves in this manner through actions even though success does not favor them. These actions need no recommendation from any subjective disposition or taste in order that they may be looked upon with immediate favor and satisfaction, nor do they have need of any immediate propensity or feeling directed to them. They exhibit the will which performs them as the object of an immediate respect, since nothing but reason is required in order to impose them on the will. The will is not to be cajoled into them, for this, in the case of duties, would be a contradiction. This esteem lets the worth of such a turn of mind be recognized as dignity and puts it infinitely beyond any price, with which it cannot in the least be brought into competition or comparison without, as it were, violating its holiness.

And what is it that justifies the morally good disposition or virtue in making such lofty claims? It is nothing less than the participation it affords the rational being in giving universal laws. He is thus fitted to be a member in a possible realm of ends to which his own nature already destined him. For, as an end in himself, he is destined to be legislative in the realm of ends, free from all laws of nature and obedient only to those which he himself gives. Accordingly, his maxims can belong to a universal legislation to which he is at the same time also subject. A thing has no worth other than that determined for it by the law. The legislation which determines all worth must therefore have a dignity, i.e., unconditional and incomparable worth. For the esteem which a rational being must have for it, only the word "respect" is a suitable expression. Autonomy is thus the basis of the dignity of both human nature and every rational nature. . . .

Questions for Analysis

1. What does Kant mean by "absolute worth"? Why do persons, but not things, have absolute worth?

2. What does it mean to treat a person as a thing rather than as an end in itself? What examples can you think of?

3. According to Kant, human autonomy lies in the fact that we are subject to the moral law of our own will, not a moral law from an external source. What does it mean to be subject to a law of our own will? Why does our subjection to it make us autonomous?

4. What is the importance of Kant's distinction between price and dignity? Why does he say that human autonomy is the basis of human dignity?

5. What does Kant mean by a "realm of ends"? What role does the concept play in his moral thought?

Utilitarianism

John Stuart Mill

In the following selection from *Utilitarianism*, John Stuart Mill argues that the principle of utility or the greatest happiness principle—choose the action that creates the greatest happiness for all concerned—is the foundation of all morality. All other moral principles, he

From John Stuart Mill, *Utilitarianism*.

says, are "secondary principles," which we adopt because following them will help us maximize happiness. Because he takes the principle of utility to be fundamental, he calls his view **utilitarianism**.

After defining *happiness* as "pleasure and the absence of pain," Mill distinguishes higher—distinctively human—pleasures from lower—animal—pleasures. The rest of the selection is devoted to defending utilitarianism from various objections, the most notable being that it amounts to expediency and selfishness.

The creed which accepts as the foundation of morals Utility, or the Greatest Happiness Principle, holds that actions are right in proportion as they tend to promote happiness, wrong as they tend to produce the reverse of happiness. By happiness is intended pleasure and the absence of pain; by unhappiness, pain and the privation of pleasure. To give a clear view of the moral standard set up by the theory, much more requires to be said, in particular, what things it includes in the ideas of pain and pleasure and to what extent this is left an open question. But these supplementary explanations do not affect the theory of life on which this theory of morality is grounded—namely, that pleasure and freedom from pain are the only things desirable as ends, and that all desirable things (which are as numerous in the utilitarian as in any other scheme) are desirable either for the pleasure inherent in themselves or as means to the promotion of pleasure and the prevention of pain.

Now, such a theory of life excites in many minds, and among them in some of the most estimable in feeling and purpose, inveterate dislike. To suppose that life has (as they express it) no higher end than pleasure—no better and nobler object of desire and pursuit—they designate as utterly mean and groveling, as a doctrine worthy only of swine, to whom the followers of Epicurus were, at a very early period, contemptuously likened; and modern holders of the doctrine are occasionally made the subject of equally polite comparisons by its German, French, and English assailants.

When thus attacked, the Epicureans have always answered that it is not they, but their accusers who represent human nature in a degrading light, since the accusation supposes human beings to be capable of no pleasures except those of which swine are capable. If this supposition were true, the charge could not be gainsaid, but would then be no longer an imputation; for if the sources of pleasure were precisely the same to human beings and to swine,

the rule of life which is good enough for the one would be good enough for the other. The comparison of the Epicurean life to that of beasts is felt as degrading precisely because a beast's pleasures do not satisfy a human being's conceptions of happiness. Human beings have faculties more elevated than the animal appetites and, when once made conscious of them, do not regard anything as happiness which does not include their gratification. I do not, indeed, consider the Epicureans to have been by any means faultless in drawing out their scheme of consequences from the utilitarian principle. To do this in any sufficient manner, many Stoic, as well as Christian, elements require to be included. But there is no known Epicurean theory of life which does not assign to the pleasures of the intellect, of the feelings and imagination, and of the moral sentiments a much higher value as pleasures than to those of mere sensation.

It must be admitted, however, that utilitarian writers in general have placed the superiority of mental over bodily pleasures chiefly in the greater permanency, safety, uncostliness, etc., of the former—that is, in their circumstantial advantages rather than in their intrinsic nature. And on all these points, utilitarians have fully proved their case; but they might have taken the other and, as it may be called, higher ground with entire consistency. It is quite compatible with the principle of utility to recognize the fact that some *kinds* of pleasure are more desirable and more valuable than others. It would be absurd that while, in estimating all other things, quality is considered as well as quantity, the estimation of pleasures should be supposed to depend on quantity alone.

If I am asked what I mean by difference of quality in pleasures or what makes one pleasure more valuable than another, merely as a pleasure, except its being greater in amount, there is but one possible answer. Of two pleasures, if there be one to which all or almost all who have experience of both give a decided preference, irrespective of any feeling of moral obligation to prefer it, that is the more desirable pleasure. If one of the two is, by those who are competently acquainted with both, placed so far above the other that they prefer it, even though knowing it to be attended with a greater amount of discontent, and would not resign it for any quantity of the other pleasure of which their nature is capable, we are justified in ascribing to the preferred enjoyment a superiority in quality so far outweighing quantity as to render it, in comparison, of small account.

Now, it is an unquestionable fact that those who are equally acquainted with and equally capable of appreciating and enjoying both do give a most marked preference to the manner of existence which employs their higher faculties. Few human creatures would consent to be changed into any of the lower animals for a promise of the fullest allowance of a beast's pleasures; no intelligent human being would consent to be a fool, no instructed person would be an ignoramus, no person of feeling and conscience would be selfish and base, even though they should be persuaded that the fool, the dunce, or the rascal is better satisfied with his lot than they are with theirs. They would not resign what they possess more than he for the most complete satisfaction of all the desires which they have in common with him. . . .

I must again repeat what the assailants of utilitarianism seldom have the justice to acknowledge, that the happiness which forms the utilitarian standard of what is right in conduct is not the agent's own happiness, but that of all concerned. As between his own happiness and that of others, utilitarianism requires him to be as strictly impartial as a disinterested and benevolent spectator. In the golden rule of Jesus of Nazareth, we read the complete spirit of the ethics of utility. To do as you would be done by and to love your neighbor as yourself constitute the ideal perfection of utilitarian morality. As the means of making the nearest approach to this ideal, utility would enjoin first that laws and social arrangements should place the happiness, or (as speaking practically it may be called) the interest, of every individual as nearly as possible in harmony with the interest of the whole; and secondly, that education and opinion, which have so vast a power over human character, should so use that power as to establish in the mind of every individual an indissoluble association

between his own happiness and the good of the whole—especially between his own happiness and the practice of such modes of conduct, negative and positive, as regard for the universal happiness prescribes, so that not only he may be unable to conceive the possibility of happiness to himself consistently with conduct opposed to the general good, but also that a direct impulse to promote the general good may be in every individual one of the habitual motives of action and the sentiments connected therewith may fill a large and prominent place in every human being's sentient existence. If the impugners of the utilitarian morality represented it to their own minds in this its true character, I know not what recommendation possessed by any other morality they could possibly affirm to be wanting to it, what more beautiful or more exalted developments of human nature any other ethical system can be supposed to foster, or what springs of action, not accessible to the utilitarian, such systems rely on for giving effect to their mandates.

The objectors to utilitarianism cannot always be charged with representing it in a discreditable light. On the contrary, those among them who entertain anything like a just idea of its disinterested character sometimes find fault with its standard as being too high for humanity. They say it is exacting too much to require that people shall always act from the inducement of promoting the general interests of society. But this is to mistake the very meaning of a standard of morals and confound the rule of action with the motive of it. It is the business of ethics to tell us what are our duties or by what test we may know them; but no system of ethics requires that the sole motive of all we do shall be a feeling of duty: on the contrary, ninety-nine hundredths of all our actions are done from other motives, and rightly so done, if the rule of duty does not condemn them. It is the more unjust to utilitarianism that this particular misapprehension should be made a ground of objection to it, inasmuch as utilitarian moralists have gone beyond almost all others in affirming that the motive has nothing to do with the morality of the action, though much with the worth of the agent. He who saves a fellow creature from drowning does what is morally right, whether his motive be duty or the hope of being paid for his trouble; he who betrays the friend that trusts him is guilty of a crime, even if his object be to serve another friend to whom he is under greater obligations. But to speak only of actions done from the motive of duty, and in direct obedience to principle: it is a misapprehension of the utilitarian mode of thought to conceive it as implying that people should fix their minds upon so wide a generality as the world or society at large. The great majority of good actions are intended not for the benefit of the world, but for that of individuals, of which the good of the world is made up; and the thoughts of the most virtuous man need not on these occasions travel beyond the particular persons concerned, except so far as is necessary to assure himself that in benefiting them he is not violating the rights, that is the legitimate and authorized expectations, of anyone else. The multiplication of happiness is, according to the utilitarian ethics, the object of virtue: the occasions on which any person (except one in a thousand) has it in his power to do this on an extended scale, in other words to be a public benefactor, are but exceptional; and on these occasions alone is he called on to consider public utility; in every other case, private utility, the interest or happiness of some few persons, is all he has to attend to. Those alone the influence of whose actions extends to society in general need concern themselves habitually about so large an object. In the case of abstinences, indeed—of things which people forbear to do from moral considerations, though the consequences in the particular case might be beneficial—it would be unworthy of an intelligent agent not to be consciously aware that the action is of a class which, if practiced generally, would be generally injurious, and that this is the ground of the obligation to abstain from it. The amount of regard for the public interest implied in this recognition is no greater than is demanded by every system of morals, for they all enjoin to abstain from whatever is manifestly pernicious to society. . . .

Again, Utility is often summarily stigmatized as an immoral doctrine by giving it the name of Expediency and taking advantage of the popular use of that term to contrast it with Principle. But the Expedient, in the sense in which it is opposed to the Right, generally means that which is expedient for the particular interest of the agent himself, as when a minister sacrifices the interests of his country to keep himself in place. When it means

anything better than this, it means that which is expedient for some immediate object, some temporary purpose, but which violates a rule whose observance is expedient in a much higher degree. The Expedient, in this sense, instead of being the same thing as the useful, is a branch of the hurtful.

Thus, it would often be expedient, for the purpose of getting over some momentary embarrassment, or attaining some object immediately useful to ourselves or others, to tell a lie. But inasmuch as the cultivation in ourselves of a sensitive feeling on the subject of veracity is one of the most useful, and the enfeeblement of that feeling one of the most hurtful, things to which our conduct can be instrumental; and inasmuch as any, even unintentional, deviation from truth does that much toward weakening the trustworthiness of human assertion, which is not only the principal support of all present social well-being, but the insufficiency of which does more than any one thing that can be named to keep back civilization, virtue, everything on which human happiness on the largest scale depends—we feel that the violation, for a present advantage, of a rule of such transcendent expediency is not expedient and that he, who for the sake of a convenience to himself or to some other individual, does what depends on him to deprive mankind of the good, and inflict upon them the evil, involved in the greater or less reliance which they can place in each other's word, acts the part of one of their worst enemies.

Yet, that even this rule, sacred as it is, admits of possible exceptions is acknowledged by all moralists, the chief of which is when the withholding of some fact (as of information from a malefactor or of bad news from a person dangerously ill) would save an individual (especially an individual other than oneself) from great and unmerited evil, and when the withholding can only be effected by denial. But in order that the exception may not extend itself beyond the need and may have the least possible effect in weakening reliance on veracity, it ought to be recognized and, if possible, its limits defined; and if the principle of utility is good for anything, it must be good for weighing these conflicting utilities against one another and marking out the region within which one or the other preponderates.

Again, defenders of utility often find themselves called upon to reply to such objections as this—that there is not time, previous to action, for calculating and weighing the effects of any line of conduct on the general happiness. This is exactly as if anyone were to say that it is impossible to guide our conduct by Christianity because there is not time, on every occasion on which anything has to be done, to read through the Old and New Testaments. The answer to the objection is that there has been ample time, namely, the whole past duration of the human species. During all that time, mankind have been learning by experience the tendencies of actions, on which experience all the prudence, as well as all the morality of life, are dependent. People talk as if the commencement of this course of experience had hitherto been put off, and as if, at the moment when some man feels tempted to meddle with the property or life of another, he had to begin considering for the first time whether murder and theft are injurious to human happiness. Even then, I do not think that he would find the question very puzzling; but, at all events, the matter is now done to his hand. It is truly a whimsical supposition that if mankind were agreed in considering utility to be the test of morality, they would remain without any agreement as to what is useful and would take no measures for having their notions on the subject taught to the young and enforced by law and opinion. There is no difficulty in proving any ethical standard whatever to work ill, if we suppose universal idiocy to be conjoined with it; but on any hypothesis short of that, mankind must by this time have acquired positive beliefs as to the effects of some actions on their happiness; and the beliefs which have thus come down are the rules of morality for the multitude, and for the philosopher until he has succeeded in finding better.

That philosophers might easily do this, even now, on many subjects; that the received code of ethics is by no means of divine right; and that mankind have still much to learn as to the effects of actions on the general happiness—I admit, or, rather, earnestly maintain. The corollaries from the principle of utility, like the precepts of every practical art, admit of indefinite improvement, and, in a progressive state of the human mind, their improvement is perpetually going on. But to consider the rules of morality as improvable is one thing; to pass over the intermediate generalizations entirely, and endeavor to test each individual action directly by the first principle, is another. It is a strange notion that the acknowledgment of a first principle is inconsistent with the admission of secondary ones. To inform a traveler respecting the place of his ultimate destination is not to forbid the use of landmarks and direction-posts on the way. The proposition that happiness is the end and aim of morality does not mean that no road ought to be laid down to that goal or that persons going thither should not be advised to take one direction, rather than another. Men really ought to leave off talking a kind of nonsense on this subject, which they would neither talk nor listen to on other matters of practical concernment. Nobody argues that the art of navigation is not founded on astronomy because sailors cannot wait to calculate the Nautical Almanack. Being rational creatures, they go to sea with it ready calculated; and all rational creatures go out upon the sea of life with their minds made up on the common questions of right and wrong, as well as on many of the far more difficult questions of wise and foolish. And this, as long as foresight is a human quality, it is to be presumed they will continue to do. Whatever we adopt as the fundamental principle of morality, we require subordinate principles to apply it by; the impossibility of doing without them, being common to all systems, can afford no argument against any one in particular; but gravely to argue as if no such secondary principles could be had, and as if mankind had remained till now, and always remain, without drawing any general conclusions from the experience of human life, is as high a pitch, I think, as absurdity has ever reached in philosophical controversy.

The remainder of the stock arguments against utilitarianism mostly consist in laying to its charge the common infirmities of human nature and the general difficulties which embarrass conscientious persons in shaping their course through life. We are told that a utilitarian will be apt to make his own particular case an exception to moral rules and, when under temptation, will see a utility in the breach of a rule greater than he will see in its observance. But is utility the only creed which is able to furnish us with excuses for evildoing and means of cheating our own conscience? They are afforded in abundance by all doctrines which recognize as a fact in morals the existence of conflicting considerations, which all doctrines do that have been believed by sane persons. It is not the fault of any creed, but of the complicated nature of human affairs, that rules of conduct cannot be so framed as to require no exceptions and that hardly any kind of action can safely be laid down as either always obligatory or always condemnable. There is no ethical creed which does not temper the rigidity of its laws by giving a certain latitude, under the moral responsibility of the agent, for accommodation to peculiarities of circumstances; and under every creed, at the opening thus made, self-deception and dishonest casuistry get in. There exists no moral system under which there do not arise unequivocal cases of conflicting obligation. These are the real difficulties, the knotty points both in the theory of ethics and in the conscientious guidance of personal conduct. They are overcome practically with greater or with less success according to the intellect and virtue of the individual; but it can hardly be pretended that anyone will be the less qualified for dealing with them from possessing an ultimate standard to which conflicting rights and duties can be referred. If utility is the ultimate source of moral obligations, utility may be invoked to decide between them when their demands are incompatible. Though the application of the standard may be difficult, it is better than none at all: while in other systems the moral laws all claiming independent authority, there is no common umpire entitled to interfere between them; their claims to precedence one over another rest on little better than sophistry, and unless determined, as they generally are, by the unacknowledged influence of considerations of utility, afford a free scope for the action of personal desires and partialities. We must remember that only in these cases of conflict between secondary principles is it requisite that first principles should be appealed to. There is no case of moral obligation in which some secondary principle is not involved; and, if only one, there can seldom be any real doubt which one it is in the mind of any person by whom the principle itself is recognized.

Questions for Analysis

1. How does Mill distinguish higher and lower pleasures? What test does he propose?

2. According to Mill, utilitarianism and the golden rule are both in the same spirit. Why? Do you agree? Why or why not?

3. What is the importance of Mill's distinction between private and public utility? What criticism is it intended to disarm?

4. Mill says that we need appeal directly to the greatest happiness principle only when secondary principles conflict. Why?

5. Mill's ethical view is often called hedonistic because it considers pleasure to be the only good desirable in itself. Can you think of goods that are desirable independent of any pleasure they might give?

The Need for More Than Justice

Annette C. Baier

In the following essay, Annette C. Baier, Professor *Emeritus* of Philosophy at the University of Pittsburgh, provides a contemporary feminist criticism of the ethical tradition that begins with Kant and continues through John Rawls. Baier's starting point is the work of psychologist

Carol Gilligan, whose studies suggest that women are more likely than men to adopt an ethics of care in addition to an ethics of Kantian respect. Baier contrasts Gilligan's studies to the earlier studies of psychologist Lawrence Kohlberg. In those studies, Kohlberg concluded that individuals go through various stages of moral development. As young children, they view right and wrong in terms of parental authority. Then they move to a conventional stage, in which right and wrong are determined by the groups they belong to. At the final stages, they move beyond conventional rules to higher moral principle, first utilitarian and then Kantian. According to Gilligan, this model of moral maturity does not reflect the experience of women, who tend to view moral decisions in terms of human interdependence and needs as well as justice and rights.

After comparing these two models of moral maturity, Baier argues that traditional justice-oriented ethics is inadequate. It masks inequalities among people, oversimplifies human relationships, and understates the moral importance of emotions like love. The best moral theory, she concludes, must place care on an equal footing with justice.

In recent decades in North American social and moral philosophy, alongside the development and discussion of widely influential theories of justice, taken as Rawls takes it as the "first virtue of social institutions,"[1] there has been a counter-movement gathering strength, one coming from some interesting sources. For some of the most outspoken of the diverse group who have in a variety of ways been challenging the assumed supremacy of justice among the moral and social virtues are members of those sections of society whom one might have expected to be especially aware of the supreme importance of justice, namely blacks and women. Those who have only recently won recognition of their equal rights, who have only recently seen the correction or partial correction of long-standing racist and sexist injustices to their race and sex, are among the philosophers now suggesting that justice is only one virtue among many, and one that may need the presence of the others in order to deliver its own undenied value. Among these philosophers of the philosophical counterculture, as it were—but an increasingly large counterculture—I include Alasdair MacIntyre,[2] Michael Stocker,[3] Lawrence Blum,[4] Michael Slote,[5] Laurence Thomas,[6] Claudia Card,[7] Alison Jaggar,[8] Susan Wolf[9] and a whole group of men and women, myself included, who have been influenced by the writings of Harvard educational psychologist Carol Gilligan, whose book *In a Different Voice* (Harvard 1982; hereafter D.V.) caused a considerable stir both in the popular press and, more slowly, in the philosophical journals.[10]

Let me say quite clearly at this early point that there is little disagreement that justice is *a* social value of very great importance, and injustice an evil. Nor would those who have worked on theories of justice want to deny that other things matter besides justice. Rawls, for example, incorporates the value of freedom into his account of justice, so that denial of basic freedoms counts as injustice. Rawls also leaves room for a wider theory of the right, of which the theory of justice is just a part. Still, he does claim that justice is the "first" virtue of social institutions, and it is only that claim about priority that I think has been challenged. It is easy to exaggerate the differences of view that exist, and I want to avoid that. The differences are as much in emphasis as in substance, or we can say that they are differences in tone of voice. But these differences do tend to make a difference in approaches to a wide range of topics not just in moral theory but in areas like medical ethics, where the discussion used to be conducted in terms of patients' rights, of informed consent, and so on, but now tends to get conducted in an enlarged moral vocabulary, which draws on what Gilligan calls the ethics of *care* as well as that of *justice*.

For "care" is the new buzz-word. It is not, as Shakespeare's Portia demanded, mercy that is to season justice, but a less authoritarian humanitarian supplement, a felt concern for the good of others and for community with them. The "cold jealous virtue of justice" (Hume) is found to be too cold, and it is "warmer" more communitarian virtues and social ideals that are being called in to supplement it. One might say that liberty and equality are being found inadequate without fraternity, except that "fraternity" will be quite the wrong word, if as Gilligan initially suggested, it is *women* who perceive this value most easily. ("Sorority" will do no better, since it is too exclusive, and English has no gender-neuter word for the mutual concern of siblings.) She has since modified this claim, allowing that there are two perspectives on moral and social issues that we all tend to alternate between, and which are not always easy to combine, one of them what she called the justice perspective, the other the care perspective. It is increasingly obvious that there are many male philosophical spokespersons for the care perspective (Laurence Thomas, Lawrence Blum, Michael Stocker) so that it cannot be the prerogative of women. Nevertheless Gilligan still wants to claim that women are most unlikely to take *only* the justice perspective, as some men are claimed to, at least until some mid-life crisis jolts them into "bifocal" moral vision (see D.V., ch. 6).

Gilligan in her book did not offer any explanatory theory of why there should be any difference between female and male moral outlook, but she did tend to link the naturalness to women of the care perspective with their role as primary caretakers of young children, that is with their parental and specifically maternal role. . . . Later, both in "The Conquistador and the Dark Continent: Reflections on the Nature of Love" (*Daedalus* [Summer 1984]), and "The Origins of Morality in Early Childhood" (Chicago: University of Chicago Press, 1987), she develops this explanation. She postulates two evils that any infant may become aware of, the evil of detachment or isolation from others whose love one needs, and the evil of relative powerlessness and weakness. Two dimensions of moral development are thereby set—one aimed at achieving satisfying community with others, the other aiming at autonomy or equality of power. The relative predominance of one over the other development will depend both upon the relative salience of the two evils in early childhood, and on early and later reinforcement or discouragement in attempts made to guard against these two evils. This provides the germs of a theory about *why,* given current customs of childrearing, it should be mainly women who are not content with only the moral outlook that she calls the justice perspective, necessary though that was and is seen by them to have been to their hard won liberation from sexist oppression. They, like the blacks, used the language of rights and justice to change their own social

position, but nevertheless see limitations in that language, according to Gilligan's findings as a moral psychologist. She reports the discontent with the individualist more or less Kantian moral framework that dominates Western moral theory and which influenced moral psychologists such as Lawrence Kohlberg,[11] to whose conception of moral maturity she seeks an alternative. Since the target of Gilligan's criticism is the dominant Kantian tradition, and since that has been the target also of moral philosophers as diverse in their own views as Bernard Williams,[12] Alasdair MacIntyre, Philippa Foot,[13] Susan Wolf, Claudia Card, her book is of interest as much for its attempt to articulate an alternative to the Kantian justice perspective as for its implicit raising of the question of male bias in Western moral theory, especially liberal democratic theory. For whether the supposed blind spots of that outlook are due to male bias, or to nonparental bias, or to early traumas of powerlessness or to early resignation to "detachment" from others, we need first to be persuaded that they *are* blind spots before we will have any interest in their cause and cure. Is justice blind to important social values, or at least only one-eyed? What is it that comes into view from the "care perspective" that is not seen from the "justice perspective"?

Gilligan's position here is most easily described by contrasting it with that of Kohlberg, against which she developed it. Kohlberg, influenced by Piaget and the Kantian philosophical tradition as developed by John Rawls, developed a theory about typical moral development which saw it to progress from a pre-conventional level, where what is seen to matter is pleasing or not offending parental authority-figures, through a conventional level in which the child tries to fit in with a group, such as a school community, and conform to its standards and rules, to a post-conventional critical level, in which such conventional rules are subjected to tests, and where those tests are of a Utilitarian, or, eventually, a Kantian sort—namely ones that require respect for each person's individual rational will, or autonomy, and conformity to any implicit social contract such wills are deemed to have made, or to any hypothetical ones they would make if thinking clearly. What was found when Kohlberg's questionnaires (mostly by verbal response to verbally sketched moral dilemmas) were applied to female as well as male subjects, Gilligan reports, is that the girls and women not only scored generally lower than the boys and men, but tended to *revert* to the lower stage of the conventional level even after briefly (usually in adolescence) attaining the post conventional level. Piaget's finding that girls were deficient in "the legal sense" was confirmed.

These results led Gilligan to wonder if there might not be a quite different pattern of development to be discerned, at least in female subjects. She therefore conducted interviews designed to elicit not just how far advanced the subjects were towards an appreciation of the nature and importance of Kantian autonomy, but also to find out what the subjects themselves saw as progress or lack of it, what conceptions of moral maturity they came to possess by the time they were adults. She found that although the Kohlberg version of moral maturity as respect for fellow persons, and for their rights as equals (rights including that of free association), did seem shared by many young men, the women tended to speak in a different voice about morality itself and about moral maturity. To quote Gilligan, "Since the reality of interconnexion is experienced by women as given rather than freely contracted, they arrive at an understanding of life that reflects the limits of autonomy and control. As a result, women's development delineates the path not only to a less violent life but also to a maturity realized by interdependence and taking care" (D.V., 172). She writes that there is evidence that "women perceive and construe social reality differently from men, and that these differences center around experiences of attachment and separation . . . because women's sense of integrity appears to be intertwined with an ethics of care, so that to see themselves as women is to see themselves in a relationship of connexion, the major changes in women's lives would seem to involve changes in the understanding and activities of care" (D.V., 171). She contrasts this progressive understanding of care, from merely pleasing others to helping and nurturing, with the sort of progression that is involved in Kohlberg's stages, a progression in the understanding, not of mutual care, but of mutual *respect,* where this has its Kantian overtones of distance, even of some fear for the respected, and where personal autonomy and *inde*pendence, rather than more satisfactory interdependence, are the paramount values.

This contrast, one cannot but feel, is one which Gilligan might have used the Marxist language of alienation to make. For the main complaint about the Kantian version of a society with its first virtue justice, construed as respect for equal rights to formal goods such as having contracts kept, due process, equal opportunity including opportunity to participate in political activities leading to policy and law-making, to basic liberties of speech, free association and assembly, religious worship, is that none of these goods do much to ensure that the people who have and mutually respect such rights will have any other relationships to one another than the minimal relationship needed to keep such a "civil society" going. They may well be lonely, driven to suicide, apathetic about their work and about participation in political processes, find their lives meaningless and have no wish to leave offspring to face the same meaningless existence. Their rights, and respect for rights, are quite compatible with very great misery, and misery whose causes are not just individual misfortunes and psychic sickness, but social and moral impoverishment. . . .

Let me try to summarize the main differences, as I see them, between on the one hand Gilligan's version of moral maturity and the sort of social structures that would encourage, express and protect it, and on the other the orthodoxy she sees herself to be challenging. I shall from now on be giving my own interpretation of the significance of her challenges, not merely reporting them.[14] The most obvious point is the challenge to the individualism of the Western tradition, to the fairly entrenched belief in the possibility and desirability of each person pursuing his own good in his own way, constrained only by a minimal formal common good, namely a working legal apparatus that enforces contracts and protects individuals from undue interference by others. Gilligan reminds us that noninterference can, especially for the relatively powerless, such as the very young, amount to neglect, and even between equals can be isolating and alienating. On her less individualist version of individuality, it becomes defined by responses to dependency and to patterns of interconnexion, both chosen and unchosen. It is not something a person *has,* and which she then chooses relationships to suit, but something that develops out of a series of dependencies and interdependencies, and responses to them. This conception of individuality is not flatly at odds with, say, Rawls' Kantian one, but there is at least a difference of tone of voice between speaking as Rawls does of each of us having our own rational life plan, which a just society's moral traffic rules will allow us to follow, and which may or may not include close association with other persons, and speaking as Gilligan does of a satisfactory life as involving "progress of affiliative relationship" (D.V., 170) where "the concept of identity expands to include the experience of interconnexion" (D.V., 173). Rawls can allow that progress to Gilligan-style moral maturity may be *a* rational life plan, but not a moral constraint on every life-pattern. The trouble is that it will not do just to say "let this version of morality be an optional extra. Let us agree on the essential minimum, that is on justice and rights, and let whoever wants to go further and cultivate this more demanding ideal of responsibility and care." For, first, it cannot be satisfactorily cultivated without closer cooperation from others than respect for rights and justice will ensure, and, second, the encouragement of some to cultivate it while others do not could easily lead to exploitation of those who do. It obviously *has* suited some in most societies well enough that others take on the responsibilities of care (for the sick, the helpless, the young) leaving them free to pursue their own less altruistic goods. Volunteer forces of those who accept an ethic of care, operating within a society where the power is exercised and the institutions designed, redesigned, or maintained by those who accept a less communal ethic of minimally constrained self-advancement, will not be the solution. The liberal individualists may be able to "tolerate" the more communally minded, if they keep the liberals' rules, but it is not so clear that the more communally minded can be content with just those rules, not be content to be tolerated and possibly exploited.

For the moral tradition which developed the concept of rights, autonomy and justice is the same tradition that provided "justifications" of the oppression of those whom the primary right-holders depended on to do the sort of work they themselves preferred not to do. The domestic work was left to women and slaves, and the liberal morality for right-holders was surreptitiously supplemented by a different set of demands made on domestic workers. As long as women could be got to assume responsibility for the care of home and children, and to train their children to continue the sexist system, the liberal morality could continue to be the official morality, by turning its eyes away from the contribution made by those it excluded. The long unnoticed moral proletariat were the domestic workers, mostly female. Rights have usually been for the privileged. Talking about laws, and the rights those laws recognize and protect, does not in itself ensure that the group of legislators and rights-holders will not be restricted to some elite. Bills of rights have usually been proclamations of the rights of some in-group, barons, landowners, males, whites, non-foreigners. The "justice perspective," and the legal sense that goes with it, are shadowed by their patriarchal past. What did Kant, the great prophet of autonomy, say in his moral theory about women? He said they were incapable of legislation, not fit to vote, that they needed the guidance of more "rational" males.[15] Autonomy was not for them, only for first class, really rational, persons. It is ironic that Gilligan's original findings in a way confirm Kant's views—it seems that autonomy really may not be for women. Many of them reject that ideal (D.V., 48), and have been found not as good at making rules as are men. But where Kant concludes—"so much the worse for women," we can conclude— "so much the worse for the male fixation on the special skill of drafting legislation, for the bureaucratic mentality of rule worship, and for the male exaggeration of the importance of independence over mutual interdependence."

It is however also true that the moral theories that made the concept of a person's rights central were not just the instruments for excluding some persons, but also the instruments used by those who demanded that more and more persons be included in the favored group. Abolitionists, reformers, women, used the language of rights to assert their claims to inclusion in the group of full members of a community. The tradition of liberal moral theory has in fact developed so as to include the women it had for so long excluded, to include the poor as well as rich, blacks and whites, and so on. Women like Mary Wollstonecraft used the male moral theories to good purpose. So we should not be wholly ungrateful for those male moral theories, for all their objectionable earlier content. They were undoubtedly patriarchal, but they also contained the seeds of the challenge, or antidote, to this patriarchal poison.

But when we transcend the values of the Kantians, we should not forget the facts of history—that those values were the values of the oppressors of women. The Christian church, whose version of the moral law Aquinas codified, in his very legalistic moral theory, still insists on the maleness of the God it worships, and jealously reserves for males all the most powerful positions in its hierarchy. Its patriarchical prejudice is open and avowed. In the secular moral theories of men, the sexist patriarchal prejudice is today often less open, not as blatant as it is in Aquinas, in the later natural law tradition, and in Kant . . . , but is often still there. No moral theorist today would say that women are unfit to vote, to make laws, or to rule a nation without powerful male advisors (as most queens had), but the old doctrines die hard. . . . Traces of the old patriarchal poison still remain in even the best contemporary moral theorizing. Few may actually say that women's place is in the home, but there is much muttering, when unemployment figures rise, about how the relatively recent flood of women into the work force complicates the problem, as if it would be a good thing if women just went back home whenever unemployment rises, to leave the available jobs for the men. We still do not really have a wide acceptance of the equal right of women to employment outside the home. Nor do we have wide acceptance of the equal duty of men to perform those domestic tasks which in no way depend on special female anatomy, namely cooking, cleaning, and the care of weaned children. All sorts of stories (maybe true stories), about children's need for one "primary" parent, who must be the mother if the mother breast feeds the child, shore up the unequal division of domestic responsibility between mothers and fathers, wives and husbands. If we are really to transvalue the values of our patriarchal past, we need to rethink all of those assumptions, really test those psychological theories. And how will men ever develop an understanding of the "ethics of care" if they continue to be shielded or kept from that experience of caring for a dependent child, which complements the experience we all have had of being cared for as dependent children?

These experiences form the natural background for the development of moral maturity as Gilligan's women saw it.

Exploitation aside, why would women, once liberated, not be content to have their version of morality merely tolerated? Why should they not see themselves as voluntarily, for their own reasons, taking on *more* than the liberal rules demand, while having no quarrel with the content of those rules themselves, nor with their remaining the only ones that are expected to be generally obeyed? To see why, we need to move on to three more differences between the Kantian liberals (usually contractarians) and their critics. These concern the relative weight put on relationships between equals, and the relative weight put on freedom of choice, and on the authority of intellect over emotions. It is a typical feature of the dominant moral theories and traditions . . . that relationships between equals or those who are deemed equal in some important sense, have been the relations that morality is concerned primarily to regulate. Relationships between those who are clearly unequal in power, such as parents and children, earlier and later generations in relation to one another, states and citizens, doctors and patients, the well and the ill, large states and small states, have had to be shunted to the bottom of the agenda, and then dealt with by some sort of "promotion" of the weaker so that an appearance of virtual equality is achieved. Citizens collectively become equal to states, children are treated as adults-to-be, the ill and dying are treated as continuers of their earlier more potent selves, so that their "rights" could be seen as the rights of equals. This pretense of an equality that is in fact absent may often lead to desirable protection of the weaker, or more dependent. But it somewhat masks the question of what our moral relationships are to those who are our superiors or our inferiors in power. A more realistic acceptance of the fact that we begin as helpless children, that at almost every point of our lives we deal with both the more and the less helpless, that equality of power and interdependency, between two persons or groups, is rare and hard to recognize when it does occur, might lead us to a more direct approach to questions concerning the design of institutions structuring these relationships between unequals (families, schools, hospitals, armies) and of the morality of our dealings with the more and the less powerful. . . .

The recognition of the importance for all parties of relations between those who are and cannot but be unequal, both of these relations in themselves and for their effect on personality formation and so on other relationships, goes along with a recognition of the plain fact that not all morally important relationships can or should be freely chosen. So far I have discussed three reasons women have not to be content to pursue their own values within the framework of the liberal morality. The first was its dubious record. The second was its inattention to relations of inequality or its pretence of equality. The third reason is its exaggeration of the scope of choice, or its inattention to unchosen relations. Showing up the partial myth of equality among actual members of a community, and of the undesirability of trying to pretend that we are treating all of them as equals, tends to go along with an exposure of the companion myth that moral obligations arise from freely *chosen* associations between such equals. Vulnerable future generations do not choose their dependence on earlier generations. The unequal infant does not choose its place in a family or nation, nor is it treated as free to do as it likes until some association is freely entered into. Nor do its parents always choose their parental role, or freely assume their parental responsibilities any more than we choose our power to affect the conditions in which later generations will live. Gilligan's attention to the version of morality and moral maturity found in women, many of whom had faced a choice of whether or not to have an abortion, and who had at some point become mothers, is attention to the perceived inadequacy of the language of rights to help in such choices or to guide them in their parental role. It would not be much of an exaggeration to call the Gilligan "different voice" the voice of the potential parents. The emphasis on care goes with a recognition of the often unchosen nature of the responsibilities of those who give care, both of children who care for their aged or infirm parents, and of parents who care for the children they in fact have. Contract soon ceases to seem the paradigm source of moral obligation once we attend to parental responsibility,

and justice as a virtue of social institutions will come to seem at best only first equal with the virtue, whatever its name, that ensures that each new generation is made appropriately welcome and prepared for their adult lives.

. . . The fourth feature of the Gilligan challenge to liberal orthodoxy is a challenge to its typical *rationalism,* or intellectualism, to its assumption that we need not worry what passions persons have, as long as their rational wills can control them. This Kantian picture of a controlling reason dictating to possibly unruly passions also tends to seem less useful when we are led to consider what sort of person we need to fill the role of parent, or indeed want in any close relationship. It might be important for father figures to have rational control over their violent urges to beat to death the children whose screams enrage them, but more than control of such nasty passions seems needed in the mother or primary parent, or parent-substitute, by most psychological theories. They need to love their children, not just to control their irritation. So the emphasis in Kantian theories on rational control of emotions, rather than on cultivating desirable forms of emotion, is challenged by Gilligan, along with the challenge to the assumption of the centrality of autonomy, or relations between equals, and of freely chosen relations. . . .

It is clear, I think, that the best moral theory has to be a cooperative product of women and men, has to harmonize justice and care. The morality it theorizes about is after all for all persons, for men and for women, and will need their combined insights. As Gilligan said (D.V., 174), what we need now is a "marriage" of the old male and the newly articulated female insights. If she is right about the special moral aptitudes of women, it will most likely be the women who propose the marriage, since they are the ones with more natural empathy, with the better diplomatic skills, the ones more likely to shoulder responsibility and take moral initiative, and the ones who find it easiest to empathize and care about how the other party feels. Then, once there is this union of male and female moral wisdom, we maybe can teach each other the moral skills each gender currently lacks, so that the gender difference in moral outlook that Gilligan found will slowly become less marked.

NOTES

1. John Rawls, *A Theory of Justice* (Cambridge: Harvard University Press, 1971).

2. Alasdair MacIntyre, *After Virtue* (Notre Dame: Notre Dame University Press).

3. Michael Stocker, "The Schizophrenia of Modern Ethical Theories," *Journal of Philosophy* 73, 14, 453–66, and "Agent and Other: Against Ethical Universalism," *Australasian Journal of Philosophy* 54, 206–20.

4. Lawrence Blum, *Friendship, Altruism and Morality* (London: Routledge & Kegan Paul 1980).

5. Michael Slote, *Goods and Virtues* (Oxford: Oxford University Press 1983).

6. Laurence Thomas, "Love and Morality" in *Epistemology and Sociobiology,* James Fetzer, ed. (1985) and "Justice, Happiness and Self Knowledge," *Canadian Journal of Philosophy* (March, 1986). Also "Beliefs and the Motivation to be Just," *American Philosophical Quarterly* 22 (4), 347–52.

7. Claudia Card, "Mercy," *Philosophical Review* 81, 1, and "Gender and Moral Luck," [in *Identity Characters, and Morality: Essays in Moral Psychology,* Owen Flanagan, ed. (Cambridge: MIT Press, 1990.)].

8. Alison Jaggar, *Feminist Politics and Human Nature* (London: Rowman and Allenheld 1983).

9. Susan Wolf, "Moral Saints," *Journal of Philosophy* 79 (August, 1982), 419–39.

10. For a helpful survey article see Owen Flanagan and Kathryn Jackson, "Justice, Care & Gender: The Kohlberg-Gilligan Debate Revisited," *Ethics.*

11. Lawrence Kohlberg, *Essays in Moral Development,* vols. I & II (New York: Harper and Row 1981, 1984).

12. Bernard Williams, *Ethics and the Limits of Philosophy* (Cambridge: Cambridge University Press 1985).

13. Philippa Foot, *Virtues and Vices* (Berkeley: University of California Press 1978).

14. I have previously written about the significance of her findings for moral philosophy in "What Do Women Want in a Moral Theory?" *Nous* 19 (March 1985), "Trust and Antitrust," *Ethics* 96 (1986), and in "Hume the Women's Moral Theorist?" in *Women and Moral Theory,* Kittay and Meyers, ed., [Totowa, N.J.: Rowman & Littlefield, 1987].

15. Immanuel Kant, *Metaphysics of Morals,* sec. 46.

Questions for Analysis

1. What does Baier mean by the ethics of care? How does it differ from the ethics of justice?

2. How, according to Baier and Gilligan, do men and women differ in moral development? How do they account for these differences? Why do they think these differences are relevant to moral theory?

3. According to Baier, the ethics of justice is compatible with "great misery" and "social and moral impoverishment." Why? How can the ethics of care correct these problems?

4. Why does Baier find fault with the traditional moral emphasis on equality and freely chosen relationships?

5. Some recent studies have cast doubt on the claim that there are distinctively masculine and feminine perspectives on morality. If correct, do these studies affect Baier's criticisms of the ethics of justice?

6. Does the ethics of justice ignore the experience of women? Why or why not?

2

GOOD REASONING

Arguments
Evaluating Moral Arguments
Summary and Conclusions

Not all opinions are equal, the first chapter concluded, and we looked at a few examples that seemed to show that some opinions are indeed better than others. However, we did not explain *why* some opinions are better than others.

Of course, given the nature of the examples, explanation might have seemed unnecessary. Let's go back to two of them. If any opinion about the best career for Mary is to be a good one, it must be based on some obvious factors—what she likes to do, what she's good at, availability of jobs, where she would like to live, and so on. Any opinion that ignores these factors is not one that will have much value to her. Similarly, any worthwhile opinion at the beginning of the baseball season regarding the outcome of the World Series must be based on equally obvious factors, like pitching and hitting.

The same can be said about any opinion. If it is to be a good one, it must be well grounded. It must be supported by good reasons. And the better the support, the better the opinion, whether it's a scientific opinion or a moral one, an opinion about what's wrong with your car, or an opinion about what's wrong with something you did. To be sure, an opinion that is not well grounded may turn out to be correct. Even the most ignorant of ignoramuses are right sometimes. But when they are, it is a matter of pure luck. Their opinions are not to be trusted in the future because they are not arrived at in a reliable way.

What makes an opinion well grounded? Well, one obvious consideration is knowledge. The more relevant details we know about a particular matter, the better grounded our opinions will be. Be sure to notice the word *relevant*. It is most important, particularly when we deal with moral problems. In fact, one of the biggest difficulties we will encounter in our dealings with the issues of Part 2 is trying to decide what the relevant details are.

Another thing is logic. A well-supported opinion is logically arrived at. It comes at the end of a reliable pattern of reasoning. Or as philosophers often put it, it is the conclusion of a strong *argument*.

ARGUMENTS

To philosophers, scientists, attorneys, and others who engage in intellectual debate, an **argument** is a collection of statements. One of the statements is the conclusion. The other statements are called *premises, reasons, evidence, supporting statements,* or *grounds.* Whatever we call them, the important point is this: Their purpose is to show that the conclusion is true or that it is reasonable to accept the conclusion as true.

Much of Part 2 will be devoted to arguments for and against various positions. And much of your task in reading Part 2 will be to do your best to evaluate these arguments. That is, you will have to decide whether the arguments for or against particular positions are the better ones. And to do that, you will have to ask yourself a variety of questions: Are the supporting statements true? If so, do they really lend support to the conclusions, or are they irrelevant to the conclusions? Are the patterns of reasoning followed by these arguments reliable ones? Has anything of importance been left out of these arguments?

In the rest of this chapter, we give you some help in answering these questions. But first, we must distinguish two kinds of argument.

Deductive Arguments

Consider the following two sentences:

1. If Clint Eastwood is a bulldog, then he has four legs.
2. Clint Eastwood is a bulldog.

Chances are, you know what comes next:

3. Therefore, Clint Eastwood has four legs.

How did you know that? Not because of anything you know about Clint Eastwood. People may have different opinions about his movies, but all of us agree that he has only two legs. Nor does your knowledge of bulldogs make a difference. Suppose the first sentence had been "If Clint Eastwood is a bulldog, then he has eight legs." Then you would have drawn a different conclusion: "Therefore, Clint Eastwood has eight legs."

What makes the difference is your knowledge of a rule of **deductive logic,** as follows:

1. If A, then B.
2. A.
3. Therefore, B.

That rule is called a **truth-preserving rule.** To say that the rule is truth preserving is to say that whenever you follow it, if the first two statements (called the **premises**) are true, the conclusion will also be true. Truth-preserving rules are also called *valid rules,* and any argument that follows only valid rules is called a **valid deductive argument.**

The notion of a valid deductive argument will prove to be very useful. Even more important is the notion of a **sound deductive argument.** To be sound, an argument must pass two tests: first, it must be valid, and second, all its premises must be true. A valid argument with false premises may or may not have a true conclusion, but the conclusion of a sound argument must be true. In other words, if we can assure ourselves that all the premises of an argument are true, and if we can also assure ourselves that the argument follows only valid deductive rules, then we can assure ourselves that the conclusion must be true.

There are many valid rules of deductive reasoning, far too many to go into here. Fortunately, we do not need to know all of them to decide whether an argument is valid. Instead, we can use a simple method for detecting invalidity. That method is known as the method of **counterexample**. Consider the following argument, which many people mistakenly think is valid:

1. If John took a shower, then he got wet.

2. John didn't take a shower.

3. Therefore, John didn't get wet.

That argument follows this rule:

1. If A, then B.

2. A is not true.

3. Therefore, B is not true.

And we can show that *that* rule is not truth preserving by giving a counterexample to the rule. To do that, we find an argument that has true premises, follows the same rule, but has a false conclusion. If we can do that, the rule is certainly not truth preserving. For instance,

1. If Rin Tin Tin had been a collie, then he'd have been a dog.

2. Rin Tin Tin was not a collie.

3. Therefore, Rin Tin Tin was not a dog.

Here's another example of an invalid argument:

1. Some baseball players are left-handed.

2. Some baseball players are pitchers.

3. Therefore, some pitchers are left-handed.

If you don't believe that the argument is invalid, consider this counterexample:

1. Some animals are human.

2. Some animals are fish.

3. Therefore, some fish are human.

And here, finally, is another:

1. All ravens are black.

2. A dove is not a raven.

3. Therefore, a dove is not black.

And here is a counterexample:

1. All ravens are black.

2. A panther is not a raven.

3. Therefore, a panther is not black.

In each of the preceding cases, we provided a counterexample by constructing an entirely new argument. Sometimes you may find it easier just to ask a few questions about the original argument. Take the argument that concluded that John didn't get wet (because he didn't take a shower). What if he'd taken a bath instead? Or take the argument that concluded that some pitchers are left-handed (because some baseball players are pitchers and some are left-handed). What if all the left-handed players are outfielders? Or take the last one. What if there are black doves?

Fortunately, you will not come upon many invalid arguments in the readings in Part 2. Unfortunately, you *will* come across many invalid arguments in other discussions of the same issues—perhaps even in class discussions—so recognizing one when you see it is an important skill.

What you are more likely to come across in the readings in Part 2 are valid but *unsound* arguments. So you must be careful to ask whether the premises are true when you evaluate the arguments you encounter.

Inductive Arguments

Most ordinary reasoning is not deductive. The supporting statements, if true, do not guarantee the truth of the conclusion. Rather, they establish that it is more reasonable than not to accept the conclusion. That is, they establish that the conclusion is likely to be true. Arguments of that kind are called **inductive arguments**. The supporting statements of inductive arguments are called *reasons, evidence,* or *grounds* instead of premises, and a good inductive argument is called a **warranted argument** instead of a sound one.

When we reason from cause to effect or from effect to cause, we generally reason inductively. If, for example, we hear a loud bang outside, we would most likely conclude that a car had just backfired. Although other explanations are possible—somebody might have shot her neighbor, say—in most neighborhoods, a backfiring car is the most probable one. Since our evidence does admit of other possibilities, though, we cannot say that we reasoned deductively. Similarly, when we put a pot of water on the stove and come back later expecting the water to be boiling, we are also reasoning inductively. Various factors may have kept the water from boiling—the gas might have been turned off, for instance—but more likely than not, the water is boiling.

Most generalizations are also examples of inductive reasoning. We examine a sample taken from a larger population, notice some features shared by a certain percentage of our sample, and then conclude that the same—or nearly the same—pattern occurs in the population at large. Thus, from a sample of green and only green emeralds, we conclude that all emeralds are green, and from a sample of Nielsen families, we conclude that more viewers watch NFL football games than NBA basketball games. These generalizations are reliable, but they are not arrived at by deductive reasoning. Because there is always some probability—however small—that the larger population does not match the sample, such reasoning is inductive.

Although inductive reasoning does not have rules in the same way that deductive reasoning does, we use a variety of criteria to evaluate inductive arguments. For our purposes, the most important are those that concern *causal* generalizations because those are the kinds of arguments that will be most prominent in Part 2.

Consider this argument:

1.   John takes two aspirin tablets every day.

2.   John never has a cold.

3.   Therefore, aspirin prevents colds.

There is much, of course, that is wrong with that argument. Two flaws are most obvious. First, a sample of one is hardly large enough to support a generalization about all human beings. Second, no care has been taken to rule out other explanations of John's good fortune. Thus, the following are important criteria for evaluating causal generalizations. First, the sample must be large enough to support the generalization. Second, it must also be representative of the larger population that's being generalized about.

Third, to help rule out other explanations, there must be a *control group*—another sample as much like the original sample (called the *experimental group*) as possible except that its members are not exposed to the factor being tested. If we are testing to see whether aspirin prevents colds, for example, we will want to study two groups, one that takes aspirin daily and one that does not. Only after the control group and the experimental group have been compared are we entitled to make our causal generalization.

But even then, we must be careful. Statistical links are not the same as causal links. Two factors may be associated without one being the cause of the other. Sneezing and coughing often go together, but one does not cause the other. Rather, both have a common cause—often a flu virus. So even after a statistical link has been established, further experiments may be necessary to establish a causal link.

To be sure, few people are ever in a position to carry out such experiments. For most of us, inductive reasoning is far less formal. We do not have the statistical techniques to evaluate the reliability of our samples, nor do we have the time and money to design and carry out tests on experimental and control groups. That's why we must rely on people who do—scientists—before we can say that a causal generalization has been established. This does not mean, however, that we can't reach reasonable conclusions before science has spoken. We can. Indeed, often we must. But when doing so, we must remember two points.

First, we must keep in mind that the more closely our reasoning resembles the scientist's, the better it is. The more numerous and representative the cases we have to generalize from, the better our evidence and the more reasonable our conclusion. And the more justified we are in ruling out other causes, the more reasonable our conclusion.

Second, no matter how reasonable our conclusion may be, we are not entitled to claim that we've established it. Inductive reasoning, unlike deductive reasoning, cannot be neatly divided into the sound and the unsound. Although it *can* be divided into the warranted and the unwarranted, warrant admits of degrees. One sound deductive argument is as conclusive as another. One warranted inductive argument is not as conclusive as another. Our confidence in our conclusions, then, should be no greater than the degree of our warrant. And as long as our inductive reasoning is informal, our degree of warrant requires a corresponding degree of humility.

Moral Arguments

A familiar position on abortion is that abortion is wrong except to save the life of the mother, and a common justification for that position is that taking an innocent life is wrong except to save a life. Proponents of broad abortion rights, on the other hand, often support their views by claiming that women have the right to control their own bodies as long as they don't harm anyone else. Like all the moral arguments we will come across in Part 2, each proceeds from a general moral principle (the first about taking an innocent life, the second about a woman's rights over her body) to a moral conclusion about a particular issue (the morality of abortion). The best way to examine such arguments is to treat them as abbreviated deductive arguments. We do that by supplying additional premises that make the arguments valid.

Consider the first argument. We are given only one premise:

1.   Taking an innocent life is wrong except to save a life.

One premise that must be added is the following:

2.   Abortion is the taking of an innocent life.

Together, those premises lead to:

3.   Therefore, abortion is wrong except to save a life.

Though that is an important conclusion of the argument, it is only an *intermediate* conclusion. To get to the *final* conclusion, we must add another premise:

4.   The only life that can be saved by an abortion is the mother's.

From that premise and the intermediate conclusion, we get the final conclusion:

5.   Therefore, abortion is wrong except to save the life of the mother.

Because the preceding argument reaches an intermediate conclusion, it is a two-step argument. Multiple-step arguments are not unusual in moral debates. In fact, the opposing argument, once the missing premises are added, turns out to be a three-step argument because it goes through two intermediate conclusions, one at line three and the other at line five:

1.   Women have the right to control their own bodies as long as they don't harm another person.

2.   A woman's right to control her body includes the right to have any medical procedure she and her doctor choose.

3.   Therefore, a woman has a right to any medical procedure she and her doctor choose as long as it doesn't harm another person.

4.   An abortion is a medical procedure.

5.   Therefore, a woman has a right to an abortion as long as it doesn't harm another person.

6.   An abortion hurts nothing but the fetus, which is not a person.

7.   Therefore, women have the right to an abortion.

Both of these arguments are valid, but since they reach opposite conclusions, they cannot both be sound. At least one of them must have at least one false premise. And that is why it is useful for us to treat moral arguments as deductive. If we do so, they become much easier to evaluate. We can lay out opposing arguments in a clear fashion, make sure that we understand the reasoning behind each one, isolate all of the premises, and then examine the premises of each to see whether they are true. The ones with true premises, or with premises more likely to be true, are the ones we should accept.

EVALUATING MORAL ARGUMENTS

Once again, one of your main tasks in dealing with the issues of Part 2 will be to evaluate arguments in favor of opposing positions. As we just saw, that task breaks down into two subtasks. The first is to try to reconstruct each argument as a valid deductive argument. The second is to examine the premises to see if they are true. Let's begin our discussion of these two tasks by looking at an example.

A Sample Evaluation

A common argument in favor of legalized abortion is often put this way: Catholics and fundamentalist Christians have no right to turn their religious beliefs into law. That is a very short argument. If we are to try to turn it into a valid argument, we must ask ourselves what premises are *assumed* by the argument but not explicitly stated by it. That is, we must ask what premises we should *add* to make the argument valid.

One way we can make it valid is by adding only one premise. Then the argument would go like this:

1. Catholics and fundamentalist Christians have no right to turn their religious beliefs into law.

2. That abortions should be banned is a religious belief of Catholics and fundamentalist Christians.

3. Therefore, Catholics and fundamentalist Christians have no right to make abortions illegal.

That is a valid argument, to be sure, but it's not very convincing as it stands. After all, why should we pick on Catholics and fundamentalist Christians? Do Presbyterians have the right to turn their religious beliefs into law? Quakers? Jews? Also, the conclusion is a very weak one. It claims that two groups have no right to make abortion illegal but not that nobody has the right to make abortion illegal.

So let's try another approach.

1. No religious group has the right to turn its religious beliefs into law.

2. Opponents of abortion are trying to turn their religious beliefs into law.

3. Therefore, opponents of abortion have no right to make abortion illegal.

That's a little better. At least it doesn't pick on two religious groups unfairly. Still, the premises are not very plausible. The trouble with the first is that *many* religious beliefs have been turned into law, often rightfully. Religious beliefs against murder, armed robbery, and rape come most readily to mind. The trouble with the second is that many opponents of abortion oppose it for nonreligious reasons. If the argument is to have any force, then, further changes must be made.

For example,

1. If there are no good nonreligious reasons for turning some group's religious beliefs into law, then nobody has the right to turn those beliefs into law.
2. That abortion should be banned is a religious belief of some groups.
3. Therefore, if there are no good nonreligious reasons for making abortion illegal, nobody has the right to make it illegal.
4. There are no good nonreligious reasons for making abortion illegal.
5. Therefore, nobody has the right to make abortion illegal.

Is that much better? Not really. For one thing, item four is not obviously true. Indeed, whether it *is* true is precisely what the debate over abortion is all about. For another thing, what the argument now boils down to is this:

1. If there are no good reasons to make abortion illegal, it should be legal.
2. There are no good reasons to make abortion illegal.
3. Therefore, abortion should be legal.

And that is not much of an argument at all. Granted, it is certainly valid, but until we have an argument in favor of premise two, opponents of abortion have no reason to take it seriously.

Reconstructing Arguments

What we did in the previous section is not nearly as difficult as it might first appear. All it takes is a little common sense plus the knowledge of a few valid rules of deductive logic. And those few rules are also common sense. One, which we already looked at in our Clint Eastwood example, is:

1. If A, then B.
2. A.
3. Therefore, B.

That is a rule that all of you already knew. No doubt you know the others as well. For example,

1. Either John is home or he's at the library.
2. He's not home.
3. Therefore, what?

The answer, obviously, is that he's at the library. And the rule is:

1. A or B.
2. A is not true.
3. Therefore, B.

Here's another:

1.   If Mary is home, she's in the den.
2.   She's not in the den.
3.   Therefore, what?

The answer here is that she's not home. And the rule is:

1.   If A, then B.
2.   B is not true.
3.   Therefore, A is not true.

There are only three others you need to know (and no doubt already know), and they are equally matters of common sense. Examples are:

1.   All dogs are mammals.
2.   Lassie is a dog.
3.   Therefore, Lassie is a mammal.

And:

1.   All dogs are mammals.
2.   My parrot is not a mammal.
3.   Therefore, my parrot is not a dog.

And:

1.   No pigs can fly.
2.   Robins can fly.
3.   Therefore, robins aren't pigs.

And the rules are:

1.   All A is B.
2.   C is A.
3.   Therefore, C is B.

And:

1.   All A is B.
2.   C is not B.
3.   Therefore, C is not A.

And:

1.   No A is B.
2.   C is B.
3.   Therefore, C is not A.

Armed with these common-sense rules, you will be able to turn any logical moral argument into a valid deductive argument. That is, as long as the argument doesn't depend on any invalid rules, you can do what we did in the previous section.

For example, we often hear that homosexuality is wrong because it's unnatural. That claim is really an abbreviated argument, as follows:

1.   Anything unnatural is morally wrong.

2.   Homosexuality is unnatural.

3.   Therefore, homosexuality is morally wrong.

Of course, few people actually put it that way. The first premise is generally left unsaid, but common sense tells us that something like the first premise is required if the argument is to be valid. Along the same lines, common sense tells us that something must be added when people claim that capital punishment is wrong because it does not deter crime any better than life imprisonment does. When we add what is needed, we get:

1.   If one punishment is more severe than another, it is wrong to impose the more severe one if it is not a better deterrent than the less severe one.

2.   Capital punishment is more severe than life imprisonment.

3.   Therefore, it is wrong to impose capital punishment if it is not a better deterrent than life imprisonment.

4.   Capital punishment is not a better deterrent than life imprisonment.

5.   Therefore, it is wrong to impose capital punishment.

How do we know which premises to add? There is no precise formula that anybody can give, but we can provide some general directions. First, we must choose premises that can be used with valid deductive rules. When we look at the claim that homosexuality is wrong because it's unnatural, for instance, we know that the conclusion is "Homosexuality is wrong" and that one premise is "Homosexuality is unnatural." What we need, then, is a premise like "If anything is unnatural, it's wrong," or "All unnatural behavior is wrong."

Second, we must make sure that our added premises are *general* enough to look like real moral principles, not prejudices. That is why we put "anything" and "all unnatural behavior" in the above premises, not "homosexuality" and "all homosexual acts." If we make the premise read "If homosexuality is unnatural, then it's wrong," somebody could justifiably ask us "Why just homosexuality?" That's why we changed "Catholics and fundamentalist Christians" to "religious groups" in an earlier example. In moral arguments, we must appeal to moral principles, and the more general a statement is, the more like a genuine moral principle and the less like an expression of prejudice it is.

Third, we must add *enough* premises to make the argument valid. That requirement is not just a matter of logic. If we are to evaluate an argument adequately, we must be able to examine all of its premises. And if we don't have enough premises to make the argument valid, we are lacking at least one assumed premise.

Fourth, we must use a little **charity**, even if we don't agree with the argument's conclusion. We must allow our opponents the best arguments we can if we are to give them a fair hearing. This means that we must do our best to give them *plausible* premises. A few pages back, for example, we looked at the claim that a woman has the right to an abortion because she has the right to control her own body. One of the premises we added was "A woman's right to control her own body includes the right to have any medical procedure she and her doctor choose." Now that may or may not be true, but it is certainly plausible. On the other hand, the following premise is most certainly not: "A woman's right to control her body includes the right to murder her children." Granted, many abortion foes believe that pro-choice advocates are claiming that, but it is most unfair to make it a premise in their arguments.

Fifth, we must do our best to make sure that the premises we add are *faithful* to the beliefs of the person putting forth the argument. Although we cannot always be sure on this point, there are ways to increase our confidence. If we add a premise that is inconsistent with sentences that appear elsewhere in the reading, we have probably failed. Of course, sometimes people are inconsistent, but if it is possible to read them in a way that makes them consistent, we should do so. (That, of course, is required of us by the principle of charity.)

Also, arguers often give us hints of their broader commitments. In his reading arguing against abortion, for example, John T. Noonan makes it clear that he agrees with much of traditional Catholic theology, although he attempts to rest his arguments on purely secular grounds. We should not supply anti-Catholic premises to Noonan.

Sixth, we must be careful not to beg any questions. To *beg a question* is to assume what you are trying to prove, and a **question-begging argument** is one that contains the conclusion as one of its premises. Sometimes that cannot be helped. If John says that he believes Mary because she's honest, and he knows she's honest because she told him so, and he believed her because she's honest, there is not much we can do to save his argument. On the other hand, we are not forced to beg any questions when reconstructing the pro-choice argument based on a woman's right to control her own body. In that case, we should not add the following:

2. A woman's right to control her body includes the right to do anything moral.

3. Abortions are moral.

4. Therefore, a woman has the right to an abortion.

Although premise three is not precisely the same as the conclusion, it is certainly close enough to qualify as question begging.

Seventh, we must be careful not to *equivocate*. That is, we must not allow the argument to turn on different meanings of the same word. For example, the word *unnatural* can mean either "perverse" or "out of the ordinary." Many things, like writing poetry or skydiving, are unnatural in the second sense of the word but not the first. Anyone who argues that skydiving is out of the ordinary, and therefore unnatural, and therefore perverse is guilty of equivocating. Of course, sometimes the arguments we are trying to reconstruct *will* turn on equivocations. Some arguments against homosexuality, for example, may turn on an equivocation on *natural* much like the one we just looked at. In those cases, we have no choice but to give up. An argument that turns on an equivocation is not a valid one, and we cannot make it valid without creating an entirely different argument.

Examining Premises

Once we have a valid argument before us, we must next ask whether it is a sound argument. The first premises to look at are the general ones because they are most likely to be questionable. Although many statements with words like *all* and *every* and *any* and *no* are true, many others are not.

Consider the general statements that appear in our pro- and anti-abortion arguments, for example. Is it really true that a woman's right to control her own body includes the right to have *any* medical procedure she and her doctor choose? What about experimental procedures that have not been approved for the general public? Or procedures that have been outlawed because they are ineffective or dangerous?

Similarly, is it really true that taking an innocent life is *always* wrong except to save another life? (The word *always* did not appear in the premise of our argument, but as in many general statements, the general word is assumed. With a sentence like "Dogs are mammals," or even "A dog is a mammal," we should understand it as being about all dogs unless we are told otherwise.) Judith Jarvis Thomson, in her defense of abortion that appears in Part 2, doesn't think so, and she provides examples to back up her point.

Thomson's examples are meant to be *counterexamples* to the generalization in the anti-abortion argument, just as the examples of unapproved medical procedures were offered as counterexamples to the generalization in the pro-abortion argument. That is, they are meant to be examples in which the generalization breaks down.

If the proposed counterexamples are genuine counterexamples, we may still be able to save the premise in a slightly altered form. Suppose we grant that a woman does not have the right to an unapproved medical procedure. All we have to do is add the phrase "medically approved" to that premise and other premises in which it is now needed to make the argument valid. The additions will not harm the argument because most abortions are medically approved.

On the other hand, the counterexamples may be decisive. That is, there may be no way to alter the premise without destroying the argument. Whether Thomson's counterexamples are decisive is not for us to decide now, but we can look at another case in which counterexamples are decisive. Take this argument:

1. Lying is wrong.
2. Telling a friend that her ugly baby is cute is lying.
3. Therefore, telling a friend that her ugly baby is cute is wrong.

Most of us agree that white lies are genuine counterexamples to the first premise. Honesty is commendable, but not when it causes our friends great hurt and the lie is an innocuous one. But once we change the first premise to exempt white lies, the argument falls apart.

One way to challenge a general premise, then, is to find a decisive counterexample. Another way is to question the assumptions it rests on. Many people, for example, take issue with premise six of the pro-abortion argument, which says that a fetus is not a person (or no fetus is a person, or all fetuses are not persons). They cannot point to a counterexample that abortion proponents will accept because the view that fetuses are not persons is based on certain assumptions about what it is to be a person—and those assumptions rule out all fetuses. What abortion opponents must do, then, is challenge the assumptions. That is, they must show that the other side is wrong about what it is to be a person and that a proper understanding would show that all or most or some fetuses are persons.

Very often, the challenged assumptions will be moral assumptions. An argument may conclude that something is right because it is justified by the principle of utility, say. Someone who disagrees with the argument, on the other hand, might feel that respect for persons must take precedence in this instance. Another argument may conclude that justice requires us to do one thing, while someone who disagrees might feel that justice requires us to do something else.

Such disagreements are, of course, very hard to settle. They often boil down to what philosophers call conflicting **moral intuitions**. By moral intuition, we do not mean some mysterious sixth sense for divining moral truths. Rather, we mean only a moral conviction arrived at after careful consideration of the relevant facts—a conviction that strikes us as right but not provable. But even though they are not provable, moral intuitions can be challenged, discussed, and even changed on reasonable grounds.

The idea is to think of a variety of cases—some ordinary, some a bit fanciful—and see if consideration of these cases has any effect on our intuitions. What these cases add is new relevant information. Many of our moral intuitions, after all, are based on a small sample of possible cases. Some of them may be generalizations we've arrived at a little too quickly. Often, we can benefit by opening them up to some careful scrutiny. So when you come across arguments that rest on moral assumptions that conflict with your intuitions, it is best to examine both the assumptions and your intuitions as carefully as possible.

Other general statements that require careful scrutiny are **causal generalizations**. Although many causal generalizations are extremely well established—friction causes heat, for example—many others are controversial at best. Among the most controversial are those that some readings in Part 2 rely on—about the deterrent effects of capital punishment or the effects of various social programs on the poor. Most of us have our own opinions on these matters, but more often than not, they are based on what we take to be common sense rather than on well-designed studies.

By well-designed studies, of course, we mean studies with large representative samples and adequate controls. Sometimes such studies exist, but they are inconclusive. Sometimes different studies on the same issue will come to conflicting conclusions. Sometimes they just don't exist. How, then, can we evaluate causal generalizations under such conditions?

First, see how they are supported. Often, they are supported by *analogies*. Many opponents of mercy killing and abortion sometimes draw analogies between those practices and what went on in Nazi death camps. When faced with such analogies, we must ask in what ways they hold up and in what ways they do not. Are there relevant differences that suggest that the compared practices will have different effects? Are there better analogies than the ones being drawn?

Causal claims might also be supported by an argument called the *slippery slope* argument. The idea here is that what at first looks like one small step is just the beginning of a series of small steps that will be difficult or impossible to stop after we've taken the first one. J. Gay-Williams, in a reading included in Part 2, argues that administering lethal injections to pain-wracked terminally ill patients who ask for them is the beginning of such a slippery slope—and that at the bottom we will find ourselves ordering the deaths of undesirables as a matter of social policy.

Whether Gay-Williams is right about that is again something that is not for us to decide here. But as a general rule, we should scrutinize such arguments carefully.

Not all slopes are as slippery as they first appear. Perhaps there are very good reasons for taking the first step and very good reasons for not taking the second. Perhaps there are principled reasons for digging in our heels somewhere along the way and nothing to stop us from doing so.

Also, causal generalizations might be "supported" by a kind of *hand waving*. That is, the argument might boil down to a nonargument, something like "Everybody knows that . . ." To be sure, there are many things that everybody *does* know, and things that everybody knows are the best premises for an argument we can find. But we must be careful, especially when dealing with causal generalizations, and even more especially when dealing with causal generalizations about human behavior, to ask whether *anybody*, let alone everybody, really knows that they're true.

Moreover, the mere fact that we don't know that they're false is insufficient support for them. The proper response to ignorance is to try to learn more. If we must decide what to do before we can learn more, we must do the same kind of calculating that's required whenever we try to make a rational decision under conditions of uncertainty. That is, we must ask ourselves what we stand to gain and lose by acting on a belief we don't know to be true. (For an example of this kind of reasoning, see Ernest Van Den Haag's defense of capital punishment in Part 2.)

Finally, causal generalizations might be supported by inductive arguments based on things we *do* know. Because these arguments will not support their conclusions as strongly as well-designed studies can, they must be approached very carefully. At best, they can establish their conclusions as reasonable, perhaps even more reasonable than their competitors, given what we now know. But what we now know, we must remember, is incomplete. That is why well-designed studies are so important. They fill in the many gaps in current knowledge, and once those gaps are filled, we may find that what was once the most reasonable conclusion is false.

Two other kinds of general premises deserve consideration here. These are generalizations about the arguer's supporters and opponents. For example, you may come across the claim that social scientists agree that such and such is true. To make the argument valid, you must add a premise like "Whatever social scientists agree on is true," or the weaker "If social scientists agree on something, we should accept it as true." You might also hear someone argue that you should not accept opponents' arguments because the opponents are untrustworthy for one reason or another. Then you must add a premise like "Arguments by untrustworthy people are unsound."

The first two of these premises appeal to the *authority* of social scientists. Are they true? Not as they now stand. On the other hand, this variation probably is: "If social scientists agree on a generalization about human behavior that is based on strong research, we should accept it as true." Of course, not being social scientists ourselves, we cannot adequately evaluate their research, but if social scientists at respectable universities claim that their agreement is based on strong research, we are certainly justified in believing them. If their agreement is just a widely shared hunch, however, then their authority is lessened. And if their agreement is on a matter other than human behavior—if it is on the best brand of toothpaste, say—then their authority evaporates.

The third of the three premises, about untrustworthy opponents, is an example of an **ad hominem argument** (from the Latin phrase for "to the man"). Like appeals to authority, they may or may not be acceptable. The premise at hand is not. Granted, untrustworthy people often do present unsound arguments, but as long as they do present arguments, we should evaluate those arguments, not the arguers. (Even paranoids have enemies, as the saying has it.) On the other hand, when someone offers us nothing better than an unsupported claim rather than an argument, all we can go on is the trustworthiness of the person making the offer.

Trying Alternative Premises

In the previous sections, we saw that we sometimes have to change an argument's premise. Often, the reason is that the premise is questionable or downright false. Why change it rather than just reject the argument? The principle of charity gives us one answer. But we are interested in more than just fairness to our opponents. We are also interested in solving moral problems, and that interest should lead us to consider the strongest arguments possible.

For example, let's return to our argument against capital punishment. The first premise read

1.   If one punishment is more severe than another, it is wrong to impose the more severe one if it is not a better deterrent than the less severe one.

There seem to be many counterexamples to that statement. Is the threat of a ten-year prison term a greater deterrent than the threat of a nine-year prison term? Is the threat of life imprisonment a greater deterrent than the threat of a thirty-year prison term? Although we can't be absolutely sure about the answers to these questions, the more plausible answer is no. Still, we see nothing wrong in giving some people thirty-year sentences and others life sentences.

More generally, though, we can say this: Deterrence is not the only consideration in determining a just sentence. Another is our concern to protect other people from individuals convicted of serious crimes. Still another is our feeling that the severity of the punishment should reflect the severity of the crime. Presumably, people who argue against capital punishment on the grounds that it does not deter know that. So we might recast the premise this way:

1.   If two punishments equally reflect the severity of the crime and offer equal protection from the convicted criminal, it is wrong to impose the more severe one if it is not a better deterrent.

Notice how this procedure helps us focus on the important issues. By exposing points that the argument takes for granted, it allows us to evaluate them as well as the points it does not take for granted. Now we must add new premises—that life imprisonment protects others from convicted criminals as well as capital punishment protects them, and that life imprisonment reflects the severity of capital crimes as adequately as capital punishment does. And we must then evaluate them.

Moreover, we might want to evaluate the new version of the first premise. Why, we might ask, must punishment *always* reflect the severity of the crime? If we really believe that it must, shouldn't we have even more awful punishments than we now have? If a man brutally rapes and tortures a half dozen women before killing them, does that mean we should subject him to something equally horrible? Or should we recognize instead that there are moral limits to the severity of punishment regardless of other factors, and maybe those limits mean we should stop short of capital punishment?

In short, trying new premises helps us do more than just evaluate arguments. It helps us think clearly and thoroughly about the problems at hand.

Another example also helps show this. Sometimes we should try new premises because the ones we first added are not the only reasonable possibilities. That reason applies to one of the premises in the pro-abortion argument we looked at:

2.   A woman's right to control her body includes the right to have any medically approved medical procedure she and her doctor choose.

Perhaps people who defend the right to an abortion on the grounds of a woman's right to control her own body mean something else, like:

2.   A woman's right to control her body includes the right not to have her body used for purposes she does not want it used for.

In that case, we get a new intermediate conclusion:

3.   A woman has the right not to have her body used for purposes she does not want it used for as long as she does not harm another person.

Then we add this premise:

4.   A woman carrying an unwanted fetus is having her body used for purposes she does not want it used for.

And then we get this intermediate conclusion:

5.   Therefore, a woman has the right not to carry an unwanted fetus as long as she does not harm another person.

Whether this version or the original version of the argument is sound is, once again, not to be decided here. But looking at both can be important. Judith Jarvis Thomson's article, for example, focuses on the new interpretation of a woman's right to control her own body, not the original one, and it might make an important difference. The reason it might is that Thomson believes a woman has the right not to have her body used in a way she doesn't want it to be used even in some cases where an innocent person *is* harmed, even fatally. Thus, she defends a woman's right to have an abortion without the premise that fetuses are not persons.

Questions of Relevance

Whether a premise is really relevant to the moral issue at hand is, of course, an important matter. Much of the advice for evaluating arguments that we've been looking at has been closely connected to the question of relevance.

Most important has been the advice about supplying and evaluating implicit general premises. If the implicit general premise turns out to be false, that is often because an explicit premise is irrelevant. To pick an obvious example, remember the implicit premise in our sample *ad hominem* argument: Arguments by untrustworthy people are unsound. Any premise that requires a general premise like that is irrelevant. That is why we need not, in general, pay any attention to *ad hominem* arguments. It is also why the arguments we will find in the readings in Part 2 will not depend on many of the emotion-laden phrases we often find in the letters columns of local newspapers, phrases like "bra burners," "Bible thumpers," "secular humanists," "bleeding hearts," and "ultra-rightists."

Irrelevancies that are intended to distract our attention from the real issues are known as **red herrings**. Because red herrings often involve appeals to our emotions, many textbooks caution their readers to be extremely wary of emotional appeals. This is good advice, if not taken too far—especially in moral arguments. When emotion takes us where reason does not, appeals to emotion are certainly out of order. On the other hand, appeals to emotion are unavoidable in moral debate. Any argument in favor of voluntary euthanasia, for example, must appeal to our sympathy for pain-wracked terminally ill patients. Any argument in favor of capital punishment must appeal to our fear and loathing of brutal murderers. Such appeals will be there even if unintended. Important moral issues are emotional ones, and there is no getting around it.

But if we cannot totally separate emotion from moral argument, we can still question particular connections in particular cases. Are our emotions being whipped up by flamboyant language? By questionable claims? By sentimental anecdotes that are unrepresentative of most relevant cases? Is our attention being diverted from relevant facts? From important moral considerations like individual rights and obligations? If so, we are being victimized by red herrings.

We must also take care not to be victimized by another kind of irrelevance—the *straw man*. Sustained arguments for a position usually include criticisms of opposing arguments. If the opposing arguments are faithfully rendered, all is as it should be. But if they are unfaithfully rendered, the arguer is attacking a straw man. And whatever defects the straw man may have, they are irrelevant to what really matters—the opponent's real arguments. So one question you must always be careful to ask is this: Is *that* what the people on the other side are *really* saying?

Fallacies

A **fallacy** is an unreliable means of arguing that does not provide good reason for accepting the argument's conclusion. **Formal fallacies** are invalid deductive rules like those we looked at in the beginning of this chapter. **Informal fallacies**, on the other hand, are a mixed bag of unreliable strategies that people commonly tend to use. In general, informal fallacies arise in arguments that rely on hidden premises that are false or irrelevant or otherwise suspect. Although we did not introduce the term earlier, we did look at various informal fallacies when we discussed how to supply and evaluate missing premises. Here, for convenience, is a list of those informal fallacies with brief definitions and examples.

Ad Hominem *Argument*.   An attack on the opponent rather than the opponent's argument. Name calling and casting doubt on an opponent's character are the most common but not the only forms. For example, to say that men have no rightful say in abortion disputes would be to commit this fallacy. The same goes for saying that a fur seller's arguments against animal rights aren't worth hearing.

Faulty Analogy.   A misuse of an **argument by analogy**, which is an argument that two things that are alike in some respects must be alike in other respects. Suppose, for example, someone notes that tigers and hard-core pornography are alike in that both can be harmful to children. This is true, as far as it goes, even if the types of harm are quite different. But if he then goes on to conclude that pornography must be controlled in the same way as tigers—banned from private homes, say—he has carried the analogy too far. For one thing, there are constitutional protections regarding expression but none regarding the ownership of dangerous animals. For another, there are less drastic ways of protecting children from pornography than banning it from private homes.

Questionable Authority.   Supporting a conclusion by depending on the judgment of someone who is not a reliable authority on the subject at hand. Citing horror stories from supermarket tabloids to back up a point—unless it's a point about the tabloids themselves, of course—is an obvious example. The same could be said about most postings on Internet bulletin boards or an athlete's paid endorsement of cereal.

Begging the Question.   Assuming as a premise what you want to prove. If, for example, someone claims that all opponents of affirmative action are racist and then defends the point by saying, "If they weren't racist, they wouldn't oppose it," that person is begging the question.

Equivocation.   Implicit reliance on two different meanings of the same word to reach a conclusion. For example, it's been said on occasion that the preamble to the Declaration of Independence does not apply to women because it says "all men are created equal" rather than "all humans" or "all persons." But the word *men* in the document refers to both male and female humans, not just to males.

Hand Waving.   Claiming that something is true (or false) because everyone knows so. A classic case of hand waving is the following: "We don't need evidence to prove that capital punishment is a better deterrent to crime than life imprisonment. Everyone knows it—it's just common sense."

Hasty Generalization.   Reaching a general conclusion from a sample that is biased or too small. Some abortion opponents, for example, have argued that women who have abortions suffer great psychological trauma but defend their assertion by pointing to only a few isolated cases.

Appeal to Ignorance.   Arguing that a claim is true (or false) because we have no evidence proving otherwise. Arguing that global warming is (or is not) a compelling threat because nobody's proved that it isn't (or is) exemplifies such an appeal.

Post Hoc, Ergo Propter Hoc (*"after this, therefore because of this"*). Claiming that one thing is caused by another because it follows the other. Politicians, for example, like to take credit for every good thing that happens after they take office, when it's not always clear that their policies are responsible.

Red Herring.   An irrelevant issue introduced to distract attention from the issue at hand. Suppose, for example, someone presents an argument in favor of increasing welfare benefits to families with children, and you respond by saying, "Look at all the babies dying in abortion clinics. If you really cared about children, you'd be doing something about that." However sincere your convictions, you'd be committing this fallacy.

Slippery Slope.   Assuming that an action will lead to an unwanted outcome as the result of many small steps that will inevitably follow. Whether such an assumption is a fallacy depends on your justification for making it. For an obvious example of when it would be a fallacy, imagine someone arguing that having sex with some-one you don't plan to marry will eventually lead you to become a streetwalker—because it's one small step to having sex with someone you don't love, and another small step to having sex with multiple partners, and another small step to accepting expensive gifts for sex, and another small step to soliciting sex for money on the street.

Straw Man.   A distortion of an opponent's actual position. This is a very com-mon tactic that can be found in any controversy that arouses passion. In environ-mental debates, for example, we often hear it from both sides. Someone will argue that a proposed regulation is too expensive and will be met by the charge that he or she advocates the poisoning of children. Or someone will argue for better protection of endangered species and will be told he or she is saying owls matter more than people.

Although it is useful to keep these fallacies in mind, we should also point out that wrongly accusing an opponent of committing a fallacy can itself be considered a fallacy. For example, the fact that an opponent appeals to an authority does not auto-matically mean she has committed a fallacy. Many appeals to authority are justified. What matters is whether the alleged authority is a good authority on the topic at hand. Similarly, whether someone commits a fallacy by drawing an analogy depends on how strong the analogy is. For a third example, whether a claim that one thing causes another is a post hoc fallacy depends on the supporting evidence. When tobacco com-pany executives argue that scientists have established only a statistical link between smoking and cancer, not a causal link, they are the ones who commit the fallacy.

SUMMARY AND CONCLUSIONS

In a play by the seventeenth-century French playwright Molière, the main character is delighted to learn that he has been speaking prose for as long as he has been talking. One thing you might have learned during the course of this chapter is that you have been reasoning logically for as long as you have been thinking. But some people speak better prose than others, and some people reason more logically than others. In each case, what often makes the difference is a bit of reflection on what distinguishes good prose or logical reasoning, followed by a little practice.

This chapter has picked out some of the features that distinguish logical reasoning, and it has applied them to various moral arguments. So should you apply them to the moral arguments of Part 2. If you do, you will provide yourself with more than just a little practice. Before we turn to Part 2, though, we should make a few final remarks.

First, don't be intimidated by the task of evaluating arguments. You don't have to write out every argument and then rewrite it every time you think of an alter-native missing premise. All you have to do is *think* as you read or listen. And that holds not just for the readings in Part 2 but for any argument you encounter—in a newspaper, a conversation, another course, or anyplace else. Passive reading or listening is never good reading or listening, especially when the writer or speaker is trying to convince you of something.

Second, the techniques for evaluating arguments we have looked at are intended not only for other people's arguments but for our own too. Whenever we arrive at a conclusion, we do so for reasons, and our reasons may be good or bad, better or worse. It is important, then, that we challenge ourselves as well as others.

Third, this is a book in applied ethics, as its title makes clear. Although every text-book is (or at least should be) an exercise in applied logic (as well as applied prose), our basic concern is to come to grips with some important moral problems. And that means you should apply the material in *both* chapters of Part 1 to the material in Part 2. We want our moral conclusions to be based on both our most general moral principles and good reasoning.

Because this chapter has said little about those principles so far, it should close by tying them to what it has said. Each of the sample moral arguments we looked at contained at least one moral principle—about a woman's rights, the taking of innocent life, or the justification of punishment, to mention just three. Some were more general than others, but none was as general as the principle of utility, say, or respect for persons. This does not mean, though, that these most general principles have no important work to do in moral arguments. Why not?

For one thing, the less general principles are based on the most general ones. We accept them because we believe the most general ones require us to accept them. If we think that some kinds of punishment are unjustified, it's because we think them unfair or inconsistent with respect for persons or because we think they will not maximize utility. Also, if we think that there are legitimate exceptions to the less general principles, it's because we think that the most general ones require the exceptions. Thus, we justify white lies, for example, because a principle more general than honesty—the principle of utility, say—requires it. So these most general principles did play an important role in our sample arguments, even though we did not make them explicit.

Sometimes, however, they *must* be made explicit. That happens when a less general principle, or a proposed exception to a less general principle, is controversial. When that does happen, we need an argument for the principle or its proposed exception, and that will take us back to the most general principles. We will have to ask whether any of our most general principles support the controversial premise. If they don't, we can reject it. If they do, then we will have to ask whether any of our other most general principles give a conflicting answer. If they don't do that, we can accept the premise. If they do, we will have to ask which of the conflicting principles should take precedence.

That last question is a particularly difficult one to answer, and moral problems that turn on it are particularly difficult to resolve to everyone's satisfaction. Men and women of good will may, in the end, come to different resolutions because they cannot agree on which principle takes precedence. Not surprisingly, many of the problems of Part 2 turn on precisely that question, which is why they are still with us. But difficult is not the same as impossible, which is why many similar problems are no longer with us.

If we were writing this book thirty years ago, we might have included a chapter on civil disobedience—we might have looked at arguments for and against the view that people have the moral right to protest laws they consider unjust by peacefully and publicly violating those laws. Also, our chapter on discrimination would have been very different. Instead of looking at arguments for and against affirmative action, we might very well have been considering whether private employers have the right to discriminate *against* minorities and women. Today, such chapters would be unthinkable. The extraordinarily powerful moral arguments of people like Martin Luther King, Jr., have made them unthinkable. Perhaps in another thirty years, we will be able to make the same statement about some of the chapters in the book you are now reading.

PART 2

ISSUES

3

Sexual Morality

The Traditional View
The Libertarian View
Treating Sex Differently
Arguments for Sexual Libertarianism
Arguments against Sexual Libertarianism
Roger Scruton, "Sexual Morality"
Alan H. Goldman, "Plain Sex"
Michael Levin, "Why Homosexuality Is Abnormal"
Timothy F. Murphy, "Homosexuality and Nature"
CASE PRESENTATION, "Deception or Joke?"
CASE PRESENTATION, "AIDS Education"
CASE PRESENTATION, "Marriage and Civil Unions"
CASE PRESENTATION, "*Lawrence v. Texas*: Private Rights and
Public Morality"

During the 1960s and 1970s, the United States was abuzz with talk of the "new morality" and the "sexual revolution." Almost everywhere, people were discussing singles bars, casual sex, one-night stands, open marriage, unwed motherhood, creative divorce, cohabitation, group sex, teen sex, and sexual preference. Traditional sexual morality was breaking or had already broken down.

To traditionalists, the changes were at best disturbing and at worst alarming. They worried about the future of their children, of the family, and of society. What they saw when they looked around was moral decline. To those caught up in the revolution, on the other hand, the changes were liberating. When they looked around, they saw new options, new freedoms, new manners of expression, and fulfillment.

Many of you are likely to take the sexual revolution as much for granted as you take the American Revolution. Some of you may even wonder what all the fuss was about. Others may think of the old morality as quaint. You might ask: Were women really supposed to remain virgins until marriage? Did people really think that living together was immoral? Could a talented and beautiful movie star like Ingrid Bergman really be run out of Hollywood for having an affair with a married man? Did parents and universities really insist on separate dorms for male and female students?

Of course, others of you do not take the new morality for granted. Some of you probably agree totally with the traditionalists, despite the pressures you might feel from your peers. Some of you probably accept parts of the new morality but not others parts. Perhaps you believe in nonmarital sex but feel that the people involved should love each other. Perhaps you find nothing wrong with premarital sex but draw the line at adultery. Perhaps you accept total freedom when it comes to heterosexual sex but believe that homosexuality is immoral.

Such differences show that the victory of the sexual revolution was not total. Moreover, certain trends in today's world suggest that we may be in store for some counterrevolutionary changes. The risk of AIDS and other sexually transmitted diseases seems to be affecting the sexual behavior of both heterosexuals and homosexuals. The large number of teenage pregnancies is also causing doubts about the new morality. And some feminists have begun calling for a "new celibacy."

For these reasons and others, debate about sexual morality continues. The issues involved are many and complex. The best place to start, no doubt, is with the two extreme positions: the traditional and the libertarian.

THE TRADITIONAL VIEW

The traditional view can be put quite simply: All sex outside marriage is wrong. Although people have held the traditional view for a variety of reasons, its most influential line of defense comes from the Roman Catholic church.

As we saw in Part 1, Catholic moral teaching was greatly influenced by Aristotle, the ancient Greek philosopher whose ideas were incorporated into church doctrine by the medieval thinker St. Thomas Aquinas. Four of Aristotle's ideas are particularly important here. First, everything in nature has a purpose. Second, everything in nature has an essential nature—certain features that constitute its defining features. Third, everything in nature has its proper good. Fourth, something's natural purpose, its essential nature, and its proper good are intimately related.

That the Roman Catholic church believes that the natural purpose of sex is reproduction is well known. Equally well known is one consequence that the church draws from that belief—that artificial means of birth control are immoral. Less well known are other, related beliefs that are also directly related to sexual morality. These beliefs are spelled out in the Vatican's 1976 "Declaration on Certain Questions Concerning Sexual Ethics."

There, the authors stress what they take to be an essential characteristic of human beings—the ability to engage in fully human love, which includes genuine caring, sincerity, respect, commitment, and fidelity. Moreover, the declaration argues, fully human love does not stop at romantic love; it naturally evolves into parental love. That is, true human love is made complete by love for the children produced by that love. These facts about human sexuality are what set it apart from mere animal sexuality. They are also what make it more valuable. Equally important, they are what give human sex and sexual relationships their special dignity.

To engage in sex without love, then, or to engage in sex not open to the possibility of procreation, is to engage in sex that violates our essential nature and dignity. And since to violate our essential nature and dignity is to turn away from the proper human good, to engage in sex without love or sex not open to procreation is to engage in wrongful sex. This does not mean, however, that unmarried sex with love and without contraception is moral in the church's view. Given the changeableness of human desire and commitment, we need added guarantees of sincerity and fidelity. And only marriage can provide those guarantees.

THE LIBERTARIAN VIEW

According to the libertarian view, sex is an activity like any other—tennis, say, or conversation or studying—and what determines whether any sexual act is moral or immoral is no different from what determines whether any other act is moral or immoral. As long as the act involves no dishonesty, exploitation, or coercion, and as long as it does not violate any obligations to others, it is not immoral.

Consider premarital sex. Many things can make it immoral. If John tells Mary that he loves her and wants to take her home to meet his parents and she goes to bed with him as a result, John acts immorally if he doesn't mean what he tells her. If Mary has a venereal disease and does not warn John ahead of time, then she acts immorally. If John tries to coerce Mary into performing sexual acts she dislikes, then he acts immorally. But if neither of them is looking for anything more than a one-night stand, and if neither holds back any important information, and if neither resorts to any coercion or breaks any promise, and if neither violates any obligation to a third person, then neither does anything wrong.

Of course, we are assuming here that both John and Mary are adults. Children are incapable of the kind of informed consent required to ensure that they are not being exploited. But there are other things we need not assume. For example, we need not assume that the adults involved are of different sexes. Whatever holds for John and Mary also holds for John and Bill or for Jane and Mary. Nor need we assume that only *two* adults are involved. Group sex that violates none of our conditions is perfectly acceptable to the libertarian. Furthermore, we need not even assume that John and Mary are not close relatives, like brother and sister. Even incest is acceptable to the libertarian, as long as there is no dishonesty, coercion, or exploitation and as long as reliable means of contraception are used.

Similar remarks hold for adultery. Even though marriage involves the promise of fidelity, husbands and wives are perfectly free to release each other from their vows, just as we are all free to release one another from any other promise. If a married couple agrees that both members would be happier if they could have extramarital affairs, then they are morally free to do so—provided, of course, that they do not keep their marriage a secret from sexual partners who do not wish to have affairs with married people.

Arguments in favor of **sexual libertarianism** are basically of the "why not" sort. Why *shouldn't* sex be treated like any other activity? Why should we consider it moral to play tennis with somebody we don't love but immoral to have sex with somebody we don't love? Why should we consider it moral to eat lunch with somebody of the same sex but immoral to have sex with that very same person? Why should we be permitted to go to a movie purely for pleasure but not have sex purely for pleasure? What's so different about sex that it requires such special rules? Why can't sexual morality be determined by the same general moral principles—the principle of utility, respect for persons, the golden rule, and so forth—that determine right and wrong in the rest of our lives?

TREATING SEX DIFFERENTLY

We have already looked at one answer to the libertarian's questions, the one offered by the Vatican. Not surprisingly, sexual libertarians reject it. Many of their reasons for rejecting it will become apparent throughout this chapter, but for now, let's just mention one. Libertarians generally feel that it is up to each individual to determine his or her own good. Human dignity lies in our capacity to pursue our own good as we see fit—provided we do not interfere with another person's pursuit of his or her own good—not in adhering to any particular sexual morality. Sex between consenting adults is a private matter, and private matters are matters of individual conscience.

Many other answers to the libertarians' arguments focus on the social context of sex. The sex lives of any particular individuals may be private, but the widespread adoption of any particular sexual morality can have far-reaching social ramifications. Let's look at several of these issues.

Venereal Diseases and AIDS

Gonorrhea, syphilis, and other venereal diseases are familiar hazards of sex. Although some can be extremely serious—even fatal—if left untreated, they *are* treatable. Because they are, fear of contracting them rarely interferes with most people's sex lives. When genital herpes burst on the scene in the seventies, however, fear did begin to play a role in many people's sexual decisions. Although not as dangerous as syphilis, herpes is a chronic condition.

In the eighties, a new and far more dangerous threat appeared—AIDS (acquired immune deficiency syndrome). There is no known cure for AIDS, nor has a vaccine been developed to prevent its spread, and that leaves its victims with the hopeless prospect of a protracted, agonizing death and leaves potential victims with a terrifying question mark.

Although there is much controversy over how AIDS is transmitted, five means of transmission are well established: anal sex, vaginal sex, intravenous needles and syringes, blood transfusions, and pregnancy. (Other feared possibilities, like "deep" kissing and eating utensils, have not been established as means of transmitting the disease.) Because of the controversy over transmission of AIDS, there is a corresponding controversy over its potential victims. Historically, the groups facing the highest risk in the United States have been male homosexuals, intravenous drug users, hemophiliacs, the sex partners of members of these three groups, and children of women at risk when pregnant.

AIDS has already taken a terrible toll among the homosexual population, and homosexual sex between men still accounts for about 42 percent of new infections according to the Centers for Disease Control. But by 2000, one-third of all new AIDS infections resulted from heterosexual sex and another one-fourth from injection drug use. The most rapid rate of increase in infection in recent years has been among young women and women of color. Whether AIDS can or cannot be spread by casual contact and whether all of us or only those of us in high-risk groups need be immediately concerned for our own safety, AIDS does raise serious concerns about sexual morality. Given what we do know, sexual promiscuity—both heterosexual and homosexual—increases the risk of AIDS, not only to ourselves, but to our partners and future children.

At the minimum, then, people who cannot be certain about their sexual partners should engage in "safe" sex. That is, they should use condoms. Even libertarians can agree on that point. Other people go further. Some argue that the threat of AIDS should cause us to return to traditional sexual morality. Others claim that we need not go that far. Perhaps we should retreat from promiscuity, they say, but monogamous relationships among unmarried people can be just as safe as among married people. Still others claim that the threat of AIDS does not even require monogamy, as long as we do not engage in sex with people in high-risk groups.

Threats to the Family

One of the most alarming trends in recent years is the sharp rise in single-parent households. Although different people find different aspects of the trend alarming, one concern is shared by all. Most single parents are women, and single women and their children are often poor. As much as 40 percent of the homeless population in the nation consists of children. Most are with single mothers, although economic difficulties also account for a recent surge in homeless families.

That many single parents are teenagers is another concern shared by all. Whether they are forced to drop out of school or manage to continue their educations, teenage motherhood places a great burden on them, their children, and society.

The causes of single parenthood are complex. Any list of contributing factors would have to include a variety of social conditions, including, most notably, poverty. But nothing can be more evident than this: no sex, no children. Another point is equally evident: the fewer the divorces, the fewer the single parents. And it is these two points that critics of sexual libertarianism stress.

Regarding the first, they say that the spread of the sexual revolution from adults to teenagers was inevitable. When unmarried rock stars and other teen heroes openly live together and have children, when the media are filled with representations of casual sex, how can teenagers not be affected? And given their lack of maturity and responsibility, the normal confusions of adolescence, and various pressures that many teens feel, how could we have expected anything less than an explosion of teen pregnancies?

The connection between the sexual revolution and divorce may seem more tenuous, but to some people, it is no less real. If sex outside marriage is freely available and without moral stigma, if sexual adventure and variety are prized at least as much as monogamy, if love and commitment are no longer seen as natural accompaniments to sex, then marital ties inevitably weaken.

What makes sex different, according to this line of argument, then, is the intimate connection between sexual behavior and the health of the family, plus the social costs that the decline of the family entails. If sexual morality concerned only the individuals involved in any particular sexual act, then perhaps we could treat sex like tennis. But it doesn't, so we can't.

Personal Fulfillment

For those of us with no aspirations to be Pete Sampras or Venus Williams, tennis is little more than an enjoyable game, a pleasant way to get fresh air and exercise, or a welcome opportunity for camaraderie. Even if such things are important to us, and even if tennis is our favorite way to get them, the role of tennis in our lives remains relatively limited.

Can we say the same about sex? Hardly. For one thing, there is a strong biological component to our sexual lives. Thus, both biological and behavioral scientists talk of sex *drives* as well as desires. For another, sexual development cannot be separated from psychological development. How we learn to deal with our sexuality is crucial to the kind of person we become, and our sexual identity is a critical feature of our personal identity. For yet another, our sexual relationships are among the most powerful and influential relationships we can have.

Critics of sexual libertarianism often charge that to treat sex like any other activity is to miss everything that is important about sex and its role in our lives. In particular, it is to ignore its importance to personal growth and fulfillment. Any sexual morality must take account of that fact. Such critics don't necessarily call for a return to traditional morality, but they do insist that we view sex as more than merely a pleasant activity. What we should do is ask ourselves questions like these: Does our sex life contribute to our sense of worth and dignity? Is it consistent with our most important goals in life? Does it reflect the kind of person we most want to be? Is it the sex life of a mature, well-adjusted person? Does it help us develop or maintain the character traits that most matter to us? Does it enhance our lives as much as it might? Does it help us build the kind of relationships we most value?

To ask such questions is to steer a middle course between the sexual traditionalist and the sexual libertarian. The questions are, after all, very much in the spirit of the Vatican declaration. The concerns they raise—fundamental values, personal dignity and fulfillment, the quality of our lives and relationships—are the same. But unlike the authors of the declaration, many people who insist that we ask these questions do not assume that our answers must follow any particular line. In that respect, they are more like the libertarians. For example, they allow that many people engaged in loving homosexual relationships can answer yes to all these questions. So can many unmarried heterosexuals with active sex lives.

People who support this way of treating sex, then, are like the traditionalists in that they do not treat sex like any other activity, but they are like the libertarians in that they make room for a variety of personal decisions about sex.

The Naturalness Argument

Another line of attack against sexual libertarianism also shares certain features with the Vatican declaration. According to this line, sex organs and sexual activity are natural phenomena, and like any other natural phenomenon, they have their own natural manifestations and purposes. In that case, we can distinguish natural from unnatural sex and natural from unnatural use of our sex organs. And since what is natural is moral and what is unnatural is immoral, we can distinguish moral from immoral sex.

Although the Vatican declaration applies this reasoning to a variety of sexual behaviors—masturbation and the use of contraception, for instance, as well as homosexuality—many people confine it to homosexuality alone.

What is it that makes homosexuality unnatural? Various answers are given. Homosexual behavior violates the laws of nature, some people say. Or it is an abnormal occurrence in nature. Or it involves an unnatural use of sex organs.

Libertarian Objections

Many libertarians share some of the concerns we have just looked at. They do not, however, conclude that these concerns justify a retreat from full sexual freedom. Sexual libertarians do not advocate moral irresponsibility, they say, but only sexual freedom. And sexual libertarianism can be just as morally responsible as sexual traditionalism.

Consider the AIDS threat. Certainly, libertarians say, we all have an obligation to avoid behavior that might cause us to become carriers of the virus and pass it on to others. And just as certainly, that obligation involves taking necessary precautions like using condoms when we cannot be sure about our sexual partners. But as long as we do take such necessary precautions, we have no obligation to turn to chastity or heterosexual monogamy.

As for teen pregnancy and single parenthood, sexual libertarians argue that the blame for these problems does not rest with them. As long as they behave responsibly, they cannot be held accountable for the irresponsibility of others. Nor should they be morally required to restrict their sex lives. The solution to such social problems lies in education, easy access to birth control counseling, and social programs to alleviate poverty and hopelessness—not in the restriction of sexual freedom.

Libertarians also point out that about half of all women and children experiencing homelessness are fleeing domestic violence. As many of those relationships were traditional marriages, there must be other explanations for this homelessness and poverty than the availability of sex outside marriage. Perhaps women are less likely now to tolerate domestic violence and instead seek other options.

What about personal fulfillment? Many libertarians might well agree with many of the remarks in that argument, as long as each individual is free to supply his or her own answers to the recommended questions. Others, though, might wonder why sex need be taken so seriously. If Jane is satisfied enough with her life, even though she takes a very casual approach to sex, why should she feel any more pressure to involve herself in any soul searching about sex than about any other aspect of her life? No doubt sex and sexual relationships are very important to many people, but if other people feel differently, who's to say they shouldn't?

Finally, there is the naturalness argument. Here, libertarians remain totally unimpressed. Does homosexuality really violate the laws of nature? No, because *nothing* can violate the laws of nature. Natural laws are not like criminal laws. They describe how the world actually works. They do not tell us how we ought to behave. Everything that happens, then, must be in accord with natural law. Is homosexuality an abnormal occurrence in nature? Perhaps, but that does not make it immoral. After all, great genius, great basketball talent, and great musical ability are even more abnormal, but we prize them when they occur, not condemn them. Does homosexuality involve the unnatural use of our sex organs? Again, perhaps, but how does that differ from using our ears for holding earrings, our eyes for giving playful winks, or our thumbs for hitching rides?

Advocates of **civil unions** for homosexual couples also point out that many of those relationships are as stable as heterosexual marriages, even though the unions are not traditional relationships. These advocates suggest that the values of traditional marriages are highly regarded in these civil unions and should be encouraged, regardless of the sexual preference of the couple. Many of these couples also adopt children who are otherwise difficult to place, including the children of drug addicts and AIDS-infected babies. Thus, they promote traditional family values, even though they are outside the definition of a traditional heterosexual marriage.

ARGUMENTS FOR
SEXUAL LIBERTARIANISM

1. *Sex is a private matter.*

POINT: "Whatever goes on between consenting adults in private is nobody's business but their own, and that holds as much for sex as for anything else. Why should anybody even care whether Mary has fifteen lovers or none, whether Jack prefers sex with Bill to sex with Jane, or whether married couples like to 'swing' with other married couples? Just because you personally disapprove of such things doesn't make them wrong. We all have the right to live our lives as we see fit as long as we don't interfere with the rights of others to live their lives as they see fit. Promiscuous people, homosexuals, and swingers don't tell you how to live your life. Don't tell them how to live theirs."

COUNTERPOINT: "Sex isn't nearly as private as you think. All of society is affected by the sexual revolution you're so fond of. Who do you think has to pick up the tab for all the illegitimate children your libertarianism is giving us? The taxpayers. And who has to pick up the tab for AIDS research? The taxpayers. And who has to live with all the abortion mills, the fear of AIDS, and the worry over how all of this free sex will affect our children? All of us."

2. *You can't turn the clock back on the sexual revolution.*

POINT: "Whether you approve of what's happened to sexual morality or not, one thing's certain: You can't turn the clock back. Once people get a taste of freedom—sexual or any other kind—they don't want to give it up. Do you really think that sexually active unmarried people are going to turn to celibacy, or that homosexuals are going to deny their sexual identity and pretend to be something they're not, or that married couples who feel that open marriage works better for them than fidelity are going to settle for fidelity? Let's face it. Human nature just doesn't work that way."

COUNTERPOINT: "Maybe not, but that doesn't make the sexual revolution right. The whole point of morality is to curb some of the excesses of human nature, to try to get people to exercise their freedoms responsibly. Besides, nobody expects to turn everything around overnight. The point is to insist that certain behavior is wrong, to make young people understand the proper place of sex in their lives, and to get them to make responsible choices about sex. It'll take some time, but eventually the changes can come."

3. *Curbing sexual freedom is unfair.*

POINT: "You're neglecting an important point here—fairness. The crux of the issue isn't just that people don't want to turn back the clock but that it's *unfair* to make them turn it back. You're comfortable with your traditional morality, but to other people, it can be a straitjacket. For them, it's impossible to live fulfilling lives under those conditions. The worst victims, of course, would be the homosexuals. What are they supposed to do—live a heterosexual lie or give up sex and love altogether? But they wouldn't be the only victims. Some people are totally unsuited to marriage. Others are totally unsuited to monogamy. They have as much right to fulfilling sex lives as you do."

COUNTERPOINT: "Nobody has the right to seek fulfillment immorally. And there's nothing unfair about making people turn away from immoral behavior. I'm not denying that traditional sexual morality is more demanding for some people than it is for others, but that doesn't make it any different from any other area of moral concern. Pathological liars and kleptomaniacs have a harder time doing right than the rest of us do, but our sympathy for them can't lead us to approve of their lies and thefts. The same holds for homosexuals. We can sympathize, but we can't condone."

4. *Traditional sexual morality is hypocritical.*

POINT: "What you're really calling for is a return to hypocrisy. Let's all pretend to be faithful heterosexual monogamists while we do whatever we feel like doing on the sly. Adultery, premarital sex, promiscuity, and homosexuality aren't new, you know. The only thing that's changed is that people are more honest about them now. And that's a change for the good."

COUNTERPOINT: "Adultery, premarital sex, promiscuity, and homosexuality may not be new, but they're sure a lot more prevalent than they used to be. And you can thank your precious honesty for that. Once people start being proud about things like that, once they start going public about them, it has to start affecting other people's behavior. They start thinking, 'If it's good enough for Dick and Jane, maybe I should give it a try.' In other words, a little bit of hypocrisy is a good thing. You don't want armed robbers telling their kids there's nothing wrong with armed robbery, do you? Well, I don't want unwed mothers telling their kids there's nothing wrong with premarital sex."

ARGUMENTS AGAINST
SEXUAL LIBERTARIANISM

1. *Sexual libertarianism undermines public morality.*

POINT: "Morality is like law. Once you encourage disrespect for a particular law, you encourage disrespect for all laws. And once you encourage disrespect for sexual morality, you encourage disrespect for all of morality. That's why it's no surprise that the sexual revolution brought with it an explosion of pornography and abortion. It's also why I wouldn't be surprised to learn that people don't care as much about loyalty and honesty as they used to. After all, a large part of your revolution is that marriage vows don't have to mean anything."

COUNTERPOINT: "Sexual libertarianism isn't about disrespect for morality. It's about moral change. If you want to talk about disrespect for morality, the real culprit is your traditional sexual morality. That's a morality that people won't adhere to, and a morality like that is bound to breed disrespect. And don't confuse sexual libertarianism with disloyalty and dishonesty. A husband and wife who agree that affairs with other people will make their marriage better aren't being disloyal to each other—and they're certainly not being dishonest."

2.   *Sex without love is empty.*

POINT: "One of the biggest problems with your view is that it erases the connection between sex and love. Even you have to admit that sex with someone you love is better than sex with someone you don't love. With someone you love, sex isn't mere empty pleasure. It's communication, it's sharing, it's an expression of affection and care. It *means* something. The sex that you advocate means nothing at all. It's sterile, and it adds nothing of worth to our lives. What you're really doing is reducing human sexuality to animal sexuality. We might as well be rabbits, according to you. But we're not rabbits, and because we're not, loveless sex can't possibly satisfy us or be fulfilling for us."

COUNTERPOINT: "First of all, I'm not advocating any kind of sex. All I'm advocating is people's moral right to engage in the kinds of sex they prefer as long as they don't hurt anyone. Second, who are you to declare that the kind of sex you prefer is the best kind of sex for anyone else? Third, even if you're right—even if loving sex is better than loveless sex—what morally important difference does that make? Some cars are better than others, but there's nothing immoral about driving the inferior ones. Or to pick an even closer analogy, celebrating good news with someone you love is probably better than celebrating good news with someone you don't love, but nobody's going to say you're doing wrong if you do celebrate good news with someone you don't love."

3.   *Sexual libertarianism undermines marriage.*

POINT: "If society adopts your position, we might as well forget about the institution of marriage. Unmarried people will have no good reason to get married because sex will be freely available. Even having children won't count as a good reason any more, as it becomes more and more acceptable to be an unmarried parent. And married people will have little reason to stay married. After all, once marital fidelity goes, there goes the most important bond between husband and wife. And even if some kind of bond remains, how can it stand up against the constant temptations that married people will face? Or the jealousies? Or the insecurities?"

COUNTERPOINT: "Aren't you being a little too cynical? People get married for lots of reasons other than sex, and they stay married because of a variety of bonds and intimacies. I'm not going to deny that sexual libertarianism can have some negative effects on marriage, but I *am* going to deny that the effects are all negative.

For one thing, people with sexual experience before marriage are less likely to confuse sex with love, and that makes it less likely that they'll choose their spouses unwisely. For another, they're less likely to feel they've missed something before getting married, and that should help protect them from temptation. And for still another, some marriages actually gain from being open to extramarital affairs. If married people feel the need for sexual variety, the possibility of having an open marriage can remove a reason for divorce."

4. *Sexual libertarianism is turning society upside down.*

POINT: "Your views have led to a number of crazy consequences. I'm not just talking about such tragedies as teen mothers, but things like the gay rights movement. First we have homosexuals demanding the right to teach in elementary schools, then we have homosexual couples demanding the right to adopt children, then we have them demanding that homosexual 'spouses' be included in family medical plans and the like. I have no idea where all this is ultimately heading, but it's certainly not in the right direction. We can't let children grow up believing that homosexuality is just another lifestyle, and we can't have society treating homosexual relationships like real marriages. No society can survive that."

COUNTERPOINT: "Why not? If homosexuality isn't immoral to begin with, what's wrong with giving homosexuals the same rights as heterosexuals? If you're afraid that we'd end up raising an entire generation of homosexual children, you're just being unrealistic. Besides, you're mixing up two different issues. Whether homosexuality is moral is one thing. Whether homosexual relationships should have the same legal status as heterosexual marriages is another."

Sexual Morality

Roger Scruton

In this essay, taken from Chapter 11 of his book *Sexual Desire,* British philosopher Roger Scruton argues for the traditional view of sexual morality. Earlier in the chapter, he develops a general moral view based on Aristotle's *Nichomachean Ethics.* Among the most important features of his view are the following:

First, morality is a constraint on practical reasoning. That is, morality rejects certain kinds of behavior even though individuals might have many prudent reasons for engaging in them.

Second, the goal of human conduct is *eudaimonia*—happiness, or fulfillment—which requires both physical health and the flourishing of the individual as a rational being. The goal of morality is to develop in the individual the dispositions—**virtues**—that lead to his or her happiness.

Third, the best model of moral reasoning is moral education. In educating our children to develop virtuous dispositions, we are teaching them to be critical of their immediate desires and to desire what is most reasonable to desire so that they will flourish and live fulfilled adult lives. In doing so, we think in terms of general human conditions as well as in terms of the individual conditions of our children. Likewise, in our own moral reasoning, we must ask ourselves not only how to achieve our own individual goals but also what goals we, as human beings, ought to have. In other words, we must think in terms of interpersonal values as well as personal preferences.

In the following selection, he applies this general view to sexual morality.

We must now attempt to apply the Aristotelian strategy to the subject-matter of this book, and ask whether there is such a thing as sexual virtue, and, if so, what is it, and how is it acquired? Clearly, sexual desire, which is an interpersonal attitude with the most far-reaching consequences for those who are joined by it, cannot be morally neutral. On the contrary, it is in the experience of sexual desire that we are most vividly conscious of the distinction between virtuous and vicious impulses, and most vividly aware that, in the choice between them, our happiness is at stake.

The Aristotelian strategy enjoins us to ignore the actual conditions of any particular person's life, and to look only at the permanent features of human nature. We know that people feel sexual desire; that they feel erotic love, which may grow from desire; that they may avoid both these feelings, by dissipation or self-restraint. Is there anything to be said about desire, other than that it falls within the general scope of the virtue of temperance, which enjoins us to desire only what reason approves?

The first, and most important, observation to be made is that the capacity for love in general, and for erotic love in particular, is a virtue. . . . I [have] tried to show that erotic love involves an element of mutual self-enhancement; it generates a sense of the irreplaceable value, both of the other and of the self, and of the activities which bind them. To receive and to give this love is to achieve something of incomparable value in the process of self-fulfillment. It is to gain the most powerful of all interpersonal *guarantees;* in erotic love the subject becomes conscious of the full reality of his personal existence, not only in his own eyes, but in the eyes of another. Everything that he is and values gains sustenance from his love, and every project receives a meaning beyond the moment. All that exists for us as mere hope and hypothesis—the attachment to life and to the body—achieves under the rule of *erōs* the aspect of a radiant certainty. Unlike the cold glances of approval, admiration and pride, the glance of love sees value

precisely in that which is the source of anxiety and doubt: in the merely contingent, merely "empirical," existence of the flesh, the existence which we did not choose, but to which we are condemned. It is the answer to man's fallen condition. . . .

To receive erotic love, however, a person must be able to give it: or if he cannot, the love of others will be a torment to him, seeking from him that which he cannot provide, and directing against him the fury of a disappointed right. It is therefore unquestionable that we have reason to acquire the capacity for erotic love, and, if this means bending our sexual impulses in a certain direction, that will be the direction of sexual virtue. Indeed, the argument of the last two chapters has implied that the development of the sexual impulse towards love may be impeded: there are sexual habits which are vicious, precisely in neutralising the capacity for love. The first thing that can be said, therefore, is that we all have reason to avoid those habits and to educate our children not to possess them.

Here it may be objected that not every love is happy, that there are many—Anna Karenina, for example, or Phaedra—whose capacity for love was the cause of their downfall. But we must remind ourselves of the Aristotelian strategy. In establishing that courage or wisdom is a virtue, the Aristotelian does not argue that the possession of these virtues is in every particular circumstance bound to be advantageous. . . .

It is not the particular personal tragedy but the generality of the human condition that determines the basis of sexual morality. Tragedy and loss are the rare but necessary outcomes of a process which we all have reason to undergo. (Indeed, it is part of the point of tragedy that it divorces in our imagination the right and the good from the merely prudential: that it sets the value of life against the value of mere survival.) We wish to know, in advance of any particular experience, which dispositions a person must have if he is successfully to express himself in sexual desire and to be fulfilled in his sexual endeavours. Love is the fulfillment of desire, and therefore love is its *telos*. A life of celibacy may also be fulfilled; but, assuming the general truth that most of us have a powerful, and perhaps overwhelming, urge to make love, it is in our interests to ensure that love—and not some other thing—is made.

Love, I have argued, is prone to jealousy, and the object of jealousy is defined by the thought of the beloved's desire. Because jealousy is one of the greatest of psychical catastrophes, involving the possible ruin of both partners, a morality based in the need for erotic love must forestall and eliminate jealousy. It is in the deepest human interest, therefore, that we form the habit of fidelity. This habit is natural and normal; but it is also easily broken, and the temptation to break it is contained in desire itself—in the element of generality which tempts us always to experiment, to verify, to detach ourselves from that which is too familiar in the interest of excitement and risk. Virtuous desire is faithful; but virtuous desire is also an artefact, made possible by a process of moral education which we do not, in truth, understand in its complexity.

If that observation is correct, a whole section of traditional sexual morality must be upheld. The fulfillment of sexual desire defines the nature of desire: *to telos phuseis estin*. And the nature of desire gives us our standard of normality. There are enormous varieties of human sexual conduct, and of "common-sense" morality: some societies permit or encourage polygamy, others look with indifference upon premarital intercourse, or regard marriage itself as no more than an episode in a relation that pre-exists and perhaps survives it. But no society, and no "common-sense" morality... looks with favour upon promiscuity or infidelity, unless influenced by a doctrine of "emancipation" or "liberation" which is dependent for its sense upon the very conventions which it defies. Whatever the institutional forms of human sexual union, and whatever the range of permitted partners, sexual desire is itself inherently "nuptial": it involves concentration upon the embodied existence of the other, leading through tenderness to the "vow" of erotic love. It is a telling observation that the civilisation which has most tolerated the institution of polygamy—the Islamic—has also, in its erotic literature, produced what are perhaps the intensest and most poignant celebrations of monogamous love, precisely through the attempt to capture, not the institution of marriage, but the human datum of desire.[1]

The nuptiality of desire suggests, in its turn, a natural history of desire: a principle of development which defines the "normal course" of sexual education. "Sexual maturity" involves incorporating the sexual impulse into the personality, and so making sexual desire into an expression of the subject himself, even though it is, in the heat of action, a force which also overcomes him. If the Aristotelian approach to these things is as plausible as I think it is, the virtuous habit will also have the character of a "mean": it will involve the disposition to desire what is desirable, despite the competing impulses of animal lust (in which the intentionality of desire may be demolished) and timorous frigidity (in which the sexual impulse is impeded altogether). Education is directed towards the special kind of temperance which shows itself, sometimes as chastity, sometimes as fidelity, sometimes as passionate desire, according to the "right judgement" of the subject. In wanting what is judged to be desirable, the virtuous person wants what may also be loved, and what may therefore be obtained without hurt or humiliation.

Virtue is a matter of degree, rarely attained in its completion, but always admired. Because traditional sexual education has pursued sexual virtue, it is worthwhile summarising its most important features, in order to see the power of the idea that underlies and justifies it.

The most important feature of traditional sexual education is summarised in anthropological language as the "ethic of pollution and taboo."[2] The child was taught to regard his body as sacred, and as subject to pollution by misperception or misuse. The sense of pollution is by no means a trivial side-effect of the "bad sexual encounter": it may involve a penetrating disgust, at oneself, one's body and one's situation, such as is experienced by the victim of rape. Those sentiments—which arise from our "fear of the obscene"—express the tension contained within the experience of embodiment. At any moment we can become "mere body," the self driven from its incarnation, and its habitation ransacked. The most important root idea of personal morality is that I am in my body, not (to borrow Descartes' image) as a pilot in a ship, but as an incarnate self. My body is identical with me, and sexual purity is the precious guarantee of this.

Sexual purity does not forbid desire: it simply ensures the status of desire as an interpersonal feeling. The child who learns "dirty habits" detaches his sex from himself, sets it outside himself as something curious and alien. His fascinated enslavement to the body is also a withering of desire, a scattering of erotic energy and a loss of union with the other. Sexual purity sustains the subject of desire, making him present as a self in the very act which overcomes him.

. . . The purely human redemption which is offered to us in love is dependent, in the last analysis, upon public recognition of the value of chastity, and of the sacrilege involved in a sexual impulse that wanders free from the controlling impulse of respect. The "pollution" of the prostitute is not that she gives herself for money, but that she gives herself to those whom she hates or despises. This is the "wound" of unchastity, which cannot be healed in solitude by the one who suffers it, but only by his acceptance into a social order which confines the sexual impulse to the realm of intimate relations. The chaste person sustains the ideal of sexual innocence, by giving honourable form to chastity as a way of life. Through his example, it becomes not foolish but admirable to ignore the promptings of a desire that brings no intimacy or fulfillment. Chastity is not a private policy, followed by one individual alone for the sake of his peace of mind. It has a wider and more generous significance: it attempts to draw others into complicity, and to sustain a social order that confines the sexual impulse to the personal sphere. . . .

The child was traditionally brought up to achieve sexual fulfillment only *through* chastity, which is the condition which surrounds him on his first entering the adult world—the world of commitments and obligations. At the same time, he was encouraged to ponder certain "ideal objects" of desire. These, presented to him under the aspect of an idealised physical beauty, were never *merely* beautiful, but also endowed with the moral attributes that fitted them for love. This dual inculcation of "pure" habits and "ideal" love might seem, on the face of it, to be unworthy of the name of education. Is it not, rather, like the mere *training* of a horse or a dog, which arbitrarily forbids some things and fosters others, without offering the first hint of

a reason why? And is it not the distinguishing mark of education that it engages with the rational nature of its recipient, and does not merely mould him indifferently to his own understanding of the process? Why, in short, is this moral education, rather than a transference into the sexual sphere—as Freud would have it—of those same processes of interdiction that train us to defecate, not in our nappies, but in a porcelain pot?

The answer is clear. The cult of innocence is an attempt to *generate* rational conduct, by incorporating the sexual impulse into the self-activity of the subject. It is an attempt to impede the impulse, until such time as it may attach itself to the interpersonal project that leads to its fulfillment: the project of union with another person, who is wanted not merely for his body, but for the person who is this body. Innocence is the disposition to avoid sexual encounter, except with the person whom one may fully desire. Children who have lost their innocence have acquired the habit of gratification through the body alone, in a state of partial or truncated desire. Their gratification is detached from the conditions of personal fulfillment and wanders from object to object with no settled tendency to attach itself to any, pursued all the while by a sense of the body's obscene dominion. "Debauching of the innocent" was traditionally regarded as a most serious offence, and one that offered genuine *harm* to the victim. The harm in question was not physical, but moral: the undermining of the process which prepares the child to enter the world of *erōs*. . . .

The personal and the sexual can become divorced in many ways. The task of sexual morality is to unite them, to sustain thereby the intentionality of desire, and to prepare the individual for erotic love. Sexual morality is the morality of embodiment: the posture which strives to unite us with our bodies, precisely in those situations when our bodies are foremost in our thoughts. Without such a morality the human world is subject to a dangerous divide, a gulf between self and body, at the verge of which all our attempts at personal union falter and withdraw. Hence the prime focus of sexual morality is not the attitude to others, but the attitude to one's own body and its uses. Its aim is to safeguard the integrity of our embodiment. Only on that condition, it is thought, can we inculcate either innocence in the young or fidelity in the adult. Such habits are, however, only one part of sexual virtue. Traditional morality has combined its praise of them with a condemnation of other things—in particular of the habits of lust and perversion. And it is not hard to find the reason for these condemnations.

Perversion consists precisely in a diverting of the sexual impulse from its interpersonal goal, or towards some act that is intrinsically destructive of personal relations and of the values that we find in them. The '"dissolution" of the flesh, which the Marquis de Sade regarded as so important an element in the sexual aim, is in fact the dissolution of the soul; the perversions described by de Sade are not so much attempts to destroy the flesh of the victim as to rid his flesh of its personal meaning, to wring out, with the blood, the rival perspective. That is true in one way or another of all perversion, which can be simply described as the habit of finding a sexual release that avoids or abolishes the *other*, obliterating his embodiment with the obscene perception of his body. Perversion is narcissistic, often solipsistic, involving strategies of replacement which are intrinsically destructive of personal feeling. Perversion therefore prepares us for a life without personal fulfillment, in which no human relation achieves foundation in the acceptance of the other, as this acceptance is provided by desire.

Lust may be defined as a genuine sexual desire, from which the goal of erotic love has been excluded, and in which whatever tends towards that goal—tenderness, intimacy, fidelity, dependence—is curtailed or obstructed. There need be nothing perverted in this. Indeed the special case of lust which I have discussed under the title of Don Juanism, in which the project of intimacy is constantly abbreviated by the flight towards another sexual object, provides one of our paradigms of desire. Nevertheless, the traditional condemnation of lust is far from arbitrary, and the associated contrast between lust and love far from a matter of convention. Lust is also a habit, involving the disposition to give way to desire, without regard to any personal relation with the object. (Thus perversions are all forms of lust even though lust is not in itself a perversion.) Naturally, we all feel the promptings of lust, but the rapidity with which sexual acts become sexual habits, and the catastrophic effect of a sexual act which cannot be remembered without shame or humiliation, give

us strong reasons to resist them, reasons that Shakespeare captured in these words:

> Th'expence of Spirit in a waste of shame
> Is lust in action, and till action, lust
> Is perjur'd, murdrous, blouddy, full of
>   blame,
> Savage, extreame, rude, cruell, not to trust,
> Injoyd no sooner but dispised straight,
> Past reason hunted, and no sooner had,
> Past reason hated as a swollowed bayt,
> On purpose layd to make the taker mad:
> Mad in pursuit and in possession so,
> Had, having, and in quest to have, extreame,
> A blisse in proofe, and prov'd, a very woe,
> Before a joy proposd, behind, a dreame,
>   All this the world well knowes, yet none
>   knowes well
>   To shun the heaven that leads men to this
>   hell.

In addition to the condemnation of lust and perversion, however, some part of traditional sexual education can be seen as a kind of sustained war against fantasy. It is undeniable that fantasy can play an important part in all our sexual doings, and even the most passionate and faithful lover may, in the act of love, rehearse to himself other scenes of sexual abandon than the one in which he is engaged. Nevertheless, there is truth in the contrast (familiar, in one version, from the writings of Freud)[3] between fantasy and reality, and in the sense that the first is in some way destructive of the second. Fantasy replaces the real, resistant, objective world with a pliant substitute—and that, indeed, is its purpose. Life in the actual world is difficult and embarrassing. Most of all it is difficult and embarrassing in our confrontation with other people, who, by their very existence, make demands that we may be unable or unwilling to meet. It requires a great force, such as the force of sexual desire, to overcome the embarrassment and self-protection that shield us from the most intimate encounters. It is tempting to take refuge in substitutes, which neither embarrass us nor resist the impulse of our spontaneous cravings. The habit grows, in masturbation, of creating a compliant world of desire, in which unreal objects become the focus of real emotions, and the emotions themselves are rendered incompetent to participate in the building of personal relations.

The fantasy blocks the passage to reality, which becomes inaccessible to the will.

Even if the fantasy can be overcome so far as to engage in the act of love with another, a peculiar danger remains. The other becomes veiled in substitutes; he is never fully himself in the act of love; it is never clearly *him* that I desire, or *him* that I possess, but always rather a composite object, a universal body, of which he is but one among a potential infinity of instances. Fantasy fills our thoughts with a sense of the obscene, and the orgasm becomes, not the possession of another, but the expenditure of energy on his depersonalised body. Fantasies are private property, which I can dispose according to my will, with no answerability to the other whom I abuse through them. He, indeed, is of no intrinsic interest to me, and serves merely as my opportunity for self-regarding pleasure. For the fantasist, the ideal partner is indeed the prostitute, who, because she can be purchased, solves at once the moral problem presented by the presence of another at the scene of sexual release.

The connection between fantasy and prostitution is deep and important. The effect of fantasy is to "commodify" the object of desire, and to replace the law of sexual relationship between people with the law of the market. Sex itself can then be seen as a commodity:[4] something that we pursue and obtain in quantifiable form, and which comes in a variety of packages: in the form of a woman or a man; in the form of a film or a dream; in the form of a fetish or an animal. In so far as the sexual act is seen in this way, it seems morally neutral—or, at best, impersonal. Such criticism as may be offered will concern merely the dangers for the individual and his partner of this or that sexual package: for some bring diseases and discomforts of which others are free. The most harmless and hygienic act of all, on this view, is the act of masturbation, stimulated by whatever works of pornography are necessary to prompt the desire for it in the unimaginative. This justification for pornography has, indeed, recently been offered.

As I have already argued, however, fantasy does not exist comfortably with reality. It has a natural tendency to realise itself: to remake the world in its own image. The harmless wanker with the video-machine can at any moment turn into the desperate rapist with a gun. The "reality principle" by which the normal sexual act is regulated is a principle of personal encounter, which enjoins us to respect the other person, and to respect, also, the sanctity of his body, as the tangible expression of another self. The world of fantasy obeys no such rule, and is governed by monstrous myths and illusions which are at war with the human world—the illusions, for example, that women wish to be raped, that children have only to be awakened in order to give and receive the intensest sexual pleasure, that violence is not an affront but an affirmation of a natural right. All such myths, nurtured in fantasy, threaten not merely the consciousness of the man who lives by them, but also the moral structure of his surrounding world. They render the world unsafe for self and other, and cause the subject to look on everyone, not as an end in himself, but as a possible means to his private pleasure. In his world, the sexual encounter has been "fetishised," to use the apt Marxian term,[5] and every other human reality has been poisoned by the sense of the expendability and replaceability of the other.

It is a small step from the preoccupation with sexual virtue, to a condemnation of obscenity and pornography (which is its published form). Obscenity is a direct assault on the sentiment of desire, and therefore on the social order that is based in desire and which has personal love as its goal and fulfillment. There is no doubt that the normal conscience cannot remain neutral towards obscenity, any more than it can remain neutral towards paedophilia and rape (which is not to say that obscenity must also be treated as a *crime*). It is therefore unsurprising that traditional moral education has involved censorship of obscene material, and a severe emphasis on "purity in thought, word and deed"—an emphasis which is now greeted with irony or ridicule.

Traditional sexual education was, despite its exaggerations and imbecilities, truer to human nature than the libertarian culture which has succeeded it. Through considering its wisdom and its shortcomings, we may understand how to resuscitate an idea of sexual virtue, in accordance with the broad requirements of the Aristotelian argument that I have, in this chapter, been presenting. The ideal of virtue remains one of 'sexual integrity': of a sexuality that is entirely integrated into the life of personal affection, and in which the self and its responsibility are centrally involved and indissolubly linked to the pleasures and passions of the body.

Traditional sexual morality has therefore been the morality of the body. Libertarian morality, by contrast, has relied almost entirely on a Kantian view of the human subject, as related to his body by no coherent moral tie. Focussing as he does on an idea of purely personal respect, and assigning no distinctive place to the body in our moral endeavour, the Kantian inevitably tends towards permissive morality. No sexual act can be wrong merely by virtue of its physical character, and the ideas of obscenity, pollution and perversion have no obvious application. His attitude to homosexuality is conveniently summarised in this passage from a Quaker pamphlet:

> We see no reason why the physical nature of the sexual act should be the criterion by which the question whether it is moral should be decided. An act which (for example) expresses true affection between two individuals and gives pleasure to them both, does not seem to us to be sinful by reason *alone* of the fact that it is homosexual. The same criteria seem to apply whether a relationship is heterosexual or homosexual.[6]

Such sentiments are the standard offering of the liberal and utilitarian moralities of our time. However much we may sympathise with their conclusions, it is not possible to accept the shallow reasoning that leads up to them. . . .

The reader may be reluctant to follow me in believing that traditional morality is largely justified by the ideal of sexual integrity. But if he accepts the main tenor of my argument, he must surely realise that the ethic of "liberation," far from promising the release of the self from hostile bondage, in fact heralds the dissipation of the self in loveless fantasy: th'expence of Spirit, in a waste of shame.

NOTES

1. Cf. the love poetry of Hafiz, of Omar Khayam, and of the Divan poets; and also the tales of faithful love in the *Thousand and One Nights.*

2. See Mary Douglas, *Implicit Meanings,* London, 1975, and *Purity and Danger,* London, 1966, for a study of the phenomena of disgust and pollution among African tribes.

3. "Formulations Regarding the Two Principles in Mental Functioning" (1911), in *Collected Papers,* tr. J. Riviere, New York, 1924–50, vol. IV.

4. An eccentric and politicised, but frequently perceptive, critique of this "commodification" of sex is contained in Stephen Heath, *The Sexual Fix,* London, 1982.

5. Karl Marx, *Capital,* tr. S. Moore and E. Aveling, ed. F. Engels, London, 1887, vol. I, Part 1, ch. 1, section 4.

6. A. Heron (ed.), *Towards a Quaker View of Sex,* London, 1963, quoted in Ronald Atkinson, *Sexual Morality,* London, 1965, p. 148.

Questions for Analysis

1. According to Scruton, sexual morality must be based on "the permanent features of human nature," not "the conditions of any particular person's life." What permanent features does he mean? Do all humans share them? If so, are they really permanent?

2. Scruton argues that masturbation is a pollution of the body. On what grounds? Do you agree?

3. Scruton bases much of his traditional sexual morality on the need to eliminate jealousy. Why? Do you consider this approach a sound one?

4. What does Scruton mean by "sexual integrity"? Why, in his view, does traditional sexual morality guarantee it and libertarian sexual morality compromise it? Do you think that there are other kinds of sexual integrity ignored by Scruton?

5. Although Scruton does not explicitly condemn homosexuality, he criticizes a common justification for it. Can his arguments in the rest of the essay be used to condemn homosexuality, or can they be used to support at least some homosexual relationships?

Plain Sex

Alan H. Goldman

In the following selection, Alan Goldman, Professor of Philosophy at the University of Miami, defends the libertarian position. Central to his argument is his rejection of what he calls "means-ends" scrutiny of sex analyses that treat sex as essentially a means to some further end like love, reproduction, or communication. To him, sexual desire is just the desire for contact with another person's body, and the goal sex is the pleasure such contact gives. Sex can also be a means of reproduction or of expressing love, he realizes, but those are extraneous purposes to the act of sex itself.

Given that analysis of sex, he concludes that sexual behavior cannot be morally evaluated by any norms other than those by which we evaluate any other kind of behavior—Kant's principle of respect for persons, for instance. We can distinguish perverted from normal sex, but perversion in this case is just a statistical notion, carrying no moral significance.

I

Several recent articles on sex herald its acceptance as a legitimate topic for analytic philosophers (although it has been a topic in philosophy since Plato). One might have thought conceptual analysis unnecessary in this area; despite the notorious struggles of judges and legislators to define pornography suitably, we all might be expected to know what sex is and to be able to identify at least paradigm sexual desires and activities without much difficulty. Philosophy is nevertheless of relevance here if for no other reason than that the concept of sex remains at the center of moral and social consciousness in our, and perhaps any, society. Before we can get a sensible view of the relation of sex to morality, perversion, social regulation, and marriage, we require a sensible analysis of the concept itself; one which neither understates its animal pleasure nor overstates its importance within a theory or system of value. I say "before," but the order is not quite so clear, for questions in this area, as elsewhere in moral philosophy, are both conceptual and normative at the same time. Our concept of sex will partially determine our moral view of it, but as philosophers we should formulate a concept that will accord with its proper moral status. What we require here, as elsewhere, is "reflective equilibrium," a goal not achieved by traditional and recent analyses together with their moral

implications. Because sexual activity, like other natural functions such as eating or exercising, has become imbedded in layers of cultural, moral, and superstitious superstructure, it is hard to conceive it in its simplest terms. But partially for this reason, it is only by thinking about plain sex that we can begin to achieve this conceptual equilibrium.

I shall suggest here that sex continues to be misrepresented in recent writings, at least in philosophical writings, and I shall criticize the predominant form of analysis which I term "means-end analysis." Such conceptions attribute a necessary external goal or purpose to sexual activity, whether it be reproduction, the expression of love, simple communication, or interpersonal awareness. They analyze sexual activity as a means to one of these ends, implying that sexual desire is a desire to reproduce, to love or be loved, or to communicate with others. All definitions of this type suggest false views of the relation of sex to perversion and morality by implying that sex which does not fit one of these models or fulfill one of these functions is in some way deviant or incomplete.

The alternative, simpler analysis with which I will begin is that sexual desire is desire for contact with another person's body and for the pleasure which such contact produces; sexual activity is activity which tends to fulfill such desire of the agent. Whereas Aristotle and Butler were correct in holding that pleasure is normally a byproduct rather than a goal of purposeful action, in the case of sex this is not so clear. The desire for another's body is, principally among other things, the desire for the

From Alan H. Goldman, "Plain Sex," *Philosophy & Public Affairs*, vol. 6, no. 3 (Spring 1977). Copyright © 1977 Princeton University Press. Reprinted by permission of Princeton University Press.

pleasure that physical contact brings. On the other hand, it is not a desire for a particular sensation detachable from its causal context, a sensation which can be derived in other ways. This definition in terms of the general goal of sexual desire appears preferable to an attempt to more explicitly list or define specific sexual activities, for many activities such as kissing, embracing, massaging, or holding hands may or may not be sexual, depending upon the context and more specifically upon the purposes, needs, or desires into which such activities fit. The generality of the definition also represents a refusal (common in recent psychological texts) to overemphasize orgasm as the goal of sexual desire or genital sex as the only norm of sexual activity (this will be hedged slightly in the discussion of perversion below).

Central to the definition is the fact that the goal of sexual desire and activity is the physical contact itself, rather than something else which this contact might express. By contrast, what I term "means-end analyses" posit ends which I take to be extraneous to plain sex, and they view sex as a means to these ends. Their fault lies not in defining sex in terms of its general goal, but in seeing plain sex as merely a means to other separable ends. I term these "means-end analyses" for convenience, although "means-separable-end analyses," while too cumbersome, might be more fully explanatory. The desire for physical contact with another person is a minimal criterion for (normal) sexual desire, but is both necessary and sufficient to qualify normal desire as sexual. Of course, we may want to express other feelings through sexual acts in various contexts; but without the desire for the physical contact in and for itself, or when it is sought for other reasons, activities in which contact is involved are not predominantly sexual. Furthermore, the desire for physical contact in itself, without the wish to express affection or other feelings through it, is sufficient to render sexual the activity of the agent which fulfills it. Various activities with this goal alone, such as kissing and caressing in certain contexts, qualify as sexual even without the presence of genital symptoms of sexual excitement. The latter are not therefore necessary criteria for sexual activity.

This initial analysis may seem to some either over- or underinclusive. It might seem too broad in leading us to interpret physical contact as sexual desire in activities such as football and other contact sports. In these cases, however, the desire is not for contact with another body per se, it is not directed toward a particular person for that purpose, and it is not the goal of the activity—the goal is winning or exercising or knocking someone down or displaying one's prowess. If the desire is purely for contact with another specific person's body, then to interpret it as sexual does not seem an exaggeration. A slightly more difficult case is that of a baby's desire to be cuddled and our natural response in wanting to cuddle it. In the case of the baby, the desire may be simply for the physical contact, for the pleasure of the caresses. If so, we may characterize this desire, especially in keeping with Freudian theory, as sexual or protosexual. It will differ nevertheless from full-fledged sexual desire in being more amorphous, not directed outward toward another specific person's body. It may also be that what the infant unconsciously desires is not physical contact per se but signs of affection, tenderness, or security, in which case we have further reason for hesitating to characterize its wants as clearly sexual. The intent of our response to the baby is often the showing of affection, not the pure physical contact, so that our definition in terms of action which fulfills sexual desire *on the part of the agent* does not capture such actions, whatever we say of the baby. (If it is intuitive to characterize our response as sexual as well, there is clearly no problem here for my analysis.) The same can be said of signs of affection (or in some cultures polite greeting) among men or women: these certainly need not be homosexual when the intent is only to show friendship, something extrinsic to plain sex although valuable when added to it.

Our definition of sex in terms of the desire for physical contact may appear too narrow in that a person's personality, not merely her or his body, may be sexually attractive to another, and in that looking or conversing in a certain way can be sexual in a given context without bodily contact. Nevertheless, it is not the contents of one's thoughts per se that are sexually appealing, but one's personality as embodied in certain manners of behavior. Furthermore, if a person is sexually attracted by another's personality, he or she will desire not just further conversation, but actual sexual contact. While looking at or conversing with someone can be interpreted as sexual in given contexts it is so when intended as preliminary to, and hence parasitic upon, elemental sexual interest. Voyeurism or viewing a pornographic movie qualifies as a sexual activity, but only as an imaginative substitute for the real thing (otherwise a deviation from the norm as expressed in our definition). The same is true of masturbation as a sexual activity without a partner.

That the initial definition indicates at least an ingredient of sexual desire and activity is too obvious to argue. We all know what sex is, at least in obvious cases, and do not need philosophers to tell us. My preliminary analysis is meant to serve as a contrast to what sex is not, at least, not necessarily. I concentrate upon the physically manifested desire for another's body, and I take as central the immersion in the physical aspect of one's own existence and attention to the physical embodiment of the other. One may derive pleasure in a sex act from expressing certain feelings to one's partner or from awareness of the attitude of one's partner, but sexual desire is essentially desire for physical contact itself: it is a bodily desire for the body of another that dominates our mental life for more or less brief periods. Traditional writings were correct to emphasize the purely physical or animal aspect of sex; they were wrong only in condemning it. This characterization of sex as an intensely pleasurable physical activity and acute physical desire may seem to some to capture only its barest level. But it is worth distinguishing and focusing upon this least common denominator in order to avoid the false views of sexual morality and perversion which emerge from thinking that sex is essentially something else.

II

We may turn then to what sex is not, to the arguments regarding supposed conceptual connections between sex and other activities which it is necessary to conceptually distinguish. The most comprehensible attempt to build an extraneous purpose into the sex act identifies that purpose as reproduction, its primary biological function. While this may be "nature's" purpose, it certainly need not be ours (the analogy with eating, while sometimes overworked, is pertinent here). While this identification may once have had a rational basis which also grounded the identification of the value and morality of sex with that applicable to reproduction and childrearing, the development of contraception ren-

dered the connection weak. Methods of contraception are by now so familiar and so widely used that it is not necessary to dwell upon the changes wrought by these developments in the concept of sex itself and in a rational sexual ethic dependent upon that concept. In the past, the ever present possibility of children rendered the concepts of sex and sexual morality different from those required at present. There may be good reasons, if the presence and care of both mother and father are beneficial to children, for restricting reproduction to marriage. Insofar as society has a legitimate role in protecting children's interests, it may be justified in giving marriage a legal status, although this question is complicated by the fact (among others) that children born to single mothers deserve no penalties. In any case, the point here is simply that these questions are irrelevant at the present time to those regarding the morality of sex and its potential social regulation. (Further connections with marriage will be discussed below.)

It is obvious that the desire for sex is not necessarily a desire to reproduce, that the psychological manifestation has become, if it were not always, distinct from its biological roots. There are many parallels, as previously mentioned, with other natural functions. The pleasures of eating and exercising are to a large extent independent of their roles in nourishment or health (as the junk-food industry discovered with a vengeance). Despite the obvious parallel with sex, there is still a tendency for many to think that sex acts which can be reproductive are, if not more moral or less immoral, at least more natural. These categories of morality and "naturalness," or normality, are not to be identified with each other, as will be argued below, and neither is applicable to sex by virtue of its connection to reproduction. The tendency to identify reproduction as the conceptually connected end of sex is most prevalent now in the pronouncements of the Catholic church. There the assumed analysis is clearly tied to a restrictive sexual morality according to which acts become immoral and unnatural when they are not oriented towards reproduction, a morality which has independent roots in the Christian sexual ethic as it derives from Paul. However, the means-end analysis fails to generate a consistent sexual ethic: homosexual and oral-genital sex is condemned while kissing or caressing, acts equally unlikely to lead in themselves to fertilization, even when properly characterized as sexual according to our definition, are not.

III

Before discussing further relations of means-end analyses to false or inconsistent sexual ethics and concepts of perversion, I turn to other examples of these analyses. One common position views sex as essentially an expression of love or affection between the partners. It is generally recognized that there are other types of love besides sexual, but sex itself is taken as an expression of one type, sometimes termed "romantic" love.[1] Various factors again ought to weaken this identification. First, there are other types of love besides that which it is appropriate to express sexually, and "romantic" love itself can be expressed in many other ways. I am not denying that sex can take on heightened value and meaning when it becomes a vehicle for the expression of feelings of love or tenderness, but so can many other usually mundane activities such as getting up early to make breakfast on Sunday, cleaning the house, and so on. Second, sex itself can be used to communicate many other emotions besides love, and, as I will argue below, can communicate nothing in particular and still be good sex.

On a deeper level, an internal tension is bound to result from an identification of sex, which I have described as a physical-psychological desire, with love as a long-term, deep emotional relationship between two individuals. As this type of relationship, love is permanent, at least in intent, and more or less exclusive. A normal person cannot deeply love more than a few individuals even in a lifetime. We may be suspicious that those who attempt or claim to love many love them weakly if at all. Yet, fleeting sexual desire can arise in relation to a variety of other individuals one finds sexually attractive. It may even be, as some have claimed, that sexual desire in humans naturally seeks variety, while this is obviously false of love. For this reason, monogamous sex, even if justified, almost always represents a sacrifice or the exercise of self-control on the part of the spouses, while monogamous love generally does not. There is no such thing as casual love in the sense in which I intend the term "love." It may occasionally happen that a spouse falls deeply in love with someone else (especially when sex is conceived in terms of love), but this is relatively rare in comparison to passing sexual desires for others; and while the former often indicates a weakness or fault in the marriage relation, the latter does not.

If love is indeed more exclusive in its objects than is sexual desire, this explains why those who view sex as essentially an expression of love would again tend to hold a repressive or restrictive sexual ethic. As in the case of reproduction, there may be good reasons for reserving the total commitment of deep love to the context of marriage and family—the normal personality may not withstand additional divisions of ultimate commitment and allegiance. There is no question that marriage itself is best sustained by a deep relation of love and affection; and even if love is not naturally monogamous, the benefits of family units to children provide additional reason to avoid serious commitments elsewhere which weaken family ties. It can be argued similarly that monogamous sex strengthens families by restricting and at the same time guaranteeing an outlet for sexual desire in marriage. But there is more force to the argument that recognition of a clear distinction between sex and love in society would help avoid disastrous marriages which result from adolescent confusion of the two when sexual desire is mistaken for permanent love, and would weaken damaging jealousies which arise in marriages in relation to passing sexual desires. The love and affection of a sound marriage certainly differs from the adolescent romantic variety, which is often a mere substitute for sex in the context of a repressive sexual ethic.

In fact, the restrictive sexual ethic tied to the means-end analysis in terms of love again has failed to be consistent. At least, it has not been applied consistently, but forms part of the double standard which has curtailed the freedom of women. It is predictable in light of this history that some women would now advocate using sex as another kind of means, as a political weapon or as a way to increase unjustly denied power and freedom. The inconsistency in the sexual ethic typically attached to the sex-love analysis, according to which it has generally been taken with a grain of salt when applied to men, is simply another example of the impossibility of tailoring a plausible moral theory in this area to a conception of sex which builds in conceptually extraneous factors.

I am not suggesting here that sex ought never to be connected with love or that it is not a more significant and valuable activity when it is. Nor am I denying that individuals need love as much as sex and perhaps emotionally need at least one complete relationship which encompasses both. Just as sex can express love and take on heightened significance when it does, so love is often naturally accompanied by an intermittent desire for sex. But again love is accompanied appropriately by desires for other shared activities as well. What makes the desire for sex seem more intimately connected with love is the intimacy which is seen to be a natural feature of mutual sex acts. Like love, sex is held to lay one bare psychologically as well as physically. Sex is unquestionably intimate, but beyond that the psychological toll often attached may be a function of the restrictive sexual ethic itself, rather than a legitimate apology for it. The intimacy involved in love is psychologically consuming in a generally healthy way, while the psychological tolls of sexual relations, often including embarrassment as a correlate of intimacy, are too often the result of artificial sexual ethics and taboos. The intimacy involved in both love and sex is insufficient in any case in light of previous points to render a means-end analysis in these terms appropriate.

IV

In recent articles, Thomas Nagel and Robert Solomon, who recognize that sex is not merely a means to communicate love, nevertheless retain the form of this analysis while broadening it. For Solomon, sex remains a means of communicating (he explicitly uses the metaphor of body language), although the feelings that can be communicated now include, in addition to love and tenderness, domination, dependence, anger, trust, and so on.[2] Nagel does not refer explicitly to communication, but his analysis is similar in that he views sex as a complex form of interpersonal awareness in which desire itself is consciously communicated on several different levels. In sex, according to his analysis, two people are aroused by each other, aware of the other's arousal, and further aroused by this awareness.[3] Such multileveled conscious awareness of one's own and the other's desire is taken as the norm of a sexual relation, and this model is therefore close to that which views sex as a means of interpersonal communication.

Solomon's analysis is beset by the same difficulties as those pointed out in relation to the narrower sex-love concept. Just as love can be communicated by many activities other than sex, which do not

therefore become properly analyzed as essentially vehicles of communication (making breakfast, cleaning the house, and so on), the same is true of the other feelings mentioned by Solomon. Domination can be communicated through economic manipulation, trust by a joint savings account. Driving a car can be simultaneously expressing anger, pride, joy, and so on. We may, in fact, communicate or express feelings in anything we do, but this does not make everything we do into language. Driving a car is not to be defined as an automotive means of communication, although with a little ingenuity we might work out an automotive vocabulary (tailgating as an expression of aggression or impatience; beating another car away from a stoplight as expressing domination) to match the vocabulary of "body language." That one can communicate various feelings during sex acts does not make these acts merely or primarily a means of communicating.

More importantly, to analyze sex as a means of communication is to overlook the intrinsic nature and value of the act itself. Sex is not a gesture or series of gestures, in fact not necessarily a means to any other end, but a physical activity intensely pleasurable in itself. When a language is used, the symbols normally have no importance in themselves; they function merely as vehicles for what can be communicated by them. Furthermore skill in the use of language is a technical achievement that must be carefully learned; if better sex is more successful communication by means of a more skillful use of body language, then we had all better be well schooled in the vocabulary and grammar. Solomon's analysis, which uses the language metaphor, suggests the appropriateness of a sex-manual approach, the substitution of a bit of technological prowess for the natural pleasure of the unforced surrender to feeling and desire.

It may be that Solomon's position could be improved by using the analogy of music rather than that of language, as an aesthetic form of communication. Music might be thought of as a form of aesthetic communicating, in which the experience of the "phonemes" themselves is generally pleasing. And listening to music is perhaps more of a sexual experience than having someone talk to you. Yet, it seems to me that insofar as music is aesthetic and pleasing in itself, it is not best conceived as primarily a means for communicating specific feelings. Such an analysis does injustice to aesthetic experience in much the same way as the sex-communication analysis debases sexual experience itself.[4]

For Solomon, sex that is not a totally self-conscious communicative art tends toward vulgarity,[5] whereas I would have thought it the other way around. This is another illustration of the tendency of means-end analyses to condemn what appears perfectly natural or normal sex on my account. Both Solomon and Nagel use their definitions, however, not primarily to stipulate moral norms for sex, as we saw in earlier analyses, but to define norms against which to measure perversion. Once again, neither is capable of generating consistency or reflective equilibrium with our firm intuitions as to what counts as subnormal sex, the problem being that both build factors into their norms which are extraneous to an unromanticized view of normal sexual desire and activity. If perversion represents a breakdown in communication, as Solomon maintains, then any unsuccessful or misunderstood advance should count as perverted. Furthermore, sex between husband and wife married for several years, or between any partners already familiar with each other, would be, if not perverted, nevertheless subnormal or trite and dull, in that the communicative content would be minimal in lacking all novelty. In fact the pleasures of sex need not wear off with familiarity, as they would if dependent upon the communicative content of the feelings. Finally, rather than a release or relief from physical desire through a substitute imaginative outlet, masturbation would become a way of practicing or rehearsing one's technique or vocabulary on oneself, or simply a way of talking to oneself, as Solomon himself says.[6]

Nagel fares no better in the implications of his overintellectualized norm. Spontaneous and heated sex between two familiar partners may well lack the complex conscious multileveled interpersonal awareness of which he speaks without being in the least perverted. The egotistical desire that one's partner be aroused by one's own desire does not seem a primary element of the sexual urge, and during sex acts one may like one's partner to be sometimes active and aroused, sometimes more passive. Just as sex can be more significant when love is communicated, so it can sometimes be heightened by an awareness of the other's desire. But at other times this awareness of an avid desire of one's partner can be merely distracting. The conscious awareness to which Nagel

refers may actually impede the immersion in the physical of which I spoke above, just as may concentration upon one's "vocabulary" or technique. Sex is a way of relating to another, but primarily a physical rather than intellectual way. For Nagel, the ultimate in degeneration or perversion would have to be what he calls "mutual epidermal stimulation"[7] without mutual awareness of each other's state of mind. But this sounds like normal, if not ideal, sex to me (perhaps only a minimal description of it). His model certainly seems more appropriate to a sophisticated seduction scene than to the sex act itself,[8] which according to the model would often have to count as a subnormal anticlimax to the intellectual foreplay. While Nagel's account resembles Solomon's means-end analysis of sex, here the sex act itself does not even qualify as a preferred or central means to the end of interpersonal communication.

V

I have now criticized various types of analysis sharing or suggesting a common means-end form. I have suggested that analyses of this form relate to attempts to limit moral or natural sex to that which fulfills some purpose or function extraneous to basic sexual desire. The attempts to brand forms of sex outside the idealized models as immoral or perverted fail to achieve consistency with intuitions that they themselves do not directly question. The reproductive model brands oral-genital sex a deviation, but cannot account for kissing or holding hands; the communication account holds voyeurism to be perverted but cannot accommodate sex acts without much conscious thought or seductive nonphysical foreplay; the sex-love model makes most sexual desire seem degrading or base. The first and last condemn extramarital sex on the sound but irrelevant grounds that reproduction and deep commitment are best confined to family contexts. The romanticization of sex and the confusion of sexual desire with love operate in both directions: sex outside the context of romantic love is repressed; once it is repressed, partners become more difficult to find and sex becomes romanticized further, out of proportion to its real value for the individual.

What all these analyses share in addition to a common form is accordance with and perhaps derivation from the Platonic-Christian moral tradition, according to which the animal or purely physical element of humans is the source of immorality, and plain sex in the sense I defined it is an expression of this element, hence in itself to be condemned. All the analyses examined seem to seek a distance from sexual desire itself in attempting to extend it conceptually beyond the physical. The love and communication analyses seek refinement or intellectualization of the desire; plain physical sex becomes vulgar, and too straightforward sexual encounters without an aura of respectable cerebral communicative content are to be avoided. Solomon explicitly argues that sex cannot be a "mere" appetite, his argument being that if it were, subway exhibitionism and other vulgar forms would be pleasing.[9] This fails to recognize that sexual desire can be focused or selective at the same time as being physical. Lower animals are not attracted by every other member of their species, either. Rancid food forced down one's throat is not pleasing, but that certainly fails to show that hunger is not a physical appetite. Sexual desire lets us know that we are physical beings and, indeed, animals; this is why traditional Platonic morality is so thorough in its condemnation. Means-end analyses continue to reflect this tradition, sometimes unwittingly. They show that in conceptualizing sex it is still difficult, despite years of so-called revolution in this area, to free ourselves from the lingering suspicion that plain sex as physical desire is an expression of our "lower selves," that yielding to our animal natures is subhuman or vulgar.

VI

Having criticized these analyses for the sexual ethics and concepts of perversion they imply, it remains to contrast my account along these lines. To the question of what morality might be implied by my analysis, the answer is that there are no moral implications whatever. Any analysis of sex which imputes a moral character to sex acts in themselves is wrong for that reason. There is no morality intrinsic to sex, although general moral rules apply to the treatment of others in sex acts as they apply to all human relations. We can speak of a sexual ethic as we can speak of a business ethic, without implying that business in itself is either moral or immoral or that special rules are required to judge business practices which are not derived from rules that apply elsewhere as well. Sex is not in itself a moral category, although like

business it invariably places us into relations with others in which moral rules apply. It gives us opportunity to do what is otherwise recognized as wrong, to harm others, deceive them or manipulate them against their wills. Just as the fact that an act is sexual in itself never renders it wrong or adds to its wrongness if it is wrong on other grounds (sexual acts towards minors are wrong on other grounds, as will be argued below), so no wrong act is to be excused because done from a sexual motive. If a "crime of passion" is to be excused, it would have to be on grounds of temporary insanity rather than sexual context (whether insanity does constitute a legitimate excuse for certain actions is too big a topic to argue here). Sexual motives are among others which may become deranged, and the fact that they are sexual has no bearing in itself on the moral character, whether negative or exculpatory, of the actions deriving from them. Whatever might be true of war, it is certainly not the case that all's fair in love or sex.

Our first conclusion regarding morality and sex is therefore that no conduct otherwise immoral should be excused because it is sexual conduct, and nothing in sex is immoral unless condemned by rules which apply elsewhere as well. The last clause requires further clarification. Sexual conduct can be governed by particular rules relating only to sex itself. But these precepts must be implied by general moral rules when these are applied to specific sexual relations or types of conduct. The same is true of rules of fair business, ethical medicine, or courtesy in driving a car. In the latter case, particular acts on the road may be reprehensible, such as tailgating or passing on the right, which seem to bear no resemblance as actions to any outside the context of highway safety. Nevertheless their immorality derives from the fact that they place others in danger, a circumstance which, when avoidable, is to be condemned in any context. This structure of general and specifically applicable rules describes a reasonable sexual ethic as well. To take an extreme case, rape is always a sexual act and it is always immoral. A rule against rape can therefore be considered an obvious part of sexual morality which has no bearing on nonsexual conduct. But the immorality of rape derives from its being an extreme violation of a person's body, of the right not to be humiliated, and of the general moral prohibition against using other persons against their wills, not from the fact that it is a sexual act.

The application elsewhere of general moral rules to sexual conduct is further complicated by the fact that it will be relative to the particular desires and preferences of one's partner (these may be influenced by and hence in some sense include misguided beliefs about sexual morality itself). This means that there will be fewer specific rules in the area of sexual ethics than in other areas of conduct, such as driving cars, where the relativity of preference is irrelevant to the prohibition of objectively dangerous conduct. More reliance will have to be placed upon the general moral rule, which in this area holds simply that the preferences, desires, and interests of one's partner or potential partner ought to be taken into account. This rule is certainly not specifically formulated to govern sexual relations; it is a form of the central principle of morality itself. But when applied to sex, it prohibits certain actions, such as molestation of children, which cannot be categorized as violations of the rule without at the same time being classified as sexual. I believe this last case is the closest we can come to an action which is wrong *because* it is sexual, but even here its wrongness is better characterized as deriving from the detrimental effects such behavior can have on the future emotional and sexual life of the naive victims, and from the fact that such behavior therefore involves manipulation of innocent persons without regard for their interests. Hence, this case also involves violation of a general moral rule which applies elsewhere as well.

Aside from faulty conceptual analyses of sex and the influence of the Platonic moral tradition, there are two more plausible reasons for thinking that there are moral dimensions intrinsic to sex acts per se. The first is that such acts are normally intensely pleasurable. According to a hedonistic, utilitarian moral theory they therefore should be at least prima facie morally right, rather than morally neutral in themselves. To me this seems incorrect and reflects unfavorably on the ethical theory in question. The pleasure intrinsic to sex acts is a good, but not, it seems to me, a good with much positive moral significance. Certainly I can have no duty to pursue such pleasure myself, and while it may be nice to give pleasure of any form to others, there is no ethical requirement to do so, given my right over my own body. The exception relates to the context of sex acts themselves, when one partner derives pleasure from the other and ought to return the favor. This duty to reciprocate takes us out of the domain

of hedonistic utilitarianism, however, and into a Kantian moral framework, the central principles of which call for just such reciprocity in human relations. Since independent moral judgments regarding sexual activities constitute one area in which ethical theories are to be tested, these observations indicate here, as I believe others indicate elsewhere, the fertility of the Kantian, as opposed to the utilitarian, principle in reconstructing reasoned moral consciousness.

It may appear from this alternative Kantian viewpoint that sexual acts must be at least prima facie wrong in themselves. This is because they invariably involve at different stages the manipulation of one's partner for one's own pleasure, which might appear to be prohibited on the formulation of Kant's principle which holds that one ought not to treat another as a means to such private ends. A more realistic rendering of this formulation, however, one which recognizes its intended equivalence to the first universalizability principle, admits no such absolute prohibition. Many human relations, most economic transactions for example, involve using other individuals for personal benefit. These relations are immoral only when they are one-sided, when the benefits are not mutual, or when the transactions are not freely and rationally endorsed by all parties. The same holds true of sexual acts. The central principle governing them is the Kantian demand for reciprocity in sexual relations. In order to comply with the principle, one must recognize the subjectivity of one's partner (not merely by being aroused by her or his desire, as Nagel describes). Even in an act which by its nature "objectifies" the other, one recognizes a partner as a subject with demands and desires by yielding to those desires, by allowing oneself to be a sexual object as well, by giving pleasure or ensuring that the pleasures of the acts are mutual. It is this kind of reciprocity which forms the basis for morality in sex, which distinguishes right acts from wrong in this area as in others. (Of course, prior to sex acts one must gauge their effects upon potential partners and take these longer range interests into account.)

VII

I suggested earlier that in addition to generating confusion regarding the rightness or wrongness of sex acts, false conceptual analyses of the means-end form cause confusion about the value of sex to the individual. My account recognizes the satisfaction of desire and the pleasure this brings as the central psychological function of the sex act for the individual. Sex affords us a paradigm of pleasure, but not a cornerstone of value. For most of us it is not only a needed outlet for desire but also the most enjoyable form of recreation we know. Its value is nevertheless easily mistaken by being confused with that of love, when it is taken as essentially an expression of that emotion. Although intense, the pleasures of sex are brief and repetitive rather than cumulative. They give value to the specific acts which generate them, but not the lasting kind of value which enhances one's whole life. The briefness of these pleasures contributes to their intensity (or perhaps their intensity makes them necessarily brief), but it also relegates them to the periphery of most rational plans for the good life.

By contrast, love typically develops over a long term relation; while its pleasures may be less intense and physical, they are of more cumulative value. The importance of love to the individual may well be central in a rational system of value. And it has perhaps an even deeper moral significance relating to the identification with the interests of another person, which broadens one's possible relationships with others as well. Marriage is again important in preserving this relation between adults and children, which seems as important to the adults as it is to the children in broadening concerns which have a tendency to become selfish. Sexual desire, by contrast, is desire for another which is nevertheless essentially self-regarding. Sexual pleasure is certainly a good for the individual, and for many it may be necessary in order for them to function in a reasonably cheerful way. But it bears little relation to those other values just discussed, to which some analyses falsely suggest a conceptual connection.

VIII

While my initial analysis lacks moral implications in itself, as it should, it does suggest by contrast a concept of sexual perversion. Since the concept of perversion is itself a sexual concept, it will always be defined relative to some definition of normal sex; and any conception of the norm will imply a contrary notion of perverse forms. The concept suggested by my account again differs sharply from those implied by the means-end analyses examined above. Perversion does not represent a deviation from the reproductive function (or kissing would be perverted), from a loving relationship (or most sexual desire and many heterosexual acts would be perverted), or from efficiency in communicating (or unsuccessful seduction attempts would be perverted). It is a deviation from a norm, but the norm in question is merely statistical. Of course, not all sexual acts that are statistically unusual are perverted—a three-hour continuous sexual act would be unusual but not necessarily abnormal in the requisite sense. The abnormality in question must relate to the *form of the desire* itself in order to constitute sexual perversion; for example, desire, not for contact with another, but for merely looking, for harming or being harmed, for contact with items of clothing. This concept of sexual abnormality is that suggested by my definition of normal sex in terms of its typical desire. However, not all unusual desires qualify either, only those with the typical physical sexual effects upon the individual who satisfies them. These effects, such as erection in males, were not built into the original definition of sex in terms of sexual desire, for they do not always occur in activities that are properly characterized as sexual, say, kissing for the pleasure of it. But they do seem to bear a closer relation to the definition of activities as perverted. (For those who consider only genital sex sexual, we could build such symptoms into a narrower definition, then speaking of sex in a broad sense as well as "proper" sex.)

Solomon and Nagel disagree with this statistical notion of perversion. For them the concept is evaluative rather than statistical. I do not deny that the term "perverted" is often used evaluatively (and purely emotively for that matter), or that it has a negative connotation for the average speaker. I do deny that we can find a norm, other than that of statistically usual desire, against which all and only activities that properly count as sexual perversions can be contrasted. Perverted sex is simply abnormal sex, and if the norm is not to be an idealized or romanticized extraneous end or purpose, it must express the way human sexual desires usually manifest themselves. Of course not all norms in other areas of discourse need be statistical in this way. Physical health is an example of a relatively clear norm which does not seem to depend upon the numbers of healthy people. But the concept in this case achieves its clarity through the connection of physical health with other clearly desirable physical functions and characteristics, for example, living longer. In the case of sex, that which is statistically abnormal is not necessarily incapacitating in other ways, and yet these abnormal desires with sexual effects upon their subject do count as perverted to the degree to which their objects deviate from usual ones. The connotations of the concept of perversion beyond those connected with abnormality or statistical deviation derive more from the attitudes of those likely to call certain acts perverted than from specifiable features of the acts themselves. These connotations add to the concept of abnormality that of *sub*normality, but there is no norm against which the latter can be measured intelligibly in accord with all and only acts intuitively called perverted.

The only proper evaluative norms relating to sex involve degrees of pleasure in the acts and moral norms, but neither of these scales coincides with statistical degrees of abnormality, according to which perversion is to be measured. The three parameters operate independently (this was implied for the first two when it was held above that the pleasure of sex is a good, but not necessarily a moral good). Perverted sex may be more or less enjoyable to particular individuals than normal sex, and more or less moral, depending upon the particular relations involved. Raping a sheep may be more perverted than raping a woman, but certainly not more condemnable morally.[10] It is nevertheless true that the evaluative connotations attaching to the term "perverted" derive partly from the fact that most people consider perverted sex highly immoral. Many such acts are forbidden by longstanding taboos, and it is sometimes difficult to distinguish what is forbidden from what is immoral. Others, such as sadistic acts, are genuinely immoral, but again not at all because of their connection with sex or abnormality. The principles which condemn these acts would condemn them equally if they were common and nonsexual. It is not true that we properly could continue to consider acts perverted which were found to be very common practice across societies. Such acts, if harmful, might continue to be condemned properly as immoral, but it was just shown that the immorality of an act does not vary with its degree of perversion. If not harmful, common acts previously considered abnormal might continue to be called perverted for a time

by the moralistic minority; but the term when applied to such cases would retain only its emotive negative connotation without consistent logical criteria for application. It would represent merely prejudiced moral judgments.

To adequately explain why there is a tendency to so deeply condemn perverted acts would require a treatise in psychology beyond the scope of this paper. Part of the reason undoubtedly relates to the tradition of repressive sexual ethics and false conceptions of sex; another part to the fact that all abnormality seems to disturb and fascinate us at the same time. The former explains why sexual perversion is more abhorrent to many than other forms of abnormality; the latter indicates why we tend to have an emotive and evaluative reaction to perversion in the first place. It may be, as has been suggested according to a Freudian line,[11] that our uneasiness derives from latent desires we are loathe to admit, but this thesis takes us into psychological issues I am not competent to judge. Whatever the psychological explanation, it suffices to point out here that the conceptual connection between perversion and genuine or consistent moral evaluation is spurious and again suggested by misleading means-end idealizations of the concept of sex.

The position I have taken in this paper against those concepts is not totally new. Something similar to it is found in Freud's view of sex, which of course was genuinely revolutionary, and in the body of writings deriving from Freud to the present time. But in his revolt against romanticized and repressive conceptions, Freud went too far—from a refusal to view sex as merely a means to a view of it as the end of all human behavior, although sometimes an elaborately disguised end. This pansexualism led to the thesis (among others) that repression was indeed an inevitable and necessary part of social regulation of any form, a strange consequence of a position that began by opposing the repressive aspects of the means-end view. Perhaps the time finally has arrived when we can achieve a reasonable middle ground in this area, at least in philosophy if not in society.

NOTES

1. Even Bertrand Russell, whose writing in this area was a model of rationality, at least for its period, tends to make this identification and to condemn plain sex in the absence of

love: "sex intercourse apart from love has little value, and is to be regarded primarily as experimentation with a view to love." *Marriage and Morals* (New York: Bantam, 1959), p. 87.

2. Robert Solomon, "Sex and Perversion," *Philosophy and Sex*, ed. R. Baker and F. Elliston (Buffalo: Prometheus, 1975).

3. Thomas Nagel, "Sexual Perversion," *The Journal of Philosophy* 66, no. 1 (16 January 1969).

4. Sex might be considered (at least partially) as communication in a very broad sense in the same way as performing ensemble music, in the sense that there is in both ideally a communion or perfectly shared experience with another. This is, however, one possible ideal view whose central feature is not necessary to sexual acts or desire per se. And in emphasizing the communication of specific feelings by means of body language, the analysis under consideration narrows the end to one clearly extrinsic to plain and even good sex.

5. Solomon, pp. 284–285.

6. Ibid., p. 283. One is reminded of Woody Allen's rejoinder to praise of his technique: "I practice a lot when I'm alone."

7. Nagel, p. 15.

8. Janice Moulton made the same point in a paper at the Pacific APA meeting, March 1976.

9. Solomon, p. 285.

10. The example is like one from Sara Ruddick, "Better Sex," *Philosophy and Sex*, p. 96.

11. See Michael Slote, "Inapplicable Concepts and Sexual Perversion," *Philosophy and Sex*.

Questions for Analysis

1. What is the significance of this essay's title?

2. According to Goldman, "We all know what sex is, at least in obvious cases, and we do not need philosophers to tell us." Do you agree? Does his analysis of sex agree with what we all know?

3. In rejecting the view that the purpose of sex is reproduction, Goldman compares sex to eating. What's the point of the comparison? Is it a good one?

4. What contrasts does Goldman draw between love and sexual desire?

5. Why does Goldman believe that perversion is not an evaluative norm against which we can judge sexual behavior?

6. Goldman claims that there is no morality intrinsic to sex. What does he mean by that? What are his reasons for claiming it?

7. In considering various means-ends analyses of sex, has Goldman missed any purpose of sex that you think important?

Why Homosexuality Is Abnormal

Michael Levin

In this selection from a much longer essay, Michael Levin defends three positions on homosexuality: that it is abnormal, that it leads to unhappiness, and that it should not be legalized.

In defending the first position, Levin gives an evolutionary definition of the function of a body part: a body part is for a given activity if it helps its host, and if this contribution is how the body part got where it is and stays there. Based on that definition, he concludes that homosexuality involves the misuse of sexual organs and is therefore abnormal. In defending the second position, he argues that homosexuals are in fact less happy than heterosexuals and that there is good evolutionary reason for their relative unhappiness. In defending the third position, he argues that legalization would convey societal approval of homosexuality, which would encourage children to take up a way of life that creates unhappiness.

From Michael Levin, "Why Homosexuality Is Abnormal," *The Monist* (Spring 1985). Copyright © 1985 *The Monist: An International Quarterly Journal of General Philosophical Inquiry*, Peru, Illinois, U.S.A. 61354. Reprinted by permission.

It is important to note that Levin is not using the unnaturalness argument discussed earlier in this chapter. He does not consider homosexuality immoral in itself, and he explicitly says that the term *abnormal* should not be taken in an evaluative or normative way.

INTRODUCTION

This paper defends the view that homosexuality is abnormal and hence undesirable—not because it is immoral or sinful, or because it weakens society or hampers evolutionary development, but for a purely mechanical reason. It is a misuse of bodily parts. Clear empirical sense attaches to the idea of *the use* of such bodily parts as genitals, the idea that they are *for* something, and consequently to the idea of their misuse. I argue on grounds involving natural selection that misuse of bodily parts can with high probability be connected to unhappiness. I regard these matters as prolegomena to such policy issues as the rights of homosexuals, the rights of those desiring not to associate with homosexuals, and legislation concerning homosexuality, issues which I shall not discuss systematically here. However, I do in the last section draw a seemingly evident corollary from my view that homosexuality is abnormal and likely to lead to unhappiness. . . .

Despite the publicity currently enjoyed by the claim that one's "sexual preference" is nobody's business but one's own, the intuition that there is something unnatural about homosexuality remains vital. The erect penis fits the vagina, and fits it better than any other natural orifice; penis and vagina seem made for each other. This intuition ultimately derives from, or is another way of capturing, the idea that the penis is not *for* inserting into the anus of another man—that so using the penis is not the way it is *supposed,* even *intended,* to be used. Such intuitions may appear to rest on an outmoded teleological view of nature, but recent work in the logic of functional ascription shows how they may be explicated, and justified, in suitable naturalist terms. . . .

ON "FUNCTION" AND ITS COGNATES

To bring into relief the point of the idea that homosexuality involves a misuse of bodily parts, I will begin with an uncontroversial case of misuse, a case in which the clarity of our intuitions is not obscured by the conviction that they are untrustworthy. Mr. Jones pulls all his teeth and strings them around his neck because he thinks his teeth look nice as a necklace. He takes puréed liquids supplemented by intravenous solutions for nourishment. It is surely natural to say that Jones is misusing his teeth, that he is not using them for what they are for, that indeed the way he is using them is incompatible with what they are for. Pedants might argue that Jones's teeth are no longer part of him and hence that he is not misusing any bodily parts. To them, I offer Mr. Smith, who likes to play "Old MacDonald" on his teeth. So devoted is he to this amusement, in fact, that he never uses his teeth for chewing—like Jones, he takes nourishment intravenously. Now, not only do we find it perfectly plain that Smith and Jones are misusing their teeth, we predict a dim future for them on purely physiological grounds; we expect the muscles of Jones's jaw that are used for—that *are* for—chewing to lose their tone, and we expect this to affect Jones's gums. Those parts of Jones's digestive tract that are for processing solids will also suffer from disuse. The net result will be deteriorating health and perhaps a shortened life. Nor is this all. Human beings enjoy chewing. Not only has natural selection selected in muscles for chewing and favored creatures with such muscles, it has selected in a tendency to find the use of those muscles reinforcing. Creatures who do not enjoy using such parts of their bodies as deteriorate with disuse, will tend to be selected out. Jones, product of natural selection that he is, descended from creatures who at least tended to enjoy the use of such parts. Competitors who didn't simply had fewer descendants. So we expect Jones sooner or later to experience vague yearnings to chew something, just as we find people who take no exercise to experience a general listlessness. Even waiving for now my apparent reification of the evolutionary process, let me emphasize how little anyone is tempted to say "each to his own" about Jones or to regard Jones's disposition of his teeth as simply a deviation from a statistical norm. This sort of case is my paradigm when discussing homosexuality.

The main obstacle to talk of what a process or organic structure is for is that, literally understood, such talk presupposes an agent who intends that structure or process to be used in a certain way. Talk of function derives its primitive meaning from the human use of artifacts, artifacts being for what purposive agents intend them for. Indeed, there is in this primitive context a natural reason for using something for what it is for: to use it otherwise would frustrate the intention of some purposeful agent. Since it now seems clear that our bodily parts were not emplaced by purposeful agency, it is easy to dismiss talk of what they are for as "theologically" based on a faulty theory of how we came to be built as we are, . . .

Until recently, philosophers of science half-countered, half-conceded such doubts by "rationally reconstructing" the locution "structure S is for function F in organism O" as—omitting inessential refinements—"S's doing F in O is necessary for the integrity or prosperity of O," . . . This, the classical analysis, suffers from two weaknesses. First, it quite severs the link stressed earlier between a structure's having a function and the inadvisability of using that structure in a way inconsistent with its function. An organism may not be interested in survival, or prosperity, or the prosperity of some genetically defined group that contains the organism. The classical analysis provides no clue as to why Jones should desist from stringing his teeth on a necklace. It must be supplemented with the premise that survival or fitness are desirable, and however strong the desire to survive may be as a *de facto* motive, there are too many cogent arguments against survival as a basic norm for this supplement to be plausible. . . .

The more decisive second objection to the classical analysis is the existence of clear counter-examples—counter-examples that turn out, on reflection, to be connected to the first objection. An accidentally incurred heart lesion might be necessary for the heart's pumping blood if it is otherwise diseased; but the lesion is not *for* pumping blood. A patient's heartbeat might be the only way his doctor can diagnose a disease that would be fatal if undiagnosed; but the beat of his heart is not *for* diagnosis. Such cases suggest that the classical analysis pays insufficient attention to how structures come to be in organisms and why they persist in

reproductive cohorts. In light of this, a more adequate explication . . . runs . . . an organ is for a given activity if the organ's performing that activity helps its host or organisms suitably related to its host, *and* if this contribution is how the organ got and stays where it is. This disqualifies the fortuitous heart lesion and the symptomatic heartbeat, which did not arise or persist by increasing (inclusive) fitness. This definition also distinguishes what something is for from what it may be *used* for on some occasion. Teeth are for chewing—we have teeth because their use in chewing favored the survival of organisms with teeth—whereas Jones is using his teeth for ornamentation. . . .

Nature is interested in making its creatures like what is (inclusively) good for them. A creature that does not enjoy using its teeth for chewing uses them less than does a toothed competitor who enjoys chewing. Since the use of teeth for chewing favors the survival of an individual with teeth, and, other things being equal, traits favorable to the survival of individuals favor survival of the relevant cohort, toothed creatures who do not enjoy chewing tend to get selected out. We today are the filtrate of this process, descendants of creature who like to chew. . . .

And here—to return to the main strand of the argument—is why it is advisable to use your organs for what they are for: you will enjoy it. Jones's behavior is ill-advised not only because of the avertible objective consequences of his defanging himself, but because he will feel that something is missing. Similarly, this is why you should exercise. It is not just that muscles are for running. We have already heard the sceptic's reply to that: "So what? Suppose I don't mind being flabby? Suppose I don't give a hang about what will propagate my genetic cohort?" Rather, running is good because nature made sure people like to run. This is, of course, the prudential "good," not the moral "good"—but I disavowed at the outset the doctrine that misuse of bodily parts is *morally* bad, at least in any narrow sense. You ought to run because running was once necessary for catching food: creatures who did not enjoy running, if there ever were any, caught less food and reproduced less frequently than competitors who enjoyed running. These competitors passed on their appetites along with their muscles *to you*. This is not to say that those who suffer the affective consequences of laziness must recognize them as such, or even be able to identify them against their general background feeling-tone. They may not realize they would feel better if they exercised. They may even doubt it. They may have allowed their muscles to deteriorate beyond the point at which satisfying exercise is possible. For all that, evolution has decreed that a life involving regular exercise is on the whole more enjoyable than a life without. The same holds for every activity that is the purpose of an organ. . . .

APPLICATIONS TO HOMOSEXUALITY

The application of this general picture to homosexuality should be obvious. There can be no reasonable doubt that one of the functions of the penis is to introduce semen into the vagina. It does this, and it has been selected in because it does this. . . . Nature has consequently made this use of the penis rewarding. It is clear enough that any proto-human males who found unrewarding the insertion of penis into vagina have left no descendants. In particular, proto-human males who enjoyed inserting their penises into each other's anuses have left no descendants. This is why homosexuality is abnormal, and why its abnormality counts prudentially against it. Homosexuality is likely to cause unhappiness because it leaves unfulfilled an innate and innately rewarding desire. And should the reader's environmentalism threaten to get the upper hand, let me remind him again of an unproblematic case. Lack of exercise is bad and even abnormal not only because it is unhealthy but also because one feels poorly without regular exercise. Nature made exercise rewarding because, until recently, we had to exercise to survive. Creatures who found running after game unrewarding were eliminated. Laziness leaves unreaped the rewards nature has planted in exercise, even if the lazy man cannot tell this introspectively. If this is a correct description of the place of exercise in human life, it is by the same token a correct description of the place of heterosexuality.

It hardly needs saying, but perhaps I should say it anyway, that this argument concerns tendencies and probabilities. Generalizations about human affairs being notoriously "true by and large and for the most

part" only, saying that homosexuals are bound to be less happy than heterosexuals must be understood as short for "Not coincidentally, a larger proportion of homosexuals will be unhappy than a corresponding selection of the heterosexual population." There are, after all, genuinely jolly fat men. To say that laziness leads to adverse affective consequences means that, because of our evolutionary history, the odds are relatively good that a man who takes no exercise will suffer adverse affective consequences. Obviously, some people will get away with misusing their bodily parts. Thus, when evaluating the empirical evidence that bears on this account, it will be pointless to cite cases of well-adjusted homosexuals. I do not say they are non-existent; my claim is that, of biological necessity, they are rare.

My argument might seem to show at most that heterosexual behavior is (self-) reinforcing, not that homosexuality is self-extinguishing—that homosexuals go without the built-in rewards of heterosexuality, but not that homosexuality has a built-in punishment. This distinction, however, is merely verbal. They are two different ways of saying that homosexuals will find their lives less rewarding than will heterosexuals. Even if some line demarcated happiness from unhappiness absolutely, it would be irrelevant if homosexuals were all happily above the line. It is the comparison with the heterosexual life that is at issue. A lazy man might count as happy by some mythic absolute standard, but he is likely to be less happy than someone otherwise like him who exercises. . . .

Talk of what is "in the genes" inevitably provokes the observation that we should not blame homosexuals for their homosexuality if it is "in their genes." True enough. Indeed, since nobody decides what he is going to find sexually arousing, the moral appraisal of sexual object "choice" is entirely absurd. However, so saying is quite consistent with regarding homosexuality as a misfortune, and taking steps—this is being within the realm of the will—to minimize its incidence, especially among children. Calling homosexuality involuntary does not place it outside the scope of evaluation. Victims of sickle cell anemia are not blameworthy, but it is absurd to pretend that there is nothing wrong with them. Homosexual activists are partial to genetic explanations and hostile to Freudian environmentalism in part because they see a genetic cause as exempting homosexuals from blame. But surely people are equally blameless for indelible traits acquired in early childhood. And anyway, a blameless condition may still be worth trying to prevent. . . .

Utilitarians must take the present evolutionary scenario seriously. The utilitarian attitude toward homosexuality usually runs something like this: even if homosexuality is in some sense unnatural, as a matter of brute fact homosexuals take pleasure in sexual contact with members of the same sex. As long as they don't hurt anyone else, homosexuality is as great a good as heterosexuality. But the matter cannot end here. Not even a utilitarian doctor would have words of praise for a degenerative disease that happened to foster a certain kind of pleasure (as sore muscles uniquely conduce to the pleasure of stretching them). A utilitarian doctor would presumably try just as zealously to cure diseases that feel good as less pleasant degenerative diseases. A pleasure causally connected with great distress cannot be treated as just another pleasure to be toted up on the felicific scoreboard. Utilitarians have to reckon with the inevitable consequences of pain-causing pleasure.

Similar remarks apply to the question of whether homosexuality is a "disease." A widely-quoted pronouncement of the American Psychiatric Association runs:

> Surely the time has come for psychiatry to give up the archaic practice of classifying the millions of men and women who accept or prefer homosexual object choices as being, by virtue of that fact alone, mentally ill. The fact that their alternative life-style happens to be out of favor with current cultural conventions must not be a basis in itself for a diagnosis.

Apart from some question-begging turns of phrase, this is right. One's taste for mutual anal intercourse is nothing "in itself" for one's psychiatrist to worry about, any more than a life of indolence is anything "in itself" for one's doctor to worry about. In fact, in itself there is nothing wrong with a broken arm or an occluded artery. The fact that my right ulna is now in two pieces is just a fact of nature, not a "basis for diagnosis." But this condition is a matter for medical science anyway, because it will lead to pain. Permitted to persist, my fracture will provoke increasingly punishing states. So if homosexuality is a reliable sign of present or future misery, it is beside the point that homosexuality is not "by virtue of the that fact alone" a mental illness. . . .

EVIDENCE AND FURTHER CLARIFICATION

I have argued that homosexuality is "abnormal" in both a descriptive and a normative sense because—for evolutionary reasons—homosexuals are bound to be unhappy. In Kantian terms, I have explained how it is possible for homosexuality to be unnatural even if it violates no cosmic purpose or such purposes as we retrospectively impose on nature. What is the evidence for my view? For one thing, by emphasizing homosexual unhappiness, my view explains a ubiquitous fact in a simple way. The fact is the universally acknowledged unhappiness of homosexuals. Even the staunchest defenders of homosexuality admit that, as of now, homosexuals are not happy. . . .

The usual environmentalist explanation for homosexuals' unhappiness is the misunderstanding, contempt and abuse that society heaps on them. But this not only leaves unexplained why society has this attitude, it sins against parsimony by explaining a nearly universal phenomenon in terms of variable circumstances that have, by coincidence, the same upshot. Parsimony urges that we seek the explanation of homosexual unhappiness in the nature of homosexuality itself, as my explanation does. Having to "stay in the closet" may be a great strain, but is does not account for all the miseries that writers on homosexuality say is the homosexual's lot. . . .

It is interesting to reflect on a natural experiment that has gotten under way in the [past] decade. . . . A remarkable change in public opinion, if not private sentiment, has occurred in America. For whatever reason—the prodding of homosexual activists, the desire not to seem like a fuddy-duddy—various organs of opinion are now hard at work providing a "positive image" for homosexuals. Judges allow homosexuals to adopt their lovers. The Unitarian Church now performs homosexual marriages. Hollywood produces highly sanitized movies like *Making Love* and *Personal Best* about homosexuality. Macmillan strongly urges its authors to show little boys using cosmetics. Homosexuals no longer fear revealing themselves, as is shown by the prevalence of the "clone look." Certain products run advertising obviously directed at the homosexual market. On the societal reaction theory, there ought to be an enormous rise in homosexual happiness. I know of no systematic study to determine if this is so, but anecdotal evidence suggests it may not be. The homosexual press has been just as strident in denouncing pro-homosexual movies as in denouncing Doris Day movies. Especially virulent venereal diseases have very recently appeared in homosexual communities, evidently spread in epidemic proportions by unabating homosexual promiscuity. One selling point for a presumably serious "gay rights" rally in Washington D.C. was an "all-night disco train" from New York to Washington. What is perhaps most salient is that, even if the changed public mood results in decreased homosexual unhappiness, the question remains of why homosexuals in the recent past, who suffered greatly for being homosexuals, persisted in being homosexuals.

But does not my position also predict—contrary to fact—that any sexual activity not aimed at procreation or at least sexual intercourse leads to unhappiness? First, I am not sure this conclusion is contrary to the facts properly understood. It is universally recognized that, for humans and the higher animals, sex is more than the insertion of the penis into the vagina. Foreplay is necessary to prepare the female and, to a lesser extent, the male. Ethologists have studied the elaborate mating rituals of even relatively simple animals. Sexual intercourse must therefore be understood to include the kisses and caresses that necessarily precede copulation, behaviors that nature has made rewarding. What my view does predict is that exclusive preoccupation with behaviors normally preparatory for intercourse is highly correlated with unhappiness. And, so far as I know, psychologists do agree that such preoccupation or "fixation" with, e.g., cunnilingus, is associated with personality traits independently recognized as disorders. In this sense, sexual intercourse really is virtually necessary for well-being. Only if one is antecedently convinced that "nothing is more natural than anything else" will one confound foreplay as a prelude to intercourse with "foreplay" that leads nowhere at all. . . .

ON POLICY ISSUES

Homosexuality is intrinsically bad only in a prudential sense. It makes for unhappiness. However, this does not exempt homosexuality from the larger categories of ethics—rights, duties, liabilities. Deontic categories apply to acts which increase or decrease happiness or expose the helpless to the risk of unhappiness.

If homosexuality is unnatural, legislation which raises the odds that a given child will become homosexual raises the odds that he will be unhappy. The only gap in the syllogism is whether legislation which legitimates, endorses or protects homosexuality does increase the chances that a child will become homosexual. If so, such legislation is *prima facie* objectionable. The question is not whether homosexual elementary school teachers will molest their charges. Pro-homosexual legislation might increase the incidence of homosexuality in subtler ways. If it does, and if the protection of children is a fundamental obligation of society, legislation which legitimates homosexuality is a dereliction of duty. I am reluctant to deploy the language of "children's rights," which usually serves as one more excuse to interfere with the prerogatives of parents. But we do have obligations to our children, and one of them is to protect them from harm. If, as some have suggested, children have a right to protection from a religious education, they surely have a right to protection from homosexuality. So protecting them limits somebody else's freedom, but we are often willing to protect quite obscure children's rights at the expenses of the freedom of others. There is a movement to ban TV commercials for sugar-coated cereals, to protect children from the relatively trivial harm of tooth decay. Such a ban would restrict the freedom of advertisers, and restrict it even though the last clear chance of avoiding the harm, and thus the responsibility, lies with the parents who control the TV set. I cannot see how one can consistently support such legislation and also urge homosexual rights, which risk much graver damage to children in exchange for increased freedom for homosexuals. . . . The right of a homosexual to work for the Fire Department is not a negligible good. Neither is fostering a legal atmosphere in which as many people as possible grow up heterosexual.

It is commonly asserted that legislation granting homosexuals the privilege or right to be firemen endorses not homosexuality, but an expanded conception of human liberation. It is conjectural how sincerely this can be said in a legal order that forbids employers to hire whom they please and demands hours of paperwork for an interstate shipment of hamburger. But in any case legislation "legalizing homosexuality" cannot be neutral. . . . Society cannot grant unaccustomed rights and privileges to homosexuals while remaining neutral about the value of homosexuality. Working from the assumption that society rests on the family and its consequences, the Judaeo-Christian tradition has deemed homosexuality a sin and withheld many privileges from homosexuals. Whether or not such denial was right, for our society to grant these privileges to homosexuals *now* would amount to declaring that it has rethought the matter and decided that homosexuality is not as bad as it had previously supposed. And unless such rethinking is a direct response to new empirical findings about homosexuality, it can only be a revaluing. Someone who suddenly accepts a policy he has previously opposed is open to the same interpretation: he has come to think better of the policy. And if he embraces the policy while knowing that this interpretation will be put on his behavior, and if he knows that others know that he knows they will so interpret it, he is acquiescing in this interpretation. He can be held to have intended, meant, this interpretation. A society that grants privileges to homosexuals while recognizing that, in the light of generally known history, this act can be interpreted as a positive re-evaluation of homosexuality, is signalling that it now thinks homosexuality is all right. Many commentators in the popular press have observed that homosexuals, unlike members of racial minorities, can always "stay in the closet" when applying for jobs. What homosexual rights activists really want, therefore, is not access to jobs but legitimation of their homosexuality. Since this is known, giving them what they want will be seen as conceding their claim to legitimacy. . . .

Questions for Analysis

1. What's the point of Levin's analogy between homosexuality and Smith's treatment of his teeth? Is the analogy a good or a bad one? Why?

2. According to Levin, the misuse of a body part is not in itself morally wrong. Why? Then why does he say that homosexuality should be discouraged by law?

3. What kind of evidence does Levin cite to show that homosexuals are less happy than heterosexuals? How persuasive is it? Why does he reject what he calls the environmentalist explanation of homosexual unhappiness?

4. Levin says, "Calling homosexuality involuntary does not place it outside the scope of evaluation." Why doesn't it? Do you agree?

5. According to Levin, laws legalizing homosexuality can't be morally neutral. Why not? Do you agree?

6. How does Levin's argument resemble the argument from nature? How does it differ from it? Does Levin's argument escape the standard objections to the argument from nature?

Homosexuality and Nature

Timothy F. Murphy

The following essay by Timothy F. Murphy, Professor of Philosophy in the Biomedical Sciences College of Medicine, University of Illinois at Chicago, is a rebuttal of Michael Levin's arguments. Evolution cannot, Murphy argues, give us a standard for normal and abnormal

From Timothy F. Murphy, "Homosexuality and Nature: happiness and the law at stake," *Journal of Applied Philosophy*, vol. 4, no. 2, 1987. Copyright © 1987 *Journal of Applied Philosophy*. Reprinted by permission.

behavior, and departures from behavior that once helped a species adapt to its environment may be beneficial today. He also disputes Levin's view that homosexuality in itself is likely to cause unhappiness, first by criticizing Levin's evidence and then by arguing that Levin fails to rule out anti-gay discrimination as the main cause.

Finally, Murphy criticizes Levin's arguments against gay rights. Using the same utilitarian reasoning as Levin, he notes that the happiness of homosexuals will be much enhanced by the removal of discrimination. Even more important, he disputes the claim that gay-rights legislation will turn children into homosexuals; homosexuality may be the result of biology, he says, or of environmental influences too early in life to be affected by the law.

The nature and legitimacy of homosexual behaviour continue to generate considerable controversy. Since 1973, the American Psychiatric Association has formally professed that homosexuality per se is no disease entity,[1] but one may still seek and find practitioners of sexual conversion therapy.[2] While some religious thinkers have become more tolerant of it,[3] others continue to conceptualize homosexuality as a sin of the first order, a sin said to be formally condemned in strong Old and New Testament language. While at present 26 states of the Union do *not* have criminal statutes for private consensual homosexual behaviour, the US Supreme Court recently held that states may criminalize such behaviours if they so choose.

There are many ways used to argue against the moral legitimacy of homosexual behaviour, whether such behaviour is transient or exclusive. Some seek recourse to concepts of sinfulness, diseases or crime in order to flesh out objections. Others appeal to the argument that homosexuality, its religious, medical, and criminal implications apart, is a kind of unnatural aberration which undermines its practitioners' prospects for happiness. I will consider this kind of argument here and contend that such an argument fails to establish that homosexuality is any significant abnormality and that neither its purported abnormality nor the unhappiness said to be associated with such behaviour can constitute a basis for criminalizing consensual homosexual behaviour or for failing to provide equal protections under the law for homosexuals in the area of public housing, service, jobs, and so on. I consider Michael Levin's "Why homosexuality is abnormal" as paradigmatic of the kind of argument I wish to investigate.[4] Although I confine myself to his specific argument and frequently use its language, my position is applicable *a fortiori* to all similar kinds of positions.

THE ARGUMENT FROM NATURE

Levin says homosexuality is abnormal because it involves a misuse of body parts, that there is "clear empirical sense" of that misuse, and that homosexual behaviour is contrary to the evolutionary adaptive order. Homosexual behaviour is abnormal, he says, because it is not the kind of behaviour which brought us to be the kind of physically constituted persons that we are today. Persons who used their penises for *coitus per anum* presumably left no ancestors. (Levin does not accept sociobiological contentions that homosexuality plays a supporting role in adaptive success.) That there are penises and vaginas today is due to the fact that they *were* used for heterosexual coitus, and hence we can infer that heterosexual coitus is indeed what such organs are for. Levin says: "an organ is for a given activity if the organ's performing that activity helps its host or organism suitable related to its host, *and* if this contribution is how the organ got and stays where it is."[5] Homosexual behaviour constitutes, according to this line of thought, an abandonment of certain functions on which species survival depended, and that abandonment is said to imply the loss of naturally occurring rewards selected for by adaptive success. This latter point does not mean that there are *no* compensatory pleasure, for just as the obese person will find gustatory rewards in his or her food, the homosexual who misuses his or her body parts can find *some* compensatory sexual rewards. It is just that the willful overeater or homosexual cannot reap the deepest rewards that nature has provided for in heterosexual usages and achievements.

Despite the effort which Levin takes to show that homosexual behaviour falls outside the behaviour upon which human adaptive success depended, I cannot say that I think this argument is even remotely convincing. Indeed, I believe it to be subject to a damning criticism. Even if it were certainly established that homosexuality was not part of originally adaptive behaviour, I do not see how that conclusion alone could establish the abnormality of homosexuality because there is neither a premise that natural selection has any kind of ultimate normative force nor a premise that human beings are bound to continue to be the kind of things that cosmic accident brought them to be. There is nothing in Levin's argument to sustain a claim that departures from a blind, accidental force of nature, or whatever metaphor of randomness is chosen, must be resisted. Without a logically prior and controlling premise that patterns of adaptive success possess ultimate, normative, force, then it seems that human beings are completely at liberty to dispose of their work, their behaviour, and even such things as their anatomy and physiology as they see fit. H. Tristam Engelhardt has made an argument along similar lines: that we human beings may choose our futures and are in no metaphysically binding sense bound to continue being the kind of persons blind determinants of nature have brought us to be.[6] Violations of a random order of nature carry no inherent penalty for there is no ultimate enforcer, or at least none is specified by this argument. Levin believes that he can show the abnormality of homosexuality without having to show that it violates some cosmic principle, by showing its inherent obstacles to adaptive success. But I think it is because no cosmic principle is invoked that we can judge that adaptive success itself is no binding force. The only guide available for human beings in respect of their lives, sexuality, and future is their will and imagination. Should the entire population of the planet choose to become exclusive homosexuals, for example, leaving the business of reproduction to ectogenesis, I cannot think of a reason *derived from nature* why they should not do so.

Levin's argument, and others like it, ignore the prospects of beneficial departures from the naturally adaptive order. His argument assumes that each departure from our adaptive heritage will be unhappy in result. The argument, too, assumes that *all* behaviour of *all* persons must serve the purpose of adaptation. Clearly, it is possible that some departures from the adaptive order are possible which do not threaten a species survival as a whole. If a species can survive if only a majority of its members use their organs in a particular fashion, then it may enjoy a surplus of adaptive protection even for those who act in wholly non-procreative fashion. Homosexuality, then, might have served some beneficial advantage (as sociobiology asserts) or it may have been (and this is more important for my argument) no impediment to selective adaptation. If this is so, it is hard to see in what sense homosexuality would have to be reckoned as a natural aberration.

Even if one were to accept Levin's suggestions regarding the abnormality of homosexuality with respect to natural selection, it seems to me that his definition of homosexuality is highly problematic. He defines homosexuality behaviourally, i.e. as something one does with one's body, specifically with one's organs. It is *behaviour* which is said to be unnatural. Since there are, after all, self-identified gay men and lesbians who have never had sexual relations with a member of the same (or opposite) sex, this definition seems ill-advised. By their own lights, adolescents and closeted adults see themselves as homosexual, their sexual continence notwithstanding. How is one to understand the nature of their sexual dispositions if there is no overt behaviour? Is their homoerotic desire itself abnormal? Or is only behaviour abnormal? I believe that homosexuality is better defined as primarily a psychic phenomenon and that specific homosexual behaviour is virtually epiphenomenal, merely a matter of what biology makes possible (this claim would also apply to heterosexuality). Most psychiatric texts follow this approach.[7] If one accepts the condition that homosexuality is primarily a psychic phenomenon, and if one wanted to argue its abnormality along the lines Levin has suggested, it would seem that one would have to argue that homoeroticism is somehow a misuse of the brain! There are arguments, of course, that attempt to show homosexuality as a result of some psychic disrepair, but even though these arguments are themselves the matter of much debate, that debate is only about psychical development, not about uses of the brain. It is hard to imagine that one could show homoeroticism as a misuse of the brain.

Finally, it is to be noted that Levin believes that homosexuality may be intuited as abnormal. He says that such an intuition "remains vital."[8] Yet however profoundly felt and however psychologically convincing intuitions may be, still they can be conceptually shallow and more importantly even dead wrong. That is, the appeal to intuition is by itself no guarantee of the accuracy of the intuition, for presumably one would, for purposes of confirmation, have to check the intuition against some other external criterion of justification. I am hard-pressed to see how this intuition of homosexuality's abnormality is to be made available to others who do not already share it. Indeed, arguments from intuition are like issues said to be self-evident: precious little can be said on their behalf, they are either seen or not. Yet Levin seems to assume that the readers of his essay *already* share the intuition. . . .

PROSPECTS FOR HAPPINESS

Levin makes a great deal of the supposed link between homosexuality and unhappiness. One may assume that he would reply to my foregoing remarks by admitting that even if it were true that humans are not bound by any ultimate metaphysical sexual directive, then it would still remain true that prudential cautions obtain against homosexuality and that these cautions are sufficient to ground legal measure designed to minimize the occurrence of homosexuality. "Homosexuality," Levin says, "is likely to cause unhappiness because it leaves unfulfilled an innate and innately rewarding desire,"[9] a desire supposedly ingrained through millennia of evolutionary selection. One might find some happy homosexuals, but Levin believes that such exceptions are inconsequential and do not disable his argument. He does not say that happy homosexuals are non-existent, only that they are rare and that their lives will be inherently less rewarding than those of heterosexuals. Moreover, "Even if some line demarcated happiness from unhappiness absolutely, it would be irrelevant if homosexuals were all happily above that line. It is the comparison with the heterosexual life that is at issue."[10] The happiest persons are practitioners of heterosexuality, therefore, even if, according to Levin, each and every homosexual was, by his or her own admission, happy. But homosexuals are not even proximately happy, Levin says. According to him,

awash in the travails of their own self-punishing promiscuity, present-day homosexuals would like to believe that all their ills are the result of an ill-constructed society, that their unhappiness is merely artifactual and in principle eliminable by the appropriate cultural and political accommodations. Levin suggests that this belief is a self-serving rationalization. . . . Happiness has not followed the work of various American organs to provide a positive image of homosexuals, judges allowing homosexuals to adopt their lovers, the Hollywood production of "highly sanitized" movies about homosexuality, publishers urging their authors to show little boys using cosmetics, or advertisers appealing directly to the homosexual market. That there has not been a resultant rise in homosexual happiness is said to be evident from (a) the gay press not liking Hollywood's movies, (b) the appearance of especially virulent diseases in homosexual populations, and (c) gay men needing frivolous enticements to get them to support important political causes on their behalf.[11]

By the way of comment on all this, I would first note that Levin has formulated his position in terms that *in principle* do not admit of refutation. He said that in principle, however happy homosexuals may be, they still cannot be as happy as heterosexuals. Of course, it is possible that a claim is unfalsifiable because the claim is indeed true. On the other hand, I think one would do better to see a definitional fiat being asserted here: human happiness, *true* human happiness is said to coextensive with the happiness of heterosexual behaviour. By definition there is nothing which could falsify this proposition, *not even* the self-asserted happiness of each and every homosexual person. I believe that this claim is no argument, avoiding as it does any potentially falsifying statement, and that it ought to be rejected as untestable rather than accepted as true by definition. As I have urged above, moreover, I do not believe that the accidental contingency of the primacy of heterosexual sexuality requires that all human happiness be sought there or that, perhaps, other kinds of happiness cannot be engineered.

Secondly, the kind of evidence that Levin uses to establish the unhappiness of homosexuals is altogether anecdotal and trivial.[12] That Hollywood continues to make bad movies, even when their subjects are "sanitized" gay men and lesbians, is no evidence that homosexuality *per se* leads to unhappiness. The existence of viral disease is a major concern of gay men, but it is not because they are gay that it is their concern; it is because these viral diseases happen by accident of fate to affect the gay population. Would one want to argue that heterosexuals qua heterosexuals are somehow intrinsically headed for unhappiness as AIDS expands into that population? Moreover, that homosexuals mix business with pleasure is no argument that they are less serious about their political agenda (let alone unhappier) than others. There is a kind of unfair asymmetry being used here in adducing Levin's evidence. If one uses such issues as he conjures up as evidence of the continuing unhappiness of homosexuals, why couldn't one equally and legitimately use similar evidence against the supposed happiness of heterosexuals? Most wars, for example, are the doing of heterosexuals. Nuclear weapons are their products. Most bad movies are also theirs. Must one infer therefore the continuing unhappiness of heterosexuals and assert prudential cautions against heterosexuality? If Levin's use of anecdotal evidence is acceptable against homosexuals, then it ought to be equally acceptable as an indictment of heterosexuality. Ironically, the case against heterosexuality would probably have to be seen as more damaging.

As for Levin's claims that homosexuals ought to be happier these days than they were in the past, it is probably the case that this is true. Anecdotal evidence may be used here since Levin uses it. The increasing success of gay pride parades ought to be taken as an indicator of some measure of increased homosexual happiness. At the very least persons who participate in them have been freed of the fear of some of the unhappy consequences that could befall them following public identification of their being gay. It is not without significance that in Boston, for example, the 1986 gay pride parade attracted some 25,000–30,000 participants whereas the first parade of 1970 had but 50! Furthermore, the heady increase in the number of gay and lesbian organizations for social, business, and political and support services indicates that homosexuals are not much inclined to wallow in despair over their sexual fate. One could go on in this vein, but I think it is important to consider that a verdict about the happiness of homosexuals would be a one-sided verdict indeed if it were to follow only from the evidence Levin puts forward.

To put specific quarrels about evidence aside, it seems to me that Levin fails almost culpably to imagine what a society would have to be like in order to be free of the oppressive elements which contribute to the putative unhappiness of homosexuals. In order to see the extent to which homosexual unhappiness is caused by social repressions and to what extent it is intrinsic, society would have to be completely free at every significant level of bias against homosexuals. To begin with—let's call this Phase I of the agenda: there should be no gratuitous assumption of heterosexuality in education, politics, advertising, and so on, just as a gender-neutral society would not presume the priority, real and symbolic, of males. For example, in education, texts and films ought to incorporate the experiences of gay men and lesbians. Educational measures should attempt to reduce anti-homosexuality in the same ways and to the same extent they educate against racism. In a society reconstructed along these lines, moreover, there would also have to be no right of access or entitlement possessed by a heterosexual that could be denied to a homosexual. *Only* in such radically restructured society would one be able to see if homosexual unhappiness were immune to social deconstruction. Even if it weren't, one could still argue that homosexuals are not necessarily unhappy but that their happiness requires social protections or accommodations unrequired by heterosexuals. That is, homosexuals might need, as Phase II of the agenda, entitlements which heterosexuals do not in the way, for example, that legally-mandated minority hiring quotas serve other specific populations. Of course, one might want to argue that such entitlements would be anti-democratic and therefore objectionable. This protestation however would not by itself diminish the point being made: that homosexual unhappiness is perhaps adventitious and that the only way of discovering this is to protect homosexuals in their lives, jobs, and interests in ways that are not presently served.

It is unlikely, of course, that the above-described experiment in social reconstruction is in any important sense immediately forthcoming. Nevertheless, that the experiment may be clearly formulated and seen as the definitive test of the social-reaction theory of homosexual unhappiness is sufficient ground to show that Levin's account of the unhappiness of homosexuals is unproved, its adduced evidence merely anecdotal. Even if it were true, I will argue later, since not all human unhappiness is tractable to social interventions, any residual unhappiness that was to survive Phase I and II of our social reformation agenda would still be no evidence against homosexuality.

ISSUES AT LAW

Levin believes that the abnormality of homosexuality and its attendant unhappiness are warrant enough to ground legal enactments against homosexuality and this is a matter of protecting citizens from lives impoverished by the loss of heterosexual rewards. Any legislation therefore that raises the odds that a child will become homosexual ought to be rejected as prima facie objectionable, as a dereliction of the duty of protecting children from the unhappy homosexual selves they might become.[13] The U.S. Supreme Court recently ruled in Bowers v. Hardwick that states may enact, if they choose, statutes proscribing private consensual homosexual behaviour since, according to the opinion, there is nothing in the Constitution making such behaviour a fundamental right.[14] Levin's argument would presumably extend further since private consensual homosexual behaviour is socially invisible and unlikely as such to influence persons to become homosexual. Although he does not specifically mention what kinds of laws ought to be called for, or what kinds of laws ought to be rejected, presumably he means denying homosexuals protections in jobs, housing, foster-parenting, and so on. In short, the law would presumably have to serve the function of rendering homosexuality entirely invisible else there would continue to exist subtle promptings to homosexuality by virtue of degree of acceptance extended to it. Levin says he does not believe that this legal scenario would put any undue burden on any actual homosexual since, unlike members of racial minorities, he or she can always stay in the closet while applying for jobs, housing and the like. Therefore to give homosexuals protections they don't really need would have to be interpreted as a de facto social legitimation of homosexuality. This implied approval might be causally involved in the production of more homosexuals and therefore ought to be rejected.

I do not believe that this argument is convincing. First of all, the "cause" or "causes" of homosexuality are a matter of continuing controversy. There are metaphysical arguments that homosexuality is the result of some cosmic principle of world ordering; Plato's *Symposium* depicts homosexuals (and heterosexuals) as the result of an angry god's punishment. Biological theories hold homosexuality to be the result of some developmental variance or organismal dysfunction. Genetic theories try to locate the origins of homosexuality at the lowest level of biological causality, the gene. The most numerous kinds of theories are psychosocial theories which see homoeroticism as the result of either original psychical constitution or some developmental influences. Even the briefest perusal of the literature of the "cause" of homosexuality leaves one with the conclusion that the "cause" is an essentially disputed concept.[15] There is not even agreement that homosexuality is a reifiable trait (any more than, say, courage) that can be explained by reference to a universally pre-existing set of conditions.[16] This dispute is important to consider since Levin seems to hold, without justification (at least without explanation), a developmental theory of homosexuality, a theory that homosexuals are made not born. This may or may not be true, but it seems wrong-headed to establish legal policy on the basis of one particular speculative theory of the origins of homosexual behaviour. If homosexuality is primarily a function of biological variance, for example, such laws and forbearances that Levin would see as desirable would have no effect whatever on the production of more homosexuals. Even if the law diligently erased all evidence of homosexual behaviour and persons from public view, one could not automatically assume a reduced number of homosexuals or a decrease in homosexual behaviour. I suspect that most persons are homosexual and become homosexual in ways completely immune to the written or enforced statutes of the various states. Children who never hear a word about homosexuality in their youth nevertheless become homosexuals. Children who walk past homosexual clubs and persons in the streets of certain American cities do not thereby automatically become homosexuals. Would it really be the case that there are more homosexuals spawned in West Virginia because there are no laws against private, consensual homosexual behaviour there than in Virginia where there are such laws?[17] The net result of efforts to criminalize and reduce the visibility of homosexuality then would be to impose burdens on those who are perhaps involuntarily homosexual. At the very least, Levin's theory gratuitously supposes a developmental theory of homosexuality, a theory which has its insistent critics. One should also point out that even if some developmental theory of homosexuality were true, it is not necessarily the case that changing statutes would halt the flow of homosexuals since there may be other pathways to homosexuality. It is also the suspicion of many psychologists that homosexual tendencies are established very early on in childhood, in which case one presumes fairly that statutes criminalizing sodomy and lacks of protection in housing on the basis of sexual orientation have little to do with either ingraining or stifling homosexual dispositions.

If the reason that Levin suggests anti-homosexual measures is to contain human unhappiness, then his argument may be turned on its head. If the reason, or part of the reason that homosexuals are unhappy is because of the existence of certain legally permissible discriminations (or what comes to the same thing: fear of such), then it can certainly be suggested that laws ought to be changed in order to protect and enlarge the happiness of homosexuals, whether their homosexuality is elective or involuntary. In the name of their happiness, they ought to be afforded protections under the law, freedom from fear of prosecution for their private consensual behaviour and freedom to occupy jobs as persons they are, not as the persons others would have them be. The law could further protect them by saving them from blackmailers who would expose their homosexuality to employers, landlords, and so on. It is eminently clear that the law could at least enlarge the happiness of gay men and lesbians in these respects even if it cannot vouchsafe them absolute satisfaction in their lives.

Interestingly enough, even if all the unhappiness said to be associated with being homosexual were not eliminated by a dogged social reconstruction that achieved full parity between homosexuality and heterosexuality, it would still not follow that the law ought to be put to the purpose of eliminating homosexuality (assuming it could). Life, sad to say, is in some of its aspects inherently tragic. For example, in some important ways, law or society could never fully compensate the atheist for the lost rewards of religion. Atheism can discover in the world no incentives to conduct, no promise of the eventual recompense for injustices borne, and no guarantee that the heart's desires will be met.[18] Society might provide such consolations as it can, but it is certainly the case that a certain tragedy antagonistic to human happiness is an irreducible element of atheistic thought. That atheism leads to this measure of unhappiness would certainly not be a reason for instituting social and legal barriers to atheism on the theory that children ought to be glowingly happy (if self-deceived) theists rather than unhappy atheists. Human dignity is not automatically overthrown by a position of atheism; the atheist accepts and honours those satisfactions that are within his or her power. That homosexuality too might lead to a certain amount of unhappiness does not thereby overthrow the dignity of homosexual persons. One realizes merely that the law is no unfailing conduit to human happiness.

Levin's conclusions that legal measures ought to be taken to minimize the possibility that children become themselves the sad new recruits of homosexuality therefore cannot stand. I believe, on the contrary, that the law ought to do what it can to protect homosexuals from socially inflicted unhappiness. Levin's point that to decriminalize homosexual behaviour and to provide legal protections for homosexual persons would be seen as social legitimization of homosexuality (and not just tolerance) is correct. But this is no point over which to despair, for this inference is precisely compatible with the underlying metaphysics of gay activism, that homosexuality is no degrading impoverishment of human life. On the contrary, it has an integrity of its own apart from invidious comparisons with heterosexuality. Therefore, lest society be a political enforcer of sexual ideology, homosexuals ought to be afforded equal standing and protections under the law, and this in the name of serving human happiness.

CONCLUSIONS

Levin has argued that homosexuality is a self-punishing maladaption likely to cause unhappiness since homosexuals do not use their organs for what they are for. Human happiness is said to attend that behaviour which follows out the natural paths plotted by evolutionary selection. As homosexuality has not thus far been shown to have contributed (*pace* sociobiology) to the kind of beings we are today, it may be assumed that homosexual behaviour is abnormal. As such behaviour, too, is linked with unhappiness it is to be rejected as both abnormal and unrewarding. The law ought to follow this conclusion through and reject any inducements to homosexuality.

I have argued against this position on a number of grounds. The most important is this: nature is represented here by Levin as without guiding or controlling force. Therefore, as pathways of evolutionary adaptation are themselves only a matter of metaphysical blind accident, nature lacks normative force and human beings are completely at liberty to dispose of the world, their behaviour, and their bodies as they see fit. One could still try to argue against homosexuality on prudential grounds, on grounds that it causes unhappiness, but I have argued that conclusions from claims about unhappiness are inconclusive because it is not clear how much homosexual unhappiness is adventitious and how much intrinsic. Levin's evidence that such unhappiness is intrinsic is anecdotal evidence of the most unconvincing kind. A complete reconstruction of society such that homosexuality was on a par with heterosexuality would be required in order to distinguish adventitious from intrinsic unhappiness and make the argument conclusive. But even if there were residual unhappiness attaching to homosexuality under socially liberating conditions of this grand experiment, such unhappiness might be likened to the irreducible tragic aspects of atheism: Such an unhappiness is no writ for legal and social measures designed to stem the genesis of either atheists or homosexuals.

On the contrary, rather than using the law as an instrument of enforcing invisibility on homosexuals, the law should, I think, be used to afford what measure of happiness it can. How far the law ought to serve the needs of gay men and lesbians is, of course, a matter of debate. But it seems to follow that at the very least, the law ought to protect gay men and lesbians from unhappiness caused by victimization and social exclusions which it is within the law's power to reject.

NOTES

1. Ronald Bayer (1981) *Homosexuality and American Psychiatry* (New York, Basic Books).

2. Mark Schwartz & William H. Masters (1984) The Masters and Johnson Program for Dissatisfied Homosexual Men, *American Journal of Psychiatry,* 141, pp. 173–181.

3. See some of the selections in Edward Batchelor, Jr. (Ed.) (1980) *Homosexuality and Ethics* (New York, Pilgrim Press).

4. Michael Levin (1985) Why homosexuality is abnormal, *Monist* (Spring) pp. 251–283.

5. Levin, p. 256.

6. See H. Tristam Engelhardt, Jr. (1986) *The Foundations of Bioethics,* pp. 375–387 (New York, OUP).

7. Michael Gelder, Dennis Gath, & Richard Mayou (1983) *Oxford Textbook of Psychiatry,* p. 468 (Oxford, OUP).

8. Levin, p. 251.

9. Levin, p. 261.

10. Levin, p. 262.

11. Levin, p. 268–269.

12. Levin's reading of the "evidence" is also suspect. At one point he refers to the narrative (1977) *The Sexual Outlaw* (New York, Grove Press), saying that even such a sympathetic observer as John Rechy admits that the immediate cause of homosexual unhappiness is a taste for promiscuity, anonymous encounters, and humiliation. This, I submit, is an embarrassing misrepresentation of Rechy's book, for that book explicitly, insistently, and frequently criticizes the hypocritical, violent sociolegal ethic which Rechy identifies itself as (the?) major cause of homosexual promiscuity and unhappiness. He says, for example: "Imagine the horror of living with that constant fear, those threats. Imagine being forbidden to seek out a sexual partner. Imagine that—and you begin to understand the promiscuous rage of the sexual outlaw" (p. 102).

13. Levin, p. 274.

14. Bowers v. Hardwick, No. 85–140 (30 June, 1986).

15. Irving Bieber, H.J. Dain, P.R. Dince, M.G. Orellich, H.G. Grand, R.H. Grundlach, M.W. Kremer, A.H. Rifkin, C.B. Wilbur & T.B. Bieber (1962) *Homosexuality: a psychoanalytic study* (New York, Basic Books). The introduction to this book reviews critically a number of theories.

16. Douglas Futuyma & Stephen J. Risch (1984) Sexual orientation, sociobiology and evolution, in J.P. DeCecco & M.G. Shively (Eds.) *Bisexual and Homosexual Identities: critical theoretical issues,* pp. 157–168 (New York, Haworth Press).

17. Sodomy laws in US (illus.), *New York Times,* 1 July 1986, p. A19.

18. Ernest Nagel (1965) A defense of atheism, in: P. Edwards & A. Pap *A Modern Introduction to Philosophy,* pp. 460–472, rev. edn (New York, Free Press).

Questions for Analysis

1. Does Murphy refute Levin's argument against gay rights? Why or why not?

2. Murphy criticizes Levin for defining homosexuality as a kind of behavior rather than a disposition. Is this a valid criticism in terms of Levin's argument?

3. How does Murphy rebut Levin's arguments about the relative unhappiness of homosexuals? How persuasive is his rebuttal?

4. According to Murphy, even if it could be shown that homosexuality had no original adaptive value, that wouldn't show that it's abnormal. Why? Do you agree?

5. How would Levin respond to Murphy's criticisms?

CASE PRESENTATION
Deception or Joke?

They were two unmarried business travelers who met in a limousine on their way to the airport. Since both had some time before their flights, he offered to buy her a drink in the airport bar. She accepted.

One of the first things they learned over their drinks was that they lived two thousand miles apart.

"Excellent," he said. "Will you marry me?"

"What?"

"Look, it'll be perfect. You'll live in your place, I'll live in mine, and we'll get together a few times a year. A marriage like that is bound to last."

He was kidding, of course, but it seemed to be an innocent enough joke. Unfortunately, she was slow to catch on.

"You think so?" she finally asked.

"Absolutely."

"Yes, maybe you're right." She pulled out her appointment book and turned a few pages. "The weekend after next I'm free. Why don't we spend it together, at my place."

And they did just that. On the appointed day, she picked him up at her city's airport and drove him back to her apartment, where they spent the next two nights.

"What next?" she asked during Sunday dinner. It was the last dinner of his visit. His plane was to leave in three hours.

"Well," he laughed, "we'll certainly keep in touch." He meant what he said. He was already looking forward to their next weekend.

"That's it?" She was not smiling. Her eyes were focused on her wine glass.

"What did you expect?"

She said nothing, nor did she look up.

"You're not thinking about what I said in the airport, are you?"

This time she did look up, with a slight smile. "I'm not?"

"But I was joking."

"I wasn't."

He explained to her all the reasons why it would be preposterous for them to get married, chief among them the fact that they hardly knew each other. She explained to him all the reasons that she'd invited him to spend the weekend with her, chief among them the fact that she'd taken his remarks about marriage seriously.

"Nobody could be serious about that," he told her.

"I was. And I thought you were too. That's what attracted me to you. You seemed adventurous, decisive, self-assured, the kind of man who'd get a crazy whim like that and act on it. You do give that impression, you know, but you're a fraud. You're just like the other men I come across. You've got a million reasons for wanting a woman to fall in love with you, and a million and one reasons not to get married."

"But—"

"But nothing. I didn't expect us to set a date, you know. I'm not a total lunatic, whatever you might think. But I certainly expected something more than 'we'll keep in touch.'"

A long period of awkwardness followed, after which she drove him to the airport. Much to his surprise, she kissed him goodbye. A few days later, she called to tell him that she didn't want to see him again.

Questions for Analysis

1. Was it unreasonable of the woman to expect more of the man than he gave her?

2. Did the man have any reason to believe that the woman would take him seriously? Should he have made it clear that he was joking?

3. What does the incident suggest about the possibility of unintentional deception in such sexual adventures?

4. Does the incident suggest that moral casual sex is rarer than the libertarian position might indicate?

CASE PRESENTATION
AIDS Education

In a statement issued by the U.S. Public Health Service in October 1986, U.S. Surgeon General C. Everett Koop said:

> Many people—especially our youth—are not receiving information that is vital to their future health and well-being because of our reticence in dealing with the subjects of sex, sexual practices, and homosexuality. This silence must end. We can no longer afford to sidestep frank, open discussion about sexual practices—homosexual and heterosexual. Education about AIDS should start at an early age so that children can grow up knowing the behaviors to avoid to protect themselves from exposure to the AIDS virus.

Considered in terms of public *health* policy, Koop's plea seems unexceptionable. In the face of any medical epidemic, the more knowledgeable the public, the safer the public. But Koop's plea has *moral* implications as well, and those implications have made it very controversial. According to his opponents, Koop was promoting the teaching of "safe sodomy" to children. They agree that children should be taught to avoid behavior that transmits the AIDS virus, but for them—including then-Secretary of Education William Bennett—that means teaching sexual abstinence.

No one doubts that abstinence is the surest way of avoiding sexual transmission of AIDS. But Koop and his supporters argue that *teaching* abstinence does not always *lead* to abstinence. Therefore, safe sex must be taught as well.

In the spring of 1988, while the debate continued, the Public Health Service mailed the pamphlet *Understanding AIDS* to every home in the country. Although the pamphlet was intended primarily for adults, the term "safe sex" does not appear anywhere in it. Also, under the heading Safe Behavior, both abstinence and monogamy with an uninfected partner are listed, but no other sexual behavior. Still, there is a section on condom use as a safety measure, including recommendations concerning what kind of condom to use and how to use it, and elsewhere in the pamphlet, mention is made of vaginal, oral, and anal sex and their role in the transmission of AIDS. Why not give the same information in the schools?

One reason given by Koop's opponents is the concern that students will interpret their instruction as *advocacy* of sexual promiscuity and homosexuality as long as condoms are used. Another involves the relative ignorance of schoolchildren. Since many do not know what oral and anal sex are, these acts must be explained to them. But schools should not be in the business of teaching children how to perform sodomy (hence the derisive term "safe sodomy").

Koop's supporters, of course, argue that the information can be conveyed without giving the impression of advocacy and that the AIDS threat requires that children receive it. But that brings us to the heart of the matter. To many people, the AIDS threat cannot require us to teach "immoral" behavior to children. They see such behavior as the problem, not the solution.

Questions for Analysis

1. Is the former surgeon general right? Should we overcome our reticence about sex in the face of the AIDS threat?

2. Do moral disagreements about sex have a legitimate role in public health matters, or should policy decisions be made purely on the grounds of effectiveness?

3. Can information about safe sex be given to children in a morally neutral way? Would moral neutrality come across as moral acceptance?

4. At what age do children become old enough to receive the information Koop thinks they should have?

5. Would learning about anal and oral sex hurt schoolchildren?

CASE PRESENTATION
Marriage and Civil Unions

Recent attention to "civil unions" has focused on same-sex relationships, especially in Vermont, which permits these by legislation passed in 2000. Under this law, eligible same-sex couples can "obtain the same benefits and protections afforded by Vermont law to married opposite-sex couples," even though Vermont reserves the word "marriage" for opposite-sex couples. Several states are considering "same-sex" civil unions modeled after the Vermont statute, including Connecticut, Rhode Island, Washington, Hawaii, and California.

In 2003, a Canadian court held that marriage laws defining marriage as the union of a man and woman were unconstitutional. The prime minister of Canada then proposed legislation recognizing gay marriage, currently recognized only in Belgium and the Netherlands.

Civil unions for opposite-sex couples are also sometimes recognized by state governments. In 2001, California enacted a law which permits both same-sex and opposite-sex couples over the age of 62 to register as domestic partners. By registering, they receive many, though not all, of the benefits of traditional marriage, including the right to sue for wrongful death, the permission to make healthcare decisions, sick leave, tax benefits, stepparent adoption, and expanded healthcare benefits for public employees.

Some have also proposed that civil union relationships be extended to blood relatives who wished to take advantage of the economic and legal benefits of marriage, such as a parent and child or two siblings.

These civil unions are sanctioned solely by government, outside the traditional religious context of

the marriage of opposite-sex couples. Traditional marriage typically has a governmental, civil element in obtaining a marriage license and government sanction, along with a variety of legal benefits not available to unmarried persons. But most people (though not all) also recognize a religious aspect to their marriages, as a ceremony or sacrament in their particular religious faith. The emergence of controversial civil unions among same-sex couples presents the question of whether these two aspects of legally sanctioned relationships—governmental and religious—might appropriately be separated to accommodate nontraditional relationships of whatever kind.

The Vermont General Assembly made several legislative findings in 2001 when it passed its Act No. 91 Relating to Civil Unions:

(1) Civil marriage under Vermont's marriage statutes consists of a union between a man and a woman. This interpretation of the state's marriage laws was upheld by the [Vermont] Supreme Court in *Baker v. State.*

(2) Vermont's history as an independent republic and as a state is one of equal treatment and respect for all Vermonters. This tradition is embodied in the Common Benefits Clause of the Vermont Constitution, Chapter I, Article 7th.

(3) The state's interest in civil marriage is to encourage close and caring families, and to protect all family members from the economic and social consequences of

abandonment and divorce, focusing on those who have been especially at risk.

(4) Legal recognition of civil marriage by the state is the primary and, in a number of instances, the exclusive source of numerous benefits, responsibilities and protections under the laws of the state for married persons and their children.

(5) Based on the state's tradition of equality under the law and strong families, for at least 25 years, Vermont Probate Courts have qualified gay and lesbian individuals as adoptive parents.

(6) Vermont was one of the first states to adopt comprehensive legislation prohibiting discrimination on the basis of sexual orientation (Act No. 135 of 1992).

(7) The state has a strong interest in promoting stable and lasting families, including families based upon a same-sex couple.

(8) Without the legal protections, benefits and responsibilities associated with civil marriage, same-sex couples suffer numerous obstacles and hardships.

(9) Despite longstanding social and economic discrimination, many gay and lesbian Vermonters have formed lasting, committed, caring and faithful relationships with persons of their same sex. These couples live together, participate in their communities together, and some raise children and care for family members together, just as do couples who are married under Vermont law.

(10) While a system of civil unions does not bestow the status of civil marriage, it does satisfy the requirements of the Common Benefits Clause. Changes in the way significant legal relationships are established under the constitution should be approached carefully, combining respect for the community and cultural institutions most affected with a commitment to the constitutional rights involved. Granting benefits and protections to same-sex couples through a system of civil unions will provide due respect for tradition and long-standing social institutions, and will permit adjustment as unanticipated consequences or unmet needs arise.

(11) The constitutional principle of equality embodied in the Common Benefits Clause is compatible with the freedom of religious belief and worship guaranteed in Chapter I, Article 3rd of the state constitution. Extending the benefits and protections of marriage to same-sex couples through a system of civil unions preserves the fundamental constitutional right of each of the multitude of religious faiths in Vermont to choose freely and without state interference to whom to grant the religious status, sacrament or blessing of marriage under the rules, practices or traditions of such faith.

Questions for Analysis

1. Do these legislative findings justify Vermont's establishment of a legally recognized civil union between same-sex couples? What additional considerations would strengthen these findings in support of civil unions? What factors does Vermont omit which argue against recognizing civil unions?

2. Which of the findings of the Vermont legislature rely on consequentialist or utilitarian reasoning to be persuasive? Which rely on an appeal to basic human rights?

3. Would these findings justify a legally recognized civil union between opposite-sex couples who did not wish to be married but did wish to establish domestic partnerships with some legal rights that single people ordinarily do not have?

4. Should the legal aspects of human relationships be separated from the religious elements of marriage for all couples, regardless of gender? Are the legal and religious elements of marriage inextricably bound together? What are the advantages and disadvantages of considering marriage to be both a legally and religiously sanctioned relationship?

5. Should other states be required to recognize the civil unions of Vermont? Of Canada?

6. Does this governmental establishment of legally sanctioned relationships, separated from the traditional religious element of marriage, undermine standards of sexual morality?

CASE PRESENTATION

Lawrence v. Texas: **Private Rights and Public Morality**

This 2003 U.S. Supreme Court decision overturned the 1986 decision *Bowers v. Hardwick*, which had held that private homosexual conduct among consenting adults was not protected under the U.S. Constitution.

MAJORITY OPINION (written by Justice Kennedy)

Liberty protects the person from unwarranted government intrusions into a dwelling or other private places. In our tradition the State is not omnipresent in the home. And there are other spheres of our lives and existence, outside the home, where the State should not be a dominant presence. Freedom extends beyond spatial bounds. Liberty presumes an autonomy of self that includes freedom of thought, belief, expression, and certain intimate conduct. The instant case involves liberty of the person both in its spatial and more transcendent dimensions.

The question before the Court is the validity of a Texas statute making it a crime for two persons of the same sex to engage in certain intimate sexual conduct. . . . The applicable state law . . . provides: "A person commits an offense if he engages in deviate sexual intercourse with another individual of the same sex." The statute defines "[d]eviate sexual intercourse" as follows:

"(A) any contact between any part of the genitals of one person and the mouth or anus of another person; or

"(B) the penetration of the genitals or the anus of another person with an object." . . .

We conclude the case should be resolved by determining whether the petitioners were free as adults to engage in the private conduct in the exercise of their liberty under the Due Process Clause of the Fourteenth Amendment to the Constitution. For this inquiry we deem it necessary to reconsider the Court's holding in *Bowers*.

. . . The Court began its substantive discussion in *Bowers* as follows: "The issue presented is whether the Federal Constitution confers a fundamental right upon homosexuals to engage in sodomy and hence invalidates the laws of the many States that still make such conduct illegal and have done so for a very long time." . . . That statement, we now conclude, discloses the Court's own failure to appreciate the extent of the liberty at stake. To say that the issue in *Bowers* was simply the right to engage in certain sexual conduct demeans the claim the individual put forward, just as it would demean a married couple were it to be said marriage is simply about the right to have sexual intercourse. The laws involved in *Bowers* and here are, to be sure, statutes that purport to do no more than prohibit a particular sexual act. Their penalties and purposes, though, have more far-reaching consequences, touching upon the most private human conduct, sexual behavior, and in the most private of places, the home. The statutes do seek to control a personal relationship that, whether or not entitled to formal recognition in the law, is within the liberty of persons to choose without being punished as criminals.

This, as a general rule, should counsel against attempts by the State, or a court, to define the meaning of the relationship or to set its boundaries absent injury to a person or abuse of an institution the law protects. It suffices for us to acknowledge that adults may choose to enter upon this relationship in the confines of their homes and their own private lives and still retain their dignity as free persons. When sexuality finds overt expression in intimate conduct with another person, the conduct can be but one element in a personal bond that is more enduring. The liberty protected by the Constitution allows homosexual persons the right to make this choice.

. . . It must be acknowledged, of course, that the Court in *Bowers* was making the broader point that for centuries there have been powerful voices to condemn homosexual conduct as immoral. The condemnation has been shaped by religious beliefs, conceptions of right and acceptable behavior, and respect for the traditional family. For many persons these are not trivial concerns but profound and deep convictions accepted as ethical and moral principles to which they aspire and which thus determine the course of their lives. These considerations do not answer the question before us, however. The issue is whether the majority may use the power of the State to enforce these views on the whole society through operation of the criminal law. . . .

. . . Equality of treatment and the due process right to demand respect for conduct protected by the substantive guarantee of liberty are linked in important respects, and a decision on the latter point advances both interests. If protected conduct is made criminal and the law which does so remains unexamined for its substantive validity, its stigma might remain even if it were not enforceable as drawn for equal protection reasons. When homosexual conduct is made criminal by the law of the State, that declaration in and of itself is an invitation to subject homosexual persons to discrimination both in the public and in the private spheres. The central holding of *Bowers* has been brought in question by this case, and it should be addressed. Its continuance as precedent demeans the lives of homosexual persons. . . .

. . . *Bowers* was not correct when it was decided, and it is not correct today. It ought not to remain binding precedent. *Bowers v. Hardwick* should be and now is overruled.

The present case does not involve minors. It does not involve persons who might be injured or coerced or who are situated in relationships where consent might not easily be refused. It does not involve public conduct or prostitution. It does not involve whether the government must give formal recognition to any relationship that homosexual persons seek to enter. The case does involve two adults who, with full and mutual consent from each other, engaged in sexual practices common to a homosexual lifestyle. The petitioners are entitled to respect for their private lives. The State cannot demean their existence or control their destiny by making their private sexual conduct a crime. Their right to liberty under the Due Process Clause gives them the full right to engage in their conduct without intervention of the government. . . . The Texas statute furthers no legitimate state interest which can justify its intrusion into the personal and private life of the individual.

Had those who drew and ratified the Due Process Clauses of the Fifth Amendment or the Fourteenth Amendment known the components of liberty in its manifold possibilities, they might have been more specific. They did not presume to have this insight. They knew times can blind us to certain truths and later generations can see that laws once thought necessary and proper in fact serve only to oppress. As the Constitution endures, persons in every generation can invoke its principles in their own search for greater freedom. . . .

Justice Scalia, dissenting

. . . The Texas statute undeniably seeks to further the belief of its citizens that certain forms of sexual behavior are "immoral and unacceptable," . . . the same interest furthered by criminal laws against fornication, bigamy, adultery, adult incest, bestiality, and obscenity. *Bowers* held that this was a legitimate state interest. The Court today reaches the opposite conclusion. The Texas statute, it says, "furthers no legitimate state interest which can justify its intrusion into the personal and private life of the individual," . . . . The Court embraces instead Justice Stevens' declaration in his *Bowers* dissent, that "the fact that the governing majority in a State has traditionally viewed a particular practice as immoral is not a sufficient reason for upholding a law prohibiting the practice," . . . . This effectively decrees the end of all morals legislation. If, as the Court asserts, the promotion of majoritarian sexual morality is not even a legitimate state interest, none of the above-mentioned laws can survive rational-basis review. . . .

One of the most revealing statements in today's opinion is the Court's grim warning that the criminalization of homosexual conduct is "an invitation to subject homosexual persons to discrimination both in the public and in the private spheres." . . . It is clear from this that the Court has taken sides in the culture war, departing from its role of assuring, as neutral observer, that the democratic rules of engagement are observed. Many Americans do not want persons who openly engage in homosexual conduct as partners in their business, as scoutmasters for their children, as teachers in their children's schools, or as boarders in their home. They view this as protecting themselves and their families from a lifestyle that they believe to be immoral and destructive. The Court views it as "discrimination" which it is the function of our judgments to deter. . . .

One of the benefits of leaving regulation of this matter to the people rather than to the courts is that the people, unlike judges, need not carry things to their logical conclusion. The people may feel that their disapprobation of homosexual conduct is strong enough to disallow homosexual marriage, but not strong enough to criminalize private homosexual acts—and may legislate accordingly. The Court today pretends that it possesses a similar freedom of action, so that we need not fear judicial imposition of homosexual marriage, as has recently occurred in Canada (in a decision that the Canadian Government has chosen not to appeal). . . . At the end of its opinion—after having laid waste the foundations of our rational-basis jurisprudence—the Court says that the present case "does not involve whether the government must give formal recognition to any relationship that homosexual persons seek to enter." . . . Do not believe it. . . . Today's opinion dismantles the structure of constitutional law that has permitted a distinction to be made between heterosexual and homosexual unions, insofar as formal recognition in marriage is concerned. If moral disapproval of homosexual conduct is "no legitimate state interest" for purposes of proscribing that conduct, . . . ; and if, as the Court coos (casting aside all pretense of neutrality), "[w]hen sexuality finds overt expression in intimate conduct with another person, the conduct can be but one element in a personal bond that is more enduring," . . . ; what justification could there possibly be for denying the benefits of marriage to homosexual couples exercising "[t]he liberty protected by the Constitution," . . . Surely not the encouragement of procreation, since the sterile and the elderly are allowed to marry. This case "does not involve" the issue of homosexual marriage only if one entertains the belief that principle and logic have nothing to do with the decisions of this Court. Many will hope that, as the Court comfortingly assures us, this is so. . . .

Questions for Analysis

1. Has the majority opinion struck the right balance between the appropriate roles of the law and of private morality? Is there any immoral behavior that should still be illegal, even if society's concerns originated in moral prohibitions?

2. Under the reasoning of the majority opinion here, should the criminal laws on fornication, bigamy, adultery, adult incest, bestiality, and obscenity also be struck down? If not, what considerations can you cite to support the continuation of those laws?

3. Does Justice Scalia engage in "slippery slope" reasoning?

4. Does the majority opinion provide a compelling basis for eventually holding that homosexual "marriage" is a constitutional right, despite the court's insistence that it has not? Is Justice Scalia right to be concerned that the reasoning of the majority makes it inevitable that homosexual "marriage" will eventually be found to be a constitutional right?

5. How would Levin and Murphy, respectively, critique *Lawrence v. Texas*?

4

Abortion

Biological Background
The Moral Problem
The Ontological Status of the Fetus
The Moral Status of the Fetus
Pro-Life Arguments (against Abortion)
Pro-Choice Arguments (for Abortion)
John T. Noonan, "An Almost Absolute Value in History"
Judith Jarvis Thomson, "A Defense of Abortion"
Mary Ann Warren, "On the Moral and
Legal Status of Abortion"
Rosalind Hursthouse, "Virtue Theory and Abortion"
CASE PRESENTATION, "Mrs. Sherri Finkbine and the
Thalidomide Tragedy"
CASE PRESENTATION, "'Conceived in Violence, Born in Hate'"
CASE PRESENTATION, "Death in Pensacola"
CASE PRESENTATION, "The Fight for Martina Greywind's Baby"

Jane Roe was an unmarried pregnant woman who wished to have an abortion, an intentional termination of a pregnancy by inducing the loss of the fetus. But Ms. Roe lived in Texas, where statutes forbade abortion except to save the life of the mother. So she went to court to prove that the statutes were unconstitutional.

The three-judge district court ruled that Jane Roe had reason to sue, that the Texas criminal abortion statutes were void on their face, and most important, that the right to choose whether to have children was protected by the right to privacy implicit in several amendments to the U.S. Constitution. Even though the word "privacy" does not appear in the Constitution, the court reasoned that privacy rights they had earlier recognized to use contraception and to permit interracial marriage extended to a right to choose whether or not to have children. Since the district court denied a number of other aspects of the suit, the case went to the U.S. Supreme Court. On January 22, 1973, in the now famous *Roe v. Wade* decision (410 U.S. 113), the Supreme Court affirmed the district court's judgment.

Expressing the views of seven members of the Court, Justice Blackmun pointed out that the right to privacy applies to a woman's decision on whether to terminate her pregnancy but that her right to terminate is not absolute. Her right may be limited by the state's legitimate interests in safeguarding the woman's health, in maintaining proper medical standards, and in protecting human life. Blackmun went on to point out that fetuses are not included within the definition of *person* as used in the Fourteenth Amendment. Most important, he indicated that prior to the end of the first trimester of pregnancy, the state may not interfere with or regulate an attending physician's decision, reached in consultation with the patient, that the patient's pregnancy should be terminated. After the first trimester and until the fetus is viable, the state may regulate the abortion procedure only for the health of the mother. After the fetus becomes viable, the state may prohibit all abortions except those necessary to preserve the health or life of the mother.

In dissenting, Justices White and Rehnquist said that nothing in the language or history of the U.S. Constitution supported the Court's judgment and that the Court had simply manufactured a new constitutional right for pregnant women. The abortion issue, they said, should have been left with the people and the political processes they had devised to govern their affairs.

So for the time being at least, the question of a woman's constitutional right to an abortion has been legally resolved. But the issue is hardly settled. Since the *Roe* decision, a number of anti-abortion movements have surfaced, and many state legislatures have passed restrictive abortion laws, some designed to narrow abortion rights and discourage abortions, others designed to challenge *Roe v. Wade* in the courts in the hope that it will be overturned.

In an important case decided July 3, 1989, *Webster v. Reproductive Health Services* (492 U.S. 490), the U.S. Supreme Court upheld a Missouri law that declared in its preamble that the "life of each human being begins at conception." The Court considered this statement to be only a "value judgment favoring childbirth over abortion" and said they would not rule on its constitutionality or unconstitutionality. The law also requires physicians to conduct viability tests on the fetuses of women twenty weeks pregnant and prohibits the use of public funds, employees, and facilities to perform, assist, or counsel abortions not necessary to save the mother's life. Moreover, four justices indicated a willingness to overturn the *Roe* decision. Since then, the Court has upheld state laws requiring parental consent for abortions on minors.

The Court's most significant decision on abortion since *Webster* was *Planned Parenthood v. Casey* (505 U.S. 833), announced June 29, 1992. The issue in this case was a Pennsylvania law regulating abortions. Although the Court again upheld the right to abortion by a 5 to 4 majority, it also upheld two of the law's restrictions. The first requires a twenty-four hour waiting period following a mandatory presentation intended to dissuade the woman from having an abortion. The second requires teenagers to have the consent of a parent or a judge. Also upheld were two other provisions: one specifying medical emergencies that exempt a woman from the restrictions, the other requiring clinics and doctors to provide the state with statistical reports on abortions performed. One other requirement, that married women first tell their husbands, was struck down as placing an "undue burden" on them.

Also significant was the Court's *Stenberg v. Carhart* decision (530 U.S. 914), announced June 28, 2000. At issue was a Nebraska law banning in all circumstances except to save the woman's life a rare but highly controversial abortion technique called *evacuation and extraction* (D&X). The law did not use that term, however. Instead, it referred to the procedure with the term commonly used by abortion opponents, "partial birth abortion," which the law defined as "deliberately and intentionally delivering into the vagina a living unborn child, or a substantial portion thereof, for the purpose of performing a procedure that the person performing such procedure knows will kill the unborn child." The majority opinion cited two chief reasons for declaring the law unconstitutional. First, the law allowed no exception to preserve the woman's health. Second, the law's definition of "partial birth abortion" was broad enough to cover another abortion procedure, the one most commonly used in the second trimester (*dilation and evacuation,* or D&E). In doing so, it placed an "undue burden on a woman's right to terminate her pregnancy before viability."

In the next section, we will explain these and other abortion procedures. For now, it's enough to say that abortion opponents are drafting new laws prohibiting D&X that are designed to withstand the Court's objections. We should also stress that the fight to overturn *Roe v. Wade,* whether through a constitutional amendment or sympathetic appointments to the Supreme Court, continues. Thus, abortion remains a live and controversial issue, both morally and legally.

Some say an abortion is right if (1) it is therapeutic—that is, if it is necessary to preserve the physical or mental health of the woman; (2) it prevents the birth of a child with a severe disability; or (3) it ends a pregnancy resulting from some criminal act of sexual intercourse. Others say that even therapeutic abortions are immoral. Still others argue that any restrictive abortion legislation is wrong and must be liberalized to allow a woman to have an abortion on demand—that is, at the request of her and her physician, regardless of or even in the absence of reasons. To evaluate such claims, it is helpful to know some biological background and to consider what sort of entities the unborn are and whether they have rights.

BIOLOGICAL BACKGROUND

Because most of the controversy surrounding the abortion issue concerns precisely when a human individual or "person" is considered to exist, it is important to have some background about the development of the human fetus and familiarity with the terms that designate the various developmental stages. Conception or fertilization occurs when a female germ cell, or *ovum,* is penetrated by a male germ cell, or *spermatozoon.* The result is a single cell containing a full genetic code of forty-six chromosomes, called the *zygote.* The zygote then journeys down the fallopian tube, which carries ova from the ovary to the uterus. This passage generally takes two or three days. During the journey, the zygote begins a process of cellular division that increases its size. Occasionally, the zygote ends its journey in the fallopian tube, where it continues to develop. Because the tube is so narrow, such a pregnancy generally must be terminated by surgery.

When the multicell zygote reaches the uterus, it floats free in the intrauterine fluid and develops into what is termed a *blastocyst,* a ball of cells surrounding a fluid-filled cavity. By the end of the second week, the blastocyst implants itself in the uterine wall. From the end of the second week until the end of the eighth week, the unborn entity is termed an *embryo.* In the interim (four to five weeks), organ systems begin to develop, and the embryo takes on distinctly human external features.

The eighth week is important in the biological development and in a discussion of abortion because it is then that brain activity generally becomes detectable. From this point until birth, the embryo is termed a *fetus*, although in common parlance *fetus* is used to designate the unborn entity at whatever stage.

Two other terms that designate events in fetal development are worth noting because they sometimes arise in abortion discussions. One is *quickening*, which refers to when the mother begins to feel the movements of the fetus. This occurs somewhere between the thirteenth and twentieth weeks. The second term is *viability*, the point at which the fetus is capable of surviving outside the womb. The fetus ordinarily reaches viability around the twenty-fourth week. Generally, then, events during pregnancy unfold as follows:

Developmental Timetable

zygote: first through third day
blastocyst: second day through second week
embryo: third week through eighth week
fetus: ninth week until birth
quickening: thirteenth week through twentieth week
viability: around twenty-fourth week

Should the unborn entity be terminated at any point in this timetable, an abortion is said to occur. Thus, *abortion simply refers to the termination of a pregnancy.*

Abortions can happen for a number of reasons. Sometimes the abortion occurs "spontaneously" because of internal biochemical factors or because of an injury to the woman. Such spontaneous abortions are ordinarily termed *miscarriages*. These generally involve no moral issues.

Abortions also can result directly from human intervention, which can occur in a variety of ways. Sometimes it happens very early, as when a woman takes a drug such as the "morning-after pill" to prevent the blastocyst from implanting in the uterine wall.

Subsequent intervention during the first trimester (through the twelfth week) usually takes the form of *vacuum aspiration*. In this procedure, the narrow opening of the uterus, the cervix, is dilated, and a small vacuum tube is inserted into the uterus to evacuate its contents through suction.

The most common abortion procedure after the twelfth week is dilation and evacuation. This procedure also involves dilation of the cervix, but the doctor uses surgical instruments, rather than a vacuum tube, to empty the uterus. How this procedure is performed depends on how advanced the pregnancy is. Up to week fifteen, fetal tissue is easily broken, so a spoon-shaped instrument known as a curette is used to scrape the uterine walls to make sure that no fetal tissue remains. After week fifteen, the fetus is generally too large to pass through the cervix, and its bones, having become more rigid, are less likely to break off. In that case, the evacuation requires that the fetus be dismembered after it has been partially pulled through the cervix.

After week sixteen, at the earliest, two other variants of D&E may be used. In the first, known as *intact D&E,* the skull of the fetus is collapsed by a sharp instrument before the entire fetus is pulled through the cervix. In the second, the position of the fetus is reversed to the breech position (feet first) and the skull is collapsed after the fetal body is pulled through the cervix. This procedure, dilation and extraction, was the one that Nebraska attempted to ban.

Before the widespread use of D&E in second trimester abortions, the most common method in use was *saline injection,* in which salt water is injected into the uterus to induce a miscarriage. The change to D&E came about because it is safer for the woman's health. Similarly, intact D&E is considered safer after the sixteenth week of pregnancy, and in a few rare cases—although there is some dispute among doctors—D&X is considered even safer.

Finally, there is one other form of abortion to consider, *mifepristone,* or RU-486, the abortion pill. Mifepristone works by blocking the action of progesterone, a steroid hormone needed to maintain a pregnancy. Approved first by France and China in 1988, and by thirteen other countries since, it did not receive approval in the United States until September 28, 2000, when the Food and Drug Administration (FDA) declared it safe and effective. Abortion by mifepristone is a three-step process. First, the woman takes the drug in her doctor's office. Second, she returns within thirty-six or forty-eight hours to take another drug, misoprostal, which forces the uterus to contract and expel the fetus. Third, she returns to the doctor's office two weeks later to make sure the pregnancy is terminated and her uterus is free of the fetal tissue.

In approving mifepristone, the FDA issued a number of restrictions. Most important, the drug cannot be used after the seventh week following the woman's last menstrual period. Since most abortions are performed later than that, no one yet knows how common its use will be.

THE MORAL PROBLEM

The key moral problem of abortion is: Under what conditions, if any, is abortion morally justifiable? In answer to this question, three positions are broadly identifiable.

(1) The so-called conservative view holds that abortion is never morally justifiable or, at most, justifiable only when the abortion is necessary to save the mother's life. This view is commonly associated with Roman Catholics, although they are certainly not the only persons who espouse it. (2) The so-called liberal view holds that abortion is always morally justifiable, regardless of the reasons or the time in fetal development. (3) The so-called intermediate or moderate views consider abortion morally acceptable up to a certain point in fetal development and/or claim that some reasons, not all, provide a sufficient justification for abortion.

While there is no consensus on the moral acceptability of abortion, there is agreement that any answer to the question depends on one's view of what sort of entities fetuses are and whether such entities have rights. These two important problems generally are referred to as the ontological and moral status of the fetus.

THE ONTOLOGICAL STATUS OF THE FETUS

In philosophy, the term **ontology** refers to the theory and nature of being and existence. When we speak of the **ontological** status of the fetus, we mean the kind of entity the fetus is. Determining the ontological status of fetuses bears directly on the issue of fetal rights and, subsequently, on permissible treatment of the fetus.

Actually, the problem of ontological status embraces a number of questions, such as: (1) whether the fetus is an individual organism; (2) whether the fetus is biologically a human being; (3) whether the fetus is psychologically a human being; (4) whether the fetus is a person.[1] Presumably, to affirm question two is to attribute more significant status to the fetus than to affirm question one, and to affirm question three is to assign even greater status. To affirm question four, that the fetus is a person, probably is to assign the most significant status to the fetus, although this, as well as the other presumptions, depends on the precise meaning of the concepts involved.

Complicating the question of the fetus's ontological status is the meaning of the expression *human life*. The concept of "human life" can be used in at least two different ways. On the one hand, it can refer to *biological* human life—that is, to a set of biological characteristics that distinguish the human species from other nonhuman species. In this sense, "human life" may be coextensive with "individual organism" as in question one. On the other hand, "human life" may refer to *psychological* human life—that is, to life that is characterized by the properties that are distinctly human. Among these properties might be the abilities to use symbols, to think, and to imagine. Abortion discussions can easily founder when these distinctions are not made. For example, many who would agree that abortion involves the taking of human life in the biological sense would deny that it involves taking human life in the psychological sense. Moreover, they might see nothing immoral about taking life exclusively in the biological sense, although they would consider taking life in the psychological sense morally unacceptable. Thus, they find nothing morally objectionable about abortion. Of course, at the root of this judgment is an assumption about the meaning of *human life*.

Intertwined with one's concept of human life is one's concept of "personhood." The concept of personhood may or may not differ from either the biological or the psychological sense of "human life." Some would argue that to be a person is simply to have the biological and/or psychological properties that make an organism human. However, others would propose additional conditions for personhood, such as consciousness, self-consciousness, rationality, even the capacities for communication and moral judgment. In this view, an entity must satisfy some or all of these criteria, even additional ones, to be a person. Still other theorists would extend the concept of personhood to include properties bestowed by human evaluation, in addition to the factual properties possessed by a person. Thus, they might argue that a person must be the bearer of legal rights and social responsibilities, and must be capable of being assigned moral responsibility, of being praised or blamed.

Clearly, the conditions that one believes are necessary for "person" status directly affect the ontological status of the fetus. For example, if the condition is only of an elementary biological nature, then the fetus can more easily qualify as a person than if the conditions include a list of factual properties. Further, if personhood must be analyzable in terms of properties bestowed by human evaluation, it becomes substantially more difficult for the fetus to qualify as a person.

---

1.   Tom L. Beauchamp and Le Roy Waiters, *Contemporary Issues in Bioethics* (Belmont, Calif.: Dickenson, 1978), p. 188.

In the final analysis, the ontological status of fetuses remains an open issue. But some viewpoint ultimately underpins any position on the morality of abortion. Whether conservative, liberal, or moderate, one must be prepared eventually to defend one's view of the ontological status of fetuses.

When Ontological Status Is Attained

Further complicating the problem of the ontological status is the question of when in fetal development the fetus gains full ontological status. Whether one claims the fetus is an individual organism, a biological human being, a psychological human being, or a full-fledged person, one must specify at what point in its biological development the fetus attains this status. It is one thing to say what status the fetus has; it is another to say *when* it has attained such status. A judgment about when the fetus has the status bears as directly on abortion views as does a judgment of the status itself.

We can identify a number of positions on when status is attained. An extreme conservative position would argue that the fetus has full ontological status from conception; at the time of conception, the fetus must be regarded as an individual person. In direct contrast to this view is the extreme liberal position, which holds that the fetus never achieves ontological status.

Viewing these as polar positions, we can identify a cluster of moderate views that fall between them. In every instance, the moderate view tries to pinpoint full ontological status somewhere between conception and birth. For example, some draw the line when brain activity is first present; others draw it at quickening; still others draw the line at viability.

Continuing progress in medicine has made these determinations increasingly difficult. With extraordinary medical support, very premature infants can be kept alive, challenging traditional views of what counts as viability. Some believe viability should be measured by an ability to live outside the womb without any medical intervention. Others believe newborn infants meet the test of viability even with the support of incubators, transfusions, and increasingly sophisticated medical assistance.

Medical advances have also challenged our definition of death, the cessation of the life of a person. Where cessation of a heartbeat once counted as death, the advent of heart transplants and mechanical hearts forced a change. Persons are now considered legally dead when all brain wave activity ceases. Some moderate abortion advocates suggest that the start of brain activity in a fetus should be the decisive point at which the fetus becomes a person and thus has the rights of persons. But there is disagreement about the extent of brain activity that would be required for such a test of personhood. And abortion foes say that the potential of a fetus for the development of brain activity—something a deceased person no longer has—makes the end of the life of a person irrelevant for determining the start of the life of a person.

THE MORAL STATUS OF THE FETUS

The issue of moral status of the fetus is generally, but not always, discussed in terms of the fetus's rights. What rights, if any, does it have? Any position on abortion must at some point address this question, and all seriously argued positions do, at least by implication.

Various views on the moral status of the fetus are currently circulating. Each view can be associated with one or another of the views on the fetus's ontological status. For example, claiming that the fetus has full ontological status at conception, the extreme conservative view also holds that it has full moral status at the same stage. From the moment of conception on, the unborn entity enjoys the same rights we attribute to any adult human. In this view, abortion would be a case of denying the unborn the right to life. Therefore, abortion could never be undertaken without reasons sufficient to override the unborn's claim to life. In other words, only conditions that would justify the killing of an adult human—for example, self-defense —would morally justify an abortion.

Liberals similarly derive their view of moral status from their theory of ontological status. The extreme liberal view would deny the fetus any moral status. In this view, abortion is not considered comparable to killing an adult person. Indeed, abortion may be viewed as removing a mass of organic material, not unlike an appendectomy. Its removal raises no serious moral problems. A somewhat less liberal view, while granting the fetus ontological status as being biologically human, claims it is not human in any significant moral sense and thus has no significant rights.

Likewise, moderates would assign moral status to the fetus at the point that the entity attained full ontological status. If brain activity is taken as the point of ontological status, for example, then abortions conducted before that time would not raise serious moral questions; those conducted subsequent to that development would. Currently, viability seems to be an especially popular point at which to assign ontological status. And so, many moderate theorists today insist that abortion raises significant moral questions only *after* the fetus has attained viability. This view is reflected in some of the opinions delivered in the *Roe v. Wade* case.

It is important to note that granting the fetus moral status does not at all deny moral status to the woman. Indeed, the question of whose rights should take precedence when a conflict develops raises thorny questions, especially for conservatives and moderates. For example, while granting the fetus full moral status, some conservatives nonetheless approve of therapeutic abortions—abortions performed to save the woman's life or to correct some life-threatening condition. These are often viewed as cases of self-defense or justifiable homicide. Since self-defense and justifiable homicide commonly are considered acceptable grounds for killing an adult person, they are also taken as moral justification for killing a fetus. But other conservatives disapprove of even therapeutic abortions.

Similarly, while moderates grant the fetus moral status at some point in development, they too must arbitrate cases of conflicting rights. They must determine just what conditions are sufficient for allowing the woman's right to override the fetus's right to life. Here the whole gamut of conditions involving the pregnancy must be evaluated, including rape, incest, fetal deformity, and of course, physical or psychological harm to the woman.

Moral Implications

Determining the moral status of the fetus, then, is directly related to determining when the fetus is actually a human. There is no question that even at the zygote stage, and from then on, the fetus is at least potentially human (until it becomes actually so).

At whatever point it becomes human, we face a set of serious moral issues regarding abortion, among which are

1.   Does the fetus have a right to be carried to full term?

2.   Under what circumstances, if ever, can we take an innocent human life?

3.   Is any other right more important than the right to life—for example, the woman's right to privacy, the woman's right not to be forced to carry a child that will make it impossible for her to have children in the future, or the woman's right not to carry the child of her rapist or her father or brother?

4.   If the woman's life is in danger because of the pregnancy, how do we decide whose right prevails?

If, as is the case at present, we can't agree at what point the fetus becomes fully human, we're confronted with another set of problems.

1.   Can we morally disregard the possibility that the fetus may be actually human (or may not)? If we do, does that imply, at best, an indifference to an important moral value? And is not such an attitude of not caring about a moral value itself morally questionable at least?

2.   Can we ever act morally on a doubt—for example, a doubt about our obligation, the morally relevant facts, the morally correct means? How are we to resolve our doubt?

3.   If reasonable people in the country hold irreconcilable moral and religious views on an issue such as abortion, is it appropriate for the government to "take sides" by forcing everyone to accept one of those views, whether through legislation or court decisions?

PRO-LIFE ARGUMENTS
(AGAINST ABORTION)

1.   *Abortion is murder.*

POINT: "The simple fact of the matter is that abortion is murder. What you call a 'fetus' is an unborn baby, a human being, and an abortion is nothing but the deliberate killing of that human being."

COUNTERPOINT: "Murder is the deliberate killing of a human person, and though a fetus is certainly a human *something,* it's hardly a person. In the earliest stages, it's nothing but a mass of cells. Even in later stages, when it begins to biologically resemble a human person, it still doesn't have anything remotely resembling a human life. It has no hopes, no plans, no concept of self, no stake in its own future. Sentimentalize it all you like, you still can't put a fetus ahead of the woman who carries it."

2.   *Abortion sets a dangerous precedent.*

POINT: "Anything that leads to disrespect for human life is wrong. Anything that leads to a casual attitude toward human life is wrong. Whatever else you say about abortion, it certainly leads to disrespect for and a casual attitude toward human life. And that doesn't just hold for abortions of convenience or for sex selection. It holds for therapeutic abortions and abortions of deformed fetuses as well. Once we decide that some human lives can be destroyed because they're inconvenient or not worth living, what's to stop us from killing individuals with severe disabilities, dysfunctions, senility, and mentally illness?"

COUNTERPOINT: "Abortion has been legal in this country for more than two decades, and we haven't started to slide down any slippery slopes because of it yet. To the contrary, in 1990 Congress passed, and the president signed, a landmark civil rights act for individuals with handicaps. We both know that abortion is a distinct issue from the treatment of various groups in society, and each has to be decided on its own merits."

3. *Abortion involves psychological risks to the woman.*

POINT: "A woman and the child she's carrying are as close to each other as any two humans can get. And I don't just mean biologically close but emotionally and psychologically close as well. Just ask any mother. A woman who intentionally harms her unborn child violates the deepest levels of her unconscious needs and desires, and she's bound to pay a psychological price for it. Plenty already have, as both psychologists and women who've had abortions can tell you."

COUNTERPOINT: "Many women, maybe even most, do want to carry their fetuses to term. And no doubt there are some women who do carry emotional scars from their abortions. But the vast majority of women who had abortions seem to have come through them quite well. The psychological portrait you paint of women and the deepest levels of their unconscious is nothing but a stereotype. And your desire to protect them from their considered decisions concerning what's best for them is insulting paternalism."

4. *Alternatives to abortion are available.*

POINT: "You abortion rights advocates make it sound as though abortion is the only alternative to rearing an unwanted child. But it's not. Countless couples and individuals are dying to have children but can't. Because of all the abortion mills throughout the country, many of them can't even adopt a healthy infant. So adoption is one alternative to abortion. Even in cases of infants with severe deformities, there are alternatives. If no one wants to adopt them, there are plenty of agencies and institutions to take care of them."

COUNTERPOINT: "Why should a woman be treated as a breeding animal for childless couples? The mere fact that other people want her child doesn't mean she has to face the health risks and discomforts of pregnancy for them. It's her body, after all. Besides, the anguish of giving up a child carried to term can be much worse than aborting a fetus. And as for infants with severe deformities, what kind of favor are you doing them by sentencing them to miserable lives in institutions?"

5. *Women must be responsible for their sexual activity.*

POINT: "No woman *has* to get pregnant. There are plenty of readily available contraceptives on the market. If a woman doesn't take advantage of them, it's her own fault and she has to take responsibility for her carelessness. To condone abortion is to condone her own irresponsibility. Even worse, it's to condone the killing of inno-cent life as an after-the-fact form of birth control."

COUNTERPOINT: "First of all, no form of birth control is 100 percent effective, except abstinence. To say that every unwanted pregnancy is the result of care-lessness is like saying that every driver struck by another car is at fault. But even if the woman was careless, that doesn't affect her right to have an abortion any more than careless driving affects the driver's right to medical treatment. To deny her that right is to engage in vindictiveness, not to uphold any principle of responsibility."

PRO-CHOICE ARGUMENTS
(FOR ABORTION)

1.   *Women have rights over their own bodies.*

POINT: "An unwanted pregnancy is an invasion of the woman's body, and to force a woman to carry a fetus to term is to force her to use her body for purposes she doesn't want to use it for. So the real issue here is whether women have the right to control their own bodies, whether they have the right to avail themselves of a simple, safe medical procedure to allow themselves to live their lives as they choose. Clearly the answer has to be yes. It's as fundamental a right as I can think of."

COUNTERPOINT: "No right is absolute. My right to swing my fist stops at your nose. My right to say whatever I please stops at yelling "fire!" in a crowded the-ater. Similarly, a woman's right to control her own body stops at taking the life of her unborn child. All your talk of 'invasion' and 'simple medical procedures' obscures the plain fact that once a woman conceives a child she's responsible for it. And that responsibility overrides her right to control her own body."

2.   *Unwanted pregnancies carry physical and emotional burdens.*

POINT: "Pregnancy isn't easy for women. Apart from the morning sickness, the back pains, the pain of childbirth, and a host of other discomforts in normal preg-nancies, the possibility of unforeseen complications poses a real risk to their phys-ical health and sometimes even their lives. To demand that a woman face all that in an unwanted pregnancy is to demand too much. And the unreasonable demands don't even stop there. Unwanted pregnancies carry emotional burdens as well as physical ones. Pregnancy can be a significant interruption in a woman's life, and motherhood can bring a serious disruption of her hopes and plans. Reproductive freedom isn't just a slogan. It's a matter of allowing a woman to control her own destiny."

COUNTERPOINT: "Yes, pregnancy can be difficult, and though I don't want to sound unsympathetic to pregnant women, I still have to insist that the woman isn't the only one involved here. Against the back pains, hemorrhoids, and varicose veins you have to balance the life of her child, which has to count for more. And as for the disruption of her hopes and plans, nobody says she has to rear the child. Don't forget—there's always adoption. The only place you may have a point is when it comes to serious risk to the woman's life. But to justify abortion for *every* woman on the grounds that she *might* face that risk is preposterous. Modern medicine has come too far for that."

3.   *The alternative to legal abortion is back alley abortion.*

POINT: "You may think that the burdens of unwanted pregnancy are minor, but many women don't. If safe, legal abortions aren't available to them, they'll resort to unsafe, illegal abortions. And if the past is any guide, that means serious infections in many cases and in some cases even death, especially for poor women who won't be able to afford anything but back alley abortions."

COUNTERPOINT: "Now you're confusing the issue. Whatever problems there may be in enforcing abortion laws is one issue. Whether abortion is moral or immoral is another. Enforcement problems might provide a reason not to ban abortions, but they certainly don't make abortions morally right. Then again, enforcement problems don't even provide a very good reason against banning abortions. As unfortunate as back alley abortions are for both the mothers and their unborn children, legalization encourages abortions; and if they're banned, there will be fewer of them."

4.   *The woman counts more than the fetus.*

POINT: "Everything you say is based on a single assumption—that the fetus counts as much as or even more than the woman. But that can't be true. A woman is a full-fledged person. She has real desires and fears, real aspirations and memories. She's connected to the world through her family and friends. She cares about her life and her future. At the very most, a fetus has only the potential for all that. And though I'm not saying the fetus's potential counts for nothing, I am saying an actual full human life out in the world has to count more than a potential full human life in the womb."

COUNTERPOINT: "Your distinction between an actual human life and a potential one just doesn't hold up. The difference between the mother and her unborn child isn't a matter of kind but of degree. Human life begins at conception. At that moment, we don't have a potential human life but a developing one. And who's to say that the more developed human life counts for more than the less developed one? If a woman doesn't count more than a ten-year-old, and if neither counts more than a two-year-old, why should any one of them count more than an unborn human life?"

An Almost Absolute Value in History

John T. Noonan

Like many authors on the subject of abortion, John T. Noonan, a judge on the U.S. Court of Appeals for the 9th Circuit, locates the central issue in the ontological status of the fetus. In his essay, Noonan assigns the fetus full ontological status at the moment of conception.

Noonan not only puts this view in the context of traditional Christian theology, but he also tests its strength compared with the other distinctions of ontological status that are commonly made: viability, experience, quickening, attitude of parents, and social visibility. Noonan shows why he thinks each of these distinctions is unsound.

From John T. Noonan, "An Almost Absolute Value in History." in *Morality of Abortion: Legal and Historical Perspectives,* ed. John T. Noonan (Cambridge, Mass: Harvard University Press, 1970). Reprinted by permission of the author.

In addition to the unique problems that each of these distinctions has, Noonan believes that they share one overriding problem: They are distinctions that appear to be arbitrary. Noonan feels that if distinctions leading to moral judgments are not to appear arbitrary, they should relate to some real difference in probabilities. He argues that his position passes this test because it recognizes the fact that 80 percent of the zygotes formed will develop into new beings. For Noonan, this probability is a most compelling reason for granting the conceptus (fetus) full ontological status.

In short, conception is the decisive moment of humanization, for it is then that the fetus receives the genetic code of the parents. These arguments lead Noonan to condemn abortion, except in cases of self-defense.

The most fundamental question involved in the long history of thought on abortion is: How do you determine the humanity of a being? To phrase the question that way is to put in comprehensive humanistic terms what the theologians either dealt with as an explicitly theological question under the heading of "ensoulment" or dealt with implicitly in their treatment of abortion. The Christian position as it originated did not depend on a narrow theological or philosophical concept. It had no relation to theories of infant baptism. It appealed to no special theory of instantaneous ensoulment. It took the world's view on ensoulment as that view changed from Aristotle to Zacchia. There was, indeed, theological influence affecting the theory of ensoulment finally adopted, and, of course, ensoulment itself was a theological concept, so that the position was always explained in theological terms. But the theological notion of ensoulment could easily be translated into humanistic language by substituting "human" for "rational soul"; the problem of knowing when a man is a man is common to theology and humanism.

If one steps outside the specific categories used by the theologians, the answer they gave can be analyzed as a refusal to discriminate among human beings on the basis of their varying potentialities. Once conceived, the being was recognized as man because he had man's potential. The criterion for humanity, thus, was simple and all-embracing: If you are conceived by human parents, you are human.

The strength of this position may be tested by a review of some of the other distinctions offered in the contemporary controversy over legalizing abortion. Perhaps the most popular distinction is in terms of viability. Before an age of so many months, the fetus is not viable, that is, it cannot be removed from the mother's womb and live apart from her. To that extent, the life of the fetus is absolutely dependent on the life of the mother. This dependence is made the basis of denying recognition to its humanity.

There are difficulties with this distinction. One is that the perfection of artificial incubation may make the fetus viable at any time: It may be removed and artificially sustained. Experiments with animals already show that such a procedure is possible. This hypothetical extreme case relates to an actual difficulty: there is considerable elasticity to the idea of viability. Mere length of life is not an exact measure. The viability of the fetus depends on the extent of its anatomical and functional development. The weight and length of the fetus are better guides to the state of its development than age, but weight and length vary. Moreover, different racial groups have different ages at which their fetuses are viable. Some evidence, for example, suggests that Negro fetuses mature more quickly than white fetuses. If viability is the norm, the standard would vary with race and with many individual circumstances.

The most important objection to this approach is that dependence is not ended by viability. The fetus is still absolutely dependent on someone's care in order to continue existence; indeed a child of one or three or even five years of age is absolutely dependent on another's care for existence; uncared for, the older fetus or the younger child will die as surely as the early fetus detached from the mother. The unsubstantial lessening in dependence at viability does not seem to signify any special acquisition of humanity.

A second distinction has been attempted in terms of experience. A being who has had experience, has lived and suffered, who possesses memories, is more human than one who has not. Humanity depends on formation by experience. The fetus is thus "unformed" in the most basic human sense.

This distinction is not serviceable for the embryo which is already experiencing and reacting. The embryo is responsive to touch after eight weeks and at least at that point is experiencing. At an earlier stage the zygote is certainly alive and responding to its environment. The distinction may also be challenged by the rare case where aphasia has erased adult memory: Has it erased humanity? More fundamentally, this distinction leaves even the older fetus or the younger child to be treated as an unformed inhuman thing. Finally, it is not clear why experience as such confers humanity. It could be argued that certain central experiences such as loving or learning are necessary to make a man human. But then human beings who have failed to love or to learn might be excluded from the class called man.

A third distinction is made by appeal to the sentiments of adults. If a fetus dies, the grief of the parents is not the grief they would have for a living child. The fetus is an unnamed "it" till birth, and is not perceived as personality until at least the fourth month of existence, when movements in the womb manifest a vigorous presence demanding joyful recognition by the parents.

Yet feeling is notoriously an unsure guide to the humanity of others. Many groups of humans have had difficulty in feeling that persons of another tongue, color, religion, sex, are as human as they. Apart from reactions to alien groups, we mourn the loss of a ten-year-old boy more than the loss of his one-day-old brother or his 90-year-old grandfather. The difference felt and the grief expressed vary with the potentialities extinguished, or the experience wiped out; they do not seem to point to any substantial difference in the humanity of baby, boy, or grandfather.

Distinctions are also made in terms of sensation by the parents. The embryo is felt within the womb only after about the fourth month. The embryo is seen only at birth. What can be neither seen nor felt is different from what is tangible. If the fetus cannot be seen or touched at all, it cannot be perceived as man.

Yet experience shows that sight is even more untrustworthy than feeling in determining humanity. By sight, color became an appropriate index for saying who was a man, and the evil of racial discrimination was given foundation. Nor can touch provide the test; a being confined by sickness, "out

of touch" with others, does not thereby seem to lose his humanity. To the extent that touch still has appeal as a criterion, it appears to be a survival of the old English idea of "quickening"—a possible mistranslation of the Latin *animatus* used in the canon law. To that extent, touch as a criterion seems to be dependent on the Aristotelian notion of ensoulment, and to fall when this notion is discarded.

Finally, a distinction is sought in social visibility. The fetus is not socially perceived as human. It cannot communicate with others. Thus, both subjectively and objectively, it is not a member of society. As moral rules are rules for the behavior of members of society to each other, they cannot be made for behavior toward what is not yet a member. Excluded from the society of men, the fetus is excluded from the humanity of men.

By force of the argument from the consequences, this distinction is to be rejected. It is more subtle than that founded on an appeal to physical sensation, but it is equally dangerous in its implications. If humanity depends on social recognition, individuals or whole groups may be dehumanized by being denied any status in their society. Such a fate is fictionally portrayed in *1984* and has actually been the lot of many men in many societies. In the Roman empire, for example, condemnation to slavery meant the practical denial of most human rights; in the Chinese Communist world, landlords have been classified as enemies of the people and so treated as nonpersons by the state. Humanity does not depend on social recognition, though often the failure of society to recognize the prisoner, the alien, the heterodox as human has led to the destruction of human beings. Anyone conceived by a man and a woman is human. Recognition of this condition by society follows a real event in the objective order, however imperfect and halting the recognition. Any attempt to limit humanity to exclude some group runs the risk of furnishing authority and precedent for excluding other groups in the name of the consciousness or perception of the controlling group in the society.

A philosopher may reject the appeal to the humanity of the fetus because he views "humanity" as a secular view of the soul and because he doubts the existence of anything real and objective which can be identified as humanity. One answer to such a philosopher is to ask how he reasons about moral questions without supposing that there is a sense in which he and the others of whom he speaks are human. Whatever group is taken as the society which determines who may be killed is thereby taken as human. A second answer is to ask if he does not believe that there is a right and wrong way of deciding moral questions. If there is such a difference, experience may be appealed to: To decide who is human on the basis of the sentiment of a given society has led to consequences which rational men would characterize as monstrous.

The rejection of the attempted distinctions based on viability and visibility, experience and feeling, may be buttressed by the following considerations: Moral judgments often rest on distinctions, but if the distinctions are not to appear arbitrary fiat, they should relate to some real difference in probabilities. There is a kind of continuity in all life, but the earlier stages of the elements of human life possess tiny probabilities of development. Consider, for example, the spermatozoa in any normal ejaculate: There are about 200,000,000 in any single ejaculate, of which one has a chance of developing into a zygote. Consider the oocytes which may become ova: There are 100,000 to 1,000,000 oocytes in a female infant, of which a maximum of 390 are ovulated. But once spermatozoon and ovum meet and the conceptus is formed, such studies as have been made show that roughly in only 20 percent of the cases will spontaneous abortion occur. In other words, the chances are about 4 out of 5 that this new being will develop. At this stage in the life of the being there is a sharp shift in probabilities, an immense jump in potentialities. To make a distinction between the rights of spermatozoa and the rights of the fertilized ovum is to respond to an enormous shift in possibilities. For about twenty days after conception, the egg may split to form twins or combine with another egg to form a chimera, but the probability of either event happening is very small.

It may be asked, What does a change in biological probabilities have to do with establishing humanity? The argument from probabilities is not aimed at establishing humanity but at establishing an objective discontinuity which may be taken into account in moral discourse. As life itself is a matter of probabilities, as most moral reasoning is an estimate of probabilities, so it seems in accord with the structure of reality and the nature of moral thought to found a moral judgment on the change in probabilities at conception. The appeal to probabilities is the most commonsensical of arguments; to a greater or smaller degree all of us base our actions on probabilities, and in morals, as in law, prudence and negligence are often measured by the account one has taken of the probabilities. If the chance is 200,000,000 to 1 that the movement in the bushes into which you shoot is a man's, I doubt if many persons would hold you careless in shooting; but if the chances are 4 out of 5 that the movement is a human being's, few would acquit you of blame. Would the argument be different if only one out of ten children conceived came to term? Of course this argument would be different. This argument is an appeal to probabilities that actually exist, not to any and all states of affairs which may be imagined.

The probabilities as they do exist do not show the humanity of the embryo in the sense of a demonstration in logic any more than the probabilities of the movement in the bush being a man demonstrate beyond all doubt that the being is a man. The appeal is a "buttressing" consideration, showing the plausibility of the standard adopted. The argument focuses on the decisional factor in any moral judgment and assumes that part of the business of a moralist is drawing lines. One evidence of the nonarbitrary character of the line drawn is the difference of probabilities on either side of it. If a spermatozoon is destroyed, one destroys a being which had a chance of far less than 1 in 200 million of developing into a reasonable being, possessed of the genetic code, a heart and other organs, and capable of pain. If a fetus is destroyed, one destroys a being already possessed of the genetic code, organs, and sensitivity to pain, and one which had an 80 percent chance of developing further into a baby, outside the womb, who, in time, would reason.

The positive argument for conception as the decisive moment of humanization is that at conception the new being receives the genetic code. It is this genetic information which determines his characteristics, which is the biological carrier of the possibility of human wisdom, which makes him a self-evolving being. A being with a human genetic code is man.

This review of current controversy over the humanity of the fetus emphasizes what a fundamental question the theologians resolved in asserting the inviolability of the fetus. To regard the fetus as possessed of equal rights with other humans was not, however, to decide every case where abortion might be employed. It did decide the case where the argument was that the fetus should be aborted for its own good. To say a being was human was to say it had a destiny to decide for itself which could not be taken from it by another man's decision. But human beings with equal rights often come in conflict with each other, and some decision must be made as to whose claims are to prevail. Cases of conflict involving the fetus are different only in two respects: the total inability of the fetus to speak for itself and the fact that the right of the fetus regularly at stake is the right to life itself.

The approach taken by the theologians to these conflicts was articulated in terms of "direct" and "indirect." Again, to look at what they were doing from outside their categories, they may be said to have been drawing lines or "balancing values." "Direct" and "indirect" are spatial metaphors: "line drawing" is another. "To weigh" or "to balance" values is a metaphor of a more complicated mathematical sort hinting at the process which goes on in moral judgments. All the metaphors suggest that, in the moral judgments made, comparisons were necessary, that no value completely controlled. The principle of double effect was no doctrine fallen from heaven, but a method of analysis appropriate where two relative values were being compared. In Catholic moral theology, as it developed, life even of the innocent was not taken as an absolute. Judgments on acts affecting life issued from a process of weighing. In the weighing, the fetus was always given a value greater than zero, always a value separate and independent from its parents. This valuation was crucial and fundamental in all Christian thought on the subject and marked it off from any approach which considered that only the parents' interests needed to be considered.

Even with the fetus weighed as human, one interest could be weighed as equal or superior: that of the mother in her own life. The casuists between 1450 and 1895 were willing to weigh this interest as superior. Since 1895, that interest was given decisive weight only in the two special cases of the cancerous uterus and the ectopic pregnancy. In both of these cases the fetus itself had little chance of survival even if the abortion were not performed. As the balance was once struck in favor of the mother whenever her life was endangered, it could be so struck again. The balance reached between 1895 and 1930 attempted prudentially and pastorally to forestall a multitude of exceptions for interests less than life.

The perception of the humanity of the fetus and the weighing of fetal rights against other human rights constituted the work of the moral analysts. But what spirit animated their abstract judgments? For the Christian community it was the injunction of Scripture to love your neighbor as yourself. The fetus as human was a neighbor; his life had parity with one's own. The commandment gave life to what otherwise would have been only rational calculation.

The commandment could be put in humanistic as well as theological terms: Do not injure your fellow man without reason. In these terms, once the humanity of the fetus is perceived, abortion is never right except in self-defense. When life must be taken to save life, reason alone cannot say that a mother must prefer a child's life to her own. With this exception, now of great rarity, abortion violates the rational humanist tenet of the equality of human lives.

For Christians the commandment to love had received a special imprint in that the exemplar proposed of love was the love of the Lord for his disciples. In the light given by this example, self-sacrifice carried to the point of death seemed in the extreme situations not without meaning. In the less extreme cases, preference for one's own interests to the life of another seemed to express cruelty or selfishness irreconcilable with the demands of love.

Questions for Analysis

1. Do you agree that considering the unborn a person from the moment of conception poses fewer problems than any of the alternative views?

2. What problems does Noonan see in distinctions based on: (a) viability, (b) experience, (c) feelings of adults, (d) social visibility?

3. Explain how Noonan used "biological probabilities" to buttress his view of the unborn as a person from the moment of conception. Is his argument persuasive?

4. On what grounds does Noonan object to abortion?

5. Is it accurate to say that Noonan finds abortion always impermissible?

A Defense of Abortion

Judith Jarvis Thomson

Philosopher Judith Jarvis Thomson, Massachusetts Institute of Technology, wrote this essay in 1971. It has since become a classic in the literature of abortion.

What makes her treatment of the pro-choice position unique is that it begins by conceding, for the sake of argument, that the fetus is a person from the moment of conception. This concession is significant because, as Thomson points out, most opposition to abortion builds on the assumption that the fetus has person status and rights from the moment of conception.

Thomson focuses her essay on an important question: Granted that the fetus is a person from the moment of conception, does it necessarily follow that abortion is always wrong? She thinks not. Relying primarily on a series of analogies, she attacks the argument that the immorality of abortion is entailed by the premise that asserts the person status of the fetus.

Toward the end of her essay, Thomson admits that anti-abortionists might object that the immorality of abortion follows not so much from the fact that the fetus is a person as from the special relationship between the fetus and the mother. Thus, anti-abortionists claim that the fetus is a person for whom the woman has a unique kind of responsibility because she is the mother.

In responding to this claim, Thomson argues that we have no responsibility for another person unless we have assumed it. If parents do not take any birth control measures, if they do not elect an abortion, if they choose to take the child home with them from the hospital, then certainly, they have a responsibility to and for the child. For they then have assumed responsibility, implicitly and explicitly, in all their actions. But if a couple has taken measures to prevent conception, this implies quite the opposite of any "special responsibility" for the unintended and unwanted fetus. Thus, in Thomson's view, the woman has no special responsibility to the fetus simply because of a biological relationship.

Ironically, as Thomson points out, many pro-choice advocates object to her argument for a couple of reasons. First, while Thomson argues that abortion is not impermissible, she does not think it is always permissible. There may be times, for example, when carrying the child to term requires only minimal inconvenience; in such cases, the woman would be required by "Minimally Decent Samaritanism" to have the child. Those supporting abortion on demand object to such a limitation of choice.

Second, while Thomson, like act utilitarians, would sanction some acts of abortion, she is not arguing for the right to kill the unborn child. That is, removing a nonviable fetus from the mother's body and thereby guaranteeing its death is not the same as removing a viable fetus from the mother's body and then killing it. In Thomson's view, the former may be permissible; the latter never is. Again, some pro-choice advocates object to this limitation of choice.

From Judith Jarvis Thomson, "A Defense of Abortion." *Philosophy & Public Affairs*, 1, no. 1 (Fall 1971). Copyright © 1971 by Princeton University Press. Reprinted by permission of Princeton University Press. Ms. Thomson acknowledges her indebtedness to James Thomson for discussion, criticism, and many helpful suggestions.

Most opposition to abortion relies on the premise that the fetus is a human being, a person, from the moment of conception. The premise is argued for, but, as I think, not well. Take, for example, the most common argument. We are asked to notice that the development of a human being from conception through birth into childhood is continuous; then it is said that to draw a line, to choose a point in this development and say "before this point the thing is not a person, after this point it is a person" is to make an arbitrary choice, a choice for which in the nature of things no good reason can be given. It is concluded that the fetus is, or anyway that we had better say it is, a person from the moment of conception. But this conclusion does not follow. Similar things might be said about the development of an acorn into an oak tree, and it does not follow that acorns are oak trees, or that we had better say they are. Arguments of this form are sometimes called "slippery slope arguments"—the phrase is perhaps self-explanatory—and it is dismaying that opponents of abortion rely on them so heavily and uncritically.

I am inclined to agree, however, that the prospects for "drawing a line" in the development of the fetus look dim. I am inclined to think also that we shall probably have to agree that the fetus has already become a human person well before birth. Indeed, it comes as a surprise when one first learns how early in its life it begins to acquire human characteristics. By the tenth week, for example, it already has a face, arms and legs, fingers and toes; it has internal organs, and brain activity is detectable.[1] On the other hand, I think that the premise is false, that the fetus is not a person from the moment of conception. A newly fertilized ovum, a newly implanted clump of cells, is no more a person than an acorn is an oak tree. But I shall not discuss any of this. For it seems to me to be of great interest to ask what happens if, for the sake of argument, we allow the premise. How, precisely, are we supposed to get from there to the conclusion that abortion is morally impermissible? Opponents of abortion commonly spend most of their time establishing that the fetus is a person, and hardly any time explaining the step from there to the impermissibility of abortion. Perhaps they think the step too simple and obvious to require much comment. Or perhaps instead they are simply being economical in argument. Many of those who defend

abortion rely on the premise that the fetus is not a person, but only a bit of tissue that will become a person at birth; and why pay out more arguments than you have to? Whatever the explanation, I suggest that the step they take is neither easy nor obvious, that it calls for closer examination than it is commonly given, and that when we do give it this closer examination we shall feel inclined to reject it.

I propose, then, that we grant that the fetus is a person from the moment of conception. How does the argument go from here? Something like this, I take it. Every person has a right to life. So the fetus has a right to life. No doubt the mother has a right to decide what shall happen in and to her body; everyone would grant that. But surely a person's right to life is stronger and more stringent than the mother's right to decide what happens in and to her body, and so outweighs it. So the fetus may not be killed; an abortion may not be performed.

It sounds plausible. But now let me ask you to imagine this. You wake up in the morning and find yourself back to back in bed with an unconscious violinist. A famous unconscious violinist. He has been found to have a fatal kidney ailment, and the Society of Music Lovers has canvassed all the available medical records and found that you alone have the right blood type to help. They have therefore kidnapped you, and last night the violinist's circulatory system was plugged into yours, so that your kidneys can be used to extract poisons from his blood as well as your own. The director of the hospital now tells you, "Look, we're sorry the Society of Music Lovers did this to you—we would never have permitted it if we had known. But still, they did it, and the violinist now is plugged into you. To unplug you would be to kill him. But never mind, it's only for nine months. By then he will have recovered from his ailment, and can safely be unplugged from you." Is it morally incumbent on you to accede to this situation? No doubt it would be very nice of you if you did, a great kindness. But do you *have* to accede to it? What if it were not nine months, but nine years? Or longer still? What if the director of the hospital says, "Tough luck, I agree, but you've now got to stay in bed, with the violinist plugged into you, for the rest of your life. Because remember this. All persons have a right to life, and violinists are persons. Granted you have a right to decide what happens in and to your body, but a person's right to life outweighs your right to decide what happens in and to your body. So you cannot ever be unplugged from him." I imagine you would regard this as outrageous, which suggests that something really is wrong with that plausible-sounding argument I mentioned a moment ago.

In this case, of course, you were kidnapped; you didn't volunteer for the operation that plugged the violinist into your kidneys. Can those who oppose abortion on the ground I mentioned make an exception for a pregnancy due to rape? Certainly. They can say that persons have a right to life only if they didn't come into existence because of rape; or they can say that all persons have a right to life, but that some have less of a right to life than others, in particular, that those who came into existence because of rape have less. But these statements have a rather unpleasant sound. Surely the question of whether you have a right to life at all, or how much of it you have, shouldn't turn on the question of whether or not you are the product of a rape. And in fact the people who oppose abortion on the ground I mentioned do not make this distinction, and hence do not make an exception in the case of rape.

Nor do they make an exception for a case in which the mother has to spend the nine months of her pregnancy in bed. They would agree that would be a great pity, and hard on the mother; but all the same, all persons have a right to life, the fetus is a person, and so on. I suspect, in fact, that they would not make an exception for a case in which, miraculously enough, the pregnancy went on for nine years, or even the rest of the mother's life.

Some won't even make an exception for a case in which continuation of the pregnancy is likely to shorten the mother's life; they regard abortion as impermissible even to save the mother's life. Such cases are nowadays very rare, and many opponents of abortion do not accept this extreme view. All the same, it is a good place to begin: A number of points of interest come out in respect to it.

1. Let us call the view that abortion is impermissible even to save the mother's life "the extreme view." I want to suggest first that it does not issue from the argument I mentioned earlier without the addition of some fairly powerful premises. Suppose a woman has become pregnant, and now learns that she has a cardiac condition such that she will die if she carries the baby to term. What may be done

for her? The fetus, being a person, has a right to life, but as the mother is a person too, so has she a right to life. Presumably they have an equal right to life. How is it supposed to come out that an abortion may not be performed? If mother and child have an equal right to life, shouldn't we perhaps flip a coin? Or should we add to the mother's right to life her right to decide what happens in and to her body, which everybody seems to be ready to grant—the sum of her rights now outweighing the fetus' right to life?

The most familiar argument here is the following. We are told that performing the abortion would be directly killing[2] the child, whereas doing nothing would not be killing the mother, but only letting her die. Moreover, in killing the child, one would be killing an innocent person, for the child has committed no crime, and is not aiming at his mother's death. And then there are a variety of ways in which this might be continued. (1) But as directly killing an innocent person is always and absolutely impermissible, an abortion may not be performed. Or, (2) as directly killing an innocent person is murder, and murder is always and absolutely impermissible, an abortion may not be performed.[3] Or, (3) as one's duty to refrain from directly killing an innocent person is more stringent than one's duty to keep a person from dying, an abortion may not be performed. Or, (4) if one's only options are directly killing an innocent person or letting a person die, one must prefer letting the person die, and thus an abortion may not be performed.[4]

Some people seem to have thought that these are not further premises which must be added if the conclusion is to be reached, but that they follow from the very fact that an innocent person has a right to life.[5] But this seems to me to be a mistake, and perhaps the simplest way to show this is to bring out that while we must certainly grant that innocent persons have a right to life, the theses in (1) through (4) are all false. Take (2), for example. If directly killing an innocent person is murder, and thus is impermissible, then the mother's directly killing the innocent person inside her is murder, and thus is impermissible. But it cannot seriously be thought to be murder if the mother performs an abortion on herself to save her life. It cannot seriously be said that she *must* refrain, that she *must* sit passively by and wait for her death. Let us look again at the case of you and the violinist. There you are, in bed with the violinist, and the director of the hospital says to you, "It's all most distressing, and I deeply sympathize, but you see this is putting an additional strain on your kidneys, and you'll be dead within the month. But you *have* to stay where you are all the same. Because unplugging you would be directly killing an innocent violinist, and that's murder, and that's impermissible." If anything in the world is true, it is that you do not commit murder, you do not do what is impermissible, if you reach around to your back and unplug yourself from that violinist to save your life.

The main focus of attention in writings on abortion has been on what a third party may or may not do in answer to a request from a woman for an abortion. This is in a way understandable. Things being as they are, there isn't much a woman can safely do to abort herself. So the question asked is what a third party may do, and what the mother may do, if it is mentioned at all, is deduced, almost as an afterthought, from what it is concluded that third parties may do. But it seems to me that to treat the matter in this way is to refuse to grant to the mother that very status of person which is so firmly insisted on for the fetus. For we cannot simply read off what a person may do from what a third party may do. Suppose you find yourself trapped in a tiny house with a growing child. I mean a very tiny house, and a rapidly growing child—you are already up against the wall of the house and in a few minutes you'll be crushed to death. The child on the other hand won't be crushed to death; if nothing is done to stop him from growing he'll be hurt, but in the end he'll simply burst open the house and walk out a free man. Now I could well understand it if a bystander were to say, "There's nothing we can do for you. We cannot choose between your life and his, we cannot be the ones to decide who is to live, we cannot intervene." But it cannot be concluded that you too can do nothing, that you cannot attack it to save your life. However innocent the child may be, you do not have to wait passively while it crushes you to death. Perhaps a pregnant woman is vaguely felt to have the status of house, to which we don't allow the right of self-defense. But if the woman houses the child, it should be remembered that she is a person who houses it.

I should perhaps stop to say explicitly that I am not claiming that people have a right to do anything whatever to save their lives. I think, rather, that there are drastic limits to the right of self defense. If someone threatens you with death unless you torture someone else to death, I think you have not the right, even to save your life, to do so. But the case under consideration here is very different. In our case there are only two people involved, one whose life is threatened, and one who threatens it. Both are innocent: The one who is threatened is not threatened because of any fault, the one who threatens does not threaten because of any fault. For this reason we may feel that we bystanders cannot intervene. But the person threatened can.

In sum, a woman surely can defend her life against the threat to it posed by the unborn child, even if doing so involves its death. And this shows not merely that the theses in (1) through (4) are false; it shows also that the extreme view of abortion is false, and so we need not canvass any other possible ways of arriving at it from the argument I mentioned at the outset.

2. The extreme view could of course be weakened to say that while abortion is permissible to save the mother's life, it may not be performed by a third party, but only by the mother herself. But this cannot be right either. For what we have to keep in mind is that the mother and the unborn child are not like two tenants in a small house which has, by an unfortunate mistake, been rented to both: The mother *owns* the house. The fact that she does adds to the offensiveness of deducing that the mother can do nothing from the supposition that third parties can do nothing. But it does more than this: It casts a bright light on the supposition that third parties can do nothing. Certainly it lets us see that a third party who says "I cannot choose between you" is fooling himself if he thinks this is impartiality. If Jones has found and fastened on a certain coat, which he needs to keep him from freezing, but which Smith also needs to keep him from freezing, then it is not impartiality that says "I cannot choose between you" when Smith owns the coat. Women have said again and again "This body is *my* body!" and they have reason to feel angry, reason to feel that it has been like shouting into the wind. Smith, after all, is hardly likely to bless us if we say to him, "Of course it's your coat, anybody would grant that it

is. But no one may choose between you and Jones who is to have it."

We should really ask what it is that says "no one may choose" in the face of the fact that the body that houses the child is the mother's body. It may be simply a failure to appreciate this fact. But it may be something more interesting, namely the sense that one has a right to refuse to lay hands on people, even where it would be just and fair to do so, even where justice seems to require that somebody do so. Thus justice might call for somebody to get Smith's coat back from Jones, and yet you have a right to refuse to be the one to lay hands on Jones, a right to refuse to do physical violence to him. This, I think, must be granted. But then what should be said is not "no one may choose," but only "*I* cannot choose," and indeed not even this, but "*I* will not *act*," leaving it open that somebody else can or should, and in particular that anyone in a position of authority, with the job of securing people's rights, both can and should. So this is no difficulty. I have not been arguing that any given third party must accede to the mother's request that he perform an abortion to save her life, but only that he may.

I suppose that in some views of human life the mother's body is only on loan to her, the loan not being one which gives her any prior claim to it. One who held this view might well think it impartiality to say "I cannot choose." But I shall simply ignore this possibility. My own view is that if a human being has any just, prior claim to anything at all, he has a just, prior claim to his own body. And perhaps this needn't be argued for here anyway, since, as I mentioned, the arguments against abortion we are looking at do grant that the woman has a right to decide what happens in and to her body.

But although they do grant it, I have tried to show that they do not take seriously what is done in granting it. I suggest the same thing will reappear even more clearly when we turn away from cases in which the mother's life is at stake, and attend, as I propose we now do, to the vastly more common cases in which a woman wants an abortion for some less weighty reason than preserving her own life.

3. Where the mother's life is not at stake, the argument I mentioned at the outset seems to have a much stronger pull. "Everyone has a right to life, so the unborn person has a right to life." And isn't the child's right to life weightier than anything other than the mother's own right to life, which she might put forward as ground for an abortion?

This argument treats the right to life as if it were unproblematic. It is not, and this seems to me to be precisely the source of the mistake.

For we should now, at long last, ask what it comes to, to have a right to life. In some views having a right to life includes having a right to be given at least the bare minimum one needs for continued life. But suppose that what in fact is the bare minimum a man needs for continued life is something he has no right at all to be given? If I am sick unto death, and the only thing that will save my life is the touch of Henry Fonda's cool hand on my fevered brow, then all the same, I have no right to be given the touch of Henry Fonda's cool hand on my fevered brow. It would be frightfully nice of him to fly in from the West Coast to provide it. It would be less nice, though no doubt well meant, if my friends flew out to the West Coast and carried Henry Fonda back with them. But I have no right at all against anybody that he should do this for me. Or again, to return to the story I told earlier, the fact that for continued life that violinist needs the continued use of your kidneys does not establish that he has a right to be given the continued use of your kidneys. He certainly has no right against you that *you* should give him continued use of your kidneys. For nobody has any right to use your kidneys unless you give him such a right; and nobody has the right against you that you shall give him this right— if you do allow him to go on using your kidneys, this is a kindness on your part, and not something he can claim from you as his due. Nor has he any right against anybody else that *they* should give him continued use of your kidneys. Certainly he had no right against the Society of Music Lovers that they should plug him into you in the first place. And if you now start to unplug yourself, having learned that you will otherwise have to spend nine years in bed with him, there is nobody in the world who must try to prevent you, in order to see to it that he is given something he has a right to be given.

Some people are rather stricter about the right to life. In their view, it does not include the right to be given anything, but amounts to, and only to, the right not to be killed by anybody. But here a related difficulty arises. If everybody is to refrain from killing that violinist, then everybody must refrain from doing a great many different sorts of things. Everybody must refrain from slitting his throat, everybody must refrain from shooting him and everybody must refrain from unplugging you from him. But does he have a right against everybody that they shall refrain from unplugging you from him? To refrain from doing this is to allow him to continue to use your kidneys. It could be argued that he has a right against us that we should allow him to continue to use your kidneys. That is, while he had no right against us that we should give him the use of your kidneys, it might be argued that he anyway has a right against us that we shall not now intervene and deprive him of the use of your kidneys. I shall come back to third-party interventions later. But certainly the violinist has no right against you that *you* shall allow him to continue to use your kidneys. As I said, if you do allow him to use them, it is a kindness on your part, and not something you owe him.

The difficulty I point to here is not peculiar to the right of life. It reappears in connection with all the other natural rights; and it is something which an adequate account of rights must deal with. For present purposes it is enough just to draw attention to it. But I would stress that I am not arguing that people do not have a right to life—quite to the contrary, it seems to me that the primary control we must place on the acceptability of an account of rights is that it should turn out in that account to be a truth that all persons have a right to life. I am arguing only that having a right to life does not guarantee having either a right to be given the use of or a right to be allowed continued use of another person's body—even if one needs it for life itself. So the right to life will not serve the opponents of abortion in the very simple and clear way in which they seem to have thought it would.

4. There is another way to bring out the difficulty. In the most ordinary sort of case, to deprive someone of what he has a right to is to treat him unjustly. Suppose a boy and his small brother are jointly given a box of chocolates for Christmas. If the older boy takes the box and refuses to give his brother any of the chocolates, he is unjust to him, for the brother has been given a right to half of them. But suppose that, having learned that otherwise it means nine years in bed with that violinist, you unplug yourself from him. You surely are not being unjust to him, for you gave him no right to

use your kidneys, and no one else can have given him any such right. But we have to notice that in unplugging yourself, you are killing him; and violinists, like everybody else, have a right to life, and thus in the view we were considering just now, the right not to be killed. So here you do what he supposedly has a right you shall not do, but you do not act unjustly to him in doing it.

The emendation which may be made at this point is this: The right to life consists not in the right not to be killed, but rather in the right not to be killed unjustly. This runs a risk of circularity, but never mind: It would enable us to square the fact that the violinist has a right to life with the fact that you do not act unjustly toward him in unplugging yourself, thereby killing him. For if you do not kill him unjustly, you do not violate his right to life, and so it is no wonder you do him no injustice.

But if this emendation is accepted, the gap in the argument against abortion stares us plainly in the face: It is by no means enough to show that the fetus is a person, and to remind us that all persons have a right to life—we need to be shown also that killing the fetus violates its right to life, that abortion is unjust killing. And is it?

I suppose we may take it as a datum that in the case of pregnancy due to rape the mother has not given the unborn person a right to the use of her body for food and shelter. Indeed, in what pregnancy should it be supposed that the mother has given the unborn person such a right? It is not as if there were unborn persons drifting about the world, to whom a woman who wants a child says "I invite you in."

But it might be argued that there are other ways one can have acquired a right to the use of another person's body than by having been invited to use it by that person. Suppose a woman voluntarily indulges in intercourse, knowing of the chance it will issue in pregnancy, and then she does become pregnant; is she not in part responsible for the presence, in fact the very existence, of the unborn person inside? No doubt she did not invite it in. But doesn't her partial responsibility for its being there itself give it a right to the use of her body?[6] If so, then her aborting it would be more like the boy's taking away the chocolates, and less like your unplugging yourself from the violinist—doing so would be depriving it of what it does have a right to, and thus would be doing it an injustice.

And then, too, it might be asked whether or not she can kill it even to save her own life: If she voluntarily called it into existence, how can she now kill it, even in self-defense?

The first thing to be said about this is that it is something new. Opponents of abortion have been so concerned to make out the independence of the fetus, in order to establish that it has a right to life, just as its mother does, that they have tended to overlook the possible support they might gain from making out that the fetus is *dependent* on the mother, in order to establish that she has a special kind of responsibility for it, a responsibility that gives it rights against her which are not possessed by any independent person—such as an ailing violinist who is a stranger to her.

On the other hand, this argument would give the unborn person a right to its mother's body only if her pregnancy resulted from a voluntary act, undertaken in full knowledge of the chance a pregnancy might result from it. It would leave out entirely the unborn person whose existence is due to rape. Pending the availability of some further argument, then, we would be left with the conclusion that unborn persons whose existence is due to rape have no right to the use of their mothers' bodies, and thus that aborting them is not depriving them of anything they have a right to and hence is not unjust killing.

And we should also notice that it is not at all plain that this argument really does go even as far as it purports to. For there are cases and cases, and the details make a difference. If the room is stuffy, and I therefore open a window to air it, and a burglar climbs in, it would be absurd to say, "Ah, now he can stay, she's given him a right to the use of her house—for she is partially responsible for his presence there, having voluntarily done what enabled him to get in, in full knowledge that there are such things as burglars, and that burglars burgle." It would be still more absurd to say this if I had had bars installed outside my windows, precisely to prevent burglars from getting in, and a burglar got in only because of a defect in the bars. It remains equally absurd if we imagine it is not a burglar who climbs in, but an innocent person who blunders or falls in. Again, suppose it were like this:

Peopleseeds drift about in the air like pollen, and if you open your windows, one may drift in and take root in your carpets or upholstery. You don't want children, so you fix up your windows with fine mesh screens, the very best you can buy. As can happen, however, and on very, very rare occasions does happen, one of the screens is defective; and a seed drifts in and takes root. Does the personplant who now develops have a right to the use of your house? Surely not—despite the fact that you voluntarily opened your windows, you knowingly kept carpets and upholstered furniture, and you knew that screens were sometimes defective. Someone may argue that you are responsible for its rooting, that it does have a right to your house, because after all you could have lived out your life with bare floors and furniture, or with sealed windows and doors. But this won't do—for by the same token anyone can avoid a pregnancy due to rape by having a hysterectomy, or anyway by never leaving home without a (reliable) army.

It seems to me that the argument we are looking at can establish at most that there are *some* cases in which the unborn person has a right to the use of its mother's body, and therefore *some* cases in which abortion is unjust killing. There is room for much discussion and argument as to precisely which, if any. But I think we should sidestep this issue and leave it open, for at any rate the argument certainly does not establish that all abortion is unjust killing.

5. There is room for yet another argument here, however. We surely must grant that there may be cases in which it would be morally indecent to detach a person from your body at the cost of his life. Suppose you learn that what the violinist needs is not nine years of your life, but only one hour: All you need do to save his life is spend one hour in that bed with him. Suppose also that letting him use your kidneys for that one hour would not affect your health in the slightest. Admittedly you were kidnapped. Admittedly you did not give anyone permission to plug him into you. Nevertheless it seems to me plain you *ought* to allow him to use your kidneys for that hour—it would be indecent to refuse.

Again, suppose pregnancy lasted only an hour, and constituted no threat to life or death [sic]. And suppose that a woman becomes pregnant as a result of rape. Admittedly she did not voluntarily do anything to bring about the existence of a child. Admittedly she did nothing at all which would give the unborn person a right to the use of her body. All the same it might well be said, as in the newly emended violinist story, that she *ought* to allow it to remain for that hour that it would be indecent in her to refuse.

Now some people are inclined to use the term "right" in such a way that it follows from the fact that you ought to allow a person to use your body for the hour he needs, that he has a right to use your body for the hour he needs, even though he has not been given that right by any person or act. They may say that it follows also that if you refuse, you act unjustly toward him. This use of the term is perhaps so common that it cannot be called wrong; nevertheless it seems to me to be an unfortunate loosening of what we would do better to keep a tight rein on. Suppose that box of chocolates I mentioned earlier had not been given to both boys jointly, but was given only to the older boy. There he sits, stolidly eating his way through the box, his small brother watching enviously. Here we are likely to say "You ought not to be so mean. You ought to give your brother some of those chocolates." My own view is that it just does not follow from the truth of this that the brother has any right to any of the chocolates. If the boy refuses to give his brother any, he is greedy, stingy, callous—but not unjust. I suppose that the people I have in mind will say it does follow that the brother has a right to some of the chocolates, and thus that the boy does act unjustly if he refuses to give his brother any. But the effect of saying this is to obscure what we should keep distinct, namely the difference between the boy's refusal in this case and the boy's refusal in the earlier case, in which the box was given to both boys jointly, and in which the small brother thus had what was from any point of view clear title to half.

A further objection to so using the term "right" that from the fact that A ought to do a thing for B, it follows that B has a right against A that A do it for him, is that it is going to make the question of whether or not a man has a right to a thing turn on how easy it is to provide him with it; and this seems not merely unfortunate, but morally unacceptable. Take the case of Henry Fonda again. I said earlier that I had no right to the touch of his cool hand on my fevered brow, even though I needed it to save my life. I said it would be frightfully nice of him to fly in from the West Coast to provide me with it, but that I had no right against him that he should do so. But suppose he isn't on the West Coast. Suppose he has only to walk across the room, place a hand briefly on my brow—and lo, my life is saved. Then surely he ought to do it, it would be indecent to refuse. Is it to be said, "Ah, well, it follows that in this case she has a right to the touch of his hand on her brow, and so it would be an unjustice in him to refuse"? So that I have a right to it when it is easy for him to provide it, though no right when it's hard? It's rather a shocking idea that anyone's rights should fade away and disappear as it gets harder and harder to accord them to him.

So my own view is that even though you ought to let the violinist use your kidneys for the one hour he needs, we should not conclude that he has a right to do so—we should say that if you refuse, you are, like the boy who owns all the chocolates and will give none away, self-centered and callous, indecent in fact, but not unjust. And similarly, that even supposing a case in which a woman pregnant due to rape ought to allow the unborn person to use her body for the hour he needs, we should not conclude that he has a right to do so; we should conclude that she is self-centered, callous, indecent, but not unjust, if she refuses. The complaints are no less grave; they are just different. However, there is no need to insist on this point. If anyone does wish to deduce "he has a right" from "you ought," then all the same he must surely grant that there are cases in which it is not morally required of you that you allow that violinist to use your kidneys, and in which he does not have a right to use them, and in which you do not do him an injustice if you refuse. And so also for mother and unborn child. Except in such cases as the unborn person has a right to demand it—and we were leaving open the possibility that there may be such cases—nobody is morally *required* to make large sacrifices, of health, of all other interests and concerns, of all other duties and commitments, for nine years, or even for nine months, in order to keep another person alive.

6. We have in fact to distinguish between the two kinds of Samaritan: the Good Samaritan and

what we might call the Minimally Decent Samaritan. The story of the Good Samaritan, you will remember, goes like this:

> A certain man went down from Jerusalem to Jericho, and fell among thieves, which stripped him of his raiment, and wounded him, and departed, leaving him half dead.
>
> And by chance there came down a certain priest that way; and when he saw him, he passed by on the other side.
>
> And likewise a Levite, when he was at the place, came and looked on him, and passed by on the other side.
>
> But a certain Samaritan, as he journeyed, came where he was; and when he saw him he had compassion on him.
>
> And went to him, and bound up his wounds, pouring in oil and wine, and set him on his own beast, and brought him to an inn, and took care of him.
>
> And on the morrow, when he departed, he took out two pence, and gave them to the host, and said unto him, "Take care of him; and whatsoever thou spendest more, when I come again, I will repay thee."
>
> (Luke 10:30–35)

The Good Samaritan went out of his way, at some cost to himself, to help one in need of it. We are not told what the options were, that is, whether or not the priest and the Levite could have helped by doing less than the Good Samaritan did, but assuming they could have, then the fact they did nothing at all shows they were not even Minimally Decent Samaritans, not because they were not Samaritans, but because they were not even minimally decent.

These things are a matter of degree, of course, but there is a difference, and it comes out perhaps most clearly in the story of Kitty Genovese, who, as you will remember, was murdered while thirty-eight people watched or listened, and did nothing at all to help her. A Good Samaritan would have rushed out to give direct assistance against the murderer. Or perhaps we had better allow that it would have been a Splendid Samaritan who did this, on the ground that it would have involved a risk of death for himself. But the thirty-eight not only did not do this, they did not even trouble to pick up a phone to call the police. Minimally Decent Samaritanism

would call for doing at least that, and their not having done it was monstrous.

After telling the story of the Good Samaritan, Jesus said, "Go, and do thou likewise." Perhaps he meant that we are morally required to act as the Good Samaritan did. Perhaps he was urging people to do more than is morally required of them. At all events it seems plain that it was not morally required of any of the thirty-eight that he rush out to give direct assistance at the risk of his own life, and that it is not morally required of anyone that he give long stretches of his life—nine years or nine months—to sustaining the life of a person who has no special right (we were leaving open the possibility of this) to demand it.

Indeed, with one rather striking class of exceptions, no one in any country in the world is *legally* required to do anywhere near as much as this for anyone else. The class of exceptions is obvious. My main concern here is not the state of the law in respect to abortion, but it is worth drawing attention to the fact that in no state in this country is any man compelled by law to be even a Minimally Decent Samaritan to any person; there is no law under which charges could be brought against the thirty-eight who stood by while Kitty Genovese died. By contrast, in most states in this country women are compelled by law to be not merely Minimally Decent Samaritans, but Good Samaritans to unborn persons inside them. This doesn't by itself settle anything one way or the other, because it may well be argued that there should be laws in this country—as there are in many European countries—compelling at least Minimally Decent Samaritanism.[7] But it does show that there is a gross injustice in the existing state of the law. And it shows also that the groups currently working against liberalization of abortion laws, in fact working toward having it declared unconstitutional for a state to permit abortion, had better start working for the adoption of Good Samaritan laws generally, or earn the charge that they are acting in bad faith.

I should think, myself, that Minimally Decent Samaritan laws would be one thing, Good Samaritan laws quite another, and in fact highly improper. But we are not here concerned with the law. What we should ask is not whether anybody should be compelled by law to be a Good Samaritan, but whether we must accede to a situation in which somebody is being compelled—by nature, perhaps—to be a Good Samaritan. We have, in other words, to look now at third-party interventions. I have been arguing that no person is morally required to make large sacrifices to sustain the life of another who has no right to demand them, and this even where the sacrifices do not include life itself; we are not morally required to be Good Samaritans or anyway Very Good Samaritans to one another. But what if a man cannot extricate himself from such a situation? What if he appeals to us to extricate him? It seems to me plain that there are cases in which we can, cases in which a Good Samaritan would extricate him. There you are, you were kidnapped, and nine years in bed with that violinist lie ahead of you. You have your own life to lead. You are sorry, but you simply cannot see giving up so much of your life to the sustaining of his. You cannot extricate yourself, and ask us to do so. I should have thought that—in light of his having no right to the use of your body—it was obvious that we do not have to accede to your being forced to give up so much. We can do what you ask. There is no injustice to the violinist in our doing so.

7. Following the lead of the opponents of abortion, I have throughout been speaking of the fetus merely as a person, and what I have been asking is whether or not the argument we began with, which proceeds only from the fetus' being a person, really does establish its conclusion. I have argued that it does not.

But of course there are arguments and arguments, and it may be said that I have simply fastened on the wrong one. It may be said that what is important is not merely the fact that the fetus is a person, but that it is a person for whom the woman has a special kind of responsibility issuing from the fact that she is its mother. And it might be argued that all my analogies are therefore irrelevant—for you do not have that special kind of responsibility for that violinist, Henry Fonda does not have that special kind of responsibility for me. And our attention might be drawn to the fact that men and women both *are* compelled by law to provide support for their children.

I have in effect dealt (briefly) with this argument in section 4 above; but a (still briefer) recapitulation now may be in order. Surely we do not have any such "special responsibility" for a person unless we have assumed it, explicitly or implicitly. If a set of parents do not try to prevent pregnancy, do not obtain an abortion, but rather take it home with them, then they have assumed responsibility for it, they have given it rights, and they cannot *now* withdraw support from it at the cost of its life because they now find it difficult to go on providing for it. But if they have taken all reasonable precautions against having a child, they do not simply by virtue of their biological relationship to the child who comes into existence have a special responsibility for it. They may wish to assume responsibility for it, or they may not wish to. And I am suggesting that if assuming responsibility for it would require large sacrifices, then they may refuse. A Good Samaritan would not refuse—or anyway, a Splendid Samaritan, if the sacrifices that had to be made were enormous. But then so would a Good Samaritan assume responsibility for that violinist; so would Henry Fonda, if he is a Good Samaritan, fly in from the West Coast and assume responsibility for me.

8. My argument will be found unsatisfactory on two counts by many of those who want to regard abortion as morally permissible. First, while I do argue that abortion is not impermissible, I do not argue that it is always permissible. There may well be cases in which carrying the child to term requires only Minimally Decent Samaritanism of the mother, and this is a standard we must not fall below. I am inclined to think it a merit of my account precisely that it does *not* give a general yes or a general no. It allows for and supports our sense that, for example, a sick and desperately frightened fourteen-year-old schoolgirl, pregnant due to rape, may of course choose abortion, and that any law which rules this out is an insane law. And it also allows for and supports our sense that in other cases resort to abortion is even positively indecent. It would be indecent in the woman to request an abortion, and indecent in a doctor to perform it, if she is in her seventh month, and wants the abortion just to avoid the nuisance of postponing a trip abroad. The very fact that the arguments I have been drawing attention to treat all cases of abortion, or even all cases of abortion in which the mother's life is not at stake, as morally on a par ought to have made them suspect at the outset.

Secondly, while I am arguing for the permissibility of abortion in some cases, I am not arguing for the right to secure the death of the unborn child. It is easy to confuse these two things in that up to a certain point in the life of the fetus it is not able to survive outside the mother's body; hence removing it from her body guarantees its death. But they are importantly different. I have argued that you are not morally required to spend nine months in bed, sustaining the life of that violinist; but to say this is by no means to say that if, when you unplug yourself, there is a miracle and he survives, you then have a right to turn around and slit his throat. You may detach yourself even if this costs him his life; you have no right to be guaranteed his death, by some other means, if unplugging yourself does not kill him. There are some people who will feel dissatisfied by this feature of my argument. A woman may be utterly devastated by the thought of a child, a bit of herself, put out for adoption and never seen or heard of again. She may therefore want not merely that the child be detached from her, but more, that it die. Some opponents of abortion are inclined to regard this as beneath contempt—thereby showing insensitivity to what is surely a powerful source of despair. All the same, I agree that the desire for the child's death is not one which anybody may gratify, should it turn out to be possible to detach the child alive.

At this place, however, it should be remembered that we have only been pretending throughout that the fetus is a human being from the moment of conception. A very early abortion is surely not the killing of a person, and so is not dealt with by anything I have said here.

NOTES

1. Daniel Callahan, *Abortion: Law, Choice and Morality* (New York, 1970), p. 373. This book gives a fascinating survey of the available information on abortion. The Jewish tradition in David M. Feldman, *Birth Control in Jewish Law* (New York, 1963), part 5; the Catholic tradition in John T. Noonan, Jr., "An Almost Absolute Value in History" in *The Morality of Abortion,* ed. John T. Noonan, Jr. (Cambridge, Mass., 1970).

2. The term "direct" in the arguments I refer to is a technical one. Roughly, what is meant by "direct killing" is either killing as an end in itself, or killing as a means to some end, for example, the end of saving someone else's life. See note 5 on this page, for an example of its use.

3. Cf. *Encyclical Letter of Pope Pius XI on Christian Marriage,* St. Paul Editions (Boston, n.d.), p. 32: "However much we may pity the mother whose health and even life is gravely imperiled in the performance of the duty allotted to her by nature, nevertheless what could ever be a sufficient reason for excusing in any way the direct murder of the innocent? This is precisely what we are dealing with here." Noonan (*The Morality of Abortion,* p. 43) reads this as follows: "What cause can ever avail to excuse in any way the direct killing of the innocent? For it is a question of that."

4. The thesis in (4) is in an interesting way weaker than those in (1), (2), and (3): They rule out abortion even in cases in which both mother *and* child will die if the abortion is not performed. By contrast, one who held the view expressed in (4) could consistently say that one needn't prefer letting two persons die to killing one.

5. Cf. the following passage from Pius XII, *Address to the Italian Catholic Society of Midwives:* "The baby in the maternal breast has the right to life immediately from God.—Hence there is no man, no human authority, no science, no medical, eugenic, social, economic or moral 'indication' which can establish or grant a valid juridical ground for a direct deliberate disposition of an innocent human life, that is a disposition which looks to its destruction either as an end or as a means to another end perhaps in itself not illicit.—The baby, still not born, is a man in the same degree and for the same reason as the mother" (quoted in Noonan, *The Morality of Abortion,* p. 45).

6. The need for a discussion of this argument was brought home to me by members of the Society for Ethical and Legal Philosophy, to whom this paper was originally presented.

7. For a discussion of the difficulties involved, and a survey of the European experience with such laws, see *The Good Samaritan and the Law,* ed. James M. Ratcliffe (New York, 1966).

Questions for Analysis

1. Does the belief that abortion is always impermissible necessarily result from the argument that the unborn is a person from the moment of conception? If not, what additional premises are necessary?

2. Why does Thomson conclude that "a woman surely can defend her life against the threat to it posed by the unborn child, even if doing so involves its death"?

3. How does Thomson answer the claim that the fetus's right to life weighs more (in the moral sense) than anything other than the mother's own right to life?

4.   Does Thomson feel that there may be cases in which it would be wrong for a
     woman to have an abortion? Explain.

5.   Distinguish between a "Good Samaritan" and a "Minimally Decent Samaritan."

On the Moral and Legal Status of Abortion

Mary Ann Warren

In the following defense of the extreme liberal position on abortion, philosopher Mary Ann
Warren challenges both John T. Noonan and Judith Jarvis Thomson. Against Thomson, she
argues that the ontological status of the fetus is crucial to any discussion of the morality of
abortion. If the fetus is a person with full moral rights, there are many situations—more than
Thomson allows—in which abortion is not morally justified. Thomson's example of a woman
involuntarily tied to a famous violinist to save his life has little in common with most pregnancies, she argues. It justifies abortion in the case of rape but not in the normal case of
unwanted pregnancy, in which the woman bears at least some responsibility for her plight.

Against Noonan, she argues that the fetus is not a person. Her argument relies on a
distinction between two senses of "human," the biological sense and the moral sense.
Noonan shows that a fetus is human in the former sense but not the latter. And Warren
argues, the fetus is not human in the moral sense. To support this claim, she gives five
criteria for being a person and argues that the fetus meets none of them. She also argues
that being a potential person does not give the fetus rights against the rights of the woman
carrying it.

In a postscript added after publication, Warren addresses the issue of infanticide. Her
arguments in favor of abortion rights do not support a right to kill newborn babies.

We will be concerned with both the moral status
of abortion, which for our purposes we may define
as the act which a woman performs in voluntarily
terminating, or allowing another person to terminate, her pregnancy, and the legal status which is
appropriate for this act. I will argue that, while it is
not possible to produce a satisfactory defense of a
woman's right to obtain an abortion without showing that a fetus is not a human being, in the morally
relevant sense of that term, we ought not to conclude that the difficulties involved in determining
whether or not a fetus is human make it impossible to produce any satisfactory solution to the problem of the moral status of abortion. For it is possible
to show that, on the basis of intuitions which we
may expect even the opponents of abortion to
share, a fetus is not a person, and hence not the
sort of entity to which it is proper to ascribe full
moral rights.

Of course, while some philosophers would
deny the possibility of any such proof,[1] others
will deny that there is any need for it, since the
moral permissibility of abortion appears to them
to be too obvious to require proof. But the inadequacy of this attitude should be evident from
the fact that both the friends and the foes of abortion consider their position to be morally self-
evident. Because pro-abortionists have never
adequately come to grips with the conceptual
issues surrounding abortion, most, if not all, of
the arguments which they advance in opposition
to laws restricting access to abortion fail to refute
or even weaken the traditional antiabortion argument, i.e., that a fetus is a human being, and therefore abortion is murder.

These arguments are typically of one of two
sorts. Either they point to the terrible side effects

From "On the Moral and Legal Status of Abortion," *The Monist*
(January 1973). Copyright ©, 1973 *The Monist: An International
Quarterly Journal of General Philosophical Inquiry*, Peru, Illinois, U.S.A.
61354. Reprinted by permission. "Postscript on Infanticide," in
Today's Moral Problems, edited by Richard Wasserstrom (1979),
pp. 135–136.

of the restrictive laws, e.g., the deaths due to illegal abortions, and the fact that it is poor women who suffer the most as a result of these laws, or else they state that to deny a woman access to abortion is to deprive her of her right to control her own body. Unfortunately, however, the fact that restricting access to abortion has tragic side effects does not, in itself, show that the restrictions are unjustified, since murder is wrong regardless of the consequences of prohibiting it; and the appeal to the right to control one's body, which is generally construed as a property right, is at best a rather feeble argument for the permissibility of abortion. Mere ownership does not give me the right to kill innocent people whom I find on my property, and indeed I am apt to be held responsible if such people injure themselves while on my property. It is equally unclear that I have any moral right to expel an innocent person from my property when I know that doing so will result in his death.

Furthermore, it is probably inappropriate to describe a woman's body as her property, since it seems natural to hold that a person is something distinct from her property, but not from her body. Even those who would object to the identification of a person with his body, or with the conjunction of his body and his mind, must admit that it would be very odd to describe, say, breaking a leg, as damaging one's property, and much more appropriate to describe it as injuring one*self*. Thus it is probably a mistake to argue that the right to obtain an abortion is in any way derived from the right to own and regulate property.

But however we wish to construe the right to abortion, we cannot hope to convince those who consider abortion a form of murder of the existence of any such right unless we are able to produce a clear and convincing refutation of the traditional antiabortion argument, and this has not, to my knowledge, been done. With respect to the two most vital issues which that argument involves, i.e., the humanity of the fetus and its implication for the moral status of abortion, confusion has prevailed on both sides of the dispute.

Thus, both pro-abortionists and antiabortionists have tended to abstract the question of whether abortion is wrong to that of whether it is wrong to destroy a fetus, just as though the rights of another person were not necessarily involved. This mistaken abstraction has led to the almost universal assumption that if a fetus is a human being, with a right to life, then it follows immediately that abortion is wrong (except perhaps when necessary to save the woman's life), and that it ought to be prohibited. It has also been generally assumed that unless the question about the status of the fetus is answered, the moral status of abortion cannot possibly be determined. . . . John Noonan is correct in saying that "the fundamental question in the long history of abortion is, How do you determine the humanity of a being?"[2] He summarizes his own antiabortion argument, which is a version of the official position of the Catholic Church, as follows:

> . . . it is wrong to kill humans, however poor, weak, defenseless, and lacking in opportunity to develop their potential they may be. It is therefore morally wrong to kill Biafrans. Similarly, it is morally wrong to kill embryos.[3]

Noonan bases his claim that fetuses are human upon what he calls the theologians' criterion of humanity: that whoever is conceived of human beings is human. But although he argues at length for the appropriateness of this criterion, he never questions the assumption that if a fetus is human then abortion is wrong for exactly the same reason that murder is wrong.

Judith Thomson is, in fact, the only writer I am aware of who has seriously questioned this assumption; she has argued that, even if we grant the antiabortionist his claim that a fetus is a human being, with the same right to life as any other human being, we can still demonstrate that, in at least some and perhaps most cases, a woman is under no moral obligation to complete an unwanted pregnancy.[4] Her argument is worth examining, since if it holds up it may enable us to establish the moral permissibility of abortion without becoming involved in problems about what entitles an entity to be considered human, and accorded full moral rights. To be able to do this would be a great gain in the power and simplicity of the proabortion position, since, although I will argue that these problems can be solved at least as decisively as can any other moral problem, we should certainly be pleased to be able to avoid having to solve them as part of the justification of abortion.

On the other hand, even if Thomson's argument does not hold up, her insight, i.e., that it requires *argument* to show that if fetuses are human then abortion is properly classified as murder, is an extremely valuable one. The assumption she attacks is particularly invidious, for it amounts to the decision that it is appropriate, in deciding the moral status of abortion, to leave the rights of the pregnant woman out of consideration entirely, except possibly when her life is threatened. Obviously, this will not do; determining what moral rights, if any, a fetus possesses is only the first step in determining the moral status of abortion. Step two, which is at least equally essential, is finding a just solution to the conflict between whatever rights the fetus may have, and the rights of the woman who is unwillingly pregnant. While the historical error has been to pay far too little attention to the second step, Ms. Thomson's suggestion is that if we look at the second step first we may find that a woman has a right to obtain an abortion *regardless* of what rights the fetus has.

Our own inquiry will also have two stages. In Section I, we will consider whether or not it is possible to establish that abortion is morally permissible even on the assumption that a fetus is an entity with a full-fledged right to life. I will argue that in fact this cannot be established, at least not with the conclusiveness which is essential to our hopes of convincing those who are skeptical about the morality of abortion, and that we therefore cannot avoid dealing with the question of whether or not a fetus really does have the same right to life as a (more fully developed) human being.

In Section II, I will propose an answer to this question, namely, that a fetus cannot be considered a member of the moral community, the set of beings with full and equal moral rights, for the simple reason that it is not a person, and that it is personhood, and not genetic humanity, i.e., humanity as defined by Noonan, which is the basis for membership in this community. I will argue that a fetus, whatever its stage of development, satisfies none of the basic criteria of personhood, and is not even enough *like* a person to be accorded even some of the same rights on the basis of this resemblance. Nor, as we will see, is a fetus's *potential* personhood a threat to the morality of abortion, since, whatever the rights of potential people may be, they are invariably overridden in any conflict with the moral rights of actual people.

I

We turn now to Professor Thomson's case for the claim that even if a fetus has full moral rights, abortion is still morally permissible, at least sometimes, and for some reasons other than to save the woman's life. Her argument is based upon a clever, but I think faulty, analogy. She asks us to picture ourselves waking up one day, in bed with a famous violinist. Imagine that you have been kidnapped, and your bloodstream hooked up to that of the violinist, who happens to have an ailment which will certainly kill him unless he is permitted to share your kidneys for a period of nine months. No one else can save him, since you alone have the right type of blood. He will be unconscious all that time, and you will have to stay in bed with him, but after the nine months are over he may be unplugged, completely cured, that is, provided that you have cooperated.

Now then, she continues, what are your obligations in this situation? The antiabortionist, if he is consistent, will have to say that you are obligated to stay in bed with the violinist: for all people have a right to life, and violinists are people, and therefore it would be murder for you to disconnect yourself from him and let him die. But this is outrageous, and so there must be something wrong with the same argument when it is applied to abortion. It would certainly be commendable of you to agree to save the violinist, but it is absurd to suggest that your refusal to do so would be murder. His right to life does not obligate you to do whatever is required to keep him alive; nor does it justify anyone else in forcing you to do so. A law which required you to stay in bed with the violinist would clearly be an unjust law, since it is no proper function of the law to force unwilling people to make huge sacrifices for the sake of other people toward whom they have no such prior obligation.

Thomson concludes that, if this analogy is an apt one, then we can grant the antiabortionist his claim that a fetus is a human being, and still hold that it is at least sometimes the case that a pregnant woman has the right to refuse to be a Good Samaritan towards the fetus, i.e., to obtain an abortion. For there is a great gap between the claim that X has a right to life, and the claim that Y is obligated to do whatever is necessary to keep X alive, let alone that he ought to be forced to do so. It is Y's duty to keep X alive only if he has somehow contracted a *special* obligation to do so; and a woman who is unwillingly pregnant, e.g., who was raped, has done nothing which obligates her to make the enormous sacrifice which is necessary to preserve the conceptus.

This argument is initially quite plausible, and in the extreme case of pregnancy due to rape is probably conclusive. Difficulties arise, however, when we try to specify more exactly the range of cases in which abortion is clearly justifiable even on the assumption that the fetus is human. Professor Thomson considers it a virtue of her argument that it does not enable us to conclude that abortion is *always* permissible. It would, she says, be "indecent" for a woman in her seventh month to obtain an abortion just to avoid having to postpone a trip to Europe. On the other hand, her argument enables us to see that "a sick and desperately frightened schoolgirl pregnant due to rape may *of course* choose abortion, and that any law which rules this out is an insane law" (p. 65). So far, so good; but what are we to say about the woman who becomes pregnant not through rape but as a result of her own carelessness, or because of contraceptive failure, or who gets pregnant intentionally and then changes her mind about wanting a child? With respect to such cases, the violinist analogy is of much less use to the defender of the woman's right to obtain an abortion.

Indeed, the choice of a pregnancy due to rape, as an example of a case in which abortion is permissible even if a fetus is considered a human being, is extremely significant; for it is only in the case of pregnancy due to rape that the woman's situation is adequately analogous to the violinist case for our intuitions about the latter to transfer convincingly. The crucial difference between a pregnancy due to rape and the *normal* case of an unwanted pregnancy is that in the normal case we cannot claim that the woman is in no way responsible for her predicament; she could have remained chaste, or taken her pills more faithfully, or abstained

on dangerous days, and so on. If, on the other hand, you are kidnapped by strangers, and hooked up to a strange violinist, then you are free of any shred of responsibility for the situation, on the basis of which it could be argued that you are obligated to keep the violinist alive. Only when her pregnancy is due to rape is a woman clearly just as nonresponsible.[5]

Consequently, there is room for the antiabortionist to argue that in the normal case of unwanted pregnancy a woman has, by her own actions, assumed responsibility for the fetus. For if X behaves in a way which he could have avoided, and which he knows involves, let us say, a 1 percent chance of bringing into existence a human being, with a right to life, and does so knowing that if this should happen then that human being will perish unless X does certain things to keep him alive, then it is by no means clear that when it does happen X is free of any obligation to what he knew in advance would be required to keep that human being alive.

The plausibility of such an argument is enough to show that the Thomson analogy can provide a clear and persuasive defense of a woman's right to obtain an abortion only with respect to those cases in which the woman is in no way responsible for her pregnancy, e.g., where it is due to rape. In all other cases, we would almost certainly conclude that it was necessary to look carefully at the particular circumstances in order to determine the extent of the woman's responsibility, and hence the extent of her obligation. This is an extremely unsatisfactory outcome, from the viewpoint of the opponents of restrictive abortion laws, most of whom are convinced that a woman has a right to obtain an abortion regardless of how and why she got pregnant.

Of course a supporter of the violinist analogy might point out that it is absurd to suggest that forgetting her pill one day might be sufficient to obligate a woman to complete an unwanted pregnancy. And indeed it *is* absurd to suggest this. As we will see, the moral right to obtain an abortion is not in the least dependent upon the extent to which the woman is responsible for her pregnancy. But unfortunately, once we allow the assumption that a fetus has full moral rights, we cannot avoid taking this absurd suggestion seriously. Perhaps we can make this point more clear by altering the violinist story just enough to make it more analogous to a normal unwanted pregnancy and less to a pregnancy due to rape, and then seeing whether it is still obvious that you are not obligated to stay in bed with the fellow.

Suppose, then, that violinists are peculiarly prone to the sort of illness the only cure for which is the use of someone else's bloodstream for nine months, and that because of this there has been formed a society of music lovers who agree that whenever a violinist is stricken they will draw lots and the loser will, by some means, be made the one and only person capable of saving him. Now then, would you be obligated to cooperate in curing the violinist if you had voluntarily joined this society, knowing the possible consequences, and then your name had been drawn and you had been kidnapped? Admittedly, you did not promise ahead of time that you would, but you did deliberately place yourself in a position in which it might happen that a human life would be lost if you did not. Surely this is at least a prima facie reason for supposing that you have an obligation to stay in bed with the violinist. Suppose that you had gotten your name drawn deliberately; surely *that* would be quite a strong reason for thinking that you had such an obligation.

It might be suggested that there is one important disanalogy between the modified violinist case and the case of an unwanted pregnancy, which makes the woman's responsibility significantly less, namely, the fact that the fetus *comes into existence* as the result of the woman's actions. This fact might give her a right to refuse to keep it alive, whereas she would not have had this right had it existed previously, independently, and then as a result of her actions become dependent upon her for its survival.

My own intuition, however, is that X has no more right to bring into existence, either deliberately or as a foreseeable result of actions he could have avoided, a being with full moral rights (Y), and then refuse to do what he knew beforehand would be required to keep that being alive, than he has to enter into an agreement with an existing person, whereby he may be called upon to save that person's life, and then refuse to do so when so called upon. Thus, X's responsibility for Y's existence does

not seem to lessen his obligation to keep Y alive, if he is also responsible for Y's being in a situation in which only he can save him.

Whether or not this intuition is entirely correct, it brings us back once again to the conclusion that once we allow the assumption that a fetus has full moral rights it becomes an extremely complex and difficult question whether and when abortion is justifiable. Thus the Thomson analogy cannot help us produce a clear and persuasive proof of the moral permissibility of abortion. Nor will the opponents of the restrictive laws thank us for anything less; for their conviction (for the most part) is that abortion is obviously *not* a morally serious and extremely unfortunate, even though sometimes justified, act comparable to killing in self-defense or to letting the violinist die, but rather is closer to being a morally neutral act, like cutting one's hair.

The basis of this conviction, I believe, is the realization that a fetus is not a person, and thus does not have a full-fledged right to life. Perhaps the reason why this claim has been so inadequately defended is that it seems self-evident to those who accept it. And so it is, insofar as it follows from what I take to be perfectly obvious claims about the nature of personhood and about the proper grounds for ascribing moral rights, claims which ought, indeed, to be obvious to both the friends and foes of abortion. Nevertheless, it is worth examining these claims, and showing how they demonstrate the moral innocuousness of abortion, since this apparently has not been adequately done before.

II

The question which we must answer in order to produce a satisfactory solution to the problem of the moral status of abortion is this: How are we to define the moral community, the set of beings with full and equal moral rights, such that we can decide whether a human fetus is a member of this community or not? What sort of entity, exactly, has the inalienable rights to life, liberty, and the pursuit of happiness? Jefferson attributed these rights to all *men,* and it may or may not be fair to suggest that he intended to attribute them *only* to men. Perhaps he ought to have attributed them to all human beings. If so, then we arrive, first, at Noonan's problem of defining what makes a being human, and, second, at the equally vital question which Noonan does not consider; namely, What reason is there for identifying the moral community with the set of all human beings, in whatever way we have chosen to define that term?

1. On the Definition of "Human"

One reason why this vital second question is so frequently overlooked in the debate over the moral status of abortion is that the term "human" has two distinct, but not often distinguished, senses. This fact results in a slide of meaning, which serves to conceal the fallaciousness of the traditional argument that since (1) it is wrong to kill innocent human beings, and (2) fetuses are innocent human beings, then (3) it is wrong to kill fetuses. For if "human" is used in the same sense in both (1) and (2) then, whichever of the two senses is meant, one of these premises is question-begging. And if it is used in two different senses then of course the conclusion doesn't follow.

Thus, (1) is a self-evident moral truth,[6] and avoids begging the question about abortion only if "human being" is used to mean something like "a full-fledged member of the moral community." (It may or may not also be meant to refer exclusively to members of the species *Homo Sapiens*.) *We may call this the moral* sense of "human." It is not to be confused with what we will call the *genetic* sense, i.e., the sense in which *any* member of the species is a human being, and no member of any other species could be. If (l) is acceptable only if the moral sense is intended, (2) is non-question-begging only if what is intended is the genetic sense.

In "Deciding Who Is Human," Noonan argues for the classification of fetuses with human beings by pointing to the presence of the full genetic code, and the potential capacity for rational thought (p. 135). It is clear that what he needs to show, for his version of the traditional argument to be valid, is that fetuses are human in the moral sense, the sense in which it is analytically true that all human beings have full moral rights. But, in the absence of any argument showing that whatever is genetically human is also morally human, and he gives none, nothing more than genetic humanity can be demonstrated by the presence of the human genetic code. And, as we will see, the *potential*

capacity for rational thought can at most show that an entity has the potential for *becoming* human in the moral sense.

2. Defining the Moral Community

Can it be established that genetic humanity is sufficient for moral humanity? I think that there are very good reasons for not defining the moral community in this way. I would like to suggest an alternative way of defining the moral community, which I will argue for only to the extent of explaining why it is, or should be, self-evident. The suggestion is simply that the moral community consists of all and only *people,* rather than all and only human beings;[7] and probably the best way of demonstrating its self-evidence is by considering the concept of personhood, to see what sorts of entity are and are not persons, and what the decision that a being is or is not a person implies about its moral rights.

What characteristics entitle an entity to be considered a person? This is obviously not the place to attempt a complete analysis of the concept of personhood, but we do not need such a fully adequate analysis just to determine whether and why a fetus is or isn't a person. All we need is a rough and approximate list of the most basic criteria of personhood, and some idea of which, or how many, of these an entity must satisfy in order to properly be considered a person.

In searching for such criteria, it is useful to look beyond the set of people with whom we are acquainted, and ask how we would decide whether a totally alien being was a person or not. (For we have no right to assume that genetic humanity is necessary for personhood.) Imagine a space traveler who lands on an unknown planet and encounters a race of beings utterly unlike any he has ever seen or heard of. If he wants to be sure of behaving morally toward these beings, he has to somehow decide whether they are people, and hence have full moral rights, or whether they are the sort of thing which he need not feel guilty about treating as, for example, a source of food.

How should he go about making this decision? If he has some anthropological background, he might look for such things as religion, art, and the manufacturing of tools, weapons, or shelters, since these factors have been used to distinguish our human from our prehuman ancestors, in what seems to be closer to the moral than the genetic sense of "human." And no doubt he would be right to consider the presence of such factors as good evidence that the alien beings were people, and morally human. It would, however, be overly anthropocentric of him to take the absence of these things as adequate evidence that they were not, since we can imagine people who have progressed beyond, or evolved without ever developing, these cultural characteristics.

I suggest that the traits which are most central to the concept of personhood, or humanity in the moral sense, are, very roughly, the following:

1. consciousness (of objects and events external and/or internal to the being), and in particular the capacity to feel pain;

2. reasoning (the *developed* capacity to solve new and relatively complex problems);

3. self-motivated activity (activity which is relatively independent of either genetic or direct external control);

4. the capacity to communicate, by whatever means, messages of an indefinite variety of types, that is, not just with an indefinite number of possible contents, but on indefinitely many possible topics;

5. the presence of self-concepts, and self-awareness, either individual or racial, or both.

Admittedly, there are apt to be a great many problems involved in formulating precise definitions of these criteria, let alone in developing universally valid behavioral criteria for deciding when they apply. But I will assume that both we and our explorer know approximately what (1)–(5) mean, and that he is also able to determine whether or not they apply. How, then, should he use his findings to decide whether or not the alien beings are people? We needn't suppose that an entity must have *all* of these attributes to be properly considered a person; (1) and (2) alone may well be sufficient for personhood, and quite probably (1)–(3) are sufficient. Neither do we need to insist that any one of these criteria is *necessary* for personhood, although once again (1) and (2) look like fairly good candidates for necessary conditions, as

does (3), if "activity" is construed so as to include the activity of reasoning.

All we need to claim, to demonstrate that a fetus is not a person, is that any being which satisfies *none* of (1)–(5) is certainly not a person. I consider this claim to be so obvious that I think anyone who denied it, and claimed that a being which satisfied none of (1)–(5) was a person all the same, would thereby demonstrate that he had no notion at all of what a person is—perhaps because he had confused the concept of a person with that of genetic humanity. If the opponents of abortion were to deny the appropriateness of these five criteria, I do not know what further arguments would convince them. We would probably have to admit that our conceptual schemes are indeed irreconcilably different, and that our dispute could not be settled objectively.

I do not expect this to happen, however, since I think that the concept of a person is one which is very nearly universal (to people), and that it is common to both pro-abortionists and antiabortionists, even though neither group has fully realized the relevance of this concept to the resolution of their dispute. Furthermore, I think that on reflection even the antiabortionists ought to agree not only that (1)–(5) are central to the concept of personhood, but also that it is apart of this concept that all and only people have full moral rights. The concept of a person is in part a moral concept; once we have admitted that X is a person we have recognized, even if we have not agreed to respect, X's right to be treated as a member of the moral community. It is true that the claim that X is a *human being* is more commonly voiced as part of an appeal to treat X decently than is the claim that X is a person, but this is either because "human being" is here used in the sense which implies personhood, or because the genetic and moral senses of "human" have been confused.

Note if (1)–(5) are indeed the primary criteria of personhood, then it is clear that genetic humanity is neither necessary nor sufficient for establishing that an entity is a person. Some human beings are not people, and there may be people who are not human beings. A man or woman whose consciousness has been permanently obliterated but who remains alive is a human being which is no longer a person; defective human beings, with no appreciable mental capacity, are not and presumably never will be people; and a fetus is a human being which is not yet a person, and which therefore cannot coherently be said to have full moral rights. Citizens of the next century should be prepared to recognize highly advanced, self-aware robots or computers, should such be developed, and intelligent inhabitants of other worlds, should such be found, as people in the fullest sense, and to respect their moral rights. But to ascribe full moral rights to an entity which is not a person is as absurd as to ascribe moral obligations and responsibilities to such an entity.

3. Fetal Development and the Right to Life

Two problems arise in the application of these suggestions for the definition of the moral community to the determination of the precise moral status of a human fetus. Given that the paradigm example of a person is a normal adult human being, then (1) How like this paradigm, in particular how far advanced since conception, does a human being need to be before it begins to have a right to life by virtue, not of being fully a person as of yet, but of being *like* a person? and (2) To what extent, if any, does the fact that a fetus has the *potential* for becoming a person endow it with some of the same rights? Each of these questions requires some comment.

In answering the first question, we need not attempt a detailed consideration of the moral rights of organisms which are not developed enough, aware enough, intelligent enough, etc., to be considered people, but which resemble people in some respects. It does seem reasonable to suggest that the more like a person, in the relevant respects, a being is, the stronger is the case for regarding it as having a right to life, and indeed the stronger its right to life is. Thus we ought to take seriously the suggestion that, insofar as "the human individual develops biologically in a continuous fashion . . . the rights of a human person might develop in the same way."[8] But we must keep in mind that the attributes which are relevant in determining whether or not an entity is enough like a person to be regarded as having some of the same moral rights are no different from those which are relevant to determining whether or not it is a fully a person—i.e., are no different

from (1)–(5)—and that being genetically human, or having recognizably human facial and other physical features, or detectable brain activity, or the capacity to survive outside the uterus, is simply not among these relevant attributes.

Thus it is clear that even though a seven- or eight-month fetus has features which make it apt to arouse in us almost the same powerful protective instinct as is commonly aroused by a small infant, nevertheless it is not significantly more personlike than is a very small embryo. It is *somewhat* more personlike; it can apparently feel and respond to pain, and it may even have a rudimentary form of consciousness, insofar as its brain is quite active. Nevertheless, it seems safe to say that it is not fully conscious, in the way that an infant of a few months is, and that it cannot reason, or communicate messages of indefinitely many sorts, does not engage in self-motivated activity, and has no self-awareness. Thus, in the *relevant* respects, a fetus, even a fully developed one, is considerably less personlike than is the average mature mammal, indeed the average fish. And I think that a rational person must conclude that if the right to life of a fetus is to be based upon its resemblance to a person, then it cannot be said to have any more right to life than, let us say, a newborn guppy (which also seems to be capable of feeling pain), and that right of that magnitude could never override a woman's right to obtain an abortion, at any stage of her pregnancy.

There may, of course, be other arguments in favor of placing legal limits upon the stage of pregnancy in which an abortion may be performed. Given the relative safety of the new techniques of artificially inducing labor during the third trimester, the danger to the woman's life or health is no longer such an argument. Neither is the fact that people tend to respond to the thought of abortion in the later stages of pregnancy with emotional repulsion, since mere emotional responses cannot take the place of moral reasoning in determining what ought to be permitted. Nor, finally, is the frequently heard argument that legalizing abortion, especially late in the pregnancy, may erode the level of respect for human life, leading, perhaps, to an increase in unjustified euthanasia and other crimes. For this threat, if it is a threat, can be better met by educating people to the kinds of moral distinctions which we are making here than by limiting access to abortion (which limitation may, in its disregard for the rights of women, be just as damaging to the level of respect for human rights).

Thus, since the fact that even a fully developed fetus is not personlike enough to have any significant right to life on the basis of its personlikeness shows that no legal restrictions upon the stage of pregnancy in which an abortion may be performed can be justified on the grounds that we should protect the rights of the older fetus; and since there is no other apparent justification for such restrictions, we may conclude that they are entirely unjustified. Whether or not it would be *indecent* (whatever that means) for a woman in her seventh month to obtain an abortion just to avoid having to postpone a trip to Europe, it would not, in itself, be *immoral*, and therefore it ought to be permitted.

4. Potential Personhood and Right to Life

We have seen that a fetus does not resemble a person in any way which can support the claim that it has even some of the same rights. But what about its *potential*, the fact that if nurtured and allowed to develop naturally it will very probably become a person? Doesn't that alone give it at least some right to life? It is hard to deny that the fact that an entity is a potential person is a strong prima facie reason for not destroying it; but we need not conclude from this that a potential person has a right to life, by virtue of that potential. It may be that our feeling that it is better, other things being equal, not to destroy a potential person is better explained by the fact that potential people are still (felt to be) an invaluable resource, not to be lightly squandered. Surely, if every speck of dust were a potential person, we would be much less apt to conclude that every potential person has a right to become actual.

Still, we do not need to insist that a potential person has no right to life whatever. There may well be something immoral, and not just imprudent, about wantonly destroying potential people, when doing so isn't necessary to protect anyone's rights. But even if a potential person does have some prima facie right to life, such a right could not possibly outweigh the right of a woman to obtain an abortion, since the rights of any actual person invariably outweigh those of any potential

person, whenever the two conflict. Since this may not be immediately obvious in the case of a human fetus, let us look at another case.

Suppose that our space explorer falls into the hand of an alien culture, whose scientists decide to create a few hundred thousand or more human beings, by breaking his body into its component cells, and using these to create fully developed human beings, with, of course, his genetic code. We may imagine that each of these newly created men will have all of the original man's abilities, skills, knowledge, and so on, and also have an individual self-concept, in short that each of them will be a bona fide (though hardly unique) person. Imagine that the whole project will take only seconds, and that its chances of success are extremely high, and that our explorer knows all of this, and also knows that these people will be treated fairly. I maintain that in such a situation he would have every right to escape if he could, and thus to deprive all of these potential people of their potential lives; for his right to life outweighs all of theirs together, in spite of the fact that they are all genetically human, all innocent, and all have a very high probability of becoming people very soon, if only he refrains from acting.

Indeed, I think he would have a right to escape even if it were not his life which the alien scientists planned to take, but only a year of his freedom, or indeed, only a day. Nor would he be obligated to stay if he had gotten captured (thus bringing all these people-potentials into existence) because of his own carelessness, or even if he had done so deliberately, knowing the consequences. Regardless of how he got captured, he is not morally obligated to remain in captivity for *any* period of time for the sake of permitting any number of potential people to come into actuality, so great is the margin by which one actual person's right to liberty outweighs whatever right to life even a hundred thousand potential people have. And it seems reasonable to conclude that the rights of a woman will outweigh by a similar margin whatever right to life a fetus may have by virtue of its potential personhood.

Thus, neither a fetus's resemblance to a person, nor its potential for becoming a person provides any basis whatever for the claim that it has any significant right to life. Consequently, a woman's right to protect her health, happiness, freedom, and even her life,[9] by terminating an unwanted pregnancy, will always override whatever right to life may be appropriate to ascribe to a fetus, even a fully developed one. And thus, in the absence of any overwhelming social need for every possible child, the laws which restrict the right to obtain an abortion, or limit the period of pregnancy during which an abortion may be performed, are a wholly unjustified violation of a woman's most basic moral and constitutional rights.[10] . . . .

POSTSCRIPT ON INFANTICIDE

Since the publication of this article, many people have written to point out that my argument appears to justify not only abortion, but infanticide as well. For a newborn infant is not significantly more personlike than an advanced fetus, and consequently it would seem that if the destruction of the latter is permissible so too must be that of the former. Inasmuch as most people, regardless of how they feel about the morality of abortion, consider infanticide a form of murder, this might appear to represent a serious flaw in my argument.

Now, if I am right in holding that it is only people who have a full-fledged right to life, and who can be murdered, and if the criteria of personhood are as I have described them, then it obviously follows that killing newborn infants isn't murder. It does *not* follow, however, that infanticide is permissible, for two reasons. In the first place, it would be wrong, at least in this country and in this period of history, and other things being equal, to kill a newborn infant, because even if its parents do not want it and would not suffer from its destruction, there are other people who would like to have it, and would, in all probability, be deprived of a great deal of pleasure by its destruction. Thus, infanticide is wrong for reasons analogous to those which make it wrong to wantonly destroy natural resources, or great works of art.

Second, most people, at least in this country, value infants and would much prefer that they be preserved, even if foster parents are not immediately available. Most of us would rather be taxed to support orphanages than allow unwanted infants to be destroyed. So long as there are people who want an infant preserved, and who are willing and able to provide the means of caring for it, under

reasonably humane conditions, it is, *ceteris parabis,* wrong to destroy it.

But, it might be replied, if this argument shows that infanticide is wrong, at least at this time and in this country, doesn't it also show that abortion is wrong? After all, many people value fetuses, are disturbed by their destruction, and would much prefer that they be preserved, even at some cost to themselves. Furthermore, as a potential source of pleasure to some foster family, a fetus is just as valuable as an infant. There is, however, a crucial difference between the two cases: so long as the fetus is unborn, its preservation, contrary to the wishes of the pregnant woman, violates her rights to freedom, happiness, and self-determination. Her rights override the rights of those who would like the fetus preserved, just as if someone's life or limb is threatened by a wild animal, his right to protect himself by destroying the animal overrides the rights of those who would prefer that the animal not be harmed.

The minute the infant is born, however, its preservation no longer violates any of its mother's rights, even if she wants it destroyed, because she is free to put it up for adoption. Consequently, while the moment of birth does not mark any sharp discontinuity in the degree to which an infant possesses the right to life, it does mark the end of its mother's right to determine its fate. Indeed, if abortion could be performed without killing the fetus, she would never possess the right to have the fetus destroyed, for the same reasons that she has no right to have an infant destroyed.

On the other hand, it follows from my argument that when an unwanted or defective infant is born into a society which cannot afford and/or is not willing to care for it, then its destruction is permissible. This conclusion will, no doubt, strike many people as heartless and immoral; but remember that the very existence of people who feel this way, and who are willing and able to provide care for unwanted infants, is reason enough to conclude that they should be preserved.

NOTES

1. For example, Roger Wertheimer, who in "Understanding the Abortion Argument" (*Philosophy and Public Affairs,* 1, no. 1 [Fall, 1971], 67–95,) argues that the problem of the moral status of abortion is insoluble, in that the dispute over the

status of the fetus is not a question of fact at all, but only a question of how one responds to the facts.

2. John Noonan, "Abortion and the Catholic Church: A Summary History," *Natural Law Forum,* 12 (1967); 125.

3. John Noonan, "Deciding Who Is Human," *Natural Law Forum,* 13 (1968), 134.

4. "A Defense of Abortion."

5. We may safely ignore the fact that she might have avoided getting raped, e.g., by carrying a gun, since by similar means you might likewise have avoided getting kidnapped, and in neither case does the victim's failure to take all possible precautions against a highly unlikely event (as opposed to reasonable precautions against a rather likely event) mean that he is morally responsible for what happens.

6. Of course, the principle that it is (always) wrong to kill innocent human beings is in need of many other modifications, e.g., that it may be permissible to do so to save a greater number of other innocent human beings, but we may safely ignore these complications here.

7. From here on, we will use "human" to mean genetically human, since the moral sense seems closely connected to, and perhaps derived from, the assumption that genetic humanity is sufficient for membership in the moral community.

8. Thomas L. Hayes, "A Biological View," *Commonweal,* 85 (March 17, 1967), 677–78; quoted by Daniel Callahan, in *Abortion, Law, Choice, and Morality* (London: Macmillan & Co., 1970).

9. That is, insofar as the death rate, for the woman, is higher for childbirth than for early abortion.

10. My thanks to the following people, who were kind enough to read and criticize an earlier version of this paper: Herbert Gold, Gene Glass, Anne Lauterbach, Judith Thomson, Mary Mothersill, and Timothy Binkley.

Questions for Analysis

1. Is Warren's objection to Thomson's analogy of the woman tied up against her will well taken?

2. According to Warren, Noonan makes no case for the position that whatever is genetically human is morally human. Do you agree? If so, what kind of case can be made?

3. Why does Warren discount the claim that being a potential person gives the fetus rights against the mother?

4. Because the fetus has no rights against the woman carrying it, Warren says, there is nothing immoral about having a late-term abortion in order to take a European vacation. Is this step warranted? Are there moral considerations she neglects?

5. Warren likens the moral reasons for not killing an infant to the moral reasons for not destroying a work of art. How persuasive is this analogy?

6. Do you agree with Warren's criteria for being human in the moral sense?

Virtue Theory and Abortion

Rosalind Hursthouse

The following selection comes from the second part of an essay by Rosalind Hursthouse. The first part, omitted here, is a general discussion of virtue theory, which she bases on Aristotle. Virtue theory, she says there, is concerned with human flourishing (*eudaimonia,* or living well), and she defines a virtue as "a character trait a human being needs to flourish or live well." She also defines a virtuous agent as a person "who has and exercises virtues" and defines a right action as "what a virtuous agent would do in the circumstances."

From Rosalind Hursthouse, "Virtue Theory and Abortion," *Philosophy & Public Affairs* (Summer 1991). Copyright © 1991 by Princeton University Press. Reprinted by permission of Princeton University.

In the section reprinted here, she applies virtue theory to the abortion debate. Her concern is the morality of abortion, not whether abortion should be legal, and she examines a number of circumstances in which a pregnant woman might consider having one. In each case, she asks whether a virtuous woman would decide to have it. Basic to her answer are two points: Aborting a fetus is a matter that must be taken seriously, and being a parent constitutes, in part, a flourishing human life.

As everyone knows, the morality of abortion is commonly discussed in relation to just two considerations: first, and predominantly, the status of the fetus and whether or not it is the sort of thing that may or may not be innocuously or justifiably killed; and second, and less predominantly (when, that is, the discussion concerns the *morality* of abortion rather than the question of permissible legislation in a just society), women's rights. If one thinks within this familiar framework, one may well be puzzled about what virtue theory, as such, could contribute. Some people assume the discussion will be conducted solely in terms of what the virtuous agent would or would not do. . . . Others assume that only justice, or at most justice and charity,[1] will be applied to the issue, generating a discussion very similar to Judith Jarvis Thomson's.[2]

Now if this is the way the virtue theorist's discussion of abortion is imagined to be, no wonder people think little of it. It seems obvious in advance that in any such discussion there must be either a great deal of extremely tendentious application of the virtue terms *just, charitable,* and so on or a lot of rhetorical appeal to "this is what only the virtuous agent knows." But these are caricatures; they fail to appreciate the way in which virtue theory quite transforms the discussion of abortion by dismissing the two familiar dominating considerations as, in a way, fundamentally irrelevant. In what way or ways, I hope to make both clear and plausible.

Let us first consider women's rights. Let me emphasize again that we are discussing the *morality* of abortion, not the rights and wrongs of laws prohibiting or permitting it. If we suppose that women do have a moral right to do as they choose with their own bodies, or, more particularly, to terminate their pregnancies, then it may well follow that a *law* forbidding abortion would be unjust. Indeed, even if they have no such right, such a law might be, as things stand at the moment, unjust, or impractical, or inhumane: on this issue I have nothing to say in this article. But,

putting all questions about the justice or injustice of laws to one side, and supposing only that women have such a moral right, *nothing* follows from this supposition about the morality of abortion, according to virtue theory, once it is noted (quite generally, not with particular reference to abortion) that in exercising a moral right I can do something cruel, or callous, or selfish, light-minded, self-righteous, stupid, inconsiderate, disloyal, dishonest—that is, act viciously.[3] Love and friendship do not survive their parties' constantly insisting on their rights, nor do people live well when they think that getting what they have a right to is of preeminent importance; they harm others, and they harm themselves. So whether women have a moral right to terminate their pregnancies is irrelevant within virtue theory, for it is irrelevant to the question "In having an abortion in these circumstances, would the agent be acting virtuously or viciously or neither?"

What about the consideration of the status of the fetus—what can virtue theory say about that? One might say that this issue is not in the province of any moral theory; it is a metaphysical question, and an extremely difficult one at that. Must virtue theory then wait upon metaphysics to come up with the answer?

At first sight it might seem so. For virtue is said to involve knowledge, and part of this knowledge consists in having the *right* attitude to things. "Right" here does not just mean "morally right" or "proper" or "nice" in the modern sense; it means "accurate, true." One cannot have the right or correct attitude to something if the attitude is based on or involves false beliefs. And this suggests that if the status of the fetus is relevant to the rightness or wrongness of abortion, its status must be known, as a truth, to the fully wise and virtuous person.

But the sort of wisdom that the fully virtuous person has is not supposed to be recondite; it does not call for fancy philosophical sophistication, and it does not depend upon, let alone wait upon, the discoveries of academic philosophers.[4] And this entails the following, rather startling, conclusion: that the status of the fetus—that issue over which so much ink has been spilt—is, according to virtue theory, simply not relevant to the rightness or wrongness of abortion (within, that is, a secular morality).

Or rather, since that is clearly too radical a conclusion, it is in a sense relevant, but only in the sense that the familiar biological facts are relevant. By "the familiar biological facts" I mean the facts that most human societies are and have been familiar with—that, standardly (but not invariably), pregnancy occurs as the result of sexual intercourse, that it lasts about nine months, during which time the fetus grows and develops, that standardly it terminates in the birth of a living baby, and that this is how we all come to be.

It might be thought that this distinction—between the familiar biological facts and the status of the fetus—is a distinction without a difference. But this is not so. To attach relevance to the status of the fetus, in the sense in which virtue theory claims it is not relevant, is to be gripped by the conviction that we must go beyond the familiar biological facts, deriving some sort of conclusion from them, such as that the fetus has rights, or is not a person, or something similar. It is also to believe that this exhausts the relevance of the familiar biological facts, that all they are relevant to is the status of the fetus and whether or not it is the sort of thing that may or may not be killed.

These convictions, I suspect, are rooted in the desire to solve the problem of abortion by getting it to fall under some general rule such as "You ought not to kill anything with the right to life but may kill anything else." But they have resulted in what should surely strike any nonphilosopher as a most bizarre aspect of nearly all the current philosophical literature on abortion, namely, that, far from treating abortion as a unique moral problem, markedly unlike any other, nearly everything written on the status of the fetus and its bearing on the abortion issue would be consistent with the human reproductive facts (to say nothing of family life) being totally different from what they are. Imagine that you are an alien extraterrestrial anthropologist who does not know that the human race is roughly 50 percent female and 50 percent male, or that our only (natural) form of reproduction involves heterosexual intercourse, viviparous birth, and the female's (and only the female's) being pregnant for nine months, or that females are capable of childbearing from late childhood to late middle age, or that childbearing is painful, dangerous, and emotionally charged—do you think you would pick up these facts from the hundreds of articles written on the status of the fetus? I am quite sure you would not. And that, I think, shows that the current philosophical literature on abortion has got badly out of touch with reality.

Now if we are using virtue theory, our first question is not "What do the familiar biological facts show—what can be derived from them about the status of the fetus?" but "How do these facts figure in the practical reasoning, actions and passions, thoughts and reactions, of the virtuous and the nonvirtuous? What is the mark of having the right attitude to these facts and what manifests having the wrong attitude to them?" This immediately makes essentially relevant not only all the facts about human reproduction I mentioned above, but a whole range of facts about our emotions in relation to them as well. I mean such facts as that human parents, both male and female, tend to care passionately about their offspring, and that family relationships are among the deepest and strongest in our lives—and, significantly, among the longest-lasting.

These facts make it obvious that pregnancy is not just one among many other physical conditions; and hence that anyone who genuinely believes that an abortion is comparable to a haircut or an appendectomy is mistaken.[5] The fact that the premature termination of a pregnancy is, in some sense, the cutting off of a new human life, and thereby, like the procreation of a new human life, connects with all our thoughts about human life and death, parenthood, and family relationships, must make it a serious matter. To disregard this fact about it, to think of abortion as nothing but the killing of something that does not matter, or as nothing but the exercise of some right or rights one has, or as the incidental means to some desirable state of affairs, is to do something callous and light-minded, the sort of thing that no virtuous and wise person would do. It is to have the wrong attitude not only to fetuses, but more generally to human life and death, parenthood, and family relationships.

Although I say that the facts make this obvious, I know that this is one of my tendentious points. In partial support of it I note that even the most dedicated proponents of the view that deliberate abortion is just like an appendectomy or haircut rarely hold the same view of spontaneous abortion, that is, miscarriage. It is not so tendentious of me to claim that to react to people's grief over miscarriage by saying, or even thinking, "What a fuss about nothing!" would be callous and light-minded, whereas to try to laugh someone out of grief over an appendectomy scar or a botched haircut would not be. It is hard to give this point due prominence within act-centered theories, for the inconsistency is an inconsistency in attitude about the seriousness of loss of life, not in beliefs about which acts are right or wrong. Moreover, an act-centered theorist may say, "Well, there is nothing wrong with *thinking* 'What a fuss about nothing!' as long as you do not say it and hurt the person who is grieving. And besides, we cannot be held responsible for our thoughts, only for the intentional actions they give rise to." But the character traits that virtue theory emphasizes are not simply dispositions to intentional actions, but a seamless disposition to certain actions and passions, thoughts and reactions.

To say that the cutting off of a human life is always a matter of some seriousness, at any stage, is not to deny the relevance of gradual fetal development. Notwithstanding the well-worn point that clear boundary lines cannot be drawn, our emotions and attitudes regarding the fetus do change as it develops, and again when it is born, and indeed further as the baby grows. Abortion for shallow reasons in the later stages is much more shocking than abortion for the same reasons in the early stages in a way that matches the fact that deep grief over miscarriage in the later stages is more appropriate than it is over miscarriage in the earlier stages (when, that is, the grief is solely about the loss of *this* child, not about, as might be the case, the loss of one's only hope of having a child or of having one's husband's child). Imagine (or recall) a woman who already has children; she had not intended to have more, but finds herself unexpectedly pregnant. Though contrary to her plans, the pregnancy, once established as a fact, is welcomed—and then she

loses the embryo almost immediately. If this were bemoaned as a tragedy, it would, I think, be a misapplication of the concept of what is tragic. But it may still properly be mourned as a loss. The grief is expressed in such terms as "I shall always wonder how she or he would have turned out" or "When I look at the others, I shall think, 'How different their lives would have been if this other one had been part of them.' " It would, I take it, be callous and light-minded to say, or think, "Well, she has already *got* four children, what's the problem?"; it would be neither, nor arrogantly intrusive in the case of a close friend, to try to correct prolonged mourning by saying, "I know it's sad, but it's not a tragedy; rejoice in the ones you have." The application of *tragic* becomes more appropriate as the fetus grows, for the mere fact that one has lived with it for longer, conscious of its existence, makes a difference. To shrug off an early abortion is understandable just because it is very hard to be fully conscious of the fetus's existence in the early stages and hence hard to appreciate that an early abortion is the destruction of life. It is particularly hard for the young and inexperienced to appreciate this, because appreciation of it usually comes only with experience.

I do not mean "with the experience of having an abortion" (though that may be part of it) but, quite generally, "with the experience of life." Many women who have borne children contrast their later pregnancies with their first successful one, saying that in the later ones they were conscious of a new life growing in them from very early on. And, more generally, as one reaches the age at which the next generation is coming up close behind one, the counterfactuals "If I, or she, had had an abortion, Alice, or Bob, would not have been born" acquire a significant application, which casts a new light on the conditionals. "If I or Alice have an abortion then some Caroline or Bill will not be born."

The fact that pregnancy is not just one among many physical conditions does not mean that one can never regard it in that light without manifesting a vice. When women are in very poor physical health, or worn out from childbearing, or forced to do very physically demanding jobs, then they cannot be described as self-indulgent, callous, irresponsible, or light-minded if they seek abortions mainly with a view to avoiding pregnancy as the physical condition that it is. To go through with a pregnancy when one is utterly exhausted, or when one's job consists of crawling along tunnels hauling coal, as many women in the nineteenth century were obliged to do, is perhaps heroic, but people who do not achieve heroism are not necessarily vicious. That they can view the pregnancy only as nine months of misery, followed by hours if not days of agony and exhaustion, and abortion only as the blessed escape from this prospect, is entirely understandable and does not manifest any lack of serious respect for human life or a shallow attitude to Motherhood. What it does show is that something is terribly amiss in the conditions of their lives, which make it so hard to recognize pregnancy and childbearing as the good that they can be. . . .

The foregoing discussion, insofar as it emphasizes the right attitude to human life and death, parallels to a certain extent those standard discussions of abortion that concentrate on it solely as an issue of killing. But it does not, as those discussions do, gloss over the fact, emphasized by those who discuss the morality of abortion in terms of women's rights, that abortion, wildly unlike any other form of killing, is the termination of a pregnancy, which is a condition of a woman's body and results in *her* having a child if it is not aborted. This fact is given due recognition not by appeal to women's rights but by emphasizing the relevance of the familiar biological and psychological facts and their connection with having the right attitude to parenthood and family relationships. But it may well be thought that failing to bring in women's rights still leaves some important aspects of the problem of abortion untouched.

Speaking in terms of women's rights, people sometimes say things like, "Well, it's her life you're talking about too, you know; she's got a right to her own life, her own happiness." And the discussion stops there. But in the context of virtue theory, given that we are particularly concerned with what constitutes a good human life, with what true happiness or *eudaimonia* is, this is no place to stop. We go on to ask, "And is this life of hers a good one? Is she living well?"

If we are to go on to talk about good human lives, in the context of abortion, we have to bring in our thoughts about the value of love and family life, and our proper emotional development through a natural life cycle. The familiar facts support the view that parenthood in general, and motherhood and childbearing in particular, are intrinsically worthwhile, are among the things that can be correctly thought to be partially constitutive of a flourishing human life.[6] If this is right, then a woman who opts for not being a mother (at all, or again, or now) by opting for abortion may thereby be manifesting a flawed grasp of what her life should be, and be about—a grasp that is childish, or grossly materialistic, or shortsighted, or shallow.

I said "*may* thereby": this need not be so. Consider, for instance, a woman who has already had several children and fears that to have another will seriously affect her capacity to be a good mother to the ones she has—she does not show a lack of appreciation of the intrinsic value of being a parent by opting for abortion. Nor does a woman who has been a good mother and is approaching the age at which she may be looking forward to being a good grandmother. Nor does a woman who discovers that her pregnancy may well kill her, and opts for abortion. . . . Nor, necessarily, does a woman who has decided to lead a life centered around some other worthwhile activity or activities with which motherhood would compete.

People who are childless by choice are sometimes described as "irresponsible," or "selfish," or "refusing to grow up," or "not knowing what life is about." But one can hold that having children is intrinsically worthwhile without endorsing this, for we are, after all, in the happy position of there being more worthwhile things to do than can be fitted into one lifetime. Parenthood, and motherhood in particular, even if granted to be intrinsically worthwhile, undoubtedly take up a lot of one's adult life, leaving no room for some other worthwhile pursuits. But some women who choose abortion rather than have their first child, and some men who encourage their partners to choose abortion, are not avoiding parenthood for the sake of other worthwhile pursuits, but for the worthless one of "having a good time," or for the pursuit of some false vision of the ideals of freedom or self-realization. And some others who say "I am not ready for parenthood yet" are making some sort of mistake about the extent to which one can manipulate the circumstances of one's life so as to make it fulfill some dream that one has. Perhaps one's dream is to have two perfect children; a girl and a boy, within a perfect marriage, in financially secure circumstances, with an interesting job of one's own. But to care too much about that dream, to demand of life that it give it to one and act accordingly, may be both greedy and foolish, and is to run the risk of missing out on happiness entirely. Not only may fate make the dream impossible, or destroy it, but one's own attachment to it may make it impossible. Good marriages, and the most promising children, can be destroyed by just one adult's excessive demand for perfection.

Once again, this is not to deny that girls may quite properly say "I am not ready for motherhood yet," especially in our society, and, far from manifesting irresponsibility or light-mindedness, show an appropriate modesty or humility, or a fearfulness that does not amount to cowardice. However, even when the decision to have an abortion is the right decision—one that does not itself fall under a vice-related term and thereby one that the perfectly virtuous could recommend—it does not follow that there is no sense in which having the abortion is wrong, or guilt inappropriate. For, by virtue of the fact that a human life has been cut short, some evil has probably been brought about,[7] and that circumstances make the decision to bring about some evil the right decision will be a ground for guilt if getting into those circumstances in the first place itself manifested a flaw in character.

What "gets one into those circumstances" in the case of abortion is, except in the case of rape, one's sexual activity and one's choices, or the lack of them, about one's sexual partner and about contraception. The virtuous woman (which here of course does not mean simply "chaste woman" but "woman with the virtues") has such character traits as strength, independence, resoluteness, decisiveness, self-confidence, responsibility, serious-mindedness, and self-determination—and no one, I think, could deny that many women become pregnant in circumstances in which they cannot welcome or cannot face the thought of having *this* child precisely because

they lack one or some of these character traits. So even in the cases where the decision to have an abortion is the right one, it can still be the reflection of a moral failing—not because the decision itself is weak or cowardly or irresolute or irresponsible or light-minded, but because lack of the requisite opposite of these failings landed one in the circumstances in the first place. Hence the common universalized claim that guilt and remorse are never appropriate emotions about an abortion is denied. They may be appropriate, and appropriately inculcated, even when the decision was the right one.

Another motivation for bringing women's rights into the discussion may be to attempt to correct the implication, carried by the killing-centered approach, that insofar as abortion is wrong, it is a wrong that only women do, or at least (given the preponderance of male doctors) that only women instigate. I do not myself believe that we can thus escape the fact that nature bears harder on women than it does on men,[8] but virtue theory can certainly correct many of the injustices that the emphasis on women's rights is rightly concerned about. With very little amendment, everything that has been said above applies to boys and men too. Although the abortion decision is, in a natural sense, the woman's decision, proper to her, boys and men are often party to it, for well or ill, and even when they are not, they are bound to have been party to the circumstances that brought it up. No less than girls and women, boys and men can, in their actions, manifest self-centeredness, callousness, and light-mindedness about life and parenthood in relation to abortion. They can be self-centered or courageous about the possibility of disability in their offspring; they need to reflect on their sexual activity and their choices, or lack of them, about their sexual partner and contraception; they need to grow up and take responsibility for their own actions and life in relation to fatherhood. If it is true, as I maintain, that insofar as motherhood is intrinsically worthwhile, being a mother is an important purpose in women's lives, being a father (rather than a mere generator) is an important purpose in men's lives as well, and it is adolescent of men to turn a blind eye to this and pretend that they have many more important things to do. . . .

NOTES

1. It seems likely that some people have been misled by Foot's discussion of euthanasia (through no fault of hers) into thinking that a virtue theorist's discussion of terminating human life will be conducted exclusively in terms of justice and charity (and the corresponding vice terms) (Philippa Foot, "Euthanasia," *Philosophy & Public Affairs* 6, no. 2 [Winter 1977]: 85–112). But the act-category *euthanasia* is a very special one, at least as defined in her article, since such an act must be done "for the sake of the one who is to die." Building a virtuous motivation into the specification of the act in this way immediately rules out the application of many other vice terms.

2. Judith Jarvis Thomson, "A Defense of Abortion," *Philosophy & Public Affairs* 1, no. 1 (Fall 1971): 47–66. One could indeed regard this article as proto-virtue theory (no doubt to the surprise of the author) if the concepts of callousness and kindness were allowed more weight.

3. One possible qualification: if one ties the concept of justice very closely to rights, then if women do have a moral right to terminate their pregnancies it *may* follow that in doing so they do not act unjustly. (Cf. Thomson, "A Defense of Abortion.") But it is debatable whether even that much follows.

4. This is an assumption of virtue theory, and I do not attempt to defend it here. An adequate discussion of it would require a separate article, since, although most moral philosophers would be chary of claiming that intellectual sophistication is a necessary condition of moral wisdom or virtue, most of us, from Plato onward, tend to write as if this were so. Sorting out which claims about moral knowledge are committed to this kind of elitism and which can, albeit with difficulty, be reconciled with the idea that moral knowledge can be acquired by anyone who really wants it would be a major task.

5. Mary Anne Warren, in "On the Moral and Legal Status of Abortion," *Monist* 57 (1973), sec. 1, says of the opponents of restrictive laws governing abortion that "their conviction (for the most part) is that abortion is not a *morally* serious and extremely unfortunate, even though sometimes justified, act, comparable to killing in self-defense or to letting the violinist die, but rather is closer to being a *morally neutral* act, like cutting one's hair" (italics mine). I would like to think that no one *genuinely* believes this. But certainly in discussion, particularly when arguing against restrictive laws or the suggestion that remorse over abortion might be appropriate, I have found that some people *say* they believe it (and often cite Warren's article, albeit inaccurately, despite its age). Those who allow that it is morally serious, and far from morally neutral, have to argue against restrictive laws, or the appropriateness of remorse, on a very different ground from that laid down by the premise "The fetus is just part of the woman's body (and she has a right to determine what happens to her body and should not feel guilt about anything she does to it)."

6. I take this as a premise here, but argue for it in some detail in my *Beginning Lives* (Oxford: Basil Blackwell, 1987). In this connection I also discuss adoption and the sense in which it may be regarded as "second best," and the difficult question of whether the good of parenthood may properly be sought, or indeed bought, by surrogacy.

7. I say "some evil has probably been brought about" on the ground that (human) life is (usually) a good and hence (human) death usually an evil. The exceptions would be (a) where death is actually a good or a benefit, because the baby that would come to be if the life were not cut short would be better off dead than alive, and (b) where death, though not a good, is not an evil either, because the life that would be led (e.g., in a state of permanent coma) would not be a good. (See Foot, "Euthanasia.")

8. I discuss this point at greater length in *Beginning Lives*.

Questions for Analysis

1. Why does Hursthouse think a woman's rights have no bearing on the morality of abortion?

2. What, according to Hursthouse, is the significance of the fetus's status to virtue theory? Why?

3. How does Hursthouse defend her claim that the early termination of a pregnancy is always a serious matter? Do you agree? What about her claim that parenthood helps to constitute human flourishing?

4. What virtues and vices does Hursthouse consider in her essay? Which do you consider the most relevant?

5. Hursthouse says that current philosophical writing about abortion is "out of touch with reality." Why? Would you say the same thing about the other selections in this chapter? How would their authors respond?

6.   According to Hursthouse, a woman who finds herself with an unwanted pregnancy lacks one or more virtues. Which virtues does she have in mind? Do you agree?

7.   Does virtue theory help to shed light on the abortion debate?

CASE PRESENTATION
Mrs. Sherri Finkbine and the Thalidomide Tragedy

In 1962, Mrs. Sherri Finkbine, the mother of four normal children, found herself pregnant. The pregnancy was going well, except that Mrs. Finkbine was experiencing trouble sleeping. Instead of consulting her physician, she simply took some of the tranquilizers her husband had brought back from a trip to Europe, where the sedative was a widely used over-the-counter drug.

A short time later, Mrs. Finkbine read an article concerning the great increase in the number of children with deformities being born in Europe. Some of the children's limbs failed to develop or developed only in malformed ways; some of the children were born blind and deaf or had seriously defective internal organs. What alarmed Mrs. Finkbine was that the birth defects had been traced to the use in pregnancy of a supposedly harmless and widely used tranquilizer, whose active ingredient was thalidomide.

A visit to her physician confirmed Mrs. Finkbine's worst fears: The tranquilizer she had taken did indeed contain thalidomide. Convinced that his patient stood little chance of delivering a baby without deformities, the physician recommended termination of the pregnancy. He explained to Mrs. Finkbine that getting approval for an abortion under such conditions should prove simple. All she had to do was explain them to the three-member medical board of Phoenix. Mrs. Finkbine followed her physician's counsel, which proved correct: The board granted approval for the abortion.

Concerned about other women who might have unwittingly taken thalidomide, Mrs. Finkbine then called a local newspaper and told her story to the editor. While agreeing not to identify her, the editor ran the story bordered in black on the front page under the headline "Baby-Deforming Drug May Cost Woman Her Child Here."

The wire services picked up the story straightaway, and it wasn't long before enterprising reporters discovered and published Mrs. Finkbine's identity. In no time, Mrs. Finkbine became the object of intense anti-abortion sentiment. *L'Oservatore Romano,* the official Vatican newspaper, condemned Mrs. Finkbine and her husband as murderers. Although she received some letters of support, many were abusive. "I hope someone takes the other four children and strangles them" one person wrote, "because it's all the same thing." Another wrote from the perspective of the fetus: "Mommy, please dear Mommy, let me live. Please please, I want to live. Let me love you, let me see the light of day, let me smell a rose, let me sing a song, let me look into your face, let me say Mommy."

In the heat of the controversy, the medical board members decided that, if challenged, their approval could not survive a court test, for Arizona statute legally sanctioned abortion only when it was required to save the mother's life. Rather than attempt to defend its judgment if asked to, it withdrew its approval.

Thwarted in her attempt to get a legal abortion in some other state, Mrs. Finkbine went to Sweden. After a rigorous investigation by a medical board there, she was given an abortion in a Swedish hospital.

Questions for Analysis

1.   Do you think Mrs. Finkbine acted rightly or wrongly in having an abortion?

2.   What bearing, if any, do you think probable or certain deformities have on the person status of the unborn?

3.   How would you assess this argument: "If you're willing to permit abortions for the reason operating in the Finkbine case, then it follows that you should permit the termination of the existence of similarly defective infants and adults."

4. Do you believe that a government has a right and perhaps even a duty to prohibit abortions in cases like Mrs. Finkbine's? Or do you believe it doesn't? Explain with reference to concepts of justice and freedom.

5. Which of the moral principles discussed in Chapter 1 do you think are especially relevant to cases like this one?

CASE PRESENTATION
Conceived in Violence, Born in Hate[1]

Shortly after returning home, a twenty-seven-year-old mother was gagged, tied up, and raped by a 220-pound guard from a nearby Air Force base who had forced his way into her home. The woman received medical treatment at a hospital and from her own physician. Nevertheless, the episode had left her pregnant.

Not wanting the child, the woman sought an abortion. Although the state's abortion law was, at the time (1955), one of the least restrictive, no hospital in her state would permit her to have an abortion.

Unable to afford to travel abroad for a legal abortion, the woman and her husband were left with two choices: a clandestine illegal abortion or having the baby. Deeply religious and law abiding, the couple chose to carry the baby to term.

During her pregnancy, the woman admitted to hating the fetus she was carrying and to eagerly awaiting the time she would be rid of it. "Thus the child, conceived in violence and born in hatred, came into the world."[2]

Questions for Analysis

1. Do you think abortion should or should not be legal in cases such as this?

2. The traditional Roman Catholic position on abortion rests on the assumption that the unborn is a person from conception. Since the fetus is an innocent person, even when a pregnancy is due to rape or incest, the fetus may not be held accountable and made to suffer through its death. According to Roman Catholicism, then, a *direct* abortion is never morally justifiable. (Although the fetus may never be deliberately killed, it may be allowed to die as a consequence of an action that is intended to save the life of the mother, such as the removal of a malignant uterus.) By this account, an abortion in the preceding case would be immoral. Evaluate this position.

3. Christian moralist Joseph Fletcher has written: "No unwanted and unintended baby should ever be born."[3] Do you think such a rule would produce the greatest social benefit?

4. Do you think Rawls's first principle of social justice has any relevance to the abortion issue?

---

1. Reported in Burton M. Leiser, *Liberty, Justice, and Morals: Contemporary Value Conflicts* (New York: Macmillan, 1973), p. 96.

2. Leiser, *Liberty, Justice, and Morals,* p. 96.

3. Joseph Fletcher, *Situation Ethics: The New Morality* (Philadelphia: Westminster Press, 1966), p. 39.

CASE PRESENTATION
Death in Pensacola

Paul J. Hill was a former Presbyterian minister who had been divested by the Orthodox Presbyterian Church. Among the reasons for his divestiture were his many quarrels with the church over abortion. Hill was strongly anti-abortion, the church moderately pro-choice. After his divestiture, he moved to Pensacola, Florida, where he became active in the pro-life movement, founding a group he called Defensive Action and leading protests at the city's two abortion clinics. One of those clinics made front-page headlines throughout the country in March 1993, when abortion doctor David Gunn was shot and killed outside it by an anti-abortion assailant. The killing, in turn, made Hill a national figure. Appearing on such talk shows as *Donahue* and *Sonya Live,* he approved of the murder as biblically justified homicide and advocated more of the same. Then, in July of the following year, he apparently put his theology into practice. Shot dead outside the city's other abortion clinic were Dr. John Britton and clinic volunteer James Barrett. Barrett's wife, June, also a volunteer, survived her wounds. Prosecutors charged Hill with the shootings the following day.

As newspaper reports over the following days made clear, Barrett was an improbable martyr for the pro-choice movement. Unlike Dr. Gunn, who had been an abortion rights advocate, he personally opposed abortions and frequently tried to discourage his patients from having them. Still, in the face of death threats and considerable harassment, he continued to work at the clinic. He wore a bullet-proof vest to and from the clinic as a precaution but refused offers of police protection.

Operation Rescue and other pro-life groups denounced the killings. President Clinton ordered federal marshalls to stand guard at abortion clinics throughout the country three days after the killings occurred. During Dr. Britton's funeral, a small group of abortion opponents demonstrated outside the church. Said one demonstrator, "May he rot in hell."

Paul Hill was executed by the state of Florida on September 3, 2003. His last words before his death included, "If you believe abortion is a lethal force, you should oppose the force and do what you have to do to stop it."

Questions for Analysis

1. Many abortion rights activists blame anti-abortion rhetoric for contributing to violence at clinics, even if the rhetoric comes from peaceful protestors. The rhetoric they have in mind includes calling abortion doctors murderers and comparing abortion to the Nazi holocaust of the Jews. Do you agree?

2. Hill and other extreme abortion foes consider abortion the moral equivalent of killing schoolchildren. What do you consider the proper level of protest for people who genuinely feel that way? What steps do you think they can justifiably take to prevent abortions?

3. The year 1994 saw the introduction of three significant legal obstacles to anti-abortion demonstrators. In one, the U.S. Supreme Court ruled that clinics can sue groups like Operation Rescue, which systematically attempt to shut clinics down, under the federal racketeering law. In another, the Court ruled that restricting peaceful demonstrators to a distance from which they cannot block access to a clinic is constitutional. In the third, Congress passed the Access to Clinic Entrances Act, making interference with a woman's right to enter a clinic a federal crime. Do such measures unfairly restrict free speech and assembly rights? Should tougher measures be enacted? Do abortion opponents have the moral right to defy the restrictions as an act of civil disobedience?

4. During the 1992 Democratic Convention in New York City that nominated Bill Clinton for president, abortion foe Harley David Belew was arrested after trying to give the nominee a plastic bag containing a fetus. In Oslo, Norway, almost two years later, thieves stole the famous Edvard Munch painting, *The Scream,* from the National Art Museum and offered to return it if the national television station aired *The Silent Scream,* an anti-abortion film. (Though the station refused, the painting was recovered.) Are such novel but illegal protests justifiable?

CASE PRESENTATION
The Fight for Martina Greywind's Baby

By the young age of twenty-eight years, Martina Greywind had already carried and delivered six children. All had been taken away from her on the grounds that she was an unfit mother. Now she was again pregnant. She was also a penniless street person and a paint-fume addict.

While serving a brief sentence in a Fargo, North Dakota, jail for sniffing paint, she met a group of prisoners doing time for an altogether different offense. Members of an anti-abortion organization called Lambs of Christ, they had come to Fargo to shut down the state's only abortion clinic. Greywind told them of her pregnancy and her plans for abortion. Seeking to change her mind, they made this offer: If she did not abort, they would give her $10,000 plus food and shelter and medical care. Greywind went ahead with the abortion anyway, after the Lamb of Christ members found five couples who were willing to adopt her baby.

Why did she reject the offer? According to those who made it, she was coerced by local prosecutors. Because her paint sniffing had continued during the pregnancy, she faced charges of reckless endangerment of a fetus; the only way to get the charges dropped was to abort. They supported their accusation by claiming she told them in jail that she didn't want the abortion. Greywind did not comment on the claim.

After the abortion, the Lamb of Christ members made another accusation. The state, they said, had violated a state law prohibiting the use of public funds for abortions when it drove Greywind in a state vehicle from a mental hospital to the clinic, a distance of 100 miles.

Questions for Analysis

1. Should Greywind have had the abortion?
2. Abortion rights activists try to frame the abortion debate as a matter of choice. Did Greywind have a real choice or was she coerced?
3. Do laws against reckless endangerment of a fetus promote abortion?
4. Were the Lambs of Christ members trying to help Greywind or merely using her in their anti-abortion crusade?

5

Euthanasia

Personhood
Death
Ordinary vs. Extraordinary Treatment
Killing vs. Allowing to Die
Meaning of *Euthanasia:* Narrow vs. Broad Interpretations
Voluntary vs. Nonvoluntary Euthanasia
Assisted Suicide
The Right to Refuse Treatment
Defective Newborns
Arguments for Voluntary (Active) Euthanasia
Arguments against Voluntary (Active) Euthanasia

J. Gay-Williams, "The Wrongfulness of Euthanasia"
James Rachels, "Active and Passive Euthanasia"
Philippa Foot, "Euthanasia"
Richard Brandt, "A Moral Principle about Killing"
Case Presentation, "I Did It Because I Loved My Son"
Case Presentation, "Myrna Is Dead. Desolation"
Case Presentation, "'A Choice Central to Personal Dignity'"
Case Presentation, "Legalized Assisted
Suicide and Decriminalized Euthanasia"

The case of Karen Ann Quinlan has probably done more than any other in recent decades to rivet public attention on the legal and moral aspects of euthanasia, which generally refers to the act of painlessly putting to death a person suffering from a terminal or incurable disease or condition. On the night of April 15, 1975, for reasons still unclear, Karen Ann Quinlan ceased breathing for at least two fifteen-minute periods. Failing to respond to mouth-to-mouth resuscitation by friends, she was taken by ambulance to Newton Memorial Hospital in New Jersey. She had a temperature of 100 degrees, her pupils were unreactive, and she did not respond even to deep pain. Physicians who examined her characterized Karen as being in a "chronic, persistent, vegetative state," and later it was judged that no form of treatment could restore her to cognitive life. Her father, Joseph Quinlan, asked to be appointed her legal guardian with the expressed purpose of discontinuing the use of the respirator by which Karen was being sustained. Eventually, the

Supreme Court of New Jersey granted the request. The respirator was turned off. However, Karen Ann Quinlan remained alive but comatose until June 11, 1985, when she died at the age of thirty-one. Although widely publicized, the Quinlan case is by no means the only one that has raised questions concerning euthanasia.

In fact, improvements in biomedical technology have made euthanasia an issue that more and more individuals and institutions must confront and that society must address. Respirators, artificial kidneys, intravenous feeding, new drugs—all have made it possible to sustain an individual's life artificially—that is, long after the individual has lost the capacity to sustain life independently. In cases like Quinlan's, individuals have fallen into a state of irreversible coma, what some health professionals term a vegetative state. In other instances, such as after severe accidents or with congenital brain disease, the individual's consciousness has been so dulled and the personality has so deteriorated that he or she lacks the capacity for development and growth. In still other cases, such as with terminal cancer, individuals vacillate between agonizing pain and a drug-induced stupor, with no possibility of ever again enjoying life. Not too long ago, "nature would have taken its course"; such patients would have died. Today, we have the technological capacity to keep them alive artificially. Should we? Or at least in some instances, are we justified in not doing this and even obliged not to?

As with abortion, euthanasia raises two basic moral issues that must be distinguished. The first deals with the morality of euthanasia itself; the second concerns the morality of euthanasia legislation. We consider both issues in this chapter.

Before discussing the arguments related to these issues, we must clarify a number of concepts central to euthanasia. Among them are the meanings of *personhood* and *death,* the difference between "ordinary" and "extraordinary" treatment, the distinctions between "killing" and "allowing to die," the various meanings of *euthanasia,* and the difference between "voluntary" and "nonvoluntary" euthanasia.

PERSONHOOD

The question of personhood bears as much on euthanasia as on abortion debates. What conditions should be used as the criteria of personhood? Can an entity be considered a **person** merely because it possesses certain biological properties? Or should other factors be introduced, such as consciousness, self-consciousness, rationality, and the capacities for communication and moral judgment? If personhood is just an elementary biological matter, then patients like Karen Ann Quinlan can qualify as persons more easily than if personhood depends on a complex list of psychosocial factors.

In part, the significance of the personhood issue lies in the assignment of basic patient rights; once the criteria for personhood are established, those qualifying presumably enjoy the same general rights as any other patient. Conversely, for those who do not qualify and have no reasonable chance of ever qualifying, the rights issue is far less problematic. This doesn't mean that a death decision necessarily follows when an entity is determined to be a nonperson. But it does mean that whatever may be inherently objectionable about allowing or causing a person to die dissolves because the entity is no longer a person. So the concept of personhood bears directly on a death decision.

DEATH

Related to personhood is the conceptual issue of death. To get some idea of the complexities enshrouding the concept of death, consider this episode, which is based on an actual case.[1]

A terrible auto accident has occurred. One of the cars was occupied by a husband and wife. Authorities on the scene pronounce the man dead and rush the unconscious woman to a hospital, where she spends the next seventeen days in a coma due to severe brain damage. On the morning of the eighteenth day, she dies. Some time afterward, a relative contesting the couple's estate claims that the two people died simultaneously. Did they?

Not too long ago, legal and medical experts would have said yes. But when this case went to the Supreme Court of Arkansas in 1958, the court ruled that since the woman was breathing after the accident, she was alive, even though unconscious. The court relied on the time-honored definition of death as "the cessation of life; the ceasing to exist; defined by physicians as a total stoppage of the circulation of blood and a cessation of the animal and vital functions consequent thereon, such as respiration, pulsation, etc."[2] By this definition, death occurs if and only if there is a total cessation of respiration and blood flow.

Using heart-lung functioning as a criterion for death served well enough until recent developments in biomedical technology made it questionable. One of these developments is the increasing and widespread use of devices that can sustain respiration and heartbeat indefinitely, even when there is no brain activity. If the traditional heart-lung criterion is applied in cases like the preceding, then these individuals are technically still alive. Yet to many—including relatives of the comatose and those who must treat them—such people are, for all intents and purposes, dead.

Another development that has cast doubt on the traditional definition of death is the need for still-viable organs in transplant surgery. In general, a transplant is most successful if the organs are removed immediately after death. Thus, there is intense pressure on transplant teams to harvest organs as soon as possible. The moral implications of this pressure are serious, as we'll see shortly.

But these developments are only part of what makes the whole issue of defining death so nettlesome. Also relevant are three distinct categories of concerns that can be identified in any discussion of death: the philosophical, the physiological, and the methical.

Philosophical Concerns

The philosophical level refers to one's basic concept of death, which inevitably springs from some view of what it means to be human. For example, if we believe it is the capacity to think and reason that makes one a human, we will likely associate the loss of personhood with the loss of rationality. If we consider consciousness as the defining characteristic, we will be more inclined to consider a person to have lost that status when a number of characteristics such as the capacities to

---

1. *Smith v. Smith,* 229 Arkansas 579, 3175. W, 2d, 275, 1958.

2. *Black's Law Dictionary,* rev. 4th ed. (St. Paul, Minn.: West Publishing), 1968, p. 488.

remember, enjoy, worry, and will are gone. Although the absence of rational or experimental capacities would not necessarily define death, it would dispose us toward such a definition, since we are already disposed to accept the absence of personhood in the absence of those criteria. So there is interplay between our concepts of personhood and death.

Physiological Concerns

These relate to the functioning of specific body systems or organs. The traditional physiological standard for recognizing death has been irreversible loss of circulatory and respiratory functions. More recent physiological standards defined by the Harvard Ad Hoc Committee (1968) and other medical groups in later years have focused on the central nervous system—the brain and spinal cord. Specifically, these standards are the irreversible loss of reflex activity mediated through the brain or spinal cord, electrical activity in the cerebral neocortex, and/or cerebral blood flow. Whether traditional or recent, these physiological standards can be used individually or in combination. The significance of the physiological category in death decisions is that a patient declared alive by one set of criteria might be ruled dead by another. If a patient is considered dead, obviously euthanasia becomes academic; if the person is considered alive, euthanasia is a real concern.

Methodical Concerns

This category refers to specific means for determining physiological standards. The method used to determine traditional heart-lung standards has been taking the pulse or reading an electrocardiogram or both. For the central nervous system, electroencephalographs can be used to measure electrical activity in the neocortex, and radioactive tracers can be injected into the circulatory system for detecting cerebral blood flow.

Moral Implications

What makes defining death so important in discussions of euthanasia and the general study of bioethics is the interplay between definitional and moral considerations. To illustrate, suppose an attacker has clubbed a woman into a comatose condition. She is rushed to a hospital, is determined to have suffered profound and irreversible brain damage, and is put on an artificial respirator. Efforts to identify her fail. As the team tending her debates whether to remove her from the respirator, one member, using one of the brain-death criteria, claims she is already dead. Therefore, withdrawing the respirator poses no special problems. Another member demurs. Using the heart-lung criterion, she insists that the woman is still alive and that the team has an obligation to sustain her life. What ought the team do?

One answer is, let the law decide. But some states lack an adequate definition of death. Complicating matters, some states allow either of the two alternative definitions. And even where the law is decisive, moral problems remain about the rightness of the standard itself. Beyond this, even when the law sanctions a brain-death criterion, as it now does in most states, it does not compel health professionals or anyone else to implement it. So although brain-death law may legally protect health professionals, it does not obligate them to act. Health professionals, presumably in consultation with others, must still wrestle with moral decisions in cases of irreversible coma.

Then there is the phenomenon of organ transplants, which promises to become of even greater concern as technology and techniques improve. A number of interests are identifiable in such cases. First, there are the interests of recipients, whose welfare depends on the availability of organs. Then there are the interests of health teams, who are obliged to provide adequate healthcare, which may include appropriate quality organs. There are also the interests of the donors, who may fear that their organs will be pirated prior to death or that their own healthcare providers will perform less than adequately in trying to sustain their lives. Moreover, there are the obligations of health teams to guard donors against physical violations as well as the psychological threat of violations and to guard themselves against developing a cannibalistic image. And finally, society at large must be watchful that the rights of its citizens to protection are not flouted, while at the same time ensuring that its ill citizens are not denied needed medical care and treatment, which may involve transplants.

ORDINARY VS. EXTRAORDINARY TREATMENT

A third issue that arises in euthanasia discussions involves the concept of ordinary as opposed to extraordinary treatment, terms used to differentiate two broad categories of medical intervention. Although the terms are often applied facilely, they elude hard-and-fast definition.

Moralist Paul Ramsey, for one, has applied *ordinary* to all medicines, treatments, and surgical procedures that offer a reasonable hope of benefit to the patient but do not involve excessive pain, expense, or other inconveniences. In contrast, he has identified *extraordinary* as measures that are unusual, extremely difficult, dangerous, inordinately expensive, or that offer no reasonable hope of benefit to the patient.[3]

Such descriptions are useful and probably find widespread acceptance. But they do raise questions. An obvious one concerns the concepts used to define *ordinary* and *extraordinary*. What can be considered "reasonable hope of benefit to the patient"? What measures qualify as "unusual"? Ramsey mentions cost, but some would claim that cost has no place in a moral calculation. And then there is always the question of whether these criteria should be used individually or in combination; if in combination, what is the proper mix? Furthermore, patient idiosyncrasies inevitably influence a determination of ordinary and extraordinary in a particular case. For example, the use of antibiotics for a pneumonia patient undoubtedly qualifies as ordinary treatment. But does it remain ordinary treatment when the patient with pneumonia happens to have terminal cancer with metastasis to the brain and liver? The institutional setting can also affect evaluations of what constitutes ordinary and extraordinary: What is

---

3. Paul Ramsey, *The Patient as Person* (New Haven, Conn.: Yale University Press, 1970), pp. 122–123.

extraordinary treatment in a small community hospital could be ordinary in a large teaching hospital.[4]

The significance of trying to pin down these two concepts is that euthanasia arguments often rely on them to distinguish the permissible from the impermissible act of euthanasia. Most moralists, both religious and secular, argue that health professionals should provide ordinary treatment for the moribund but not extraordinary, which may be withheld or never started. Others insist that health professionals initiate extraordinary measures. Indeed, the medical profession itself makes similar operational distinctions in making death decisions.

KILLING VS. ALLOWING TO DIE

A fourth conceptual issue that we should try to clarify is what some consider to be the difference between killing a person and allowing a person to die. Presumably, "killing" a person refers to a definite action taken to end someone's life, as in the case of the physician who, out of mercy, injects a terminally ill patient with air or a lethal dose of a medication. Killing is an act of commission. In contrast, "allowing to die" presumably is an act of omission, whereby the steps needed to preserve someone's life simply are not taken. For example, a doctor, again out of mercy, fails to give an injection of antibiotics to a terminally ill patient who has contracted pneumonia. As a result of this omission, the patient dies.

Those making this distinction, such as the American Medical Association (AMA), say that the distinction is reasonable because in ordinary language and everyday life we distinguish between causing someone harm and permitting the harm to happen to them. If, in cases of euthanasia, the distinction is not made between killing and allowing to die, we lose the important distinction between causing someone harm and permitting that harm to happen.

Proponents also claim that the distinction acknowledges cases in which additional curative treatment would serve no purpose and in fact would interfere with a person's natural death. It recognizes that medical science will not initiate or sustain extraordinary means to preserve the life of a dying patient when such means would obviously serve no useful purpose for the patient or the patient's family.

Finally, some argue that the distinction is important in determining causation of death and ultimate responsibility. In instances where the patient dies following nontreatment, the proximate cause of death is the patient's disease, not the treatment or the person who did not provide it. If we fail to differentiate between killing and allowing to die, we blur this distinction. If allowing to die is subsumed under the category of euthanasia, then the nontreatment is the cause of the death, not the disease.

Not everyone, however, agrees that the distinction is a logical one. Some argue that withholding extraordinary treatment or suspending heroic measures in terminal cases is tantamount to the intentional termination of the life of one human being by another; that is, it is an act of killing. Thus, they claim that no logical distinction can be made between killing and allowing to die.

---

4. See A. J. Davis and M. A. Aroskar, *Ethical Dilemmas and Nursing Practice* (New York: Appleton-Century-Crofts, 1978), p. 117.

Whether or not the distinction between the two can be sustained logically is only one question raised by the killing vs. letting die debate. Another is the moral relevance of such a distinction. Even if the distinction is logical, does it have any bearing on the rightness or wrongness of acts commonly termed *euthanasia?*

On the one hand, for those making the distinction, allowing a patient to die under carefully circumscribed conditions could be moral. On the other hand, they seemingly would regard the killing of a patient, even out of mercy, an immoral act. But those opposing the killing–letting die distinction would not necessarily accept the close connection between killing a dying patient and an immoral act. For them, while killing is generally wrong, in some cases it may be the right thing to do. What determines the morality of killing a patient, what is of moral relevance and importance, is not the manner of causing the death but the circumstances in which the death is caused.

In summary, those distinguishing killing from allowing to die claim that the distinction is logically and morally relevant. Generally, they would condemn any act of killing a patient, while recognizing that some acts of allowing a patient to die may be moral (as, for example, in cases where life is being preserved heroically and death is imminent). In contrast are those who hold that the killing-letting die distinction is not logical and that allowing to die is in effect killing. They claim that killing a patient may be morally justifiable depending on the circumstances and not the manner in which the death is caused. The debate that surrounds the killing vs. allowing to die question is basic to the very meaning of euthanasia, a fifth conceptual issue that needs clarification.

MEANING OF *EUTHANASIA:* NARROW VS. BROAD INTERPRETATIONS

Construing euthanasia (from the Greek, meaning "good or happy death") narrowly, some philosophers have taken it to be the equivalent of killing. Since allowing someone to die does not involve killing, allowing to die would not actually be an act of euthanasia at all. By this account, then, there are acts of allowing to die, which may be moral, and acts of euthanasia, which are always wrong.

Other philosophers interpret the meaning of **euthanasia** more broadly. For them, euthanasia includes not only acts of killing but also acts of allowing to die. In other words, euthanasia can take an active or passive form. **Active** (sometimes termed positive) **euthanasia** refers to the act of painlessly putting to death persons suffering from incurable conditions or diseases. Injecting a lethal dosage of medication into a terminally ill patient would constitute active euthanasia. **Passive euthanasia**, in contrast, refers to any act of allowing a patient to die. Not providing a terminally ill patient the needed antibiotics to survive pneumonia would be an example of passive euthanasia.

It is tempting to view the debate between the narrow and the broad interpretations of euthanasia largely in terms of semantics. While the meaning of euthanasia certainly is a factor in the disagreement, the issue involves more than mere word definition.

One side, the narrow interpretation, considers killing a patient always morally wrong. Since euthanasia, by this definition, is killing a patient, euthanasia is always morally wrong. But allowing a patient to die does not involve killing a patient. Therefore, allowing a patient to die does not fall under the moral prohibition that euthanasia does; allowing a patient to die may be morally right.

The other side, the broad interpretation, considers acts of allowing patients to die acts of euthanasia, albeit passive euthanasia. They argue that if euthanasia is wrong, then so is allowing patients to die (since it is a form of euthanasia). But if allowing patients to die is not wrong, then euthanasia is not always wrong. Generally, those favoring the broad interpretation in fact claim that allowing patients to die is not always wrong and that euthanasia, therefore, may be morally justifiable. With the possible moral justifiability of euthanasia established, it is conceivable that acts of active euthanasia, as well as passive, may be moral. What determines their morality are the conditions under which the death is caused and not the manner in which it is caused. It's within these broad interpretations that the most problematic cases of death decisions fall—including the Quinlan case.

VOLUNTARY VS. NONVOLUNTARY EUTHANASIA

In addition to the preceding, there is another conceptual issue that arises in discussions of euthanasia. It concerns the difference between voluntary and nonvoluntary decisions about death.

Voluntary decisions about death refer to cases in which a competent adult patient requests or gives informed consent to a particular course of medical treatment or nontreatment. Generally speaking, informed consent exists when patients can understand what they are agreeing to and voluntarily choose it. Voluntary decisions also include cases in which persons take their own lives either directly or by refusing treatment and cases where patients deputize others to act in their behalf. For example, a woman who is terminally ill instructs her husband and family not to permit antibiotic treatment should she contract pneumonia or not to use artificial support systems should she lapse into a coma and be unable to speak for herself. Similarly, a man requests that he be given a lethal injection after an industrial explosion has left him with third-degree burns over most of his body and no real hope of recovery. For a decision about death to be voluntary, the individual must give explicit consent.

A nonvoluntary decision about death refers to cases in which the decision is not made by the person who is to die. Such cases would include situations where, because of age, mental impairment, or unconsciousness, patients are not competent to give informed consent to life-or-death decisions and where others make the decisions for them. For example, suppose that as a result of an automobile accident, a man suffers massive and irreparable brain damage, falls into unconsciousness, and can be maintained only by artificial means. Should he regain consciousness, he would likely be little more than a vegetable. Given this prognosis, the man's family, in consultation with his physicians, decides to suspend artificial life-sustaining means and allows him to die.

In actual situations, the difference between voluntary and nonvoluntary decisions about death is not always clear. For example, take the case of a man who has heard his mother say that she would never want to be kept alive with "machines and pumps and tubes." Now that she is in fact being kept alive that way and is unable to express a life-or-death decision, the man is not sure that his mother actually would choose to be allowed to die. Similarly, a doctor might not be certain that the tormented cries of a stomach-cancer patient to be "put out of my misery" are an expression of informed consent or of profound pain and momentary despair.

The voluntary–nonvoluntary distinction is relevant to both the narrow and the broad interpretations of the meaning of euthanasia. Each interpretation seemingly distinguishes four kinds of death decisions in which the voluntary–nonvoluntary distinction plays a part. Thus, the narrow interpretation recognizes cases of

1. **Voluntary euthanasia**
2. Nonvoluntary euthanasia
3. Voluntary allowing to die
4. Nonvoluntary allowing to die

By this account, the first two generally are considered immoral; instances of the second two may be moral under carefully circumscribed conditions.

Recognizing no logical or morally relevant distinction between euthanasia and allowing to die, the broad interpretation allows four forms of euthanasia:

1. Voluntary active euthanasia
2. Nonvoluntary active euthanasia
3. Voluntary passive euthanasia
4. Nonvoluntary passive euthanasia

By this account, any of these types of euthanasia may be morally justifiable under carefully circumscribed conditions.

The narrow and the broad interpretations differ sharply in their moral judgment of *deliberate* acts taken to end or shorten a patient's life—that is, acts that the narrow interpretation terms voluntary or nonvoluntary euthanasia and that the broad interpretation terms voluntary or nonvoluntary *active* euthanasia. Generally, the narrow interpretation considers such acts always morally repugnant; the broad interpretation views them as being morally justifiable under carefully circumscribed conditions.

Some discussions of euthanasia distinguish nonvoluntary euthanasia from involuntary euthanasia. Nonvoluntary in these discussions is limited to euthanasia in which the patient is not able now to make a meaningful decision about euthanasia but has previously made preferences clear to a caretaker or family member, usually through a **living will** or directive. **Involuntary euthanasia** involves a decision made by someone else that the person's life should end, even though that person has never made these preferences known to anyone. This might be a decision by a hospital ethics committee that the person should be euthanized, even though no such wishes were ever expressed by that person. In the discussion here, **nonvoluntary euthanasia** includes all situations where the decision for euthanasia is made by someone other than the patient, whether or not that patient had previously expressed a preference for this course of action.

ASSISTED SUICIDE

Closely related to the issue of euthanasia is that of **assisted suicide**, which has become one of the most debated moral and legal issues of recent years. Most of the debate centers on *physician*-assisted suicide—whether to allow doctors to assist terminally ill patients in taking their own lives, usually by prescribing a lethal dose of drugs. For all the similarities between assisted suicide and voluntary active euthanasia, there is one crucial if subtle difference: In the former, the physician does not directly cause the patient's death but enables the patient to choose the time and circumstances of his or her own death. Because of this difference, proponents of physician-assisted suicide see it as a moral solution to the problem posed by the suffering of the terminally ill. If the terminally ill have the right to end their suffering, which proponents feel they do, then they also have the right to seek their doctors' assistance. Opponents counter that the terminally ill have no right to take their own lives and that assisting in suicide is not the proper role of physicians.

The debate was sparked by Dr. Jack Kervorkian and his "suicide machine," an invention of his that enables patients to give themselves lethal injections. The Michigan doctor first provided the device in 1990 to a woman who suffered from Alzheimer's disease. Because Michigan had no law forbidding assisted suicide at the time, he was not charged. But then, after assisting in the suicides of two other women the following year, he was charged with two counts of murder, both of which a judge dismissed. These dismissals led the state's legislature to enact a temporary ban on assisted suicide. Undeterred, Kervorkian continued to make his machine available, and he was consequently charged with violating the new law. On May 3, 1994, a jury acquitted him. Since then, he has assisted or been present at dozens of suicides. After the temporary ban expired, he faced five more prosecutions, each for violating Michigan common law. Not once was a jury willing to convict him.

Kervorkian's persistence and legal troubles generated enormous attention and controversy, which quickly turned to action as voters in various states petitioned for ballot initiatives either to allow assisted suicide or to ban it. In states with existing legislation banning the practice, terminally ill patients went to court asking that the laws be declared unconstitutional. Twice the issue reached the U.S. Supreme Court. In June 1997, the Court upheld the constitutionality of two state laws, Washington's and New York's, that ban assisted suicide (*Washington v. Glucksberg* and *Vacco v. Quill*). Then in October of that year, the Court refused to hear a challenge to an Oregon law—this one passed by voters in a 1994 ballot initiative—that legalizes assisted suicide. After a legal challenge, Oregon voters passed another ballot initiative permitting assisting suicide in 1997. Since the Oregon Death with Dignity Act went into effect in 1998, at least ninety-one persons have ended their lives, most of them suffering from cancer. In 2002, efforts by the U.S. Department of Justice to prosecute doctors who participated in Oregon's assisted suicide program were halted by a federal court. So far, attempts to pass a ban on assisted suicide by the U.S. Congress have failed. Thus, the issue is left to the states for now. The terminally ill have no constitutional right to commit suicide, but states may allow them to do so with the assistance of their doctors.

THE RIGHT TO REFUSE TREATMENT

Though the right to refuse medical treatment has long been widely recognized, and though many state courts (as in the Karen Ann Quinlan case) have upheld the right of family members to refuse life-preserving treatment, it was not until the summer of 1990 that the U.S. Supreme Court, in *Cruzan v. Missouri Health Services,* recognized the right of a competent patient to refuse life-preserving medical treatment, including artificial (nonoral) delivery of nutrition and water. The court also ruled that when the patient is not competent to make the decision, it may be made by a surrogate acting according to the patient's wishes.

Thus, the court established a constitutional basis for voluntary passive euthanasia (or allowing to die) in some cases. But the court also ruled that states may require clear and convincing evidence that the surrogate is in fact acting in accordance with the patient's wishes. Thus, even though the court upheld the right, it did not rule that treatment be stopped in the case at issue because of the lack of clear and convincing evidence.

One likely consequence of the ruling is the legal validity of *living wills,* documents that direct physicians not to apply artificial means of preserving life. A model living will, Directive to Physicians, was created by the California legislature in 1977 as part of the state's Natural Death Act (see Figure 1). Living wills have long been advocated by many Americans, including those who advocate not only the right to refuse treatment but also a broader right, the right to die, which also includes the right to voluntary active euthanasia. That broader right has not been recognized by the courts, and most current controversy surrounding euthanasia concerns whether it should be.

DEFECTIVE NEWBORNS

The legal and moral questions of refusing treatment become more complicated in cases of newborns with defects, babies born with serious birth defects, such as Tay-Sachs, a fatal degenerative disease; Down's syndrome, which manifests itself in mental retardation and various physical abnormalities; and duodenal atresia, in which the upper part of the small intestine, the duodenum, is closed off, therefore preventing the passage and digestion of food. (Although duodenal atresia can usually be treated through surgery, it often is accompanied by other serious birth defects.)

One complication concerns the treatment in question. Allowing defective newborns to die often includes the withholding of ordinary treatment, such as simple nourishment. Another concerns the defects themselves. Although some birth defects, such as anencephalus (the partial or total absence of the brain), guarantee a life in a vegetative state, children with others, such as Down's syndrome, often lead meaningful, if limited, lives.

It is possible to identify three broad positions on the moral acceptability of allowing defective newborns to die. Underpinning each are controversial value assumptions.

The first and most permissive position is that allowing seriously defective newborns to die is morally permissible not only when there is no significant potential for meaningful human existence but also when the emotional or financial hardship of caring for the child would place a grave burden on the family. Adherents to this view argue their case on the grounds that newborns are not yet persons, which, as we saw in Chapter 4, is a controversial assumption.

The second position is that it is permissible only if there is no significant potential for meaningful human existence. Clearly implied here is a quality-of-life judgment, which often elicits debate. Should we make such judgments? And if so, what

---

DIRECTIVE TO PHYSICIANS

Directive made this _____ day of _____ _____ (month, year).

I, _____ being of sound mind, willfully and voluntarily make known my desire that my life shall not be artificially prolonged under the circumstances set forth below, do hereby declare:

1. If at any time I should have an incurable injury, disease, or illness certified to be a terminal condition by two physicians, and where the application of life-sustaining procedures would serve only to artificially prolong the moment of my death and where my physician determines that my death is imminent whether or not life-sustaining procedures are utilized, I direct that such procedures be withheld or withdrawn, and that I be permitted to die naturally.

2. In the absence of my ability to give directions regarding the use of such life-sustaining procedures, it is my intention that this directive shall be honored by my family and physician(s) as the final expression of my legal right to refuse medical or surgical treatment and accept the consequences from such refusal.

3. If I have been diagnosed as pregnant and that diagnosis is known to my physician, this directive shall have no force or effect during the course of my pregnancy.

4. I have been diagnosed and notified at least 14 days ago as having a terminal condition by _____, M.D., whose address is _____ and whose telephone number is _____.
I understand that if I have not filled in the physician's name and address, it shall be presumed that I did not have a terminal condition when I made out this directive.

5. This directive shall have no force or effect five years from the date filled in above.

6. I understand the full import of this directive and I am emotionally and mentally competent to make this directive.

Signed _____

City, County and State of Residence _____

The declarant has been personally known to me and I believe him or her to be of sound mind.

Witness _____

Witness _____

Figure 1

should count as a meaningful human existence? The degree of retardation associated with Down's syndrome, for example, can vary widely. At what point can we separate a meaningful from a meaningless human existence?

The third position asserts that it is never morally permissible to allow a defective newborn to die. Stated more cautiously, it is never moral to withhold from a defective newborn any treatment that would be provided to a normal one. The clear implication here is that the defective infant has full personhood and must be treated accordingly. Just as clearly, this view rejects any quality-of-life or cost factors in determining the acceptability of allowing a defective infant to die. Like the other positions, this one is fraught with debatable value judgments, and in cases of duodenal atresia, it ignores that normal infants would not require corrective surgery to digest food.

It is quite apparent, then, that whether cases involve defective newborns or adults who are terminally ill, the central moral question concerns the acceptability of a death decision and subsequent action. But there are additional moral problems relating to death decisions in the institutional setting that are worth considering.

ARGUMENTS FOR
VOLUNTARY (ACTIVE) EUTHANASIA

1. *Individuals have the right to decide about their own lives and deaths.*

POINT: "What more basic right is there than the right of terminally ill patients to control the circumstances of their own deaths? To decide whether they'll spend their last days in great pain or not, hooked up to machines or not, conscious or not, drugged to a stupor or not? If they wish to spare themselves the agony of a drawn-out death and their families the agony of watching them go through it, who are we to deny them the right to do so?"

COUNTERPOINT: "What you're really saying is that all of us have the right to commit suicide. But we don't have that right and we shouldn't have it. It's one thing to say that we have the right to refuse medical treatment, but it's quite another to say that we have the right to decide when our lives are no longer bearable and then end them. If we follow your reasoning, we'd also have to say that the nonterminally ill have the right to determine the circumstances of their death too. After all, we're all going to die some day anyway."

2. *Denying terminally ill patients the right to die is unfair and cruel.*

POINT: "We allow terminally ill patients to refuse life-preserving treatment out of compassion. We allow them to refuse to be hooked up to respirators or intravenous feeding tubes, to refuse treatment for pneumonia. But what can be crueler than to let suffering cancer patients starve to death or wait for pneumonia when we can end their misery immediately? Besides, denying suffering patients the right to active euthanasia isn't fair to those who aren't on life support. Why should they be denied the right to die when it's not denied to those who are on life support?"

COUNTERPOINT: "The issue isn't the right to die but the right to refuse extraordinary means of treatment, the right of all patients, including the terminally ill, to decide that further medical treatment won't benefit them. There's also another issue at stake, the role of healthcare professionals. When they disconnect life-support systems, they're respecting the autonomy of their patients. If they give them lethal injections, they'll be committing an act of deliberately killing a fellow human being. Everyone feels compassion for these patients, but you can't justify everything in the name of compassion."

3.   *The golden rule requires that we allow active euthanasia for terminally ill patients.*

POINT: "The simplest way to put the matter is like this: If you were in a terminal cancer ward and found the suffering to be more than you could bear, you'd want your doctor to give you a lethal injection if you asked for it, wouldn't you? Then how can you justify not allowing the same for others? It's a straightforward application of the golden rule. Do unto others as you would have them do unto you."

COUNTERPOINT: "For all I know, I might end up exactly as you describe, but that still doesn't change anything. Just because we *want* someone to do something for us doesn't mean that we have the *right* to have it done. And it certainly doesn't mean that others have the obligation or even the right to do it. The golden rule applies only to moral actions, and neither suicide nor deliberate killing is moral."

4.   *People have a right to die with dignity.*

POINT: "Not everyone wants to spend his or her last days lying in a hospital bed wasting away to something hardly recognizable as a human being, let alone his or her former self. To constantly fight horrible pain, to be hooked up to an intravenous machine that supplies painkilling narcotics, to drift up and back between a dream state and reality, not to recognize family and friends, to waste away to nothing while dying of dehydration or starvation—to some people that's an unacceptable affront to their dignity. Out of respect for the dignity of others, we allow them to *live* with dignity. Why not allow them to *die* with dignity?"

COUNTERPOINT: "The phrase 'death with dignity' makes perfect sense when we're talking about allowing people to die a natural death instead of being kept alive against their will by artificial means. But you're talking about avoiding natural death instead of facing it. And there's nothing undignified about facing a natural death."

ARGUMENTS AGAINST
VOLUNTARY (ACTIVE) EUTHANASIA

1.   *Active euthanasia is the deliberate taking of a human life.*

POINT: "The deliberate killing of a human being is wrong, pure and simple, whether the person wants to die or not. And calling it 'euthanasia' doesn't change the fact that what we're talking about is the deliberate taking of a human life."

COUNTERPOINT: "Certainly, under normal circumstances, taking a human life is wrong, but we're not talking about normal circumstances. The circumstances here involve terminally ill patients who can't bear their pointless suffering. If we're willing to disconnect the life-support systems of such patients if they request it, we should be willing to give them lethal injections if they request it. In both cases, the intention is the same—to respect their wish to be put out of their misery."

2. *We can't be sure consent is voluntary.*

POINT: "We can't ever be sure consent is voluntary. In fact, the circumstances surrounding most terminally ill patients make voluntary consent impossible. Either they're in terrible pain or they're drugged. In any case, they can't be thinking clearly enough to understand the full impact of what they're consenting to. And that hardly counts as rational free choice."

COUNTERPOINT: "Maybe not, but suppose the patient requests to be euthanized before he or she reaches that point. Or suppose the family feels the patient really wants the lethal injection. We disconnect life-support systems from patients who are no longer capable of giving informed consent in those circumstances. Why not give them lethal injections in the same circumstances?"

3. *Allowing active euthanasia will lead to abuses.*

POINT: "Killing terminally ill patients who ask for it is a dangerous step. Once you accept the principle of the right to die, what stops you from extending it to the nonterminally ill? Does an athlete who becomes a quadriplegic have the right to be put out of his misery? Someone suffering from chronic depression? Severe arthritis? Alzheimer's disease? And what happens when people like that don't request lethal injections but their families do? Are we to 'euthanize' them too?"

COUNTERPOINT: "I'm not advocating a general right to die, just the right of terminally ill patients to choose the way they die. To suggest that complying with a terminally ill cancer patient's request for a lethal injection will lead to the kind of abuses you mention is to confuse distinct and separate issues. Certainly, nobody's calling for nonvoluntary euthanasia."

4. *There's always the possibility of mistaken diagnosis, a new cure, or spontaneous remission.*

POINT: "The judgment that a patient is terminally ill isn't always the last word, you know. The diagnosis may be mistaken, a new cure may come along, and cancer patients have been known to go into spontaneous remission. But death is the last word. Once you've killed a patient, he or she is beyond all hope. How would you feel if a wonder drug turned up the next day or if the doctors discovered their diagnosis was wrong?"

COUNTERPOINT: "The judgment that a patient is terminally ill may not always be the last word, but it usually is. Despite what you say, many patients are already beyond hope. No new cure is going to come along in time to save people after cancer has metastasized throughout their bodies. And to hope for spontaneous remission or mistaken diagnosis at that point is absurd. Besides, everything you say holds for passive as well as active euthanasia. When a terminally ill cancer patient comes down with pneumonia, few, if any, people are willing to treat the pneumonia in hopes of finding a wonder drug for cancer. To do so would be outright cruelty. And that's what denying a lethal injection to a patient without pneumonia amounts to—outright cruelty."

The Wrongfulness of Euthanasia

J. Gay-Williams

In this essay, professor of philosophy J. Gay-Williams defines euthanasia as intentionally taking the life of a person suffering from some illness or injury from which recovery cannot reasonably be expected. While rejecting *voluntary* euthanasia as a *name* for actions that are usually designated by the phrase, Gay-Williams seems to approve of the actions themselves. He argues that euthanasia as intentional killing goes against natural law because it violates the natural inclination to preserve life. Furthermore, in Gay-Williams's view, both self-interest and possible practical effects of euthanasia provide reasons for rejecting it.

My impression is that euthanasia—the idea, if not the practice—is slowly gaining acceptance within our society. Cynics might attribute this to an increasing tendency to devalue human life, but I do not believe this is the major factor. The acceptance is much more likely to be the result of unthinking sympathy and benevolence. Well-publicized, tragic stories like that of Karen Quinlan elicit from us deep feelings of compassion. We think to ourselves, "She and her family would be better off if she were dead." It is an easy step from this very human response to the view that if someone (and others) would be better off dead, then it must be all right to kill that person.[1] Although I respect the compassion that leads to this conclusion, I believe the conclusion is wrong. I want to show that euthanasia is wrong. It is inherently wrong, but it is also wrong judged from the standpoints of self-interest and of practical effects.

Before presenting my arguments to support this claim, it would be well to define "euthanasia." An essential aspect of euthanasia is that it involves taking a human life, either one's own or that of another. Also, the person whose life is taken must be someone who is believed to be suffering from some disease or injury from which recovery cannot reasonably be expected. Finally, the action must be deliberate and intentional. Thus, euthanasia is intentionally taking the life of a presumably hopeless person. Whether the life is one's own or that of another, the taking of it is still euthanasia.

It is important to be clear about the deliberate and intentional aspect of the killing. If a hopeless person is given an injection of the wrong drug by mistake and this causes his death, this is wrongful killing but not euthanasia. The killing cannot be the result of accident. Furthermore, if the person is given an injection of a drug that is believed to be necessary to treat his disease or better his condition and the person dies as a result, then this is neither wrongful killing nor euthanasia. The intention was to make the patient well, not kill him. Similarly, when a patient's condition is such that it is not reasonable to hope that any medical procedures or treatments will save his life, a failure to implement the procedures or treatments is not euthanasia. If the person dies, this will be as a result of his injuries or disease and not because of his failure to receive treatment.

The failure to continue treatment after it has been realized that the patient has little chance of benefitting from it has been characterized by some as "passive euthanasia." This phrase is misleading and mistaken.[2] In such cases, the person involved is not killed (the first essential aspect of euthanasia), nor is the death of the person intended by the withholding of additional treatment (the third essential aspect of euthanasia). The aim may be to spare the person additional and unjustifiable pain, to save him from the indignities of hopeless manipulations, and to avoid increasing the financial and emotional burden on his family. When I buy a pencil it is so that I can use it to write, not to contribute to an increase in the gross national product. This may be the unintended consequence of my action, but it is not the aim of my action. So it is with failing to continue the treatment of a dying person. I intend his death no more than I intend to reduce the GNP by not using medical supplies. His is an unintended dying, and so-called "passive euthanasia" is not euthanasia at all.

1. THE ARGUMENT FROM NATURE

Every human being has a natural inclination to continue living. Our reflexes and responses fit us to fight attackers, flee wild animals, and dodge out of the way of trucks. In our daily lives we exercise the caution and care necessary to protect ourselves. Our bodies are similarly structured for survival right down to the molecular level. When we are cut, our capillaries seal shut, our blood clots, and fibrogen is produced to start the process of healing the wound. When we are invaded by bacteria, antibodies are produced to fight against the alien organisms, and their remains are swept out of the body by special cells designed for clean-up work.

Euthanasia does violence to this natural goal of survival. It is literally acting against nature because all the processes of nature are bent towards the end of bodily survival. Euthanasia defeats these subtle mechanisms in a way that, in a particular case, disease and injury might not.

It is possible, but not necessary, to make an appeal to revealed religion in this connection.[3] Man as trustee of his body acts against God, its rightful possessor, when he takes his own life. He also violates the commandment to hold life sacred and never to take it without just and compelling cause. But since this appeal will persuade only those who are prepared to accept that religion has access to revealed truths, I shall not employ this line of argument.

It is enough, I believe, to recognize that the organization of the human body and our patterns of behavioral responses make the continuation of life a natural goal. By reason alone, then, we can recognize that euthanasia sets us against our own nature.[4] Furthermore, in doing so, euthanasia does violence to our dignity. Our dignity comes from seeking our ends. When one of our goals is survival, and actions are taken that eliminate that goal, then our natural dignity suffers. Unlike animals, we are conscious through reason of our nature and our ends. Euthanasia involves acting as if this dual nature—inclination towards survival and awareness of this as an end—did not exist. Thus, euthanasia denies our basic human character and requires that we regard ourselves or others as something less than fully human.

2. THE ARGUMENT FROM SELF-INTEREST

The above arguments are, I believe, sufficient to show that euthanasia is inherently wrong. But there are reasons for considering it wrong when judged by standards other than reason. Because death is final and irreversible, euthanasia contains within it the possibility that we will work against our own interest if we practice it or allow it to be practiced on us.

Contemporary medicine has high standards of excellence and a proven record of accomplishment, but it does not possess perfect and complete knowledge. A mistaken diagnosis is possible, and so is a mistaken prognosis. Consequently, we may believe that we are dying of a disease when, as a matter of fact, we may not be. We may think that we have no hope of recovery when, as a matter of fact, our chances are quite good. In such circumstances, if euthanasia were permitted, we would die needlessly. Death is final and the chance of error too great to approve the practice of euthanasia.

Also, there is always the possibility that an experimental procedure or a hitherto untried technique will pull us through. We should at least keep this option open, but euthanasia closes it off. Furthermore, spontaneous remission does occur in many cases. For no apparent reason, a patient simply recovers when those all around him, including his physicians, expected him to die. Euthanasia would just guarantee their expectations and leave no room for the "miraculous" recoveries that frequently occur.

Finally, knowing that we can take our life at any time (or ask another to take it) might well incline us to give up too easily. The will to live is strong in all of us, but it can be weakened by pain and suffering and feelings of hopelessness. If during a bad time we allow ourselves to be killed, we never have a chance to reconsider. Recovery from a serious illness requires that we fight for it, and anything that weakens our determination by suggesting that there is an easy way out is ultimately against our own interest. Also, we may be inclined towards euthanasia because of our concern for others. If we see our sickness and suffering as an emotional and financial burden on our family, we may feel that to leave our life is to make their lives easier.[5] The very presence of the possibility of euthanasia may keep us from surviving when we might.

3. THE ARGUMENT FROM PRACTICAL EFFECTS

Doctors and nurses are, for the most part, totally committed to saving lives. A life lost is, for them, almost a personal failure, an insult to their skills and knowledge. Euthanasia as a practice might well alter this. It could have a corrupting influence so that in any case that is severe doctors and nurses might not try hard enough to save the patient. They might decide that the patient would simply be "better off dead" and take the steps necessary to make that come about. This attitude could then carry over to their dealings with patients less seriously ill. The result would be an overall decline in the quality of medical care.

Finally, euthanasia as a policy is a slippery slope. A person apparently hopelessly ill may be allowed to take his own life. Then he may be permitted to deputize others to do it for him should he no longer be able to act. The judgment of others then becomes the ruling factor. Already at this point euthanasia is not personal and voluntary, for others are acting "on behalf of" the patient as they see fit. This may well incline them to act on behalf of other patients who have not authorized them to exercise their judgment. It is only a short step, then, from voluntary euthanasia (self-inflicted or authorized), to directed euthanasia administered to a patient who has given no authorization, to involuntary euthanasia conducted as part of a social policy.[6] Recently many psychiatrists and sociologists have argued that we define as "mental illness" those forms of behavior that we disapprove of.[7] This gives us license then to lock up those who display the behavior. The category of the "hopelessly ill" provides the possibility of even worse abuse. Embedded in a social policy, it would give society or its representatives the authority to eliminate all those who might be considered too "ill" to function normally any longer. The dangers of euthanasia are too great to all to run the risk of approving it in any form. The first slippery step may well lead to a serious and harmful fall.

I hope that I have succeeded in showing why the benevolence that inclines us to give approval of euthanasia is misplaced. Euthanasia is inherently wrong because it violates the nature and dignity of human beings. But even those who are not convinced by this must be persuaded that the potential personal and social dangers inherent in euthanasia are sufficient to forbid our approving it either as a personal practice or as a public policy.

Suffering is surely a terrible thing, and we have a clear duty to comfort those in need and to ease their suffering when we can. But suffering is also a natural part of life with values for the individual and for others that we should not overlook. We may legitimately seek for others and for ourselves an easeful death, as Arthur Dyck has pointed out.[8] Euthanasia, however, is not just an easeful death. It is a wrongful death. Euthanasia is not just dying. It is killing.

NOTES

1. For a sophisticated defense of this position see Philippa Foot, "Euthanasia," *Philosophy & Public Affairs,* vol. 6 (1977), pp. 85–112. Foot does not endorse the radical conclusion that euthanasia, voluntary and involuntary, is always right.

2. James Rachels rejects the distinction between active and passive euthanasia as morally irrelevant in his "Active and Passive Euthanasia," *New England Journal of Medicine,* vol. 292, pp. 78–80. But see the criticism by Foot, pp. 100–103.

3. For a defense of this view see J. V. Sullivan, "The Immorality of Euthanasia," in *Beneficent Euthanasia,* ed. Marvin Kohl (Buffalo, New York: Prometheus Books, 1975), pp. 34–44.

4. This point is made by Ray V. McIntyre in "Voluntary Euthanasia: The Ultimate Perversion," *Medical Counterpoint,* vol. 2, 26–29.

5. See McIntyre, p. 28.

6. See Sullivan, "Immorality of Euthanasia," pp. 34–44, for a fuller argument in support of this view.

7. See, for example, Thomas S. Szasz, *The Myth of Mental Illness,* rev. ed. (New York: Harper & Row, 1974).

8. Arthur Dyck, "Beneficent Euthanasia and Benemortasia," in Kohl, op. cit., pp. 117–129.

Questions for Analysis

1. Why doesn't Gay-Williams consider "passive euthanasia" an act of euthanasia? Do you agree with his distinction?

2. Would it be accurate to say that Gay-Williams applies both religious and non-religious interpretations to argue against euthanasia? Explain.

3. State his arguments from self-interest.

4. State his arguments from practical effects. Which moral principle or type of ethical theory does this reflect?

5. What critical inquiries, if any, would you make about the author's arguments against euthanasia?

6. Can Gay-Williams's arguments be equally applied against passive euthanasia?

Active and Passive Euthanasia

James Rachels

The traditional view that there is an important moral difference between active and passive euthanasia is one that was endorsed by J. Gay-Williams in the preceding essay. Active euthanasia involves killing and passive euthanasia letting die, and this fact has led many physicians and philosophers to reject active euthanasia as morally wrong, even while approving of passive euthanasia.

In this essay, professor of philosophy James Rachels (1941–2003) challenges both the use and moral significance of this distinction for several reasons. First, active euthanasia is in many cases more humane than passive. Second, the conventional doctrine leads to decisions concerning life and death on irrelevant grounds. Third, the doctrine rests on a distinction between killing and letting die that itself has no moral significance. Fourth, the most common arguments in favor of the doctrine are invalid. Therefore, in Rachels's view, the American Medical Association's policy statement endorsing the active–passive distinction is unwise.

The distinction between active and passive euthanasia is thought to be crucial for medical ethics. The idea is that it is permissible, at least in some cases, to withhold treatment and allow a patient to die, but it is never permissible to take any direct action designed to kill the patient. This doctrine seems to be accepted by most doctors, and it is endorsed in a statement adopted by the House of Delegates of the American Medical Association on December 4, 1973:

From James Rachels. "Active and Passive Euthanasia," *New England Journal of Medicine,* 292 (January 9, 1975), 78–80. Reprinted by permission of the publisher.

The intentional termination of the life of one human being by another—mercy killing—is contrary to that for which the medical profession stands and is contrary to the policy of the American Medical Association.

The cessation of the employment of extraordinary means to prolong the life of the body when there is irrefutable evidence that biological death is imminent is the decision of the patient and/or his immediate family. The advice and judgment of the physician should be freely available to the patient and/or his immediate family.

However, a strong case can be made against this doctrine. In what follows I will set out some of the relevant arguments, and urge doctors to reconsider their views on this matter.

To begin with a familiar type of situation, a patient who is dying of incurable cancer of the throat is in terrible pain, which can no longer be satisfactorily alleviated. He is certain to die within a few days, even if present treatment is continued, but he does not want to go on living for those days since the pain is unbearable. So he asks the doctor for an end to it, and his family joins in the request.

Suppose the doctor agrees to withhold treatment, as the conventional doctrine says he may. The justification for his doing so is that the patient is in terrible agony, and since he is going to die anyway, it would be wrong to prolong his suffering needlessly. But now notice this. If one simply withholds treatment, it may take the patient longer to die, and so he may suffer more than he would if more direct action were taken and a lethal injection given. This fact provides strong reason for thinking that, once the initial decision not to prolong his agony has been made, active euthanasia is actually preferable to passive euthanasia, rather than the reverse. To say otherwise is to endorse the option that leads to more suffering rather than less, and is contrary to the humanitarian impulse that prompts the decision not to prolong his life in the first place.

Part of my point is that the process of being "allowed to die" can be relatively slow and painful, whereas being given a lethal injection is relatively quick and painless. Let me give a different sort of example. In the United States about one in 600 babies is born with Down's syndrome. Most of

these babies are otherwise healthy—that is, with only the usual pediatric care, they will proceed to an otherwise normal infancy. Some, however, are born with congenital defects such as intestinal obstructions that require operations if they are to live. Sometimes, the patients and the doctor will decide not to operate, and let the infant die. Anthony Shaw describes what happens then:

> . . .When surgery is denied [the doctor] must try to keep the infant from suffering while natural forces sap the baby's life away. As a surgeon whose natural inclination is to use the scalpel to fight off death, standing by and watching a salvageable baby die is the most emotionally exhausting experience I know. It is easy at a conference, in a theoretical discussion, to decide that such infants should be allowed to die. It is altogether different to stand by in the nursery and watch as dehydration and infection wither a tiny being over hours and days. This is a terrible ordeal for me and the hospital staff—much more so than for the parents who never set foot in the nursery.[1]

I can understand why some people are opposed to all euthanasia, and insist that such infants must be allowed to live. I think I can also understand why other people favor destroying these babies quickly and painlessly. But why should anyone favor letting "dehydration and infection wither a tiny being over hours and days"? The doctrine that says that a baby may be allowed to dehydrate and wither, but may not be given an injection that would end its life without suffering, seems so patently cruel as to require no further refutation. The strong language is not intended to offend, but only to put the point in the clearest possible way.

My second argument is that the conventional doctrine leads to decisions concerning life and death made on irrelevant grounds.

Consider again the case of the infants with Down's syndrome who need operations for congenital defects unrelated to the syndrome to live. Sometimes, there is no operation, and the baby dies, but when there is no such defect, the baby lives on. Now, an operation such as that to remove an intestinal obstruction is not prohibitively difficult. The reason why such operations are not performed in these cases is, clearly, that the child has

Down's syndrome and the parents and the doctor judge that because of that fact it is better for the child to die.

But notice that this situation is absurd, no matter what view one takes of the lives and potentials of such babies. If the life of such an infant is worth preserving, what does it matter if it needs a simple operation? Or, if one thinks it better that such a baby should not live on, what difference does it make that it happens to have an unobstructed intestinal tract? In either case, the matter of life and death is being decided on irrelevant grounds. It is the Down's syndrome, and not the intestines, that is the issue. The matter should be decided, if at all, on that basis, and not be allowed to depend on the essentially irrelevant question of whether the intestinal tract is blocked.

What makes this situation possible, of course, is the idea that when there is an intestinal blockage, one can "let the baby die," but when there is no such defect there is nothing that can be done, for one must not "kill" it. The fact that this idea leads to such results as deciding life or death on irrelevant grounds is another good reason why the doctrine should be rejected.

One reason why so many people think that there is an important moral difference between active and passive euthanasia is that they think killing someone is morally worse than letting someone die. But is it? Is killing, in itself, worse than letting die? To investigate this issue, two cases may be considered that are exactly alike except that one involves killing whereas the other involves letting someone die. Then, it can be asked whether this difference makes any difference to the moral assessments. It is important that the cases be exactly alike, except for this one difference, since otherwise one cannot be confident that it is this difference and not some other that accounts for any variation in the assessments of the two cases. So, let us consider this pair of cases:

In the first, Smith stands to gain a large inheritance if anything should happen to his six-year-old cousin. One evening while the child is taking his bath, Smith sneaks into the bathroom and drowns the child, and then arranges things so that it will look like an accident.

In the second, Jones also stands to gain if anything should happen to his six-year-old cousin.

Like Smith, Jones sneaks in planning to drown the child in his bath. However, just as he enters the bathroom Jones sees the child slip and hit his head, and fall face down in the water. Jones is delighted; he stands by, ready to push the child's head back under if it is necessary, but it is not necessary. With only a little thrashing about, the child drowns all by himself, "accidentally" as Jones watches and does nothing.

Now Smith killed the child, whereas Jones "merely" let the child die. That is the only difference between them. Did either man behave better, from a moral point of view? If the difference between killing and letting die were in itself a morally important matter, one should say that Jones's behavior was less reprehensible than Smith's. But does one really want to say that? I think not. In the first place, both men acted from the same motive, personal gain, and both had exactly the same end in view when they acted. It may be inferred from Smith's conduct that he is a bad man, although that judgment may be withdrawn or modified if certain further facts are learned about him—for example, that he is mentally deranged. But would not the very same thing be inferred about Jones from his conduct? And would not the same further considerations also be relevant to any modification of this judgment? Moreover, suppose Jones pleaded, in his own defense, "After all, I didn't do anything except just stand there and watch the child drown. I didn't kill him; I only let him die." Again, if letting die were in itself less bad than killing, this defense should have at least some weight. But it does not. Such a "defense" can only be regarded as a grotesque perversion of moral reasoning. Morally speaking, it is no defense at all.

Now, it may be pointed out, quite properly, that the cases of euthanasia with which doctors are concerned are not like this at all. They do not involve personal gain or the destruction of normal healthy children. Doctors are concerned only with cases in which the patient's life is of no further use to him, or in which the patient's life has become or will soon become a terrible burden. However, the point is the same in these cases: The bare difference between killing and letting die does not, in itself, make a moral difference. If a doctor lets a patient die, for humane reasons, he is in the same moral position as if he had given the patient a lethal injection for humane reasons. If his decision was wrong—if, for example, the patient's illness was in fact curable—the decision would be equally regrettable no matter which method was used to carry it out. And if the doctor's decision was the right one, the method used is not in itself important.

The AMA policy statement isolates the crucial issue very well: The crucial issue is "the intentional termination of the life of one human being by another." But after identifying this issue, and forbidding "mercy killing," the statement goes on to deny that the cessation of treatment is the intentional termination of a life. This is where the mistake comes in, for what is the cessation of treatment, in these circumstances, if it is not "the intentional termination of the life of one human being by another"? Of course it is exactly that, and if it were not, there would be no point to it.

Many people will find this judgment hard to accept. One reason, I think, is that it is very easy to conflate the question of whether killing is, in itself, worse than letting die, with the very different question of whether most actual cases of killing are more reprehensible than most actual cases of letting die. Most actual cases of killing are clearly terrible (think, for example, of all the murders reported in the newspapers), and one hears of such cases everyday. On the other hand, one hardly ever hears of a case of letting die, except for the actions of doctors who are motivated by humanitarian reasons. So one learns to think of killing in a much worse light than of letting die. But this does not mean that there is something about killing that makes it in itself worse than letting die, for it is not the bare difference between killing and letting die that makes the difference in these cases. Rather, the other factors—the murderer's motive of personal gain, for example, contrasted with the doctor's humanitarian motivation—account for different reactions to the different cases.

I have argued that killing is not in itself any worse than letting die; if my contention is right, it follows that active euthanasia is not any worse than passive euthanasia. What arguments can be given on the other side? The most common, I believe, is the following:

"The important difference between active and passive euthanasia is that in passive euthanasia, the doctor does not do anything to bring about the patient's death. The doctor does nothing, and the patient dies of whatever ills already afflict him. In active euthanasia, however, the doctor does something to bring about the patient's death: He kills him. The doctor who gives the patient with cancer a lethal injection has himself caused his patient's death; whereas if he merely ceases treatment, the cancer is the cause of death."

A number of points need to be made here. The first is that it is not exactly correct to say that in passive euthanasia the doctor does nothing, for he does do one thing that is very important: He lets the patient die. "Letting someone die" is certainly different, in some respects, from other types of action—mainly in that it is a kind of action that one may perform by way of not performing certain other actions. For example, one may let a patient die by way of not giving medication, just as one may insult someone by way of not shaking his hand. But for any purpose of moral assessment, it is a type of action nonetheless. The decision to let a patient die is subject to moral appraisal in the same way that a decision to kill him would be subject to moral appraisal: It may be assessed as wise or unwise, compassionate or sadistic, right or wrong. If a doctor deliberately let a patient die who was suffering from a routinely curable illness, the doctor would certainly be to blame for what he had done, just as he would be to blame if he had needlessly killed the patient. Charges against him would then be appropriate. If so, it would be no defense at all for him to insist that he didn't "do anything." He would have done something very serious indeed, for he let his patient die.

Fixing the cause of death may be very important from a legal point of view, for it may determine whether criminal charges are brought against the doctor. But I do not think that this notion can be used to show a moral difference between active and passive euthanasia. The reason why it is considered bad to be the cause of someone's death is that death is regarded as a great evil—and so it is. However, if it has been decided that euthanasia—even passive euthanasia—is desirable in a given case, it has also been decided that in this instance death is no greater an evil than the patient's continued existence. And if this is true, the usual reason for not wanting to be the cause of someone's death simply does not apply.

Finally, doctors may think that all of this is only of academic interest—the sort of thing that philosophers may worry about but that has no practical bearing on their own work. After all, doctors must be concerned about the legal consequences of what they do, and active euthanasia is clearly forbidden by the law. But even so, doctors should also be concerned with the fact that the law is forcing upon them a moral doctrine that may well be indefensible, and has a considerable effect on their practices. Of course, most doctors are not now in the position of being coerced in this matter, for they do not regard themselves as merely going along with what the law requires. Rather, in statements such as the AMA policy statement that I have quoted, they are endorsing this doctrine as a central point of medical ethics. In that statement, active euthanasia is condemned not merely as illegal but as "contrary to that for which the medical profession stands," whereas passive euthanasia is approved. However, the preceding considerations suggest that there is really no moral difference between the two, considered in themselves (there may be important moral differences in some cases in their consequences, but, as I pointed out, these differences may make active euthanasia, and not passive euthanasia, the morally preferable option). So, whereas doctors may have to discriminate between active and passive euthanasia to satisfy the law, they should not do any more than that. In particular, they should not give the distinction any added authority and weight by writing it into official statements of medical ethics.

NOTE

1. A. Shaw, "Doctor, Do We Have a Choice?" *The New York Times Magazine,* January 30, 1972, p. 54.

Questions for Analysis

1. Early in his essay, Rachels sets up a familiar situation involving a throat-cancer patient. What is the point of the example? Do you think that suspending pain-relieving drugs is what people generally understand by "withholding treatment"?

2. Explain, through Rachels's own example of the infant with Down syndrome, why he thinks the distinction between active and passive euthanasia leads to life-or-death decisions made on irrelevant grounds.

3. Do you agree with Rachels that the cessation of treatment is tantamount to the intentional termination of life?

4. Rachels claims that killing is not necessarily any worse than allowing a person to die. What are the implications of this claim for the morality of active euthanasia?

5. Rachels believes it is inaccurate and misleading to say that a doctor who allows a patient to die does "nothing" to cause the death. Do you agree?

Euthanasia

Philippa Foot

Griffin Professor of Philosophy Philippa Foot, as part of her general concerns in this essay, develops a distinction between active and passive euthanasia by using the notion of a "right to life." She disagrees with Rachels, who criticizes the distinction between active and passive as morally irrelevant and inhumane in application. In contrast, Foot offers cases to show the value of making and using the distinction.

Philippa Foot, "Euthanasia," from *Philosophy & Public Affairs,* vol. 6, no. 2 (Winter 1977). Copyright © 1977 by Philippa Foot. Reprinted by permission of the author.

The basic issue Foot considers, however, is whether one is ever morally justified in killing people for their own good. Replying, Foot examines the idea of "ordinary human life" and explores the question of when someone's life might be regarded as not worth living any longer. She doesn't believe that it's legitimate for us to decide that for someone else. In her view, everyone has a right to life in the sense she specifies; it is what a person wants that counts. Thus, even if someone would be better off dead, if that person wants to live, we aren't justified in killing him or her. In short, Foot cannot support nonvoluntary active euthanasia. Furthermore, if a person both wants to live and has a right to medical treatment, then involuntary passive euthanasia isn't justified either.

But what of cases involving those whose wishes we don't know—for example, patients in a comatose state? Foot argues that taking the lives of such people would infringe their rights. So she rejects nonvoluntary active euthanasia in these cases. But she does concede that there are cases in which the comatose, were they able, would not want to be kept alive artificially. This leads her to conclude that nonvoluntary passive euthanasia may be sometimes morally permissible.

Although Foot does endorse both forms of voluntary euthanasia (active and passive) as morally legitimate, she doesn't believe that we have a duty to kill people who have decided their lives are no longer worth living. For Foot, the explicit consent by such people merely guarantees that we would not be infringing their right to life by following their wishes.

The widely used *Shorter Oxford English Dictionary* gives three meanings for the word "euthanasia": the first, "a quiet and easy death"; the second, "the means of procuring this"; and the third, "the action of inducing a quiet and easy death." It is a curious fact that no one of the three gives an adequate definition of the word as it is usually understood. For "euthanasia" means much more than a quiet and easy death, or the means of procuring it, or the action of inducing it. The definition specifies only the manner of the death, and if this were all that was implied, a murderer, careful to drug his victim, could claim that his act was an act of euthanasia. We find this ridiculous because we take it for granted that in euthanasia it is death itself, not just the manner of death, that must be kind to the one who dies.

To see how important it is that "euthanasia" should not be used as the dictionary definition allows it to be used, merely to signify that a death was quiet and easy, one has only to remember that Hitler's "euthanasia" program traded on this ambiguity. Under this program, planned before the War but brought into full operation by a decree of 1 September 1939, some 275,000 people were gassed in centers which were to be a model for those in which Jews were later exterminated. Anyone in a state institution could be sent to the gas chambers if it was considered that he could not be "rehabilitated" for useful work. As Dr. Leo Alexander reports, relying on the testimony of a neuropathologist who received 500 brains from one of the killing centers,

> In Germany the exterminations included the mentally defective, psychotics (particularly schizophrenics), epileptics and patients suffering from infirmities of old age and from various organic neurological disorders such as infantile paralysis, Parkinsonism, multiple sclerosis and brain tumors. . . . In truth, all those unable to work and considered nonrehabilitable were killed.[1]

These people were killed because they were "useless" and "a burden on society"; only the manner of their deaths could be thought of as relatively easy and quiet.

Let us insist, then, that when we talk about euthanasia we are talking about a death understood as a good or happy event for the one who dies. This stipulation follows etymology, but is itself not exactly in line with current usage, which would be captured by the condition that the death should *not* be an evil rather than that it *should* be a good. That this is how people talk is shown by the fact that the case of Karen Ann Quinlan and others in a state of permanent coma is often discussed under the heading of "euthanasia." Perhaps it is not too late to object to the use of the word "euthanasia" in this sense. Apart from the break with the Greek origins of the word, there are other unfortunate aspects of this extension of the term. For if we say that the death must be supposed to be a good to the subject, we can also specify that it shall be for his sake that an act of euthanasia is performed. If we say merely that death shall not be an evil to him, we cannot stipulate that benefiting him shall be the motive where euthanasia is in question. Given the importance of the question, For whose sake are we acting? it is good to have a definition of euthanasia which brings under this heading only cases of opting for death for the sake of the one who dies. Perhaps what is most important is to say either that euthanasia is to be for the good of the subject or at least that death is to be no evil to him, thus refusing to talk Hitler's language. However, in this paper it is the first condition that will be understood, with the additional proviso that by an act of euthanasia we mean one of inducing or otherwise opting for death for the sake of the one who is to die.

A few lesser points need to be cleared up. In the first place it must be said that the word "act" is not to be taken to exclude omission; we shall speak of an act of euthanasia when someone is deliberately allowed to die, for his own good, and not only when positive measures are taken to see that he does. The very general idea we want is that of a choice of action or inaction directed at another man's death and causally effective in the sense that, in conjunction with actual circumstances, it is a sufficient condition of death. Of complications such as overdetermination, it will not be necessary to speak.

A second, and definitely minor, point about the definition of an act of euthanasia concerns the question of fact versus belief. It has already been implied that one who performs an act of euthanasia thinks that death will be merciful for the subject since we have said that it is on account of this thought that the act is done. But is it enough that he acts with this thought, or must things actually be as he thinks them to be? If one man kills another, or allows him to die, thinking that he is in the last stages of a terrible disease, though in fact he could have been cured, is this an act of euthanasia or not? Nothing much seems to hang on our decision about this. The same condition has got to enter into the definition whether as an element in reality or only as an element in the agent's belief. And however we define an act of euthanasia, culpability or justifiability will be the same: if a man acts

through ignorance, his ignorance may be culpable or it may not.[2]

These are relatively easy problems to solve, but one that is dauntingly difficult has been passed over in this discussion of the definition, and must now be faced. It is easy to say, as if this raised no problems, that an act of euthanasia is by definition one aiming at the *good* of the one whose death is in question, and that it is *for his sake* that his death is desired. But how is this to be explained? Presumably we are thinking of some evil already with him or to come on him if he continues to live, and death is thought of as a release from this evil. But this cannot be enough. Most people's lives contain evils such as grief or pain, but we do not therefore think that death would be a blessing to them. On the contrary, life is generally supposed to be a good even for someone who is unusually unhappy or frustrated. How is it that one can ever wish for death for the sake of the one who is to die? This difficult question is central to the discussion of euthanasia, and we shall literally not know what we are talking about if we ask whether acts of euthanasia defined as we have defined them are ever morally permissible without first understanding better the reason for saying that life is a good, and the possibility that it is not always so.

If a man should save my life he would be my benefactor. In normal circumstances this is plainly true; but does one always benefit another in saving his life? It seems certain that he does not. Suppose, for instance, that a man were being tortured to death and was given a drug that lengthened his sufferings; this would not be a benefit but the reverse. Or suppose that in a ghetto in Nazi Germany a doctor saved the life of someone threatened by disease, but that the man once cured was transported to an extermination camp; the doctor might wish for the sake of the patient that he had died of the disease. Nor would a longer stretch of life always be a benefit to the person who was given it. Comparing Hitler's camps with those of Stalin, Dmitri Panin observes that in the latter the method of extermination was made worse by agonies that could stretch out over months.

> Death from a bullet would have been bliss compared with what many millions had to endure while dying of hunger. The kind of death to which they were condemned has nothing to equal it in treachery and sadism.[3]

These examples show that to save or prolong a man's life is not always to do him a service: it may be better for him if he dies earlier rather than later. It must therefore be agreed that while life is normally a benefit to the one who has it, this is not always so.

The judgment is often fairly easy to make—that life is or is not a good to someone—but the basis for it is very hard to find. When life is said to be a benefit or a good, on what grounds is the assertion made?

The difficulty is underestimated if it is supposed that the problem arises from the fact that one who is dead has nothing, so that the good someone gets from being alive cannot be compared with the amount he would otherwise have had. For why should this particular comparison be necessary? Surely it would be enough if one could say whether or not someone whose life was prolonged had more good than evil in the extra stretch of time. Such estimates are not always possible, but frequently they are; we say, for example, "He was very happy in those last years," or, "He had little but unhappiness then." If the balance of good and evil determined whether life was a good to someone, we would expect to find a correlation in the judgments. In fact, of course, we find nothing of the kind. First, a man who has no doubt that existence is a good to him may have no idea about the balance of happiness and unhappiness in his life, or of any other positive and negative factors that may be suggested. So the supposed criteria are not always operating where the judgment is made. And secondly, the application of the criteria gives an answer that is often wrong. Many people have more evil than good in their lives; we do not, however, conclude that we would do these people no service by rescuing them from death.

To get around this last difficulty Thomas Nagel has suggested that experience itself is a good which must be brought in to balance accounts.

> . . . life is worth living even when the bad elements of experience are plentiful, and the good ones too meager to outweigh the bad ones on their own. The additional positive weight is supplied by experience itself, rather than by any of its contents.[4]

This seems implausible because if experience itself is a good it must be so even when what we experience is wholly bad, as in being tortured to death. How should one decide how much to count for this experiencing; and why count anything at all?

Others have tried to solve the problem by arguing that it is a man's desire for life that makes us call life a good: if he wants to live, then anyone who prolongs his life does him a benefit. Yet someone may cling to life where we would say confidently that it would be better for him if he died, and he may admit it too. Speaking of those same conditions in which, as he said, a bullet would have been merciful, Panin writes,

> I should like to pass on my observations concerning the absence of suicides under the extremely severe conditions of our concentration camps. The more that life became desperate, the more a prisoner seemed determined to hold on to it.[5]

One might try to explain this by saying that hope was the ground of this wish to survive for further days and months in the camp. But there is nothing unintelligible in the idea that a man might cling to life though he knew those facts about his future which would make any charitable man wish that he might die.

The problem remains, and it is hard to know where to look for a solution. Is there a conceptual connection between *life* and *good?* Because life is not always a good we are apt to reject this idea, and to think that it must be a contingent fact that life is usually a good, as it is a contingent matter that legacies are usually a benefit, if they are. Yet it seems not to be a contingent matter that to save someone's life is ordinarily to benefit him. The problem is to find where the conceptual connection lies.

It may be good tactics to forget for a time that it is euthanasia we are discussing and to see how *life* and *good* are connected in the case of living beings other than men. Even plants have things done to them that are harmful or beneficial, and what does them good must be related in some way to their living and dying. Let us therefore consider plants and animals, and then come back to human beings. At least we shall get away from the temptation to think that the connection between life and benefit must everywhere be a matter of happiness and unhappiness or of pleasure and pain; the idea being absurd in the case of animals and impossible even to formulate for plants.

In case anyone thinks that the concept of the beneficial applies only in a secondary or analogical way to plants, he should be reminded that we speak quite straightforwardly in saying, for instance, that a certain amount of sunlight is beneficial to most plants. What is in question here is the habitat in which plants of particular species flourish, but we can also talk, in a slightly different way, of what does them good, where there is some suggestion of improvement or remedy. What has the beneficial to do with sustaining life? It is tempting to answer, "everything," thinking that a healthy condition just is the one apt to secure survival. In fact, however, what is beneficial to a plant may have to do with reproduction rather than the survival of the individual member of the species. Nevertheless there is a plain connection between the beneficial and the life-sustaining even for the individual plant; if something makes it better able to survive in conditions normal for that species, it is ipso facto good for it. We need go no further, and could go no further, in explaining why a certain environment or treatment is good for a plant than to show how it helps this plant to survive.[6]

This connection between the life-sustaining and the beneficial is reasonably unproblematic, and there is nothing fanciful or zoomorphic in speaking of benefiting or doing good to plants. A connection with its survival can make something beneficial to a plant. But this is not, of course, to say that we count life as a good to a plant. We may save its life by giving it what is beneficial; we do not benefit it by saving its life.

A more ramified concept of benefit is used in speaking of animal life. New things can be said, such as that an animal is better or worse off for something that happened, or that it was a good or bad thing for it that it did happen. And new things count as benefit. In the first place, there is comfort, which often is, but need not be, related to health. When loosening a collar which is too tight for a dog we can say, "That will be better for it." So we see that the words "better for it" have two different meanings which we mark when necessary by a difference of emphasis, saying "better *for* it" when health is involved. And secondly, an animal can be benefited by having its life saved. "Could you do

anything for it?" can be answered by, "Yes, I managed to save its life." Sometimes we may understand this, just as we would for a plant, to mean that we had checked some disease. But we can also do something for an animal by scaring away its predator. If we do this, it is a good thing for the animal that we did, unless of course it immediately meets a more unpleasant end by some other means. Similarly, on the bad side, an animal may be worse off for our intervention, and this is not because it pines or suffers but simply because it gets killed.

The problem that vexes us when we think about euthanasia comes on the scene at this point. For if we can do something for an animal—can benefit it—by relieving its suffering but also by saving its life, where does the greater benefit come when only death will end pain? It seemed that life was a good in its own right; yet pain seemed to be an evil with equal status and could therefore make life not a good after all. Is it only life without pain that is a good when animals are concerned? This does not seem a crazy suggestion when we are thinking of animals, since unlike human beings they do not have suffering as part of their normal life. But it is perhaps the idea of ordinary life that matters here. We would not say that we had done anything for an animal if we had merely kept it alive, either in an unconscious state or in a condition where, though conscious, it was unable to operate in an ordinary way; and the fact is that animals in severe and continuous pain simply do not operate normally. So we do not, on the whole, have the option of doing the animal good by saving its life though the life would be a life of pain. No doubt there are borderline cases, but that is no problem. We are not trying to make new judgments possible, but rather to find the principle of the ones we do make.

When we reach human life, the problems seem even more troublesome. For now we must take quite new things into account, such as the subject's own view of his life. It is arguable that this places extra constraints on the solution: might it not be counted as a necessary condition of life's being a good to a man that he should see it as such? Is there not some difficulty about the idea that a benefit might be done to him by saving or prolonging his life even though he himself wished for death? Of course he might have a quite mistaken view of his own prospects, but let us ignore this and think only of cases where it is life as he knows it that is in question. Can we think that the prolonging of this life would be a benefit to him even though he would rather have it end than continue? It seems that this cannot be ruled out. That there is no simple incompatibility between life as a good and the wish for death is shown by the possibility that a man should wish himself dead, not for his own sake, but for the sake of someone else. And if we try to amend the thesis to say that life cannot be a good to one who wishes *for his own sake* that he should die, we find the crucial concept slipping through our fingers. As Bishop Butler pointed out long ago, not all ends are either benevolent or self-interested. Does a man wish for death for his own sake in the relevant sense if, for instance, he wishes to revenge himself on another by his death? Or what if he is proud and refuses to stomach dependence or incapacity even though there are many good things left in life for him? The truth seems to be that the wish for death is sometimes compatible with life's being a good and sometimes not, which is possible because the description "wishing for death" is one covering diverse states of mind from that of the determined suicide, pathologically depressed, to that of one who is surprised to find that the thought of a fatal accident is viewed with relief. On the one hand, a man may see his life as a burden but go about his business in a more or less ordinary way; on the other hand, the wish for death may take the form of a rejection of everything that is in life, as it does in severe depression. It seems reasonable to say that life is not a good to one permanently in the latter state, and we must return to this topic later on.

When are we to say that life is a good or a benefit to a man? The dilemma that faces us is this. If we say that life as such is a good, we find ourselves refuted by the examples given at the beginning of this discussion. We therefore incline to think that it is as bringing good things that life is a good, where it is a good. But if life is a good only because it is the condition of good things, why is it not equally an evil when it brings bad things? And how can it be a good even when it brings more evil than good?

It should be noted that the problem has here been formulated in terms of the balance of good and evil, not that of happiness and unhappiness, and that it is not to be solved by the denial (which may be reasonable enough) that unhappiness is the only evil or happiness the only good. In this paper no view has been expressed about the nature of goods other than life itself. The point is that on any view of the goods and evils that life can contain, it seems that a life with more evil than good could still itself be a good.

It may be useful to review the judgments with which our theory must square. Do we think that life can be a good to one who suffers a lot of pain? Clearly we do. What about severely handicapped people; can life be a good to them? Clearly it can be, for even if someone is almost completely paralyzed, perhaps living in an iron lung, perhaps able to move things only by means of a tube held between his lips, we do not rule him out of order if he says that some benefactor saved his life. Nor is it different with mental handicap. There are many fairly severely handicapped people—such as those with Down's Syndrome (Mongolism)—for whom a simple affectionate life is possible. What about senility? Does this break the normal connection between life and good? Here we must surely distinguish between forms of senility. Some forms leave a life which we count someone as better off having than not having, so that a doctor who prolonged it would benefit the person concerned. With some kinds of senility this is, however, no longer true. There are some in geriatric wards who are barely conscious, though they can move a little and swallow food put into their mouths. To prolong such a state, whether in the old or in the very severely mentally handicapped, is not to do them a service or confer a benefit. But of course it need not be the reverse: only if there is suffering would one wish for the sake of the patient that he should die.

It seems, therefore, that merely being alive even without suffering is not a good, and that we must make a distinction similar to that which we made when animals were our topic. But how is the line to be drawn in the case of men? What is to count as ordinary human life in the relevant sense? If it were only the very senile or very ill who were to be said not to have this life, it might seem right to describe it in terms of *operation*. But it will be hard to find the sense in which the men described by Panin were not operating, given that they dragged themselves out to the forest to work. What is it about the life that the prisoners were living that makes us put it on the other side of the dividing line from that of some severely ill or suffering patients, and from most of the physically or mentally handicapped? It is not that they were in captivity, for life in captivity can certainly be a good. Nor is it merely the unusual nature of their life. In some ways the prisoners were living more as other men do than the patient in an iron lung.

The suggested solution to the problem is, then, that there is a certain conceptual connection between *life* and *good* in the case of human beings as in that of animals and even plants. Here, as there, however, it is not the mere state of being alive that can determine, or itself count as, a good, but rather life coming up to some standard of normality. It was argued that it is as part of ordinary life that the elements of good that a man may have are relevant to the question of whether saving his life counts as benefiting him. Ordinary human lives, even very hard lives, contain a minimum of basic goods, but when these are absent the idea of life is no longer linked to that of good. And since it is in this way that the elements of good contained in a man's life are relevant to the question of whether he is benefited if his life is preserved, there is no reason why it should be the balance of good and evil that counts.

It should be added that evils are relevant in one way when, as in the examples discussed above, they destroy the possibility of ordinary goods, but in a different way when they invade a life from which the goods are already absent for a different reason. So, for instance, the connection between *life* and *good* may be broken because consciousness has sunk to a very low level, as in extreme senility or severe brain damage. In itself this kind of life seems to be neither good nor evil, but if suffering sets in, one would hope for a speedy end.

The idea we need seems to be that of life which is ordinary human life in the following respect—that it contains a minimum of basic human goods. What is ordinary in human life—even in very hard lives— is that a man is not driven to work far beyond his capacity; that he has the support of a family or community; that he can more or less satisfy his hunger; that he has hopes for the future; that he can lie down to rest at night. Such things were denied to the men in the Vyatlag camps described by Panin; not even rest at night was allowed them when they were tormented by bed-bugs, by noise and stench, and by routines such as body-searches

and bath-parades—arranged for the night time so that work norms would not be reduced. Disease too can so take over a man's life that the normal human goods disappear. When a patient is so overwhelmed by pain or nausea that he cannot eat with pleasure, if he can eat at all, and is out of the reach of even the most loving voice, he no longer has ordinary human life in the sense in which the words are used here. And we may now pick up a thread from an earlier part of the discussion by remarking that crippling depression can destroy the enjoyment of ordinary goods as effectively as external circumstances can remove them.

This, admittedly inadequate, discussion of the sense in which life is normally a good, and of the reasons why it may not be so in some particular case, completes the account of what euthanasia is here taken to be. An act of euthanasia, whether literally act or rather omission, is attributed to an agent who opts for the death of another because in his case life seems to be an evil rather than a good. The question now to be asked is whether acts of euthanasia are ever justifiable. But there are two topics here rather than one. For it is one thing to say that some acts of euthanasia considered only in themselves and their results are morally unobjectionable, and another to say that it would be all right to legalize them. Perhaps the practice of euthanasia would allow too many abuses, and perhaps there would be too many mistakes. Moreover, the practice might have very important and highly undesirable side effects, because it is unlikely that we could change our principles about the treatment of the old and the ill without changing fundamental emotional attitudes and social relations. The topics must, therefore, be treated separately. In the next part of the discussion, nothing will be said about the social consequences and possible abuses of the practice of euthanasia, but only about acts of euthanasia considered in themselves.

What we want to know is whether acts of euthanasia, defined as we have defined them, are ever morally permissible. To be more accurate, we want to know whether it is ever sufficient justification of the choice of death for another that death can be counted a benefit rather than harm, and that this is why the choice is made.

It will be impossible to get a clear view of the area to which this topic belongs without first marking the distinct grounds on which objection may lie when one man opts for the death of another. There are two different virtues whose requirements are, in general, contrary to such actions. An unjustified act of killing, or allowing to die, is contrary to justice or to charity, or to both virtues, and the moral failings are distinct. Justice has to do with what men *owe* each other in the way of noninterference and positive service. When used in this wide sense, which has its history in the doctrine of the cardinal virtues, justice is not especially connected with, for instance, law courts but with the whole area of rights, and duties corresponding to rights. Thus murder is one form of injustice, dishonesty another, and wrongful failure to keep contracts a third; chicanery in a law court or defrauding someone of his inheritance are simply other cases of injustice. Justice as such is not directly linked to the good of another, and may require that something be rendered to him even where it will do him harm, as Hume pointed out when he remarked that a debt must be paid even to a profligate debauchee who "would rather receive harm than benefit from large possessions."[7] Charity, on the other hand, is the virtue which attaches us to the good of others. An act of charity is in question only where something is not demanded by justice, but a lack of charity and of justice can be shown where a man is denied something which he both needs and has a right to; both charity and justice demand that widows and orphans are not defrauded, and the man who cheats them is neither charitable nor just.

It is easy to see that the two grounds of objection to inducing death are distinct. A murder is an act of injustice. A culpable failure to come to the aid of someone whose life is threatened is normally contrary, not to justice, but to charity. But where one man is under contract, explicit or implicit, to come to the aid of another, injustice too will be shown. Thus injustice may be involved either in an act or an omission, and the same is true of a lack of charity; charity may demand that someone be aided, but also that an unkind word not be spoken.

The distinction between charity and justice will turn out to be of the first importance when voluntary and nonvoluntary euthanasia are distinguished later on. This is because of the connection between justice and rights, and something should now be said about this. I believe it is true to say that wherever a man acts unjustly he has infringed

a right, since justice has to do with whatever a man is owed, and whatever he is owed is his as a matter of right. Something should therefore be said about the different kinds of rights. The distinction commonly made is between having a right in the sense of having a liberty, and having a "claim-right" or "right of recipience."[8] The best way to understand such a distinction seems to be as follows. To say that a man has a right in the sense of a liberty is to say that no one can demand that he do not do the thing which he has a right to do. The fact that he has a right to do it consists in the fact that a certain kind of objection does not lie against his doing it. Thus a man has a right in this sense to walk down a public street or park his car in a public parking space. It does not follow that no one else may prevent him from doing so. If for some reason I want a certain man not to park in a certain place I may lawfully park there myself or get my friends to do so, thus preventing him from doing what he has a right (in the sense of a liberty) to do. It is different, however, with a claim-right. This is the kind of right which I have in addition to a liberty when, for example, I have a private parking space; now others have duties in the way of noninterference, as in this case, or of service, as in the case where my claim-right is to goods or services promised to me. Sometimes one of these rights gives other people the duty of securing to me that to which I have a right, but at other times their duty is merely to refrain from interference. If a fall of snow blocks my private parking space, there is normally no obligation for anyone else to clear it away. Claim-rights generate duties; sometimes these duties are duties of noninterference; sometimes they are duties of service. If your right gives me the duty not to interfere with you, I have "no right" to do it; similarly, if your right gives me the duty to provide something for you, I have "no right" to refuse to do it. What *I* lack is the right which is a liberty; I am not "at liberty" to interfere with you or to refuse the service.

Where in this picture does the right to life belong? No doubt people have the right to live in the sense of a liberty, but what is important is the cluster of claim-rights brought together under the title of the right to life. The chief of these is, of course, the right to be free from interferences that threaten life. If other people aim their guns at us or try to pour poison into our drink we can, to put it mildly, demand that they desist. And then there are the services we can claim from doctors, health officers, bodyguards, and firemen; the rights that depend on contract or public arrangement. Perhaps there is no particular point in saying that the duties these people owe us belong to the right to life; we might as well say that all the services owed to anyone by tailors, dressmakers, and couturiers belong to a right called the right to be elegant. But contracts such as those understood in the patient–doctor relationship come in an important way when we are discussing the rights and wrongs of euthanasia, and are therefore mentioned here.

Do people have the right to what they need in order to survive, apart from the right conferred by special contracts into which other people have entered for the supplying of these necessities? Do people in the underdeveloped countries in which starvation is rife have the right to the food they so evidently lack? Joel Feinberg, discussing this question, suggests that they should be said to have "a claim," distinguishing this from a "valid claim," which gives a claim-right.

> The manifesto writers on the other side who seem to identify needs, or at least basic needs, with what they call "human rights," are more properly described, I think, as urging upon the world community the moral principle that *all* basic human needs ought to be recognized as *claims* (in the customary *prima facie* sense) worthy of sympathy and serious consideration right now, even though, in many cases, they cannot yet plausibly be treated as *valid* claims, that is, as grounds of any other people's duties. This way of talking avoids the anomaly of ascribing to all human beings now, even those in pre-industrial societies, such "economic and social rights" as "periodic holidays with pay."[9]

This seems reasonable, though we notice that there are some actual rights to service which are not based on anything like a contract, as for instance the right that children have to support from their parents and parents to support from their children in old age, though both sets of rights are to some extent dependent on existing social arrangements.

Let us now ask how the right to life affects the morality of acts of euthanasia. Are such acts sometimes or always ruled out by the right to life? This

is certainly a possibility; for although an act of euthanasia is, by our definition, a matter of opting for death for the good of the one who is to die, there is, as we noted earlier, no direct connection between that to which a man has a right and that which is for his good. It is true that men have the right only to the kind of thing that is, in general, a good: we do not think that people have the right to garbage or polluted air. Nevertheless, a man may have the right to something which he himself would be better off without; where rights exist, it is a man's will that counts, not his or anyone else's estimate of benefit or harm. So the duties complementary to the right to life—the general duty of noninterference and the duty of service incurred by certain persons—are not affected by the quality of a man's life or by his prospects. Even if it is true that he would be, as we say, "better off dead," so long as he wants to live this does not justify us in killing him and may not justify us in deliberately allowing him to die. All of us have the duty of noninterference, and some of us may have the duty to sustain his life. Suppose, for example, that a retreating army has to leave behind wounded or exhausted soldiers in the wastes of an arid or snowbound land where the only prospect is death by starvation or at the hands of an enemy notoriously cruel. It has often been the practice to accord a merciful bullet to men in such desperate straits. But suppose that one of them demands that he should be left alive? It seems clear that his comrades have no right to kill him, though it is a quite different question as to whether they should give him a life-prolonging drug. The right to life can sometimes give a duty of positive service, but does not do so here. What it does give is the right to be left alone.

Interestingly enough, we have arrived by way of a consideration of the right to life at the distinction normally labeled "active" versus "passive" euthanasia, and often thought to be irrelevant to the moral issue.[10] Once it is seen that the right to life is a distinct ground of objection to certain acts of euthanasia, and that this right creates a duty of noninterference more widespread than the duties of care, there can be no doubt about the relevance of the distinction between passive and active euthanasia. Where everyone may have the duty to leave someone alone, it may be that no one has the duty to maintain his life, or that only some people do.

Where then do the boundaries of the "active" and "passive" lie? In some ways the words are themselves misleading, because they suggest the difference between act and omission which is not quite what we want. Certainly the act of shooting someone is the kind of thing we were talking about under the heading of "interference" and omitting to give him a drug a case of refusing care. But the act of turning off a respirator should surely be thought of as no different from the decision not to start it; if doctors had decided that a patient should be allowed to die, either course of action might follow, and both should be counted as passive rather than active euthanasia if euthanasia were in question. The point seems to be that interference in a course of treatment is not the same as other interference in a man's life, and particularly if the same body of people are responsible for the treatment and for its discontinuance. In such a case we could speak of the disconnecting of the apparatus as killing the man, or of the hospital as allowing him to die. By and large, it is the act of killing that is ruled out under the heading of noninterference, but not in every case.

Doctors commonly recognize this distinction, and the grounds on which some philosophers have denied it seem untenable. James Rachels, for instance, believes that if the difference between active and passive is relevant anywhere, it should be relevant everywhere, and he has pointed to an example in which it seems to make no difference which is done. If someone saw a child drowning in a bath it would seem just as bad to let it drown as to push its head under water.[11] If "it makes no difference" means that one act would be as iniquitous as the other, this is true. It is not that killing is *worse* than allowing to die, but that the two are contrary to distinct virtues, which gives the possibility that in some circumstances one is impermissible and the other permissible. In the circumstances invented by Rachels, both are wicked: it is contrary to justice to push the child's head under the water—something one has no right to do. To leave it to drown is not contrary to justice, but it is a particularly glaring example of lack of charity. Here it makes no practical difference because the requirements of justice and charity coincide; but in the case of the retreating army they did not: charity would have required that the wounded soldier be killed had not justice required that he be left alive.[12] In such a case it makes all the difference whether a man opts for the death of another in a positive action, or whether he allows him to die. An analogy with the right to property will make the point clear. If a man owns something, he has the right to it even when its possession does him harm, and we have no right to take it from him. But if one day it should blow away, maybe nothing requires us to get it back for him; we could not deprive him of it, but we may allow it to go. This is not to deny that it will often be an unfriendly act or one based on an arrogant judgment when we refuse to do what he wants. Nevertheless, we would be within our rights, and it might be that no moral objection of any kind would lie against our refusal.

It is important to emphasize that a man's rights may stand between us and the action we would dearly like to take for his sake. They may, of course, also prevent action which we would like to take for the sake of others, as when it might be tempting to kill one man to save several. But it is interesting that the limits of allowable interference, however uncertain, seem stricter in the first case than the second. Perhaps there are no cases in which it would be all right to kill a man against his will *for his own sake* unless they could equally well be described as cases of allowing him to die, as in the example of turning off the respirator. However, there are circumstances, even if these are very rare, in which one man's life would justifiably be sacrificed to save others, and "killing" would be the only description of what was being done. For instance, a vehicle which had gone out of control might be steered from a path on which it would kill more than one man to a path on which it would kill one.[13] But it would not be permissible to steer a vehicle towards someone in order to kill him, against his will, for his own good. An analogy with property rights illustrates the point. One may not destroy a man's property against his will on the grounds that he would be better off without it; there are, however, circumstances in which it could be destroyed for the sake of others. If his house is liable to fall and kill him, that is his affair; it might, however, without injustice be destroyed to stop the spread of a fire.

We see then that the distinction between active and passive, important as it is elsewhere, has a special importance in the area of euthanasia. It should also be clear why James Rachels' other argument, that it is often "more humane" to kill than to allow to die, does not show that the distinction between active and passive euthanasia is morally irrelevant. It might be "more humane" in this sense to deprive a man of the property that brings evils on him, or to refuse to pay what is owed to Hume's profligate debauchee; but if we say this we must admit that an act which is "more humane" than its alternative may be morally objectionable because it infringes rights.

So far we have said very little about the right to service as opposed to the right to noninterference, though it was agreed that both might be brought under the heading of "the right to life." What about the duty to preserve life that may belong to special classes of persons such as bodyguards, firemen, or doctors? Unlike the general public, they are not within their rights if they merely refrain from interfering and do not try to sustain life. The subject's claim-rights are twofold as far as they are concerned, and passive as well as active euthanasia may be ruled out here if it is against his will. This is not to say that he has the right to any and every service needed to save or prolong his life; the rights of other people set limits to what may be demanded, both because they have the right not to be interfered with and because they may have a competing right to services. Furthermore, one must inquire just what the contract or implicit agreement amounts to in each case. Firemen and bodyguards presumably have a duty which is simply to preserve life, within the limits of justice to others and of reasonableness to themselves. With doctors it may, however, be different, since their duty relates not only to preserving life but also to the relief of suffering. It is not clear what a doctor's duties are to his patient if life can be prolonged only at the cost of suffering or suffering relieved only by measures that shorten life. George Fletcher has argued that what the doctor is under contract to do depends on what is generally done, because this is what a patient will reasonably expect.[14] This seems right. If procedures are part of normal medical practice, then it seems that the patient can demand them however much it may be against his interest to do so. Once again, it is not a matter of what is "most humane."

That the patient's right to life may set limits to permissible acts of euthanasia seems undeniable. If he does not want to die, no one has the right to practice active euthanasia on him, and passive euthanasia may also be ruled out where he has a right to the services of doctors or others.

Perhaps few will deny what has so far been said about the impermissibility of acts of euthanasia simply because we have so far spoken about the case of one who positively wants to live, and about his rights, whereas those who advocate euthanasia are usually thinking either about those who wish to die or about those whose wishes cannot be ascertained either because they cannot properly be said to have wishes or because, for one reason or another, we are unable to form a reliable estimate of what they are. The question that must now be asked is whether the latter type of case, where euthanasia though not involuntary would again be nonvoluntary, is different from the one discussed so far. Would we have the right to kill someone for his own good so long as we had no idea that he positively wished to live? And what about the life-prolonging duties of doctors in the same circumstances? This is a very difficult problem. On the one hand, it seems ridiculous to suppose that a man's right to life is something which generates duties only where he has signaled that he wants to live; as a borrower does indeed have a duty to return something lent on indefinite loan only if the lender indicates that he wants it back. On the other hand, it might be argued that there is something illogical about the idea that a right has been infringed if someone incapable of saying whether he wants it or not is deprived of something that is doing him harm rather than good. Yet on the analogy of property we would say that a right has been infringed. Only if someone had earlier told us that in such circumstances he would not want to keep the thing could we think that his right had been waived. Perhaps if we could make confident judgments about what anyone in such circumstances would wish, or what he would have wished beforehand had he considered the matter, we could agree to consider the right to life as "dormant," needing to be asserted if the normal duties were to remain. But as things are, we cannot make any such assumption; we simply do not know what most people would want, or would have wanted, us to do unless they tell us. This is certainly the case so far as active measures to end life are concerned. Possibly it is different, or will become different, in the matter of being kept alive, so general is the feeling against using sophisticated procedures on moribund patients, and so much is this dreaded by people who are old or terminally ill. Once again the distinction between active and passive euthanasia has come on the scene, but this time because most people's attitudes to the two are so different. It is just possible that we might presume, in the absence of specific evidence, that someone would not wish, beyond a certain point, to be kept alive; it is certainly not possible to assume that he would wish to be killed.

In the last paragraph we have begun to broach the topic of voluntary euthanasia, and this we must now discuss. What is to be said about the case in which there is no doubt about someone's wish to die: either he has told us beforehand that he would wish it in circumstances such as he is now in, and has shown no sign of a change of mind, or else he tells us now, being in possession of his faculties and of a steady mind. We should surely say that the objections previously urged against acts of euthanasia, which it must be remembered were all on the ground of rights, had disappeared. It does not seem that one would infringe someone's right to life in killing him with his permission and in fact at his request. Why should someone not be able to waive his right to life, or rather, as would be more likely to happen, to cancel some of the duties of noninterference that this right entails? (He is more likely to say that he should be killed by this man at this time in this manner, than to say that anyone may kill him at any time and in any way.) Similarly, someone may give permission for the destruction of his property, and request it. The important thing is that he gives a critical permission, and it seems that this is enough to cancel the duty normally associated with the right. If someone gives you permission to destroy his property, it can no longer be said that you have no right to do so, and I do not see why it should not be the case with taking a man's life. An objection might be made on the ground that only God has the right to take life, but in this paper religious as opposed to moral arguments are being left aside. Religion apart, there seems to be no case to be made out for an infringement of rights if a

man who wishes to die is allowed to die or even killed. But of course it does not follow that there is no moral objection to it. Even with property, which is after all a relatively small matter, one might be wrong to destroy what one had the right to destroy. For, apart from its value to other people, it might be valuable to the man who wanted it destroyed, and charity might require us to hold our hand where justice did not.

Let us review the conclusion of this part of the argument, which has been about euthanasia and the right to life. It has been argued that from this side come stringent restrictions on the acts of euthanasia that could be morally permissible. Active nonvoluntary euthanasia is ruled out by that part of the right to life which creates the duty of noninterference, though passive nonvoluntary euthanasia is not ruled out, except where the right to life-preserving action has been created by some special condition such as a contract between a man and his doctor, and it is not always certain just what such a contract involves. Voluntary euthanasia is another matter: as the preceding paragraph suggested, no right is infringed if a man is allowed to die or even killed at his own request.

Turning now to the other objection that normally holds against inducing the death of another, that it is against charity, or benevolence, we must tell a very different story. Charity is the virtue that gives attachment to the good of others, and because life is normally a good, charity normally demands that it should be saved or prolonged. But as we so defined an act of euthanasia that it seeks a man's death for his own sake—for his good—charity will normally speak in favor of it. This is not, of course, to say that charity can require an act of euthanasia which justice forbids, but if an act of euthanasia is not contrary to justice—that is, it does not infringe rights—charity will rather be in its favor than against.

Once more the distinction between nonvoluntary and voluntary euthanasia must be considered. Could it ever be compatible with charity to seek a man's death although he wanted to live, or at least had not let us know that he wanted to die? It has been argued that in such circumstances active euthanasia would infringe his right to life, but passive euthanasia would not do so, unless he had some special right to life-preserving service from the one who allowed him to die. What would charity dictate? Obviously when a man wants to live there is a presumption that he will be benefited if his life is prolonged, and if it is so the question of euthanasia does not arise. But it is, on the other hand, possible that he wants to live where it would be better for him to die: perhaps he does not realize the desperate situation he is in, or perhaps he is afraid of dying. So, in spite of a very proper resistance to refusing to go along with a man's own wishes in the matter of life and death, someone might justifiably refuse to prolong the life even of someone who asked him to prolong it, as in the case of refusing to give the wounded soldier a drug that would keep him alive to meet a terrible end. And it is even more obvious that charity does not always dictate that life should be prolonged where a man's own wishes, hypothetical or actual, are not known.

So much for the relation of charity to nonvoluntary passive euthanasia, which was not, like nonvoluntary active euthanasia, ruled out by the right to life. Let us now ask what charity has to say about voluntary euthanasia, both active and passive. It was suggested in the discussion of justice that if of sound mind and steady desire, a man might give others the *right* to allow him to die or even to kill him, where otherwise this would be ruled out. But it was pointed out that this would not settle the question of whether the act was morally permissible, and it is this that we must now consider. Could not charity speak against what justice allowed? Indeed it might do so. For while the fact that a man wants to die suggests that his life is wretched, and while his rejection of life may itself tend to take the good out of the things he might have enjoyed, nevertheless his wish to die might here be opposed for his own sake just as it might be if suicide were in question. Perhaps there is hope that his mental condition will improve. Perhaps he is mistaken in thinking his disease incurable. Perhaps he wants to die for the sake of someone else on whom he feels he is a burden, and we are not ready to accept this sacrifice whether for ourselves or others. In such cases, and there will surely be many of them, it could not be for his own sake that we will him or allow him to die, and therefore euthanasia as defined in this paper would not be in question. But this is not to deny that there could be acts of voluntary euthanasia both

passive and active against which neither justice nor charity would speak.

We have now considered the morality of euthanasia both voluntary and nonvoluntary, and active and passive. The conclusion has been that nonvoluntary active euthanasia (roughly, killing a man against his will or without his consent) is never justified; that is to say, that a man's being killed for his own good never justifies the act unless he himself has consented to it. A man's rights are infringed by such an action, and it is therefore contrary to justice. However, all the other combinations, nonvoluntary passive euthanasia, voluntary active euthanasia, and voluntary passive euthanasia, are sometimes compatible with both justice and charity. But the strong condition carried in the definition of euthanasia adopted in this paper must not be forgotten; an act of euthanasia as here understood is one whose purpose is to benefit the one who dies.

In the light of this discussion let us look at our present practices. Are they good or are they bad? And what changes might be made, thinking now not only of the morality of particular acts of euthanasia but also of the indirect effects of instituting different practices, of the abuses to which they might be subject and of the changes that might come about if euthanasia became a recognized part of the social scene.

The first thing to notice is that it is wrong to ask whether we should introduce the practice of euthanasia as if it were not something we already had. In fact we do have it. For instance, it is common, where the medical prognosis is very bad, for doctors to recommend against measures to prolong life, and particularly where a process of degeneration producing one medical emergency after another has already set in. If these doctors are not certainly within their legal rights, this is something that is apt to come as a surprise to them as to the general public. It is also obvious that euthanasia is often practiced where old people are concerned. If someone very old and soon to die is attacked by a disease that makes his life wretched, doctors do not always come in with life-prolonging drugs. Perhaps poor patients are more fortunate in this respect than rich patients, being more often left to die in peace; but it is in any case a well-recognized piece of medical practice, which is a form of euthanasia.

No doubt the case of infants with mental or physical defects will be suggested as another example of the practice of euthanasia as we already have it, since such infants are sometimes deliberately allowed to die. That they are deliberately allowed to die is certain; children with severe spina bifida malformations are not always operated on even where it is thought that without the operation they will die; and even in the case of children with Down's Syndrome who have intestinal obstructions, the relatively simple operation that would make it possible to feed them is sometimes not performed.[15] Whether this is euthanasia in our sense or only as the Nazis understood it is another matter. We must ask the crucial question, "Is it for the sake of the child himself that the doctors and parents choose his death?" In some cases the answer may really be yes, and, what is more important, it may really be true that the kind of life which is a good is not possible or likely for this child, and that there is little but suffering and frustration in store for him.[16] But this must presuppose that the medical prognosis is wretchedly bad, as it may be for some spina bifida children. With children who are born with Down's Syndrome it is, however, quite different. Most of these are able to live on for quite a time in a reasonably contented way, remaining like children all their lives but capable of affectionate relationships and able to play games and perform simple tasks. The fact is, of course, that the doctors who recommend against lifesaving procedures for handicapped infants are usually thinking not of them but rather of their parents and of other children in the family or of the "burden on society" if the children survive. So it is not for their sake but to avoid trouble to others that they are allowed to die. When brought out into the open this seems unacceptable: at least we do not easily accept the principle that adults who need special care should be counted too burdensome to be kept alive. It must in any case be insisted that if children with Down's Syndrome are deliberately allowed to die this is not a matter of euthanasia except in Hitler's sense. And for our children, since we scruple to gas them, not even the manner of their death is "quiet and easy"; when not treated for an intestinal obstruction a baby simply starves to death. Perhaps some will take this as an argument for allowing active euthanasia, in which

case they will be in the company of an S.S. man stationed in the Warthgenau who sent Eichmann a memorandum telling him that "Jews in the coming winter could no longer be fed" and submitting for his consideration a proposal as to whether "it would not be the most humane solution to kill those Jews who were incapable of work through some quicker means."[17] If we say we are *unable* to look after children with handicaps, we are no more telling the truth than was the S.S. man who said that the Jews could not be fed.

Nevertheless, if it is ever right to allow deformed children to die because life will be a misery to them, or not to take measures to prolong for a little the life of a newborn baby whose life cannot extend beyond a few months of intense medical intervention, there is a genuine problem about active as opposed to passive euthanasia. There are well-known cases in which the medical staff has looked on wretchedly while an infant died slowly from starvation and dehydration because they did not feel able to give a lethal injection. According to the principles discussed in the earlier part of this paper they would indeed have had no right to give it, since an infant cannot ask that it should be done. The only possible solution—supposing that voluntary active euthanasia were to be legalized—would be to appoint guardians to act on the infant's behalf. In a different climate of opinion this might not be dangerous, but at present, when people so readily assume that the life of a handicapped baby is of no value, one would be loath to support it.

Finally, on the subject of handicapped children, another word should be said about those with severe mental defects. For them too it might sometimes be right to say that one would wish for death for their sake. But not even severe mental handicap automatically brings a child within the scope even of a possible act of euthanasia. If the level of consciousness is low enough it could not be said that life is a good to them, any more than in the case of those suffering from extreme senility. Nevertheless, if they do not suffer it will not be an act of euthanasia by which someone opts for their death. Perhaps charity does not demand that strenuous measures are taken to keep people in this state alive, but euthanasia does not come into the matter, any more than it does when someone is, like Karen Ann Quinlan, in a state of permanent coma. Much could be said about this last case. It might even be suggested that in the case of unconsciousness this "life" is not the life to which "the right to life" refers. But that is not our topic here.

What we must consider, even if only briefly, is the possibility that euthanasia, genuine euthanasia, and not contrary to the requirements of justice or charity, should be legalized over a wider area. Here we are up against the really serious problem of abuse. Many people want, and want very badly, to be rid of their elderly relatives and even of their ailing husbands or wives. Would any safeguards ever be able to stop them describing as euthanasia what was really for their own benefit? And would it be possible to prevent the occurrence of acts which were genuinely acts of euthanasia but morally impermissible because infringing the rights of a patient who wished to live?

Perhaps the furthest we should go is to encourage patients to make their own contracts with a doctor by making it known whether they wish him to prolong their life in case of painful terminal illness or of incapacity. A document such as the Living Will seems eminently sensible, and should surely be allowed to give a doctor following the previously expressed wishes of the patient immunity from legal proceedings by relatives.[18] Legalizing active euthanasia is, however, another matter. Apart from the special repugnance doctors feel towards the idea of a lethal injection, it may be of the very greatest importance to keep a psychological barrier up against killing. Moreover, it is active euthanasia which is the most liable to abuse. Hitler would not have been able to kill 275,000 people in his "euthanasia" program if he had had to wait for them to need life-saving treatment. But there are other objections to active euthanasia, even voluntary active euthanasia. In the first place, it would be hard to devise procedures that would protect people from being persuaded into giving their consent. And secondly, the possibility of active voluntary euthanasia might change the social scene in ways that would be very bad. As things are, people do, by and large, expect to be looked after if they are old or ill. This is one of the good things that we have, but we might lose it, and be much worse off without it. It might come to be expected that someone likely to need a lot of looking after should call for the doctor and demand his own death.

Something comparable could be good in an extremely poverty-stricken community where the children genuinely suffered from lack of food; but in rich societies such as ours it would surely be a spiritual disaster. Such possibilities should make us very wary of supporting large measures of euthanasia, even where moral principle applied to the individual act does not rule it out.

NOTES

I would like to thank Derek Parfit and the editors of *Philosophy & Public Affairs* for their very helpful comments.

1. Leo Alexander, "Medical Science under Dictatorship," *New England Journal of Medicine,* 14 July 1949, p. 40.

2. For a discussion of culpable and nonculpable ignorance see Thomas Aquinas, *Summa Theologica,* First Part of the Second Part, Question 6, article 8, and Question 19, articles 5 and 6.

3. Dmitri Panin, *The Notebooks of Sologdin* (London, 1976), pp. 66–67.

4. Thomas Nagel, "Death," in James Rachels, ed., *Moral Problems* (New York, 1971), p. 362.

5. Panin, *Sologdin,* p. 85.

6. Yet some detail needs to be filled in to explain why we should not say that a scarecrow is beneficial to the plants it protects. Perhaps what is beneficial must either be a feature of the plant itself, such as protective prickles, or else must work on the plant directly, such as a line of trees which give it shade.

7. David Hume, *Treatise,* Book III, Part II, Section 1.

8. See, for example, D. D. Raphael, "Human Rights Old and New," in D. D. Raphael, ed., *Political Theory and the Rights of Man* (London, 1967), and Joel Feinberg, "The Nature and Value of Rights," *The Journal of Value Inquiry* 4, no. 4 (Winter 1970): 243–257. Reprinted in Samuel Gorovitz, ed., *Moral Problems in Medicine* (Englewood Cliffs, New Jersey, 1976).

9. Feinberg, "Human Rights," *Moral Problems in Medicine,* p. 465.

10. See, for example, James Rachels, "Active and Passive Euthanasia," *New England Journal of Medicine* 292, no. 2 (9 Jan. 1975): 78–80.

11. Ibid.

12. It is not, however, that justice and charity conflict. A man does not lack charity because he refrains from an act of injustice which would have been for someone's good.

13. For a discussion of such questions, see my article "The Problem of Abortion and the Doctrine of Double Effect," *Oxford Review,* no. 5 (1967); reprinted in Rachels, *Moral Problems,* and Gorovitz, *Moral Problems in Medicine.*

14. George Fletcher, "Legal Aspects of the Decision not to Prolong Life," *Journal of the American Medical Association* 203, no. 1 (1 Jan. 1968): 119–122. Reprinted in Gorovitz.

15. I have been told this by a pediatrician in a well-known medical center in the United States. It is confirmed by Anthony M. Shaw and Iris A. Shaw, "Dilemma of Informed Consent in Children," *The New England Journal of Medicine* 289, no. 17 (25 Oct. 1973): 885–890. Reprinted in Gorovitz.

16. It must be remembered, however, that many of the social miseries of spina bifida children could be avoided.

Professor R. B. Zachary is surely right to insist on this. See, for example, "Ethical and Social Aspects of Spina Bifida," *The Lancet,* 3 Aug. 1968, pp. 274–276. Reprinted in Gorovitz.

17. Quoted by Hannah Arendt, *Eichmann in Jerusalem* (London 1963), p. 90.

18. Details of this document are to be found in J. A. Behnke and Sissela Bok, eds., *The Dilemmas of Euthanasia* (New York, 1975), and in A. B. Downing, ed., *Euthanasia and the Right to Life: The Case for Voluntary Euthanasia* (London, 1969).

Questions for Analysis

1. What does Foot mean by "right to life," and how does she use this notion to distinguish between active and passive euthanasia?

2. Under what conditions might a person's life be regarded as no longer worth living?

3. Why does Foot believe it is not legitimate for us to decide when someone else's life is no longer worth living?

4. Which forms of euthanasia does Foot regard as legitimate and which illegitimate? Cite her reasons.

5. Why does Foot believe we don't have a duty to kill a person who has decided his or her life is no longer worth living?

A Moral Principle about Killing

Richard Brandt

The preceding writers, either explicitly or implicitly, dealt with the moral principle "It is morally wrong to kill innocent human beings." In this essay, philosopher Richard Brandt observes that this principle is really more useful in determining blame than for guiding us in making decisions. Brandt thinks a more appropriate principle can be based on the presumed obligation not to kill any human being except in justifiable self-defense—unless we have an even stronger moral obligation to do something that cannot be done without killing. In Brandt's view, that other overriding obligation is not to cause injury to another.

Brandt is distinguishing, then, between killing and causing injury, so that not every act of killing is an act of injury. After citing examples of what he believes are noninjurious killings and specifying conditions under which an act is noninjurious, Brandt argues that a person in irreversible coma is "beyond injury." If such a person has left instructions that his or her life should be ended, then, in Brandt's view, we are under a *prima facie* obligation to do so. In the absence of explicit instructions, we may attempt to determine what the person's wishes likely would be and carry them out. Of course, if a person has left instructions to be maintained under any circumstances, then we have an obligation to respect that preference.

Throughout the essay, Brandt uses the term *"prima facie* duty" or "obligation," which he has borrowed from the English philosopher William David Ross. *Prima facie* means "at

This article first appeared in the book *Beneficent Euthanasia*, ed. Marvin Kohl (Buffalo, N.Y.: Prometheus Books, 1975). Reprinted by permission of the publisher.

first sight" or "on the surface." Accordingly, a ***prima facie* duty** is one that dictates what I should do when other relevant factors aren't considered. For example, I have a *prima facie* duty not to lie in every case in which lying is possible. Likewise, I have a *prima facie* duty to prevent the needless suffering of others. In other words, all things being equal, this is what I ought to try to do.

In this essay, Brandt is taking issue with the commonplace view that killing a person is something that is *prima facie* wrong in itself. In his view, killing is wrong *only if* and *because* it is an injury to someone, or *if* and *because* it runs counter to the person's known preference. In short, Brandt believes that a principle about the *prima facie* wrongness of killing derives from principles about when we are *prima facie* obligated not to injure and when we are *prima facie* obligated to respect a person's wishes..

One of the Ten Commandments states: "Thou shalt not kill." The commandment does not supply an object for the verb, but the traditional Catholic view has been that the proper object of the verb is "innocent human beings" (except in cases of extreme necessity), where "innocent" is taken to exclude persons convicted of a capital crime or engaged in an unjust assault aimed at killing, such as members of the armed forces of a country prosecuting an unjust war. Thus construed, the prohibition is taken to extend to suicide and abortion. (There is a qualification: that we are not to count cases in which the death is not wanted for itself or intended as a *means* to a goal that is wanted for itself, provided that in either case the aim of the act is the avoidance of some evil greater than the death of the person.) Can this view that all killing of innocent human beings is morally wrong be defended, and if not, what alternative principle can be?

This question is one the ground rules for answering which are far from a matter of agreement. I should myself be content if a principle were identified that could be shown to be one that would be included in any moral system that rational and benevolent persons would support for a society in which they expected to live. Apparently others would not be so content; so in what follows I shall simply aim to make some observations that I hope will identify a principle with which the consciences of intelligent people will be comfortable. I believe the rough principle I will suggest is also one that would belong to the moral system rational and benevolent people would want for their society.

Let us begin by reflecting on what it is to kill. The first thing to notice is that *kill* is a biological term. For example, a weed may be killed by being sprayed with a chemical. The verb *kill* involves essentially the broad notion of death—the change from the state of being biologically alive to the state of being dead. It is beyond my powers to give any general characterization of this transition, and it may be impossible to give one. If there is one, it is one that human beings, flies, and ferns all share; and to kill is in some sense to bring that transition about. The next thing to notice is that at least human beings do not live forever, and hence killing a human being at a given time must be construed as *advancing the date* of its death, or as *shortening its life*. Thus it may be brought about that the termination of the life of a person occurs at the time t instead of at the time $t + k$. Killing is thus shortening the span of organic life of something.

There is a third thing to notice about *kill*. It is a term of causal agency and has roots in the legal tradition. As such, it involves complications. For instance, suppose I push a boulder down a mountainside, aiming it at a person X and it indeed strikes X, and he is dead after impact and not before (and not from a coincidental heart attack); in that case we would say that I killed X. On the other hand, suppose I tell Y that X is in bed with Y's wife, and Y hurries to the scene, discovers them, and shoots X to death; in that case, although the unfolding of events from my action may be as much a matter of causal law as the path of the boulder, we should not say that I killed X. Fortunately, for the purpose of principles of the morally right, we can sidestep such complications. For suppose I am choosing whether to do A or B (where one or the other of these "acts" may be construed as essentially *inaction*—for example, *not* doing what I know is the one thing that will *prevent* someone's death); then it is enough if I know, or have reason to think it highly probable, that were I to do A, a state of the world including the death of some person or persons would ensue, whereas were I to do *B*, a state of the world of some specified different sort would ensue. If a moral principle will tell me in this case whether I am to do *A* or *B*, that is all I need. It could be that a moral principle would tell me that I am absolutely never to perform any action *A*, such that were I to do it the death of some innocent human being would ensue, provided there is some alternative action I might perform, such that were I to do it no such death would ensue.

It is helpful, I think, to reformulate the traditional Catholic view in a way that preserves the spirit and intent of that view (although some philosophers would disagree with this assessment) and at the same time avoids some conceptions that are both vague and more appropriate to a principle about when a person is morally blameworthy for doing something than to a principle about what a person ought morally to do. The terminology I use goes back, in philosophical literature, to a phrase introduced by W. D. Ross, but the conception is quite familiar. The alternative proposal is that there is a *strong prima facie obligation* not to kill any human being except in justifiable self-defense; in the sense (of prima facie) that it is morally *wrong* to kill any human being except in justifiable self-defense *unless* there is an even stronger prima facie moral obligation to do something that cannot be done without killing. (The term *innocent* can now be omitted, since if a person is not innocent, there may be a stronger moral obligation that can only be discharged by killing him; and this change is to the good since it is not obvious that we have no prima facie obligation to avoid killing people even if they are not innocent.) This formulation has the result that sometimes, to decide what is morally right, we have to compare the stringencies of conflicting moral obligations—and that is an elusive business; but the other formulation either conceals the same problem by putting it in another place, or else leads to objectionable implications. (Consider one implication of the traditional formulation for a party of spelunkers in a cave by the oceanside. It is found that a rising tide is bringing water into the cave and all will be drowned unless they escape at once. Unfortunately, the first man to try to squeeze through the exit is fat and gets wedged inextricably in the opening, with his head inside the cave. Somebody in the party has a stick of dynamite. Either they blast the fat man out, killing him, or all of them, including him, will drown. The traditional formulation leads to the conclusion that all must drown.)

Let us then consider the principle: "There is a strong prima facie moral obligation not to kill any human being except in justifiable self-defense." I do not believe we want to accept this principle without further qualification; indeed, its status seems not to be that of a basic principle at all, but derivative from some more-basic principles. W. D. Ross listed what he thought were the main basic prima facie moral obligations; it is noteworthy that he listed a prima facie duty not to *cause injury,* but he did not include an obligation not to kill. Presumably this was no oversight. He might have thought that killing a human being is always an injury, so that the additional listing of an obligation not to kill would be redundant; but he might also have thought that killing is sometimes not an injury and that it is prima facie obligatory not to kill only when, and because, so doing would injure a sentient being.

What might be a noninjurious killing? If I come upon a cat that has been mangled but not quite killed by several dogs and is writhing in pain, and I pull myself together and put it out of its misery, I have killed the cat but surely not *injured* it. I do not injure something by relieving its pain. If someone is being tortured and roasted to death and I know he wishes nothing more than a merciful termination of life, I have not injured him if I shoot him; I have done him a favor. In general, it seems I have not injured a person if I treat him in a way in which he would want me to treat him if he were fully rational, or in a way to which he would be indifferent if he were fully rational. (I do not think that terminating the life of a human fetus in the third month is an injury; I admit this view requires discussion.[1])

Consider another type of killing that is not an injury. Consider the case of a human being who has become unconscious and will not, it is known, regain consciousness. He is in a hospital and is being kept alive only through expensive supportive measures. Is there a strong prima facie moral obligation not to withdraw these measures and not to take positive steps to terminate his life? It seems obvious that if he is on the only kidney machine and its use could *save* the life of another person, who could lead a normal life after temporary use, it would be wrong not to take him off. Is there an obligation to continue, or not to terminate, if there is no countering obligation? I would think not, with an exception to be mentioned; and this coincides with the fact that he is *beyond* injury. There is also not an obligation *not* to preserve his life, say, in order to have his organs available for use when they are needed.

There seems, however, to be another morally relevant consideration in such a case—knowledge of the patient's own wishes when he was conscious and in possession of his faculties. Suppose he had feared such an eventuality and prepared a sworn statement requesting his doctor to terminate his life at once in such circumstances. Now, if it is morally obligatory to some degree to carry out a person's wishes for disposal of his body and possessions after his death, it would seem to be equally morally obligatory to respect his wishes in case he becomes a "vegetable." In the event of the existence of such a document, I would think that if he can no longer be injured we are free to withdraw life-sustaining measures and also to take positive steps to terminate life—and are even morally bound, prima facie, to do so. (If, however, the patient had prepared a document directing that his body be preserved alive as long as possible in such circumstances, then there would be a prima facie obligation *not* to cease life-sustaining measures and not to terminate. It would seem obvious, however, that such an obligation would fall far short of giving the patient the right to continued use of a kidney machine when its use by another could save that person's life.) Some persons would not hesitate to discontinue life-sustaining procedures in such a situation, but would balk at more positive measures. But the hesitation to use more positive procedures, which veterinarians employ frequently with animals, is surely nothing but squeamishness; if a person is in the state described, there can be no injury to him in positive termination more than or less than that in allowing him to wither by withdrawing life-supportive procedures.

If I am right in my analysis of this case, we must phrase our basic principle about killing in such a way as to take into account (1) whether the killing would be an injury and (2) the person's own wishes and directives. And perhaps, more important, any moral principle about killing must be viewed simply as an implicate of more basic principles about these matters.

Let us look for corroboration of this proposal to how we feel about another type of case, one in which termination would be of positive benefit to the agent. Let us suppose that a patient has a terminal illness and is in severe pain, subject only to brief remissions, with no prospect of any event that could make his life good, either in the short or long term. It might seem that here, with the patient in severe pain, at least life-supportive measures should be discontinued, or positive termination adopted. But I do not think we would accept this inference, for in this situation the patient, let us suppose, has his preferences and is able to express them. The patient may have strong religious convictions and prefer to go on living despite the pain; if so, surely there is a prima facie moral obligation not positively to terminate his life. Even if, as seemingly in this case, the situation is one in which it would be *rational* for the agent, from the point of view of his own welfare, to direct the termination of his life,[2] it seems that if he (irrationally) does the opposite, there is a prima facie moral obligation not to terminate and some prima facie obligation to sustain it. Evidently a person's own expressed wishes have moral force. (I believe, however, that we think a person's expressed wishes have *less* moral force when we think the wishes are irrational.)

What is the effect, in this case, if the patient himself expresses a preference for termination and would, if he were given the means, terminate his own existence? Is there a prima facie obligation to sustain his life—and pain—against his will? Surely not. Or is there an obligation *not* to take positive measures to terminate his life immediately, thereby saving the patient much discomfort? Again, surely not. What possible reason could be offered to justify the claim that the answer is affirmative, beyond theological ones about God's will and our being bound to stay alive at His pleasure? The only argument I can think of is that there is some consideration of public policy, to the effect that a recognition of such moral permission might lead to abuses or to some other detriment to society in the long run. Such an argument does seem weak.

It might be questioned whether a patient's request should be honored, if made at a time when he is in pain, on the grounds that it is not rational. (The physician may be in a position to see, however, that the patient is quite right about his prospects and that his personal welfare would be maximized by termination.) It might also be questioned whether a patient's formal declaration, written earlier, requesting termination if he were ever in his present circumstances should be honored, on the grounds that at the earlier time he did not know what it would be like to be in his present situation. It would seem odd, however, if *no* circumstances are identifiable in which a patient's request for termination is deemed to have moral force, when his request *not* to terminate is thought morally weighty in the same circumstances even when this request is clearly irrational. I think we may ignore such arguments and hold that, in a situation in which it is rational for a person to choose termination of his life, his expressed wish is morally definitive and removes both the obligation to sustain life and the obligation not to terminate.

Indeed, there is a question whether or not in these circumstances a physician has not a moral obligation at least to withdraw life-supporting measures, and perhaps positively to terminate life. At least there seems to be a general moral obligation to render assistance when a person is in need, when it can be given at small cost to oneself, and when it is requested. The obligation is the stronger when one happens to be the only person in a position to receive such a request or to know about the situation. Furthermore, the physician has acquired a special obligation if there has been a long-standing personal relationship with the patient—just as a friend or relative has special obligations. But since we are discussing not the possible obligation to terminate but the obligation *not* to terminate, I shall not pursue this issue.

The patient's own expression of preference or consent, then, seems to be weighty. But suppose he is unable to express his preference; suppose that his terminal disease not only causes him great pain but has attacked his brain in such a way that he is incapable of thought and of rational speech. May the physician, then, after consultation, take matters into his own hands? We often think we know what is best for another, but we think one person should not make decisions for another. Just as we must respect the decision of a person who has decided after careful reflection that he wants to commit suicide, so we must not take the liberty of deciding to bring another's life to a close contrary to his wishes. So

what may be done? Must a person suffer simply because he cannot express consent? There is evidence that can be gathered about what conclusions a person would draw if he were in a state to draw and express them. The patient's friends will have some recollection of things he has said in the past, of his values and general ethical views. Just as we can have good reason to think, for example, that he would vote Democratic if voting for president in a certain year, so we can have good reason to think he would take a certain stand about the termination of his own life in various circumstances. We can know of some persons who because of their religious views would want to keep on living until natural processes bring their lives to a close. About others we can know that they decidedly would not take this view. We can also know what would be the *rational* choice for them to make, and our knowledge of this can be *evidence* about what they would request if they were able. There are, of course, practical complications in the mechanics of a review board of some kind making a determination of this sort, but they are hardly insurmountable.

I wish to consider one other type of case, that of a person who, say, has had a stroke and is leading, and for some time can continue to lead, a life that is comfortable but one on a very low level, *and* who has antecedently requested that his life be terminated if he comes, incurably, into such a situation. May he then be terminated? In this case, unlike the others, there are probably ongoing pleasant experiences, perhaps on the level of some animals, that seem to be a good thing. One can hardly say that *injury* is being done such a person by keeping him alive; and one might say that some slight injury is being done him by terminating his existence. There is a real problem here. Can the (slight) goodness of these experiences stand against the weight of an earlier firm declaration requesting that life be terminated in a situation of hopeless senility? There is no *injury* in keeping the person alive despite his request, but there seems something *indecent* about keeping a mind alive after a severe stroke, when we know quite well that, could he have anticipated it, his own action would have been to terminate his life. I think that the person's own request should be honored; it should be if a person's expressed preferences have as much moral weight as I think they should have.

What general conclusions are warranted by the preceding discussion? I shall emphasize two. First, there is a prima facie obligation *not* to terminate a person's existence when this would injure him (except in cases of self-defense or of senility of a person whose known wish is to be terminated in such a condition) *or* if he wishes not to be terminated. Second, there is *not* a prima facie obligation not to terminate when there would be *no* injury, or when there would be a positive benefit (release from pain) in so doing, provided the patient has not declared himself otherwise or there is evidence that his wishes are to that effect. Obviously there are two things that are decisive for the morality of terminating a person's life: whether so doing would be an *injury* and whether it conforms to what is known of his *preferences*.

I remarked at the outset that I would be content with some moral principles if it could be made out that rational persons would want those principles incorporated in the consciences of a group among whom they were to live. It is obvious why rational persons would want these principles. They would want injury avoided both because they would not wish others to injure them and because, if they are benevolent, they would not wish others injured. Moreover, they would want weight given to a person's own known preferences. Rational people do want the decision about the termination of their lives, where that is possible; for they would be uncomfortable if they thought it possible that others would be free to terminate their lives without consent. The threat of serious illness is bad enough without that prospect. On the other hand, this discomfort would be removed if they knew that termination would not be undertaken on their behalf without their explicit consent, except after a careful inquiry had been made, both into whether termination would constitute an injury and whether they would request termination under the circumstances if they were in a position to do so.

If I am right in all this, then it appears that killing a person is not something that is just prima facie wrong *in itself;* it is wrong roughly only if and because it is an *injury* of someone, or if and because it is contrary to the *known preferences* of someone. It would seem that a principle about the prima facie wrongness of killing is *derivative* from principles about when we are prima facie obligated not to injure and when we are prima facie obligated to respect a person's wishes, at least about what happens to his own body. I do not, however, have any suggestions for a general statement of principles of this latter sort.

NOTES

1. See my "The Morality of Abortion" in *The Monist,* 56 (1972), pp. 503–26; and, in revised form, in *Abortion: Pro and Con,* ed. R. L. Perkins (General Learning Press, 1975).

2. See my "The Morality and Rationality of Suicide," in James Rachels, ed., *Moral Problems* (Harper & Row, 1975); and, in revised form, in E. S. Shneidman, ed., *Suicidology: Current Developments* (Grune & Stratton, 1976).

Questions for Analysis

1. Under what conditions, according to Brandt, can one person be said to injure another?

2. Give an example of killing that causes injury and of killing that doesn't.

3. How do we determine what a comatose person's wishes are if the person has left no directions about terminating his or her life?

4. According to Brandt, under what conditions are we *prima facie* obligated not to terminate a person's existence? Under what conditions is there no at such *prima facie* obligation?

5. Explain the significance (with respect to mercy deaths) of Brandt's deriving a principle about the *prima facie* wrongness of killing from principles about when we are *prima facie* obligated not to injure and when we are *prima facie* obligated to respect a person's wishes.

6. Would you say that Brandt's analysis is consistent or inconsistent with a Kantian view of the morality of euthanasia? (To answer this question, you of course should first try to apply Kant's ethics to the problem of euthanasia. Under what conditions, if ever, do you think Kant would approve of a mercy death?)

CASE PRESENTATION
"I Did It Because I Loved My Son"

In early May 1989, Rudolfo Linares visited his son Samuel in a Chicago hospital, where the fifteen-month-old boy, partially brain dead, lay connected to a respirator. Samuel's coma had begun nine months earlier, when he'd suffocated after swallowing an uninflated balloon at a birthday party.

Along with his wife, Tamara, Rudolfo had been pleading with hospital officials to disconnect the respirator, but always to no avail. Once, in December, he disconnected it himself, but security officers reconnected it. After that, he decided to hire a lawyer to challenge the hospital in court.

Apparently, Rudolfo was growing impatient with the legal process. On this visit to the hospital, he brought a hand gun, which he used to hold off nurses, doctors, and police officers as he disconnected the respirator and held his son in his arms. Crying all the while, he sat with his son for a full forty minutes, long after hospital instruments showed that he was dead.

"I did it because I loved my son," he said.

Prosecutors immediately charged Linares with first degree murder, but following a storm of national publicity, charges were dropped.

Questions for Analysis

1. Who should decide whether to "pull the plug" in cases like this one: the parents, the attending physician, a hospital committee, or the courts?

2. In its *Cruzan* decision, the U.S. Supreme Court ruled that states can forbid family members to refuse treatment of an incompetent patient without clear evidence that the patient, if competent, would refuse it. Should its ruling apply to patients who, like Samuel, never were competent?

3. Suppose the patient in this case had been an adult who had never expressed an opinion about refusing or accepting treatment in such circumstances. Would his family have the moral right to refuse treatment for him?

4. If hospital officials refuse to stop treatment, do family members have the moral right to take matters into their own hands, as Rudolfo Linares did?

CASE PRESENTATION
"Myrna Is Dead. Desolation"

It was Independence Day 1995. George Delury and his wife, Myrna Lebov, who suffered from multiple sclerosis, were in their New York apartment. As planned, he dissolved several pills of the anti-depressant amitriptyline (sold under the brand name Elavil) in water and sweetened the mixture with honey. Then he handed it to her, she drank it, and soon afterward she was dead.

Although New York State has a law banning assisted suicide, few cases are prosecuted. Still, Manhattan's district attorney charged Delury with second-degree manslaughter, claiming that Delury coerced his wife into suicide. As evidence, he had the statements of her sister, Beverly Sloane, who insisted that Lebov did not want to die. The district attorney also had Delury's diary, which he had kept for four months preceding her death. Following are some excerpts:

FEB. 27 Myrna's on the lower side of a downswing. It will get worse before it gets better. She worries about every little thing, even denying the evidence of the senses in order to express worry. . . . She expressed special concern about her incapacity to express herself well. It is unclear whether this is an inability to hold onto a thought, an inability to find the words needed to express a thought, or both.

MARCH 30 Nothing done. Myrna spent her time reading the paper and watching the movie again. We talked in the evening, or rather, I talked. Myrna is more or less rational. Able to see but not accept the reality of the situation. She is only vaguely aware of the degree to which she is now adrift, with little autonomy left. She will admit in one moment that the situation is bad, that she can't write a book, that suicide might be the best solution, but moments later, it's as if nothing of this was said or was real. We can go through the same round again and again with no change. I doubt that anything will come of all this. The drift will get worse, until she's gone.

APRIL 1 It is now 11:30 P.M. Since 10:30 last night, I have had about 11 hours' sleep. I'm rested and it's good to have Myrna back for a bit. We talked some more about suicide and method today. She agreed to test a solution of cran juice and Elavil for taste and consistency for tonight.

Reviewing this memoir this evening, I was surprised that the last time we talked of suicide was only a month ago; it seems much longer—probably a sign of the emotional rollercoaster we're on.

MAY 1 Sheer hell. Myrna is more or less euphoric. She spoke of writing a book today. She's interested in everything, wants everything explained and believes that every bit of bad news has some way out; e.g., our back tax bills:

there must be something that can be done to make them less. She is encouraged in all this by her sister, Cleopatra, the Queen of Denial, who appears to believe that everything difficult here is my fault: Myrna's moods—the dysphoria is my fault, the euphoria is the good old Myrna; the Medicaid problem; the shortage of money, etc. It became an old-fashioned screaming match today, with me marching out saying I was going to get drunk. (Just a threat.) When I came back, dry as ever, I told Myrna to tell Cleo that if she wishes to speak to me she will speak with respect or not at all.

It's all just too much. I'm not going to come out of this in one piece or with any honor. I'm so tired of it all; maybe I should kill myself.

MAY 19 My problem: if she asks for the poison now but seems very depressed, should I comply? Is she still autonomous? If I comply, I may be serving my own interests more than hers. If I don't, she may be losing her last chance to make the decision. She's mentioned July 4 as "independence day," a possible suicide date, but at the rate her mind is deteriorating, she may not still be a whole, autonomous person by that time. I believe I will comply—on the rationale (rationalization?) that I will be saving her from a fate worse than death. (What an ironic cliche in this context!)

JULY 3 3:30 P.M. Myrna has pushed up the schedule to tonight. She seems mostly concerned about whether she can keep the amitriptyline down and whether it will work. She told me that when she set up her pills on Saturday night, she only set them up as far as Tuesday. . . . She was going to try to work on her suicide note, but at the last minute decided to watch "Forrest Gump" instead.

7:30 P.M. Myrna is now questioning the efficacy of the solution, a sure sign that she will not take it tonight and doesn't want to. So, confusion and hesitation strike again. If she changes her mind tonight and does decide to go ahead, I will be surprised.

JULY 4 12:30 A.M. Myrna has just consumed about 3,000 to 4,000 mg. of the amitriptyline. Her courage was remarkable. Once begun, she went ahead as long as she could before it began to threaten the heaves. About 14 oz. of liquid, about half of what I had prepared. She said very little. Very direct and businesslike. No tearful goodbyes, no jokes, just a let's-get-this-done approach. All rather anticlimactic.

Before we cathed and she took the solution, she expressed regret that she couldn't write letters to Beverly and Alison [Lebov's niece]. I said, Leave a message with me. She said, as if dictating, "I love you both very much. Please don't feel hurt; I know you did all you could for me. I'm bored with my bodily functions and my mind is going. It's better to end it now, while I still can do something."

We sat up together on the bed for about a half-hour. She's soundly asleep now. I'll check back in about an hour. I'm disappointed that she was finally so direct and single-minded about it. I wish she had said goodbye. I think there was an element of desperation there that simply blocked out everything else.

2:15 A.M. Myrna is sleeping very soundly, breathing heavily. I'm going to grab an hour's sleep.

5:30 A.M. Slept through the alarm. It's over. Myrna is dead. Desolation.

When indicted, Delury pleaded not guilty, but after the ensuing plea-bargaining, he agreed to plead guilty to a lesser charge and spend six months in prison. (Second-degree manslaughter carries a sentence of five to fifteen years in New York.) At his sentencing in May of 1996, he said, "I regret that my wife's spirit has been impugned and her courage dishonored because society and the government have provided no way to deal with these situations openly with due respect for individual freedom of conscience and individual dignity."

Questions for Analysis

1. Do the excerpts from Delury's diary support the D.A.'s decision to prosecute?

2. Supporters of assisted suicide argue that if New York had passed a law providing a clear protocol to follow before assisting a suicide, Delury would not have gone to prison. If true, does the claim show the benefits or the dangers of such a law?

3. After his release from prison, Delury revealed that he had suffocated his wife with a plastic bag to hasten her death. He hadn't admitted it earlier, he said, because he wanted to avoid prosecution for murder. Did his use of the bag and his initial silence about it affect the morality of his actions? If so, how?

4. If you think assisted suicide should be legal, does the Delury case suggest that the practice should be limited to physician-assisted suicide?

CASE PRESENTATION
"A Choice Central to Personal Dignity"

It was the first time a law banning assisted suicide had come before a federal judge. The setting was the U.S. District Court in Seattle. The federal judge was Judge Barbara Rothstein. Three terminally ill patients seeking assistance in ending their lives, along with five doctors and an organization named Compassion in Dying, were challenging a Washington State law that forbade them to do so. Judge Rothstein's decision came May 3, 1994: The Washington law, which had been on the books for 140 years, was unconstitutional.

As noteworthy as the ruling itself was the reasoning behind it. In declaring the law in violation of the Fourteenth Amendment, Judge Rothstein cited the Supreme Court's *Planned Parenthood v. Casey* decision, which upheld a woman's right to abortion. "Like the abortion decision," she wrote, "the decision of a terminally ill patient to end his or her life 'involves the most intimate and personal choice a person can make in a lifetime,' and constitutes a 'choice central to personal dignity and autonomy.'" Drawing on these similarities, she concluded that "The suffering of a terminally ill person cannot be deemed . . . any less deserving of protection from unwarranted governmental interference than that of a pregnant woman."

For one of the patients, a cancer victim who had already died, the ruling came too late. The other two were now free to seek help. And Compassion in Dying, which for two years had been referring terminally ill patients to doctors for prescription drugs they could take to end their lives, was now free to act more openly.

In a front-page story two days after the ruling, *The New York Times* quoted Ralph Mero, the group's director and a Unitarian minister, as follows: "Today, every time I pick up the phone, there are three more people on voice mail asking for help." The report also quoted a statement by the Roman Catholic Bishops of Washington, who said of the ruling, "It undermines the moral integrity of the medical profession, whose duty is to heal and comfort, not kill. And it tramples on our conviction that life, no matter how feeble or impaired, is a sacred gift from God."

The state appealed the decision, and three years later, in *Washington v. Glucksberg,* the U.S. Supreme Court ruled the law constitutional.

Questions for Analysis

1. Do you agree with Judge Rothstein's analogy between the decision of a pregnant woman to abort and a terminally ill patient to take his or her own life?

2. Judge Rothstein's ruling applied only to terminally ill patients. Can you think of other cases where a decision to commit suicide might be justified by the same reasoning? If so, has she put us at the top of a slippery slope? Does her ruling suggest that Supreme Court decisions upholding abortion rights have already put us there?

3. In their statement, the bishops claimed that a physician's duty is "to heal and comfort, not kill." When healing is impossible, what kind of comfort does the patient deserve? Does it include prescribing lethal drugs when asked?

4. The Fourteenth Amendment says that states cannot deprive people of life, liberty, or property without due process of law. Do laws banning assisted suicide of the terminally ill violate that provision? If so, why not ban assisted suicide of the nonterminally ill?

CASE PRESENTATION
Legalized Assisted Suicide and Decriminalized Euthanasia

Fewer than three years after the U.S. Supreme Court provided a constitutional basis for voluntary passive euthanasia, one European country took a much bolder step. By a vote of 91 to 45, the parliament of the Netherlands decriminalized active euthanasia and doctor-assisted suicide under a set of strict conditions. As reported by the Associated Press, these conditions are:

Voluntary Nature. The request for euthanasia must be made "entirely of the patient's own free will" and not under pressure from others.

Weighing Alternatives. The patient must be well informed and must be able to consider the alternatives.

Certain Decision. The patient must have a "lasting longing for death." Requests made on impulse or based on a temporary depression cannot be considered.

Unacceptable Suffering. "The patient must experience his or her suffering as perpetual, unbearable and hopeless." The physician must be reasonably able to conclude that the suffering experienced is unbearable.

Consultation.   The doctor must consult at least one colleague who has faced the question of euthanasia before.

Reporting.   A documented written report must be drawn up stating the history of the patient's illness and declaring that the rules have been met.

The vote followed what *The New York Times* called "two decades of tormented national debate." It also followed a significant increase in doctor-reported cases of active euthanasia and assisted suicide from 1990 to 1992. According to the *Times,* Dutch legal and medical experts attributed the increase to "more open discussion of the issue and a clearer agreement on the rules that protect doctors from prosecution."

Soon after the measure passed, many observers expected the Dutch parliament to go even further by legalizing active euthanasia and assisted suicide by physicians, and in 2000, that's exactly what the parliament did.

The significance of that step is twofold. First, it means that Dutch physicians who help their patients die are no longer technically committing a crime. Second, these physicians are no longer accountable to a prosecutor but to a panel of medical, legal, and ethical experts.

In 1994, as we have seen, voters in Oregon took a similar step when they passed a ballot initiative legalizing doctor-assisted suicide. That measure too contains restrictions. Among the most important are these: (1) the means of assistance are limited to a prescription for a lethal dose of medication to be taken orally; (2) two doctors must determine that the patient has six months or less to live; (3) the patient must be of sound mind; (4) the patient's request must be made in writing; (5) the prescription must be written no less than fifteen days after the request; (6) the patient, not the doctor, must administer the pills.

Questions for Analysis

1.   The Dutch rules are obviously intended to prevent abuses. Are they sufficiently strict and clear? Do any of the rules seem too vague? Do any need to be made more precise?

2.   As reported by the *Times,* a Dutch study found that in 1992 doctors ended the lives of a thousand patients "without an explicit recent request." In most cases, the *Times* reported, "the patient had only days or hours to live, was often in great pain, and was either in a coma or not fully conscious. In more than half the cases the patient had either talked about euthanasia to the doctor or others." Do these findings support J. Gay-Williams's contention that active euthanasia is a slippery slope? Will the new Dutch rules prevent such sliding in the future?

3.   Nowhere do the rules say that a patient must be suffering from a terminal illness or that death must be near. Should either condition be added?

4.   After the vote, one pro-life Dutch physician declared, "Today the Netherlands abolished the Hippocratic Oath." Do you agree?

5.   In many areas of moral controversy—for instance, drugs and prostitution—the Netherlands has pursued a more liberal social policy than the United States. Do you think the Dutch rules for euthanasia and assisted suicide are appropriate for the United States?

6.   One forceful opponent of the Oregon measure is the American Medical Association, which argues that doctors cannot reliably determine that a patient has six months or less to live. Is this a serious flaw in the law?

7.   The Oregon requirement that the patient, not the doctor, administer the pills is meant to ensure that the patient's death results from suicide, not euthanasia. Is this distinction morally significant?

6

Human Cloning

The 1990s brought a number of astonishing technological developments, many of them highly controversial. Perhaps the most controversial came from the field of biotechnology, and among them, none created more controversy than the birth of a lamb named Dolly. By all outward appearances a perfectly ordinary lamb, she was the product of the first successful cloning of an adult mammal. Ian Wilmut, who headed the team of Scottish scientists that produced her, announced the feat in 1997, and a staple of fiction suddenly loomed as an imminent reality: the successful cloning of an adult human being.

Not surprisingly, people began talking in earnest about the dangers and promises this startling development raised, whether—as in the book and movie versions of *The Boys from Brazil*—it was the mass production of Hitler clones in a fanatical attempt to resurrect the Third Reich or maybe a U.S. Olympic basketball team composed entirely of Michael Jordan clones. And in the face of such possibilities came a raft of questions: Should the technology be made available when scientists are able to extend it to human beings? If so, to whom? And what kinds of legal restrictions, if any, should we place on its availability? More generally, is there something fundamentally immoral and frightening about human cloning, or is it—like sperm donorship, in vitro fertilization, or surrogate motherhood—

a benign form of reproductive technology that individuals have a moral and legal right to use?

A number of national governments took the lead in this discussion. In the United States, for example, President Bill Clinton placed an immediate ban on all federal funding for attempts to clone humans. He also asked the National Bioethics Advisory Commission (NBAC) to issue a report within ninety days on the legal and ethical issues that surround human cloning. The resulting document, citing both safety concerns and moral concerns, called for a continuation of the president's ban. It also called on Congress to pass legislation banning all attempts to clone human beings, whether in clinical settings or research settings. The proposed legislation should, the report added, contain a "sunset clause," which would cause the ban to expire within three to five years; at some time before that point, the status of cloning technology and the ethical and social issues involved should be reevaluated.

President George W. Bush has repeatedly called for a complete ban on cloning, saying, "We must not create life to destroy life. Human beings are not research material to be used in a cruel and reckless experiment." Although the House of Representatives has passed the Human Cloning Prohibition Act that would ban all cloning, the proposed ban is still pending in the Senate.

Because of the safety concerns, many have supported the proposed bans, even if they did not have ethical qualms about cloning for purposes of medical research. But many of those safety concerns are being overcome. In fact, as we'll see in the next section, one of the most serious safety problems has already been overcome. The moral concerns, however, which are the subject of this chapter, will no doubt continue long after.

HOW CLONING WORKS: A BRIEF HISTORY

A **clone** is an exact genetic copy of a molecule, cell, plant, or animal.[1] Though the term is a relatively recent one, the phenomenon itself is as old as the simplest forms of life; whenever single-celled organisms like bacteria reproduce by cell division, the resultant cells are natural clones of the originals. In the laboratory, the cloning of molecules and cells has been a routine part of molecular biology for decades, as when scientists regularly clone DNA fragments in recombinant DNA technology (popularly known as "genetic engineering"). Outside the laboratory, the cloning of plants—a more complex form of cloning—has been a commonplace in ordinary households for a much longer time; whenever we take a cutting of a plant, place it in water, and grow a complete new plant from it, we produce a clone of the original plant.

Animal cloning too has been around a long time. At one end of the animal kingdom—with such invertebrates as worms, for example—an organism can be divided into two parts, and each will regenerate itself into a full genetic duplicate of the original. At the other end, we have the phenomenon of identical human twins, the result of separated embryos in the womb. In both cases, we have examples of natural animal cloning.

---

1. This definition and much of what follows in this section are adapted from the second chapter of the NBAC report, *Cloning Human Beings, U.S. Government,* Washington, D.C, 1997.

In the laboratory, scientists have been successfully cloning animals since the early 1980s, using a technique known as *nuclear transplantation cloning*. In its earliest form, this technique involved removing the nucleus from an unfertilized egg and replacing it with the nucleus of a somatic cell from an embryo. (A **somatic cell** is any cell other than a sperm or an egg, both of which are known as **germ cells**.) The product of the transplant, an embryo, is then implanted into a female for normal gestation.

The significance of Dolly is that the somatic cell used in the transplant came from an adult animal rather than from an embryo. And what makes that difference so important is this: As cells develop and divide after fertilization, they *differentiate* into specific tissues—muscle and bone, for example. That's why embryo cells were used in the earlier cases of cloning—because they had not yet differentiated. Mature cells, on the other hand, are cells that have differentiated, and before Dolly came along, scientists didn't know if the genes of these cells could be reprogrammed to an undifferentiated state. Previous attempts had provided discouraging results. In one series of experiments, in which the nuclei of adult frog skin cells replaced the nuclei of frog eggs, only 4 percent of the embryos resulted in tadpoles, and none of the tadpoles developed into an adult frog. In another series, using cells from adult mice, no successes occurred. With the successful cloning of Dolly, however, it seemed that mature cells could indeed be reprogrammed.

Even so, some doubts remained. The lingering uncertainty centered on the source of the cells that Wilmut's team had used for the transplant: the udder of a six-year-old female sheep in the late stages of pregnancy. Breasts of pregnant mammals grow much larger in the late stages of pregnancy, and a cell taken from one may be quite unusual in a relevant way. As the scientist Stephen J. Gould put it:

> some mammary cells, though technically adult, may remain unusually labile or even 'embryo-like' and thus able to proliferate rapidly to produce new breast tissue at an appropriate stage of pregnancy. Consequently, we may only be able to clone only from unusual adult cells with effectively embryonic potential and not from any stray cheek cell, hair follicle, or drop of blood that happens to fall in the clutches of a mad Xeroxer.[2]

This uncertainty was resolved almost three years later, when scientists at the University of Connecticut at Storrs and the Prefectural Cattle Breeding Development Institute in Japan announced that they had cloned four calves from cells scraped from the ear of a bull—cells without, to use Gould's term, "effectively embryonic potential." This development was significant for another reason as well: the number of successful clones. (Dolly had been a single success among a large number of failures. Of 277 fusions between cell and egg, only twenty-nine became embryos; of those twenty-nine, which Wilmut's team implanted into ewes, only the embryo that produced Dolly resulted in a pregnancy.) Adding to these advances, the same team announced weeks later that it had successfully cloned one of the original clones.

The next major step in animal cloning came in April 2000, when a serious obstacle, particularly important for the prospect of human cloning, was overcome.

---

2.   "Dolly's Fashion and Louis's Passion," *Natural History* vol. 106, no. 5 (June 1997): 21.

That obstacle first came to light after an examination of Dolly's chromosomes. The tips of her chromosomes, called *telomeres*, were shorter than those of a sheep produced by sexual reproduction. What was troubling about the finding is that telomeres grow shorter each time a cell divides. So the younger the animal in normal cases, the longer the telomeres; the older the animal, the shorter the telomeres. The implication, then, was that Dolly would not live as long as a sheep conceived through sexual reproduction. And the resulting implication for the ethics of human cloning was obvious. Clearly, most people thought, it would be immoral to produce a human being in that way if he or she could not live a normal human life span. But then scientists at a Massachusetts company called Advanced Cell Technology, who had produced six cloned calves, announced that the telomeres of all the clones were not shorter than normal. To the team's surprise, they were actually longer than normal, suggesting that the calves would have an unusually long life span. So one of the most prominent of the safety issues seems no longer a problem. Others, however, remain, including the dangers of genetic mutation to the clone and other biological damage.

WHY CLONE HUMANS?

Although modern cloning technology is still too young to ensure the safe cloning of humans, many researchers think that eventually it can and will be done. When scientists have the technology to accomplish something, the common line of reasoning goes, they will use it. Besides, even if most scientists oppose its use—and even if its use is outlawed in most corners of the world—all it takes is one millionaire persistent enough to find one scientist willing to clone him. But before we discuss whether scientists ought to use this technology, we should first discuss why anyone would want to.

Some reasons have nothing to do with the aim of producing a fully developed human being. For instance, many scientists (including those at Advanced Cell Technology) see great hope in using cloning to create replacement tissue—spare parts, you might say—for humans. This is not, as some have feared, a matter of keeping a mindless clone in a closet to be "harvested" for parts when needed but of producing an embryo that can be used to generate an organ for transplant. Being an exact genetic match with the host, the organ would not be rejected. For another example, cloning not aimed at producing a fully developed human being would almost certainly bring great gains in scientific knowledge—concerning cell division, say, or genetic differentiation.

But why use cloning for human reproduction? The most obvious reasons concern couples in which one or both partners are infertile. For at least some of them, cloning might be a welcome reproductive technology, a new technique for producing genetic offspring. Similarly, there are cases in which sexual reproduction carries the risk of passing on an inheritable disease, most commonly when both parties carry the same regressive gene for the disease. Also, many homosexuals see cloning as an opportunity for homosexual couples to have children. True, in all these cases, the couples have other options—adoption or sperm donorship, for example—but they may also want their children to be genetically related to at least one of them without having to introduce the genes of some unwanted third party.

Another reason is suggested by the case of Abe and Mary Ayala, a California couple who conceived a child in 1989—seventeen years after the birth of their second and presumed last child—in the hope of providing a compatible bone marrow donor for their leukemia-stricken daughter. Although the child did prove to be a compatible donor, they had no guarantee of success. With the availability of cloning, parents in similar situations could be certain of success, since the clone would be an exact genetic match of the recipient. Then there are those couples who have lost a child in a car accident, say, and want their next child to be as much like the first as possible—a later identical twin of the lost child—or couples who may want a later identical twin of someone else dear to them, such as a parent, a grandparent, or a sibling.

Still other reasons have been given for wanting to clone human beings, some more or less fanciful than others. We may want to pass on specific traits of specific people with the hope of producing another Jordan, Mozart, Gandhi, or Martin Luther King. Or vanity may be a factor in the case of people who want to see a world inhabited by genetic copies of themselves. In other cases, the motivation may be curiosity. How, some may wonder, would they (or some other individual) have turned out if born and reared in another time and environment? Pushing this kind of reasoning even further, we can imagine scientists who specialize in twin research wanting to create clones as subjects in controlled experiments.

MORAL AND LEGAL ISSUES

No doubt many of you find yourselves uncomfortable with at least some of these possibilities, maybe even repulsed by them. And in some cases, the discomfort is fully justified. Consider the last possibility we mentioned, creating clones for experimentation. Given that human clones would have claim to all the rights of any other human being, it would clearly be immoral to experiment on them without their consent. But what about the moral status of human cloning itself?

Perhaps the most important question to ask here is whether people have the moral and legal right to reproduce by any safe means available, including cloning, which may be considered a form of asexual reproduction. Do we have a fundamental right to choose whether and how to reproduce? Notwithstanding the importance of this question, how we answer it will not settle the matter by itself. Even our most fundamental rights are not absolute. Some other factor may override them. That's why we have libel laws, for example, which limit our fundamental right to free expression. Furthermore, someone might grant that we do have a fundamental right to reproduce but deny that cloning is a form of reproduction. Many critics of human cloning say just that. To them, cloning is better described as replication or manufacturing, and they insist that we do not have a right to manufacture human beings.

What if we decide that reproduction is not a fundamental right? We might still say that our general right to freedom allows us the right to take advantage of human cloning. After all, we claim all sorts of rights that are not fundamental as long as there's no rational basis for restricting them. For example, no one would claim a fundamental right to wear socks of a particular color, but what rational basis could there be for banning brown, blue, or white socks?

Other moral issues concern the possible psychological effects of human cloning. Various commentators have wondered how the later twin will feel about his or her worth and future. Will clones feel that their right to their own identity has been infringed upon? Will they feel that their futures are foreclosed, that the limitations they see in their earlier twins, whether physical or mental, unfairly narrow their own choices in life? Will they wonder if they are loved for themselves instead of being valued as a copy of someone else, that they are merely replacements for the previous twins who were really loved? And at least in the earliest cases of human clones, will they feel like freaks?

These questions concern the psychological effects on the later twins. Other questions concern the effects on humanity as a whole. How will the availability of cloning affect humankind's understanding of itself? Will we come to see people as fundamentally different once we know they can be manufactured as well as sexually conceived? Will our view of the role that sex plays in our lives fundamentally change? Will we no longer view individual humans as unique and irreplaceable?

Beyond all that, there are more practical concerns. If, for example, cloning becomes prevalent, what will that do to the genetic diversity of the human species? Or for another example, what if scientists make multiple clones of a great artist, scientist, or moral or political leader? Do we really want some "mad Xeroxer" to produce a run of thirty or more Mozarts, Einsteins, or Kings? Or to return to the fears raised by *The Boys from Brazil,* a run of thirty or more Hitlers?

Another practical issue concerns family relationships. If a woman bears her husband's clone, is he the father to the son she bears, his twin brother, or is he both? And is she both the mother of her child and his sister-in-law? Or suppose instead that she bears her own clone. Is she both mother and twin sister to the child? Then there are cases in which the cell donor is a third party—a relative, say, or some unrelated genius. As an earlier twin, would he or she be the clone's sibling? Related to these questions are questions of legal rights and responsibilities. If the donor is a third party, what responsibilities does he have for his later twin? And what rightful claims does the clone have against his earlier twin?

These last questions raise another concern about human cloning. Once cloning is made available, it will be easy to clone humans without their consent. All it will take is one stray cell, easily obtainable without the person's knowledge or consent. Many of us, presumably, will not want to be cloned. Do we have the right not to be? And if so, how can the right be enforced?

Still other moral issues are familiar from debates surrounding other topics in this book. Just as critics of homosexuality argue that homosexual behavior is immoral because it's unnatural, many opponents of human cloning claim the same about it. Unlike other forms of reproductive technology, such as in vitro fertilization, cloning takes us out of the realm of sex altogether, and that difference, opponents say, presents a fundamental break with natural reproduction. Two other issues arise from the abortion debates. To those who feel that a human embryo is a person, a morally significant being with the right to life, creating a human embryo for scientific research or the generation of organs for transplant is every bit as wrong as abortion. In both cases, they say, a human life is being destroyed. Cloning proponents, on the other hand, argue that the constitutional right to privacy comes into play here. Just as a woman's right to privacy guarantees her right to terminate a pregnancy, so does it guarantee her the right to reproduce by cloning.

ARGUMENTS AGAINST HUMAN CLONING

1. *Cloning is unfair to the clone.*

POINT: "Imagine what it would be like to be a clone, especially if the person you were cloned from were still alive. Your whole life would be laid out before you. You'd be able to see yourself as an adult, what you'll look like, what you'll be capable of doing and won't be capable of doing, the aches and pains and diseases you'll suffer from, the personality quirks you and others will have to put up with. And you'd know you could never grow up to be all sorts of things you might want to be because you'd see that the person you were cloned from is not capable of any of them. And that's just not fair to the clone. Every human being has a right to an open future."

COUNTERPOINT: "Sorry, but I don't see any unfairness here. First of all, we'd be two different people, just as identical twins are two different people. Genetic makeup isn't everything, you know. How we age, what abilities we have, our health and our personalities depend as much on our environment and choices as they do on our genes. Second, if there are some biological limits on what I can be and do in life, then I might as well know about them in advance. Self-knowledge is good, right? Then why not have it as soon as I can?"

2. *Cloning is dangerous.*

POINT: "But what about the dangers of cloning? If there were ever something open to the worst kinds of abuse, this is it. Think about some mad scientist intent on producing an army of clones of some ruthless killer or some other mad scientist producing a bunch of human research subjects. And think about all the people who'd be tempted to clone themselves for all the wrong reasons—out of vanity, maybe, or the desire for spare parts. And even without the abuses, there's a host of other dangers. Most important, the more popular cloning becomes, the more we'll have clones of clones of clones of clones, and once that happens, the human race will lose much of its genetic diversity. We'll be like those interbred strains of lab mice used for medical experiments."

COUNTERPOINT: "You can make up horror stories about any new technology, but that doesn't mean they'll come true. And as for people cloning themselves for the wrong reasons, so what? People have children the old-fashioned way for all sorts of reasons, many of them selfish, and nobody's trying to put an end to that. And you can't really believe cloning will come even close to driving out the old-fashioned way of making babies. People *like* the old-fashioned way. I can't imagine them giving it up. Cloning will be like all the other forms of reproductive technology—there for people who need it, but not a replacement for normal sexual reproduction."

3. *Cloning is repugnant.*

POINT: "Doesn't the idea of human cloning make you even just a little bit sick? It should, because it's repugnant, unnatural, disgusting. What we're talking about here is children with only one biological parent, children being the genetic twins of one of their parents or maybe even some stranger, children created not by a sperm and an egg but by a cheek cell nucleus and an egg. That's just not the way things ought to be."

COUNTERPOINT: "Maybe you find it repugnant, but I don't. A clone is nothing but a later identical twin, and there's nothing repugnant about it. Besides, your repugnance is morally irrelevant in any case. Personally, I find a lot of things repugnant—certain kinds of movies and music, for example—but that doesn't give me the right to deny them to others."

ARGUMENTS FOR HUMAN CLONING

1. *People have a right to reproduce.*

POINT: "Both morally and legally, we have the right to reproduce. Except under the most extreme situations, you wouldn't countenance forced sterilization, would you? Of course not. Nor would you countenance forced abortion, or deny sperm donorship to a woman married to an infertile man, or the opportunity to find a surrogate mother for a woman who can't bear a child herself. So how can you deny anyone the option of cloning, which is just another form of reproductive technology?"

COUNTERPOINT: "Cloning is not just another form of reproductive technology. In fact, it's not reproduction at all, but a means of manufacturing humans, even of mass manufacturing them. No one has the right to do that. And even if you could convince me that cloning is a form of reproduction, I'd still say it's wrong because of the dangers it poses to both the clone and society."

2. *Cloning offers many benefits to individuals.*

POINT: "First of all, you're wrong about the dangers. But even more important, you're ignoring all the benefits cloning offers—to infertile couples, couples in which both the man and the woman carry a recessive gene for the same illness, and to gay couples too, and to couples who have lost a child and would dearly love its identical twin. Not only that, but cloning can also guarantee successful matches for life-saving transplants. How can anyone be against that?"

COUNTERPOINT: "There are alternatives to cloning, you know—sperm donorship, surrogate motherhood, adoption. Nobody has to resort to cloning to have a child. And even the last benefit you mentioned, cloning to ensure successful matches for transplants, won't be necessary. Scientists are already at work on using cloning technology to generate organs without having to bring the embryo to term, and it won't be long before they're successful. As for cloning a dead child, that's just sick. It's one thing to want another one, but to manufacture an exact replica of the dead one? How do you think the clone would feel about that?"

3. *Cloning offers many benefits to society.*

POINT: "But what about the benefits to society? I'm thinking about two in particular. First, think of all we can learn about the respective contributions of our genes and environment to our personalities, intelligence, and skills. Research on identical twins has been of some help here, but there just aren't that many of them, and cloning can give us more twins to study. Second, there are the advantages we can get by cloning great people from a variety of fields—scientists, political leaders, artists, athletes. Wouldn't it be great to have clones of Jonas Salk working on vaccines for diseases like AIDS?"

COUNTERPOINT: "Now you're getting into *Brave New World* territory, manufacturing people to serve some preset purpose or other—scientific research or the mass production of great people. Besides, you already admitted that our choices and the environment play a big role in shaping who we are. What makes you think a Salk clone would have any interest in searching for an AIDS vaccine?"

The Wisdom of Repugnance

Leon R. Kass

Leon R. Kass was appointed chairman of the President's Council on Bioethics by President George W. Bush in 2001. In this excerpt from a longer essay, Kass lays out a broad case against human cloning and calls for an absolute ban on it. Taking his cue from the repugnance that many people feel at the prospect of making exact human genetic copies, he argues that this repugnance reveals the deeper immorality of the technology: its violation of human individuality, its transformation of the role that sex plays in our lives, its confounding of family relationships and their moral ties, and its transformation of "begetting" into "making."

In arguing his case, Kass criticizes three perspectives on cloning that its proponents have taken. The first, the technological perspective, sees cloning as a harmless extension of current reproductive technologies. The second, the liberal perspective, sees cloning in the context of human rights and liberties. The third, the meliorist perspective, sees cloning as a way to improve human beings through advances in health and the elimination of genetic defects. All three, he argues, neglect the profound differences that the availability of cloning would bring about.

Offensive, grotesque, revolting, repugnant, and *repulsive*—those are the words most commonly heard regarding the prospect of human cloning. Such reactions come both from the man or woman in the street and from the intellectuals, from believers and atheists, from humanists and scientists. Even Dolly's creator has said he "would find it offensive" to clone a human being.

People are repelled by many aspects of human cloning. They recoil from the prospect of mass production of human beings, with large clones of look-alikes, compromised in their individuality; the idea of father-son or mother-daughter twins; the bizarre prospects of a woman's giving birth to and rearing a genetic copy of herself, her spouse, or even her deceased father or mother; the grotesqueness of conceiving a child as an exact replacement for another who has died; the utilitarian creation of embryonic genetic duplicates of oneself, to be frozen away or created when necessary, in case of need for homologous tissues or organs for transplantation; the narcissism of those who would clone themselves and the arrogance of others who think they know who deserves to be cloned or which genotype any child-to-be should be thrilled to receive; the Frankensteinian hubris to create human life and increasingly to control its destiny; man playing God. Almost no one finds any of the suggested reasons for human cloning compelling; almost everyone anticipates its possible misuses and abuses. Moreover, many people feel oppressed by the sense that there is probably nothing we can do to prevent it from happening. That makes the prospect all the more revolting.

From Leon R. Kass, "The Wisdom of Repugnance," from Leon R. Kass and James Q. Wilson, *The Ethics of Human Cloning*, pp. 17–59. Reprinted with the permission of the American Enterprise Institute for Public Policy Research, Washington, D.C.

Revulsion is not an argument; and some of yesterday's repugnances are today calmly accepted—though, one must add, not always for the better. In crucial cases, however, repugnance is the emotional expression of deep wisdom, beyond reason's power fully to articulate it. Can anyone really give an argument fully adequate to the horror which is father-daughter incest (even with consent), or having sex with animals, or mutilating a corpse, or eating human flesh, or raping or murdering another human being? Would anybody's failure to give full rational justification for his revulsion at those practices make that revulsion ethically suspect? Not at all. On the contrary, we are suspicious of those who think that they can rationalize away our horror, say, by trying to explain the enormity of incest with arguments only about the genetic risks of inbreeding.

The repugnance at human cloning belongs in that category. We are repelled by the prospect of cloning human beings not because of the strangeness or novelty of the undertaking, but because we intuit and feel, immediately and without argument, the violation of things that we rightfully hold dear. Repugnance, here as elsewhere, revolts against the excesses of human willfulness, warning us not to transgress what is unspeakably profound. Indeed, in this age in which everything is held to be permissible so long as it is freely done, in which our given human nature no longer commands respect, in which our bodies are regarded as mere instruments of our autonomous rational wills, repugnance may be the only voice left that speaks up to defend the central core of our humanity. Shallow are the souls that have forgotten how to shudder.

The goods protected by repugnance are generally overlooked by our customary ways of approaching all new biomedical technologies. The way we evaluate cloning ethically will in fact be shaped by how we characterize it descriptively, by the context into which we place it, and by the perspective from which we view it. The first task for ethics is proper description. And here is where our failure begins.

Typically, cloning is discussed in one or more of three familiar contexts, which one might call the technological, the liberal, and the meliorist. Under the first, cloning will be seen as an extension of existing techniques for assisting reproduction and determining the genetic makeup of children. Like them, cloning is to be regarded as a neutral technique, with no inherent meaning or goodness, but subject to multiple uses, some good, some bad. The morality of cloning thus depends absolutely on the goodness or badness of the motives and intentions of the cloners. As one bioethicist defender of cloning puts it, "The ethics must be judged [only] by the way the parents nurture and rear their resulting child and whether they bestow the same love and affection on a child brought into existence by a technique of assisted reproduction as they would on a child born in the usual way."

The liberal (or libertarian or liberationist) perspective sets cloning in the context of rights, freedoms, and personal empowerment. Cloning is just a new option for exercising an individual's right to reproduce or to have the kind of child that he wants. Alternatively, cloning enhances our liberation (especially women's liberation) from the confines of nature, the vagaries of chance, or the necessity for sexual mating. Indeed, it liberates women from the need for men altogether, for the process requires only eggs, nuclei, and (for the time being) uteri—plus, of course, a healthy dose of our (allegedly "masculine") manipulative science that likes to do all those things to mother nature and nature's mothers. For those who hold this outlook, the only moral restraints on cloning are adequately informed consent and the avoidance of bodily harm. If no one is cloned without her consent, and if the clonant is not physically damaged, then the liberal conditions for licit, hence moral, conduct are met. Worries that go beyond violating the will or maiming the body are dismissed as "symbolic"—which is to say, unreal.

The meliorist perspective embraces valetudinarians and also eugenicists. The latter were formerly more vocal in those discussions, but they are now generally happy to see their goals advanced under the less threatening banners of freedom and technological growth. These people see in cloning a new prospect for improving human beings—minimally, by ensuring the perpetuation of healthy individuals by avoiding the risks of genetic disease inherent in the lottery of sex, and maximally, by producing "optimum babies," preserving outstanding genetic material, and (with the help of soon-to-come techniques for precise genetic engineering) enhancing inborn human capacities on many fronts. Here the morality of cloning as a means is justified solely by the excellence of the end, that is, by the outstanding traits of individuals cloned—beauty, or brawn, or brains.

These three approaches, all quintessentially American and all perfectly fine in their places, are sorely wanting as approaches to human procreation. It is, to say the least, grossly distorting to view the wondrous mysteries of birth, renewal, and individuality, and the deep meaning of parent-child relations, largely through the lens of our reductive science and its potent technologies. Similarly, considering reproduction (and the intimate relation of family life!) primarily under the political-legal, adversarial, and individualistic notion of rights can only undermine the private yet fundamentally social, cooperative, and duty-laden character of child-bearing, child-rearing, and their bond to the covenant of marriage. Seeking to escape entirely from nature (to satisfy a natural desire or a natural right to reproduce!) is self-contradictory in theory and self-alienating in practice. For we are erotic beings only because we are embodied beings and not merely intellects and wills unfortunately imprisoned in our bodies. And, though health and fitness are clearly great goods, there is something deeply disquieting in looking on our prospective children as artful products perfectible by genetic engineering, increasingly held to our willfully imposed designs, specifications, and margins of tolerable error.

The technical, liberal, and meliorist approaches all ignore the deeper anthropological, social, and indeed, ontological meanings of bringing forth a new life. To this more fitting and profound point of view cloning shows itself to be a major violation of our given nature as embodied, gendered, and engendering beings—and of the social relations built on this natural ground. Once this perspective is recognized, the ethical judgment on cloning can no longer be reduced to a matter of motives and intentions, rights and freedoms, benefits and harms, or even means and ends. It must be regarded primarily as a matter of meaning: Is cloning a fulfillment of human begetting and belonging? Or is cloning rather, as I contend, their pollution and perversion? To pollution and perversion the fitting response can only be horror and revulsion; and conversely, generalized horror and revulsion are prima facie evidence of foulness and violation. The burden of

moral argument must fall entirely on those who want to declare the widespread repugnances of humankind to be mere timidity or superstition.

Yet repugnance need not stand naked before the bar of reason. The wisdom of our horror at human cloning can be partially articulated, even if this is finally one of those instances about which the heart has its reasons that reason cannot entirely know.

THE PROFUNDITY OF SEX

To see cloning in its proper context, we must begin not, as I did before, with laboratory technique, but with the anthropology—natural and social—of sexual reproduction.

Sexual reproduction—by which I mean the generation of new life from (exactly) two complementary elements, one female, one male, (usually) through coitus—is established (if that is the right term) not by human decision, culture, or tradition, but by nature; it is the natural way of all mammalian reproduction. By nature, each child has two complementary biological progenitors. Each child thus stems from and unites exactly two lineages. In natural generation, moreover, the precise genetic constitution of the resulting offspring is determined by a combination of nature and chance, not by human design: each human child shares the common natural human species genotype, each child is genetically (equally) kin to each (both) parent(s), yet each child is also genetically unique.

Those biological truths about our origins foretell deep truths about our identity and about our human condition altogether. Every one of us is at once equally human, equally enmeshed in a particular familial nexus of origin, and equally individuated in our trajectory from birth to death—and, if all goes well, equally capable (despite our mortality) of participating, with a complementary other, in the very same renewal of such human possibility through procreation. Though less momentous than our common humanity, our genetic individuality is not humanly trivial. It shows itself forth in our distinctive appearance through which we are everywhere recognized; it is revealed in our "signature" marks of fingerprints and our self-recognizing immune system; it symbolizes and foreshadows exactly the unique, never-to-be repeated character of each human life.

Human societies virtually everywhere have structured child-rearing responsibilities and systems of identity and relationship on the bases of those deep natural facts of begetting. The mysterious yet ubiquitous "love of one's own" is everywhere culturally exploited, to make sure that children are not just produced but well cared for and to create for everyone clear ties of meaning, belonging, and obligation. But it is wrong to treat such naturally rooted social practices as mere cultural constructs (like left- or right-driving, or like burying or cremating the dead) that we can alter with little human cost. What would kinship be without its clear natural grounding? And what would identity be without kinship? We must resist those who have begun to refer to sexual reproduction as the "traditional method of reproduction," who would have us regard as merely traditional, and by implication arbitrary, what is in truth not only natural but most certainly profound.

Asexual reproduction which produces "single-parent" offspring, is a radical departure from the natural human way, confounding all normal understandings of father, mother, sibling, and grandparent and all moral relations tied thereto. It becomes even more of a radical departure when the resulting offspring is a clone derived not from an embryo, but from a mature adult to whom the clone would be an identical twin; and when the process occurs not by natural accident (as in natural twinning), but by deliberate human design and manipulations; and when the child's (or children's) genetic constitution is preselected by the parent(s) (or scientists). Accordingly, as we shall see, cloning is vulnerable to three kinds of concerns and objections, related to these three points: cloning threatens confusion of identity and individuality, even in small-scale cloning; cloning represents a giant step (though not the first one) toward transforming procreation into manufacture, that is, toward the increasing depersonalization of the process of generation and, increasingly, toward the "production" of human children as artifacts, products of human will and design (what others have called the problem of "commodification " of new life); and cloning—like other forms of eugenic engineering of the next generation—represents a form of despotism of the cloners over the cloned, and thus (even in benevolent cases) represents a blatant violation of the

inner meaning of parent-child relations, of what it means to have a child, of what it means to say yes to our own demise and "replacement."

Before turning to those specific ethical objections, let me test my claim of the profundity of the natural way by taking up a challenge recently posed by a friend. What if the given natural human way of reproduction were asexual, and we now had to deal with a new technological innovation—artificially induced sexual dimorphism and the fusing of complementary gametes—whose inventors argued that sexual reproduction promised all sorts of advantages, including hybrid vigor and the creation of greatly increased individuality? Would one then be forced to defend natural asexuality because it was natural? Could one claim that it carried deep human meaning?

The response to that challenge broaches the ontological meaning of sexual reproduction. For it is impossible, I submit, for there to have been human life—or even higher forms of animal life—in the absence of sexuality and sexual reproduction. We find asexual reproduction only in the lowest forms of life; bacteria, algae, fungi, some lower invertebrates. Sexuality brings with it a new and enriched relationship to the world. Only sexual animals can seek and find complementary others with whom to pursue a goal that transcends their own existence. For a sexual being, the world is no longer an indifferent and largely homogeneous *otherness,* in part edible, in part dangerous. It also contains some very special and related and complementary beings, of the same kind but of opposite sex, toward whom one reaches out with special interest and intensity. In higher birds and mammals, the outward gaze keeps a lookout not only for food and predators, but also for prospective mates; the beholding of the many-splendored world is suffused with desire for union—the animal antecedent of human eros and the germ of sociality. Not by accident is the human animal both the sexiest animal—whose females do not go into heat but are receptive throughout the estrous cycle and whose males must therefore have greater sexual appetite and energy to reproduce successfully—and also the most aspiring, the most social, the most open, and the most intelligent animal.

The soul-elevating power of sexuality is, at bottom, rooted in its strange connection to mortality, which it simultaneously accepts and tries to overcome. Asexual reproduction may be seen as a continuation of the activity of self-preservation. When one organism buds or divides to become two, the original being is (doubly) preserved, and nothing dies. Sexuality, by contrast, means perishability and serves replacement; the two that come together to generate one soon will die. Sexual desire, in human beings as in animals, thus serves an end that is partly hidden from, and finally at odds with, the self-serving individual. Whether we know it or not, when we are sexually active we are voting with our genitalia for our own demise. The salmon swimming upstream to spawn and die tell the universal story: sex is bound up with death, to which it holds a partial answer in procreation.

The salmon and the other animals evince that truth blindly. Only the human being can understand what it means. As we learn so powerfully from the story of the Garden of Eden, our humanization is coincident with sexual self-consciousness, with the recognition of our sexual nakedness and all that it implies: shame at our needy incompleteness, unruly self-division, and finitude; awe before the eternal; hope in the self-transcending possibilities of children and a relationship to the divine. In the sexually self-conscious animal, sexual desire can become eros, lust can become love. Sexual desire humanly regarded is thus sublimated into erotic longing for wholeness, completion, and immortality, which drives us knowingly into the embrace and its generative fruit—as well as into all the higher human possibilities of deed, speech, and song.

Through children, a good common to both husband and wife, male and female achieve some genuine unification (beyond the mere sexual "union," which fails to do so). The two become one through sharing generous (not needy) love for that third being as good. Flesh of their flesh, the child is the parents' own commingled being externalized and given a separate and persisting existence. Unification is enhanced also by their commingled work of rearing. Providing an opening to the future beyond the grave, carrying not only our seed but also our names, our ways, and our hopes that they will surpass us in goodness and happiness, children are a testament to the possibility of transcendence. Gender duality and sexual

desire, which first draws our love upward and outside of ourselves, finally provide for the partial overcoming of the confinement and limitation of perishable embodiment altogether.

Human procreation, in sum, is not simply an activity of our rational wills. It is a more complete activity precisely because it engages us bodily, erotically, and spiritually as well as rationally. There is wisdom in the mystery of nature that has joined the pleasure of sex, the inarticulate longing for union, the communication of the loving embrace, and the deep-seated and only partly articulate desire for children in the very activity by which we continue the chain of human existence and participate in the renewal of human possibility. Whether or not we know it, the severing of procreation from sex, love, and intimacy is inherently dehumanizing, no matter how good the product.

We are now ready for the more specific objections to cloning.

THE PERVERSITIES OF CLONING

First, an important if formal objection: Any attempt to clone a human being would constitute an unethical experiment upon the resulting child-to-be. As the animal experiments (frog and sheep) indicate, there are grave risks of mishaps and deformities. Moreover, because of what cloning means, one cannot presume a future cloned child's consent to be a clone, even a healthy one. Thus, ethically speaking, we cannot even get to know whether or not human cloning is feasible.

I understand, of course, the philosophical difficulty of trying to compare a life with defects against nonexistence. Several bioethicists, proud of their philosophical cleverness, use that conundrum to embarrass claims that one can injure a child in its conception, precisely because it is only thanks to that complained-of conception that the child is alive to complain. But common sense tells us that we have no reason to fear such philosophisms. For we surely know that people can harm and even maim children in the very act of conceiving them, say, by paternal transmission of the AIDS virus, maternal transmission of heroin dependence, or, arguably, even by bringing them into being as bastards or with no capacity or willingness to look after them properly. And we believe that to do that intentionally, or even negligently, is inexcusable and clearly unethical.

The objection about the impossibility of presuming consent may even go beyond the obvious and sufficient point that a clonant, were he subsequently to be asked, could rightly resent having been made a clone. At issue are not just benefits and harms, but doubts about the very independence needed to give proper (even retroactive) consent, that is, not just the capacity to choose but the disposition and ability to choose freely and well. It is not at all clear to what extent a clone will fully be a moral agent. For, as we shall see, in the very fact of cloning, and especially of rearing him *as a clone,* his makers subvert the cloned child's independence, beginning with that aspect that comes from knowing that one was an unbidden surprise, a gift, to the world, rather than the designed result of someone's artful project.

Cloning creates serious issues of identity and individuality. The cloned person may experience concerns about his distinctive identity not only because he will be in genotype and appearance identical to another human being, but, in this case, because he may also be twin to the person who is his "father" or "mother"—if one can still call them that. What would be the psychic burdens of being the "child" or "parent" of your twin? The cloned individual, moreover, will be saddled with a genotype that has already lived. He will not be fully a surprise to the world. People are likely always to compare his performance in life with that of his alter ego. True, his nurture and his circumstance in life will be different; genotype is not exactly destiny. Still, one must also expect parental and other efforts to shape that new life after the original—or at least to view the child with the original version always firmly in mind. Why else did they clone from the star basketball player, mathematician, and beauty queen—or even dear old dad—in the first place?

Since the birth of Dolly, there has been a fair amount of doublespeak on the matter of genetic identity. Experts have rushed in to reassure the public that the clone would in no way be the same person or have any confusions about his identity: as previously noted, they are pleased to point out that the clone of Mel Gibson would not be Mel Gibson. Fair enough. But one is shortchanging the truth by emphasizing the additional importance of the intrauterine environment, rearing, and social setting: genotype obviously matters plenty. That, after all, is the only reason to clone, whether human beings or sheep. The odds that clones of Wilt Chamberlain will play in the NBA are, I submit, infinitely greater than they are for clones of Robert Reich.

Curiously, this conclusion is supported, inadvertently, by the one ethical sticking point insisted on by friends of cloning: no cloning without the donor's consent. Though an orthodox liberal objection, it is in fact quite puzzling when it comes from people (such as Ruth Macklin) who also insist that genotype is not identity or individuality and who deny that a child could reasonably complain about being made a genetic copy. If the clone of Mel Gibson would not be Mel Gibson, why should Mel Gibson have grounds to object that someone had been made his clone? We already allow researchers to use blood and tissue samples for research purposes of no benefit to their sources: my falling hair, my expectorations, my urine, and even my biopsied tissues are "not me" and not mine. Courts have held that the profit gained from uses to which scientists put my discarded tissues do not legally belong to me. Why, then, no cloning without consent—including, I assume, no cloning from the body of someone who just died? What harm is done the donor, if genotype is "not me"? Truth to tell, the only powerful justification for objecting is that genotype really does have something to do with identity, and everybody knows it. If not, on what basis could Michael Jordan object that someone cloned "him," say, from cells taken from a "lost" scraped-off piece of his skin? The insistence on donor consent unwittingly reveals the problem of identity in all cloning.

Genetic distinctiveness not only symbolizes the uniqueness of each human life and the independence of its parents that each human child rightfully attains. It can also be an important support for living a worthy and dignified life. Such arguments apply with great force to any large-scale replication of human individuals. But they are sufficient, in my view, to rebut even the first attempts to clone a human being. One must never forget that these are human beings upon whom our eugenic or merely playful fantasies are to be enacted.

Troubled psychic identity (distinctiveness), based on all-too-evident genetic identity (sameness), will be made much worse by the utter confusion of social identity and kinship ties. For, as already noted, cloning radically confounds lineage and social relations, for "offspring" as for "parents." As bioethicist James Nelson has pointed out, a female child cloned from her "mother" might develop a desire for a relationship to her "father" and might understandably seek out the father of her "mother," who is after all also her biological twin sister. Would "grandpa," who thought his paternal duties concluded, be pleased to discover that the clonant looked to him for paternal attention and support?

Social identity and social ties of relationship and responsibility are widely connected to, and supported by, biological kinship. Social taboos on incest (and adultery) everywhere serve to keep clear who is related to whom (and especially which child belongs to which parents), as well as to avoid confounding the social identity of parent-and-child (or brother-and-sister) with the social identity of lovers, spouses, and coparents. True, social identity is altered by adoption (but as a matter of the best interest of already living children: we do not deliberately produce children for adoption). True, artificial insemination and in vitro fertilization with donor sperm, or whole embryo donation, are in some way forms of "prenatal adoption"—a not altogether unproblematic practice. Even here, though, there is in each case (as in all sexual reproduction) a known male source of sperm and a known single female source of egg—a genetic father and a genetic mother—should anyone care to know (as adopted children often do) who is genetically related to whom.

In the case of cloning, however, there is but one "parent." The usually sad situation of the "single-parent child" is here deliberately planned, and with a vengeance. In the case of self-cloning, the "offspring" is, in addition, one's twin; and so the dreaded result of incest—to be parent to one's sibling—is here brought about deliberately, albeit without any act of coitus. Moreover, all other relationships will be confounded. What will *father, grandfather, aunt, cousin,* and *sister* mean? Who will bear what ties and what burdens? What sort of social identity will someone have with one whole side—"father's" or "mother's"—necessarily excluded? It is no answer to say that our society, with its high incidence of divorce, remarriage, adoption, extramarital childbearing, and the rest, already confounds lineage and confuses kinship and responsibility for children (and everyone else), unless one also wants to argue that this is, for children, a preferable state of affairs.

Human cloning would also represent a giant step toward turning begetting into making, procreation into manufacture (literally, something "handmade"), a process already begun with in vitro fertilization and genetic testing of embryos. With cloning, not only is the process in hand, but the total genetic blueprint of the cloned individual is selected and determined by the human artisans. To be sure, subsequent development will take place according to natural processes; and the resulting children will still be recognizably human. But we here would be taking a major step into making man himself simply another one of the man-made things. Human nature becomes merely the last part of nature to succumb to the technological project, which turns all of nature into raw material at human disposal, to be homogenized by our rationalized technique according to the subjective prejudices of the day.

How does begetting differ from making? In natural procreation, human beings come together, complementarily male and female, to give existence to another being who is formed, exactly as we were, *by what we are:* living, hence perishable, hence aspiringly erotic, human beings. In clonal reproduction, by contrast, and in the more advanced forms of manufacture to which it leads, we give existence to a being not by what we are but by what we intend and design. As with any product of our making, no matter how excellent, the artificer stands above it, not as an equal but as a superior, transcending it by his will and creative prowess. Scientists who clone animals make it perfectly clear that they are engaged in instrumental making; the animals are, from the start, designed as means to serve rational human purposes. In human cloning scientists and prospective "parents" would be adopting the same technocratic mentality to human children: human children would be their artifacts.

Such an arrangement is profoundly dehumanizing, no matter how good the product. Mass-scale cloning of the same individual makes the point vividly; but the violation of human equality, freedom, and dignity is present even in a single planned clone. And procreation dehumanized into manufacture is further degraded by commodification, a virtually inescapable result of allowing baby-making to proceed under the banner of commerce. Genetic and reproductive biotechnology companies are already growth industries, but they will go into commercial orbit once the Human Genome Project nears completion. Supply will create enormous demand. Even before the capacity for human cloning arrives, established companies will have invested in the harvesting of eggs from ovaries obtained at autopsy or through ovarian surgery, practiced embryonic genetic alteration, and initiated the stockpiling of prospective donor tissues. Through the rental of surrogate-womb services and through the buying and selling of tissues and embryos, priced according to the merit of the donor, the commodification of nascent human life will be unstoppable.

Finally, and perhaps most important, the practice of human cloning by nuclear transfer—like other anticipated forms of genetic engineering of the next generation—would enshrine and aggravate a profound and mischievous misunderstanding of the meaning of having children and of the parent-child relationship. When a couple now chooses to procreate, the partners are saying yes to the emergence of new life in its novelty, saying yes not only to having a child but also, tacitly, to having whatever child the child turns out to be. In accepting our finitude and opening ourselves to our replacement, we are tacitly confessing the limits of our control. In this ubiquitous way of nature, embracing the future by procreating means precisely that we are relinquishing our grip, in the very activity of taking up our own share in what we hope will be the immortality of human life and the human species. This means that our children are not *our* children: they are not our property, not our possessions. Neither are they supposed to live our lives for us, or anyone else's life but their own. To be sure, we seek to guide them on their way, imparting to them not just life but nurturing, love, and a way of life; to be sure, they bear our hopes that they will live fine and flourishing lives, enabling us in small measure to transcend our own limitations. Still, their genetic distinctiveness and independence are the natural foreshadowing of the deep truth that they have their own and never-before-enacted life to

live. They are sprung from a past, but they take an uncharted course into the future.

Much harm is already done by parents who try to live vicariously through their children. Children are sometimes compelled to fulfill the broken dreams of unhappy parents; John Doe, Jr., or John Doe III is under the burden of having to live up to his forebear's name. Still, if most parents have hopes for their children, cloning parents will have expectations. In cloning, such overbearing parents take at the start a decisive step that contradicts the entire meaning of the open and forward-looking nature of parent-child relations. The child is given a genotype that has already lived, with full expectation that the blueprint of a past life ought to be controlling of the life that is to come. Cloning is inherently despotic, for it seeks to make one's children (or someone else's children) after one's own image (or an image of one's choosing) and their future according to one's will. In some cases the despotism may be mild and benevolent. In other cases it will be mischievous and downright tyrannical. But despotism—the control of another through one's will—it inevitably will be.

MEETING SOME OBJECTIONS

The defenders of cloning, of course, are not wittingly friends of despotism. Indeed, they regard themselves mainly as friends of freedom: the freedom of individuals to reproduce, the freedom of scientists and inventors to discover and devise and to foster "progress" in genetic knowledge and technique. They want large-scale cloning only for animals, but they wish to preserve cloning as a human option for exercising our "right to reproduce"—our right to have children, and children with" desirable genes." As law professor John Robertson points out, under our "right to reproduce" we already practice early forms of unnatural, artificial, and extramarital reproduction, and we already practice early forms of eugenic choice. For that reason, he argues, cloning is no big deal.

We have here a perfect example of the logic of the slippery slope, and the slippery way in which it already works in that area. Only a few years ago, slippery-slope arguments were advanced to oppose artificial insemination and in vitro fertilization using unrelated sperm donors. Principles used to justify those practices, it was said, will be used to justify more artificial and more eugenic practices, including cloning. Not so, the defenders retorted, since we can make the necessary distinctions. And now, without even a gesture at making the necessary distinctions, the continuity of practice is held by itself to be justificatory.

The principle of reproductive freedom as currently enunciated by the proponents of cloning logically embraces the ethical acceptability of sliding down the entire rest of the slope—to producing children ectogenetically from sperm to term (should it become feasible) and to producing children whose entire genetic makeup will be the product of parental eugenic planning and choice. If reproductive freedom means the right to have a child of one's own choosing, by whatever means, it knows and accepts no limits.

But, far from being legitimated by a "right to reproduce," the emergence of techniques of assisted reproduction and genetic engineering should compel us to reconsider the meaning and limits of such a putative right. In truth, a "right to reproduce" has always been a peculiar and problematic notion. Rights generally belong to individuals, but this is a right that (before cloning) no one can exercise alone. Does the right then inhere only in couples? Only in married couples? Is it a (woman's) right to carry or deliver or a right (of one or more parents) to nurture and rear? Is it a right to have your own biological child? Is it a right only to attempt reproduction or a right also to succeed? Is it a right to acquire the baby of one's choice?

The assertion of a negative "right to reproduce" certainly makes sense when it claims protection against state interference with procreative liberty, say, through a program of compulsory sterilization. But surely it cannot be the basis of a tort claim against nature, to be made good by technology, should free efforts at natural procreation fail. Some insist that the right to reproduce embraces also the right against state interference with the free use of all technological means to obtain a child. Yet such a position cannot be sustained: for reasons having to do with the means employed, any community may rightfully prohibit surrogate pregnancy, polygamy, or the sale of babies to infertile couples without violating anyone's basic human "right to reproduce." When the exercise of a previously innocuous freedom now involves or impinges on troublesome practices that the original freedom never was intended to reach, the general presumption of liberty needs to be reconsidered.

We do indeed already practice negative eugenic selection, through genetic screening and prenatal diagnosis. Yet our practices are governed by a norm of health. We seek to prevent the birth of children who suffer from known (serious) genetic diseases. When and if gene therapy becomes possible, such diseases could then be treated, in utero or even before implantation. I have no ethical objection in principle to such a practice (though I have some practical worries), precisely because it serves the medical goal of healing existing individuals. But therapy, to be therapy, implies not only an existing "patient." It also implies a norm of health. In this respect, even germline gene "therapy," though practiced not on a human being but on egg and sperm, is less radical than cloning, which is in no way therapeutic. But once one blurs the distinction between health promotion and genetic enhancement, between so-called negative and positive eugenics, one opens the door to all future eugenic designs. "To make sure that a child will be healthy and have good chances in life": that is Robertson's principle, and, owing to its latter clause, it is an utterly elastic principle, with no boundaries. Being over eight feet tall will likely produce some very good chances in life, and so will having the looks of Marilyn Monroe, and so will a genius-level intelligence.

Proponents want us to believe that there are legitimate uses of cloning that can be distinguished from illegitimate uses, but by their own principles no such limits can be found. (Nor could any such limits be enforced in practice.) Reproductive freedom, as they understand it, is governed solely by the subjective wishes of the parents-to-be (plus the avoidance of bodily harm to the child). The sentimentally appealing case of the childless married couple is, on those grounds, indistinguishable from the case of an individual (married or not) who would like to clone someone famous or talented, living or dead. Further, the principle here endorsed justifies not only cloning but, indeed, all future artificial attempts to create (manufacture) "perfect" babies.

A concrete example will show how, in practice no less than in principle, the so-called innocent case will merge with, or even turn into, the more troubling ones. In practice, the eager parent-to-be will necessarily be subject to the tyranny of expertise. Consider an infertile married couple, she lacking eggs or he lacking sperm, that wants a child of their (genetic) own and proposes to clone either husband or wife. The scientist-physician (who is also coowner of the cloning company) points out the likely difficulties: A cloned child is not really their (genetic) child, but the child of only *one* of them; that imbalance may produce strains on the marriage; the child might suffer identity confusion; there is a risk of perpetuating the cause of sterility. The scientist-physician also points out the advantages of choosing a donor nucleus. Far better than a child of their own would be a child of their own choosing. Touting his own expertise in selecting healthy and talented donors, the doctor presents the couple with his latest catalog containing the pictures, the health records, and the accomplishments of his stable of cloning donors, samples of whose tissues are in his deep freeze. Why not, dearly beloved, a more perfect baby?

The "perfect baby," of course, is the project not of the infertility doctors, but of the eugenic scientists and their supporters. For them, the paramount right is not the so-called right to reproduce but what biologist Bentley Glass called, a quarter of a century ago, "the right of every child to be born with a sound physical and mental constitution, based on a sound genotype . . . the inalienable right to a sound heritage." But to secure that right and to achieve the requisite quality control over new human life, human conception and gestation will need to be brought fully into the bright light of the laboratory, beneath which the child-to-be can be fertilized, nourished, pruned, weeded, watched, inspected, prodded, pinched, cajoled, injected, tested, rated, graded, approved, stamped, wrapped, sealed, and delivered. There is no other way to produce the perfect baby.

Yet we are urged by proponents of cloning to forget about the science fiction scenarios of laboratory manufacture and multiple-copied clones and to focus only on the homely cases of infertile couples exercising their reproductive rights. But why, if the single cases are so innocent, should multiplying their performance be so off-putting? (Similarly, why do others object to people's making money from that practice if the practice itself is perfectly

acceptable?) When we follow the sound ethical principle of universalizing our choice—would it be right if everyone cloned a Wilt Chamberlain (with his consent, of course)? would it be right if everyone decided to practice asexual reproduction?—we discover what is wrong with such seemingly innocent cases. The so-called science fiction cases make vivid the meaning of what looks to us, mistakenly, to be benign.

Though I recognize certain continuities between cloning and, say, in vitro fertilization, I believe that cloning differs in essential and important ways. Yet those who disagree should be reminded that the "continuity" argument cuts both ways. Sometimes we establish bad precedents and discover that they were bad only when we follow their inexorable logic to places we never meant to go. Can the defenders of cloning show us today how, on their principles, we shall be able to see producing babies ("perfect babies") entirely in the laboratory or exercising full control over their genotypes (including so-called enhancement) as ethically different, in any essential way, from present forms of assisted reproduction? Or are they willing to admit, despite their attachment to the principle of continuity, that the complete obliteration of "mother" or "father," the complete depersonalization of procreation, the complete manufacture of human beings, and the complete genetic control of one generation over the next would be ethically problematic and essentially different from current forms of assisted reproduction? If so, where and how will they draw the line, and why? I draw it at cloning, for all the reasons given.

BAN THE CLONING OF HUMANS

What, then, should we do? We should declare that human cloning is unethical in itself and dangerous in its likely consequences. In so doing, we shall have the backing of the overwhelming majority of our fellow Americans, of the human race, and (I believe) of most practicing scientists. Next, we should do all that we can to prevent the cloning of human beings. We should do that by means of an international legal ban if possible and by a unilateral national ban at a minimum. Scientists may secretly undertake to violate such a law, but they will be deterred by not being able to stand up proudly to claim the credit for their technological bravado and success. Such a ban on clonal baby-making, moreover, will not harm the progress of basic genetic science and technology. On the contrary, it will reassure the public that scientists are happy to proceed without violating the deep ethical norms and intuitions of the human community.

That still leaves the vexed question about laboratory research using early embryonic human clones, specially created only for such research purposes, with no intention to implant them into a uterus. There is no question that such research holds great promise for gaining fundamental knowledge about normal (and abnormal) differentiation and for developing tissue lines for transplantation that might be used, say, in treating leukemia or in repairing brain or spinal cord injuries—to mention just a few of the conceivable benefits. Still, unrestricted clonal embryo research will surely make the production of living human clones much more likely. Once the genies put the cloned embryos into the bottles, who can strictly control where they go, especially in the absence of legal prohibitions against implanting them to produce a child?

I appreciate the potentially great gains in scientific knowledge and medical treatment available from embryo research, especially with cloned embryos. At the same time, I have serious reservations about creating human embryos for the sole purpose of experimentation. There is something deeply repugnant and fundamentally transgressive about such a utilitarian treatment of prospective human life. Such total, shameless exploitation is worse, in my opinion, than the "mere" destruction of nascent life. But I see no added objections, as a matter of principle, to creating and using *cloned* early embryos for research purposes, beyond the objections that I might raise to doing so with embryos produced sexually.

And yet, as a matter of policy and prudence, any opponent of the manufacture of cloned humans must, I think, in the end oppose also the creating of cloned human embryos. Frozen embryonic clones (belonging to whom?) can be shuttled around without detection. Commercial ventures in human cloning will be developed without adequate oversight. To build a fence around the law, prudence dictates that one oppose—for that reason alone—all production of cloned human embryos, even for

research purposes. We should allow all cloning research on animals to go forward, but the only defensible barrier we can erect against the slippery slide, I suspect, is to insist on the inviolable distinction between animal and human cloning.

Some readers and certainly most scientists will not accept such prudent restraints, since they desire the benefits of research. They will prefer, even in fear and trembling, to allow human embryo cloning research to go forward.

Very well. Let us test them. If the scientists want to be taken seriously on ethical grounds, they must at the very least agree that embryonic research may proceed if and only if it is preceded by an absolute and effective ban on all attempts to implant into a uterus a cloned human embryo (cloned from an adult) to produce a living child. Absolutely no permission for the former without the latter.

The National Bioethics Advisory Commission's recommendations regarding these matters were a step in the right direction, but a step made limpingly and without adequate support. To its credit, the commission has indeed called for federal legislation to prevent anyone from attempting to create a child through cloning. That was, frankly, more than I expected. But the *moral basis* for the commission's opposition to cloning is, sadly, much less than expected and needed, and the ban it urges is to be only temporary. Trying to clone a human being, says the commission, is "morally unacceptable" "*at this time*" because the technique has not been perfected to the point of safe usage. In other words, once it becomes readily feasible to clone a human being, with little risk of bodily harm to the resulting child, the commission has offered not one agreed-upon reason to object. Indeed, anticipating such improvements in technique, the commission insists that "it is critical" that any legislative ban on baby-making through cloning "should include a sunset clause to ensure that Congress will review the issue after a specified time period (three to five years) to decide whether the prohibition continues to be needed." Although it identifies other ethical concerns (beyond the issue of safety), that blue-ribbon ethics commission takes no stand on any of them! It says only that those issues "require much more widespread and careful public deliberation *before this technology may be used*"—not to decide *whether* the technology *should* be used. Relativistically, the commission wants to ensure only that such ethical and social issues be regularly reviewed "in light of public understandings at that time." This is hardly the sort of opposition to cloning that could be made the basis of any lasting prohibition.

Almost as worrisome, the report is silent on the vexed question of creating cloned human embryos for use in research. Silence is, of course, not an endorsement, but neither is it opposition. Given the currently existing ban on the use of federal funds for any research that involves creating human embryos for experimentation, the commission may have preferred to avoid needless controversy by addressing that issue. Besides, those commissioners (no doubt a big majority) who favor proceeding with cloned embryo research have in fact gained their goal precisely by silence: Both the moratorium on federal funding and the legislative ban called for by the commission are confined *solely* to attempts to *create a child* through cloning. The commission knows well how vigorously and rapidly embryo research is progressing in the private sector, and the commission surely understands that its silence on the subject—along with Congress's—means that the creation of human embryonic clones will proceed and perhaps is already proceeding in private or commercial laboratories. Indeed, the report expects and tacitly welcomes such human embryo research: for by what other means shall we arrive at the expected improvements in human cloning technology that would require the recommended periodic reconsideration of any legislative ban?

In the end, the report of the commission turns out to be a moral and (despite its best efforts) a practical failure. Morally, this ethics commission has waffled on the main ethical question by refusing to declare the production of human clones unethical (or ethical). Practically, the moratorium and ban on baby-making that it calls for, while welcome as temporary restraints, have not been given the justification needed to provide a solid and lasting protection against the production of cloned human beings. To the contrary, the commission's weak ethical stance may be said to undermine even its limited call for restraint. Do we really need a federal law solely to protect unborn babies from bodily harm?

Opponents of cloning need therefore to be vigilant. They should press for legislation to *permanently* prohibit baby-making through cloning, and they should take steps to make such a prohibition effective.

The proposal for such a legislative ban is without American precedent, at least in technological matters, though the British and others have banned cloning of human beings, and we ourselves ban incest, polygamy, and other forms of "reproductive freedom." Needless to say, working out the details of such a ban, especially a global one, would be tricky, what with the need to develop appropriate sanctions for violators. Perhaps such a ban will prove ineffective; perhaps it will eventually be shown to have been a mistake. But it would at least place the burden of practical proof where it belongs: on the proponents of this horror, requiring them to show very clearly what great social or medical good can be had only by the cloning of human beings.

We Americans have lived by, and prospered under, a rosy optimism about scientific and technological progress. The technological imperative—if it can be done, it must be done—has probably served us well, though we should admit that there is no accurate method for weighing benefits and harms. Even when, as in the cases of environmental pollution, urban decay, or the lingering deaths that are the unintended byproducts of medical success, we recognize the unwelcome outcomes of technological advance, we remain confident in our ability to fix all the "bad" consequences—usually by means of still newer and better technologies. How successful we can continue to be in such post hoc repairing is at least an open question. But there is very good reason for shifting the paradigm around, at least regarding those technological interventions into the human body and mind that will surely effect fundamental (and likely irreversible) changes in human nature, basic human relationships, and what it means to be a human being. Here we surely should not be willing to risk everything in the naïve hope that, should things go wrong, we can later set them right.

The president's call for a moratorium on human cloning has given us an important opportunity. In a truly unprecedented way, we can strike a blow for the human control of the technological project, for wisdom, prudence, and human dignity. The prospect of human cloning, so repulsive to contemplate, is the occasion for deciding whether we shall be slaves of unregulated progress, and ultimately its artifacts, or whether we shall remain free human beings who guide our technique toward the enhancement of human dignity. If we are to seize the occasion, we must, as the late Paul Ramsey wrote,

> raise the ethical questions with a serious and not a frivolous conscience. A man of frivolous conscience announces that there are ethical quandaries ahead that we must urgently consider before the future catches up with us.

By this he often means that we need to devise a new ethics that will provide the rationalization for doing in the future what men are bound to do because of new actions and interventions science will have made possible. In contrast a man of serious conscience means to say in raising urgent ethical questions that there may be some things that men should never do. The good things that men do can be made complete only by the things they refuse to do.

Questions for Analysis

1. Kass writes that the "technical, liberal, and meliorist approaches all ignore the deeper anthropological, social, and indeed, ontological meanings of bringing forth a new life." What are these deeper meanings, and why does he think those approaches ignore them?

2. According to Kass, cloning "represents a form of despotism." Why? Is he right? Why or why not?

3. Why does Kass believe that higher forms of animal life would have been impossible without sexual reproduction? What role does this belief play in his criticism of cloning?

4. According to Kass, cloning "creates serious issues of identity and individuality." What are those issues? How serious do you think they are?

5. When discussing the view that our right to reproductive freedom guarantees the right to clone, Kass calls it "a perfect example of the logic of the slippery slope." Why? Do you agree?

6. Although he concedes that research on early embryonic clones holds great promise, Kass believes that such research should be banned. Why? Do you think his reasons adequately support his belief?

7. Is cloning more rightly thought of as reproduction or manufacture?

Moral Status of Cloning Humans

Michael Tooley

The following selection by Michael Tooley, a professor of philosophy at the University of Colorado, is the second part of a longer essay. The first part examines the safety issues of human cloning and concludes that a temporary legal ban on cloning to produce humans is fully justified. The second part examines the moral issues and reaches two major conclusions: (1) there is nothing intrinsically immoral about human cloning, and (2) it promises to be very beneficial for society.

From *Human Cloning*, James M. Humber and Robert F. Almeder (Totowa, N.J.: Humanities Press, 1998), pp. 77–100.

Along the way, Tooley addresses many of the moral issues raised by cloning's opponents, from the possible psychological harm to clones to the fears raised by what he calls *Brave New World* scenarios, and he finds none of them compelling. In fact, he even argues that there is nothing morally wrong with using cloning to produce "mindless organ banks" to be harvested for transplants. Since these clones would not be persons, he contends, using them that way would not violate respect for persons.

IS IT INTRINSICALLY WRONG TO PRODUCE A PERSON BY CLONING?

Let us now turn to the question of whether the use of cloning to produce a person is, in principle, morally acceptable or not. In this section, I shall focus on the question of whether cloning, so used, is intrinsically wrong. Then, in a later section, I shall consider whether cloning to produce persons necessarily has consequences that render it morally wrong.

How might one attempt to argue that the production of persons via cloning is intrinsically wrong? Here it seems to me that Dan Brock is right when he suggests that there are basically two lines of argument that deserve examination.[1] First, there is an argument that appeals to what might initially be described as the right of a person to be a unique individual, but which, in the end, must be characterized instead as the right of a person to a genetically unique nature. Second, there is an argument that appeals to the idea that a person has a right to a future that is, in a certain sense, open.

Does a Person Have a Right to a Genetically Unique Nature?

Many people feel that being a unique individual is important, and the basic thrust of this first attempt to show that cloning is intrinsically wrong involves the idea that the uniqueness of individuals would be in some way impaired by cloning. In response, I think that one might very well question whether uniqueness is important. If, for example, it turned out that there was, perhaps on some distant planet, an individual that was qualitatively identical to oneself, down to the last detail, both physical and psychological, would that really make one's own life less valuable, less worth living?

In thinking about this issue, it may be important to distinguish two different cases: first, the case in which the two lives are qualitatively identical because of the operation of deterministic causal laws; second, the case in which it just happens that both individuals are always in similar situations in which they freely decide upon the same actions, have the same thoughts and feelings, and so on. The second of these scenarios, I suggest, is not troubling. The first, on the other hand, may be. But if it is, is it because there is a person who is qualitatively indistinguishable from oneself, or, rather, because one's life is totally determined?

I am inclined to question, accordingly, the perhaps rather widely held view that uniqueness is an important part of the value of one's life. Fortunately, however, one need not settle that issue in the present context, since cloning does not, of course, produce a person who is qualitatively indistinguishable from the individual who has been cloned, for, as is shown by the case of identical twins, two individuals with the same genetic makeup, even if raised within the same family at the same time, will differ in many respects, because of the different events that make up their life histories.

How great are those differences? The result of one study was as follows:

On average, our questionnaires show that the personality traits of identical twins have a 50 percent correlation. The traits of fraternal twins, by contrast, have a correlation of 25 percent, non-twin siblings a correlation of 11 percent and strangers a correlation of close to zero.[2]

Consequently, the personality traits of an individual and his or her clone should, on average, exhibit no more that a 50 percent correlation, and presumably, the correlation will generally be even less, given that an individual and his or her clone will typically be raised at different times, and in generations that may differ quite substantially in terms of basic beliefs and fundamental values.

The present argument, accordingly, if it is to have any chance, must shift from an appeal to the claim that a person has a right to absolute uniqueness to an appeal to the very different claim that a person has a right to a genetically unique nature. How, then, does the argument fare when reformulated in that way?

An initial point worth noticing is that any appeal to a claimed right to a genetically unique nature poses a difficulty for a theist: if there is such a right, why has God created a world where identical twins can arise? But there are, of course, many features of the world that are rather surprising, if our world is one that was created by an omnipotent, omniscient, and morally perfect person, and so the theist who appeals to a right to a genetically unique nature may simply reply that the presence of twins is just another facet of the general problem of evil.

How can one approach the question of whether persons have a right to a genetically unique nature? Some writers, I think, are content to rest with a burden of proof approach. Here the idea is that, although it may be the case that many people do think that being a unique individual, in the sense of not being qualitatively identical with anyone else, is an important part of what is valuable about being a person, the idea that persons have a right to a genetically unique identity is one that, by contrast, has been introduced only recently, and so those who advance the latter claim really need to offer some reasons for thinking that it is true.

There are, however, other ways of approaching this question that involve offering positive arguments against the claim. One possibility for example, is to appeal to the intuitions that one has upon reflection. Thus, one can consider the case of identical twins, and ask oneself whether, upon reflection, one thinks that it would be prima facie wrong to reproduce if one somehow knew that doing so would result in identical twins. I think it would be surprising if many people felt that this was so.

Another way of approaching the issue is by appealing to some plausible general theory of rights. Thus, for example, I am inclined to think that rights exist when there are serious, self-regarding interests that deserve to be protected. If some such view is correct, then one can approach the question of whether persons have a right to a genetically unique nature by asking whether one has some serious, self-regarding interest that would be impaired if one were a clone. Is the latter the case? The initial

reason for thinking that it is not is that the existence of a clone does not seem to impinge on a person in the same way in which being prevented from performing some action that harms no one, or being tortured, or being killed, does: A distant clone might have no impact at all upon one's life.

In response, it might be argued that, while the mere existence of a clone need have no impact on, and so need not impair in any way, one's self-regarding interests, the situation might be very different if one knew of the existence of the clone, since that knowledge might, for example, be damaging to one's sense of individuality. But why should this be so, given that individuals can differ greatly, although sharing the same genetic makeup? It seems to me that if the knowledge that a clone of oneself exists were disturbing to one, this would probably be because of the presence of some relevant, false belief, such as a belief in genetic determinism. But if this is so, then the question arises as to whether rights exist when the interests that they protect are ones that will be harmed only if the potential subjects of the harm have certain false, and presumably irrational, beliefs. My own feeling is that the responsibility for such harm is properly assigned to the individual who has acquired the irrational beliefs whose presence is necessary if there is to be any harm. Consequently, it seems to me that the actions of others should not be constrained in order to prevent such harm from occurring, and thus that there is no right that is violated in such a case.

A third way of thinking about this question of whether there is a right to a genetically unique nature is to consider a scenario in which individuals with the same genetic makeup are very common indeed, and to consider whether such a world would, for example, be inferior to the present world. Imagine, for example, that it is the year 4004 B.C.E., and that God is contemplating creating human beings. He has already considered the idea of letting humans come into being via evolution, but has rejected that plan on the grounds that a lottery approach to such a vital matter as bringing humans into existence hardly seems appropriate. He also considers creating an original human pair that are genetically distinct, and who will then give rise to humans who will be genetically quite diverse. Upon reflection, however, that idea also seems flawed, since the random shuffling of genes will result in individuals who may be physically impaired, or disposed to unpleasant diseases, such as cancer, that will cause them enormous suffering and lead to premature deaths. In the end, accordingly, the Creator decides upon a genetic constitution with the following two properties. First, it will not lead to serious physical handicaps and diseases, and it will allow an individual, who makes wise choices, to grow in mind and spirit. Second, all of the genes involve identical alleles. God then creates one person with that genetic makeup—call her Eve—and a second individual, Adam, whose only genetic difference is that he has one X chromosome, and one Y chromosome, where Eve has two X chromosomes. The upshot will then be that when Adam and Eve reproduce, they will breed true, because of the fact that they have, aside from the one difference, the same genetic makeup, with identical alleles for every inherited character, and so all of their descendants will be genetically identical to either Adam or Eve.

How would such a world compare with the actual world? If one were choosing from behind the Rawlsian veil of ignorance, would it be rational to prefer the actual world, or the alternative world? This is not, perhaps, an easy question. But it is clear that there would be some significant pluses associated with the alternative world. First, unlike the actual world, one would be assured of a genetic makeup that would be free of dispositions to various unwelcome and life-shortening diseases, or to other debilitating conditions such as depression, schizophrenia, and so on. Secondly, inherited traits would be distributed in a perfectly equitable fashion, and no one would start out, as is the case in the actual world, severely disadvantaged, and facing an enormous uphill battle. Third, aside from the differences between men and women, everyone would be physically the same, and so people would differ only with regard to the quality of their "souls", and thus one would have a world in which judgments of people might well have a less superficial basis than is often the case in the actual world. So there would seem to be some serious reasons for preferring the alternative world over the actual world.

The third advantage just mentioned also points, of course, to an obvious practical drawback of the alternative world: knowing who was who would be a rather more difficult matter than it is in the actual world. But this problem can be dealt with by variants on the above scenario. One variant, for

example, would involve having identity of genetic makeup, except regarding the genes that determine the appearance of face and hair. Then one would be able to identify individuals in just the way that one typically does in the actual world. This change would mean, of course, that one was no longer considering an alternative world in which there was widespread identity with respect to genetic makeup. Nevertheless, if this other alternative world would be preferable to the actual world, I think that it still provides an argument against the view that individuals have a right to a unique genetic makeup. For, first of all, the preferability of this other alternative world strongly suggests that genetic difference, rather than being desirable in itself, is valuable only to the extent that it is needed to facilitate the easy identification of people. Second, is it plausible to hold that, although genetic uniqueness is crucial, a very high degree of genetic similarity is not? But in the alternative world we are considering here, the degree of genetic similarity between any two individuals would be extraordinarily high. Third, the alternative world is one in which the genes that determine the initial structure of one's brain are not merely very similar, but absolutely the same in all individuals. But, then, can one plausibly hold that genetic uniqueness is morally crucial, while conceding that a world in which individuals do not differ regarding the genes that determine the initial nature of their brains might be better than the actual world?

These three considerations, I suggest, provide good reasons for holding that one cannot plausibly maintain that individuals have a right to a genetically unique nature, without also holding that the actual world is to be preferred to the alternative world just described. The identification problem can, however, also be addressed without shifting to a world where people differ genetically, since one could instead suppose that a different mechanism for identifying other people is built into human beings. God could, for example, incorporate special circuitry into the human brain, which broadcasts both one's name and appropriate identifying information about one, and which picks up the information that is broadcast by other humans within one's perceptual field. The information is then checked against a memory bank containing information about everyone one knows, and if it turns out that one is in perceptual contact with some person with whom one is acquainted, and if one would like to know who the person in question is, one would automatically find oneself in possession of the relevant information.

The result would be a world where all individuals will have exactly the same genetic makeup, aside from an X and a Y chromosome, and all of the attractive features of the original alternative world would be present, without there being any problem of determining who was who. One can then ask how this world compares with the actual world, and whether, in particular, the fact that all people in this alternative world would have essentially the same genetic makeup really seems to be, upon reflection, a reason for preferring the actual world.

The Open Future Argument

Dan Brock mentions a second argument for the view that cloning that aims at producing persons is intrinsically wrong.[3] The argument, which is based upon ideas put forward by Joel Feinberg, who speaks of a right to an open future,[4] and by Hans Jonas, who refers to a right to ignorance of a certain sort,[5] is essentially as follows. One's genetic makeup may very well determine to some extent the possibilities that lie open to one, and so it may constrain the course of one's future life. If there is no one with the same genetic makeup, or if there is such a person, but one is unaware of the fact, or, finally, if there is such a person, but the person is either one's contemporary, or someone who is younger, then one will not be able to observe the course of the life of someone with the same genetic makeup as oneself. But what if one does know of a genetically identical person whose life precedes one's own? Then one could have knowledge that one might well view as showing that certain possibilities were not really open to one, and so one would have less of a sense of being able to choose the course of one's life.

To see why this argument is unsound, one needs to ask about the reasoning that might be involved if someone, observing the earlier life of someone with the same genetic makeup, concludes that his or her own life is subject to certain constraints. One possibility is that one may have observed someone striving very hard, over a long period of time, to achieve some goal and failing to get anywhere near it. Perhaps the earlier, genetically identical individual wanted to be the first person to run the marathon in under two hours, and after several hears of intense and well-designed training, attention to diet, and so one, never got below two and one-half hours. One would then surely be justified in viewing that particular goal as not really open to one. But would that knowledge be a bad thing, as Jonas seems to be suggesting? I would think that, on the contrary, such knowledge would be valuable, since it would make it easier for one to choose goals that one could successfully pursue.

A very different possibility is that one might observe the course of the life of the genetically identical individual, and conclude that no life significantly different from that life could really be open to one. Then one would certainly feel that one's life was constrained to a very unwelcome extent. But in drawing the conclusion that one's life could not be significantly different from that of the other individual, one would be drawing a conclusion for which there is not only no evidence, but one that there is excellent evidence against: The lives of identical twins demonstrate that very different lives indeed are possible, given the same genetic makeup.

In short, the idea that information about the life of a person genetically identical to oneself would provide grounds for concluding that only a narrow range of alternatives was open to one would only be justified if genetic determinism, or a close approximation thereto, was correct. But nothing like genetic determinism is true. This second argument for the view that cloning with the goal of producing persons is intrinsically wrong is, accordingly, unsound.

CONSIDERATIONS IN SUPPORT OF THE CLONING OF PERSONS

Whether it is desirable to produce persons by cloning depends, as we noticed earlier, upon the outcome of an issue that is not yet decided: the aging question. Here, however, I shall simply assume that it will become possible to clone an adult individual in such a way that one winds up with a cell whose chromosomes have full-length telomeres, so that the individual who results will have a normal life expectancy. Given that assumption, I want to argue that there are a number of important benefits that may result from the cloning of humans that is done with the goal of producing persons.

In setting out what I take to be benefits of cloning, I shall not address possible objections. These will be discussed, instead, under "Objections to the Cloning of Humans."

Scientific Knowledge: Psychology and the Heredity-vs-Environment Issue

A crucial theoretical task for psychology is the construction of a satisfactory theory that will explain the acquisition of traits of character, and central to the development of such a theory is information about the extent to which various traits are inherited, or alternatively, dependent on aspects of the environment that are controllable, or, finally, dependent on factors, either in the brain or in the environment, that have a chancy quality. But such knowledge is not just theoretically crucial to psychology. Knowledge of the contributions that are, and are not, made to the individual's development by his or her genetic makeup, by the environment in which he or she is raised, and by chance events, will enable one to develop approaches to child-rearing that will increase the likelihood that one can raise people with desirable traits, people who will have a better chance of realizing their potentials, and of leading happy and satisfying lives. So this knowledge is not merely of great theoretical interest: it is also potentially very beneficial to society.

In the attempt to construct an adequate theory of human development, the study of identical twins has been very important, and has generated considerable information on the nature/nurture issue. But adequate theories still seem rather remote. Cloning would provide a powerful way of speeding up scientific progress in this area, since society could produce a number of individuals with the same genetic makeup, and then choose adoptive parents who would provide those individuals with good, but significantly different environments, in which to mature.

Cloning to Benefit Society

One very familiar suggestion is that one might benefit mankind by cloning individuals who have made very significant contributions to society. In the form in which it is usually put, when it is assumed that, if, for example, one had been able to clone Albert Einstein, the result would be an individual who would also make some very significant contribution to science, the suggestion is surely unsound. In the first place, whether an individual will do highly creative work surely depends on traits whose acquisitions is a matter of the environment in which the individual is raised, rather than on being determined simply by his or her genetic makeup. But could it not be argued in response that one could control the environment as well, raising a clone of Einstein, for example, in an environment that was as close as possible to the sort of environment in which Einstein was raised? That, of course, might prove difficult. But even if it could be done, it is not clear that it would be sufficient, because there is a second point that can be made here, namely, that great creative achievements may depend on things that are to some extent accidental, and whose occurrence is not ensured by the combination of a certain genetic makeup and a certain general sort of environment. Many great mathematicians, for example, have developed an intense interest in numbers at an early age. Is there good reason to think that, had one been able to clone Carl Friedrich Gauss, and reared that person in an environment similar to Gauss's, that person would have developed a similar interest in numbers, and gone on to achieve great things in mathematics? Or is it likely that a clone of Einstein, raised in an environment similar to that in which Einstein was raised, would have wondered, as Einstein did, what the world would look like if one could travel as fast as light, and then gone on to reflect on the issues that fascinated Einstein, and that led ultimately to the development of revolutionary theories in physics?

I think that there are, then, some serious problems with the present suggestion in the form in which it is usually put. On the other hand, I am not convinced that a slightly more modest version cannot be sustained. Consider, for example, the Polgar sisters. There we have a case in which the father of three girls succeeded in creating an environment in which all three of his daughters became very strong chess players, and one of them, Judit Polgar, is now the strongest female chess player who has ever lived. Is it not reasonable to think that if one were to make a number of clones of Judit Polgar, and then raise them in an environment very similar to that in which the Polgar sisters were raised, the result would be a number of very strong chess players?

More generally, I think it is clear that there is a strong hereditary basis for intelligence,[6] and I also believe that there is good reason for thinking that other traits that may play a crucial role in creativity, such as extreme persistence, determination, and confidence in one's own abilities, are such as are likely to be produced by the right combination of heredity and environment. So, although the chance that the clone of an outstandingly creative individual will also achieve very great things is perhaps, at least in many areas, not especially high, I think that there is reason for thinking that, given an appropriate environment, the result will be an individual who is likely to accomplish things that may benefit society in significant ways.

Happier and Healthier Individuals

A third benefit of cloning is that it should make it possible to increase the likelihood that the person that one is bringing into existence will enjoy a healthy and happy life. For, to the extent that one's genetic constitution has a bearing on how long one is likely to live, on what diseases, both physical and mental, one is likely to suffer from, and on whether one will have traits of character or temperament that make for happiness, or for unhappiness, by cloning a person who has enjoyed a very long life, who has remained mentally alert, and not fallen prey to Alzheimer's disease, who has not suffered from cancer, arthritis, heart attacks, stroke, high blood pressure, and so on, and who has exhibited no tendencies to depression, or schizophrenia, and so on, one is increasing the chances that the individual that one is producing will also enjoy a healthy and happy life.

More Satisfying Childrearing: Individuals with Desired Traits

Many couples would prefer to raise children who possess certain traits. In some cases they may want children who have a certain physical appearance. In other cases, they might like to have children who have the physical abilities that would enable them to have a better chance of performing at a high level in certain physical activities. Or they might prefer to have children who would have the intellectual capabilities that would enable them to enjoy mathematics or science. Or they might prefer to have children who possess traits that would enable

them to engage in, and enjoy, various aesthetic pursuits. Some of the traits that people might like their children to have presumably have a very strong hereditary basis; others are such as a child, given both the relevant genes, and the right environment, would be very likely to acquire. To the extent that the traits in question fall into either of these categories, the production of children via cloning would enable more couples to raise children with traits that they judge to be desirable.

More Satisfying Childrearing: Using Self-Knowledge

There is a second way in which cloning could make childrearing more satisfying, and it emerges if one looks back on one's own childhood. Most people, when they do this, remember things that they think were good, and other things that they think would have been better if they had been different. In some cases, of course, one's views may be unsound, and it may be that some of the things that one's parents did, and which one did not like, actually had good effects on one's development. On the whole, however, it seems plausible that most people have reasonably sound views on which features of the way in which they were raised had good effects overall, and which did not.

The idea, then, is that if a couple raises a child who is a clone of one of the parents, the knowledge that the relevant parent has of the way in which he or she was raised can be used to bring up the child in a way that fits better with the individual psychology of the child. In addition, given the greater psychological similarity that will exist between the child and one of his parents in such a case, the relevant parent will better be able, at any point, to appreciate how things look from the child's point of view. So it would seem that there is a good chance both that such a couple will find childrearing a more rewarding experience, and that the child will have a happier childhood through being better understood.

Infertility

Since the successful cloning that resulted in Dolly, at least one person has expressed the intention of pushing ahead with the idea of using cloning to help infertile couples. For reasons that emerged under the second heading, "Cloning in the Present

Context", the idea that cloning should be so used in the near future seems morally very problematic. In principle, however, the general idea would seem to have considerable merit. One advantage, for example, as Dan Brock and others have pointed out, is that "cloning would allow women who have no ova or men who have no sperm to produce an offspring that is biologically related to them."[7] Another advantage, also noted by Brock, is that "embryos might be cloned, either by nuclear transfer or embryo splitting, in order to increase the number of embryos for implantations and improve the chances of successful conception."[8]

Children for Homosexual Couples

Many people, especially in the United States, believe that homosexuality is deeply wrong, and that homosexuals should not be allowed either to marry or to raise children. These opinions, however, would be rejected, I think, by most philosophers, who would hold, on the contrary, that homosexuality is not morally wrong, and that homosexuals should be allowed both to marry, and to raise children. Assume, for the sake of the present discussion, that the latter views are correct. Then, as Philip Kitcher and others have noted, cloning would seem to be a promising method of providing a homosexual couple with children that they could raise, since, in the case of a gay couple, each child could be a clone of one person; in the case of a lesbian couple, every child could, in a sense, be biologically connected with both people:

> A lesbian couple wishes to have a child. Because they would like the child to be biologically connected to each of them, they request that a cell nucleus from one of them be inserted into an egg from the other, and that the embryo be implanted in the uterus of the woman who donated the egg.[9]

Cloning to Save Lives

A final possibility is suggested by the well-known case of the Ayala parents in California, who decided to have another child in the hope, which turned out to be justified, that the resulting child would be able to donate bone marrow for a transplant operation that would save the life of their teenage daughter, who was suffering from leukemia. If cloning had been possible at the time, a course of action would have been available to them that unlike having another child in the normal way, would not have been chancy: If they could have cloned the child who was ill, a tissue match would have been certain.

OBJECTIONS TO THE CLONING OF HUMANS

The Cloning of Mindless Organ Banks

Certain objections to the cloning of humans to produce mindless human organisms that would serve as a source of organs for others are perfectly intelligible. If someone objects to this idea on the grounds that one is destroying a person, the concern that is being expressed here is both completely clear and serious. The same is true if the objection is, instead, that such cloning is seriously wrong, since, in preventing a human organism from developing a functioning brain, one is depriving an immaterial soul associated with the organism in question of the possibility of experiencing life in this world. And, finally, the same is also true if someone holds that such cloning would be wrong, because it involves the destruction of an active potentiality for personhood.

The problem with these objections, accordingly, is not that they are in any way incoherent. Nor is it the case that the points raised are unimportant. The problem is simply that all of these objections are, in the end, unsound, for reasons that emerged earlier. Thus, the problem with the first objection is that there are excellent reasons for holding that human embryos do not possess those capacities, such as the capacity for thought and self-consciousness, that something must have, at some point, if it is to be a person. The problem with the second objection is that there are strong reasons for holding that the ontological basis for the capacities involved in consciousness, self-consciousness, thought, and other mental processes resides in the human brain, and not in any immaterial soul. Finally, the problem with the third objection lies in the assumption that the destruction of an active potentiality for personhood is morally wrong, for that claim is, on the one hand, unsupported by any satisfactory argument, and, on the other hand, exposed to decisive objections, one of which was set out earlier.

Often, however, it seems that people who would agree that the above objections are unsound, and who, moreover, do not view abortion as morally problematic, still express uneasiness about the idea of producing mindless human organ banks. Such uneasiness is rarely articulated, however, and it usually takes the form simply of describing the idea of mindless organ banks as a ghoulish scenario. This sort of dismissal of the use of cloning to produce organ banks is very puzzling. For what we are considering here is a way in which lives can be saved, and so, if one rejects this use of cloning, one is urging a course of action that will result in the deaths of innocent people. To do this on the grounds that mindless organ banks strike one as ghoulish seems morally irresponsible in the extreme: If this use of cloning is to be rejected, serious moral argument is called for.

The Cloning of Humans to Produce Persons
Violation of Rights Objections

Some people oppose cloning that is done with the goal of producing a person, on the grounds that such cloning involves a violation of some right of the person who is produced. The most important versions of this first sort of objection are those considered earlier, namely, that there is a violation either of a person's right to be a unique individual, or, more accurately, to be a genetically unique individual, or, alternatively, of a person's right to enjoy an open future that is not constrained by knowledge of the course of the life of some individual with the same genetic makeup. But for the reasons set out earlier, neither of these objections is sound.

Brave New World Style Objections

Next, there is a type of objection that is not frequently encountered in scholarly discussions, but which is rather common in the popular press, and which involves scenarios in which human beings are cloned in large numbers to serve as slaves, or as enthusiastic soldiers in a dictator's army. Such scenarios, however, do not seem very plausible. Is it really at all likely that, were cloning to become available, society would decide that its rejection of slavery had really been a mistake? Or that a dictator who was unable to conscript a satisfactory army from the existing citizens would be able to induce people to undertake a massive cloning program, in order that, 18 years or so down the line, he would finally have the army he had always wanted?

Psychological Distress

This objection is closely related to the earlier, violation of rights objections, because the idea is that, even if cloning does not violate a person's right to be a unique individual, or to have a unique genetic makeup, or to have an open and unconstrained future, nevertheless, people who are clones may feel that their uniqueness is compromised, or that their future is constrained, and this may cause substantial psychological harm and suffering.

There are two reasons for rejecting this objection as unsound. The first arises once one asks what one is to say about the beliefs in question, that is, the belief that one's uniqueness is compromised by the existence of a clone, and the belief that one's future is constrained if one has knowledge of the existence of a clone. Both beliefs are, as we have seen, false. But, in addition, it also seems clear that such beliefs would be, in general, irrational, since it is hard to see what grounds one could have for accepting either belief, other than something like genetic determinism, against which, as we saw earlier, there is conclusive evidence.

Once it is noted that the feelings that may give rise to psychological distress are irrational, one can appeal to the point that I made earlier, when we considered the question of whether knowledge of the existence of a clone might, for example, be damaging to one's sense of individuality, and whether, if this were so, such damage would be grounds for holding that there was a corresponding right that would be violated by cloning. What I argued at that point was that harm to an individual that arises because the individual has an irrational belief has a different moral status from harm that is not dependent on the presence of an irrational belief, and that, in particular, the possibility of the former sort of harm should not be taken as morally constraining others. The responsibility for such harm should, instead, be assigned to the individual who has the irrational belief, and the only obligation that falls on others is to point out to the person in question why the belief is an irrational one.

The second reason why the present objection cannot be sustained is also connected with the fact that the feelings in question are irrational, since the irrationality of the feelings means that they would not be likely to persist for very long, once cloning had become a familiar occurrence. For example, suppose that John feels that he is no longer a unique individual, or that his future is constrained, given that he is a clone of some other individual. Mary may also be a clone of some individual, and she may point out to John that she is very different from the person with whom she is genetically identical, and that she has not been constrained by the way the other person lived her life. Will John then persist in his irrational belief? This does not really seem very likely. If so, any distress that is produced will not be such as is likely to persist for any significant period of time.

Failing to Treat Individuals as Ends in Themselves

A fourth objection is directed, not against the cloning of persons in general, but against certain cases, such as those in which parents clone a child who is suffering from some life-threatening condition, in order to produce another child who will be able to save the first child's life. The thrust of this objection is that such cases involve a failure to view individuals as ends in themselves. Thus Philip Kitcher, referring to such cases, says that "a lingering concern remains," and he goes on to ask whether such scenarios "can be reconciled with Kant's injunction to 'treat humanity, whether in your own person or in the person of another, always at the same time as an end and never simply as a means.'"[10]

What is one to say about this objection? It may be important to be explicit about what sacrifices the child who is being produced is going to have to make to save his or her sibling. When I set out this sort of case under the subheading "Cloning to Save Lives," I assumed that what was involved was a bone marrow transplant. Kitcher, in his formulation, assumes that it will be a kidney transplant. I think that one might well be inclined to take different views of these two cases, given that, in the kidney donation case, but not the bone marrow case, the donor is making a sacrifice that may have unhappy consequences for that person in the future.

To avoid this complicated factor, let us concentrate, then, on the bone marrow case. In such a case, would there be a violation of Kant's injunction? There could be, if the parents were to abandon, or

not really care for the one child, once he or she had provided bone marrow to save the life of the other child. But this, surely, would be a very unlikely occurrence. After all, the history of the human race is mostly the history of unplanned children, often born into situations in which the parents were anything but well off, and yet, typically, those children were deeply loved by their parents.

In short, though this sort of case is, by hypothesis, one in which the parents decide to have a child with a goal in mind that has nothing to do with the well being of that child, this is no reason for supposing that they are therefore likely to treat that child merely as a means, and not also as an end in itself. Indeed, surely there is good reason to think, on the contrary, that such a child will be raised in no less loving a way than is normally the case.

Interfering with Personal Autonomy

The final objection that I shall consider is also one that has been advanced by Philip Kitcher, and he puts it as follows: "If the cloning of human beings is undertaken in the hope of generating a particular kind of person, then cloning is morally repugnant. The repugnance arises not because cloning involves biological tinkering but because it interferes with human autonomy."[11]

This objection would not apply to all of the cases that I mentioned in "Considerations in Support of the Cloning of Persons" as ones in which the cloning of a person would be justified. It does, however, apply to many of them. Is the objection sound? I cannot see that it is. First, notice that, in some cases, when one's goal is to produce "a particular kind of person," what one is aiming at is simply a person who will have certain potentialities. Parents might, for example, want to have children who are capable of enjoying intellectual pursuits. The possession of the relevant capacities does not force the children to spend their lives engaged in such pursuits, and so it is hard to see how cloning that is directed at that goal would interfere with human autonomy.

Second, consider cases in which the goal is not to produce a person who will be *capable* of doing a wider range of things, but an individual who will be *disposed* in certain directions. Perhaps it is this sort of case that Kitcher has in mind when he speaks of interfering with human autonomy. But is it really morally problematic to attempt to create persons who will be disposed in certain directions, and not in others? To answer this question, one needs to consider concrete cases, such as the sorts of cases that I mentioned earlier. Is it morally wrong, for example, to attempt to produce, via cloning, individuals who will, because of their genetic makeup, be disposed not to suffer from conditions that may cause considerable pain, such as arthritis, or from life-threatening diseases, such as cancer, high blood pressure, strokes, and heart attacks? Or to attempt to produce individuals who will have a cheerful temperament, or who will not be disposed to depression, to anxiety, to schizophrenia, or to Alzheimer's disease?

It seems unlikely that Kitcher, or others, would want to say that attempting to produce individuals who will be constitutionally disposed in the ways just indicated is a case of interfering with human autonomy. But then, what are the traits that are such that attempting to create a person with those traits is a case of interfering with human autonomy? Perhaps Kitcher, when he speaks about creating a particular kind of person, is thinking not just of any properties that persons have, but, more narrowly, of such things as personality traits, or traits of character, or having certain interests? But again one can ask whether there is anything morally problematic about attempting to create persons with such properties. Some personality traits are desirable, and parents typically encourage their children to develop those traits. Some character traits are virtues, and others are vices, and both parents and society attempt to encourage the acquisition of the former, and to discourage the acquisition of the latter. Finally, many interests, such as music, art, mathematics, science, games, physical activities, can add greatly to the quality of one's life, and once again, parents typically expose their children to relevant activities, and help their children to achieve levels of proficiency that will enable them to enjoy those pursuits.

The upshot is that, if cloning that aimed at producing people who would be more likely to possess various personality traits, or traits of character, or who would be more likely to have certain interests, was wrong because it was a case of interfering with personal autonomy, then the childrearing practices of almost all parents would stand condemned on precisely the same grounds. But such a claim, surely, is deeply counterintuitive.

In addition, however, one need not rest content with an appeal to intuitions here. The same conclusion follows on many high-order moral theories. Suppose, for example, that one is once again behind the Rawlsian veil of ignorance, and that one is deciding among societies that differ regarding their approaches to the rearing of children. Would it be rational to choose a society in which parents did not attempt to encourage their children to develop personality traits that would contribute to the latters' happiness? Or a society in which parents did not attempt to instill in their children a disposition to act in ways that are morally right? Or one in which parents made no attempt to develop various interests in their children? It is, I suggest, hard to see how such a choice could be a rational one, given that one would be opting, it would seem, for a society in which one would be likely to have a life that, on average, would be less worth living.

I conclude, therefore, that, contrary to what Philip Kitcher has claimed, it is not true that most cloning scenarios are morally repugnant, and that, in particular, there is, in general, nothing morally problematic about aiming at creating a child with specific attributes.

CONCLUSION

In this essay, I have distinguished between two very different cases involving the cloning of a human being—one that aims at the production of mindless human organisms that are to serve as organ banks for the people who are cloned, and another that aims at the creation of persons. Regarding the former, the objections that can be advanced are just the objections that can be directed against abortion, and, for reasons that I briefly outlined above, those objections can be shown to be unsound.

Very different objections arise in the case of cloning whose aim is the production of persons. Concerning this second sort of cloning, I argued that it is important to distinguish between the question of whether such cloning is, in principle, morally acceptable, and whether it is acceptable at the present time. Regarding the latter question, I argued that the present use of cloning to produce persons would be morally problematic. By contrast, concerning the question of whether such cloning is in principle morally acceptable, I argued, first, that such cloning is not intrinsically wrong; second, that there are a number of reasons why the cloning of persons would be desirable; and, third, that the objections that have been directed against such cloning cannot be sustained.

My overall conclusion, in short, is that the cloning of human beings, both to produce mindless organ banks, and to produce persons, is both morally acceptable, in principle, and potentially very beneficial for society.

NOTES

1. Brock, D. W. (1998) Cloning human beings: an assessment of the ethical issues pro and con, in *Clones and Clones,* Nussbaum, M. C. and Sunstein, C. R., eds., Norton, New York. *See* the section entitled "Would the use of human cloning violate important human rights?"

2. Bouchard, T. J., Jr. (1997) Whenever the twain shall meet. *The Sciences* 37, 52–57.

3. Brock, D. in the section entitled "Would the use of human cloning violate important human rights?"

4. Feinberg, J. (1980) The child's right to an open future, in *Whose Child? Children's Rights, Parental Authority, and State Power,* Aiken, W. and LaFollette, H., eds., Rowan and Littlefield, Totowa, NJ.

5. Jonas, H. (1974) *Philosophical Essay: From Ancient Creed to Technological Man,* Prentice-Hall, Englewood Cliffs, NJ.

6. *See,* for example, the discussion of this issue in Bouchard, pp. 55, 56.

7. Brock, D., in the subsection entitled "Human cloning would be a new means to relieve the infertility some persons now experience."

8. *Ibid.*

9. Kitcher, P. (1998) Whose self is it, anyway? *The Sciences* 37, 58–62. It should be noted that, although Kitcher mentions this idea as initially attractive, in the end he concludes that it is problematic, for a reason that will be considered in the subsection "The Cloning of Humans to Produce Persons."

10. *Ibid.,* p. 61.

11. *Ibid.,* p. 61.

Questions for Analysis

1. Tooley asks us to compare the world as it is to an imaginary world in which God decided to make Adam and Eve genetically identical except for the Y chromosome. What is the point of this thought experiment?

2. What benefits does Tooley think cloning would bring? Are they equally beneficial?

3. Does Tooley adequately rebut the objections to human cloning? Why or why not?

4. Do you agree with Tooley that there is nothing immoral about creating mindless human clones as organ banks?

5. Although Tooley addresses many of the objections that Kass raises against human cloning, he fails to address others. Do you think that adequate rebuttals are available to them?

Genetic Encores: The Ethics of Human Cloning

Robert Wachbroit

Like the previous reading, this essay by Robert Wachbroit defends cloning against a variety of objections. Two features of his defense are particularly noteworthy. First, he argues that a clone is not an identical copy of another individual but rather a delayed identical twin. Even though they carry the same genes, they will be distinct persons with distinctly different traits.

From Robert Wachbroit, "Genetic Encores: the Ethics of Human Cloning," in *Report from the Institute for Philosophy and Public Policy,* Fall 97. Copyright © 1997 Institute for Philosophy and Public Policy. Reprinted by permission.

To think otherwise, Wachbroit says, is to accept the false view that our genes alone determine all of our traits. Second, he compares cloning to other assisted reproductive technologies—including sperm donorship, surrogate motherhood, and genetic engineering—and finds it no more troubling. In some cases, he argues, it presents even fewer moral problems.

The successful cloning of an adult sheep, announced in Scotland this past February, is one of the most dramatic recent examples of a scientific discovery becoming a public issue. During the last few months, various commentators—scientists and theologians, physicians and legal experts, talk-radio hosts and editorial writers—have been busily responding to the news, some calming fears, others raising alarms about the prospect of cloning a human being. At the request of the President, the National Bioethics Advisory Commission (NBAC) held hearings and prepared a report on the religious, ethical, and legal issues surrounding human cloning. While declining to call for a permanent ban on the practice, the Commission recommended a moratorium on efforts to clone human beings, and emphasized the importance of further public deliberation on the subject.

An interesting tension is at work in the NBAC report. Commission members were well aware of the "widespread public discomfort, even revulsion, about cloning human beings." Perhaps recalling the images of Dolly the ewe that were featured on the covers of national news magazines, they noted that "the impact of these most recent developments on our national psyche has been quite remarkable." Accordingly, they felt that one of their tasks was to articulate, as fully and sympathetically as possible, the range of concerns that the prospect of human cloning had elicited.

Yet it seems clear that some of these concerns, at least, are based on false beliefs about genetic influence and the nature of the individuals that would be produced through cloning. Consider, for instance, the fear that a clone would not be an "individual" but merely a "carbon copy" of someone else—an automaton of the sort familiar from science fiction. As many scientist have pointed out, a clone would not in fact be an identical *copy*, but more like a delayed identical *twin*. And just as identical twins are two separate people—biologically, psychologically, morally and legally, though not genetically—so, too, a clone would be a separate person from her non-contemporaneous twin. To think otherwise is to embrace a belief in genetic determinism—the view

that genes determine everything about us, and the environmental factors or the random events in human development are insignificant.

The overwhelming scientific consensus is that genetic determinism is false. In coming to understand the ways in which genes operate, biologists have also become aware of the myriad ways in which the environment affects their "expression." The genetic contribution to the simplest physical traits, such as height and hair color, is significantly mediated by environmental factors (and possibly by stochastic events as well). And the genetic contribution to the traits we value most deeply, from intelligence to compassion, is conceded by even the most enthusiastic genetic researchers to be limited and indirect.

It is difficult to gauge the extent to which "repugnance" toward cloning generally rests on a belief in genetic determinism. Hoping to account for the fact that people "instinctively recoil" from the prospect of cloning, James Q. Wilson wrote, "There is a natural sentiment that is offended by the mental picture of identical babies being produced in some biological factory." Which raises the question: once people learn that this picture is mere science fiction, does the offense that cloning presents to "natural sentiment" attenuate, or even disappear? Jean Bethke Elshtain cited the nightmare scenarios of "the man and woman on the street," who imagine a future populated by "a veritable army of Hitlers, ruthless and remorseless bigots who kept reproducing themselves until they had finished what the historic Hitler failed to do: annihilate us." What happens, though, to the "pity and terror" evoked by the topic of cloning when such scenarios are deprived (as they deserve to be) of all credibility?

Richard Lewontin has argued that the critics' fears—or at least, those fears that merit consideration in formulating public policy—dissolve once genetic determinism is refuted. He criticizes the NBAC report for excessive deference to opponents of human cloning, and calls for greater public education on the scientific issues. (The Commission in fact makes the same recommendation, but Lewontin seems unimpressed.) Yet even if a public education campaign succeeded in eliminating the most egregious misconceptions about genetic influence, that wouldn't settle the matter. People might continue to express concerns about the interests and rights of human clones, about the social and moral consequences of the cloning process, and about the possible motivations for creating children in this way.

INTERESTS AND RIGHTS

One set of ethical concerns about human clones involves the risks and uncertainties associated with the current state of cloning technology. This technology has not yet been tested with human subjects, and scientists cannot rule out the possibility of mutation or other biological damage. Accordingly, the NBAC report concluded that "at this time, it is morally unacceptable for anyone in the public or private sector, whether in a research or clinical setting, to attempt to create a child using somatic cell nuclear transfer cloning." Such efforts, it said, would pose "unacceptable risks to the fetus and/or potential child."

The ethical issues of greatest importance in the cloning debate, however, do not involve possible failures of cloning technology, but rather the consequences of its success. Assuming that scientists were able to clone human beings without incurring the risks mentioned above, what concerns might there be about the welfare of clones?

Some opponents of cloning believe that such individuals would be wronged in morally significant ways. Many of these wrongs involve the denial of what Joel Feinberg has called "the right to an open future." For example, a child might be constantly compared to the adult from whom he was cloned, and thereby burdened with oppressive expectations. Even worse, the parents might actually limit the child's opportunities for growth and development: a child cloned from a basketball player, for instance, might be denied any educational opportunities that were not in line with a career in basketball. Finally, regardless of his parents' conduct or attitudes, a child might be burdened by the *thought* that he is a copy and not an "original." The child's sense of self-worth or individuality or dignity, so some have argued, would thus be difficult to sustain.

How should we respond to these concerns? On the one hand, the existence of a right to an open future has a strong intuitive appeal. We are troubled by parents who radically constrict their children's possibilities for growth and development. Obviously, we would condemn a cloning parent for crushing a child with oppressive expectations, just as we might condemn fundamentalist parents for utterly isolating their children from the modern world, or the parents of twins for inflicting matching wardrobes and rhyming names. But this is not enough to sustain an objection to cloning itself. Unless the claim is that cloned parents cannot help but be oppressive, we would have cause to say they had wronged their children only because of their subsequent, and avoidable, sins of bad parenting—not because they had chosen to create the child in the first place. (The possible reasons for making this choice will be discussed below.)

We must also remember that children are often born in the midst of all sorts of hopes and expectations; the idea that there is a special burden associated with the thought "There is someone who is genetically just like me" is necessarily speculative. Moreover, given the falsity of genetic determinism, any conclusions a child might draw from observing the person from whom he was cloned would be uncertain at best. His knowledge of his future would differ only in degree from what many children already know once they begin to learn parts of their family's (medical) history. Some of us knew that we would be bald, or to what diseases we might be susceptible. To be sure, the cloned individual might know more about what he or she could become. but because our knowledge of the effect of environment on development is so incomplete, the clone would certainly be in for some surprises.

Finally, even if we were convinced that clones are likely to suffer particular burdens, that would not be enough to show that it is wrong to create them. The child of a poor family can be expected to suffer specific hardships and burdens, but we don't thereby conclude that such children shouldn't be born. Despite the many hardships, poor children can experience parental love and many of the joys of being alive: the deprivations of poverty, however painful, are not decisive. More generally, no one's life is entirely free of some difficulties or burdens. In order for these considerations to have decisive weight, we have to be able to say that life doesn't offer any compensating benefits. Concerns expressed about the welfare of human clones do not appear to justify such a bleak assessment. Most such children can be expected to have lives well worth living; many of the imagined harms are no worse than those faced by children acceptably produced by more conventional means. If there is something deeply objectionable about cloning, it is more likely to be found by examining implications of the cloning process itself, or the reasons people might have for availing themselves of it.

CONCERNS ABOUT PROCESS

Human cloning falls conceptually between two other technologies. At one end we have the assisted reproductive technologies, such as in vitro fertilization, whose primary purpose is to enable couples to produce a child with whom they have a biological connection. At the other end we have the emerging technologies of genetic engineering—specifically, gene transplantation technologies—whose primary purpose is to produce a child that has certain traits. Many proponents of cloning see it as part of the first technology: cloning is just another way of providing a couple with a biological child they might otherwise be unable to have. Since this goal and these other technologies are acceptable, cloning should be acceptable as well. On the other hand, many opponents of cloning see it as part of the second technology: even though cloning is a transplantation of an entire nucleus and not of specific genes, it is nevertheless an attempt to produce a child with certain traits. The deep misgivings we may have about the genetic manipulation of offspring should apply to cloning as well.

The debate cannot be resolved, however, simply by determining which technology to assimilate cloning to. For example, some opponents of human cloning see it as continuous with assisted reproductive technologies; but since they find those technologies objectionable as well, the assimilation does not indicate approval. Rather than argue for grouping cloning with one technology or another, I wish to suggest that we can best understand the significance of the cloning process by comparing it with these other technologies, and thus broadening the debate.

To see what can be learned from such a comparative approach, let us consider a central argument that has been made against cloning—that it undermines the structure of the family by making identities and lineages unclear. On the one hand, the relationship between an adult and the child cloned from her could be described as that between a parent and offspring. Indeed, some commentators have called cloning "asexual reproduction," which clearly suggests that cloning is a way of generating *descendants.* The clone, on this view, has only one biological parent. On the other hand, from the point of view of genetics, the clone is a *sibling,* so that cloning is more accurately described as "delayed twinning" rather than as asexual reproduction. The clone, on this view, has two biological parents, not one—they are the same parents as those of the person from whom that individual was cloned.

Cloning thus results in ambiguities. Is the clone an offspring or a sibling? Does the clone have one biological parent or two? The moral significance of these ambiguities lies in the fact that in many societies, including our own, lineage identifies responsibilities. Typically, the parent, not the sibling, is responsible for the child. But if no one is unambiguously the parent, so the worry might go, who is responsible for the clone? Insofar as social identity is based on biological ties, won't this identity be blurred or confounded?

Some assisted reproductive technologies have raised similar questions about lineage and identity. An anonymous sperm donor is thought to have no parental obligations towards his biological child. A surrogate mother may be required to relinquish all parental claims to the child she bears. In these cases, the social and legal determination of "who is the parent" may appear to proceed in defiance of profound biological facts, and to subvert attachments that we as a society are ordinarily committed to upholding. Thus, while the *aim* of assisted reproductive technologies is to allow people to produce or raise a child to whom they are biologically connected, such technologies may also involve the creation of social ties that are permitted to override biological ones.

In the case of cloning, however, ambiguous lineages would seem to be less problematic, precisely because no one is being asked to relinquish a claim on a child to whom he or she might otherwise acknowledge a biological connection. What, then, are the critics afraid of? It does not seem plausible that someone would have herself cloned and then hand the child over to her parents, saying, "You take care of her! She's *your* daughter!" Nor is it likely that, if the cloned individual did raise the child, she would suddenly refuse to pay for college on the grounds that this was not a sister's responsibility. Of course, policymakers should address any confusion in the social or legal assignment of responsibility resulting from cloning. But there are reasons to think that this would be *less* difficult than in the case of other reproductive technologies.

Similarly, when we compare cloning with genetic engineering, cloning may prove to be the less troubling of the two technologies. This is true even though the dark futures to which they are often alleged to lead are broadly alike. For example, a recent *Washington Post* article examined fears that the development of genetic enhancement technologies might "create a market in preferred physical traits." The reporter asked, "Might it lead to a society of DNA haves and have-nots, and the creation of a new underclass of people unable to keep up with the genetically fortified Joneses?" Similarly, a member of the National Bioethics Advisory Commission expressed concern that cloning might become "almost a preferred practice," taking its place "on the continuum of providing the best for your child." As a consequence, parents who chose to "play the lottery of old-fashioned reproduction would be considered irresponsible."

Such fears, however, seem more warranted with respect to genetic engineering than to cloning. By offering some people—in all probability, members of the upper classes—the opportunity to acquire desired traits through genetic manipulation, genetic engineering could bring about a biological reinforcement (or accentuation) of existing social divisions. It is hard enough already for disadvantaged children to compete with their more affluent counterparts, given the material resources and intellectual opportunities that are often available only to children of privilege. This unfairness would almost certainly be compounded if genetic manipulation came into the picture. In contrast, cloning does not bring about "improvements" in the genome: it is, rather, a way of *duplicating* the genome—with all its imperfections. It wouldn't enable certain groups of people to keep getting better and better along some valued dimension.

To some critics, admittedly, this difference will not seem terribly important. Theologian Gilbert Meilaender, Jr., objects to cloning on the grounds that children created through this technology would be "designed as a product" rather than "welcomed as a gift." The fact that the design process would be more selective and nuanced in the case of genetic engineering would, from this perspective, have no moral significance. To the extent that this objection reflects a concern about the commodification of human life, we can address it in part when we consider people's reasons for engaging in cloning.

REASONS FOR CLONING

This final area of contention in the cloning debate is as much psychological as it is scientific or philosophical. If human cloning technology were safe and widely available, what use would people make of it? What reasons would they have to engage in cloning?

In its report to the President, the Commission imagined a few situations in which people might avail themselves of cloning. In one scenario, a husband and wife who wish to have children are both carriers of a lethal recessive gene:

> Rather than risk the one in four chance of conceiving a child who will suffer a short and painful existence, the couple considers the alternatives: to forego rearing children; to adopt; to use prenatal diagnosis and selective abortion; to use donor gametes free of the recessive trait; or to use the cells of one of the adults and attempt to clone a child. To avoid donor gametes and selective abortion, while maintaining a genetic tie to their child, they opt for cloning.

In another scenario, the parents of a terminally ill child are told that only a bone marrow transplant can save the child's life. "With no other donor available, the parents attempt to clone a human being from the cells of the dying child. If successful, the new child will be a perfect match for bone marrow transplant, and can be used as a donor without significant risk or discomfort. The net result: two healthy children, loved by their parents, who happen [sic] to be identical twins of different ages."

The Commission was particularly impressed by the second example. That scenario, said the

NBAC report, "makes what is probably the strongest possible case for cloning a human being, as it demonstrates how this technology could be used for lifesaving purposes." Indeed, the report suggests that it would be a "tragedy" to allow "the sick child to die because of a moral or political objection to such cloning." Nevertheless, we should note that many people would be morally uneasy about the use of a minor as a donor, regardless of whether the child were a result of cloning. Even if this unease is justifiably overridden by other concerns, the "transplant scenario" may not present a more compelling case for cloning than that of the infertile couple desperately seeking a biological child.

Most critics, in fact, decline to engage the specifics of such tragic (and presumably rare) situations. Instead, they bolster their case by imagining very different scenarios. Potential users of the technology, they suggest, are narcissists or control freaks—people who will regard their children not as free, original selves but as products intended to meet more or less rigid specifications. Even if such people are not genetic determinists, their recourse to cloning will indicate a desire to exert all possible influence over the "kind" of child they produce.

The critics' alarm at this prospect has in part to do, as we have seen, with concerns about the psychological burdens such a desire would impose on the clone. But it also reflects a broader concern about the values expressed, and promoted, by a society's reproductive policies. Critics argue that a society that enables people to clone themselves thereby endorses the most narcissistic reason for having children—to perpetuate oneself through a genetic encore. The demonstrable falsity of genetic determinism may detract little, if at all, from the strength of this motive. Whether or not clones will have a grievance against their parents for producing them with this motivation, the societal indulgence of that motivation is improper and harmful.

It can be argued, however, that the critics have simply misunderstood the social meaning of a policy that would permit people to clone themselves even in the absence of the heartrending exigencies described in the NBAC report. This country has developed a strong commitment to reproductive autonomy. (This commitment emerged in response to the dismal history of eugenics—the very history that is sometimes invoked to support restrictions on cloning.) With the exception of practices that risk coercion and exploitation—notably baby-selling and commercial surrogacy—we do not interfere with people's freedom to create and acquire children by almost any means, for almost any reason. This policy does not reflect a dogmatic libertarianism. Rather, it recognizes the extraordinary personal importance and private character of reproductive decisions, even those with significant social repercussions.

Our willingness to sustain such a policy also reflects a recognition of the moral complexities of parenting. For example, we know that the motives people have for bringing a child into the world do not necessarily determine the manner in which they raise him. Even when parents start out as narcissists, the experience of childrearing will sometimes transform their initial impulses, making them caring, respectful, and even self-sacrificing. Seeing their child grow and develop, they learn that she is not merely an extension of themselves. Of course, some parents never make this discovery; others, having done so, never forgive their children for it. The pace and extent of moral development among parents (no less than among children) is infinitely variable. Still, we are justified in saying that those who engage in cloning will not, by virtue of this fact, be immune to the transformative effects of parenthood—even if it is the case (and it won't always be) that they begin with more problematic motives than those of parents who engage in the "genetic lottery."

Moreover, the nature of parental motivation is itself more complex than the critics often allow. Though we can agree that narcissism is a vice not to be encouraged, we lack a clear notion of where pride in one's children ends and narcissism begins. When, for example, is it unseemly to bask in the reflected glory of a child's achievements? Imagine a champion gymnast who takes delight in her daughter's athletic prowess. Now imagine that the child was actually cloned from one of the gymnast's somatic cells. Would we have to revise our moral assessment of her pleasure in her daughter's success? Or suppose a man wanted to be cloned and to give his child opportunities he himself had never enjoyed. And suppose that, rightly or wrongly, the man took the child's success as a measure of his own untapped potential—an indication of the flourishing life he might have had. Is *this* sentiment blamable? And is it all that different from what many natural parents feel?

CONCLUSION

Until recently, there were few ethical, social, or legal discussions about human cloning via nuclear transplantation, since the scientific consensus was that such a procedure was not biologically possible. With the appearance of Dolly, the situation has changed. But although it now seems more likely that human cloning will become feasible, we may doubt that the practice will come into widespread use.

I suspect it will not, but my reasons will not offer much comfort to the critics of cloning. While the technology for nuclear transplantation advances, other technologies—notably the technology of genetic engineering—will be progressing as well. Human genetic engineering will be applicable to a wide variety of traits; it will be more powerful than cloning, and hence more attractive to more people. It will also, as I have suggested, raise more troubling questions than the prospect of cloning has thus far.

SOURCES

National Bioethics Advisory Commission, "Cloning Human Beings: Report and Recommendations" (June 9, 1997).

James Q. Wilson, "The Paradox of Cloning," *Weekly Standard* (May 26, 1997).

Jean Bethke Elshtain, "Ewegenics," *New Republic* (March 31, 1997); R. C. Lewontin, "The Confusion over Cloning," *New York Review of Books* (October 23, 1997).

Leon Kass, "The Wisdom of Repugnance," *New Republic* (June 2, 1997).

Susan Cohen, "What Is a Baby? Inside America's Unresolved Debate about the Ethics of Cloning," *Washington Post Magazine* (October 12, 1997).

Rick Weiss, "Genetic Enhancements' Thorny Ethical Traits," *Washington Post* (October 12, 1997).

Questions for Analysis

1. What is genetic determinism? Why does Wachbroit claim that it's false? What bearing does it have on the morality of cloning?

2. Against the claim that cloning carries many psychological burdens on the clone, Wachbroit argues that "no one's life is entirely free of some difficulties or burdens." How relevant is this point?

3. In his discussion of the problems of lineage and identity associated with cloning, Wachbroit argues that the same problems have arisen in other assisted reproductive technologies. He also argues that they are more problematic in those technologies than in cloning. Is he right?

4. How does Wachbroit respond to the criticism that a clone would be a designed product? How adequate is his response?

5. How many of Kass's three perspectives on cloning does Wachbroit take?

The Constitution and the Clone

Cass R. Sunstein

In the following selection, law professor Cass R. Sunstein imagines that "some time in the future" a group of American citizens challenges state and federal laws against human cloning on the grounds that the U.S. Constitution guarantees a right to clone. He further imagines that the case has reached the U.S. Supreme Court. Rather than predicting how the

From *Clones and Clones,* Martha C. Nussbaum and Cass R. Sunstein, eds. (New York: Norton, 1998), pp. 207–220.

Court would rule on such a case, he offers two contrasting majority opinions, one upholding the right and one declining to uphold it.

As presented by Sunstein, the case involves two central issues: whether precedents involving contraception and abortion set the foundations for a constitutional right to reproductive privacy, and if so, whether any compelling government interests override that right when it comes to cloning. The first opinion answers yes and no to these questions, respectively. The second opinion comes to the opposite conclusion: There is no constitutional right to clone, and even if there were, the government's interest in preventing human clones is compelling enough to override that right.

"My decision to clone myself should not be the government's business, or Cardinal O'Connor's, any more than a woman's decision to have an abortion is. Cloning is hugely significant. It's part of the reproductive rights of every human being."

—Randolfe Wicker, head of the Cloning Rights United Front of New York, *New York Times Magazine*, May 25, 1997, at 18.

It is some time in the future. Federal and state laws forbid the practice of cloning human beings; but a number of American citizens are claiming that the Constitution guarantees a "right to clone." Some infertile couples contend that cloning provides their "best option for having children." Some couples who have lost their first child are seeking a biologically identical replacement via cloning. Some homosexual groups are insisting on a right to clone.

An especially prominent case was brought by Kristina Martin and Ronald Martin. Kristina is 38 and Ronald is 42; Ronald is infertile. Kristina seeks to carry Ronald's cloned child. In a case brought by the Martins and several other married couples, a court of appeals held that the Constitution protects the right to clone. The constitutional issue has come before the Supreme Court of the United States.

But now there is a fork in the road: two possible but very different paths for constitutional law. Path A contains the Supreme Court's reasoning in its dramatic decision firmly recognizing a constitutional right to reproductive privacy, including the right to clone. Path B summarizes the Supreme Court's reasoning in its unambiguous denial of any such right. There are intersections between the two divergent paths. The reasoning of the two Supreme Courts has been organized to allow comparisons between the two paths—and to facilitate choices between them.

KRISTINA MARTIN AND RONALD MARTIN, ET AL. V. MARTIN BALLINGER, SECRETARY OF HEALTH AND HUMAN SERVICES, ET AL.

On Petition for Writ of Certiorari to the United States Court of Appeals for the Eight Circuit
No. 99–1099

Justice Monroe delivered the opinion of the Court.

In this case American citizens seeking to clone human beings have challenged federal and state prohibitions on cloning. The plaintiffs are married couples. They argue that these prohibitions violate their right to free reproductive choice.

The plaintiffs make two arguments. They argue, first, that the right to clone is part and parcel of the right of reproductive privacy. They claim that this right is akin to the rights to use contraception and to have an abortion, firmly recognized under our prior cases. They therefore urge that the right to clone qualifies, under the due process clause of the Fifth and Fourteenth Amendments, as a "fundamental interest," which may be invaded only if the government can satisfy "strict scrutiny," by showing the most compelling of justifications.

The plaintiffs argue, second, that even if the right to clone does not qualify as a "fundamental interest," the legal prohibition on cloning is unconstitutional, because the government cannot show a "rational basis" for the restriction. The plaintiffs claim that the government has no legitimate reason for interfering with private decisions about whether to have a child via cloning.

The government makes several arguments in response. It urges that the right to clone is very different from the right to use contraceptives or to have an abortion, and that it does not qualify as a fundamental right under the Constitution. The government also claims that there are compelling reasons to ban human cloning even if the right to clone does qualify as a fundamental right. Finally, the government insists that there is a "rational basis" for restricting human cloning, to prevent a wide range of social harms.

We reject the government's arguments and hold today that under the Constitution as it has come to be understood, there is a constitutional right to clone. The Court's cases firmly recognize the individual right to control reproduction—to decide whether or not to have a child. This right lies at the very heart of the constitutional right of "privacy"; it is part of the liberty protected by the due process clause of the Fifth and Fourteenth Amendments.

To be sure, the government can override that right if it has an extremely good reason for doing so. But in the context of cloning, the government's arguments are far too weak. Certainly the government cannot satisfy the "strict scrutiny" standard that governs this Court's review of restrictions on fundamental rights. Indeed, we do not believe that the government's interests are strong enough to overcome "rational basis" review, the most deferential standard the Court now uses.

I

There is an acknowledged constitutional right to some form of individual control over decisions involving reproduction. In *Griswold v. Connecticut*, 381 U.S. 479 (1965), this Court held that a state could not ban a married couple from using contraceptives. In the Court's view, a right of "privacy" forecloses state interference with that decision. In *Eisenstadt v. Baird*, 405 U.S. 438 (1972), the Court extended *Griswold* to invalidate a law forbidding the distribution of contraceptives to unmarried people. In the key passage of its opinion, the Court said, "If the right of privacy means anything, it is the right of the individual, married or single, to be free from unwarranted governmental intrusion into matters so affecting a person as the decision whether to bear or beget a child." And in *Roe v. Wade*, 410 U.S. 113 (1973), the Court held that there is a constitutional right to have an abortion. This decision the Court strongly reaffirmed in *Casey v. Planned Parenthood*, 505 U.S. 833 (1992).

On the other hand, we have held that there is no general right against government interference with important private choices. Thus in *Washington v. Glucksberg,* 116 U.S. 2021 (1997), we held that under ordinary circumstances, there is no general right to physician-assisted suicide. We emphasized that this right is quite foreign to the traditions of American law and policy, which strongly discourage suicide, assisted or otherwise.

These cases clearly establish a basic principle: The Constitution creates a presumptive individual right to decide whether and when to reproduce. The precise dimensions of this right will inevitably change over time. Of course new technologies are expanding the methods by which reproduction is possible. New technologies have been especially prominent in the last decades, and undoubtedly scientific progress will continue, producing unforeseeable developments. The Constitution provides the basic right, which is itself constant; but the specific content of the right necessarily changes with relevant technology.

We think it very plain that the government would need an exceptionally powerful justification to ban couples with serious fertility problems from using methods other than sexual intercourse to produce a child between husband and wife. It has become quite ordinary for couples to use new methods and technologies, and governments have generally refrained from interfering with individual freedom to choose. A governmental ban on in vitro fertilization, to take one example, would have to be powerfully justified, certainly if the ban prevented couples from having children in the only way they could. Cloning is of course a new technology. But for some couples, including the plaintiffs here, it is the only or the best reproductive option. If the government wishes to limit or restrict that choice, it must come up with an exceptionally strong justification.

II

The closest precedent for our decision today is *Roe v. Wade,* reaffirmed in *Casey v. Planned Parenthood,* and these decisions strongly support a right to clone. In fact the argument for a right to clone is far stronger, in many ways, than the argument for a right to abortion. Cloning produces life where abortion destroys it. Abortion is contested on the ground that it destroys the fetus, which many people consider to be equivalent to, or nearly equivalent to, a human being. If there is a right to abort fetal life, there must be a parallel right to create life. Of course the morality of abortion, like that of cloning, is socially contested. *Roe* demonstrates that the fact that people have moral reservations, whether or not inspired by religion, is by itself an insufficient reason to allow interference with a decision about whether to bear or beget a child.

In any case the right to have an abortion reflects a judgment that the choice about whether to reproduce lies with the individual, not the government. That judgment strongly supports the plaintiffs' claim here.

III

If a ban on cloning is subject to the most stringent forms of constitutional review, it is clear that the ban cannot be upheld. The government's interests are speculative in the extreme. The government notes that there is a risk of psychological harm to the clone, who will know that it is the genetic equivalent of someone else, with a known life; perhaps this knowledge will be hard to bear. We acknowledge that psychological harm may occur. But psychological harm is a risk in many settings, and it is not a reason to allow the government to control reproductive choices, to ban adoption, or (for that matter) to outlaw twins, for whom there is in any case no decisive evidence of trauma.

The government argues that it fears the outcomes of unsuccessful medical experiments; it says that children with various physical defects are likely to occur. This too is possible, especially at the early stages, but it is a reason for regulation, not prohibition. The government refers as well to the need for a large stock of genetic diversity. The interest in a large gene pool is, we may acknowledge, compelling; but it is utterly implausible to think that the existence of cloning, bound to be a relatively unusual practice, will compromise the genetic diversity of mankind.

Finally, the government attempts to justify its ban with the legal equivalent of tales from science fiction or horror movies—thus, the government refers to dozens or even hundreds of genetically equivalent people, or of clones of especially abhorrent historical figures. The government fears that narcissistic or ill-motivated people will produce armies of "selves."

We think it plain that these fanciful speculations, far afield from the case at hand, do not justify a total ban. If problems of this kind arise, they should be controllable through more fine-tuned regulations. The government's emphasis on unlikely scenarios of this kind simply confirms our belief that the government has been unable to find a "compelling" interest to override the presumptive right to control one's reproductive processes.

IV

Even if the right to clone did not qualify as a fundamental interest, we believe that a wholesale ban on cloning would be unconstitutional, because it cannot survive rational basis review. In the end the government's justifications are best understood as a form of unmediated and highly emotional repugnance—produced not by evidence, arguments, or reality, but by the simple novelty of the practice under review.

Repugnance frequently accompanies new technological developments; and repugnance tends to underlie the worst forms of prejudice and irrationality. We need not repeat the details about our nation's long-standing practices of discrimination on the basis of race and sex—now understood to violate our deepest constitutional ideals—in order to establish the point. Nor should it be necessary to stress that the most solemn obligation of this Court is to uphold constitutional principles against popular prejudice and irrationality, which often take the form of "repugnance." And to the extent that the ban on cloning has foundations in religious convictions, it should be unnecessary to say that religious convictions, standing alone, are not, in a pluralistic society, a sufficient basis for the coercion of law. It does not deprecate religious conviction to say that its appropriate place is not in the statute books, and to emphasize that religious arguments must have secular equivalents in order to provide the basis for law.

V

Our conclusions are fortified by a simple, widely recognized point: A ban on cloning will simply drive the practice of human cloning both abroad and underground. At this stage in our history, it is altogether clear that prohibitions on cloning will not operate as prohibitions, but will simply force people who are determined to clone to act unlawfully or in other nations. Thus, the prohibition at issue here cannot be supported by the government's justifications, which would lose what little force they have if the prohibition cannot operate in practice as it does on paper.

We hold, in sum, that the right to clone, however novel as a matter of technology, is part and parcel of a time-honored individual right to control the circumstances and event of reproduction; that the government has pointed to no sufficient justification for overriding that fundamental right; and that on inspection, the government's grounds for concern dissolve into a simple statement of repugnance and disgust, lacking scientific or ethical foundations and fed mostly by imaginative literature. Because they invade the right to privacy in its most fundamental form, legal bans on cloning violate the due process clause of the Constitution.

The judgment of the court of appeals is affirmed.

It is so ordered.

KRISTINA MARTIN AND RONALD MARTIN, ET AL. V. MARTIN BALLINGER, SECRETARY OF HEALTH AND HUMAN SERVICES, ET AL.

On Petition for Writ of Certiorari to the United States Court of Appeals for the Eighth Circuit
No. 99–1099

Justice Winston delivered the opinion of the Court.

In this case a group of American citizens seeking to clone human beings have challenged federal and state prohibitions on cloning. The plaintiffs are married couples. They argue that these prohibitions violate their right to free reproductive choice.

The plaintiffs make two arguments. They argue, first, that the right to clone is part and parcel of the right to reproductive privacy, closely akin to the rights to use contraception and to have an abortion, recognized under our prior cases. They therefore urge that the right to clone qualifies, under the due process clause of the Fifth and Fourteenth Amendments, as a "fundamental interest," which may be invaded only if the government can satisfy "strict scrutiny," by showing the most compelling of justifications.

The plaintiffs argue, second, that even if the right to clone does not qualify as a "fundamental interest,"

the legal prohibition is unconstitutional, because the government cannot show a "rational basis" for the restriction. The plaintiffs claim that the government has no legitimate reason for interfering with private decisions about whether to have a child via cloning.

The government makes several arguments in response. It urges that the right to clone is very different from the right to use contraceptives or to have an abortion, and that it does not qualify as a fundamental right under the Constitution. The government also claims that there are compelling reasons to ban human cloning even if the right to clone does qualify as a fundamental right. Finally, the government insists that there is a "rational basis" for restricting human cloning, to prevent a wide range of social harms.

We accept the government's arguments and hold today that under the Constitution as it is now understood, there is no constitutional right to clone. The Court's cases recognize an individual right to control reproduction, as part of the liberty protected by the due process clause of the Fifth and Fourteenth Amendments. But it is facetious, at best, to say that anything in our precedents recognizes an individual right to replicate oneself through the new technology of cloning.

To override the individual interest in replicating other human beings, the government needs only a "rational basis." But the government has far more than this. We believe that the government has exceptionally powerful grounds for controlling cloning. Indeed, the government's justifications are strong enough to override the individual's interest even if the government needs to overcome "strict scrutiny," the least deferential standard the Court now uses.

I

There is an acknowledged constitutional right to some form of individual control over decisions involving reproduction. In *Griswold v. Connecticut,* 381 U.S. 479 (1965), this Court held that a state could not ban a married couple from using contraceptives. In the Court's view, a right of "privacy" forecloses state interference with that decision. In *Eisenstadt v. Baird,* 405 U.S. 438 (1972), the Court extended *Griswold* to invalidate a law forbidding the distribution of contraceptives to unmarried people. In the key passage of its opinion, the Court said, "If the right of privacy means anything, it is the right of the individual, married or single, to be free from unwarranted governmental intrusion into matters so affecting a person as the decision whether to bear or beget a child." And in *Roe v. Wade,* 410 U.S. 113 (1973), the Court held that there is a constitutional right to have an abortion. This decision the Court strongly reaffirmed in *Casey v. Planned Parenthood,* 505 U.S. 833 (1992).

On the other hand, we have held that there is no general right against government interference with important private choices. Thus in *Washington v. Glucksberg,* 116 U.S. 2021 (1997), we held that under ordinary circumstances, there is no general right to physician-assisted suicide. We emphasized that this right is quite foreign to the traditions of American law and policy, which strongly discourage suicide, assisted or otherwise.

These cases clearly establish a basic principle: The Constitution creates a presumptive individual right to decide whether and when to reproduce. Thus, government cannot prevent people from choosing not to have a child, and we agree with the plaintiffs that serious issues would also be raised by (for example) a legal requirement of abortion, or a restriction on the number of children a married couple might have. But the constitutional right is far from unbounded. It lies in a specific judgment about *reproduction,* understood by our traditions as a distinctive human interest with a distinctive human meaning.

Our traditions rebel against the idea that the state, rather than the individual, can make the decision whether a person is to bear or beget a child. But it defies common sense to suggest that *replication* falls in the same category. No tradition supports a right to replicate. This is not merely a matter of technological limitations. The human meaning of replication, of creating genetically identical beings, is fundamentally different from that of reproduction, and replication is to many people horrifying. Centuries of culture, of myth and literature, confirm this basic fact. It is not the business of this Court to say whether replication of human beings should or should not be permitted. But when the people of the country, and their elected representatives, conclude that it should be banned, no fundamental right is invaded. We require only a rational justification.

II

The plaintiffs rely most fundamentally on *Roe v. Wade,* but there is an enormous difference between the right to clone and the right to an abortion. The Court has come to see that the decision in *Roe* turned in large part on the interest in equality on the basis of sex. As a matter of history, governments have denied the right to abortion because they seek to preserve women's traditional role. Moreover, the denial of the right to have an abortion tends to fortify that traditional role and thus to undermine equality on the basis of sex. No equality interest supports the right to clone. With respect to sex equality, cloning is a very complex matter— reasonable people have set forth competing views— and we do not believe that it is plausible to argue that the right to clone finds a justification in principles of equality on the basis of sex.

There is a further point. *Roe v. Wade* did not create a general right to decide whether to have a child through whatever technological means may be available. It is far narrower than that: an outgrowth of cases establishing a right to decide whether to reproduce, a time-honored right in Anglo-American law. The right to replicate stands on much weaker ground.

III

Even if the ban on cloning were subject to the most stringent forms of judicial review, it would be upheld. Physical difficulties and even deformities are highly likely. The government has an exceptionally strong interest in protecting young children against disease and disability, and both of these are likely products of experiments in human cloning. The government has pointed to considerable evidence of this risk, and this Court is in no position to second-guess the scientific evidence.

It is highly likely as well that the practice of cloning would have undesirable effects on the "people" who result. There is some evidence of psychological difficulties faced by human twins; the practice of cloning will inevitably risk far more severe problems from people who know that they are genetic equivalents of people with known lives, including known problems, known successes, and known failures. Similarly, the government reasonably fears that the parent-child relationship, between genetic equivalents, would be unrecognizable, and permeated by difficulties of various sorts. It may well be that especially wealthy people, or especially narcissistic people, would fund large numbers of replications of themselves. Who would rear the resulting children? With what motivations? The government has the strongest possible reasons to fear the outcomes of such a situation.

There is a further consideration. The government has an extremely powerful interest in preserving the stock of biological diversity. Widespread cloning could compromise that interest to the detriment of humanity as a whole. We think that these points confirm our belief that the government has a wide range of compelling interests sufficient to override any presumptive right to clone.

IV

If the decision whether to clone does not qualify as a fundamental right, the only question is whether the government's ban is "rational." Certainly it qualifies as such. As we have indicated, the government might reasonably believe that there would be adverse psychological effects on "clones." It might believe that the process of cloning human beings would result in physical deformities for the "products" of the relevant scientific practices. It might even believe that the existence of clones would have adverse psychological effects on many children and even adults who might fear that they would be cloned against their will. All of these speculations are reasonable.

This Court does not sit to second-guess reasonable judgments by the elected representatives of the American people, especially when there is no defect in the system of democratic deliberation that gave rise to the law under review. And it should not be necessary to say that the religious convictions that may underlie legal bans on cloning are not, in a pluralistic society, at all troublesome from the standpoint of constitutional democracy, where everyone's convictions are entitled to count.

Our conclusions are not undermined in the least by the possibility that people determined to defy the law will do so, either here or by seeking refuge abroad. It is not an argument against the criminal law that criminal prohibitions may be violated or circumvented. If bans on human replication do not operate in practice as they do on paper, Congress and the legislatures of the several states are entitled to respond as they choose.

We hold, in sum, that the right to clone has no basis in our constitutional traditions, which involve human reproduction, not replication; that the government has ample grounds for restricting individual choice in light of the novelty of the relevant technology and its unpredictable and potentially damaging effects on the most basic human values and in particular on those involved in the relevant "experiments." Because they do not implicate the right to privacy or any other constitutionally protected interest, legal bans on cloning are entirely consistent with the due process clause of the Constitution.

The judgment of the court of appeals is reversed. It is so ordered.

Questions for Analysis

1. What different lines of reasoning do these opinions take in determining that there is or is not a constitutional right to reproductive privacy? Which do you think is closer to the cited precedents?

2. What government interests in preventing cloning are discussed in these opinions? Why does the first opinion call them speculative? Why does the second consider them compelling enough to survive "strict scrutiny"? Which opinion do you agree with on this point?

3. If a case like the one Sunstein imagines does come before the Supreme Court, how do you think it will rule? How do you think it should rule?

4. In what ways is the decision to bear a clone like the decision to use contraception or the decision to abort a pregnancy? In what ways is it unlike these other decisions? What bearing do these differences have on the moral and legal issues surrounding cloning?

CASE PRESENTATION
Recommendations of the President's Council on Bioethics[1]

For the past five years, the prospect of human cloning has been the subject of considerable public attention and sharp moral debate, both in the United States and around the world. Since the announcement in February 1997 of the first successful cloning of a mammal (Dolly the sheep), several other species of mammals have been cloned. Although a cloned human child has yet to be born, and although the animal experiments have had low rates of success, the production of functioning mammalian cloned offspring suggests that the eventual cloning of humans must be considered a serious possibility.

In November 2001, American researchers claimed to have produced the first cloned human embryos, though they reportedly reached only a six-cell stage before they stopped dividing and died. In addition, several fertility specialists, both here and abroad, have announced their intention to clone human beings. The United States Congress has twice taken up the matter, in 1998 and again in 2001–2002, with the House of Representatives in July 2001 passing a strict ban on all human cloning, including the production of cloned human embryos. As of this writing, several cloning-related bills are under consideration in the Senate. Many other nations have banned human cloning, and the United Nations is considering an international convention on the subject. . . .

Public Policy Options

The Council recognizes the challenges and risks of moving from moral assessment to public policy. Reflections on the "social contract" between science and society highlight both the importance of scientific freedom and the need for boundaries. We note that other countries often treat human cloning in the context of a broad area of biomedical technology, at the intersection of reproductive technology, embryo research, and genetics, while the public policy debate in the United States has treated cloning largely on its own. We recognize the special difficulty in formulat-

ing sound public policy in this area, given that the two ethically distinct matters—cloning-to-produce-children and cloning-for-biomedical-research—will be mutually affected or implicated in any attempts to legislate about either. Nevertheless, our ethical and policy analysis leads us to the conclusion that some deliberate public policy at the federal level is needed in the area of human cloning.

We reviewed the following seven possible policy options and considered their relative strengths and weaknesses: (1) Professional self-regulation but no federal legislative action ("self-regulation"); (2) A ban on cloning-to-produce-children, with neither endorsement nor restriction of cloning-for-biomedical-research ("ban plus silence"); (3) A ban on cloning-to-produce-children, with regulation of the use of cloned embryos for biomedical research ("ban plus regulation"); (4) Governmental regulation, with no legislative prohibitions ("regulation of both"); (5) A ban on all human cloning, whether to produce children or for biomedical research ("ban on both"); (6) A ban on cloning-to-produce-children, with a moratorium or temporary ban on cloning-for-biomedical-research ("ban plus moratorium"); or (7) A moratorium or temporary ban on all human cloning, whether to produce children or for biomedical research ("moratorium on both").

The Council's Policy Recommendations

Having considered the benefits and drawbacks of each of these options, and taken into account our discussions and reflections throughout this report, the Council recommends two possible policy alternatives, each supported by a portion of the Members.

Majority Recommendation: Ten Members of the Council recommend a ban on cloning-to-produce-children combined with a four-year moratorium on cloning-for-biomedical-research. We also call for a federal review of current and projected practices of human embryo research, pre-implantation genetic diagnosis, genetic modification of human embryos and gametes, and related matters, with a view to recommending and shaping ethically sound policies for the entire field. Speaking only for ourselves, those of us who support this recommendation do so for some or all of the following reasons:

---

1.   This is excerpted from the executive summary of the Council's report, *Human Cloning and Human Dignity: An Ethical Inquiry*, U.S. Government, Washington, 2002. Other chapters in the report include discussions of the historical, scientific, and ethical issues surrounding cloning. The full text is available on the Web:

http://www.bioethics.gov/reports/cloning/cloningreport/index.html

- By permanently banning cloning-to-produce-children, this policy gives force to the strong ethical verdict against cloning-to-produce-children, unanimous in this Council (and in Congress) and widely supported by the American people. And by enacting a four-year moratorium on the creation of cloned embryos, it establishes an additional safeguard not afforded by policies that would allow the production of cloned embryos to proceed without delay.

- It calls for and provides time for further democratic deliberation about cloning-for-biomedical research, a subject about which the nation is divided and where there remains great uncertainty. A national discourse on this subject has not yet taken place in full, and a moratorium, by making it impossible for either side to cling to the status-quo, would force both to make their full case before the public. By banning all cloning for a time, it allows us to seek moral consensus on whether or not we should cross a major moral boundary (creating nascent cloned human life solely for research) and prevents our crossing it without deliberate decision. It would afford time for scientific evidence, now sorely lacking, to be gathered—from animal models and other avenues of human research—that might give us a better sense of whether cloning-for-biomedical-research would work as promised, and whether other morally nonproblematic approaches might be available. It would promote a fuller and better-informed public debate. And it would show respect for the deep moral concerns of the large number of Americans who have serious ethical objections to this research.

- Some of us hold that cloning-for-biomedical-research can never be ethically pursued, and endorse a moratorium to enable us to continue to make our case in a democratic way. Others of us support the moratorium because it would provide the time and incentive required to develop a system of national regulation that might come into use if, at the end of the four-year period, the moratorium were not reinstated or made permanent. Such a system could not be developed overnight, and therefore even those who support the research but want it regulated should see that at the very least a pause is required. In the absence of a moratorium, few proponents of the research would have much incentive to institute an effective regulatory system. Moreover, the very process of proposing such regulations would clarify the moral and prudential judgments involved in deciding whether and how to proceed with this research.

- A moratorium on cloning-for-biomedical-research would enable us to consider this activity in the larger context of research and technology in the areas of developmental biology, embryo research, and genetics, and to pursue a more comprehensive federal regulatory system for setting and executing policy in the entire area.

- Finally, we believe that a moratorium, rather than a lasting ban, signals a high regard for the value of biomedical research and an enduring concern for patients and families whose suffering such research may help alleviate. It would reaffirm the principle that science can progress while upholding the community's moral norms, and would therefore reaffirm the community's moral support for science and biomedical technology.

The decision before us is of great importance. Creating cloned embryos for any purpose requires crossing a major moral boundary, with grave risks and likely harms, and once we cross it there will be no turning back. Our society should take the time to make a judgment that is well-informed and morally sound, respectful of strongly held views, and representative of the priorities and principles of the American people. We believe this ban-plus-moratorium proposal offers the best means of achieving these goals. . . .

Minority Recommendation: Seven Members of the Council recommend a ban on cloning-to-produce-children, with regulation of the use of cloned embryos for biomedical research. Speaking only for ourselves, those of us who support this recommendation do so for some or all of the following reasons:

- By permanently banning cloning-to-produce-children, this policy gives force to the strong ethical verdict against cloning-to-produce-children, unanimous in this Council (and in Congress) and widely supported by the American people. We believe that a ban on the transfer of cloned embryos to a woman's uterus would be a sufficient and effective legal safeguard against the practice.

- It approves cloning-for-biomedical-research and permits it to proceed without substantial delay. This is the most important advantage of this proposal. The research shows great promise, and its actual value can only be determined by allowing it to go forward now. Regardless of how much time we allow it, no amount of experimentation with animal models can provide the needed understanding of human diseases. The special benefits from working with stem cells from cloned human embryos cannot be obtained using embryos obtained by IVF. We believe this research could provide relief to millions of Americans, and that the government should therefore support it, within sensible limits imposed by regulation.

- It would establish, as a condition of proceeding, the necessary regulatory protections to avoid abuses and misuses of cloned embryos.

These regulations might touch on the secure handling of embryos, licensing and prior review of research projects, the protection of egg donors, and the provision of equal access to benefits.

- Some of us also believe that mechanisms to regulate cloning-for-biomedical-research should be part of a larger regulatory program governing all research involving human embryos, and that the federal government should initiate a review of present and projected practices of human embryo research, with the aim of establishing reasonable policies on the matter.

Permitting cloning-for-biomedical-research now, while governing it through a prudent and sensible regulatory regime, is the most appropriate way to allow important research to proceed while insuring that abuses are prevented. We believe that the legitimate concerns about human cloning expressed throughout this report are sufficiently addressed by this ban-plus-regulation proposal, and that the nation should affirm and support the responsible effort to find treatments and cures that might help many who are suffering. . . .

Questions for Analysis

1. All members of the council agree on recommending a permanent ban on cloning-to-produce-children. Are there developments in medical research that might someday justify permitting such cloning? Are the ethical concerns about cloning-to-produce-children sufficiently strong that no scientific advances would ever justify permitting such cloning?

2. A majority of the council recommends a four-year moratorium on cloning-for-biomedical-research to allow the nation time for further deliberation on the moral issues presented by such research. What additional ethical issues should be examined in an effort to reach the moral consensus sought by these council members? As some of these members state that they do not believe cloning-for-biomedical-research can ever be ethically pursued, is this recommendation just a stalling tactic?

3. A minority of the council recommends allowing cloning-for-biomedical-research immediately, with appropriate government regulation to avoid abuses and misuses of cloned embryos. Why is this group of council members eager to permit this research? Would government regulation be sufficient to protect against possible abuses and overcome the ethical concerns of the majority?

CASE PRESENTATION

Clonaid

It's a truly bizarre mixture. Start with Rael, once a French sportswriter named Claude Vorilhon, then a singer-songwriter named Claude Cellar, and now the leader of a UFO-worshiping cult called the Raelians, which claims to have more than 50,000 members in eighty-five countries. Among the cult's tenets is the belief that human life is the product of the Elohim, a group of alien scientists who cloned themselves and transported the clones to Earth; among its practices, free love; among its assets, a Montreal theme park named UFOland; among its planned projects, a welcome center for visiting scientists from other planets.

Next add Clonaid, a Bahamian corporation the Raelians founded in 1997 to create clones for homosexual couples who want to start families. Bridgette Boisselier, a French-born chemical engineer who now lives in New York State, is the corporation's scientific director. She claims to have hired a team of three American-trained scientists—a physician, a geneticist, and a biochemist—to create the clones. She also claims to have enlisted fifty young Raelian volunteers, including her daughter, to serve as surrogate mothers for Clonaid's homosexual clients.

Now add to this list a wealthy American couple who lost their ten-month-old daughter due to a tragic medical error. In October 2000, Clonaid announced that the unidentified couple would be the corporation's first clients—not just clients but business partners as well, since they had agreed to fork over a total of $1 million to Clonaid, half as a cloning fee and the other half as an investment in the corporation. (The fee for future clients was set at $200,000.) The procedure was to be performed somewhere in the United States, where human cloning had not been banned, reportedly Nevada.

Whether Clonaid actually has the ability to clone humans, or whether the American couple even exists, has not been confirmed, but scientists around the world expressed reactions ranging from concern to alarm. Ian Wilmut, for example, the scientist who headed the team that created Dolly and knows as well as anyone the risks involved in trying to clone humans at this time, told England's *Sunday Times* that the program was "absolutely criminal." Meanwhile, in the United States, the Food and Drug Administration, which has the authority to regulate human cloning, began to monitor the program.

Despite the risks, Clonaid claims that more than 100 couples have signed up for the program, not only homosexuals but also infertile couples and couples who have lost a child. In 2003, Clonaid claimed that it had produced five cloned babies and that they were developing normally. Scientists and news organizations remain skeptical that the cloned babies even exist.

Questions for Analysis

1. Because of a presidential order banning the use of federal funds for human cloning, such research is left to private sources like Clonaid. Which would be better, to reverse the order or to enact an outright ban on all efforts to clone humans?

2. Does the existence of Clonaid help to show that the cloning of humans is inevitable? If so, how should that affect the moral and legal debates on the issue?

3. Much of the alarm caused by Clonaid is a result of the nature of the Raelians and what they believe in. Much of it is also a result of the unresolved safety issues of current cloning technology. Suppose that a scientifically respectable team of scientists were to demonstrate that human cloning is indeed safe. Should they be allowed to offer the procedure to the public?

4. According to news reports, Clonaid is preparing to offer another service, Clonapet. What, if any, moral objections would you have to that service?

CASE PRESENTATION
A Birth to Save a Life

When Louise Brown, the world's first "test-tube" baby, was born in Oldham, England, she and her parents became instant international celebrities. But that was back in 1978, an entirely different era in terms of reproductive technology. Today, by contrast, in vitro fertilization is an everyday aid in helping women to conceive, not just in the industrialized West but also in such countries as Egypt, Malaysia, and Pakistan. Whether the sperm comes from the woman's husband or an anonymous donor, it is routinely joined with her egg in a laboratory, and just as routinely the newly formed embryo is implanted in the woman's womb. Rarely do these procedures make news.

But the *Washington Post* found one such case newsworthy when it reported in October 2000 that Adam Nash, a test-tube baby, had been conceived and born to save his sister's life. The sister, six-year-old Molly Nash, was born with Franconi anemia, an inherited disease that prevents the production of bone marrow cells. Children who suffer from the condition usually die from leukemia or some other complication by the age of seven, and Molly had already developed a blood condition her doctors called "preleukemia." The only effective treatment for Franconi anemia is a successful cell transplant.

Unlike Louise's conception, Adam's involved another, more recent technique as well: preimplantation genetic diagnosis, which allows scientists to examine the genes of an embryo before it's implanted in the womb. Fifteen embryos were created for the Nashes, and researchers at Illinois Masonic Medical Center tested each of them for two genetic traits. First, it had to be free of Franconi anemia; second, it had to be a perfect match for Molly. Two embryos passed, one was implanted, and on August 29, 2000, Adam was born in a Denver hospital, where doctors painlessly removed the needed donor cells from his umbilical cord. A month later, they were introduced into his sister's bloodstream. According to the director of medical genetics at the center that performed the tests, Molly had an 85 to 90 percent chance of being free of the disease. And in an article that appeared in *The New York Times* the following day, the doctor who performed the transplant said that Molly's blood tests had already begun to improve.

What made the story newsworthy was the Nashes' reason for using preimplantation genetic diagnosis. In previous cases, it had been used to select genes that were best for the health of the future child. In this case, it was used for Molly's benefit. That makes Adam's conception and birth the first case in which modern reproductive technology and genetic testing combined to create a suitable donor for a transplant. It will not, however, be the last. Before the story was even reported, ten other families had begun preparing for the same procedure.

Despite the procedure's promise for such families, the articles in both newspapers raised identical ethical questions. As bioethicist Jeffrey P. Kahn told the *Times,* "We've crossed the line that we really never crossed before, selecting based on characteristics that are not best for the child being born, but for somebody else." Dr. Kahn also posed a moral dilemma that goes well beyond the technologies used for the Nashes: "Nobody wants babies to be born strictly for the parts they could create, but by the same token, I don't think we're willing as a society to ask people why they're having children and to say, 'That's not a good enough reason.'"

The other ethical question concerns "designer" babies. "You could say it's like buying a new car, where you decide which package of accessories you want," said Dr. Kahn, this time speaking to the *Post*. "I suppose it's only because we don't yet have the tests that we're not having parents asking for embryos without a predisposition to homosexuality or for kids who will grow to more than six feet tall."

Questions for Analysis

1. Is it morally wrong to create a child for "parts," as the Nashes did? Would it be wrong to use cloning for the same purpose?

2. Are there good and bad reasons for having children? For using reproductive technologies or the genetic testing of embryos? If so, what distinguishes the good from the bad? How closely does the distinction parallel the distinction between good and bad reasons for creating a clone?

3. What, if any, moral concerns does the prospect of choosing embryos for a variety of traits—beauty, say, or athletic ability—raise? How close are they to the moral concerns raised by cloning?

4. Earlier in this chapter, we discussed the case of Abe and Mary Ayala, who conceived and bore a child to provide a compatible donor for their leukemia-stricken daughter. Do you see any important difference between what they did and what the Nashes did?

5. For whatever reasons the Nashes and Ayalas conceived their youngest children, they ended up loving them as much as their other children. Does that make the reasons irrelevant?

CASE PRESENTATION

Therapeutic Human Cloning in Britain

In our discussion of why anyone would want to clone humans, we noted that some reasons have nothing to do with creating a fully developed human being. One reason mentioned is to create embryos that could be used to generate compatible organs for transplants. Although not possible now, scientists believe that research in the area will eventually prove successful. What makes this research so promising is that early-stage embryos contain unprogrammed master cells, called stem cells, which can produce any kind of tissue in the body.

Despite the potential of such research, it remains highly controversial because it involves the creation and destruction of a human embryo, and for those who believe that a human embryo is a person, that amounts to murder. That's why U.S. law bans scientists who receive federal funds from pursuing stem cell research, even if the embryos are not the product of cloning but are left over from in vitro fertilization (IVF) clinics. The ban does not affect scientists who receive no federal funds, but it does have the practical consequences of severely restricting stem cell research. Because of the significant reliance of academic and many other researchers on federal grants, the number of scientists free to pursue the research is limited.

In Britain, however, matters are different. On December 19, 2000, the British House of Commons voted to allow researchers to clone human embryos and to keep them alive for fourteen days to extract stem cells, not just for research into generating organs for transplant but for other therapeutic purposes as well, including the prevention and treatment of such conditions as paralysis and diabetes. The vote followed a call by the country's chief medical officer to allow the research.

In the United States, the National Institutes of Health (NIH) had called for a change in the law to allow government-funded scientists to perform the same research well before the British vote. Because of powerful opposition in Congress, however, such a change seems unlikely.

Questions for Analysis

1. Since cloning for stem cell research is legal in the United States, should government funds be made available to stem cell researchers?

2. Is there a moral difference between using cloned embryos in research and using leftover embryos from IVF clinics? Would you support legalization of either? Why or why not?

3. The NIH call for a change in U.S. policy is based on scientific considerations, while congressional resistance is based on moral and religious considerations. Which should take precedence here?

7

Capital Punishment

The Nature and Definition of Punishment
The Moral Acceptability of Punishment
Aims of Punishment
Retentionist and *Abolitionist* Defined
Capital Punishment as Deterrent
Abolitionist Arguments (against Capital Punishment)
Retentionist Arguments (for Capital Punishment)

John Stuart Mill, "Speech in Favor of
Capital Punishment"
Sidney Hook, "The Death Sentence"
Ernest Van Den Haag, "On Deterrence and the Death Penalty"
Hugo Adam Bedau, "Capital Punishment and Social Defense"
CASE PRESENTATION, "J. D. Autry: Death in Texas"
CASE PRESENTATION, "Karla Faye Tucker:
The Pickax Murderer"
CASE PRESENTATION, "A Failed Experiment?"
CASE PRESENTATION, "Warren McClesky"

Late on the night of October 4, 1983, in Huntsville, Texas, convicted killer J. D. Autry was taken from his death-row cell in the penitentiary and strapped to a wheeled cot. Intravenous tubes were connected to both arms, ready to administer a dose of poison.

Outside, a crowd shouted "Kill him, kill him, kill him!" whenever television lights were turned on.

In Washington, Supreme Court Justice Byron White waited for a last-minute application for a stay of execution. The application, written on three sheets of a yellow pad, made a new argument related to another case due to be heard by the Court. Shortly after midnight, White granted the stay. The intravenous tubes were disconnected, the straps unbuckled. Autry was returned to his cell. Only in March of 1984 was the execution carried out.

The U.S. Supreme Court decision that paved the way for Autry's execution was *Gregg v. Georgia* (1976). In an earlier decision, *Furman v. Georgia* (1972), the Court had ruled that capital punishment as then administered was cruel and unusual punishment and therefore unconstitutional. The issue in that case was *standardless discretion*—the freedom of a jury (or in some cases, a judge) to use its own discretion in determining a sentence without explicit legal standards to guide its decision. In their attempts to get around the decision, some states passed laws making the death penalty mandatory for certain crimes, while others enacted legal standards to guide the discretion of the sentencing jury or judge. In *Woodson v. North Carolina* (1976), the Supreme Court ruled laws of the first type unconstitutional. In *Gregg v. Georgia*, it upheld laws of the second type for the crime of murder.

Since that decision, capital punishment has withstood another major legal challenge—*McClesky v. Kemp* (1987). In that case, the Supreme Court ruled against Warren McClesky, a black man who had been sentenced to death for killing a white policeman. McClesky argued that the imposition of the death penalty was unconstitutionally affected by racial bias, and in support of his claim, he offered studies showing that convicted killers of white victims were more likely to receive the death penalty than were convicted killers of black victims. Although the Court did not dispute the studies, it rejected his argument. With almost 1,900 convicted killers waiting on death row, the constitutionality of the death penalty was upheld by a 5 to 4 majority.

The application of the death penalty has been narrowed, however. In 2002, in *Atkins v. Virginia,* the U.S. Supreme Court held that execution of people with mental retardation violated the constitutional protection against cruel and unusual punishment. This decision reversed a 1989 decision, *Perry v. Lynaugh,* which said that executing mentally retarded individuals did not violate the Constitution. In the *Atkins* decision, the Court said that executing people mentally retarded does not meet the deterrent nor the retributive purpose of the death penalty. They also noted a growing national consensus that executing mentally retarded people is wrong. Of the thirty-eight states that permit capital punishment, eighteen had banned execution of mentally retarded people.

Execution of minors under eighteen remains permissible, however. In 2002, the Court declined to hear a case asking that execution of minors be declared unconstitutional, even though four justices said they wanted to hear the case and would have held such executions unconstitutional. Sixteen states currently allow the execution of minors.

Scientific developments, especially DNA testing, have further complicated public debate over the appropriateness of the death penalty. In 2000, the governor of Illinois announced a moratorium on executions, as DNA testing had shown that thirteen people on death row were innocent. Maryland has also instituted a moratorium, and efforts are underway in Congress to pass a nationwide moratorium.

Support for the death penalty remains strong in the United States, with recent polls indicating more than half the population supports it and most of those believing it should be used more often. More than 600 prisoners have been executed since the *Gregg v. Georgia* decision in 1976. Internationally, however, support for capital punishment has been steadily declining. It has been abolished in Canada, Mexico, Russia, South Africa, and most industrialized nations. Amnesty International claims that more than half the nations in the world have abolished the death penalty in law or in practice.

The death penalty is a form of punishment. Consequently, one's view of the morality of the death penalty usually is influenced by one's view of punishment generally. So the specific moral question under discussion in this chapter is: Is capital punishment ever a justifiable form of punishment?

THE NATURE AND
DEFINITION OF PUNISHMENT

Generally, philosophers discuss punishment in terms of five elements. For something to be punishment, it must (1) involve pain, (2) be administered for an offense against a law or rule, (3) be administered to someone who has been judged guilty of an offense, (4) be imposed by someone other than the offender, and (5) be imposed by rightful authority. Whether a punishment is commensurate with an offense, whether it is fair and equitable—these are very important moral and legal questions. But they must be distinguished from the question of what punishment is.

1. *Punishment must involve pain, harm, or some other consequence normally considered unpleasant.* For example, if convicted robbers were sentenced to "five to twenty" in a Beverly Hills country club, this would not be considered punishment, since ordinarily it would not involve pain or other unpleasant consequences (unless the robbers had to pick up the tab). If they were sentenced to have their hands cut off, this could constitute punishment, though draconian by many people's standards.

2. *The punishment must be administered for an offense against a law or rule.* While punishment involves pain, obviously not all pain involves punishment. If robbers break into your house and steal your stereo, they are not "punishing" you, even though their action satisfies element one. Although it caused you pain, their action is not taken to punish an offense against a law or rule. However, should the robbers subsequently be sent to prison for the crime, then that action would be administered for breaking a law and thus satisfy element two.

3. *The punishment must be administered to someone who has been judged guilty of an offense.* Suppose the robbers are apprehended and imprisoned, although never judged guilty of the robbery. This would not be considered punishment. However, if they are imprisoned after their conviction for stealing your stereo, then they are being punished.

4. *The punishment must be imposed by someone other than the offender.* It is true that people sometimes speak of "punishing themselves" for a transgression. This, however, is not punishment in the strict sense but a self-imposed act of atonement. Suffering from a twinge of conscience as they listen to the latest Willie Nelson album on your stereo, the robbers decide to "punish" themselves by listening to Robert Goulet, whom they detest, for two hours each day for a year. Properly speaking, this would not be punishment, although it might qualify as masochism.

5. *The punishment must be imposed by rightful authority.* In a strictly legal sense, "rightful authority" would be that constituted by a legal system against whom the offense is committed. In the case of the robbers, "rightful authority" would likely be a court judge and jury. In a less legal sense, the authority might be a parent, a teacher, or some official who has a right to harm a person in a particular way for having done something or failed to do something.

These five elements, then, generally constitute the nature of punishment. Combining them produces a useful definition of punishment. Thus, a punishment is harm inflicted by a rightful authority on a person who has been judged to have violated a law or rule.[1]

THE MORAL ACCEPTABILITY OF PUNISHMENT

Is punishment ever morally acceptable? This may seem a foolish question to ask, because it is hard to imagine society functioning without an established legal system of punishment. In fact, philosophers generally agree that punishment is morally acceptable. They, like most others, view punishment as a part of the rule and law necessary to minimize the occurrence of forbidden acts. In short, law without punishment is toothless.

Still, there are people who do not share this view. They argue that society should be restructured so that a legal system of punishment is unnecessary. Just how this can or should be done remains problematic. The method most often proposed involves some form of therapeutic treatment or behavior modification for antisocial behavior rather than a traditional form of punishment. Among the most morally controversial procedures for modifying undesirable social behavior are those associated with some startling advances in biomedicine. Such cases rarely can be resolved by a simple appeal to the individual's right to obtain appropriate treatment on request, and they are even less likely to be resolved by an appeal to society's right to order such treatment.

Consider one case provided by a leading research scientist in the field, Dr. J. R. Delgado. A number of years ago, Delgado recalls, an attractive twenty-four-year-old woman of average intelligence and education and a long record of arrests for disorderly conduct approached him and his associates. The patient explained that she had been repeatedly involved in bar brawls in which she would entice men to fight over her. Having spent a number of years in jail and mental institutions, the woman expressed a strong desire but inability to change her behavior. Because past psychological therapy had proved ineffective, both she and her mother urgently requested that some sort of brain surgery be performed to control her antisocial and destructive behavior. As Delgado said: "They asked specifically that electrodes be implanted to orient a possible electrocoagulation of a limited cerebral area; and if that wasn't possible, they wanted a lobotomy."[2]

At that time, medical knowledge could not determine whether such procedures could help resolve the woman's problem, so the physicians rejected surgical intervention. When Delgado and his colleagues explained their decision to the woman and her mother, the two reacted with disappointment and anxiety: "What is the future? Only jail or the hospital?"[3]

1.   See Burton M. Leiser, *Liberty, Justice, and Morals* (New York: Macmillan, 1973), pp. 195–197.

2.   J. R. Delgado, *Physical Control of the Mind: Toward a Psycho-Civilized Society* (New York: Harper & Row, 1969), p. 85.

3.   Ibid.

What is the future, indeed? The day could very well come when such therapeutic treatment renders traditional kinds of punishment obsolete, perhaps barbaric. But even then, pressing moral questions will remain concerning society's right to alter an individual's personality against his or her will. For now, most agree that punishment is a morally acceptable practice. What they do not agree on, however, is the aim of punishment.

AIMS OF PUNISHMENT

The aims of punishment can be divided into two categories: (1) in terms of giving people what they deserve or (2) in terms of its desirable consequences. The first category includes retributive theories of punishment; the second includes preventive, deterrent, and reformative theories.

Retribution

The term **retribution** refers to punishment given in return for some wrong done. This view of punishment holds that we should punish people simply because they deserve it. Traditionally, retributive theorists have considered punishment a principle of justice, often referred to as retributory justice, whereby offenders are made to suffer in kind for the harm they have caused others. Arguments in favor of capital punishment commonly make this point.

But another version of retribution associates punishment not with revenge but with respect for persons, both noncriminals and criminals. Proponents of this theory argue that robbers, for example, like everyone else in society, ought to live under the same limitations of freedom. When robbers steal your stereo, they are taking unfair advantage of you, disrupting the balance of equal limitations. When the state subsequently punishes them, the punishment is viewed as an attempt to restore this disrupted balance, to reaffirm society's commitment to fair treatment for all. This version of retribution focuses on the noncriminal generally and the victim in particular, claiming that respect for the parties who abide by society's limitations requires punishment of those who flout those limitations.

The other side of the respect–retribution theory concerns respect for the offender. Proponents of retribution sometimes argue that failure to punish is tantamount to treating offenders with disrespect because it denies them autonomy and responsibility for their actions. Showing respect entails giving people what they deserve, whether that be reward or punishment. To deny praise to a deserving person is disrespectful. By the same token, to deny punishment to a deserving person is equally disrespectful. Both views of respect–retribution can be used in defense of capital punishment.

Prevention

The prevention view of punishment holds that we should punish to ensure that offenders do not repeat their offense and so further injure society. Thus, robbers should be punished, perhaps imprisoned, so that they will not steal anything else. Prevention is one of the most common justifications for capital punishment.

Deterrence

The **deterrence** view holds that we should punish to discourage others from committing similar offenses. Like the prevention theory, it aims to minimize the crime rate. Thus, when other potential thieves see that the robber has been punished for the crime, they will be less likely to steal. Deterrence is perhaps the most common argument made on behalf of capital punishment and thus is the one that those against capital punishment often focus on. For the moment, we will simply observe that if a punishment is to function effectively as a deterrent, it must be severe enough to be undesirable, and just as important, it must be known and certain. Thus, potential offenders must be aware of the kind and severity of the punishment that awaits them, and they must be convinced that they will receive it if they commit the offense.

Reform

The reform theory holds that one should punish to induce people to conform to standards of behavior they have tended to ignore or violate. The idea is that people will emerge from punishment better than they were before, insofar as they will be less likely to breach conventional standards of behavior.

Although rehabilitation often accompanies reform, the aims of each are different. Rehabilitation aims not to punish but to offer the offenders opportunities to find a useful place in society on release from prison. Modern penal institutions attempt to accomplish this goal by providing various recreational, educational, and vocational services for prisoners.

It's important to keep in mind that the aforementioned aims of punishment are not mutually exclusive. It's possible for more than one purpose of punishment to be morally legitimate. In fact, perhaps all four, in varying degrees, might be called for.

RETENTIONIST AND *ABOLITIONIST* DEFINED

Having briefly examined some aspects of punishment, including its nature and definition, its moral acceptability, and its aims, let us now turn to the particular form of punishment that is the topic of this chapter: capital punishment. The central moral question that concerns us is: Is capital punishment ever a justifiable form of punishment?

Those who support retaining or reinstituting capital punishment can be termed **retentionists**. Retentionists are not agreed that all the arguments supporting capital punishment are acceptable or on the conditions under which capital punishment should be imposed. But they do agree that capital punishment is at least sometimes morally justifiable. Those who oppose capital punishment are commonly termed **abolitionists**. Like retentionists, abolitionists disagree among themselves about which arguments against capital punishment are acceptable. But all abolitionists share the belief that capital punishment is never morally justifiable.

One common argument enlisted by both retentionists and abolitionists concerns capital punishment as a deterrent. As we'll see, retentionists sometimes claim that capital punishment deters potential murderers and therefore should be kept. For their part, some abolitionists claim that capital punishment does not serve as a deterrent and offer this—usually with other reasons—for abolishing the death penalty. Because the deterrent argument figures so prominently in capital punishment debates, we should inspect it before beginning this chapter's dialogues.

CAPITAL PUNISHMENT AS DETERRENT

Does capital punishment succeed in deterring potential murderers? At first glance, the answer seems to be a resounding yes. After all, virtually everyone seems deterred from lawbreaking by relatively mild intimidation—for example, being towed away for illegal parking or losing one's driver's license for recklessness. How much more, common sense suggests, must potential murderers be intimidated by the threat of their own death at the executioner's hand. In this instance, however, common sense misleads by failing to recognize that murderers differ from the rest of us in important respects.

First, there's the large category of murderers who kill in a fit of rage or passion. A barroom brawl escalates and one man kills another; in a gang fight, a member of one group kills a member of another, perhaps to save face or avenge a harm; in a family quarrel, a person kills a relative when things get out of hand. The list goes on and on. Such murders, of which there are many, are committed not with forethought of the consequences but in a moment of white-hot anger. Hence, not even the death penalty is likely to deter these murderers. (In fact, in instances of gang killings, it might have the opposite effect: In risking their own lives at the hands of the state, killers might feel they're proving their mettle or giving ultimate evidence of gang loyalty.)

Then there's the category of so-called professional criminals, those who deliberately calculate when, where, and how to commit crimes. It's not at all clear that this type of criminal is deterred by the death penalty. In fact, if professional criminals perceive the likely punishment for nonhomicidal crimes (e.g., robbery, burglary, rape, and so forth) as overly severe, they might be encouraged to kill their victims and witnesses rather than risk getting caught: Killing these people greatly increases the criminals' chances of getting away with their crimes, and so they may not in the least be deterred by the threat of the death penalty.

Besides these kinds of potential murderers are those who seemingly have a death wish. The annals of psychiatry are replete with cases of people so emotionally disturbed that they kill to win the death penalty and end their tortured existence. In effect, their murderous acts are expressions of suicidal impulses. Since they lack the nerve to kill themselves, they want someone else to do it for them—in this case, the state.

But what about cases of so-called normal, nonsuicidal persons who carefully weigh the risks before killing? Are these potential murderers deterred by the death penalty? Even here, the deterrent effect of capital punishment is by no means obvious or certain. What's required is a determination of how many, if any, calculating potential murderers (a small class to begin with) who are not deterred by the threat of life imprisonment would be deterred by the threat of death. Even if such a determination is possible, it's not obvious or certain that there would be any such people at all or much more than a small number annually.

A further complication in assessing the death penalty as deterrent relates not to factual questions such as the preceding but to the moral and legal costs of deterrence. Some claim there's a basic incompatibility between the deterrent efficacy of the death penalty and due process, which refers to a constitutionally guaranteed, specific, systematic procedure of appeal. The death penalty can be deterrent, the argument goes, only if due process is sacrificed. Conversely, due process can govern the inflicting of capital punishment but at the cost of deterrence. When human life is at issue—as of course it is in capital punishment cases—the courts have been understandably scrupulous in reviewing cases for error and ensuring that basic rights have been respected. The consequences of this process of rigorous judicial review are quite apparent: increasing delays of execution, an ever-increasing percentage of those convicted who are never executed, and large numbers of convictions overturned. When fully exercised, the right of appeal can lead to costly, protracted litigation, in which a criminal's fate may hinge as much on the quality of legal representation as on any other factor. Given the delay between murder and the death penalty, and the uncertainty that a death sentence will ever be carried out, one wonders about the death penalty's deterrent effect. On the other hand, to ensure swiftness and certainty mocks one of the most cherished ideals of our system of justice: due process.

Currently, the consensus among social scientists is that no statistical studies on the deterrent effect of capital punishment yield a conclusive answer. We simply don't know whether the threat of death deters people from killing. Given this picture, some argue that since there is a moral presumption against the taking of life, the burden of proving capital punishment is a deterrent should fall on those who advocate the taking of life in the form of capital punishment. But by the same token, one could contend that abolitionists should bear the burden of proof: Since we don't know for sure whether the death penalty is a deterrent, we should give the benefit of doubt to the lives of potential victims of murderers rather than to the murderers. This tack is especially forceful when applied to measures intended to reserve the death penalty for the intentional killings of law enforcement agents and others who need special protection, which they might get from the threat of the death penalty.

ABOLITIONIST ARGUMENTS
(AGAINST CAPITAL PUNISHMENT)

1. *Every human life has dignity and worth.*

POINT: "Capital punishment is nothing more than legalized cold-blooded murder. Whatever crime a person has committed, he or she is still a human being, and every human life has inherent dignity and worth. Don't get me wrong—I'm not advocating leniency toward vicious murderers. We have to protect ourselves from them, and we have to send a clear signal to other would-be murderers that society will not tolerate heinous crime. But life imprisonment without the possibility of parole is sufficient punishment and deterrent. To strap a fellow human being into a chair and give a lethal dose of gas, a lethal jolt of electricity, or a lethal injection is unworthy of a civilized society. Capital punishment should have gone the way of legalized torture and mutilation years ago. It too is 'cruel and unusual punishment,' and like them it's morally unacceptable in today's world."

COUNTERPOINT: "I have no quarrel with a general commitment to respect for human life, but imposing the death penalty on depraved murderers who have no respect for human life themselves is the strongest commitment to that principle a society can make. First-degree murder is the ultimate crime, and anyone who commits it deserves to pay the ultimate price. As for capital punishment being 'cruel and unusual' in today's world, whether a punishment falls into that category depends on prevailing moral standards. And as long as democratically elected legislatures are willing to enact it and citizen juries are willing to impose it, it can hardly be considered cruel and unusual."

2. *Capital punishment is imposed with class and racial bias.*

POINT: "Statistics show two very disturbing facts about the way capital punishment is imposed in our society. First, the poor, the underprivileged, and members of minority groups are far more likely to be executed than the rich, the influential, and whites. Second, the death penalty is far more likely to be imposed when the victim is white than when the victim is the member of a minority group. Regardless of your high-minded principles, capital punishment shows at best a respect for affluent white life, not human life in general. Because its implementation is patently discriminatory and therefore unjust, it must be stopped."

COUNTERPOINT: "Though the bias you mention is indeed unjust, it's irrelevant to the morality of capital punishment. After all, the same charges have often been made against our criminal justice systems in general. Of course, such bias should be rooted out wherever it exists; and of course, comparable crimes should bring the same punishment. But whether capital punishment is justified for the worst of crimes is one issue. Whether it's currently implemented in a justifiable way is another."

3. *The innocent may die.*

POINT: "The innocent are often convicted of crimes. As tragic as that is when the sentence is a prison term, the tragedy is far worse when the sentence is death. In the former case, society can at least make *some* reparation for time unjustly served, but no fact is more obvious than the fact that nothing can be done for the dead. To execute even one innocent person is inexcusable, and there's no way in the world that we can rule that possibility out without abolishing the death penalty."

COUNTERPOINT: "I can't deny that the execution of an innocent human being is a terrible tragedy. Nor can I deny that the possibility will always be there. That's why we require such safeguards as the automatic right of appeal after capital convictions. But given these safeguards, the possibility remains extremely slim. And as unfortunate as that slim risk is, like many other unfortunate risks, it's one worth taking. The thousands of murders committed in the United States each year require us to take it."

4. *Capital punishment compromises the judicial system.*

POINT: "Capital punishment compromises our judicial system in two ways. First, though the point of capital punishment is to present a tough stance against crime, it sometimes has the opposite effect. Juries have been known to strain the evidence to convict defendants of lesser charges—or even to acquit them—when a conviction of first-degree murder carries a mandatory death sentence. Second, cases of capital punishment invariably involve years of costly appeals. Not only does that delay justice, but it also subjects the victims' families, as well as the convicts', to years of cruel and unusual punishment."

COUNTERPOINT: "Again, the problem isn't capital punishment itself but the way it's implemented. And again, the answer is to improve the judicial system, not to abolish the death penalty. We need greater care in jury selection and a more efficient appeals process. What we don't need is to keep vicious murderers alive as wards of the state."

RETENTIONIST ARGUMENTS
(FOR CAPITAL PUNISHMENT)

1. *Capital punishment deters crime.*

POINT: "Simple common sense tells us that capital punishment is a more powerful deterrent against crime than prison. The more severe the punishment, the greater the risk to the would-be criminal; and the greater the risk, the more reason not to commit the crime. I'm not saying that every would-be killer is rational enough to weigh the pros and cons before deciding whether to kill, but it certainly stands to reason that some are. And as long as that's true, capital punishment serves its purpose—saving innocent lives."

COUNTERPOINT: "Regardless of what your common sense tells you, the statistics offer no support. There just isn't any conclusive evidence that the death penalty is a more powerful deterrent than prison. Besides, my common sense doesn't agree with yours. Mine tells me that very few murderers follow any kind of rational weighing of pros and cons. And in the rare cases when they do, the murderer isn't thinking that a life sentence won't be too high a price to pay. It's far more likely that the murderer doesn't expect to get caught in the first place."

2. *Capital punishment keeps the convicted murderer from killing again.*

POINT: "Capital punishment guarantees at least one thing. We don't have to worry that an executed murderer will kill again. Even if every murderer sentenced to imprisonment for life without possibility of parole never leaves prison alive, which is highly doubtful, we still have to worry about murders committed in prison. The rest of society may be protected from these killers, but prison guards and fellow inmates aren't. Don't forget: Since they're already serving the maximum sentence, they have nothing to fear from killing again."

COUNTERPOINT: "The truth of the matter is that convicted murderers rarely do kill again, whether in prison or in society after release or parole. Since we can never know which ones will kill again, we'd have to execute hundreds who would-n't just to prevent one who would. Clearly, that can't be just. We might as well execute everyone who might conceivably commit a murder."

3. *Capital punishment balances the scales of justice.*

POINT: "Murder being the ultimate crime, simple justice requires that the murderer pay the ultimate penalty. After all, deterrence and prevention aren't the only purposes of punishing criminals. An equally important purpose is to see that justice is done, that moral retribution is taken. That's why we insist that the punishment must fit the crime. Furthermore, society has both the right and the obligation to express its moral outrage over the most heinous crimes committed against it. And both purposes are best served by capital punishment. Prison is just too weak a punishment for many murderers, and a prison term cannot satisfy society's moral outrage over vicious murders."

COUNTERPOINT: "You call it retribution and the expression of moral outrage, but I call it revenge. Certainly, justice requires that the guilty be punished for their crimes. It also requires that more severe crimes be met by more severe penalties. But there are moral limits to what we can inflict on even the cruelest criminals. We don't torture murderers who tortured their victims. We don't rape murderers who raped their victims. To do either wouldn't be justice but a gross perversion of justice. It would be bloodthirsty revenge, pure and simple. And that's what the death penalty is."

4. *Society shouldn't have to pay the economic costs of life sentences for murders.*

POINT: "When you put murderers away for life, you give up all hope of reforming them. That leaves society with the heavy cost of supporting the worst criminals in maximum security prisons until they die. Why should innocent taxpayers have to foot the bill for the care of depraved criminals who've demonstrated that they have no respect for society's laws or human life?"

COUNTERPOINT: "Because the rest of us do have—or at least should have—respect for human life. But if we continue to execute our fellow human beings because it's cheaper than keeping them alive, we demonstrate that our respect for human life isn't much stronger than theirs. Besides, don't be so sure that capital punishment is cheaper than life imprisonment. The costs of executing a convict, including the costs of the lengthy appeals process and the high costs of keeping a convict on death row, are enormous."

Speech in Favor of Capital Punishment

John Stuart Mill

The English philosopher John Stuart Mill (1806–1873) is best known for his development of utilitarianism, as well as his sweeping defense of the importance of free speech in the development of democracies. Routinely characterized as a "liberal," he supported capital punishment on what he perceived to be humanitarian grounds drawn from his theory of utilitarianism. He delivered this speech to the English Parliament in 1868 in opposition to a bill introduced by Mr. Gilpin that would ban capital punishment.

. . . It would be a great satisfaction to me if I were able to support this Motion. It is always a matter of regret to me to find myself, on a public question, opposed to those who are called—sometimes in the way of honour, and sometimes in what is intended for ridicule—the philanthropists. Of all persons who take part in public affairs, they are those for whom, on the whole, I feel the greatest amount of respect; for their characteristic is, that they devote their time, their labour, and much of their money to objects purely public, with a less admixture of either personal or class selfishness, than any other class of politicians whatever.

On almost all the great questions, scarcely any politicians are so steadily and almost uniformly to be found on the side of right; and they seldom err, but by an exaggerated application of some just and highly important principle. On the very subject that is now occupying us we all know what signal service they have rendered. It is through their efforts that our criminal laws—which within my memory hanged people for stealing in a dwelling house to the value of 40s.–laws by virtue of which rows of human beings might be seen suspended in front of Newgate by those who ascended or descended Ludgate Hill—have so greatly relaxed their most revolting and most impolitic ferocity, that aggravated murder is now practically the only crime which is punished with death by any of our lawful tribunals; and we are even now deliberating whether the extreme penalty should be retained in that solitary case. This vast gain, not only to humanity, but to the ends of penal justice, we owe to the philanthropists; and if they are mistaken, as I cannot but think they are, in the present instance, it is only in not perceiving the right time and place for stopping in a career hitherto so eminently beneficial.

Sir, there is a point at which, I conceive, that career ought to stop. When there has been brought home to any one, by conclusive evidence, the greatest crime known to the law; and when the attendant circumstances suggest no palliation of the guilt, no hope that the culprit may even yet not be unworthy to live among mankind, nothing to make it probable that the crime was an exception to his general character rather than a consequence of it, then I confess it appears to me that to deprive the criminal of the life of which he has proved himself to be unworthy—solemnly to blot him out

from the fellowship of mankind and from the catalogue of the living—is the most appropriate as it is certainly the most impressive, mode in which society can attach to so great a crime the penal consequences which for the security of life it is indispensable to annex to it.

I defend this penalty, when confined to atrocious cases, on the very ground on which it is commonly attacked—on that of humanity to the criminal; as beyond comparison the least cruel mode in which it is possible adequately to deter from the crime. If, in our horror of inflicting death, we endeavour to devise some punishment for the living criminal which shall act on the human mind with a deterrent force at all comparable to that of death, we are driven to inflictions less severe indeed in appearance, and therefore less efficacious, but far more cruel in reality. Few, I think, would venture to propose, as a punishment for aggravated murder, less than imprisonment with hard labor for life; that is the fate to which a murderer would be consigned by the mercy which shrinks from putting him to death.

But has it been sufficiently considered what sort of a mercy this is, and what kind of life it leaves to him? If, indeed, the punishment is not really inflicted—if it becomes the sham which a few years ago such punishments were rapidly becoming—then, indeed, its adoption would be almost tantamount to giving up the attempt to repress murder altogether. But if it really is what it professes to be, and if it is realized in all its rigour by the popular imagination, as it very probably would not be, but as it must be if it is to be efficacious, it will be so shocking that when the memory of the crime is no longer fresh, there will be almost insuperable difficulty in executing it.

What comparison can there really be, in point of severity, between consigning a man to the short pang of a rapid death, and immuring him in a living tomb, there to linger out what may be a long life in the hardest and most monotonous toil, without any of its alleviations or rewards—debarred from all pleasant sights and sounds, and cut off from all earthly hope, except a slight mitigation of bodily restraint, or a small improvement of diet? Yet even such a lot as this, because there is no one moment at which the suffering is of terrifying intensity, and, above all, because it does not contain the element, so imposing to the imagination, of the unknown, is universally reputed a milder punishment than death—stands in all codes as a mitigation of the capital penalty, and is thankfully accepted as such. For it is characteristic of all punishments which depend on duration for their efficacy—all, therefore, which are not corporal or pecuniary—that they are more rigorous than they seem; while it is, on the contrary, one of the strongest recommendations a punishment can have, that it should seem more rigorous than it is; for its practical power depends far less on what it is than on what it seems.

There is not, I should think, any human infliction which makes an impression on the imagination so entirely out of proportion to its real severity as the punishment of death. The punishment must be mild indeed which does not add more to the sum of human misery than is necessarily or directly added by the execution of a criminal. As my hon. Friend the Member for Northampton (Mr. Gilpin) has himself remarked, the most that human laws can do to anyone in the matter of death is to hasten it; the man would have died at any rate; not so very much later, and on the average, I fear, with a considerably greater amount of bodily suffering. Society is asked, then, to denude itself of an instrument of punishment which, in the grave cases to which alone it is suitable, effects its purposes at a less cost of human suffering than any other; which, while it inspires more terror, is less cruel in actual fact than any punishment that we should think of substituting for it.

My hon. Friend says that it does not inspire terror, and that experience proves it to be a failure. But the influence of a punishment is not to be estimated by its effect on hardened criminals. Those whose habitual way of life keeps them, so to speak, at all times within sight of the gallows, do grow to care less about it; as, to compare good things with bad, an old soldier is not much affected by the chance of dying in battle. I can afford to admit all that is often said about the indifference of professional criminals to the gallows. Though of that indifference one-third is probably bravado and another third confidence that they shall have the luck to escape, it is quite probable that the remaining third is real. But the efficacy of a punishment which acts principally through the imagination,

is chiefly to be measured by the impression it makes on those who are still innocent; by the horror with which it surrounds the first promptings of guilt; the restraining influence it exercises over the beginning of the thought which, if indulged, would become a temptation; the check which it exerts over the graded declension towards the state—never suddenly attained—in which crime no longer revolts, and punishment no longer terrifies.

As for what is called the failure of death punishment, who is able to judge of that? We partly know who those are whom it has not deterred; but who is there who knows whom it has deterred, or how many human beings it has saved who would have lived to be murderers if that awful association had not been thrown round the idea of murder from their earliest infancy? Let us not forget that the most imposing fact loses its power over the imagination if it is made too cheap. When a punishment fit only for the most atrocious crimes is lavished on small offences until human feeling recoils from it, then, indeed, it ceases to intimidate, because it ceases to be believed in.

The failure of capital punishment in cases of theft is easily accounted for; the thief did not believe that it would be inflicted. He had learnt by experience that jurors would perjure themselves rather than find him guilty; that Judges would seize any excuse for not sentencing him to death, or for recommending him to mercy; and that if neither jurors nor Judges were merciful, there were still hopes from an authority above both. When things had come to this pass it was high time to give up the vain attempt.

When it is impossible to inflict a punishment, or when its infliction becomes a public scandal, the idle threat cannot too soon disappear from the statute book. And in the case of the host of offences which were formerly capital, I heartily rejoice that it did become impracticable to execute the law. If the same state of public feeling comes to exist in the case of murder; if the time comes when jurors refuse to find a murderer guilty; when Judges will not sentence him to death, or will recommend him to mercy; or when, if juries and Judges do not flinch from their duty, Home Secretaries, under pressure of deputations and memorials, shrink from theirs, and the threat becomes, as it became in the other cases, a mere *brutum fulmen*;[1] then, indeed, it may become necessary to do in this case what has been done in those—to abrogate the penalty.

That time may come—my hon. Friend thinks that it has nearly come. I hardly know whether he lamented it or boasted of it; but he and his Friends are entitled to the boast; for if it comes it will be their doing, and they will have gained what I cannot but call a fatal victory, for they will have achieved it by bringing about, if they will forgive me for saying so, an enervation, an effeminancy, in the general mind of the country. For what else than effeminancy is it to be so much more shocked by taking a man's life than by depriving him of all that makes life desirable or valuable? Is death, then, the greatest of all earthly ills? *Usque adeone mori miserum est?*[2] Is it, indeed, so dreadful a thing to die? Has it not been from of old one chief part of a manly education to make us despise death—teaching us to account it, if an evil at all, by no means high in the list of evils; at all events, as an inevitable one, and to hold, as it were, our lives in our hands, ready to be given or risked at any moment, for a sufficiently worthy object?

I am sure that my hon. Friends know all this as well, and have as much of all these feelings as any of the rest of us; possibly more. But I cannot think that this is likely to be the effect of their teaching on the general mind. I cannot think that the cultivating of a peculiar sensitiveness of conscience on this one point, over and above what results from the general cultivation of the moral sentiments, is permanently consistent with assigning in our own minds to the fact of death no more than the degree of relative importance which belongs to it among the other incidents of our humanity.

The men of old cared too little about death, and gave their own lives or took those of others with equal recklessness. Our danger is of the opposite kind, lest we should be so much shocked by death, in general and in the abstract, as to care too much about it in individual cases, both those of other people and our own, which call for its being risked. And I am not putting things at the worst, for it is proved by the experience of other countries that horror of the executioner by no means

necessarily implies horror of the assassin. The stronghold, as we all know, of hired assassination in the 18th century was Italy; yet it is said that in some of the Italian populations the infliction of death by sentence of law was in the highest degree offensive and revolting to popular feeling.

Much has been said of the sanctity of human life, and the absurdity of supposing that we can teach respect for life by ourselves destroying it. But I am surprised at the employment of this argument, for it is one which might be brought against any punishment whatever. It is not human life only, not human life as such, that ought to be sacred to us, but human feelings. The human capacity of suffering is what we should cause to be respected, not the mere capacity of existing.

And we may imagine somebody asking how we can teach people not to inflict suffering by ourselves inflicting it? But to this I should answer—all of us would answer—that to deter by suffering from inflicting suffering is not only possible, but the very purpose of penal justice. Does fining a criminal show want of respect for property, or imprisoning him, for personal freedom? Just as unreasonable is it to think that to take the life of a man who has taken that of another is to show want of regard for human life. We show, on the contrary, most emphatically our regard for it, by the adoption of a rule that he who violates that right in another forfeits it for himself, and that while no other crime that he can commit deprives him of his right to live, this shall.

There is one argument against capital punishment, even in extreme cases, which I cannot deny to have weight—on which my hon. Friend justly laid great stress, and which never can be entirely got rid of. It is this—that if by an error of justice an innocent person is put to death, the mistake can never be corrected; all compensation, all reparation for the wrong is impossible. This would be indeed a serious objection if these miserable mistakes—among the most tragical occurrences in the whole round of human affairs—could not be made extremely rare.

The argument is invincible where the mode of criminal procedure is dangerous to the innocent, or where the Courts of Justice are not trusted. And this probably is the reason why the objection to an irreparable punishment began (as I believe it did) earlier, and is more intense and more widely diffused, in some parts of the Continent of Europe

---

1. A display of force.
2. Is it so hard a thing to die?

than it is here. There are on the Continent great and enlightened countries, in which the criminal procedure is not so favorable to innocence, does not afford the same security against erroneous conviction, as it does among us; countries where the Courts of Justice seem to think they fail in their duty unless they find somebody guilty; and in their really laudable desire to hunt guilt from its hiding places, expose themselves to a serious danger of condemning the innocent.

If our own procedure and Courts of Justice afforded ground for similar apprehension, I should be the first to join in withdrawing the power of inflicting irreparable punishment from such tribunals. But we all know that the defects of our procedure are the very opposite. Our rules of evidence are even too favorable to the prisoner; and juries and Judges carry out the maxim, "It is better that ten guilty should escape than that one innocent person should suffer," not only to the letter, but beyond the letter. Judges are most anxious to point out, and juries to allow for, the barest possibility of the prisoner's innocence. No human judgment is infallible; such sad cases as my hon. Friend cited will sometimes occur; but in so grave a case as that of murder, the accused, in our system, has always the benefit of the merest shadow of a doubt.

And this suggests another consideration very germane to the question. The very fact that death punishment is more shocking than any other to the imagination, necessarily renders the Courts of Justice more scrupulous in requiring the fullest evidence of guilt. Even that which is the greatest objection to capital punishment, the impossibility of correcting an error once committed, must make, and does make, juries and Judges more careful in forming their opinion, and more jealous in their scrutiny of the evidence. If the substitution of penal servitude for death in cases of murder should cause any declaration in this conscientious scrupulosity, there would be a great evil to set against the real, but I hope rare, advantage of being able to make reparation to a condemned person who was afterwards discovered to be innocent.

In order that the possibility of correction may be kept open wherever the chance of this sad contingency is more than infinitesimal, it is quite right that the Judge should recommend to the Crown a commutation of the sentence, not solely when the proof of guilt is open to the smallest suspicion, but whenever there remains anything unexplained and mysterious in the case, raising a desire for more light, or making it likely that further information may at some future time be obtained. I would also suggest that whenever the sentence is commuted the grounds of the commutation should, in some authentic form, be made known to the public.

Thus much I willingly concede to my hon. Friend; but on the question of total abolition I am inclined to hope that the feeling of the country is not with him, and that the limitation of death punishment to the cases referred to in the Bill of last year will be generally considered sufficient. The mania which existed a short time ago for paring down all our punishments seems to have reached its limits, and not before it was time. We were in danger of being left without any effectual punishment, except for small of offences.

What was formerly our chief secondary punishment—transportation—before it was abolished, had become almost a reward. Penal servitude, the substitute for it, was becoming, to the classes who were principally subject to it, almost nominal, so comfortable did we make our prisons, and so easy had it become to get quickly out of them. Flogging—a most objectionable punishment in ordinary cases, but a particularly appropriate one for crimes of brutality, especially crimes against women—we would not hear of, except, to be sure, in the case of garotters, for whose peculiar benefit we reestablished it in a hurry, immediately after a Member of Parliament had been garrotted. With this exception, offences, even of an atrocious kind, against the person, as my hon. and learned Friend the Member for Oxford (Mr. Neate) well remarked, not only were, but still are, visited with penalties so ludicrously inadequate, as to be almost an encouragement to the crime.

I think, Sir, that in the case of most offences, except those against property, there is more need of strengthening our punishments than of weakening them; and that severer sentences, with an apportionment of them to the different kinds of offences which shall approve itself better than at present to the moral sentiments of the community, are the kind of reform of which our penal system now stands in need. I shall therefore vote against the Amendment.

Questions for Analysis

1. Mill defends capital punishment as the "most humane" punishment available for those who deserve severe punishment compared to the alternatives. Considering the options he weighs, is execution really the most humane? Given the punishments we typically use today, would Mill likely reach the same conclusion if he were alive now?

2. How does Mill rely on his principles of utilitarian reasoning in his consideration of capital punishment?

3. How are Mill's arguments similar to and different from contemporary debates?

4. How does he respond to concerns that innocent people might be executed? Does his answer adequately address concerns today, now that DNA testing is showing that many on death row are innocent?

The Death Sentence

Sidney Hook

In this essay, professor of philosophy Sidney Hook suggests that much of the debate about capital punishment suffers from vindictiveness and sentimentality. For example, abolitionists often argue that capital punishment is no more than an act of revenge, that it is the ultimate inhumanity. Hook is no more sympathetic, however, to the thrust of retentionist arguments. He points out that capital punishment has never been established as a deterrent to crime. Furthermore, he rejects as question-begging the retentionist argument that capital punishment is justified because it fulfills a community need or that it is the only appropriate punishment for certain unspeakable offenses.

So where does Hook stand on the issue? Despite his feelings that no valid case for capital punishment has thus far been made, Hook is not categorically opposed to it. Indeed, he cites two conditions under which he believes capital punishment is justified. The first is in cases where criminals facing a life imprisonment sentence request it. The second involves cases of convicted murderers who murder again. Hook regards the abolitionist objections to these exceptions as expressions of sentimentalism, even cruelty.

Is there anything new that can be said for or against capital punishment? Anyone familiar with the subject knows that unless extraneous issues are introduced, a large measure of agreement about it can be, and has been, won. For example, during the last 150 years the death penalty for criminal offenses has been abolished, or remains unenforced, in many countries; just as important, the number of crimes punishable by death has been sharply reduced in all countries. But while the progress has been encouraging, it still seems to me that greater clarity on the issues involved is desirable. Much of the continuing polemic still suffers from one or the other of the twin evils of vindictiveness and sentimentality.

Sentimentality, together with a great deal of confusion about determinism, is found in Clarence Darrow's speeches and writings on the subject. Darrow was an attractive and likable human being but a very confused thinker. He argued against capital punishment on the ground that the murderer was always a victim of heredity and environment—and therefore it was unjust to execute him.

From Sidney Hook, "The Death Sentence," *The New Leader,* vol. 44 (April 3, 1961). Copyright © The American Labor Conference on International Affairs, Inc. Reprinted, with three paragraphs added, by permission of the publisher. Cf. the original version which appeared in *The New York Law Forum* (August 1961), pp. 278–83, as an address before the New York State District Attorneys' Association.

("Back of every murder and back of every human act are sufficient causes that move the human machine beyond their control.") The crucifiers and the crucified, the lynch mob and its prey are equally moved by causes beyond their control and the relevant differences between them are therewith ignored. Although Darrow passionately asserted that no one knows what justice is and that no one can measure it, he nonetheless was passionately convinced that capital punishment was unjust.

It should be clear that if Darrow's argument were valid, it would be an argument not only against capital punishment but against all punishment. Very few of us would be prepared to accept this. But the argument is absurd. Even if we are all victims of our heredity and environment, it is still possible to alter the environment by meting out capital punishment to deter crimes of murder. If no one can help doing what he does, if no one is responsible for his actions, then surely this holds just as much for those who advocate and administer capital punishment as for the criminal. The denunciation of capital punishment as unjust, therefore, would be senseless. The question of universal determinism is irrelevant. If capital punishment actually were a deterrent to murder, and there existed no other more effective deterrent, and none as effective but more humane, a case could be made for it.

Nor am I impressed with the argument against capital punishment on the ground of its inhumanity. Of course it is inhumane. So is murder. If it could be shown that the inhumanity of murder can be decreased in no other way than by the inhumanity of capital punishment acting as a deterrent, this would be a valid argument for such punishment.

I have stressed the hypothetical character of these arguments because it makes apparent how crucially the wisdom of our policy depends upon the alleged facts. Does capital punishment serve as the most effective deterrent we have against murder? Most people who favor its retention believe that it does. But any sober examination of the facts will show that this has never been established. It seems plausible, but not everything which is plausible or intuitively credible is true.

The experience of countries and states which have abolished capital punishment shows that there has been no perceptible increase of murders after abolition—although it would be illegitimate to infer from this that the fear of capital punishment never deterred anybody. The fact that "the state with the very lowest murder rate is Maine, which abolished capital punishment in 1870" may be explained by the hypothesis that fishermen, like fish, tend to be cold-blooded, or by some less fanciful hypothesis. The relevant question is: What objective evidence exists which would justify the conclusion that if Maine had not abolished capital punishment, its death rate would have been higher? The answer is: No evidence exists.

The opinion of many jurists and law enforcement officers from Cesare Beccaria (the eighteenth-century Italian criminologist) to the present is that swift and certain punishment of some degree of severity is a more effective deterrent of murder than the punishment of maximum severity when it is slow and uncertain. Although this opinion requires substantiation, too, it carries the weight which we normally extend to pronouncements by individuals who report on their life experience. And in the absence of convincing evidence that capital punishment is a more effective and/or humane form of punishment for murder than any other punishment, there remains no other reasonable ground for retaining it.

This is contested by those who speak of the necessity for capital punishment as an expression of the "community need of justice" or as the fulfillment of "an instinctive urge to punish injustice." Such views lie at the basis of some forms of the retributive theory. It has been alleged that the retributive theory is nothing more than a desire for revenge, but it is a great and arrogant error to assume that all who hold it are vindictive. The theory has been defended by secular saints like G. E. Moore and Immanuel Kant, whose dispassionate interest in justice cannot reasonably be challenged. Even if one accepted the retributive theory or believed in the desirability of meeting the community need of justice, it doesn't in the least follow that this justifies capital punishment. Other forms of punishment may be retributive, too.

I suppose that what one means by community need or feeling and the necessity of regarding it is that not only must justice be done, it must be seen to be done. A requirement of good law is that it must be consonant with the feeling of the community something which is sometimes called "the living law." Otherwise it is unenforceable and brings the whole system of law into disrepute. Meeting community feeling is a necessary condition for good law, but not a sufficient condition for good law. This is what Justice Holmes meant when he wrote in *The Common Law* that "The first requirement of a sound body of law is that it should correspond with the actual feelings and demands of the community, whether right or wrong." But I think he would admit that sound law is sounder still if in addition to being enforceable it is also just. Our moral obligation as citizens is to build a community feeling and demand which is right rather than wrong.

Those who wish to retain capital punishment on the ground that it fulfills a community need or feeling must believe either that community feeling *per se* is always justified, or that to disregard it in any particular situation is inexpedient because of the consequences, *viz.*, increase in murder. In either case they beg the question—in the first case, the question of justice, and in the second, the question of deterrence.

One thing is incontestable. From the standpoint of those who base the argument for retention of capital punishment on the necessity of satisfying community needs there could be no justification whatsoever for any *mandatory* death sentence. For a mandatory death sentence attempts to determine in advance what the community need and feeling will be, and closes the door to fresh inquiry about the justice as well as the deterrent consequences of any proposed punishment.

Community need and feeling are notoriously fickle. When a verdict of guilty necessarily entails a death sentence, the jury may not feel the sentence warranted and may bring in a verdict of not guilty even when some punishment seems to be legally and morally justified. Even when the death sentence is not mandatory, there is an argument, not decisive but still significant, against any death sentence. This is its incorrigibility. Our judgment of a convicted man's guilt may change. If he has been executed in the meantime, we can only do him "posthumous justice." But can justice ever really be posthumous to the victim? Rarely has evidence, even when it is beyond reasonable doubt, the same finality about its probative force

as the awful finality of death. The weight of this argument against capital punishment is all the stronger if community need and feeling are taken as the prime criteria of what is just or fitting.

What about heinous political offenses? Usually when arguments fail to sustain the demand for capital punishment in ordinary murder cases, the names of Adolf Hitler, Adolf Eichmann, Joseph Stalin and Ilse Koch are introduced and flaunted before the audience to inflame their feelings. Certain distinctions are in order here. Justice, of course, requires severe punishment. But why is it assumed that capital punishment is, in these cases, the severest and most just of sentences? How can any equation be drawn between the punishment of one man and the sufferings of his numerous victims? After all, we cannot kill Eichmann six million times or Stalin twelve million times (a conservative estimate of the number of people who died by their order).

If we wish to keep alive the memory of political infamy, if we wish to use it as a political lesson to prevent its recurrence, it may be educationally far more effective to keep men like Eichmann in existence. Few people think of the dead. By the same token, it may be necessary to execute a politically monstrous figure to prevent him from becoming the object of allegiance of a restoration movement. Eichmann does not have to be executed. He is more useful alive if we wish to keep before mankind the enormity of his offense. But if Hitler had been taken alive, his death would have been required as a matter of political necessity, to prevent him from becoming a living symbol or rallying cry of Nazi diehards and irreconcilables.

There is an enormous amount of historical evidence which shows that certain political tyrants, after they lose power, become the focus of restoration movements that are a chronic source of bloodshed and civil strife. No matter how infamous a tyrant's actions, there is usually some group which has profited by it, resents being deprived of its privileges, and schemes for a return to power. In difficult situations, the dethroned tyrant also becomes a symbol of legitimacy around which discontented elements rally who might otherwise have waited for the normal processes of government to relieve their lot. A *mystique* develops around the tyrant, appeals are made to the "good old days" when his bread and circuses were used to distract attention from the myriads of his tortured victims, plots seethe around him until they boil over into violence and blood-shed again. I did not approve of the way Mussolini was killed. Even he deserved due process. But I have no doubt whatsoever that had he been sentenced merely to life imprisonment, the Fascist movement in Italy today would be a much more formidable movement, and that sooner or later, many lives would have been lost in consequence of the actions of Fascist legitimists.

Where matters of ordinary crime are concerned these political considerations are irrelevant. I conclude, therefore, that no valid case has so far been made for the retention of capital punishment, that the argument from deterrence is inconclusive and inconsistent (in the sense that we do not do other things to reinforce its deterrent effect if we believe it has such an effect), and that the argument from community feeling is invalid.

However, since I am not a fanatic or absolutist, I do not wish to go on record as being categorically opposed to the death sentence in all circumstances. I should like to recognize two exceptions. A defendant convicted of murder and sentenced to life should be permitted to choose the death sentence instead. Not so long ago a defendant sentenced to life imprisonment made this request and was rebuked by the judge for his impertinence. I can see no valid grounds for denying such a request out of hand. It may sometimes be denied, particularly if a way can be found to make the defendant labor for the benefit of the dependents of his victim, as is done in some European countries. Unless such considerations are present, I do not see on what reasonable ground the request can be denied, particularly by those who believe in capital punishment. Once they argue that life imprisonment is either a more effective deterrent or more justly punitive, they have abandoned their position.

In passing, I should state that I am in favor of permitting *any* criminal defendant, sentenced to life imprisonment, the right to choose death. I can understand why certain jurists, who believe that the defendant wants thereby to cheat the state out of its mode of punishment, should be indignant at the idea. They are usually the ones who believe that even the attempt at suicide should be deemed a crime—in effect saying to the unfortunate person that if he doesn't succeed in his act of suicide, the state will punish him for it. But I am baffled to understand why the absolute abolitionist, dripping with treacly humanitarianism, should oppose this proposal. I have heard some people actually oppose capital punishment in certain cases on the ground that: "Death is too good for the vile wretch! Let him live and suffer to the end of his days." But the absolute abolitionist should be the last person in the world to oppose the wish of the lifer, who regards this form of punishment as torture worse than death, to leave our world.

My second class of exceptions consists of those who having been sentenced once to prison for premeditated murder, murder again. In these particular cases we have evidence that imprisonment is not a sufficient deterrent for the individual in question. If the evidence shows that the prisoner is so psychologically constituted that, without being insane, the fact that he can kill again with impunity may lead to further murderous behavior, the court should have the discretionary power to pass the death sentence if the criminal is found guilty of a second murder.

In saying that the death sentence should be *discretionary* in cases where a man has killed more than once, I am *not* saying that a murderer who murders again is more deserving of death than the murderer who murders once. Bluebeard was not twelve times more deserving of death when he was finally caught. I am saying simply this: that in a sub-class of murderers, those who murder several times, there may be a special group of sane murderers who, knowing that they will not be executed, will not hesitate to kill again and again. For them the argument from deterrence is obviously valid. Those who say that there must be no exceptions to the abolition of capital punishment cannot rule out the existence of such cases on *a priori* grounds. If they admit that there is a reasonable probability that such murderers will murder again or attempt to murder again, a probability which usually grows with the number of repeated murders, and still insist they would *never* approve of capital punishment, I would conclude that they are indifferent to the lives of the human beings doomed, on their position, to be victims. What fancies itself as a humanitarian attitude is sometimes an expression of sentimentalism. The reverse coin of sentimentalism is often cruelty.

Our charity for all human beings must not deprive us of our common sense. Nor should our charity be less for the future or potential victims of the murderer than for the murderer himself. There are crimes in this world which are, like acts of nature, beyond the power of men to anticipate or control. But not all or most crimes are of this character. So long as human beings are responsible and educable, they will respond to praise and blame and punishment. It is hard to imagine it, but even Hitler and Stalin were once infants. Once you can imagine them as infants, however, it is hard to believe that they were already monsters in their cradles. Every confirmed criminal was once an amateur. The existence of confirmed criminals testifies to the defects of our education—where they can be reformed—and of our penology—where they cannot. That is why we are under the moral obligation to be intelligent about crime and punishment. Intelligence should teach us that the best educational and penological system is the one which prevents crimes rather than punishes them; the next best is one which punishes crime in such a way as to prevent it from happening again.

Questions for Analysis

1. Why does Hook say that if Darrow's argument were valid, it would be an argument not against capital punishment but against all punishment?

2. Why is Hook not impressed by the claim that capital punishment is inhumane? Do you agree with him?

3. Why does Hook feel that those who justify capital punishment by appeal to community feeling beg the question? Do you accept his argument?

4. How does Hook respond to the retentionist claim that capital punishment is justified for politically heinous offenses?

5. Do you agree that a "lifer's" request for capital punishment ought to be honored? Is Hook's justification for his position utilitarian or nonutilitarian? Explain.

6. Why does Hook believe capital punishment is justified when a convicted murderer murders again? Is his defense utilitarian? Explain.

7. Do you agree with Hook that what are called "humanitarian" objections to his two exceptions are really expressions of sentimentalism, even cruelty?

On Deterrence and the Death Penalty

Ernest Van Den Haag

Professor of social philosophy Ernest Van Den Haag begins his essay by conceding that capital punishment cannot be defended on grounds of rehabilitation or protection of society from unrehabilitated offenders. But he does believe that the ultimate punishment can be justified on grounds of deterrence.

To make his point, Van Den Haag at some length provides a psychological basis for deterrence. He associates deterrence with human responses to danger. Law functions to change social dangers into individual ones: Legal threats are designed to deter individuals from actions that threaten society. Most of us, Van Den Haag argues, transfer these external penalty dangers into internal ones; that is, we each develop a conscience that threatens us if

Reprinted by special permission of the *Journal of Criminal Law, Criminology, and Police Science,* © 1969 by Northwestern University School of Law, vol. 60, no. 2.

we do wrong. But this conscience is and needs to be reinforced by external authority, which imposes penalties for antisocial behavior.

Van Den Haag then critically examines the reason punishment has fallen into disrepute as a deterrent to crime: the claim that slums, ghettos, and personality disorders are the real causes of crime. He dismisses these as spurious explanations and insists that only punishment can deter crime. In Van Den Haag's view, whether individuals will commit crimes depends exclusively on whether they perceive the penalty risks as worth it.

While he concedes that the death penalty cannot be proven to deter crime, Van Den Haag observes that this in no way means capital punishment lacks a deterrent value. Indeed, it is this very uncertainty about its deterrence that impels Van Den Haag to argue for its retention. In the last analysis, he believes that retaining capital punishment leads to a net gain for society, notwithstanding the occasional abuse of it. In arguing for capital punishment, then, Van Den Haag takes a utilitarian viewpoint.

I

If rehabilitation and the protection of society from unrehabilitated offenders were the only purposes of legal punishment, the death penalty could be abolished: It cannot attain the first end, and is not needed for the second. No case for the death penalty can be made unless "doing justice" or "deterring others" is among our penal aims.[1] Each of these purposes can justify capital punishment by itself; opponents, therefore, must show that neither actually does, while proponents can rest their case on either.

Although the argument from justice is intellectually more interesting, and, in my view, decisive enough, utilitarian arguments have more appeal: The claim that capital punishment is useless because it does not deter others is most persuasive. I shall, therefore, focus on this claim. Lest the argument be thought to be unduly narrow, I shall show, nonetheless, that some claims of injustice rest on premises which the claimants reject when arguments for capital punishment are derived therefrom; while other claims of injustice have independent standing: Their weight depends on the weight given to deterrence.

II

Capital punishment is regarded as unjust because it may lead to the execution of innocents, or because the guilty poor (or disadvantaged) are more likely to be executed than the guilty rich.

Regardless of merit, these claims are relevant only if "doing justice" is one purpose of punishment. Unless one regards it as good, or, at least,

better, that the guilty be punished rather than the innocent, and that the equally guilty be punished equally,[2] unless, that is, one wants penalties to be just, one cannot object to them because they are not. However, if one does include justice among the purposes of punishment, it becomes possible to justify any one punishment—even death—on grounds of justice. Yet, those who object to the death penalty because of its alleged injustice usually deny not only the merits, or the sufficiency, of specific arguments based on justice, but the propriety of justice as an argument: They exclude "doing justice" as a purpose of legal punishment. If justice is not a purpose of penalties, injustice cannot be an objection to the death penalty, or to any other; if it is, justice cannot be ruled out as an argument for any penalty.

Consider the claim of injustice on its merits now. A convicted man may be found to have been innocent; if he was executed, the penalty cannot be reversed. Except for fines, penalties never can be reversed. Time spent in prison cannot be returned. However, a prison sentence may be remitted once the prisoner serving it is found innocent; and he can be compensated for the time served (although compensation ordinarily cannot repair the harm). Thus, though (nearly) all penalties are irreversible, the death penalty, unlike others, is irrevocable as well.

Despite all precautions, errors will occur in judicial proceedings: The innocent may be found guilty,[3] or the guilty rich may more easily escape conviction, or receive lesser penalties than the guilty poor. However, these injustices do not reside in the penalties inflicted but in their maldistribution.

It is not the penalty—whether death or prison—which is unjust when inflicted on the innocent, but its imposition on the innocent. Inequity between poor and rich also involves distribution, not the penalty distributed.[4] Thus injustice is not an objection to the death penalty but to the distributive process—the trial. Trials are more likely to be fair when life is at stake—the death penalty is probably less often unjustly inflicted than others. It requires special consideration not because it is more, or more often, unjust than other penalties, but because it is always irrevocable.

Can any amount of deterrence justify the possibility of irrevocable injustice? Surely injustice is unjustifiable in each actual individual case; it must be objected to whenever it occurs. But we are concerned here with the process that may produce injustice, and with the penalty that would make it irrevocable—not with the actual individual cases produced, but with the general rules which may produce them. To consider objections to a general rule (the provision of any penalties by law) we must compare the likely net result of alternative rules and select the rule (or penalty) likely to produce the least injustice. For however one defines justice, to support it cannot mean less than to favor the least injustice. If the death of innocents because of judicial error is unjust, so is the death of innocents by murder. If some murders could be avoided by a penalty conceivably more deterrent than others—such as the death penalty—then the question becomes: Which penalty will minimize the number of innocents killed (by crime and by punishment)? It follows that the irrevocable injustice sometimes inflicted by the death penalty would not significantly militate against it, if capital punishment deters enough murders to reduce the total number of innocents killed so that fewer are lost than would be lost without it.

In general, the possibility of injustice argues against penalization of any kind only if the expected usefulness of penalization is less important than the probable harm (particularly to innocents) and the probable inequities. The possibility of injustice argues against the death penalty only inasmuch as the added usefulness (deterrence) expected from irrevocability is thought less important than the added harm. (Were my argument specifically concerned with justice, I could compare the injustice inflicted by the courts with the injustice—outside the courts—avoided by the judicial process. "Iimportant" here may be used to include everything to which importance is attached.)

We must briefly examine now the general use and effectiveness of deterrence to decide whether the death penalty could add enough deterrence to be warranted.

III

Does any punishment "deter others" at all? Doubts have been thrown on this effect because it is thought to depend on the incorrect rationalistic psychology of some of its 18th- and 19th-century proponents. Actually deterrence does not depend on rational calculation, on rationality or even on capacity for it; nor do arguments for it depend on rationalistic psychology. Deterrence depends on the likelihood and on the regularity—not on the rationality—of human responses to danger; and further on the possibility of reinforcing internal controls by vicarious external experiences.

Responsiveness to danger is generally found in human behavior; the danger can, but need not, come from the law or from society; nor need it be explicitly verbalized. Unless intent on suicide, people do not jump from high mountain cliffs, however tempted to fly through the air; and they take precautions against falling. The mere risk of injury often restrains us from doing what is otherwise attractive; we refrain even when we have no direct experience, and usually without explicit computation of probabilities, let alone conscious weighing of expected pleasure against possible pain. One abstains from dangerous acts because of vague, inchoate, habitual and, above all, preconscious fears. Risks and rewards are more often felt than calculated; one abstains without accounting to oneself, because "it isn't done," or because one literally does not conceive of the action one refrains from. Animals as well refrain from painful or injurious experiences presumably without calculation; and the threat of punishment can be used to regulate their conduct.

Unlike natural dangers, legal threats are constructed deliberately by legislators to restrain actions which may impair the social order. Thus legislation transforms social into individual dangers.

Most people further transform external into internal danger: They acquire a sense of moral obligation, a conscience, which threatens them, should they do what is wrong. Arising originally from the external authority of rulers and rules, conscience is internalized and becomes independent of external forces. However, conscience is constantly reinforced in those whom it controls by the coercive imposition of external authority on recalcitrants and on those who have not acquired it. Most people refrain from offenses because they feel an obligation to behave lawfully. But this obligation would scarcely be felt if those who do not feel or follow it were not to suffer punishment.

Although the legislators may calculate their threats and the responses to be produced, the effectiveness of the threats neither requires nor depends on calculations by those responding. The predictor (or producer) of effects must calculate; those whose responses are predicted (or produced) need not. Hence, although legislation (and legislators) should be rational, subjects, to be deterred as intended, need not be: They need only be responsive.

Punishments deter those who have not violated the law for the same reasons—and in the same degrees (apart from internalization: moral obligation) as do natural dangers. Often natural dangers—all dangers not deliberately created by legislation (*e.g.,* injury of the criminal inflicted by the crime victim) are insufficient. Thus, the fear of injury (natural danger) does not suffice to control city traffic; it must be reinforced by the legal punishment meted out to those who violate the rules. These punishments keep most people observing the regulations. However, where (in the absence of natural danger) the threatened punishment is so light that the advantage of violating rules tends to exceed the disadvantage of being punished (divided by the risk), the rule is violated (*i.e.,* parking fines are too light). In this case the feeling of obligation tends to vanish as well. Elsewhere punishment deters.

To be sure, not everybody responds to threatened punishment. Non-responsive persons may be (a) self-destructive or (b) incapable of responding to threats, or even of grasping them. Increases in the size, or certainty, of penalties would not affect these two groups. A third group (c) might respond to more certain or more severe penalties.[5] If the punishment threatened for burglary, robbery, or rape

were a $5 fine in North Carolina, and 5 years in prison in South Carolina, I have no doubt that the North Carolina treasury would become quite opulent until vigilante justice would provide the deterrence not provided by law. Whether to increase penalties (or improve enforcement) depends on the importance of the rule to society, the size and likely reaction of the group that did not respond before, and the acceptance of the added punishment and enforcement required to deter it. Observation would have to locate the points—likely to differ in different times and places—at which diminishing, zero, and negative returns set in. There is no reason to believe that all present and future offenders belong to the *a priori* non-responsive groups, or that all penalties have reached the point of diminishing, let alone zero returns.

IV

Even though its effectiveness seems obvious, punishment as a deterrent has fallen into disrepute. Some ideas which help explain this progressive heedlessness were uttered by Lester Pearson, then Prime Minister of Canada, when, in opposing the death penalty, he proposed that instead "the state seek to eradicate the causes of crime—slums, ghettos and personality disorders."[6]

"Slums, ghettos, and personality disorders" have not been shown, singly or collectively, to be "the causes" of crime.

(1) The crime rate in the slums is indeed higher than elsewhere; but so is the death rate in hospitals. Slums are no more "causes" of crime than hospitals are of death; they are locations of crime, as hospitals are of death. Slums and hospitals attract people selectively; neither is the "cause" of the condition (disease in hospitals, poverty in slums) that leads to the selective attraction.

As for poverty which draws people into slums, and, sometimes, into crime, any relative disadvantage may lead to ambition, frustration, resentment and, if insufficiently restrained, to crime. Not all relative disadvantages can be eliminated; indeed very few can be, and their elimination increases the resentment generated by the remaining ones; not even relative poverty can be removed altogether. (Absolute poverty—whatever that may be—hardly affects crime.) However, though contributory, relative disadvantages are not a necessary or sufficient cause of crime: Most poor people do not commit crimes, and some rich people do. Hence, "eradication of poverty" would, at most, remove one (doubtful) cause of crime.

In the United States, the decline of poverty has not been associated with a reduction of crime. Poverty measured in dollars of constant purchasing power, according to present government standards and statistics, was the condition of ½ of all our families in 1920; of ⅕ in 1962; and of less than ⅙ in 1966. In 1967, 5.3 million families out of 49.8 million were poor—⅑ of all families in the United States. If crime has been reduced in a similar manner, it is a well-kept secret.

Those who regard poverty as a cause of crime often draw a wrong inference from a true proposition: The rich will not commit certain crimes—Rockefeller never riots; nor does he steal. (He mugs, but only on T.V.) Yet while wealth may be the cause of not committing (certain) crimes, it does not follow that poverty (absence of wealth) is the cause of committing them. Water extinguishes or prevents fire; but its absence is not the cause of fire. Thus, if poverty could be abolished, if everybody had all "necessities" (I don't pretend to know what this would mean), crime would remain, for, in the words of Aristotle, "the greatest crimes are committed not for the sake of basic necessities but for the sake of superfluities." Superfluities cannot be provided by the government; they would be what the government does not provide.

(2) Negro ghettos have a high, Chinese ghettos have a low crime rate. Ethnic separation, voluntary or forced, obviously has little to do with crime; I can think of no reason why it should.[7]

(3) I cannot see how the state could "eradicate" personality disorders even if all causes and cures were known and available. (They are not.) Further, the known incidence of personality disorders within the prison population does not exceed the known incidence outside—though our knowledge of both is tenuous. Nor are personality disorders necessary or sufficient causes for criminal offenses, unless these be identified by means of (moral, not clinical) definition with personality disorders. In this case, Mr. Pearson would have proposed to "eradicate" crime by eradicating crime—certainly a sound, but not a helpful idea.

Mr. Pearson's views are part as well of the mental furniture of the former U.S. Attorney General Ramsey Clark, who told a congressional committee that ". . . only the elimination of the causes of crime can make a significant and lasting difference in the incidence of crime." Uncharitably interpreted, Mr. Clark revealed that only the elimination of causes eliminates effects—a sleazy cliché and wrong to boot. Given the benefit of the doubt, Mr. Clark probably meant that the causes of crime are social; and that therefore crime can be reduced "only" by non-penal (social) measures.

This view suggests a fireman who declines fire-fighting apparatus by pointing out that "in the long run only the elimination of the causes" of fire "can make a significant and lasting difference in the incidence" of fire, and that fire-fighting equipment does not eliminate "the causes"—except that such a fireman would probably not rise to fire chief. Actually, whether fires are checked depends on equipment and on the efforts of the firemen using it no less than on the presence of "the causes": inflammable materials. So with crimes. Laws, courts and police actions are no less important in restraining them than "the causes" are in impelling them. If firemen (or attorneys general) pass the buck and refuse to use the means available, we may all be burned while waiting for "the long run" and "the elimination of the causes."

Whether any activity—be it lawful or unlawful—takes place depends on whether the desire for it, or for whatever is to be secured by it, is stronger than the desire to avoid the costs involved. Accordingly people work, attend college, commit crimes, go to the movies—or refrain from any of these activities. Attendance at a theatre may be high because the show is entertaining and because the price of admission is low. Obviously the attendance depends on both—on the combination of expected gratification and cost. The wish, motive or impulse for doing anything—the experienced, or expected, gratification—is the cause of doing it; the wish to avoid the cost is the cause of not doing it. One is no more and no less "cause" than the other. (Common speech supports this use of "cause" no less than logic: "Why did you go to Jamaica?" "*Because* it is such a beautiful place." "Why didn't you go to Jamaica?" "*Because* it is too expensive."—"Why do you buy this?" "*Because* it is so cheap." "Why don't you buy that?"*"Because* it is too expensive.") Penalties (costs) are causes of lawfulness, or (if too low or uncertain) of unlawfulness, of crime. People do commit crimes because, given their conditions, the desire for the satisfaction sought prevails. They refrain if the desire to avoid the cost prevails. Given the desire, low cost (penalty) causes the action, and high cost restraint. Given the cost, desire becomes the causal variable. Neither is intrinsically more causal than the other. The crime rate increases if the cost is reduced or the desire raised. It can be decreased by raising the cost or by reducing the desire.

The cost of crime is more easily and swiftly changed than the conditions producing the inclination to it. Further, the costs are very largely within the power of the government to change, whereas the conditions producing propensity to crime are often only indirectly affected by government action, and some are altogether beyond the control of the government. Our unilateral emphasis on these conditions and our undue neglect of costs may contribute to an unnecessarily high crime rate.

V

The foregoing suggests the question posed by the death penalty: Is the deterrence added (return) sufficiently above zero to warrant irrevocability (or other, less clear, disadvantages)? The question is not only whether the penalty deters, but whether it deters more than alternatives and whether the difference exceeds the cost of irrevocability. (I shall assume that the alternative is actual life imprisonment so as to exclude the complication produced by the release of the unrehabilitated.)

In some fairly infrequent but important circumstances the death penalty is the only possible deterrent. Thus, in case of acute *coups d'état,* or of acute substantial attempts to overthrow the government, prospective rebels would altogether discount the threat of any prison sentence. They would not be deterred because they believe the swift victory of the revolution will invalidate a prison sentence and turn it into an advantage. Execution would be the only deterrent because, unlike prison sentences, it cannot be revoked by victorious rebels. The same reasoning applies to deterring spies or traitors in wartime. Finally, men who, by virtue of past acts, are already serving, or are threatened, by

a life sentence could be deterred from further offenses only by the threat of the death penalty.[8]

What about criminals who do not fall into any of these (often ignored) classes? Prof. Thorsten Sellin has made a careful study of the available statistics: He concluded that they do not yield evidence for the deterring effect of the death penalty.[9] Somewhat surprisingly, Prof. Sellin seems to think that this lack of evidence for deterrence is evidence for the lack of deterrence. It is not. It means that deterrence has not been demonstrated statistically—not that non-deterrence has been.

It is entirely possible, indeed likely (as Prof. Sellin appears willing to concede), that the statistics used, though the best available, are nonetheless too slender a reed to rest conclusions on. They indicate that the homicide rate does not vary greatly between similar areas with or without the death penalty, and in the same area before and after abolition. However, the similar areas are not similar enough; the periods are not long enough; many social differences and changes, other than the abolition of the death penalty, may account for the variation (or lack of it) in homicide rates with and without, before and after abolition; some of these social differences and changes are likely to have affected homicide rates. I am unaware of any statistical analysis which adjusts for such changes and differences. And logically, it is quite consistent with the postulated deterrent effect of capital punishment that there be less homicide after abolition: With retention there might have been still less.

Homicide rates do not depend exclusively on penalties any more than do other crime rates. A number of conditions which influence the propensity to crime, demographic, economic or generally social changes or differences—even such matters as changes of the divorce laws or of the cotton price—may influence the homicide rate. Therefore variation or constancy cannot be attributed to variations or constancy of the penalties, unless we know that no other factor influencing the homicide rate has changed. Usually we don't. To believe the death penalty deterrent does not require one to believe that the death penalty, or any other, is the only or the decisive causal variable; this would be as absurd as the converse mistake that "social causes" are the only or always the decisive factor. To favor capital punishment, the efficacy of neither variable need be denied. It is enough to affirm that the severity of the penalty may influence some potential criminals, and that the added severity of the death penalty adds to deterrence, or may do so. It is quite possible that such a deterrent effect may be offset (or intensified) by nonpenal factors which affect propensity; its presence or absence therefore may be hard, and perhaps impossible to demonstrate.

Contrary to what Prof. Sellin *et al.* seem to presume, I doubt that offenders are aware of the absence or presence of the death penalty state by state or period by period. Such unawareness argues against the assumption of a calculating murderer. However, unawareness does not argue against the death penalty if by deterrence we mean a preconscious, general response to a severe, but not necessarily specifically and explicitly apprehended, or calculated threat. A constant homicide rate, despite abolition, may occur because of unawareness and not because of lack of deterrence: People remain deterred for a lengthy interval by the severity of the penalty in the past, or by the severity of penalties used in similar circumstances nearby.

I do not argue for a version of deterrence which would require me to believe that an individual shuns murder while in North Dakota, because of the death penalty, and merrily goes to it in South Dakota since it has been abolished there; or that he will start the murderous career from which he had hitherto refrained, after abolition. I hold that the generalized threat of the death penalty may be a deterrent, and the more so, the more generally applied. Deterrence will not cease in the particular areas of abolition or at the particular times of abolition. Rather, general deterrence will be somewhat weakened, through local (partial) abolition. Even such weakening will be hard to detect owing to changes in many offsetting, or reinforcing, factors.

For all of these reasons, I doubt that the presence or absence of a deterrent effect of the death penalty is likely to be demonstrable by statistical means. The statistics presented by Prof. Sellin *et al.* show only that there is no statistical proof for the deterrent effect of the death penalty. But they do not show that there is no deterrent effect. Not to demonstrate presence of the effect is not the same as to demonstrate its absence; certainly not when there are plausible explanations for the non-demonstrability of the effect.

It is on our uncertainty that the case for deterrence must rest.[10]

VI

If we do not know whether the death penalty will deter others, we are confronted with two uncertainties. If we impose the death penalty, and achieve no deterrent effect thereby, the life of a convicted murderer has been expended in vain (from a deterrent viewpoint). There is a net loss. If we impose the death sentence and thereby deter some future murderers, we spared the lives of some future victims (the prospective murderers gain too; they are spared punishment because they were deterred). In this case, the death penalty has led to a net gain, unless the life of a convicted murderer is valued more highly than that of the unknown victim, or victims (and the non-imprisonment of the deterred non-murderer).

The calculation can be turned around, of course. The absence of the death penalty may harm no one and therefore produce a gain—the life of the convicted murderer. Or it may kill future victims of murderers who could have been deterred, and thus produce a loss—their life.

To be sure, we must risk something certain—the death (or life) of the convicted man, for something uncertain—the death (or life) of the victims of murderers who may be deterred. This is in the nature of uncertainty—when we invest, or gamble, we risk the money we have for an uncertain gain. Many human actions, most commitments—including marriage and crime—share this characteristic with the deterrent purpose of any penalization, and with its rehabilitative purpose (and even with the protective).

More proof is demanded for the deterrent effect of the death penalty than is demanded for the deterrent effect of other penalties. This is not justified by the absence of other utilitarian purposes such as protection and rehabilitation; they involve no less uncertainty than deterrence.[11]

Irrevocability may support a demand for some reason to expect more deterrence than revocable penalties might produce, but not a demand for more proof of deterrence, as has been pointed out above. The reason for expecting more deterrence lies in the greater severity, the terrifying effect inherent in finality. Since it seems more important to spare victims than to spare murderers, the burden of proving that the greater severity inherent in irrevocability adds nothing to deterrence lies on those who oppose capital punishment. Proponents of the death penalty need show only that there is no more uncertainty about it than about greater severity in general.

The demand that the death penalty be proved more deterrent than alternatives cannot be satisfied any more than the demand that six years in prison be proved to be more deterrent than three. But the uncertainty which confronts us favors the death penalty as long as by imposing it we might save future victims of murder. This effect is as plausible as the general idea that penalties have deterrents which increase with their severity. Though we have no proof of the positive deterrence of the penalty, we also have no proof of zero or negative effectiveness. I believe we have no right to risk additional future victims of murder for the sake of sparing convicted murderers; on the contrary, our moral obligation is to risk the possible ineffectiveness of executions. However rationalized, the opposite view appears to be motivated by the simple fact that executions are more subjected to social control than murder. However, this applies to all penalties and does not argue for the abolition of any.

NOTES

1. Social solidarity of "community feeling" (here to be ignored) might be dealt with as a form of deterrence.

2. Certainly a major meaning of *suum cuique tribue*.

3. I am not concerned here with the converse injustice, *which I regard as no less grave.*

4. Such inequity, though likely, has not been demonstrated. Note that, since there are more poor than rich, there are likely to be more guilty poor; and, if poverty contributes to crime, the proportion of the poor who are criminals also should be higher than of the rich.

5. I neglect those motivated by civil disobedience or, generally, moral or political passion. Deterring them depends less on penalties than on the moral support they receive,

though penalties play a role. I also neglect those who may belong to all three groups listed, some successively, some even simultaneously, such as drug addicts. Finally, I must altogether omit the far-from-negligible role that problems of apprehension and conviction play in deterrence—beyond saying that, by reducing the government's ability to apprehend and convict, courts are able to reduce the risks of offenders.

6. I quote from the *New York Times* (November 24, 1967, p. 22). The actual psychological and other factors which bear on the disrepute—as distinguished from the rationalizations—cannot be examined here.

7. Mixed areas, incidentally, have higher crime rates than segregated ones. See, e.g., R. Ross and E. van den Haag, *The Fabric of Society* (New York: Harcourt, Brace & Co., 1957), pp. 102–4. Because slums are bad (morally) and crime is, many people seem to reason that "slums spawn crime"—which confuses some sort of moral with a causal relation.

8. Cautious revolutionaries, uncertain of final victory, might be impressed by prison sentences—but not in the acute stage, when faith in victory is high. And one can increase even the severity of a life sentence in prison. Finally, harsh punishment of rebels can intensify rebellious impulses. These points, though they qualify it, hardly impair the force of the argument.

9. Sellin considered mainly homicide statistics. His work may be found in his *Capital Punishment* (New York: Harper & Row, 1967); or, most conveniently, in H. A. Bedau, *The Death Penalty in America* (Garden City, N.Y.: Doubleday & Co., 1964), which also offers other material, mainly against the death penalty.

10. In view of the strong emotions aroused (itself an indication of effectiveness to me: Might not murderers be as upset over the death penalty as those who wish to spare them?) and because I believe penalties must reflect community feeling to be effective, I oppose mandatory death sentences and favor optional, and perhaps binding, recommendations by juries after their finding of guilt. The opposite course risks the non-conviction of guilty defendants by juries who do not want to see them executed.

11. Rehabilitation or protection are of minor importance in our actual penal system (though not in our theory). We confine many people who do not need rehabilitation and against whom we do not need protection (e.g., the exasperated husband who killed his wife); we release many unrehabilitated offenders against whom protection is needed. Certainly rehabilitation and protection are not, and deterrence is, the main actual function of legal punishment if we disregard non-utilitarian ones.

Questions for Analysis

1. Van Den Haag claims that injustice is an objection not to the death penalty but to the distributive process. What does he mean? Is his distinction between penalty and distribution germane?

2. What does deterrence depend on, in Van Den Haag's view?

3. How does punishment differ from natural dangers?

4. What kinds of people do not respond to threatened punishment? Would you be persuaded by the anti–capital punishment argument that insists the death penalty simply does not deter certain people?

5. What determines whether penalties ought to be increased? Explain how this is a utilitarian argument.

6. Does Van Den Haag convince you that slums and ghettos are "no more 'causes' of crimes than hospitals are of death"?

7. In Van Den Haag's view, what is the sole determinant of whether people will or will not commit crimes? Do you agree?

8. Why does Van Den Haag not believe that the presence or absence of a deterrent effect of the death penalty is likely to be proved statistically? Does this weaken, strengthen, or have no effect on his own retentionist position?

9. Explain why Van Den Haag believes there is more to be gained by retaining the death penalty than by abolishing it.

Capital Punishment and Social Defense

Hugo Adam Bedau

In this selection from a longer essay, abolitionist Hugo Adam Bedau discusses the death penalty as a means of preventing convicted murderers from murdering again and as a means of deterring others from murdering. Neither, he concludes, justifies capital punishment.

When it comes to prevention, Bedau argues that few convicted murderers will murder again, and we cannot predict which ones will. Therefore, we would have to execute all convicted murderers, which is unacceptable. As for deterrence, the evidence does not show that capital punishment is a stronger deterrent than long prison terms. There are, however, significant social costs to the death penalty, including the executions of innocent people.

Bedau also argues that the courts do not apply the death penalty equitably. We do not execute the "worst of the bad," he says. Instead, we execute defendants who are put at a disadvantage by race, sex, poverty, and other unjust factors.

THE ANALOGY WITH SELF-DEFENSE

Capital punishment, it is sometimes said, is to the body politic what self-defense is to the individual. If the latter is not morally wrong, how can the former be morally wrong? In order to assess the strength of this analogy, we need first to inspect the morality of self-defense.

Except for absolute pacifists, who believe it is morally wrong to use violence even to defend themselves or others from unprovoked and undeserved aggression, most of us believe that it is not morally wrong and may even be our moral duty to use violence to prevent aggression directed either against ourselves or against innocent third parties. The law has long granted persons the right to defend themselves against the unjust aggressions of others, even to the extent of using lethal force to kill a would-be assailant. It is very difficult to think of any convincing argument that would show it is

From *Matters of Life and Death*, 2nd ed., Tom Regan. © 1986 McGraw-Hill, Inc. Reprinted by permission of the publisher.

never rational to risk the death of another in order to prevent death or grave injury to oneself. Certainly self-interest dictates the legitimacy of self defense. So does concern for the well-being of others. So also does justice. If it is unfair for one person to inflict violence on another, then it is hard to see how morality could require the victim to acquiesce in the attempt by another to hurt him or her, rather than to resist it, even if that resistance involves or risks injury to the assailant.

The foregoing account assumes that the person acting in self-defense is innocent of any provocation of the assailant. It also assumes that there is no alternative to victimization except resistance. In actual life, both assumptions—especially the second—are often false, because there may be a third alternative: escape, or removing oneself from the scene of danger and imminent aggression. Hence, the law imposes on us the "duty to retreat." Before we use violence to resist aggression, must try to get out of the way, lest unnecessary violence be used to resist aggression. Now suppose that unjust aggression is imminent, and there is no path open for escape. How much violence may justifiably be used to ward off aggression? The answer is: No more violence than is necessary to prevent the aggressive assault. Violence beyond that is unnecessary and therefore unjustified. We may restate the principle governing the use of violence in self-defense in terms of the use of "deadly force" by the police in the discharge of their duties. The rule is this: Use of deadly force is justified only to prevent loss of life in immediate jeopardy where a lesser use of force cannot reasonably be expected to save the life that is threatened.

In real life, violence in self-defense in excess of the minimum necessary to prevent aggression, even though it is not justifiable, is often excusable. One cannot always tell what will suffice to deter or prevent becoming a victim, and so the law looks with a certain tolerance upon the frightened and innocent would-be victim who in self-protection turns upon a vicious assailant and inflicts a fatal injury even though a lesser injury would have been sufficient. What is not justified is deliberately using far more violence than is necessary to prevent becoming a victim. It is the deliberate, not the impulsive or the unintentional use of violence that

is relevant to the death-penalty controversy, since the death penalty is enacted into law and carried out in each case only after ample time to weigh alternatives. Notice that we are assuming that the act of self-defense is to protect one's person or that of a third party. The reasoning outlined here does not extend to the defense of one's property. Shooting a thief to prevent one's automobile from being stolen cannot be excused or justified in the way that shooting an assailant charging with a knife pointed at one's face can be. In terms of the concept of "deadly force," our criterion is that deadly force is never justified to prevent crimes against property or other violent crimes not immediately threatening the life of an innocent person.

The rationale for self-defense as set out above illustrates two moral principles of great importance to our discussion. . . . One is that if a life is to be risked, then it is better that it be the life of someone who is guilty (in our context, the initial assailant) rather than the life of someone who is not (the innocent potential victim). It is not fair to expect the innocent prospective victim to run the added risk of severe injury or death in order to avoid using violence in self-defense to the extent of possibly killing his assailant. It is only fair that the guilty aggressor run the risk.

The other principle is that taking life deliberately is not justified so long as there is any feasible alternative. One does not expect miracles, of course, but in theory, if shooting a burglar through the foot will stop the burglary and enable one to call the police for help, then there is no reason to shoot to kill. Likewise, if the burglar is unarmed, there is no reason to shoot at all. In actual life, of course, burglars are likely to be shot at by aroused householders because one does not know whether they are armed, and prudence may dictate the assumption that they are. Even so, although the burglar has no right to commit a felony against a person or a person's property, the attempt to do so does not give the chosen victim the right to respond in whatever way one pleases, and then to excuse or justify such conduct on the ground that one was "only acting in self-defense." In these ways the law shows a tacit regard for the life of even a felon and discourages the use of unnecessary violence even by the innocent; morality can hardly do less.

PREVENTING VERSUS DETERRING CRIME

The analogy between capital punishment and self-defense requires us to face squarely the empirical questions surrounding the preventive and deterrent effects of the death penalty. Executing a murderer in the name of punishment can be seen as a crime-*preventive* measure just to the extent it is reasonable to believe that if the murderer had not been executed he or she would have committed other crimes (including, but not necessarily confined to, murder). Executing a murderer can be seen as a crime *deterrent* just to the extent it is reasonable to believe that by the example of the execution other persons would be frightened off from committing murder. Any punishment can be a crime preventive without being a crime deterrent, just as it can be a deterrent without being a preventive. It can also be both or neither. Prevention and deterrence are theoretically independent because they operate by different methods. Crimes can be prevented by taking guns out of the hands of criminals, by putting criminals behind bars, by alerting the public to be less careless and less prone to victimization, and so forth. Crimes can be deterred only by making would-be criminals frightened of being arrested, convicted, and punished for crimes—that is, making persons overcome their desire to commit crimes by a stronger desire to avoid the risk of being caught and punished.

THE DEATH PENALTY AS A CRIME PREVENTIVE

Capital punishment is unusual among penalties because its preventive effects limit its deterrent effects. The death penalty can never deter the executed person from further crimes. At most, it can prevent a person from committing them. Popular discussions of the death penalty are frequently confused because they so often assume that the death penalty is a perfect and infallible deterrent so far as the executed criminal is concerned, whereas nothing of the sort is true. What is even more important, it is also wrong to think that in every execution the death penalty has proved to be an infallible crime preventive. What is obviously true is that once an offender has been executed, it is physically impossible for that person to commit any further crimes, since the punishment is totally incapacitative. But incapacitation is not identical with prevention. Prevention by means of incapacitation occurs only if the executed criminal would have committed other crimes if he or she had not been executed and had been punished only in some less incapacitative way (e.g., by imprisonment).

What evidence is there that the incapacitative effects of the death penalty are an effective crime preventive? From the study of imprisonment, parole, release records, this much is clear: If the murderers and other criminals who have been executed are like the murderers who were convicted but not executed, then (1) executing all convicted murderers would have prevented many crimes, but not many murders (less than one convicted murderer in five hundred commits another murder); and (2) convicted murderers, whether inside prison or outside after release, have at least as good a record of no further criminal activity as any other class of convicted felon.

These facts show that the general public tends to overrate the danger and threat to public safety constituted by the failure to execute every murderer who is caught and convicted. While it would be quite wrong to say that there is no risk such criminals will repeat their crimes—or similar ones—if they are not executed, it would be equally erroneous to say that by executing every convicted murderer many horrible crimes will be prevented. All we know is that a few such crimes will never be committed; we do not know how many or by whom they would have been committed. (Obviously, if we did know we would have tried to prevent them!) This is the nub of the problem. There is no way to know in advance which if any of the incarcerated or released murderers will kill again. It is useful in this connection to remember that the only way to guarantee that no horrible crimes ever occur is to execute *everyone* who might conceivably commit such a crime. Similarly, the only way to guarantee that no convicted murderer ever commits another murder is to execute them all. No modern society has ever done this, and for two hundred years ours has been moving steadily in the opposite direction.

These considerations show that our society has implicitly adopted an attitude toward the risk of murder rather like the attitude it has adopted toward the risk of fatality from other sources, such as automobile accidents, lung cancer, or drowning. Since no one knows when or where or upon whom any of these lethal events will fall, it would be too great an invasion of freedom to undertake the severe restrictions that alone would suffice to prevent any such deaths from occurring. It is better to take the risks and keep our freedom than to try to eliminate the risks altogether and lose our freedom in the process. Hence, we have lifeguards at the beach, but swimming is not totally prohibited; smokers are warned, but cigarettes are still legally sold; pedestrians may be given the right of way in a crosswalk, but marginally competent drivers are still allowed to operate motor vehicles. Some risk is therefore imposed on the innocent; in the name of our right to freedom, our other rights are not protected by society at all costs.

THE DEATH PENALTY AS A CRIME DETERRENT

Determining whether the death penalty is an effective deterrent is even more difficult than determining its effectiveness as a crime preventive. In general, our knowledge about how penalties deter crimes and whether in fact they do—whom they deter, from which crimes, and under what conditions—is distressingly inexact. Most people nevertheless are convinced that punishments do deter, and that the more severe a punishment is the better it will deter. For half a century, social scientists have studied the questions whether the death penalty is a deterrent and whether it is a better deterrent than the alternative of imprisonment. Their verdict, while not unanimous, is nearly so. Whatever may be true about the deterrence of lesser crimes by other penalties, the deterrence achieved by the death penalty for murder is not measurably any greater than the deterrence achieved by long-term imprisonment. In the nature of the case, the evidence is quite indirect. No one can identify for certain any crimes that did not occur because the would-be offender was deterred by the threat of the death penalty and could not have been deterred by a less severe threat. Likewise, no one can identify any crimes that did occur

because the offender was not deterred by the threat of prison even though he would have been deterred by the threat of death. Nevertheless, such evidence as we have fails to show that the more severe penalty (death) is really a better deterrent than the less severe penalty (imprisonment) for such crimes as murder.

If the conclusion stated above is correct, and the death penalty and long-term imprisonment are equally effective (or ineffective) as deterrents to murder, then the argument for the death penalty on grounds of deterrence is seriously weakened. One of the moral principles identified earlier now comes into play. It is the principle that unless there is a good reason for choosing a more rather than a less severe punishment for a crime, the less severe penalty is to be preferred. This principle obviously commends itself to anyone who values human life and who concedes that, all other things being equal, less pain and suffering is always better than more. Human life is valued in part to the degree that it is free of pain, suffering, misery, and frustration, and in particular to the extent that it is free of such experiences when they serve no purpose. If the death penalty is not a more effective deterrent than imprisonment, then its greater severity is gratuitous, purposeless suffering and deprivation. Accordingly, we must reject it in favor of some less severe alternative, unless we can identify some more weighty moral principle that the death penalty protects better than any less severe mode of punishment does. Whether there is any such principle is unclear.

A COST/BENEFIT ANALYSIS OF THE DEATH PENALTY

A full study of the costs and benefits involved in the practice of capital punishment would not be confined solely to the question of whether it is a better deterrent or preventive of murder than imprisonment. Any thoroughgoing utilitarian approach to the death-penalty controversy would need to examine carefully other costs and benefits as well, because maximizing the balance of all the social benefits over all the social costs is the sole criterion of right and wrong according to utilitarianism. . . . Let us consider, therefore, some of the other costs and benefits to be calculated. Clinical psychologists have presented evidence to suggest that the death penalty actually incites some persons of unstable mind to murder others, either because they are afraid to take their own lives and hope that society will punish them for murder by putting them to death, or because they fancy that they, too, are killing with justification analogously to the lawful and presumably justified killing involved in capital punishment. If such evidence is sound, capital punishment can serve as a counter-preventive or even an incitement to murder; such incited murders become part of its social cost. Imprisonment, however, has not been known to incite any murders or other crimes of violence in a comparable fashion. (A possible exception might be found in the imprisonment of terrorists, which has inspired other terrorists to take hostages as part of a scheme to force the authorities to release their imprisoned comrades.) The risks of executing the innocent are also part of the social cost. The historical record is replete with innocent persons arrested, indicted, convicted, sentenced, and occasionally legally executed for crimes they did not commit. This is quite apart from the guilty persons unfairly convicted, sentenced to death, and executed on the strength of perjured testimony, fraudulent evidence, subernation of jurors, and other violations of the civil rights and liberties of the accused. Nor is this all. The high costs of a capital trial and of the inevitable appeals, the costly methods of custody most prisons adopt for convicts on "death row," are among the straightforward economic costs that the death penalty incurs. Conducting a valid cost/benefit analysis of capital punishment is extremely difficult, and it is impossible to predict exactly what such a study would show. Nevertheless, based on such evidence as we do have, it is quite possible that a study of this sort would favor abolition of all death penalties rather than their retention.

WHAT IF EXECUTIONS DID DETER?

From the moral point of view, it is quite important to determine what one should think about capital punishment if the evidence were clearly to show that the death penalty is a distinctly superior method of social defense by comparison with less severe alternatives. Kantian moralists . . . would have no use for such knowledge, because their entire case for the morality of the death penalty rests on the way it is thought to provide just retribution, not on the way it is thought to provide social defense. For a utilitarian, however, such knowledge would be conclusive. Those who follow Locke's reasoning would also be gratified, because they defend the morality of the death penalty both on the ground that it is retributively just and on the ground that it provides needed social defense.

What about the opponents of the death penalty, however? To oppose the death penalty in the face of incontestable evidence that it is an effective method of social defense violates the moral principle that where grave risks are to be run, it is better that they be run by the guilty than by the innocent. Consider in this connection an imaginary world in which by executing the murderer his victim is invariably restored to life, whole and intact, as though the murder had never occurred. In such a miraculous world, it is hard to see how anyone could oppose the death penalty on moral grounds. Why shouldn't a murderer die if that will infallibly bring the victim back to life? What could possibly be morally wrong with taking the murderer's life under such conditions? The death penalty would now be an instrument of perfect restitution, and it would give a new and better meaning to *lex talionis,* "a life for a life." The whole idea is fanciful, of course, but it shows as nothing else can how opposition to the death penalty cannot be both moral and wholly unconditional. If opposition to the death penalty is to be morally responsible, then it must be conceded that there are conditions (however unlikely) under which that opposition should cease.

But even if the death penalty were known to be a uniquely effective social defense, we could still imagine conditions under which it would be reasonable to oppose it. Suppose that in addition to being a slightly better preventive and deterrent than imprisonment, executions also have a slight incitive effect (so that for every ten murders an execution prevents or deters, it also incites another murder). Suppose also that the administration of criminal justice in capital cases is inefficient, unequal, and tends to secure convictions and death sentences only for murderers who least "deserve" to be sentenced to death (including some death sentences and a few executions of the innocent). Under such conditions, it would still be reasonable to oppose the death penalty, because on the facts supposed more (or not fewer) innocent lives are being threatened and lost by using the death penalty than would be risked by abolishing it. It is important to remember throughout our evaluation of the deterrence controversy that we cannot ever apply the principle . . . that advises us to risk the lives of the guilty in order to save the lives of the innocent. Instead, the most we can do is weigh the risk for the general public against the execution of those who are *found* guilty by an imperfect system of criminal justice. These hypothetical factual assumptions illustrate the contingencies upon which the morality of opposition to the death penalty rests. And not only the morality of opposition; the morality of any defense of the death penalty rests on the same contingencies. This should help us understand why, in resolving the morality of capital punishment one way or the other, it is so important to know, as well as we can, whether the death penalty really does deter, prevent, or incite crime, whether the innocent really are ever executed, and how likely is the occurrence of these things in the future.

HOW MANY GUILTY LIVES IS ONE INNOCENT LIFE WORTH?

The great unanswered question that utilitarians must face concerns the level of social defense that executions should be expected to achieve before it is justifiable to carry them out. Consider three possible situations: (1) At the level of a hundred executions per year, each additional execution of a convicted murderer reduces the number of murder victims by ten. (2) Executing every convicted murderer reduces the number of murders to 5,000 victims annually, whereas executing only one out of ten reduces the number to 5,001. (3) Executing every convicted murderer reduces the murder rate no more than does executing one in a hundred and no more than does a random pattern of executions.

Many people contemplating situation (1) would regard this as a reasonable trade-off: The execution of each further guilty person saves the lives of ten innocent ones. (In fact, situation [1] or something like it may be taken as a description of what most of those who defend the death penalty on grounds of social defense believe is true.) But suppose that, instead of saving 10 lives, the number dropped to 0.5, i.e, one victim avoided for each two additional executions. Would that be a reasonable price to pay? We are on the road toward the situation described in situation (2), where a drastic 90 percent reduction in the number of persons executed causes the level of social defense to drop by only 0.0002 percent. Would it be worth it to execute so many more murderers at the cost of such a slight decrease in social defense? How many guilty lives is one innocent life worth? (Only those who think that guilty lives are *worthless* can avoid facing this problem.) In situation (3), of course, there is no basis for executing all convicted murderers, since there is no gain in social defense to show for each additional execution after the first out of each hundred has been executed. How, then, should we determine which out of each hundred convicted murderers is the unlucky one to be put to death?

It may be possible, under a complete and thoroughgoing cost/benefit analysis of the death penalty, to answer such questions. But an appeal merely to the moral principle that if lives are to be risked then let it be the lives of the guilty rather than of the innocent will not suffice. (We have already noticed . . . that this abstract principle is of little use in the actual administration of criminal justice, because the police and the courts do not deal with the guilty as such but only with those *judged* guilty.) Nor will it suffice to agree that society deserves all the crime prevention and deterrence it can get as a result of inflicting severe punishments. These principles are consistent with too many different policies. They are too vague by themselves to resolve the choice on grounds of social defense when confronted with hypothetical situations like those proposed above.

Since no adequate cost/benefit analysis of the death penalty exists, there is no way to resolve these questions from that standpoint at this time. Moreover, it can be argued that we cannot have such an analysis without already establishing in some way or other the relative value of innocent lives versus guilty lives. Far from being a product of cost/benefit analysis, a comparative evaluation of lives would have to be available to us before we undertook any such analysis. Without it, no cost/benefit analysis can get off the ground. Finally, it must be noted that our knowledge at present does not approximate to anything like the situation described above in (1). On the contrary, from the evidence we do have it seems we achieve about the same deterrent and preventive effects whether we punish murder by death or by imprisonment.... Therefore, something like the situation in (2) or in (3) may be correct. If so, this shows that the choice between the two policies of capital punishment and life imprisonment for murder will probably have to be made on some basis other than social defense; on that basis alone, the two policies are equivalent and therefore equally acceptable....

EQUAL JUSTICE AND CAPITAL PUNISHMENT

During the past generation, the strongest practical objection to the death penalty has been the inequities with which it has been applied. As the late Supreme Court Justice William O. Douglas once observed, "One searches our chronicles in vain for the execution of any member of the affluent strata of this society."[1] One does not search our chronicles in vain for the crime of murder committed by the affluent. All the sociological evidence points to the conclusion that the death penalty is the poor man's justice; hence the slogan, "Those without the capital get the punishment." The death penalty is also racially sensitive. Every study of the death penalty for rape (unconstitutional only since 1977) has confirmed that black male rapists (especially where the victim is a white female) are far more likely to be sentenced to death and executed than white male rapists. Convicted black murderers are more likely to end up on "death row" than are others, and the killers of whites (whether white or nonwhite) are more likely to be sentenced to death than are the killers of nonwhites.

Let us suppose that the factual basis for such a criticism is sound. What follows for the morality of capital punishment? Many defenders of the death penalty have been quick to point out that since there is nothing intrinsic about the crime of murder or rape dictating that only the poor or only racial-minority males will commit it, and since there is nothing overtly racist about the statutes that authorize the death penalty for murder or rape, capital punishment itself is hardly at fault if in practice it falls with unfair impact on the poor and the black. There is, in short, nothing in the death penalty that requires it to be applied unfairly and with arbitrary or discriminatory results. It is at worst a fault in the system of administering criminal justice. (Some, who dispute the facts cited above, would deny even this.) There is an adequate remedy—execute more whites, women, and affluent murderers.

Presumably, both proponents and opponents of capital punishment would concede that it is a fundamental dictate of justice that a punishment should not be unfairly—inequitably or unevenly—enforced and applied. They should also be able to agree that when the punishment in question is the extremely severe one of death, then the requirement to be fair in using such a punishment becomes even more stringent. There should be no dispute in the death penalty controversy over these principles of justice. The dispute begins as soon as one attempts to connect the principles with the actual use of this punishment.

In this country, many critics of the death penalty have argued, we would long ago have got rid of it entirely if it had been a condition of its use that it be applied equally and fairly. In the words of the attorneys who argued against the death penalty in the Supreme Court during 1972, "It is a freakish aberration, a random extreme act of violence, visibly arbitrary and discriminatory—a penalty reserved for unusual application because, if it were usually used, it would affront universally shared standards of public decency."[2] It is difficult to dispute this judgment, when one considers that there have been in the United States during the past fifty years about half a million criminal homicides but only about 3,900 executions (all but 33 of which were of men).

We can look at these statistics in another way to illustrate the same point. If we could be assured that the nearly 4,000 persons executed were the worst of the bad, repeated offenders incapable of safe incarceration, much less of rehabilitation, the most dangerous murderers in captivity—the ones who had killed more than once and were likely to kill again, and the least likely to be confined in prison without chronic danger to other inmates and the staff—then one might accept half a million murders and a few thousand executions with a sense that rough justice had been done. But the truth is otherwise. Persons are sentenced to death and executed not because they have been found to be uncontrollably violent or hopelessly poor confinement and release risks. Instead, they are executed because they have a poor defense (inexperienced or overworked counsel) at trial; they have no funds to bring sympathetic witnesses to court; they are transients or strangers in the community where they are tried; the prosecuting attorney wants the publicity that goes with "sending a killer to the chair"; there are no funds for an appeal or for a transcript of the trial record; they are members of a despised racial or political minority. In short, the actual study of why particular persons have been sentenced to death and executed does not

show any careful winnowing of the worst from the bad. It shows that the executed were usually the unlucky victims of prejudice and discrimination, the losers in an arbitrary lottery that could just as well have spared them, the victims of the disadvantages that almost always go with poverty. A system like this does not enhance human life; it cheapens and degrades it. However heinous murder and other crimes are, the system of capital punishment does not compensate for or erase those crimes. It only tends to add new injuries of its own to the catalogue of human brutality.

NOTES

1. *Furman v. Georgia,* 408 U.S. 238 (1972), at pp. 251–252.

2. NAACP Legal Defense and Educational Fund, Brief for Petitioner in *Aikens v. California,* O.T. 1971, No. 68-5027, reprinted in Philip English Mackey, ed., *Voices Against Death: American Opposition to Capital Punishment, 1787–1975* (1975), p. 288.

Questions for Analysis

1. According to Bedau, our attitude toward the risks of murder is like our attitude toward the risks of swimming. We do not outlaw swimming even though some swimmers will drown. Similarly, we do not execute all murderers even though some will murder again. In both cases, he says, the reasoning is the same: We allow some risk to the innocent in order to protect our freedoms. Do you agree with this analogy? Why or why not?

2. Bedau argues that a cost-benefit analysis of the death penalty would show that the costs outweigh the benefits. Why? What assumptions does he make? Do you accept these assumptions?

3. Even if the death penalty did deter some would-be murderers, Bedau says, there would still be good reasons to oppose it in some conditions. What conditions? Do they obtain today?

4. According to Van Den Haag, it is better to risk the lives of the guilty than the lives of the innocent. Bedau says that this principle will "not suffice" to justify the death penalty. Why not?

5. Bedau argues that "the strongest practical objection to the death penalty has been the inequities with which it has been applied." What inequities? How strong do you think the objection is?

6. Does Bedau provide a convincing refutation of Van Den Haag? Why or why not?

CASE PRESENTATION

J. D. Autry: Death in Texas

High on booze, pot, and pills, James David (J. D.) Autry and his companion John Alton Sandifer had been bumping around Port Arthur, Texas, in a borrowed pickup one warm Sunday night in April 1980, when they stopped at a convenience store for more beer. What then happened is unclear. But a jury concluded, and a succession of appellate courts affirmed, that there had been a drunken attempt at a robbery and that Autry had shot the cashier between the eyes when she resisted. Then, fleeing the store, Autry had run into two men, both of whom he shot. One was killed, and the other was disabled for life in mind and body. Autry's net profit for the bloodshed was a $2.70 six-pack.

Before the year was out, Autry was convicted of capital murder and delivered in chains to death row—protesting his innocence all the way.

A half hour before his scheduled death by lethal injection in October 1983, Autry was plucked off the gurney. Supreme Court Justice Byron White had granted a last-minute reprieve, a chance to re-examine and re-argue the question of whether a killer should die. The reprieve meant that not only Autry but all death row inmates in Texas and California, who account for about one-quarter of the nation's condemned population, might not even be considered for execution until the spring of 1984.

In the following months, the Supreme Court heard arguments in a case from California that posed the question of a condemned prisoner's being entitled to a judicial review of his or her sentence to determine whether it is "proportional"—that is, whether like crimes typically warrant the death penalty. In the 1976 decisions that restored the death penalty, the Court noted with approval that both the Georgia and Florida courts made proportionality reviews to make sure the penalty wouldn't be imposed arbitrarily. Since then, the Court has struck down as "disproportional" death sentences for rapists and defendants who neither killed nor attempted to kill the victim. At the same time, it has upheld state statutes like that in Texas which make no mention of comparative sentence review. The Court decided that the absence of a proportionality review is not grounds to stay an execution. Shortly thereafter, on the morning of March 14, 1984, J. D. Autry was executed by lethal injection.

Questions for Analysis

1. Do you think states should have proportionality reviews to ensure that the death penalty is not imposed arbitrarily? Do you think justice requires this?

2. Critics say proportionality review systems don't work. They point out that the state courts have failed to set standards for real comparisons, collect complete information on the sentences of all killers, and provide other judges with guidance. Discuss the implications of these charges with regard to the equitable administration of the death penalty.

3. Do you think proportionality is relevant to whether the death penalty is ever morally permissible? Explain.

4. Some say the Autry case is just another example of delay that results in a denial of justice. Both retentionists and abolitionists view such delays as support for their positions. For example, retentionists argue that the obvious difficulties in carrying out the death penalty undermine confidence in the legal system. For their part, abolitionists claim that the very tortuousness of the appeals process demonstrates there is no way to make capital punishment work. On various occasions, the Supreme Court has expressed its own concern with the delays. Justice William Rehnquist charged in 1987 that his colleagues were making a mockery of the criminal justice system by countenancing extended appeals. In 1983, Justice Lewis F. Powell, Jr., told a group of federal judges that unless the judiciary can find

a more efficient way to handle death cases, capital punishment should be abolished. And in granting Autry his last-minute stay, Justice White called for a change in the law to limit repetitive appeals. Despite the high court's impatience, it is obligated to keep reviewing death penalty cases. Do you think that delays do, in fact, result in a denial of justice? Explain. Do they make stronger the retentionist or the abolitionist position?

CASE PRESENTATION
Karla Faye Tucker: The Pickax Murderer

They were only two of 556 homicides recorded in Houston that year and received little initial attention, but they were surely two of the most sensational slayings in the city's history. One the night of June 14, 1983, Karla Faye Tucker and David Garrett climaxed a three-day drug binge by hacking to death Jerry Lynn Dean and Deborah Thornton. They had broken into Dean's apartment to steal motorcycle parts. Upon finding Dean at home, Garrett attacked him with a hammer. Tucker joined in with a pickax that belonged to Dean. Then she used it to kill Thornton, Dean's overnight visitor, who lay shivering in his bed. Far from feeling regret over the murders, the twenty-three-year-old former teenage prostitute boasted to friends that she felt a surge of sexual gratification with every thrust of the pickax. A year later, Tucker and Garrett were sentenced to death.

Garrett, who was Tucker's boyfriend at the time of the murders, died in prison before he could be executed. Tucker's case went on to become a worldwide controversy. While awaiting trial at the Harris County Jail, she claimed to have found God; she was now, she said, a born-again Christian who repented her crimes. At their trials, she confessed to the murders and then testified against Garrett; while on death row, she counseled her fellow inmates and married her own spiritual counselor.

Following the customary appeals through the courts, her execution was set for February 3, 1998. As the date neared, she attracted numerous supporters, including Pope John Paul II, television evangelist Pat Robertson, Jesse Jackson, the National Council of Churches, the European Parliament, and Ronald Carlson, Deborah Thornton's brother. Nearly 2,400 others sent letters to Texas Governor George W. Bush asking that her sentence be commuted to life. For many of her supporters, the issue was her religious conversion. She was not, they argued, the same woman who had committed the lurid murders. Nor was she a threat to society. Tucker argued the same point in her appeal for clemency before the Texas Board of Pardons and Parole, saying "If you decide you must carry out this execution, do it based solely on the brutality and heinousness of my crime. But please don't do it based on me being a future threat to our society, because I am definitely no longer a threat to our society, and in fact I believe I am a positive contributor to our society and helping others." Still, the board voted 16 to 0, with two abstentions, to deny her appeal.

Compounding the controversy was the fact that Tucker was a woman. Texas had not executed a woman since 1863, and the last U.S. execution of a woman—the only execution of a woman since 1976, when the Supreme Court allowed the states to resume capital punishment—had occurred in 1984 in North Carolina.

On February 3, the Supreme Court refused Tucker's last-minute appeal for a stay of execution. Governor Bush, who had the option to grant a one-time-only thirty-day stay, refused to do so, and the execution was carried out that evening by lethal injection. In her final statement, Tucker said, "I would like to say to all of you, the Thornton family and Jerry Dean's family, that I am sorry. I hope God will give you peace with this."

Questions for Analysis

1. Many death row prisoners claim they have found God and been rehabilitated. If true, should their sentences be commuted? How can we decide if the claims are true?

2. Would a man in Tucker's position have attracted so many supporters?

3. Between 1976 and Tucker's execution in 1998, 432 people were executed in the United States, only one a woman. Does the enormous disparity in the numbers of executed men and women show bias in favor of women? If so, what should be done about it?

4. Given her heinous, brutal crimes, did Tucker deserve the death penalty?

CASE PRESENTATION

A Failed Experiment?

Callins v. Collins was a routine decision for the U.S. Supreme Court. With no written opinion, the Court declined to review the death sentence of Bruce Edwin Callins, who had been convicted of murder by a Texas jury. What was not routine was Justice Harry A. Blackmun's headline-making dissent. When he first joined the Court more than twenty years earlier, he had been a supporter of the death penalty. But on February 22, 1994, during his final term, Justice Blackmun announced in a lone dissent that "the death penalty experiment has failed."

In arguing that it had failed, he claimed that two constitutional requirements for imposing the death penalty are incompatible. The requirement that it must be imposed consistently (from *Furman v. Georgia*), he wrote, clashes with other precedents that require individualized sentencing. Excerpts follow:

> . . . Twenty years have passed since this Court declared that the death penalty must be imposed fairly and with reasonable consistency or not at all (see *Furman v. Georgia,* 1972), and, despite the effort of the states and courts to devise legal formulas and procedural rules to meet this daunting challenge, the death penalty remains fraught with arbitrariness, discrimination, caprice and mistakes. . . .
>
> Experience has taught us that the constitutional goal of eliminating arbitrariness and discrimination from the administration of death . . . can never be achieved without compromising an equally essential component of fundamental fairness: individualized sentencing. (See *Lockett v. Ohio,* 1978.)
>
> It is tempting, when faced with conflicting constitutional commands, to sacrifice one for the other, or to assume that an acceptable

balance between them already has been struck. In the context of the death penalty, however, such jurisprudential maneuvers are wholly inappropriate. The death penalty must be imposed "fairly, and with reasonable consistency, or not at all." (*Eddings v. Oklahoma,* 1982.)

> To be fair, capital sentencing schemes must treat each person convicted of a capital offense with that "degree of respect for the uniqueness of the individual. . . ." That means affording the sentencer the power and discretion to grant mercy in a particular case, and providing avenues for the consideration of any and all relevant mitigating evidence that would justify a sentence less than death.
>
> Reasonable consistency, on the other hand, requires that the death penalty be inflicted evenhandedly, in accordance with reason and objective standards, rather than by whim, caprice or prejudice.
>
> . . . [T]his Court, in my opinion, has engaged in a futile effort to balance these constitutional demands, and now is retreating not only from the *Furman* promise of consistency and rationality, but from the requirement of individualized sentencing as well. . . .
>
> From this day forward, I no longer shall tinker with the machinery of death. . . . Rather than continue to coddle the Court's delusion that the desired level of fairness be achieved and the need for regulation eviscerated, I feel morally and intellectually obligated to concede that the death penalty experiment has failed. . . .
>
> It seems that the decision whether a human being should live or die is so inherently subjective, rife with all of life's understandings, experiences, prejudices, and passions, that it

inevitably defies the rationality and consistency required by the Constitution. . . .

Justice Antonin Scalia, in a rebutting opinion, responded as follows:

> . . . As Justice Blackmun describes . . . this court has attached to the imposition of the death penalty two quite incompatible sets of commands: the sentencer's discretion to impose death must be closely confined (see *Furman v. Georgia,* 1972) but the sentencer's discretion not to impose death (to extend mercy) must be unlimited (*Eddings v. Oklahoma,* 1982; *Lockett v. Ohio,* 1978). These commands were invented without benefit of any textual support; they are the product of just such "intellectual, moral and personal" perceptions as Justice Blackmun expressed today. . . .
>
> Though Justice Blackmun joins those of us who have acknowledged the incompatibility of the Court's *Furman* and *Lockett-Eddings* lines of jurisprudence . . . he unfortunately draws the wrong conclusion from the acknowledgment. . . .
>
> Surely a different conclusion commends itself to wit, that at least one of the judicially announced irreconcilable commands which cause the Constitution to prohibit what its text [the Fifth Amendment] explicitly permits must be wrong. . . .

Questions for Analysis

1. Justices Blackmun and Scalia agree that past Supreme Court decisions regarding the death penalty are incompatible. To the former, the incompatibility shows that the death penalty cannot be imposed constitutionally. To the latter, it shows that the Court has erred. Which justice do you agree with?

2. Along with Justice Scalia, many critics have accused Justice Blackmun of reading his personal views into the Constitution. Do you agree?

3. Regardless of the constitutional issue, does Justice Blackmun have a strong moral position? That is, does justice require both evenhandedness and consideration for the uniqueness of the individual when we impose the death penalty? If so, are the two really incompatible?

4. Is the decision to impose the death penalty "inherently subjective"?

CASE PRESENTATION
Warren McClesky

Warren McClesky was black. The fatally wounded police officer was white. Their paths crossed in the Dixie Furniture Store near downtown Atlanta on May 13, 1978. McClesky was robbing the store at gunpoint; officer Frank Schlatt had responded to a silent alarm. Whether McClesky or one of his accomplices fired the bullet that killed Officer Schlatt is unknown, but in Georgia, as in many other states, McClesky could be charged with the murder nonetheless. He was tried, convicted, and sentenced to death.

On appeal, McClesky argued that his sentence was the result of racial bias. To back up the claim, the defense offered two studies by University of Iowa Professor David Baldus. These studies examined racial factors in the imposition of the death penalty in Georgia between 1973, when the state's capital punishment law took effect, and 1979. Among the results were the following:[1]

1. Although whites were victims of fewer than 40 percent of all homicides studied, they were victims in 87 percent that resulted in the death penalty for the killer.

---

1. Cited in Anthony G. Amsterdam, "Race and the Death Penalty," *Criminal Justice Ethics,* Vol. 7, No 1 (1988), pp. 84–86.

2 Twenty-two percent of blacks convicted of killing whites received the death penalty, compared to only 8 percent of white defendants convicted of killing whites.

3. The racial disparities were greatest in cases that fell between the most heinous and least heinous murders. The death penalty was imposed in 34 percent of such cases when the victim was white, but only 14 percent when the victim was black.

4. The disparities cannot be explained by nonracial factors.

In 1987, *McClesky v. Kemp* reached the Supreme Court, which upheld the sentence. The Court accepted the studies' findings, but it ruled that they did not prove discrimination in McClesky's case. Only proof that the jury, the prosecutor, or some other decision maker in his case was influenced by racial bias could do so. Wrote Justice Lewis F. Powell in his majority opinion, "Because discretion is essential to the criminal justice process, we would demand exceptionally clear proof before we infer that the discretion has been abused."

Questions for Analysis

1. One of the studies' significant implications is that a white life counts for more than a black life when it comes to imposing the death penalty. If the implication is correct, does it taint the way capital punishment is imposed in Georgia?

2. Between 1973 and 1980, seventeen defendants were charged with killing police officers in Fulton County. In only two cases did the prosecution seek the death penalty. One was McClesky's. In the other case, the slain officer was black, and his killer was sentenced to life. Is it reasonable to suspect that racial bias played a role in the decision to seek the death penalty in McClesky's case? In his being sentenced to death?

3. In 1994, the U.S. Congress passed a massive anti-crime package that increased the number of federal crimes punishable by death. The Congressional Black Caucus had proposed a bill known as the Racial Justice Act, allowing convicts on death row to use statistical evidence to argue that race played a role in their sentencing. The bill was not part of the final package. Should it have been?

4. Suppose similar disparities could be found throughout the country. Would that justify the abolition of capital punishment?

8

Terrorism and Civil Liberties

Just War Theory
Preemptive Wars
Violence and Terrorism
Jihadism
Pacifism
Civil Liberties
Arguments for Trading Civil Liberties for Safety
Arguments against Trading Civil Liberties for Safety

David Luban, "Just War and Human Rights"
Jean Bethke Elshtain, "Reflections on War and Political
Discourse: Realism, Just War, and
Feminism in a Nuclear Age"
R. G. Frey and Christopher W. Morris, "Violence,
Terrorism, and Justice"
David Cole, "Enemy Aliens"
CASE PRESENTATION, "Preemptive War"
CASE PRESENTATION, "Driving While Veiled"
CASE PRESENTATION, "Fear of Flying"
CASE PRESENTATION, "Racial Profiling before and
after 9/11"

Did the tragic events of 9/11 "change everything," as many have said in the years since? At a minimum, the attacks and our national response to them have led us to reexamine our views of terrorism, violence, war, and when, if ever, they can be justified. America had experienced terrorist attacks before, including the bombing of the Federal Building in Oklahoma City. But most people in this country seemed to feel largely immune from the random attacks on civilians that are all too familiar in countries such as England, which has experienced years of terrorist attacks from the Irish Republican Army over issues in Northern Ireland. The ease of international travel reminded us that broad expanses of oceans on our borders do not insulate us from violent attacks by outsiders.

Historically, we often have had to address the justifiability of military action by the nation. Few seem to doubt that the attack on American naval installations in Pearl Harbor in 1941 justified a declaration of war against Japan, but the decision to drop nuclear bombs on two Japanese cities a few years later, killing or maiming many civilians, remains controversial. The decision to intervene on the side of the Allies in Europe during World War II was controversial at the time to many Americans who thought we should remain neutral. The American role in the Vietnam War remains perennially controversial, as do attempts by some to compare the recent invasion of Iraq to Vietnam.

In this chapter, we consider traditional and recent views on what counts as a "just war" in an age of often-frightening terrorism. We also consider a pervasive concern in our responses to terrorism, namely, the balancing of our safety and security with our tradition of freedom and civil liberties. In a well-known quotation, Benjamin Franklin said, "Those who would give up essential Liberty, to purchase a little temporary Safety, deserve neither Liberty nor Safety." Is this as true today as it was in the eighteenth century?

JUST WAR THEORY

Throughout history, people have developed justifications for their participation in war, and recent developments raise anew these issues for the American role in Afghanistan and Iraq. These theories of "just war" are often described as **jus ad bellum**, proposals to justify the use of force in a particular type of situation. Another theory, **jus in bello**, considers the justice of particular types of actions within a war, whether or not that war itself was justified. For example, a theory of *jus ad bellum* would ask whether the United States invasion of Iraq was justified. A theory of *jus in bello* would address whether it was justifiable to drop bombs on civilian areas during that war.

In the thirteenth century, St. Thomas Aquinas developed one of the most influential theories of just war in his work *Summa Theologica*, an approach which remains much debated even today. Much of Aquinas's work is rooted in that of the classic Greek philosopher Aristotle and is devoted to reconciling Aristotelian insights with Christian theology. Aquinas asked whether it is always sinful to wage war. In response, he argued, in part:

> In order for a war to be just, three things are necessary. First, the authority of the sovereign by whose command the war is to be waged. For it is not the business of a private individual to declare war, because he can seek for redress of his rights from the tribunal of his superior. Moreover it is not the business of a private individual to summon together the people, which has to be done in wartime. And as the care of the common weal is committed to those who are in authority, it is their business to watch over the common weal of the city, kingdom or province subject to them. And just as it is lawful for them to have recourse to the sword in defending that common weal against internal disturbances, when they punish evil-doers, . . . so too, it is their business to have recourse to the sword of war in defending the common weal against external enemies. . . .

Secondly, a just cause is required, namely that those who are attacked, should be attacked because they deserve it on account of some fault. . . .

Thirdly, it is necessary that the belligerents should have a rightful intention, so that they intend the advancement of good, or the avoidance of evil. . . . For it may happen that the war is declared by the legitimate authority, and for a just cause, and yet be rendered unlawful through a wicked intention.[1]

In summary, Aquinas believes we should first ask whether the entity declaring war is a legitimate sovereign. We might ask whether these sovereigns should include all recognized nations, regardless of how their leaders came to power, or whether we should also consider the legitimacy of those governments and perhaps limit recognized sovereigns to democratically elected governments. In his article here, David Luban is troubled that the United Nations recognizes many nations whose leaders came to power in violent and perhaps illegitimate ways and suggests that they should not benefit from the defense of just war theory.

Second, Aquinas says that the people we attack should deserve it because of "some fault" of theirs, and we can ask what faults would legitimately support war against that country. Should we limit those faults to aggression against another nation? What if that aggression was an attempt to reclaim land that the aggressor believes was wrongfully seized centuries earlier? In the 1991 Gulf War, Iraq claimed that it was simply retaking land in Kuwait that was rightfully Iraq's anyway. In the wars in the Balkans, combatants have said they were merely reclaiming land wrongfully taken from their ancestors long ago. Who should decide who properly deserves to have this land? Should there be a statute of limitations or time limit against reclaiming land?

Are there other faults that would justify initiating war against another nation? Would knowledge of the concentration camps and the extermination of 6 million Jews in Nazi Germany have justified initiating war against that nation? If Timothy McVeigh, the Oklahoma City bomber, had been a citizen of Canada, would that alone have justified American initiation of war against Canada? If we had indisputable evidence that the Canadian government had provided McVeigh with financial assistance to carry out the bombing, would that have justified initiation of war against Canada? McVeigh, of course, was an American citizen, and there is not a shred of evidence of Canadian involvement. But it can be helpful in reasoning about a just war to imagine different hypothetical situations to test our views on the applicability of these theories.

Aquinas's third requirement for a just war is a "rightful intention," either "the advancement of good, or the avoidance of evil." How should we determine what a rightful intention is? By whose standards should we judge the advancement of "good"? Can we use the utilitarian theories of Mill or the human rights views of Kant to make these assessments? What other considerations should be brought to bear in making these decisions?

In the recent debates over the American invasion of Iraq, some argue that a well-founded belief that Saddam Hussein possessed weapons of mass destruction

---

1.   Literal translation by Fathers of the English Dominican Province, 1920. The complete text of the *Summa* can be found online: http://www.newadvent.org/summa/

(WMD), which posed an imminent threat to the safety of Americans, is adequate justification for this war, even if it is later determined that those weapons did not exist. Another argument in support of the Iraq war noted that Hussein had committed genocide against his own Iraqi citizens and thus deserved to be deposed by a nation with the military power to accomplish that. How would you assess these claims using Aquinas's three requirements for a just war? Some critics of the war claim that it had a hidden agenda of gaining control over the Iraq oil fields to meet America's needs for oil. If that were true, would it constitute a violation of Aquinas's third condition?

PREEMPTIVE WARS

In 2002, President George W. Bush articulated a new theory of the justifiability of war, which has come to be known as "preemptive" war. (Excerpts from his announcement of this policy can be found in the Case Presentations.) He observes that the United States has traditionally engaged in war only in defense of aggression by other nations against us. Otherwise, we pursued a policy of deterrence from war, efforts to discourage other nations from attacking us with threats, for example, of "mutually assured destruction" from the dropping of nuclear bombs.

At the heart of the justification of preemptive war is the claim that changes in warfare and the character of our enemies throughout the world make preemption necessary in some circumstances. We can no longer wait for our adversaries to attack us, if those attacks might be nuclear bombs and other devastating attacks by terrorists that would make it impossible for us to even respond. Instead, we must strike first, the theory goes, to destroy those adversaries who pose a serious risk of attacking us first with weapons of mass destruction.

Supporters of the president's approach emphasize that the nature of warfare has changed, especially since the attacks of 9/11. The unpredictability of rogue states and the proliferation of nuclear arsenals, as well as biological weapons with enormous destructive potential, they argue, dictate that we take steps to protect ourselves that we might have found inappropriate in an earlier time. Critics are troubled by this change in longstanding national policy to become an aggressor nation. They wonder if this theory of preemptive wars will encourage other nations to initiate aggression, perhaps against us, if they suspect that we present an imminent threat to them.

VIOLENCE AND TERRORISM

Violence in the world is nothing new, and neither is terrorism. In considering these concepts, it is important to carefully scrutinize what we mean by these terms, an essential first step in good reasoning about when, if ever, they might be justifiable. Although everyone has an intuitive sense of how they understand these terms, under close scrutiny we might find that one person's justifiable aggression is another person's unjustifiable terrorism.

War itself seems necessarily to involve violence, but most people consider such violence justified, at least against military combatants, if the war itself was justified.

Violence would include physical death and injury, but we also sometimes speak of "violence" to intellectual and conceptual ideas of cultural identity, economic well-being, and state of mind. Further, not all situations where physical injury might be involved seem appropriately labeled "violence."

R. G. Frey and Christopher W. Morris consider different definitions of "terrorism" in their essay in this chapter. They suggest that terrorism is included within violence but that not all violence is terrorism. One characteristic of terrorism, they suggest, is randomness or surprise. But modern warfare also depends on an element of surprise, yet that does not necessarily seem to make it terrorism. Another characteristic of terrorism is attack on nonmilitary personnel, innocent civilians, yet in war, innocent civilians often die as so-called "collateral damage," even if their deaths were not the intention of the military action. The attack of 9/11 on the Pentagon was typically called terrorism, even though most of the people killed were members or employees of the military.

If an act of violence can also be called terrorism, should this justify a change in our response to the behavior? Should we assess punishment or blame based on other factors, such as the claimed justification for the attack or the supposed involvement of the persons attacked in causing hardship to the attackers? Even if some violence can be justified—for example, violence in self-defense or violence in a justified war—can any terrorism be justified? Has the United States ever engaged in activities that others believe constituted terrorism? Are historic attacks on the United States that we considered war more appropriately reconsidered now as terrorism?

JIHADISM

After 9/11, a concept called *jihadism* has been the source of much controversy. Some use it to describe a campaign of violence against the West by a militant, extremist form of Islam, noting that all nineteen hijackers claimed Islam as their religion. However, many scholars of Islamic religion, especially practitioners living in the West, have insisted that this is a perversion of the Islamic faith. Some people seem to use jihadism as synonymous with terrorism, even though much of the terrorism in the world has been committed by persons who had no affiliation with any version of Islam and made no claim of engaging in a religious war against the West.

A passage in the Qur'an, the sacred text of Islam, has caused special concern and debate:

Against them make ready your strength to the utmost of your power, including steeds of war, to strike terror into (the hearts of) the enemies, of God and your enemies, and others besides, whom ye may not know, but whom God doth know.

—Holy Qur'an—Sura 8:60

Taken literally, this passage might seem to authorize—indeed, to order—physical violence against anyone who does not support the Muslim religion. This might mean violence against one's own government if it does not support Islam or perhaps violence against other nations that are a threat to Islam. But many adherents of Islam insist that this passage should be considered only metaphorically and not as an authorization for physical terror against non–Muslims. They suggest that Islam cannot be forced on people and that war would be justified only in self-defense. They also cite passages in the Qur'an that prohibit suicide and the harming of innocent civilians. After 9/11, dozens of prominent Islamic world leaders and scholars criticized the attacks as contrary to the teachings of Islam. Some noted that, under Islamic law, the 9/11 terrorism constituted the crime of *hirabah* (waging war against society).

In popular literature since 9/11, the word *jihadism* has taken on a pervasive meaning of aggressive terrorism against innocent civilians for religious purposes, especially for purportedly Islamic interests. As with so many other important concepts in our understanding of these contemporary challenges, care in clarifying our understanding of terms in such a way that our dialogue is clear and not laced with fallacies of reasoning is paramount.

PACIFISM

The tradition of pacifism can be traced back thousands of years, often with religious underpinnings and sometimes as a result of philosophical and ethical views. In general, pacifists believe that violence is always wrong, although adherents might emphasize their interests in different settings. Pacifism in war promotes an absolute ban on violence among nations and urges instead peaceful, nonviolent resolution of political and social differences. A consistent pacifist would also urge that all violence is wrong, such as the killing of a human being in any setting, whether as individuals, in self-defense, or as capital punishment.

Absolutist pacifism can result in other ethical dilemmas, however. If pacifists refuse to fight to defend their country in war, are they relying instead on others to fight those wars, likely benefitting the pacifists in the end? If pacifists urge a national policy that we should never respond to any aggression against us—whether Pearl Harbor or 9/11—are they actually encouraging aggressor nations to attack us on the belief that we will not respond? Is pacifism "unilateral disarmament" that makes us vulnerable to attack by nations that do not adhere to pacifism?

Self-defense in individual situations also presents ethical dilemmas for consistent pacifists. It is one thing to believe that you should never respond to an attack on your own life in self-defense and that it is better to die consistently with your moral views than to live in violation of your pacifist convictions. But what about situations where the pacifist is in a good position to intervene to protect someone else's innocent life? If a young child is being beaten to death by an insane person and the pacifist could easily kill the attacker with a club and save the life of the child, which is the more ethical conduct—to be consistent with pacifism and watch the child murdered or to murder the wrongdoer and save the child's life? It is one thing to sacrifice your own life in the name of ethical principles, but is it equally justifiable to sacrifice the life of another in the name of those principles?

The nature of violence is important here too. We earlier discussed active, aggressive violence against the lives and health of persons. But violence might also be passive, such as in allowing someone to starve to death when we have the means to provide food or knowingly letting someone die from lack of medical attention. Does the pacifist, to be consistent, have a moral obligation to stop passive violence as well, for example, with an affirmative obligation to provide food to the starving or medicine to the sick?

Is pacifism a viable ethical alternative to just war, preemptive war, terrorism, or jihadism? In our deliberations, clarity in our understanding of these concepts is paramount, as is the avoidance of slippery language that distorts and blurs our fair consideration of these issues. One can object to preemptive war without necessarily being a pacifist. One can support preemptive war without necessarily being a terrorist. As in all areas of public dialogue, name-calling and *ad hominems* accomplish nothing.

CIVIL LIBERTIES

"The Constitution is not a suicide pact." This somewhat sarcastic remark about the role of the liberties accorded to us under the Constitution (attributed to two U.S. Supreme Court Justices, Robert Jackson and, later, Arthur Goldberg) has become a familiar refrain since 9/11. And the statistics about the terrorist dangers in the United States can be frightening. Some 300,000 foreign nationals are in this country, even though they have already been ordered deported, according to the attorney general. Even just a small number of persons could cause massive destruction in our country. The Department of Justice claims to have broken up terrorist cells in Buffalo, Detroit, Seattle, and Portland that could have caused disastrous harm to American citizens on our own soil. The popular press buzzes with accounts of thousands of "sleeper cells" in the United States, preparing to launch attacks on everything from water supplies, bridges, and tunnels to oil pipelines, nuclear power plants, and shopping centers. In the face of such uncertainty and fear, it is no wonder that many Americans have rushed to insist that everything possible be done to round up these potential terrorists, even at the expense of sacrificing their own civil liberties, guaranteed under the U.S. Constitution.

How much are people willing to give up to find the terrorists supposedly in our midst? Quite a bit it seems! David Cole, in his article here, explains that the civil liberties of legal residents who are noncitizens have been the most heavily trampled but that the risks to law-abiding citizens are also in jeopardy. In a *Newsweek* poll in November 2002, 72 percent said the restrictions on civil liberties by the Bush administration's war on terrorism were "about right."[2] In this poll 51 percent thought the Bill of Rights should apply only to U.S. citizens, excluding the many noncitizens who are in this country legally. In a poll taken two months after 9/11, Americans overwhelmingly favored restrictions on free speech if it would help the war on terrorism; 61 percent said that people who had expressed support for the terrorists should not be allowed to give a speech at a college; 40 percent would permit

---

2. Jennifer Barrett, "*Newsweek* Poll: Public Backs Military Tribunals; Most Americans Support New Restrictions on Civil Liberties and Expanded Government Powers—Up to a Point," December 1, 2002, *Newsweek Web Exclusive*.

censorship of news reporting about war protests; and 36 percent approved of censorship of negative news reports about presidential conduct of the military.[3]

Which civil liberties are at stake? The Bill of Rights, the first ten amendments to the U.S. Constitution, is a good starting point for review of provisions that are at issue in the new anti-terrorist measures. The First Amendment protects our right of free speech, freedom of association, and academic freedom. Efforts to censor public speeches, even if supportive of terrorism in the minds of some, would be protected under this constitutional right. If a college wants to sponsor a debate on the meaning of jihadism, should restrictions be placed on how wide-ranging the debate can be? If a local school raises money to donate to a charity and later learns that it has been linked with terrorist activities, should that school lose its right of freedom of association? Freedom of religion is also protected under the First Amendment. But in the interest of protecting us against terrorism, should the government be allowed to place special restrictions on religious schools that it suspects might promote anti-American views?

The Fourth Amendment protects us against "unreasonable searches and seizures" by the government. Yet the anti-terrorism provisions make it considerably easier for the government to conduct secret searches of homes and to tap cell phones with much greater ease if it asserts a "foreign intelligence" need.

The Sixth Amendment guarantees our right to "a speedy and public trial" yet the anti-terrorist measures ordered by President Bush after 9/11 allow secret military tribunals of persons who are not American citizens. The Seventh Amendment guarantees our right to a jury trial in a criminal proceeding, yet this is also denied in the secret military tribunals of persons who are not American citizens.

The Eighth Amendment guarantees that "Excessive bail shall not be required, nor excessive fines imposed, nor cruel and unusual punishments inflicted," yet thousands of immigrants, especially those of Middle Eastern descent, are being held in detention centers without formal charges being brought against them for months, even years, at a time.

The challenge ahead is to determine how best to protect the country and its residents from future terrorist attacks without jettisoning those liberties that our forefathers and so many generations of Americans fought to preserve.

ARGUMENTS FOR TRADING CIVIL LIBERTIES FOR SAFETY

1.   *Only terrorists need to worry about searches by the government, not law-abiding citizens.*

POINT: "People who have done nothing wrong have nothing to hide. If government officials want to search my house, let them. They won't find anything. If conducting a lot of searches means the government finds the terrorists and brings them to justice, then I say, let them search all of us."

---

3.   The survey was conducted by National Public Radio News, the Kaiser Family Foundation, and the Harvard University Kennedy School of Government. http://www.npr.org/news/specials/civillibertiespoll/011130.poll.html

COUNTERPOINT: "We all have a right to privacy in our homes. I don't want the government searching my home on a fishing expedition. I'm not a terrorist, but I don't think my life should be an open book to government officials. And what if they find things that are perfectly innocent but might be taken out of context and make me look guilty of something I didn't do?"

2.   *I'll never go on trial, as I follow the law, so the right to a public trial with a jury is irrelevant to me.*

POINT: "Most people who are arrested are probably guilty anyway. And the terrorists who aren't even American citizens don't deserve the same rights citizens have under the Bill of Rights. Most countries in the world don't even have juries, so this is a luxury that people from those countries don't deserve if they do something wrong here."

COUNTERPOINT: "Innocent people are arrested too, sometimes, and I want to know those rights will always be available to me to have a fair public trial with a jury. Further, our Bill of Rights is an important symbol we hold out to the world of our respect for human rights and human dignity. We should insist on upholding those rights, regardless of who commits a crime in our country, whether or not they are a citizen of this country."

3.   *Good citizens should not speak ill of the president and the government in a time of war anyway.*

POINT: "These are unusual times and we should all rally behind the president and the military. Publicly criticizing them is demoralizing to the nation and only encourages our enemies. Loyal Americans won't mind giving up some of their rights to free speech if it means we're more likely to defeat terrorism. Free speech is a luxury we can afford only during peacetime."

COUNTERPOINT: "Free speech is our best insurance that all viewpoints about the best way to proceed against terrorism are heard and discussed. We should never assume that one viewpoint from the government or the military is necessarily the right one. For centuries, the United States has stood for free speech and public debate on important issues, and in difficult times, we should not abandon that important debate."

4.   *Those religious schools that teach Islam are a breeding ground for terrorists and should be closed down in this country.*

POINT: "All nineteen of the hijackers on 9/11 were Muslims, and they thought they were carrying out the command of their religion. Religious schools in Saudi Arabia and Pakistan are teaching hatred of the West. I realize that most Muslims do not share those views, but while we are in danger from terrorism, we should be safe and close down the religious schools in this country that might be breeding more terrorism right here at home."

COUNTERPOINT: "Islamic leaders in the United States and around the world have denounced the teachings espoused by the hijackers. Most Muslims love peace and condemn terrorism. We should encourage more of that. Closing down religious schools because they might have some terrorists working at them is a dangerous precedent. Timothy McVeigh was raised as a Christian, but nobody thought we should close down all the Christian schools in the country because of what he did."

ARGUMENTS AGAINST TRADING CIVIL LIBERTIES FOR SAFETY

1.   *Our forefathers fought hard to give us precious civil liberties and we should value and protect them, even when times are frightening because of the threats of terrorism.*

POINT: "Our Bill of Rights is over 200 years old and it provides a cornerstone of our country and its values. We should not so readily abandon it just because we are experiencing difficult times and fears of terrorism. Our forefathers would be disappointed to see us so readily agree to give up our liberties because we are afraid."

COUNTERPOINT: "George Washington and the framers of the Constitution never could have envisioned a world in which we are threatened by terrorists, nuclear bombs, and hijacked airplanes flying into tall buildings. They would surely understand that we need to back away from some of their idealistic vision of liberty in the different and much more frightening world we live in today."

2.   *Our protection of civil liberties and freedom is what sets us apart from other countries. We should set an example for the world and show how a free democracy really works.*

POINT: "If we want the rest of the world to emulate our high standards of democracy, we must be vigilant to protect the liberties of a free and open society. If we start to curtail our own liberties because we are afraid, we encourage other countries to curtail what liberties they give their citizens now or to continue to refuse to provide their citizens with any of the liberties we take for granted."

COUNTERPOINT: "No other country provides the degree of freedom and liberty to its citizens that we do in America. Cutting back a little to keep ourselves safe from terrorism won't discourage other countries from experimenting with democracy. And even if it does, it's more important to protect our nation from total devastation than to worry about setting an example for countries who don't like us anyway."

3.   *We might think we're only hurting the terrorists and other criminals when we chip away at civil liberties, but we're putting ourselves at risk too.*

POINT: "Innocent people are sometimes arrested wrongly. Civil liberties in the Constitution protect us in ways that innocent people are not protected in other countries. If we look the other way at the diminishment of civil liberties for some people, it's a slippery slope before they start coming after the rest of us for no good reason."

COUNTERPOINT: "As long as you stay out of trouble, the government won't waste time searching your home or throwing you into jail for no good reason.

Most people who are searched by the police or arrested are probably guilty anyway. Where there's smoke, there's fire!"

4. *Religious freedom is another hallmark of our nation, and we should continue to promote religious diversity and tolerance.*

POINT: "As a nation, we have always treasured our religious freedom, and this is no time to try to restrict some religions just because some of the terrorists belong to them. Many religions have promoted tolerance and understanding of each other, a message we desperately need in this day and age. If we have serious reason to believe terrorists plots are being developed anywhere, then go after them under the law, but don't assume an entire religion is plotting against us."

COUNTERPOINT: "Religious freedom is fine, but not when it preaches intolerance and breeds hatred against American values. We need to take whatever steps are necessary to protect us from the seething violence that is being fomented against us. Religion should not be a shield behind which terrorists can hide. Whether they are hiding in churches or charities or social groups, we need to go after them in any way we can."

Just War and Human Rights

David Luban

David J. Luban, the Frederick J. Haas Professor of Law and Philosophy at Georgetown University Law Center, has written extensively on social justice, legal ethics, and jurisprudence. In this essay, he rejects the traditional approach of understanding "just" and "unjust" war in terms of aggression against another nation. He proposes reconceptualizing just war in terms of the moral dimensions of basic human rights.

Doctrines of just war have been formulated mainly by theologians and jurists in order to provide a canon applicable to a variety of practical situations. No doubt these doctrines originate in a moral understanding of violent conflict. The danger exists, however, that when the concepts of the theory are adopted into the usage of politics and diplomacy their moral content is replaced by definitions which are merely convenient. If that is so, the concepts of the traditional theory of just war could be exactly the wrong starting point for an attempt to come to grips with the relevant moral issues.

This is the case, I wish to argue, with the moral assessment of the justice of war (*jus ad bellum*)[1]. My

argument is in four parts. First I show that the dominant definition in international law is insensitive to one morally crucial dimension of politics. Secondly, I connect this argument with classical social contract theory. Thirdly, I propose an alternative definition which attempts to base itself more firmly on the moral theory of human rights. And finally, I apply this definition to two hard cases.

I UNJUST WAR AS AGGRESSION

International law does not speak of just or unjust war as such, but rather of legal or illegal war. For the purpose of the present discussion I shall assume that the latter distinction expresses a theory of just war and treat the two distinctions as equivalent. The alternative would be to claim that international law is simply irrelevant to the theory of just war, a claim which is both implausible and question-begging.

From David Luban, "Just War and Human Rights," *Philosophy and Public Affairs*, Vol. 9, No. 2 (Winter 1980), 160–81. Copyright © 1980 *Philosophy and Public Affairs*. Reprinted by permission.

Several characterizations of illegal war exist in international law. The Kellogg-Briand Pact of 1928, for example, condemns any use of war as an instrument of national policy except in the case of self-defense; and Brierly maintained that it did not lapse among its signers.[2] It is a very wide criterion for unjust war—wider, it may at first appear, than the United Nations Charter, which reads:

> All members shall refrain in their international relations from the threat or use of force against the territorial integrity or political independence of any State, or in any other manner inconsistent with the purposes of the United Nations.[3]

Presumably an act of war could exist which violated neither the political independence nor the territorial integrity of any state—say, a limited sea war. Or, to take another example, two states could agree to settle an issue by fighting a series of prearranged battles with prior agreements protecting their political independence and territorial integrity. Such acts would be barred by the Kellogg-Briand Pact; whether they are prohibited by Article 2(4) depends on how one reads the phrase "inconsistent with the purposes of the United Nations." I believe that on the most plausible reading, they would be prohibited.[4] Moreover, they would most likely constitute violations of the *jus cogens*, the overriding principles of general international overriding principles of general international law.[5] Thus, Article 2(4) is in fact roughly equivalent to the Kellogg-Briand Pact.

In any case, the provisions of Article 2(4) are subsumed under the definition of aggression adopted by the UN General Assembly in 1974. It includes the clause:

> Aggression is the use of armed force by a State against the sovereignty, territorial integrity or political independence of another State, or in any other manner inconsistent with the Charter of the United Nations.[6]

That this is a characterization of unjust war may be seen from the fact that it terms aggression "the most serious and dangerous form of the illegal use of force."[7] The definition of aggression differs from Article 2(4) in that it includes a reference to sovereignty not present in the latter. This does not, however, mean that it is a wider characterization of unjust war than Article 2(4), for an armed attack on a state's sovereignty would be barred by the latter's catchall phrase "inconsistent with the purposes of the United Nations." Thus, the definition of aggression is not really an emendation of Article 2(4). Rather, it should be viewed as an attempt to conceptualize and label the offense at issue in Article 2(4). It attempts to give a sharp statement of principle.

Matters are further complicated by the fact that the General Assembly in 1946 adopted the Charter of the Nuremberg Tribunal as UN policy. Article 6 of this Charter includes among the crimes against peace "waging of a war of aggression or a war in violation of international treaties, agreements, or assurances. . . ."[8] This appears to be wider in scope than the definition of aggression, in that a war of aggression is only one type of criminal war. However, an argument similar to the one just given can be made here. Wars in violation of international treaties, agreements, or assurances are without question "inconsistent with the Charter of the United Nations," and hence fall under the definition of aggression; the Nuremberg Charter and the definition of aggression are thus extensionally equivalent.

It appears, then, that the definition of aggression captures what is essential in the Kellogg-Briand Pact, Article 2(4) of the UN Charter, and the relevant clause in the Nuremberg Charter. Thus, we may say that the UN position boils down to this:

(1) A war is unjust if and only if it is aggressive.

This gives us a characterization of unjust war, which is half of what we want. The other half emerges from Article 51 of the UN Charter:

> Nothing in the present Charter shall impair the inherent right of individual or collective self-defense if an armed attack occurs against a member of the United Nations. . . .[9]

This tells us, at least in part, what a just war is. Thus, we have

(2) A war is just if it is a war of self-defense (against aggression).

We note that "just" and "unjust" do not, logically speaking, exhaust the possibilities, since it is (just barely) possible that a war which is not fought in self-defense also does not threaten the sovereignty, territorial integrity, or political independence of any state, nor violate international treaties, agreements, or assurances. Now the expression "just war" suggests "permissible war" rather than "righteous war"; if so, then any war which is not specifically proscribed should be just. It is perhaps better, then, to make the two characterizations exhaustive of the possibilities. This can be done in two ways. Either (1) can be expanded to

(1′) A war is unjust if and only if it is not just,

used in conjunction with (2), or (2) can be relaxed to

(2′) A war is just if an only if it is not unjust,

used in conjunction with (1). Overall, it appears that the conjunction of (1′) and (2), which makes every war except a war of self-defense unjust, is more in the spirit of the UN Charter than the more permissive conjunction of (1) and (2′).

Thus, (1′) and (2) capture pretty much what we want, namely the extant conception of *jus ad bellum*. In what follows I will refer to the conjunction of (1′) and (2) as "the UN definition," although it must be emphasized that it is not formulated in these words in any United Nations document.

THE UN DEFINITION AND THE DOCTRINE OF SOVEREIGNTY: A CRITIQUE

As it is formulated in the UN definition, the crime of aggressive war is a crime of state against state. Each state, according to international law, has a duty of non-intervention into the affairs of other states: indeed, this includes not just military intervention, but, in Lauterpacht's widely accepted definition, any "dictatorial interference in the sense of action amounting to the denial of the independence of the State."[10] At the basis of this duty lies the concept of state sovereignty, of which in fact the duty of non-intervention is considered a "corollary."[11] Now the concept of sovereignty has been interpreted in a multitude of ways, and has at different times covered a multitude of sins (in such forms as the notorious doctrine that sovereign states are above the law and entitled to do anything); but in its original use by Bodin, it meant that there can be only one ultimate source of law in a nation, namely the sovereign.[12] This doctrine suffices to explain why intervention is a crime, for "dictatorial interference" of one state in another's affairs in effect establishes a second legislator.

The doctrine does not, however, explain why the duty of non-intervention is a moral duty. For the recognition of a state as sovereign means in international law only that it in fact exercises sovereign power,[13] and it is hard to see how that fact could confer moral rights on it. Might, or so we are told, does not make right. Rather, one should distinguish mere de facto exercise of sovereign power from legitimate exercise of it. The natural argument would then be that the duty of non-intervention exists only toward states which are legitimate (in the sense of the term employed in normative political theory).

Before accepting this argument, however, we must consider another possibility, namely that the duty of non-intervention in a state's affairs is not a duty owed to that state, but to the community of nations as a whole. This, in fact, seems to be one idea behind the United Nations Charter. The experience of World War II showed the disastrous nature of escalating international violence, and an absolute ban on the initiation of warfare is justified on what we would now call rule-utilitarian grounds: regardless of the moral stature of a state, or the empirical likelihood of escalation in a given case, military intervention in the state's affairs is forbidden for the sake of international security.

I want to reject this argument as the basis for a theory of just war, however. For by giving absolute primacy to the world community's interest in peace, it does not really answer the question of when a war is or can be just; rather, it simply refuses to consider it. Obviously, the dangers posed by a war in the volatile political configuration of the nuclear era must weigh heavily into the question of *jus ad bellum*. But to make this the only factor is to refuse a priori to consider the merits of particular issues, and this is simply to beg the question of *jus ad bellum*.

Thus, I return to the claim that a state must be legitimate in order for a moral duty of non-intervention in its affairs to exist. If this is so, it pulls the rug out from under the UN definition, which is simply indifferent to the question of legitimacy, and thus to the whole moral dimension of the issue. We may put this in more graphic terms. When State *A* recognizes State *B*'s sovereignty it accepts a duty of non-intervention in *B*'s internal affairs. In other words, it commits itself to pass over what *B* actually does to its own people unless *B* has entered into international agreements regulating its domestic behavior; and even in this case *A* cannot intervene militarily to enforce these agreements.[14] No matter if *B* is repulsively tyrannical; no matter if it consists of the most brutal torturers or sinister secret police; no matter if its ruling generals make its primary export bullion shipped to Swiss banks. If *A* recognizes *B*'s sovereignty it recognizes *B*'s right to enjoy its excesses without "dictatorial interference" from outside.

Really, however, the point retains its force no matter what the character of *B*. The concept of sovereignty is morally flaccid, not because it applies to illegitimate regimes, but because it is insensitive to the entire dimension of legitimacy.

Can the UN definition be repaired, then, by restricting the concepts of sovereignty and aggression to legitimate states? This would certainly be a step in the right direction; but the attempt underlines a puzzle about the whole strategy of defining *jus ad bellum* as a crime against states. Wars are not fought by states, but by men and women. There is, therefore, a conceptual lacuna in such a definition. It can be bridged only by explaining how a crime against a state is also a crime against its citizens, that is, by relating men and women to their states in a morally cogent fashion. This, I take it, is what the concept of legitimacy is supposed to do. A legitimate state has a right against aggression because people have a right to their legitimate state. But if so we should be able to define *jus ad bellum* directly in terms of human rights, without the needless detour of talk about states. Nor is this simply a question of which terms are logically more basic. If the rights of states are derived from the rights of humans, and are thus in a sense one kind of human rights, it will be important to consider their possible conflicts with other human rights. Thus, a doctrine of *jus ad bellum* formulated in terms of human rights may turn out not to consider aggression the sole crime of war. Indeed, this is what I shall argue in Section III.

First, however, it will be helpful to consider more closely the connection between a state's rights and those of its citizens. For I have criticized the UN definition (and the doctrine of sovereignty) by suggesting that its focus on the former shows indifference to the latter.

II CONTRACT, NATION AND STATE

This argument may be clarified by examining social contract theory, the canonical modern account of legitimacy. The key feature of contract theory for our present discussion is its conception of the rights of political communities, particularly their right against aggression. According to contract theory, a political community is made legitimate by the consent (tacit or explicit) of its members; it thereby acquires rights which derive from the rights of its members. Thus the rights of political communities are explained by two rather harmless assumptions: that people have rights, and that those rights may be transferred through freely given consent. Contract theory, then, appears to offer a particularly clear account of how aggression against a political community is a crime against its members.

However, it is important to note the term "political community" has two radically distinct meanings, corresponding to two very different conceptions of the social contract. The seventeenth-century theorists distinguished between a contract by which people bind themselves into a community prior to any state—Locke's version—and a contract by which people set a sovereign over them—Hobbes' version. Let us call the former a "horizontal" and the latter a "vertical" contract.[15]

A horizontal contract may be explicit: Arendt, in introducing the terms, suggests the Mayflower Compact as a paradigm case of a horizontal contract to which consent was explicitly rendered. More often, however, the consent is given tacitly through the process of everyday living itself. In Walzer's words:

> Over a long period of time, shared experiences and cooperative activity of many different kinds shape a common life. 'Contract' is a metaphor for a process of association and mutuality. . . .[16]

Such a contract gives rise to a *people* or, as I shall say in order to emphasize the people's existence as a political community, to a *nation*. But only the vertical contract can legitimate a *state*. A state is an ongoing institution of rule over, or government of, its nation. It is a drastic error to confuse the two; for while every government loudly asserts, "Le peuple, c'est moi!" [I am the people] it is clear that this is never literally true and seldom plausible even as a figure of speech. And it is equally obvious what ulterior motives and interests lie behind the assertion.

A state's rights can be established only through a vertical contract, which according to social-contract theory means nothing more or less than that the state is legitimate. This, too, requires consent, and this will be consent over and above that which establishes the horizontal contract. For the nation is prior to the state. Political communities, not sets of atomic individuals, consent to be governed. . . .

THE MODERN MORAL REALITY OF WAR

Modern international law is coeval with the rise of the European nation-state in the seventeenth and eighteenth centuries. As the term suggests, it is within the historical context of nation-states that a theory will work whose tendency is to equate the rights of nations with the rights of states. It is plausible to suggest that an attack on the French state amounts to an attack on the French nation (although even here some doubts are possible: a Paris Communard in 1871 would hardly have agreed). But when nations and states do not characteristically coincide, a theory of *jus ad bellum* which equates unjust war with aggression, and aggression with violations of state sovereignty, removes itself from the historical reality of war.

World politics in our era is marked by two phenomena: a breakup of European hegemony in the Third World which is the heritage of nineteenth-century imperialism; and maneuvering for hegemony by the (neo-imperialist) superpowers, perhaps including China. The result of this process is a political configuration in the Third World in which states and state boundaries are to an unprecedented extent the result of historical accident (how the European colonial powers parceled up their holdings) and political convenience (how the contending superpowers come to terms with

each other). In the Third World the nation-state is the exception rather than the rule. Moreover, a large number of governments possess little or no claim to legitimacy. As a result of these phenomena, war in our time seems most often to be revolutionary war, war of liberation, civil war, border war between newly established states, or even tribal war, which is in fact a war of nations provoked largely by the noncongruence of nation and state.

In such circumstances a conception of *jus ad bellum* like the one embodied in the UN definition fails to address the moral reality of war. It reflects a theory that speaks to the realities of a bygone era. The result is predictable. United Nations debates—mostly ineffectual in resolving conflicts—and discussions couched in terms of aggression and defense, have deteriorated into cynical and hypocritical rhetoric and are widely recognized as such. Nor is this simply one more instance of the well-known fact that politicians lie in order to dress up their crimes in sanctimonious language. For frequently these wars are fought for reasons which are recognizably moral. It is just that their morality cannot be assessed in terms of the categories of the UN definition; it must be twisted and distorted to fit a conceptual **Procrustes' bed**.

III HUMAN RIGHTS AND THE NEW DEFINITION

What, then, are the terms according to which the morality of war is to be assessed? In order to answer this question, let me return to my criticism of the contractarian derivation of the rights of states from the rights of individuals. States—patriots and Rousseau to the contrary—are not to be loved, and seldom to be trusted. They are, by and large, composed of men and women whose interests are consequently at least slightly at variance with those of the rest of us. When we talk of the rights of a state, we are talking of rights—"privileges" is a more accurate word—which those men and women possess over and above the general rights of man; and this is why they demand a special justification.

I have not, however, questioned the framework of individual rights as an adequate language for moral discourse. It is from this framework that we may hope to discover the answer to our question. Although I accept the vocabulary of individual rights for the purpose of the present discussion, I do not mean to suggest that its propriety cannot be questioned. Nevertheless, talk of individual rights does capture much of the morality of contemporary politics, as talk of sovereignty and states' rights does not. This is a powerful pragmatic reason for adopting the framework.

To begin, let me draw a few elementary distinctions. Although rights do not necessarily derive from social relations, we do not have rights apart from them, for rights are always claims on other people. If I catch pneumonia and die, my right to life has not been violated unless other humans were directly or indirectly responsible for my infection or death. To put this point in syntactic terms, a right is not to be thought of as a one-place predicate, but rather a two-place predicate whose arguments range over the class of beneficiaries and the class of obligors. A human right, then, will be a right whose beneficiaries are all humans and whose obligors are all humans in a position to effect the right. (The extension of this latter class will vary depending on the particular beneficiary.)[17] Human rights are the demands of all of humanity on all of humanity. This distinguishes human rights from, for example, civil rights, where the beneficiaries and obligors are specified by law.

By a *socially basic human right* I mean a right whose satisfaction is necessary to the enjoyment of any other rights.[18] Such rights deserve to be called "basic" because, while they are neither intrinsically more valuable nor more enjoyable than other human rights, they are means to the satisfaction of all rights, and thus they must be satisfied even at the expense of socially non-basic human rights if that is necessary. In Shue's words, "Socially basic human rights are everyone's minimum reasonable demands upon the rest of humanity." He goes on to argue that socially basic human rights include security rights—the right not to be subject to killing, torture, assault, and so on—and subsistence rights, which include the rights to healthy air and water, and adequate food, clothing, and shelter.[19]

Such rights are worth fighting for. They are worth fighting for not only by those to whom

they are denied but, if we take seriously the obligation which is indicated when we speak of human rights, by the rest of us as well (although how strictly this obligation is binding on "neutrals" is open to dispute). This does not mean that any infringement of socially basic human rights is a *causes belli*: here as elsewhere in the theory of just war the doctrine of proportionality applies. But keeping this reservation in mind we may formulate the following, to be referred to henceforth as the "new definition":

> (3) A just war is (i) a war in defense of socially basic human rights (subject to proportionality); or (ii) a war of self-defense against an unjust war.
>
> (4) An unjust war is (i) a war subversive of human rights, whether socially basic or not, which is also (ii) not a war in defense of socially basic human rights.

I shall explain. The intuition here is that any proportional struggle for socially basic human rights is justified, even one which attacks the non-basic rights of others. An attack on human rights is an unjust war *unless* it is such a struggle. This is why clause (4) (ii) is necessary: without it a war could be both just and unjust. Clause (3) (ii) is meant to capture the moral core of the principle of self-defense, formulated above as (2). And it is worth noting that clause (4)(i) is an attempt to reformulate the concept of aggression as a crime against people rather than states; an aggressive war is a war against human rights. Since the rights of nations may be human rights (I shall not argue the pros or cons of this here), this notion of aggression may cover ordinary cases of aggression against nations.

Let me emphasize that (3) and (4) refer to *jus ad bellum*, not *jus in bello* [the law within a war, regardless of the justifiability of the war itself]. When we consider the *manner* in which wars are fought, of course, we shall always find violations of socially basic human rights. One might well wonder, in that case, whether a war can ever be justified. Nor is this wonder misplaced, for it addresses the fundamental horror of war. The answer, if there is to be one, must emerge from the doctrine of proportionality; and here I wish to suggest that the new definition is able to make sense of this doctrine in a way which the UN definition is not.[20] For the UN definition would have us measure the rights of states against socially basic human rights, and this may well be a comparison of incommensurables. Under the new definition, on the other hand, we are asked only to compare the violations of socially basic human rights likely to result from the fighting of a war with those which it intends to rectify. Now this comparison, like the calculus of utilities, might be Benthamite pie-in-the-sky; but if it is nonsense, then proportionality under the UN definition is what Bentham once called the theory of human rights: "nonsense on stilts."

IV TWO HARD CASES

The new definition differs in extension from the UN definition in two ways: on the one hand, an aggressive war may be intended to defend socially basic human rights, and thus be just according to (3); on the other, a war of self-defense may be fought in order to preserve a status quo which subverts human rights, and thus be unjust according to (4). But, I suggest, this is no objection, because (3) and (4) accord more with the moral reality of war in our time than do (1) or (1') and (2).

There are two situations which are of particular interest for the theory of *jus ad bellum* because they exhibit marked differences between the UN definition and the new definition. The first concerns a type of economic war, the second an armed intervention in a state's internal affairs.

What I have in mind in the first case is a war for subsistence. Consider this example: A and B are neighboring countries of approximately the same military capability, separated by a mountain range. A is bordered by the ocean and receives plentiful rainfall; however, the mountains prevent rain clouds from crossing over to B, which is consequently semi-arid. One year the lack of rain causes a famine in B which threatens millions of lives. A, on the other hand, has a large food surplus; but for a variety of cultural, historical, and economic reasons it makes none of this food available to B. Can B go to war with A to procure food?

According to the UN definition such a war would constitute an aggression, and consequently be unjust; but according to (3), since the war would be an attempt to procure socially basic human rights

for B's people, it would be just. Indeed, A is morally obligated to give food to B, and assuming that B's sole purpose in fighting is to procure food, a defense by A would be an unjust war.

This, I suggest, is a position fully in accord with moral decency. Indeed, it is interesting to note that Walzer adopts a similar position, despite the fact that it runs counter to his basic argument concerning the criminality of aggression. Discussing the case of barbarian tribes who, driven west by invaders, demanded land from the Roman Empire on which to settle, Walzer quotes Hobbes with approval: "he that shall oppose himself against [those doing what they must do to preserve their own lives], for things superfluous is guilty of the war that thereupon is to follow."[21] A fight for life is a just fight.

An important qualification must be made to this argument, however. If A itself has a food shortage it cannot be obligated to provide food to B, for its own socially basic human rights are in jeopardy. Thus B loses its claim against A. And if a third nation, C, can supply food to A or B but not both, it is unclear who has a right to it. Socially basic human rights can conflict, and in such cases the new definition of just war will not yield clear-cut answers. Nor, however, do we have reason to expect that clear-cut answers might exist.

There are less clear examples. What about a fight against impoverishment? In the 1960s and 1970s Great Britain and Iceland were repeatedly embroiled in a conflict over fishing grounds. This resulted in an act of war on the part of Iceland, namely, a sea attack on British ships. Of course, Iceland's belligerance may have been merely theatrical; moreover, on Iceland's interpretation of the limits of fisheries jurisdiction, she was simply defending her own right, since the British vessels were within the two-hundred mile fisheries zone claimed by Iceland. But the moral issue had to do with the fact that Iceland's economy is built around the fishing industry, and thus a threat to this industry presented a threat of impoverishment. Now no socially basic human rights are at issue here: impoverishment is not starvation. Nevertheless, there is a certain moral plausibility to the Icelanders' position, and it clearly resembles the position of country B in our previous example. But if we weaken the definition of unjust war to include struggles against economic collapse, the door is opened to allowing any economic war. For example, do industrialized countries have a right to go to war for OPEC oil?

One way to handle this would be to claim that while nations have no socially basic right to any given economic level beyond subsistence, they do possess a socially basic right not to have their economic position worsened at a catastrophic rate. There is a certain plausibility to this suggestion, inasmuch as a collapsing economy will undoubtedly cause social disruption sufficient to prevent the enjoyment of other rights. The point is nevertheless debatable. Without pretending to settle it, I would, however, claim that we are now on the right moral ground for carrying out the debate, whereas a discussion couched in terms of aggression and sovereignty would miss the point entirely.

The other case I wish to discuss concerns foreign intervention into a country's internal affairs. The point is that if such an intervention is on behalf of socially basic human rights it is justified according to the new definition.

Here again it will be useful to look at Walzer's position. He begins by endorsing an argument of Mill's which is based on the right of national self-determination. Mill's point is that this is a right of nations to set their own house in order *or fail to* without outside interference. If a people struggles against a dictatorship but loses, it is still self-determining; whereas if it wins due to the intervention of an outside power, its right to self-determination has been violated. Walzer admits only three exceptions: (i) a secession, when there are two or more distinct political communities contending within the same national boundary; (ii) a situation in which another foreign power has already intervened; and (iii) a situation in which human rights violations of great magnitude—massacres or enslavements—are occurring. Only in these cases may intervention be justified.[22]

Now Mill's argument employs a somewhat Pickwickian conception of self-determination. A self-determining people, it suggests, fights its own battles, even if it loses them. But then one might infer that a self-determining people fights its own wars as well, even if it loses them. Thus, a nation's conquest by a foreign power would become an instance of its self-determination[23] Surely that fact

that it is a foreign rather than a domestic oppressor is not a morally relevant factor, for that would imply that oppressions can be sorted on moral grounds according to the race or nationality of the oppressor. Yet something is clearly wrong with an argument which leads to this doublethink concept of self-determination.[24]

The problem with Mill's position is that it takes the legitimacy of states too much at face value. "Mill generally writes as if he believes that citizens get the government they deserve. . . ."[25] That is, somehow oppression of domestic vintage carries a prima facie claim to legitimacy which is not there in the case of foreign conquest. It seems that Mill suspects that the state would not be there if the people did not secretly want it. This seems to me to be an absurd, and at times even obscene view, uncomfortably reminiscent of the view that women are raped because secretly they want to be. The only argument for Mill's case, I believe, is the improbable claim that the fact that people are not engaged in active struggle against their state shows tacit consent. Even granting this, however, there remains one case in which Mill's position is unacceptable on its own terms. That is when there is overwhelming evidence that the state enjoys no legitimacy—when there is active and virtually universal struggle against it. Such struggles do not always succeed, and after each bloody suppression the possibility of another uprising grows less. Heart and flesh can bear only so much. In such a case an argument against intervention based on the people's right of self-determination is merely perverse. It makes the "self" in "self-determination" mean "other"; it reverses the role of people and state. One thinks of Brecht's poem "Die Lösung," written after the rebellion of East German workers in 1953: "After the rebellion of the seventeenth of June . . . one could read that the people had forfeited the government's confidence and could regain it only by redoubling their work efforts. Would it not be simpler for the government to dissolve the people and elect another one?"[26] I might add that in fact Walzer grants the point: "a state (or government) established against the will of its own people, ruling violently, may well forfeit its right to defend itself even against a foreign invasion."[27] Thus, it would appear that in such a case intervention is morally justified, even in the absence of massacres and slavery.

And, to make a long story short, the new definition will endorse this view. For the kind of evidence which demonstrates a government's illegitimacy must consist of highly visible signs that it does not enjoy consent, for example, open insurrection or plain repression. And this necessitates violations of security rights, which are socially basic human rights. Obedience which is not based on consent is based on coercion; thus the more obvious it is that a government is illegitimate, the more gross and widespread will its violations of security rights be, reaching even those who do not actively oppose it. This is akin to a law of nature. And thus an intervention becomes morally justified, or even morally urgent.

No definition of just war is likely to address all of the difficult cases adequately—and there is no realm of human affairs in which difficult cases are more common. Seat-of-the-pants practical judgment is a necessary supplement to one's principle in such matters: in this respect I fully agree with Walzer that "The proper method of practical morality is casuistic in character."[28] Thus, while I do not doubt that troubling examples may be brought against the new definition, it seems to me that if it corresponds with our moral judgments in a large number of cases, and can be casuistically stretched to address others, it serves its purpose. My claim is that, whatever its deficiencies, the new definition of *jus ad bellum* offered in (3) and (4) is superior to the existing one in this respect.

NOTES

1. I follow the traditional distinction between the justice of war, that is, which side is in the right with respect to the issues over which they are fighting, and justice in war (*jus in bello*), which pertains to the way the war is fought.

2. J. L. Brierly, *The Law of Nations*, 6th ed., ed. Humphrey Waldock (Oxford: Oxford University Press, 1963), p. 409.

3. Article 2(4), quoted in Brierly, p. 415.

4. This is Brierly's claim, p. 409. The relevant Article of the Charter is I(1).

5. This point was suggested to me by Professor Boleslaw Boczek.

6. Quoted in Yehuda Melzer, *Concepts of Just War* (Lewyden: A. W. Sijthoff, 1975), pp. 28–29.

7. Ibid.

8. Quoted in Ian Brownlie, *Principles of Public International Law*, 2nd ed. (Oxford: Clarendon Press, 1973), p. 545.

9. Quoted in Melzer, *Concepts of Just War*, p. 18. I have omitted a clause which does not bear on the present argument.

10. Hersch Lauterpacht, *International Law and Human Rights* (London: Stevens, 1950), p. 167.

11. The term is used in Brownlie, *Public International Law*, p. 280.

12. Brierly, *Law of Nations*, pp. 7–16. See Bodin, *République* (n.p.: Scientia Aalen, 1961), Book One, Chap. 8.

13. This is discussed in Brownlie, chap. 5, pp. 89–108.

14. On the relation of international agreements with the duty of non-intervention, particularly in the case of human rights, see Louis Henkin, "Human Rights and 'Domestic Jurisdiction,'" in Thomas Buergenthal, ed., *Human Rights, International Law and the Helsinki Accords* (New York: Universe Books, 1977), pp. 21–40, and Thomas Buergenthal, "Domestic Jurisdiction, Intervention, and Human Rights: The International Law Perspective," in Peter G. Brown and Douglas Maclean, eds., *Human Rights and U.S. Foreign Policy* (Lexington, Mass.: Lexington Books, 1979), pp. 111–120. Both agree that even when the right of domestic jurisdiction over human rights has been "signed away" by a state, military intervention against it is proscribed. This doctrine, a product of the United Nations era, has replaced the nineteenth-century doctrine which permitted humanitarian intervention on behalf of oppressed peoples. The legal issues are discussed in the readings collected in Richard B. Lillich and Frank C. Newman, eds., *International Human Rights: Problems of Law and Policy* (Boston: Little, Brown and Company, 1979), pp. 484–544. The case analyzed there is India's 1971 intervention into Bangladesh; on this see also Oriana Fallaci's interview with Zulfikar Ali Bhutto, in *Interview with History* (Boston: Houghton Mifflin Co., 1976), pp. 182–209.

15. I adopt this terminology from Hannah Arendt, "Civil Disobedience," in *Crises of the Republic* (New York: Harcourt, Brace, Jovanovich, 1972), pp. 85–87. See also her *On Revolution* (New York: Viking, 1965), pp. 169–171. It appears also in Michael Walzer, "The Problem of Citizenship," *Obligations* (New York: Simon and Schuster, 1970), p. 207.

16. Walzer, *Just and Unjust Wars* (New York: Basic Books, 1977), p. 54.

17. Other analyses of the concept of "human right" are possible. Walzer, for example, makes the interesting suggestion that the beneficiary of human rights is not a person but humanity itself (*Just and Unjust Wars*, p. 158). Such an analysis has much to recommend it, but it does not concern us here, for humanity will still enjoy its rights through particular men and women.

18. I take this concept from Henry Shue, "Foundations for a Balanced U.S. Policy on Human Rights: The Significance of

Subsistence Rights" (College Park, Maryland: Center for Philosophy and Public Policy Working Paper HRFP-1, 1977), pp. 3–4. Shue discusses it in detail in *Basic Rights: Subsistence, Affluence, and U.S. Foreign Policy* (Princeton: Princeton University Press, in press), chap.I.

19. Ibid., pp. 3, 6–12.

20. The new definition also allows us to make sense of an interesting and plausible suggestion by Melzer, namely that a just war (in the sense of *jus ad bellum*) conducted in an unjust way (*jus in bello*) becomes unjust (*jus ad bellum*), in other words, that the *jus ad bellum* is "anchored" in the *jus in bello*. On the new definition this would follow from the fact that a war conducted in a sufficiently unjust way would violate proportionality. See Melzer, pp. 87–93.

21. Walzer, *Just and Unjust Wars*, p. 57. See also Charles R. Beitz, *Political Theory in International Relations* (Princeton: Princeton University Press, 1979), pp. 175–176.

22. Walzer, *Just and Unjust Wars*, pp. 87–91.

23. As Walzer expressly denies, p. 94.

24. I take Doppelt to be making a similar point when he suggests that a people can be "aggressed" against by its own state as well as by a foreign state, "Walzer's Theory," p. 8. My argument in this section is quite in sympathy with Doppelt's, pp. 10–13.

25. Walzer, p. 88.

26. Quoted by Hannah Arendt, *Men in Dark Times* (New York: Harcourt, Brace and World, 1968), p. 213.

27. Walzer, *Just and Unjust Wars*, p. 82n.

28. Ibid., p. xvi.

Some of the ideas in Sections II and III were suggested to me by George Friedman. I received helpful criticism of an early draft of this paper from Boleslaw Boczek and my colleagues Douglas Maclean and Henry Shue. Any resemblance between my remaining mistakes and their beliefs is wholly accidental. Finally, I wish to thank the Editors of *Philosophy & Public Affairs*, who spared the reader some rococo diction and bad arguments.

Questions for Analysis

1. Luban begins by arguing that the United Nations Charter, in effect, defines "just war" as a war of self-defense against aggression, with all other wars "unjust." Using this definition, how would you assess the justness of recent wars waged by the United States, including Afghanistan, Iraq, and the Balkans? Do you find this understanding of just war adequate to analyze the participation of the United States in these wars? What additional considerations would you add to this understanding of just war?

2. What problems with the UN concept of just war does Luban identify? Are these fair criticisms? Are there additional criticisms you would raise of the UN concept? How would you defend the UN against Luban's criticisms?

3. Is the UN approach to just war too deferential to states which are themselves illegitimate exercises of power, including tyrannical dictatorships? Do you agree with Luban that we have a moral obligation of nonintervention only to states that behave morally toward their own people? How should we determine the morality of other governments to make these judgments? How should we assess the legitimacy of governments? Should we define "legitimate government" as limited only to democratically elected governments?

4. Luban proposes reconceptualizing just war in terms of the rights of individuals, not the rights of sovereign nations. Is this a realistic proposal? What standard of human rights should we use in such an approach? Should we only recognize an American standard of human rights or are there alternative ways we might frame this test? Using this approach to just war, analyze the participation of the United States in wars in Afghanistan, Iraq, and the Balkans.

5. Critique Luban's proposal that a war is just if it is "in defense of socially basic human rights"? Is a war of aggression just if it is necessary to protect the basic

human right of the citizens to food? A right to avoid impoverishment? A right to preserve one's economic standard of living? Would Luban's proposal justify more wars of aggression than you believe are truly warranted?

Reflections on War and Political Discourse: Realism, Just War, and Feminism in a Nuclear Age

Jean Bethke Elshtain

Political philosopher Jean Bethke Elshtain is the Laura Spelman Rockefeller Professor of Social and Political Ethics at the University of Chicago Divinity School. Her books include *Public Man, Private Woman: Women in Social Thought; The Family in Political Thought; Meditations on Modern Political Thought; Women and War; Democracy on Trial; Augustine and the Limits of Politics; Real Politics: At the Center of Everyday Life; New Wine in Old Bottles: Politics and Ethical Discourse; Who Are We? Critical Reflections; Hopeful Possibilities; Jane Addams and the Dream of American Democracy;* and most recently, *Just War against Terror: The Burden of American Power in a Violent World.*

In the first part of her article, omitted here, she discussed a realist approach to understanding political discourse, supposedly free of moral judgment, and focused instead on sovereign states, each seeking to enhance or secure its own power. She laments the resignation of the realist approach to the inevitability of international conflict. In the excerpt here, she first critiques the cultural images of males and females in "just war" discourse, with the men seen as warriors, fighters, and defenders of righteous causes and the women seen as virtuous and nonviolent, stereotypes which do not account for contemporary conditions of war with nuclear and other powerful weapons of mass destruction. Finally, she considers the proposals of political philosopher Hannah Arendt that reconstitute both men and women as citizens who share alike a "faculty of action."

. . . Just war theory grows out of a complex genealogy, beginning with the pacifism and withdrawal from the world of early Christian communities through later compromises with the world as Christianity took institutional form. The Christian saviour was a "prince of peace" and the New Testament Jesus deconstructs the powerful metaphor of the warrior central to Old Testament narrative. He enjoins Peter to sheath his sword; he devirilizes the image of manhood; he tells his followers to go as sheep among wolves and to offer their lives, if need be, but never to take the life of another in violence. From the beginning, Christian narrative presents a pacific ontology, finding in the "paths of peace" the most natural as well as the most desir-

From Jean Bethke Elshtain, "Reflections on War and Political Discourse: Realism, Just War, and Feminism in a Nuclear Age," *Political Theory,* Vol. 13, No. 1 (February 1985), 39–57. Copyright © 1985 Sage Publications, Inc. Reprinted by permission.

able way of being. Violence must justify itself before the court of nonviolence.

Classic just war doctrine, however, is by no means a pacifist discourse.[1] St. Augustine's *The City of God,* for example, distinguishes between legitimate and illegitimate use of collective violence. Augustine denounces the *Pax Romana* as a false peace kept in place by evil means and indicts Roman imperialist wars as paradigmatic instances of unjust war. But he defends, with regret, the possibility that a war may be just if it is waged in defense of a common good and to protect the innocent from certain destruction. As elaborated over the centuries, noncombatant immunity gained a secure niche as the most important of *jus in bello* rules, responding to unjust aggression is the central *jus ad bellum.* Just war thinking requires that moral considerations center into all determinations of collective violence, not as a post hoc gloss but as a serious ground for making political judgments.

In common with realism, just war argument secretes a broader worldview, including a vision of domestic politics. Augustine, for example, sees human beings as innately social. It follows that all ways of life are laced through with moral rules and restrictions that provide a web of social order not wholly dependent on external force to keep itself intact. Augustine's household, unlike Machiavelli's private sphere, is "the beginning or element of the city" and domestic peace bears a relation to "civic peace."[2] The sexes are viewed as playing complementary roles rather than as segregated into two separate normative systems governed by wholly different standards of judgment depending upon whether one is a public man or a private woman.

Just war discourse, like realism, has a long and continuing history; it is a gerrymandered edifice scarred by social transformation and moral crisis. A specific strength embedded in its ontology of peace is the vantage point it affords with reference to social arrangements, one from which its adherents frequently assess what the world calls peace and find it wanting. From Augustine's thunderings against the *Pax Romana* to John Paul II's characterization of our present armed-to-the-teeth peace as the continuation of war by other means—not war's opposite but one of the forms war takes in the modern world—just war thinking has, from time to time, offered a critical discursive edge.[3]

My criticisms of just war are directed to two central concerns: One flows directly from just war teaching; the other involves less explicit filiations. I begin with the latter, with cultural images of males and females rooted, at least in part, in just war discourse. Over time, Augustine's moral householders (with husbands cast as just, meaning neither absolute nor arbitrary heads) gave way to a discourse that more sharply divided males and females, their honored activities, and their symbolic force. Men were constituted as just Christian warriors, fighters, and defenders of righteous causes. Women, unevenly and variously depending upon social location, got solidified into a culturally sanctioned vision of virtuous, nonviolent womanhood that I call the "beautiful soul," drawing upon Hegel's *Phenomenology*.

The tale is by no means simple but, by the late eighteenth century, "absolute distinctions between men and women in regard to violence" had come to prevail.[4] The female beautiful soul is pictured as frugal, self-sacrificing, and, at times, delicate. Although many women empowered themselves to think and to act on the basis of this ideal of female virtue, the symbol easily slides into sentimentalism. To "preserve the purity of its heart," writes Hegel, the beautiful soul must flee "from contact with the actual world."[5] In matters of war and peace, the female beautiful soul cannot put a stop to suffering, cannot effectively fight the mortal wounding of sons, brothers, husbands, fathers. She continues the long tradition of women as weepers, occasions for war, and keepers of the flame of nonwarlike values.

The just warrior is a complex construction, an amalgam of Old Testament, chivalric, and civic republican traditions. He is a character we recognize in all the statues on all those commons and greens of small New England towns: the citizen-warrior who died to preserve the union and to free the slaves. Natalie Zemon Davis shows that the image of warlike manliness in the later Middle Ages and through the seventeenth century, was but one male ideal among many, having to compete, for example, with the priest and other religious who foreswore use of their "sexual instrument" and were forbidden to shed blood. However, "male physical force could sometimes be moralized" and "thus could provide the foundation for an ideal of warlike manliness."[6] This moralization of collective male violence held sway and continues to exert a powerful fascination and to inspire respect.

But the times have outstripped beautiful souls and just warriors alike; the beautiful soul can no longer be protected in her virtuous privacy. Her world, and her children, are vulnerable in the face of nuclear realities. Similarly, the just warrior, fighting fair and square by the rules of the game, is a vision enveloped in the heady mist of an earlier time. War is more and more a matter of remote control. The contemporary face of battle is anomic and impersonal, a technological nightmare, as weapons technology obliterates any distinction between night and day, between the "front" and the "rear." Decades before laser weapons, however, the reality of battle had undermined the ideal of the warrior. World War I constituted the foot-soldier as cannon-fodder. In the first day of the Battle of the Somme, July 1, 1916, 110,000 British men got out of the trenches and began to walk forward along a thirteen-mile front. They had no visible enemy to fight; they wore number tags hung around their necks; 60,000 were dead by the end of the day.

A just war requires agents to carry out its purposes. But if the warrior no longer serves as an avatar of justice, how is war itself to claim this imprimatur? If the present human condition can be described as the continuation of war by other means, a false peace, how can human agents legitimate their aims in the waging of a real war rather than the maintenance of a bogus peace? Does it make sense any longer to construe war as a coherent entity at all? These questions take me to my criticisms of just war argument in our time.

Just war discourse from its inception recognized the rights of political entities to self-defense. The moral requirements for waging war have also remained essentially unchanged from the fourth century to the present. Over time, of course, much has changed including the nature of political bodies, the context of international life, and the totalistic deadliness of weapons. Faced with historic transformations of such awesome magnitude, just war thinkers seek valiantly to apply the appropriate rules to cover increasingly horrific situations. All agree that violence is regrettable, tragic, and to be avoided devoutly. But much slips through the cracks when one gets down to hard cases.

For example, in Michael Walzer's *Just and Unjust Wars*, the most lucid modern treatment of the topic by a nontheologian, queries concerning past practice (the British decision to engage in saturation bombing of German cities during World War II) and present policy (nuclear deterrence theory) are assessed on consequentalist criteria that frequently override the deontological formulae of classic just war teaching (though it, too, required projections of consequence in certain situations). For example, Walzer justifies, with regret, British saturation bombing of German cities in light of the Nazi threat and given the predictable outcome should Britain fall to Germany. Present threat and future danger override *jus in bello* rules.[7] By declaring Nazism an "immeasurable evil," Walzer foreordains his judgment: "Immeasurable" is an absolute and the "determinate crime" of terror bombing is clearly a lesser evil—it must be the way the issues get framed.

By continually adjusting to the realities of total war, just war discourse is hard to distinguish from

modified realism. I noted the example from World War II above in part because Walzer proclaims the present moment one of continuing "supreme emergency," analogous to the Nazi peril. If what we've got is supreme emergency, what we need—nuclear deterrence—is inexorable. Once again, Walzer regrets his own conclusion. Deterrence is a "bad way" of "coping" with supreme emergency but "there may well be no other that is practical in a world of sovereign and suspicious states. We threaten evil in order not to do it."[8]

Despite the impressive and determined efforts of Walzer, the U.S. Catholic Bishops, and others, the just war frame is stretched to the breaking point as it can no longer provide a coherent picture of its discursive object—war in any conventional sense. Take, for example, Walzer's discussion of American use of the atomic bombs on Hiroshima and Nagasaki, unjustifiable, he argued, within a just war frame. He goes on to ask: "How did the people of Hiroshima forfeit their rights?"[9] The language of rights and their forfeiture is impoverished in this context, inadequate to describe what happened on those dreadful days. The shakiness of just war discourse, then, is forced upon us by "the nature of the modern state combined with the nature of modern total war."[10] In a twilight zone of false peace, with war deeply rooted inside the infrastructure of the modern state, the discourses of just war and realism link up to confront jointly the seemingly intractable present. I return to this matter in part three.

Few feminist writers on war and peace take up just war discourse explicitly. There is, however, feminist theorizing that may aptly be situated inside the broader frames of beautiful souls and just warriors as features of inherited discourse. The strongest contemporary feminist statement of a beautiful soul position involves celebrations of a "female principle" as ontologically given and superior to its dark opposite, masculinism. (The male "other" in this vision is not a just warrior but a dangerous beast.) The evils of the social world are traced in a free-flowing conduit from masculinism to environmental destruction, nuclear energy, wars, militarism, and states. In utopian evocations of "cultural feminism," women are enjoined to create separate communities to free themselves from the male surround and to create a "space" based on the values they embrace. An essentially Manichean vision, the discourse of feminism's beautiful souls contrasts images of "caring" and "connected" females in opposition to "callous" and "disconnected" males. Deepening sex segregation, the separatist branch of cultural feminism draws upon, yet much exaggerates received understandings of the beautiful soul.[11]

A second feminist vision indebted implicitly to the wider discursive universe of which just war thinking is a part features a down-to-earth female subject, a soul less beautiful than virtuous in ways that locate her as a social actor. She shares just war's insistence that politics must come under moral scrutiny. Rejecting the hard-line gendered epistemology and metaphysic of an absolute beautiful soul, she nonetheless insists that ways of knowing flow from ways of being in the world and that hers have vitality and validity in ways private and public. The professed ends of feminists in this loosely fitting frame locate the woman as a moral educator and a political actor. She is concerned with "mothering," whether or not she is a biological mother, in the sense of protecting society's most vulnerable members without patronizing them. She thinks in terms of human dignity as well as social justice and fairness. She also forges links between "maternal thinking" and pacifist or nonviolent theories of conflict without presuming that it is possible to translate easily particular maternal imperatives into a public good.[12]

The pitfalls of this feminism are linked to its intrinsic strengths. By insisting that women are in and of the social world, its framers draw explicit attention to the context within which their constituted subjects act. But this wider surround not only derogates maternal women, it bombards them with simplistic formulae that equate "being nice" with "doing good." Even as stereotypic maternalisms exert pressure to sentimentalize, competing feminisms are often sharply repudiating, finding in any evocation of "maternal thinking" a trap and a delusion. A more robust concept of the just (female) as citizen is needed to shore up this disclosure, a matter I take up below.

RESCUING POLITICS FROM WAR: HANNAH ARENDT'S HOPE

Hannah Arendt's attempt to rescue politics from war deepens an important insight of just war theory—underdeveloped in the theory itself—by insisting that the problem lies not only in the compulsions of international relations but in that ordering of modern, technological society just war thinkers call a "false" or "armed" peace. Dulled by the accretion of tropes, truths, necessities, and concepts that help us talk ourselves into war, situated inside a world of armed peace, Norman Mailer's claim in 1948 that "the ultimate purpose" of modern society is continuation of the army by other means seems exaggerated but not altogether far-fetched.[13] Michel Foucault, too, argues that 'politics' (the single quotes are his) "has been conceived as a continuation, if not exactly and directly of war, at least of the military model as a fundamental means of preventing civil disorder. Politics . . . sought to implement the mechanisms of the perfect army, of the disciplined mass, of the docile, useful troop," and so on.[14]

In an over-coordinated social world, violence may promise a release from inner emptiness or a temporary escape from overplanned pointlessness. Paradoxically, on this view, the routinization of everyday life, much at odds with a heroic or warrior society, nevertheless feeds rather than sates a deeper will to warfare as the prospect of escape from "impersonality, monotony, standardization," the chance to take and to share risks, to act rather than to persist in predetermined behavior.[15] That promise, however, is itself a victim of our armed peace. War technology devirilizes war fighting. The fighter exists for, and is eclipsed by, his weapons and an awesome nuclear arsenal.

More problematic than the inadequacies of just war doctrine in light of social mimesis of military order, however, is the discourse of "disassociation" evident in contemporary rationalist, scientized realism. Such realists portray themselves as clear-sighted, unsentimental analysts describing the world as it is. At present, hundreds of think tanks, universities, and government bureaucracies support the efforts of "scientifically minded brain trusters" who should be criticized, argues Arendt, not because they are thinking the unthinkable, but rather because "they do not *think* at all."[16] The danger is this: a world of self-confirming theorems invites fantasies of control over events that we do not have. The scientization of rationalist realism eclipses the strengths classical realists could claim, including awareness of the intractability of events and a recognition that relations between and among states are necessarily alienated. Through abstracted models and logic, hyper-rationalism reduces states and their relations to games that can be simulated. Consider the following depiction of Western Europe by a strategic analyst: "Western Europe amounts geographically to a peninsula projecting out from the Eurasian land mass from which large continents of military force can emerge on relatively short notice to invade the peninsula."[17] Western Europe, reduced to an undifferentiated, manageable piece of territory, becomes (theoretically) expendable or indiscriminately usable for our strategic planning.

Modern thinkers of the abstracted unthinkable are not alone in doing violence to complex realities. "If truth is the main casualty in war, ambiguity is another," notes Paul Fussell, and one of the legacies of war is a "habit of simple distinction, simplification, and opposition."[18] Mobilized language, wartime's rhetoric of "binary deadlock," may persist and do much of our thinking for us. The absorption of politics by the language and imperatives of war becomes a permanent rhetorical condition.[19] J. Glenn Gray reminds us that one basic task of a state at war is to portray the enemy in terms as absolute and abstract as possible in order to distinguish as sharply as possible the act of killing from the act of murder. It is always "*the enemy*," a "pseudoconcrete universal." This moral absolutism is constituted through language: there is no other way to do it. We are invited to hate without limit and told we are good citizens for doing so.

At one time war fighting often served, paradoxically, to deconstruct war rhetoric as soldiers rediscovered concreteness and particularity in tragic and terrifying ways. For example, Eric Maria Remarque's protagonist in *All Quiet on the Western Front*, bayonets a frightened French soldier who, seeking refuge, has leapt into the trench beside him. Four agonizing hours later the Frenchman dies and when he has died, Remarque's hero, his capacity to perceive and to judge concretely restored, speaks to the man he has killed: "Comrade, I did not want to kill you. . . . but you were only an idea to me before, an abstraction that lived in my mind and called forth its appropriate response. It was that abstraction I stabbed."[20] Grey, similarly, observes that the abstract bloodthirstiness expressed by civilians furthest removed from war fighting was often

in contrast to the thinking of front-line soldiers whose moral absolutism dissolved once they met "the enemy" face to face.[21] Because it is now possible for us to destroy the enemy without ever seeing him or her, abstract hatreds are less likely to rub against concrete friction.

If realism's modern offspring invites dangerous disassociations, an alternative discourse should be one less available for such purposes even as it offers a compelling orientation to the systemic imperatives at work in a world of "sovereign and suspicious states." Too often alternatives to "thinking war" reproduce problematic features of the discourse they oppose, for example, by insisting that we love (rather than hate) abstract collectives. But "the human race" is a pseudoconcrete universal much like "the enemy." Pitched at a level of abstract universals, the discourse of "the victims" falls apart if one moves to specify connections between its grand vision and political exigencies. Also, an alternative discourse must problematize war narratives with their teleological assurance of triumphant endings and their prototypical figurations of fighting men and weeping women, even as it acknowledges the attraction of the narrative.[22] Admitting rather than denying what Grey calls "the communal enthusiasm and ecstasies of war," we are invited to ask if we might not enlist our energies in some other way. Peace discourse that denies the violent undercurrents and possibilities in everyday life and in each one of us, perhaps by projecting that violence outward into others ("masculinism") is but the opposite side of the hard-line realist coin.

Hannah Arendt's *On Violence* responds to these concerns by exposing our acceptance of politics as war by other means. Arendt asks what historic transformations and discursive practices made possible a consensus "among political theorists from Left to Right . . . that violence is nothing more than the most flagrant manifestation of power?"[23] (The violence Arendt has in mind is that of groups or collectives, not individual outrage culminating in a single violent act; Melville's *Billy Budd* is her example.) Her answer is multiple: teleological constructions of historic inevitability (known to us as Progress); theories of absolute power tied to the emergence of the nation-state; the Old Testament tradition of God's Commandments that fed command-obedience conceptions of law in

Judaeo-Christian discourse; the infusion of biologism into political discourse, particularly the notion that destruction is a law of nature and violence a "life promoting force" through which men purge the old and rotten. All these "time-honored opinions have become dangerous." Locked into dangerously self-confirming ways of thinking, embracing "progress" as a standard of evaluation, we manage to convince ourselves that good will come out of horrendous things; that somehow, in history, the end does justify the means. Both classical liberals and their Marxist adversaries share this discursive terrain, Arendt argues, though she is especially critical of "great trust in the dialectical 'power of negation'" that soothes its adherents into believing that evil "is but a temporary manifestation of a still-hidden good."

By conflating the crude instrumentalism of violence with power, defined by Arendt as the human ability to act in concert and to begin anew, we guarantee further loss of space within which authentic empowerment is possible. In this way violence nullifies power and stymies political being. One important step away from the instrumentalism of violence and toward the possibility of politics is to resist the reduction of politics to domination. Arendt evokes no image of isolated heroism here; rather, she underscores the ways in which centralized orders dry up power and political possibility. If we recognize the terms through and means by which this happens, we are less susceptible to unreflective mobilization and more open to finding and creating public space in the current order. As citizens through their actions break repetitive cycles of behavior, power as the "true opposite" of violence reveals itself.

Arendt's discourse constitutes its subjects as citizens: neither victims nor warriors. She paints no rosy picture of her rescue effort. Just as Grey argues that the will to war is deepened by the emptiness of a false peace, Arendt believes that the greater a society's bureaucratization, the greater will be secret fantasies of destruction. She repudiates grandiose aims and claims, refusing to dictate what politics should do or accomplish instrumentally, for that would undermine her exposé of the future oriented teleologies on which violence and progress feed. To the extent that we see what she is doing and let it work on us, her symbolic alternative for political being offers a plenary jolt to our reining

political metaphors and categories—state of nature, sovereignty, statism, bureaucratization, contractualism, nationalist triumphalism, and so on. If we remain entrapped in this cluster of potent typifications, each of them suffused with violent evocations or built on fears of violence, we will face only more, and deadlier, of what we've already got. Contrastingly, Arendt locates as central a powerful but pacific image that engenders hope, the human capacity that sustains political being.

Evidence of hopelessness is all around us. The majority of young people say they do not believe there will be a future of any sort. We shake our heads in dismay, failing to see that our social arrangements produce hopelessness and require it to hold themselves intact. But the ontological possibility for hope is always present, rooted, ultimately, in "the fact of natality." Arendt's metaphor, most fully elaborated in the following passage from *The Human Condition*, is worth quoting in full:

> The miracle that saves the world, the realm of human affairs, from its normal, "natural" ruin is ultimately the fact of natality, in which the faculty of action is ontologically rooted. It is, in other words, the birth of new human beings and the new beginning, the action they are capable of by being born. *Only the full experience of this capacity can bestow upon human affairs faith and hope, those two essential characteristics of human existence* . . . that found perhaps their most glorious and most succinct expression in the new words with which the Gospels accounted their "glad tiding": 'A Child has been born unto us.'[24]

The infant, like all beginnings is vulnerable. We must nurture that beginning, not knowing and not being able to control the "end" of the story.

Arendt's evocation of natal imagery through its most dramatic ur-narrative is not offered as an abstraction to be endorsed abstractly. Rather, she invites us to restore long atrophied dispositions of commemoration and awe; birth, she declares, is a "miracle," a beginning that renews and irreversibly alters the world. Hers is a fragile yet haunting figuration that stirs recognition of our own vulnerable beginnings and our necessary dependency on others. Placed alongside the reality of human beginnings, many accounts of political beginnings construed as the actions of male hordes or contractualists seem parodic in part because of the massive denial (of "the female") on which they depend. A "full experience" of the "capacity" rooted in birth helps us to keep before our mind's eye the living reality of singularities, differences, and individualities rather than a human mass as objects of possible control or manipulation.[25]

By offering an alternative genealogy that problematizes collective violence and visions of triumph, Arendt devirilizes discourse, not in favor of feminization (for the feminized and masculinized emerged in tandem and both embody dangerous distortions), but politicalization, constituting her male and female objects as citizens who share alike the "faculty of action."[26] At this juncture, Arendt's discourse makes contact with that feminism I characterized as a modified vision of the beautiful soul. Her bracing ideal of the citizen adds political robustness to a feminist picture of women drawn to action from their sense of being and their epistemic and social location. Arendt's citizen, for example, may act from her maternal thinking but not as a mother—an important distinction that could help to chasten sentimentalism or claims of moral superiority.

But war is the central concern of this essay. Does Arendt's discourse offer a specifiable orientation toward international relations? Her discourse shifts the ground on which we stand when we think about states and their relations. We become skeptical about the forms and the claims of the sovereign state; we deflate fantasies of control inspired by the reigning teleology of progress; we recognize the (phony) parity painted by a picture of equally "sovereign states" and are thereby alert to the many forms hegemony can take. Additionally, Arendt grants "forgiveness" a central political role as the only way human beings have to break remorseless cycles of vengeance. She embraces an "ascesis," a refraining or withholding that allows refusal to bring one's force to bear to surface as a strength not a weakness.

Take the dilemma of the nuclear arms race that seems to have a life and dynamic of its own. From an Arendtian perspective, we see current arms control efforts for what they are—the arms race under another name negotiated by a bevy of experts with a vested interest in keeping the race alive so they can "control" it. On the other hand, her recognition of the limiting conditions internal to the international political order precludes a leap into utopian

fantasies of world order or total disarmament. For neither the arms control option (as currently defined) nor calls for immediate disarmament are bold—the first because it is a way of doing business as usual; the second because it covertly sustains business as usual by proclaiming "solutions" that lie outside the reach of possibility.

Instead, Arendt's perspective invites us—as a strong and dominant nation of awesome potential force—to take unilateral initiatives in order to break symbolically the cycle of vengeance and fear signified by our nuclear arsenals. Just as action from an individual or group may disrupt the automisms of everyday life, action from a single state may send shock waves that reverberate throughout the system. Arendt cannot be pegged as either a "systems dominance" nor "sub-systems dominance" thinker—a form of argumentation with which she has no patience in any case. She recognizes systemic imperatives yet sees space for potentially effective change from "individual (state) action." The war system is so deeply rooted that to begin to dismantle it in its current and highly dangerous form requires bold strokes.

At this juncture, intimations of an alternative genealogy emerge. Freeman Dyson suggests the *Odyssey* or the theme of homecoming rather than the *Iliad* or the theme of remorseless force as a dominant ur-political myth if we break the deadlock of victims versus warriors. Socrates, Jesus of Nazareth, and Nietzsche, in some of his teachings, emerge as articulators of the prototypical virtues of restraint and refusal to bring all one's power to bear. For it was Nietzsche, from his disillusionment, who proclaimed the only way out of "armed peace" to be a people, distinguished by their wars and victories who, from strength, not weakness, "break the sword" thereby giving peace a chance. "Rather perish than hate and fear," he wrote, "and twice rather perish than make oneself hated and feared."[27] Historic feminist thinkers and movements who rejected politics as force take center stage rather than being relegated to the periphery in this alternative story.

To take up war-as-discourse compels us to recognize the powerful sway of received narratives and reminds us that the concepts through which we think about war, peace, and politics get repeated endlessly, shaping debates, constraining consideration of alternatives, often reassuring us that things cannot really be much different than they are. As we nod an automatic yes when we hear the truism (though we may despair of the truth it tells) that "there have always been wars," we acknowledge tacitly that "there have always been war stories," for wars are deeded to us as texts. We cannot identify "war itself" as an entity apart from a powerful literary tradition that includes poems, epics, myths, official histories, first-person accounts, as well as the articulated theories I have discussed. War and the discourse of war are imbricated, part and parcel of political reality. Contesting the discursive terrain that identifies and gives meaning to what we take these realities to be does not mean one grants a self-subsisting, unwarranted autonomy to discourse; rather, it implies a recognition of the ways in which received doctrines, "war stories," may lull our critical faculties to sleep, blinding us to possibilities that lie within our reach.

NOTES

1. The 1983 Pastoral Letter of the U.S. Bishops on War and Peace restored the pacifist tradition to a place of importance, however. The pastoral is printed in full in *Origins* (May 19, 1983), pp. 1–32.

2. Henry Paolucci, ed., *The Political Writings of St. Augustine* (Chicago: Henry Regnery, 1967), p. 151.

3. John Paul II, "On Pilgrimage: The UN Address" *Origins* 9, no. 42, pp. 675–680.

4. Natalie Zemon Davis, "Men, Women, and Violence: Some Reflections on Equality," *Smith Alumnae Quarterly* (April, 1972), p.15.

5. G. W. F. Hegel, *The Phenomenology of Spirit*, trans. A.V. Miller (Oxford: Clarendon Press, 1977), pp. 399–400.

6. Davis, "Men, Women, and Violence," p. 13.

7. Michael Walzer, *Just and Unjust Wars* (New York: Basic Books, 1977), pp. 251–263. A different view of the process is found in Freeman Dyson's *Disturbing the Universe* (New York: Harper Colophon, 1979). Dyson served in the "Operational Research Section" of British Bomber Command during the war, calculating probabilities for bombing raids without much of a "feeling of personal responsibility. None of us ever saw the people we killed. None of us particularly cared" (p. 30). But his reflections after the fact are mordant. He writes: "I began to look backward and to ask myself how it happened that I got involved in this crazy game of murder. Since the beginning of the war I had been retreating step by step from one

moral position to another, until at the end I had no moral position at all" (pp. 30–31).

8. Walzer, *Just and Unjust Wars*, p. 274.

9. Ibid., p. 264.

10. Gordon Zahn, *Another Part of the War. The Camp Simon Story* (Amherst, MA: University of Massachusetts Press, 1979), p. 251.

11. The separatist literature is vast but the strongest statement of its theory remains Mary Daly's works, including *Gyn/Ecology: The Metaethics of Radical Feminism* (Boston: Beacon Press, 1979). A softer version in which men may be redeemable is Helen Caldicott, *Missile Envy* (New York: William Morrow, 1984).

12. This perspective has past and present elaborations. See, for example, Jane Addams, *The Long Road of Women's Memory* (New York: Macmillan, 1916) and Sara Ruddick, "Maternal Thinking," which appears most recently in Joyce Trebilcot, ed., *Mothering: Essays in Feminist Theory* (Totowa, NJ: Rowman and Allanheld, 1984), p. 213–230. I have evoked Ruddick's formulation in several of my essays. The strengths and weaknesses of "maternal thinking" as a basis for political action are described in historic depth by Amy Swerdlow in her forthcoming work on the Mothers Strike for Peace.

13. Cited in Paul Fussell, *The Great War and Modern Memory* (Oxford: Oxford University Press, 1975): 320.

14. Michel Foucault, *Discipline and Punish* (New York: Vintage Books,1979), pp. 168–169.

15. J. Glenn Gray, *The Warriors. Reflections on Men in Battle* (New York: Harper Colophon, 1970), p. 224.

16. Arendt, *On Violence*, p. 12.

17. Cited in E. P. Thompson, *Beyond the Cold War* (New York: Pantheon, 1982), p. 10.

18. Fussell, *Great War and Modern Memory*, p. 79.

19. See Fussell's discussion in *Great War and Modern Memory*, p. 108.

20. Eric Maria Remarque, *All Quiet on the Western Front* (New York: Fawcett, 1975), p. 195.

21. Gray, *The Warriors*, p. 135.

22. Huston's "Tales of War, Tears of Women" reminds us of the antiquity and pervasiveness of this narrative in Western history.

23. Arendt, *On Violence*, p. 81.

24. Hannah Arendt, *The Human Condition* (Chicago: University of Chicago Press, 1958), p. 247.

25. Arendt, *On Violence*, p. 81.

26. Arendt makes no gender-based distinction in this faculty though some commentators have argued—I am one of them—that the way she construes social arrangements contains its own built-in, unacceptable restrictions on action

for particular groups and classes. I am not as persuaded of the thorough soundness of this criticism as I once was. The most complete treatment of a strategic doctrine based on neither "warrior" nor "victim" thinking, but drawing from each is Freeman Dyson's recent *Weapons and Hope* (New York: Basic Books, 1984).

27. Grey cites in full the paragraph from Nietzsche's *The Wanderer and His Shadow* in which he repudiates the corruptions that flow from being hated and feared, pp.

225–26. To be sure, one could count twenty declarations by Nietzsche in praise of war for every one condemning it but even in such passages an ironic ambivalence may be at work. A genealogy that locates Jesus and Nietzsche on the "same side" is provocative and I cannot make a full argument here. But see René Girard, "The Extinction of Social Order," *Salmagundi* (Spring–Summer, 1984), pp. 204–237 for a discussion of the Gospel deconstruction of mimetic (violent) rivalries and the mechanism of the scapegoat on which rests the "false transcendence" of violent systems.

Questions for Analysis

1. What, if anything, would be different in the United States's conduct of the wars in Iraq or Afghanistan if most high-ranking positions in the government were held by women (e.g., the secretary of defense, secretary of state, president, vice-president)? How would Elshtain answer this question?

2. Can the U.S. war in Afghanistan be justified under the just war theory? The U.S. war in Iraq? Do any of the criticisms Elshtain raises of just war theory weaken or strengthen your conclusions about the justifiability of these wars?

3. What role have "abstract hatreds" played in the violence of 9/11 and its aftermath? Have the individual fighters of classic just war theory been eclipsed by modern weapons, whether jet airplanes or computer-guided "smart" bombs or nuclear weapons? Can just war theory be salvaged to justify contemporary war?

4. As explained by Elshtain, Hannah Arendt urges that we "break symbolically the cycle of vengeance and fear signified by our nuclear arsenals." What specific changes might that involve for U.S. policy in our current world conditions? Would these changes be wise?

Violence, Terrorism, and Justice

R. G. Frey and Christopher W. Morris

R. G. Frey is professor of philosophy at Bowling Green State University. Christopher W. Morris is professor of philosophy at the University of Maryland. Each has written extensively on social and political theory, ethical theory, and applied ethics. This essay introduces discussions of violence and terrorism from a conference they organized in 1988.

Unless one is a pacifist, one is likely to find it relatively easy to think of scenarios in which the use of force and violence against others is justified.

Killing other people in self-defense, for example, seems widely condoned, but so, too, does defending our citizens abroad against attack from violent regimes. Violence in these cases appears reactive, employed to defeat aggression against or violence toward vital interests. Where violence comes to be seen as much more problematic, if not simply prohibited, is in its direct use for social/political ends. It then degenerates into terrorism, many people seem to think, and terrorism, they hold is quite wrong. But what exactly is terrorism? And why is it wrong?

Most of us today believe terrorism to be a serious problem, one that raises difficult and challenging questions. The urgency of the problem, especially to North Americans and Western Europeans, may appear to be that terrorism is an issue that we confront from outside—that, as it were, it is an issue for us, not because violence for political ends is something approved of in our societies, but because we are the objects of such violence. The difficulty of the questions raised by contemporary terrorism has to do, we may suppose, with the complexity of issues having to do with the use of violence generally for political ends.

The first question, that of the proper characterization of terrorism, is difficult, in part because it is hard to separate from the second, evaluative question, that of the wrongness of terrorism. We may think of terrorism as a type of violence, that is, a kind of force that inflicts damage or harm on people and property. Terrorism thus broadly understood raises the same issues raised generally by the use of violence by individuals or groups. If we think of violence as being a kind of force, then the more general issues concern the evaluation of the use of force, coercion, and the like: When may we restrict people's options so that they have little or no choice but to do what we wish them to do? Violence may be used as one would use force, in order to obtain some end. But violence inflicts harm or damage and consequently adds a new element to the nonviolent use of force. When, then, if ever, may we inflict harm or damage on someone in the pursuit of some end? This question and the sets of issues it raises are familiar topics of moral and political philosophy.

Without preempting the varying characterizations of terrorism developed by the authors in this volume, however, we can think of it more narrowly; that is, we can think of it as a particular use of violence, typically for social/political ends, with several frequently conjoined characteristics. On this view, terrorism, as one would expect from the use of the term, usually involves creating terror or fear, even, perhaps, a sense of panic in a population. This common feature of terrorism is related to another characteristic, namely, the seemingly random or arbitrary use of violence. This in turn is related to a third feature, the targeting of the innocent of "noncombatants." This last, of course, is a more controversial feature than the others, since many terrorists attempt to justify their acts by arguing that their victims are not (wholly) innocent.

Thus characterized, terrorism raises specific questions that are at the center of contemporary philosophical debate. When, if ever, may one intentionally harm the innocent? Is the justification of terrorist violence to be based entirely on consequences, beneficial or other? Or are terrorist acts among those that are wrong independently of their consequences? What means may one use in combating people who use violence without justification? Other questions, perhaps less familiar, also arise. What does it mean for people to be innocent, that is, not responsible for the acts, say of their governments? May there not be some justification in terrorists' targeting some victims but not others? May terrorist acts be attributed to groups or to states? What sense, if any, does it make to think of a social system as terrorist?

Additionally, there are a variety of issues that specifically pertain to terrorists and their practices. What is the moral standing generally of terrorists? That is, what, if any duties do we have to them? How do their acts, and intentions, affect their standing? How does that standing affect our possible responses to them? May we, for instance, execute terrorists or inflict forms of punishment that would, in the words of the American Constitution, otherwise be "cruel and unusual"? What obligations might we, or officials of state, have in our dealings with terrorists? Is bargaining, of the sort practiced by virtually all Western governments, a justified response to terrorism? How, if at all, should our responses to terrorists be altered in the event that we admit or come to admit, to some degree, the justice of their cause?

Considered broadly, as a type of violence, or even more generally, as a type of force, terrorism is difficult to condemn out of hand. Force is a common feature of political life. We secure compliance with law by the use and threat of force. For many, this may be the sole reason for compliance. Force is used, for instance, to ensure that people pay their taxes, and force, even violence, is commonplace in the control of crime. In many such instances, there is not much controversy about the general justification of the use of force. The matter, say, of military conscription, though endorsed by many, is more controversial. In international contexts, however, the uses of force, and of violence, raise issues about which there is less agreement. Examples will come readily to mind.

More narrowly understood, involving some or all of the three elements mentioned earlier (the creation of terror, the seemingly random use of violence, and the targeting of the innocent or of noncombatants), the justification of terrorism is more problematic, as a brief glance at several competing moral theories will reveal.

Act-consequentialists, those who would have us evaluate actions solely in terms of their consequences, would presumably condone some terrorist acts. Were some such act to achieve a desirable goal, with minimal costs, the consequentialist might approve. Care, however, must be taken in characterizing the terrorists' goals and means. For contemporary consequentialists invariably are universalists; the welfare or ends of all people (and, on some accounts, all sentient beings) are to be included. Thus, terrorists cannot avail themselves of such theories to justify furthering the ends of some small group at the cost of greater damage to the interests of others. Merely to argue that the ends justify the means, without regard to the nature of the former, does not avail to one the resources of consequentialist moral theory.

Two factors will be further emphasized. First, consequentialist moral theory will focus upon effectiveness and efficiency, upon whether terrorist acts are an effective, efficient means to achieving desirable goals. The question naturally arises, then, whether there is an alternative means available, with equal or better likelihood of success in achieving the goals at a reduced cost. If resort to terrorism is a tactic, is there another tactic, just as likely to achieve the goal, at a cost more easy for us to bear? It is here, of course, that alternatives such as passive resistance and nonviolent civil disobedience will arise and need to be considered. It is here also that account must be taken of the obvious fact that terrorist acts seem often to harden the resistance of those the terrorists oppose. Indeed, the alleged justice of the terrorists' cause can easily slip into the background, as the killing and maiming come

to preoccupy and outrage the target population. Second, consequentialist moral theory will focus upon the goal to be achieved: Is the goal that a specific use of terrorism is in aid of desirable enough for us to want to see it realized in society, at the terrible costs it exacts? It is no accident that terrorists usually portray their cause as concerned with the rectification and elimination of injustice; for *this* goal seems to be one the achievement of which we might just agree was desirable enough for us to tolerate significant cost. And it is here, of course, that doubts plague us, because we are often unsure where justice with respect to some issue falls. In the battle over Ireland, and the demand of the Irish Republican Army for justice, is there nothing to be said on the English side? Is the entire matter black and white? Here, too, a kind of proportionality rule may intrude itself. Is the reunification of Ireland worth all the suffering and loss the IRA inflicts? Is this a goal worth, not only members of the IRA's dying for, but also their making other people die for? For consequentialists, it typically will not be enough that members of the IRA think so; those affected by the acts of the IRA cannot be ignored.

Finally, consequentlist moral theory will stress how unsure we sometimes are about what counts as doing justice. On the one hand, we sometimes are genuinely unsure about what counts as rectifying an injustice. For instance, is allowing the Catholics of Northern Ireland greater and greater control over their lives part of the rectification process? For the fact remains that there are many more Protestants than Catholics in the North, so that *democratic* votes may well not materially change the condition of the latter, whatever their degree of participation in the process. On the other hand, we sometimes are genuinely unsure whether we can rectify or eliminate one injustice without perpetrating another. In the Arab-Israeli conflict, for example, can we remove one side's grievances without thereby causing additional grievances on the other side? Is there *any* way of rectifying an injustice in that conflict without producing another?

Thus, while consequentialist moral theory can produce a justification of terrorist acts, it typically will do so here, as in other areas, only under conditions that terrorists in the flesh will find it difficult to satisfy.

It is the seeming randomness of the violence emphasized by terrorism, understood in the narrower sense, that leads many moral theorists to question its legitimacy. Many moral traditions, especially nonconsequentialist ones, impose strict limits on the harm that may be done to the innocent. Indeed, some theories such as those associated with natural law and Kantian traditions, will impose an indefeasible prohibition on the intentional killing of the innocent, which "may not be overriden, whatever the consequences." Sometimes this prohibition is formulated in terms of the rights of the innocent not to be killed (e.g., the right to life), other times in terms merely of our duties not to take their lives. Either way the prohibition is often understood to be indefeasible.

If intentionally killing the innocent is indefeasibly wrong, that is, if it may never be done whatever the consequences, then many, if not most, contemporary terrorists stand condemned. Killing individuals who happen to find themselves in a targeted store, café, or train station may not be done, according to these traditions. Contemporary terrorists, who intend to bring about the deaths of innocent people by their acts, commit one of the most serious acts of injustice, unless, of course, they can show that these people are not innocent. Much turns on their attempts, therefore, to attack the innocence claim.

Just as natural law and Kantian moral theories constrain our behavior and limit the means we may use in the pursuit of political ends, so they constrain our responses to terrorists. We may not, for instance, intentionally kill innocent people (e.g., bystanders, hostages) while combating those who attack us. Our hands may thus be tied in responding to terrorism. Many commentators have argued that a morally motivated reluctance to use the nondiscriminating means of terrorists makes us especially vulnerable to them.

Some natural law or Kantian thinking invoke the notions of natural or of human rights to understand moral standing, where these are rights which we possess simply by virtue of our natures or of our humanity. Now if our nature or our humanity is interpreted, as it commonly is in these traditions, as something we retain throughout our lives, at least to the extent that we retain those attributes and capacities that are characteristic of humans, then even those who violate the strictest prohibitions of justice will retain their moral standing. According to this view, a killer acts wrongly without thereby ceasing to be the sort of being that possesses moral standing. Terrorists, then, retain their moral standing, and consequently, there are limits to what we may do to them, by way either of resistance or of punishment. Conversely, though there is reason to think consequentialists, including those who reject theories of rights to understand moral standing, would not deny terrorists such standing, what may be done to terrorists may not be so easily constrained. For harming those who harm the innocent seems less likely to provoke outrage and opposition and so negative consequences.

Certainly, not every member of these consequentialist traditions will agree with this analysis. John Locke, for instance, believed that a murderer has "by the unjust Violence and Slaughter he hath committed upon one, declared War against all Mankind, and therefore may be destroyed as a *Lyon* or a *Tyger*, one of those wild Savage Beasts, with whom Men can have no Society nor Security."[1] It may, however, be argued that the analysis accords with many parts of these traditions, as well as with much of ordinary, commonsense morality.

Whether we follow these theories in understanding the prohibition on the intentional killing of the innocent to be indefeasible or not, this principle figures importantly in most moral traditions. Care, however, must be taken in its interpretation and application. Even if we understand terrorism narrowly, as involving attacks on the innocent, it may not be clear here as elsewhere exactly who is innocent. As made clear in the just war and abortion literature, the term "innocent" is ambiguous. The usual sense is to designate some individual who is not guilty of moral or legal wrongdoing, a sense usually called the moral or juridical sense of the term. By contrast, in discussing what are often called "innocent threats"—for instance, an approaching infant who unwittingly is boobytrapped with explosives, a fetus whose continued growth threatens the life of the woman—it is common to distinguish a "technical" or "causal" sense of "innocence." People lack innocence in this second sense insofar as they threaten, whatever their culpability.

Determining which sense of "innocence" is relevant (and this is not to prejudge the issue of still further, different senses) is controversial. In discussions of the ethics of war, it is often thought that "noncombatants" are not legitimate targets, because of their innocence. Noncombatants, however, may share some of the responsibility for the injustice of a war or the injustice of the means used to prosecute the war, or they may threaten the adversary in certain ways. In the first case, they would not be fully innocent in the moral or juridical sense; in the second, they would lack, to some degree, causal innocence.

This distinction is relevant to the moral evaluation of terrorist acts aimed at noncombatants. Sometimes attempts are made at justification by pointing to the victims' lack of innocence, in the first sense. Perhaps this is what Emile Henry meant when he famously said, in 1894, after exploding a bomb in a Paris café, "There are no innocents." Presumably in such cases, where the relevant notion of innocence is that of nonculpability, terrorists would strike only at members of certain national or political groups. Other times it might be argued that the victims in someway (for instance, by their financial, electoral, or tacit support for a repressive regime) posed a threat. In these cases, terrorists would view themselves as justified in striking at anyone who, say, was present in a certain location. The distinction may also be of importance in discussions of the permissibility of various means that might be used in response to terrorist acts. If the relevant sense of innocence is causal, then certain means, those endangering the lives of victims, might be permissible.

Of course it is hard to understand how the victims of the Japanese Red Army attack at Israel's Lod airport in 1972 or of a bomb in a Paris department store in 1986 could be thought to lack innocence in either sense. In the first case, the victims were travelers (e.g., Puerto Rican Christians); in the second case, the store in question was frequented by indigent immigrants and, at that time of year, by mothers and children shopping for school supplies. It is this feature of some contemporary terrorism that has lead many commentators to distinguish it from earlier forms and from other political uses of violence.

The analogies here with another issue that has preoccupied moral theorists recently, that of the ethics of nuclear deterrence and conflict, are significant. The United States, of course, dropped atomic weapons on two Japanese cities at the end of the last world war. For several decades now, American policy has been to threaten the Soviet Union with a variety of kinds of nuclear strikes in the event that the latter attacked the United States or its Western allies with nuclear or, in the case of an invasion of Western Europe, merely with conventional weapons. These acts or practices involve killing or threatening to kill noncombatants in order to achieve certain ends: unconditional surrender in the case of Japan, deterrence of aggression in that of the Soviet Union. The possible analogies with terrorism have not gone unnoticed. Furthermore, just as some defenders of the atomic strikes against the Japanese have argued, those we attack, or threaten to attack, with nuclear weapons are themselves sufficiently similar to terrorists to justify our response.

A still different perspective on these issues may be obtained by turning from the usual consequentialist and natural law or Kantian theories to forms of contractarianism in ethics. Although this tradition has affinities with natural law and Kantian theories, especially with regard to the demands of justice or the content of moral principles, there are differences that are especially noteworthy in connection with the issues that are raised by terrorist violence.

According to this tradition, justice may be thought of as a set of principles and dispositions that bind people insofar as those to whom they are obligated reciprocate. In the absence of constraint by others, one has little or no duty to refrain from acting toward them in ways that normally would be unjust. Justice may be thus thought, to borrow a phrase from John Rawls, to be a sort of "cooperative venture for mutual advantage." According to this view, justice is not binding in the absence of certain conditions, one of which would be others' cooperative behavior and dispositions.

Adherents to this tradition might argue that we would be in a "state of nature," that is, a situation where few if any constraints of justice would bind us, with regard to terrorists who attack those who are innocent (in the relevant sense). As Hume argues in the *Second Enquiry*, when in "the society of ruffians, remote from the protection of laws and government," or during the "rage and violence of public war," the conventions of justice are suspended:

The laws of war, which then succeed to those of equity and justice, are rules calculated for the advantage and utility of that particular state, in which men are now placed. And were a civilized nation engaged with barbarians, who observed no rules even of war, the former must also suspend their observance of them, where they no longer serve to any purpose; and must render every action or rencounter as bloody and pernicious as possible to the first aggressors.[2]

Unlike the earlier views, then, this view holds that terrorists who, by act or by intent, forswear the rules of justice may thereby lose the protection of those rules, and so a major part of their moral standing.

Similarly, partisans of terrorism might argue that it is the acts of their victims or of their governments that make impossible cooperative relations of fair dealing between themselves and those they attack. The acts, or intentions, of the latter remove them from the protection of the rules of justice.

In either case, the acts of terrorists and our response to them take place in a world beyond, or prior to, justice. Students of international affairs and diplomacy will recognize here certain of the implications of a family of skeptical positions called "realism."

Consequentialists, it should be noted, are likely to find this exclusive focus on the virtue of justice to be misguided, and they are likely to be less enamored of certain distinctions involving kinds of innocence or types of violence that are incorporated into contractarianism. In general, they will argue, as noted earlier, that terrorism *can* be justified by its consequences, where these must include the effects not merely on the terrorists but also on their victims (and others). As terrorist acts appear often not to produce sufficient benefits to outweigh the considerable costs they inevitably exact, there will most likely be a moral presumption, albeit defeasible, against them. But wrongful terrorism will be condemned, not because of the existence of mutually advantageous conventions of justice, but because of the overall harm or suffering caused. Consequentialists, then, will doubtless stand out as much against contractarian views here as they do against natural law or Kantian ones.

The foregoing, then, is a sketch of different ways terrorism may be understood and of different types of moral theories in which its justification may be addressed. There is serious controversy on both counts, and this fact alone, whatever other differences may exist, makes the works of philosophers and political and social scientists on terrorism contentious even among themselves. . . .

NOTES

1. John Locke, *Second Treatise of Government*, in *Two Treatises of Government*, ed. Peter Laslett (Cambridge: Cambridge University Press, 1988), p. 274 (chap. 2, sec. 11).

2. David Hume, *An Enquiry concerning the Principles of Morals*, in *Enquiries concerning Human Understanding and the Principles of Morals*, ed. L. A. Selby-Bigge, 3d ed., ed. P. H. Nidditch (Oxford: Clarendon, 1975), pp. 187–8 (sec. 3, pt. 1).

Questions for Analysis

1. How would you define "terrorism" using ideas from Frey and Morris? Is it "violence against innocent civilians for social and political purposes"? Is it only a particular type of violence? How is violence different from force? Does terrorism include all social and political purposes or only some? During war, innocent civilians are often killed or injured, even if that is not the intent of the attacks. How is this different from terrorism?

2. Test your definition of terrorism by considering the attacks of 9/11 on the World Trade Center and the Pentagon, the attack on the Oklahoma City Federal Building, the spread of anthrax through the U.S. mail, the attack on the American ship the U.S.S. *Cole*, and the truck bombings of the U.S. Embassy and the U.S. Marine Barracks in Beirut. Does your definition explain everything that you consider terrorism? Does it cover things you do not ordinarily consider terrorism?

3. Can terrorism ever be justified using consequentialist or utilitarian ethical reasoning? Is this a weakness of consequentialist theories or a misuse of those theories?

4. What are the advantages and disadvantages of a Kantian or a natural law approach to terrorism, under which the taking of innocent life is always wrong, whether by a terrorist or in response to a terrorist attack?

Enemy Aliens

David Cole

David Cole* is a professor at Georgetown University Law Center and attorney for the Center for Constitutional Rights. In Sections IV and V, omitted here, he reviews extensive examples from the past century of how measures designed to target noncitizen aliens also curtailed the civil liberties of many citizens.

Come on, let us deal wisely with them; lest they multiply, and it come to pass, that, when there falleth out any war, they join also unto our enemies, and fight against us, and so get them up out of the land.

—Exodus 1:10

To those who pit Americans against immigrants and citizens against non-citizens, to those who scare peace-loving people with phantoms of lost liberty, my message is this: Your tactics only aid terrorists, for they erode our national unity and diminish our resolve. They give ammunition to America's enemies, and pause to America's friends.

—Attorney General John Ashcroft Dec. 6, 2001[1]

I. INTRODUCTION

. . . It is often said that civil liberties are the first casualty of war. It would be more accurate to say that noncitizens' liberties are the first to go. The current war on terrorism is no exception.

In the wake of September 11, we plainly need to rethink the balance between liberty and security. The attacks, which killed more than 3,000 people and did immeasurable damage to the human spirit, succeeded beyond our worst nightmares and their perpetrators' wildest dreams in wreaking destruction and spreading fear throughout the nation. We all feel a profound and deeply unfamiliar sense of vulnerability in their wake and have a correspondingly urgent need for security and reassurance. The anthrax scare that followed underscored the gravity of the threats we face, vividly demonstrating that scientific and technological advances have made instruments of mass destruction far too widely accessible. And as Attorney General John Ashcroft's statement quoted as an epigraph to this article illustrates, many argue that the demands of waging war—here, a war without an articulable endpoint—require that civil liberties not stand in the way of victory.[2]

There is undoubtedly a balance to be struck between liberty and security, but there are also several reasons to be cautious about too readily sacrificing liberty in the name of security. First, as a historical matter, we have often overreacted in times of crisis. In World War I, we imprisoned people for years at a time merely for speaking out against the war effort.[3] In World War II, we interned more than 110,000 persons solely because of their Japanese ancestry.[4] And during the Cold War, thousands of innocent persons lost their jobs, were subjected to congressional investigations, or were incarcerated for their mere association with the Communist Party.[5] In hindsight, these responses are generally viewed as shameful excesses; but in their day, they were considered reasonable and necessary.

Second, there is reason to think that as a general matter in times of crisis, we will overestimate our security needs and discount the value of liberty. Liberty is almost by definition abstract; it is measured by the *absence* of control or restraint. Fear, by contrast, is immediate and palpable; it takes physical form as stress, anxiety, depression, a pit in the stomach, a bad taste in the mouth. It is easy to take liberty for granted, and to presume that government powers to intrude on liberty are not likely to be directed at one's *own* liberty. Fear affects us all, especially after an attack like that of September 11.

Third, liberty and security are not necessarily mutually exclusive values in a zero-sum game. Liberty often plays a critical role in maintaining security. One of the justifications for guaranteeing political freedoms is that a free people are less likely to be driven to extreme violence. A political process that treats people with equal dignity and allows dissidents to voice their views and organize to change the rules through political means is likely to be more stable in the long run. Recent experience in England and Israel has shown that cracking down on civil liberties does not necessarily reduce violence, and may simply inspire more violence.[6] As Justice Brandeis wrote, the Framers knew "that fear breeds repression; that repression breeds hate; [and] that hate menaces stable government."[7]

Understanding both the importance of liberty and the temptation to restrict it that government authorities and democratic majorities would face in times of crisis, the Framers sought to protect our basic liberties from the momentary passions of the majority by inscribing them in the Constitution. But with few exceptions, constitutional rights are not absolute; a balance must be struck. As Justice Goldberg famously put it, "[the Constitution] is not a suicide pact."[8]

Thus, while the tension between liberty and security should not be overstated, it cannot be denied. We love liberty and security, but recognize that sometimes we must limit one to enjoy the other.[9] When a democratic society strikes that balance in ways that impose the costs and benefits uniformly on all, one might be relatively confident that the political process will ultimately achieve a proper balance. But all too often we seek to avoid the difficult trade-offs by striking an illegitimate balance, sacrificing the liberties of a minority group in order to further the majority's security interests. In the wake of September 11, citizens and their elected representatives have repeatedly chosen to sacrifice the liberties of noncitizens in furtherance of the citizenry's purported security. Because noncitizens have no vote, and thus no direct voice in the democratic process, they are a particularly vulnerable minority. And in the heat of the nationalistic and nativist fervor engendered by war, noncitizens' interests are even less likely to weigh in the balance.

In this essay, I will show how this double standard has operated, both in the wake of September 11 and at critical moments in our history. Since September 11, immigrants have been the targets of a massive preventive detention campaign conducted under unprecedented secrecy. Congress has enacted new laws that subject noncitizens to guilt by association, ideological exclusion, and unilateral executive detention. And federal and local officials have engaged in ethnic profiling, treating immigrants as suspect based on little more than their Arab ethnicity or national origin.

Some argue that a "double standard" for citizens and noncitizens is perfectly justified. The attacks of September 11 were perpetrated by 19 Arab noncitizens, and we have reason to believe that other Arab noncitizens are associated with the attackers and will seek to attack again. Citizens, it is said, are presumptively loyal; noncitizens are not. Thus, it is not irrational to focus on Arab noncitizens. Moreover, on a normative level, if citizens and noncitizens were treated identically, citizenship itself might be rendered meaningless. The very essence of war involves the drawing of lines in the sand between citizens of our nation and those against whom we are fighting. Surely in that setting it makes sense to treat noncitizens differently from citizens.

I will suggest that such reasoning should be resisted on three grounds: It is normatively and constitutionally wrong; it undermines our security interests; and it will pave the way for future inroads on citizens' liberties. First, properly understood, the Constitution imposes substantial limits on sacrificing immigrants' liberties for citizens' purported security. The basic rights at stake—political freedom, due process, and equal protection of the laws—are not limited to citizens, but apply to all "persons" subject to our laws. These rights are best understood not as special privileges stemming from a specific social contract, but from what it means to be a person with free and equal dignity. They are human rights, not privileges of citizenship, and ought to apply whenever we seek to impose legal obligations on persons. The Constitution reserves relatively few rights to citizens, the principal one being the right to vote. And precisely because noncitizens do not enjoy the franchise, and therefore cannot rely on the political process for their protection, it is all the more critical that they be accorded basic human rights enforceable in court.

The fact that we are waging a "war on terrorism" does not alter these basic constitutional principles. This war is more akin to the metaphorical (and indefinite) "war on drugs" or "war on crime" than to a conventional war. As yet, it finds no nation on the other side. We are fighting an international criminal organization, Al Qaeda, and those who aid it, including, thus far, the Taliban. But we have declared war on no nation. Moreover, as the Japanese internment of World War II illustrated, it is perilous to predicate suspicion on ethnic identity even with respect to persons associated with a specific country on which we have declared war. It is another matter entirely to apply such treatment to citizens from a wide range of Arab countries, most of which are fighting *on our side* in the war on terrorism.

Second, as a security matter, employing a double standard with respect to the basic rights accorded citizens and noncitizens is likely to be counterproductive at home and abroad, because it undermines our legitimacy in both spheres. At home, law enforcement is more effective when it works with rather than against communities. If authorities have reason to believe that there might be potential terrorists lurking in the Arab immigrant community, they would do better to work with the millions of law-abiding members of that community to obtain their assistance in identifying potential threats, than to alienate the community by

treating many of its members as suspect because of their ethnicity or national origin and pursuing others under conditions of secrecy that invite fear and paranoia.

Legitimacy is essential at the international level as well. As September 11 illustrated, terrorism is a transnational phenomenon, and it demands a transnational response. We must maintain a broad coalition if we are to succeed in our efforts, not only because we need the cooperation of many different nations' intelligence and law enforcement apparatuses, but also because if we are seen as fighting for our own parochial interests and not for the interests of justice and peace more broadly, we are likely to inspire more people to take up the mantle of terrorism against us. As the critical responses of our allies to the military tribunals and the Guantanamo detentions illustrate, our credibility on matters of international law and human rights is already at a low ebb.[10] This is in large part our own fault; as the world's most powerful nation, we have too often acted as if we are free to ignore international norms whenever it serves our interests.[11] But doing so will surely undermine the multilateral coalition we desperately need to fight the war against terrorism effectively. Secretary of State Colin Powell's reported objections to the United States' stance on the Guantanamo prisoners reflects precisely that concern.[12]

Finally, what we are willing to allow our government to do to immigrants creates precedents for how it treats citizens. In 1798, for example, Congress enacted the Enemy Alien Act, which remains on the books to this day and authorizes the President during wartime to detain, deport, or otherwise restrict the liberties of any citizen over 14 years of age of a country with which we are at war, without any individualized showing of disloyalty, criminal conduct, or even suspicion. In World War II, the government extended that logic to intern 110,000 persons of Japanese ancestry, about two-thirds of whom were U.S. citizens. Similarly, while we think of the McCarthy era as beginning in the 1940s, it was in fact preceded by several decades of targeting immigrants for their purportedly subversive political associations using immigration law. Joe McCarthy simply applied to citizens techniques developed in the 1910s under the leadership of a young J. Edgar Hoover, head of the Justice Department's "Alien Radical" division.

Measures initially targeted at noncitizens may well come back to haunt us all.

In short, when we balance liberty and security, we should do so in ways that respect the equal dignity and basic human rights of all persons and not succumb to the temptation of purchasing security at the expense of noncitizens' basic rights. In the wake of September 11, we have failed to follow that mandate. But our long-term success in the campaign against terrorism prompted by the September 11 attacks will turn on our treating immigrants as we would want to be treated ourselves. In the end, the true test of justice in a democratic society is not how it treats those with a political voice, but how it treats those who have no voice in the democratic process.

II. SACRIFICING THEIR LIBERTY FOR OUR SECURITY: THE POST-9/11 RESPONSE

"[S]omebody who comes into the United States of America illegally, who conducts a terrorist operation killing thousands of innocent Americans—men, women, and children—is not a lawful combatant.... They don't deserve the same guarantees and safeguards that would be used for an American citizen going through the normal judicial process."[13] With these words Vice President Dick Cheney defended the president's military order of November 13, 2001,[14] which authorizes trial by military commission of any noncitizen whom the president accuses of engaging in international terrorism or belonging to Al Qaeda. The vice president's view captures much of the administration's response to the attacks of September 11. It has repeatedly targeted noncitizens, selectively denying them liberties that citizens take for granted. Each of its initiatives raises serious constitutional concerns, and each imposes burdens on noncitizens' basic rights that citizens do not bear.

A. Secret Preventive Detention

Perhaps the most troubling feature of the government's response to the attacks of September 11 has been its campaign of mass preventive detention. The actual number detained is a mystery, because in early November 2001, when the number was 1147, the government responded to growing criticism of the number of persons it was detaining by halting its practice of issuing a running tally.[15] If one assumes that the numbers of newly arrested persons decreased by half in the five months since the government stopped announcing a running tally, the number would be over 2,000 detained as of April 2002. Yet only a single person—Zaccarias Moussaoui—has been charged with any involvement in the crimes under investigation. And he was arrested before September 11. Government officials have claimed that 10 or 11 of the detainees, presumably including Moussaoui, may be members of Al Qaeda.[16] But that simply raises the question of why the other 1,990 or so individuals were detained.

The detentions have been carried out under an unprecedented veil of secrecy. Initially, the government refused to release any details regarding the identity of the detainees. After substantial public pressure, a Freedom of Information Act (FOIA) lawsuit, and requests from members of Congress, the Justice Department released limited information in November regarding the approximately 600 persons then still in federal custody. The vast majority of the detainees were being held on immigration charges. About fifty were held on federal criminal charges, and an undisclosed but assertedly small number were held as material witnesses. The government refused to disclose how many were being held on state or local charges, and refused to reveal the identities of any of the immigration or material witness detainees.[17] In February 2002, the government announced that 327 persons remained in INS custody in connection with the September 11 investigation, but continued to refuse to provide the identities or charges for any of these persons.[18] This secrecy makes it difficult to assess the extent to which the government is adhering to or violating the law in its detention policy. . . .

None of these measures apply to citizens. Citizens are entitled to a public trial. They may be subjected to "preventive detention," but only if brought before an independent judge within 48 hours of arrest for a hearing to determine whether there is probable cause that they have committed a crime, and only if they are shown to be a flight risk or danger to the community.[19] The "speedy trial" requirement means that unless a citizen agrees to an extension, preventive detention is limited to a matter of weeks.[20] Citizens cannot be held simply because the government entertains vague suspicions about them and has not yet convinced itself that they are innocent. And if a judge rules that a citizen should be released on bail pending trial, the prosecutor cannot keep him in jail simply by filing an appeal. In other words, we have imposed on foreign citizens widespread human rights deprivations that we would not likely tolerate if imposed on ourselves.

B. The USA PATRIOT Act

The targeting of noncitizens is further reflected in the USA PATRIOT Act,[21] an omnibus antiterrorism bill enacted just six weeks after September 11. The Act makes many changes to criminal, immigration, banking, and intelligence law, but it reserves its most extreme measures for noncitizens. It makes noncitizens deportable for wholly innocent associational activity, excludable for pure speech, and detainable on the Attorney General's say-so, without a hearing and without a finding that they pose a danger or a flight risk.

1. Guilt by Association

Section 411 of the USA PATRIOT Act imposes guilt by association on aliens. This McCarthy-era philosophy, which the Supreme Court has since condemned as "alien to the traditions of a free society and the First Amendment itself,"[22] has made a strong comeback in recent years under the guise of cutting off funding for terrorism.[23] Before September 11, however, aliens were deportable for engaging in or supporting terrorist activity, but not for mere association.[24] Aliens could be deported for providing material support to an organization only if they knew or reasonably should have known that their activity would support the organization "in conducting a terrorist activity."[25] In other words, the government had to demonstrate a nexus between the alien's conduct and terrorist activity. The USA PATRIOT Act eliminates that nexus requirement. It makes aliens deportable for wholly innocent associational activity with a "terrorist organization," whether or not there is any connection between the alien's associational conduct and any act of violence, much less terrorism.[26] Because the new law defines "terrorist activity" to include virtually any use or threat to use a weapon, and defines "terrorist organization" as any group of two or more persons

that has used or threatened to use a weapon, the Act's proscription on associational activity potentially encompasses every organization that has ever been involved in a civil war or a crime of violence, from a pro-life group that once threatened workers at an abortion clinic, to the African National Congress, the Irish Republican Army, or the Northern Alliance in Afghanistan. . . .

2. Ideological Exclusion

The USA PATRIOT Act also resurrects ideological exclusion, the practice of denying entry to aliens for pure speech. It bars admission to aliens who "endorse or espouse terrorist activity," or who "persuade others to support terrorist activity or a terrorist organization," in ways determined by the Secretary of State to undermine U.S. efforts to combat terrorism.[27] It also excludes aliens who are representatives of groups that "endorse acts of terrorist activity" in ways that similarly undermine U.S. efforts to combat terrorism. Because of the breadth of the definitions of "terrorist activity" and "terrorist organizations," this authority would empower the government to deny entry to any alien who advocated support for the ANC, for the Contras during the war against the Sandinistas, or for opposition forces in Iraq and Iran today. Because all of these groups have used force or violence, they would be terrorist organizations, and anyone who urged people to support them could be denied entry on the Secretary of State's say-so.

Citizens have a constitutional right to endorse terrorist organizations or terrorist activity, so long as their speech is not intended and likely to produce imminent lawless action.[28] While the Supreme Court has long ruled that aliens outside our borders—in contrast to those living among us—have limited constitutional rights,[29] such ideological exclusions nonetheless raise constitutional concerns.[30] The First Amendment is designed to protect a robust public debate, and if our government can keep out persons who espouse disfavored ideas, our opportunity to hear and consider those ideas will be diminished. More broadly, excluding people for their ideas is contrary to the spirit of political freedom for which the United States stands. It was for that reason that Congress removed all such grounds from the Immigration and Nationality

Act (INA) in 1990, after years of embarrassing visa denials for political reasons.[31] We are a strong enough country, and our resolve against terrorism is strong enough, to make such censorship unnecessary. Yet we have now returned to the much-criticized ways of the McCarran-Walter Act, targeting aliens not for their acts but for their words, and for words that would be fully protected if uttered by United States citizens.

3. Unilateral Executive Detention

The USA PATRIOT Act radically revises the rules governing detention of immigrants. Prior to its enactment, aliens in removal proceedings were subject to preventive detention under essentially the same standards that apply to defendants in criminal proceedings: They could be detained without bond if they posed a danger to the community or a risk of flight.[32] Unless the government could make such a showing in a hearing before an immigration judge, aliens were entitled to release on bond.

The USA PATRIOT Act gives the Attorney General unprecedented power to detain aliens *without* a hearing and *without* a showing that they pose a threat to national security or a flight risk. He need only certify that he has "reasonable grounds to believe" that the alien is "described in" various anti-terrorism provisions of the INA, and the alien is then subject to potentially indefinite "mandatory detention."[33] The INA's anti-terrorism provisions in turn include persons who are mere members of designated "terrorist organizations,"[34] and persons who have supported the lawful activities of such organizations.[35] Because the INA defines "engage in terrorist activity" so broadly as to include the use of, or threat to use, a weapon with intent to endanger person or property,[36] it would encompass a permanent resident alien who brandished a kitchen knife in a domestic dispute with her abusive husband, or an alien who found himself in a barroom brawl, picked up a bottle, and threatened another person with it. Surely all such persons do not pose a danger or flight risk necessitating mandatory preventive detention, yet the USA PATRIOT Act empowers the Attorney General to detain such persons without any showing that they pose a danger or flight risk. . . .

4. Secret Searches Without Probable Cause

The USA PATRIOT Act also made substantial changes to the rules that govern the collection and sharing of information by law enforcement and intelligence agencies. Many of these changes potentially affect citizens and immigrants alike, although their principal targets, at least initially, are likely to be Arab and Muslim immigrants. One of the most significant changes has the effect of authorizing warrants for secret searches (so-called "black bag jobs") and wiretaps in criminal investigations without probable cause of criminal conduct.[37] The Fourth Amendment generally permits the government to conduct searches or wiretaps only where it has probable cause that an individual is engaged in criminal activity or that evidence of a crime would be found. But the USA PATRIOT Act allows the government to evade that requirement wherever it says that its investigation also has a significant foreign intelligence purpose. . . .

C. Ethnic Profiling

One of the most dramatic responses to the attack of September 11 was a swift reversal in public attitudes about racial and ethnic profiling as a law enforcement tool. Before September 11, about 80 percent of the American public considered racial profiling wrong.[38] State legislatures, local police departments, and the President had condemned the practice and ordered data collection on the racial patterns of stops and searches.[39] The U.S. Customs Service, sued for racial profiling, had instituted measures to counter racial and ethnic profiling at the borders. A federal law on racial profiling seemed likely.

After September 11, however, polls reported that nearly 60 percent of the American public favored ethnic profiling, at least as long as it was directed at Arabs and Muslims.[40] The fact that the perpetrators of the September 11 attack were all male Arab immigrants and that the attack was apparently orchestrated by Al Qaeda has led many to believe that it is only common sense to pay closer attention to Arab-looking men boarding airplanes and elsewhere. The high stakes make the case for engaging in profiling stronger here than in routine drug interdiction stops on highways. Thus, Stuart

Taylor, a columnist for *Newsweek*, the *National Journal*, and *Legal Times*, who had previously been highly critical of racial profiling, wrote shortly after the attacks in favor of ethnic profiling of Arab men on airplanes.[41] Press accounts made clear that, whether as a matter of official policy or not, law enforcement officials were paying closer attention to those who appear to be Arabs and Muslims.[42]

While the Bush Administration has been careful to speak out against ethnic and religious intolerance and hate crimes, it has sent mixed messages through its own enforcement policies. In November, the Justice Department announced its intention to interview 5,000 young immigrant men, based solely on their age, date of arrival, and the country from which they came.[43] The countries singled out were said to be those where support for Al Qaeda was believed to exist, mostly Arab nations. In any event it appeared that virtually all of those interviewed were Arabs or Muslims. Several police departments around the country refused to participate in the interviews on the grounds that the practice appeared to constitute ethnic profiling.[44]

In January 2002, the *Washington Post* reported that the Justice Department had decided to prioritize the deportation of 6,000 aliens, selected from more than 300,000 foreign nationals who have remained in the country after being ordered deported.[45] The basis for their selection? Once again, nothing more than that they are young men from countries where Al Qaeda support is thought to exist, i.e., Arab countries. There is no question that the immediate aftermath of September 11 called for greater urgency than the ongoing war on drugs. But that does not demonstrate that ethnic profiling is a legal, much less an effective, response. The argument that we cannot afford to rely on something other than racial or ethnic proxies for suspicion, after all, is precisely the rationale used to intern 110,000 persons of Japanese ancestry during World War II. While subjecting an individual to closer inspection and a possible search is far less extreme than detention, the underlying rationale—that we must use ethnicity as a proxy for suspicion—is the same.

Precisely because of the history of racial discrimination in this country, the Equal Protection Clause of the Constitution presumptively forbids government authorities from relying on such racial or ethnic categories. Such actions trigger "strict scrutiny," requiring the government to show that its distinctions are "narrowly tailored" to further a "compelling government interest."[46] There is no question that protecting citizens from terrorism is a compelling government interest, but so too is drug interdiction—in fact, all criminal law enforcement would likely be viewed as a compelling state interest. The real question from a constitutional perspective is whether the means adopted—reliance on ethnic appearance as a proxy for suspicion—is narrowly tailored to further that interest. It is highly unlikely that profiling could satisfy that scrutiny.

First, the vast majority of persons who appear Arab and Muslim—probably well over 99.9 percent—have no involvement with terrorism. Arab and Muslim appearance, in other words, is a terribly inaccurate proxy. In the sex discrimination context, where the Supreme Court applies less stringent scrutiny than it does to ethnic or racial discrimination, the Court has held that statistics showing that 2 percent of young men between the ages of 18 and 21 had been arrested for drunk driving did not justify denying men of that age the right to purchase an alcoholic beverage.[47] Surely the percentage of terrorists among men of Arab appearance is far smaller than the percentage of drunk drivers among college-age men.

Second, the use of ethnic stereotypes, far from being "necessary" for effective law enforcement, is likely to be ineffective. When one treats a whole group of people as presumptively suspicious, it means that agents are more likely to miss dangerous persons who do not to fit the profile, such as Richard Reid, the British citizen who boarded a plane in Paris headed for Miami with a bomb in his shoe.[48] In addition, the fact that the vast majority of those targeted on the basis of their Arab or Muslim appearance will prove to be innocent will inevitably cause agents to let their guard down.[49] Overbroad ethnic generalizations, in other words, are not only not narrowly tailored to furthering effective law enforcement, but may actually undermine effectiveness.

D. Military Tribunals

The final example of the double standard at work in our response to September 11 is President Bush's order creating military tribunals to try alleged terrorists and Al Qaeda members.[50] As noted at the outset, the Constitution imposes no bar on using the tribunals to try any person who qualifies as an unlawful combatant, irrespective of citizenship. Yet the president opted to limit the application of the tribunals to noncitizens. As there is no legal reason for that justification, one has to wonder why the president chose to delimit the tribunals in this way, particularly as in all other respects the order recognized virtually no limits. It seems all too likely that this was a politically opportunistic decision, fully in keeping with the rest of the post-September 11 response that I have described above. If citizens were subject to the tribunals, citizens would have a much more immediate interest in overseeing and limiting the president's assertion of power. The president's military tribunals are extraordinary, as they do away with any independent judicial review, and make the determination of guilt a matter of military judgment. Moreover, they permit the use of classified evidence, presented **ex parte** and *in camera*, to convict suspects, and do not permit access to that evidence by anyone outside the military chain of command.[51] Such measures may or may not be justified in wartime, but the important point for purposes of this article is that it was politics, not law, that limited exposure to the tribunals to noncitizens. . . .

III. THE BILL OF RIGHTS AS HUMAN RIGHTS

The critique leveled above presumes that there is something wrong with treating immigrants differently from citizens. But is there? If aliens are differently situated from citizens, then treating them differently would not violate basic norms of equality and dignity, but would simply reflect that they are in fact different. There is nothing wrong with a double standard where relevant considerations warrant the application of separate rules.

Defenders of the administration maintain that we need not extend the same rights to foreigners that we extend to citizens. Aliens have taken no oath of loyalty to this country and presumably maintain their principal fidelity elsewhere. And surely it is not irrational to treat Arab and Muslim aliens differently now, in light of the fact that Al Qaeda, the organization apparently responsible for

the September 11 attacks, is comprised almost exclusively of Arab and Muslim noncitizens and has threatened to carry out further terrorist acts against American civilians. Al Qaeda doesn't issue identify cards or passports, so we can't easily identity its members, but we do know that they are likely to consist of young Arab or Muslim men.

But the fact that it may not be *irrational* to focus more closely on Arab and Muslim immigrants than on other persons does not resolve whether it is *fair* to deny those immigrants basic constitutional rights. In particular, it does not justify denying them the basic guarantees of due process, political freedom, and equal protection. Were an Asian-American gang to launch a series of violent attacks on residents of New York City, it might justify paying more attention to those who might be members of the gang, but it would not warrant denying gang members, much less those who merely share their ethnic identity, basic constitutional rights.

Similarly, the issue of loyalty and oaths is a red herring. Most citizens do not take an oath of loyalty either; they become citizens by the accident of birth, not by passing any test of commitment. And while one might roughly presume that citizens will be loyal to the countries of which they are citizens, where we are at war with no nation, there is no basis for a presumption of conflicting loyalties based on national origin. Most fundamentally, there is simply nothing in the nature of the rights of due process, political freedom, and equal protection that would warrant imposing a threshold requirement of loyalty.

The Constitution does distinguish in some respects between the rights of citizens and noncitizens. But in fact, relatively little turns on citizenship status. The right to vote and the right to run for federal elective office are restricted to citizens, but all of the other rights are written without such limitation. Thus, the First and Fourth Amendments protect the rights of "the people," while the Fifth and Fourteenth Amendment Due Process Clauses, as well as the Equal Protection Clause, extend their protections to all "persons." The rights attaching to criminal trials apply to "the accused." As the Court has noted, the fact that the Framers knew how to limit rights to citizens, and chose to so limit only the right to vote and run for office, indicates that the other rights are not so limited. Specifically, the Court has stated that neither the First nor the

Fifth Amendment "acknowledges any distinction between citizens and resident aliens."[52] For more than a century, the Court has recognized that the Equal Protection Clause is "universal in [its] application to all persons within the territorial jurisdiction, without regard to differences of ... nationality."[53] Similarly, the Court has repeatedly stated that "the Due Process Clause applies to all 'persons' within the United States, including aliens, whether their presence here is lawful, unlawful, temporary, or permanent."[54] And when noncitizens, no matter what their status, are tried for crimes, they are entitled to all of the rights that attach to the criminal process.[55]

There are good reasons for this. First, the rights articulated in the Bill of Rights were viewed by many at the time not as a set of optional contractual provisions enforceable because they were agreed upon by a group of states and extending only to the contracting parties, but as inalienable natural rights that find their provenance in God.[56] While natural law theories no longer hold much influence, the human rights movement of the last 50 years reflects a similar understanding that there are certain basic rights to which all persons are entitled, simply by virtue of being persons.[57] The rights of political freedom, due process, and equal protection, in other words, are part of the minimal set of rights that the world has come to demand of any free society. In the words of the Supreme Court, these rights are "implicit in the concept of ordered liberty."[58]

Second, as Alexander Bickel has argued, our experience with delimiting rights on the basis of citizenship should give us pause.[59] The Supreme Court's decision in *Dred Scott v. Sandford*[60] sought to define away Dred Scott's rights by concluding that "persons who are descendants of Africans who were imported into this country, and sold as slaves," were not citizens and therefore could not invoke federal court jurisdiction.[61] The Court reasoned that when the Constitution was adopted, blacks were not protected by its provisions, because they were "considered as a subordinate and inferior class of beings, who had been subjugated by the dominant race, and, whether emancipated or not, yet remained subject to their authority, and had no rights or privileges but such as those who held the power and the Government might choose to grant them."[62] With the express intent of overruling that

reasoning, Congress provided in the Civil Rights Act of 1866 that "all persons born in the United States and not subject to any foreign power, excluding Indians not taxed, are hereby declared to be citizens of the United States. . . ."[63] The same Congress enacted the Fourteenth Amendment, which provided that all persons born or naturalized in the United States are citizens, and further guaranteed to all persons in the United States—whether citizen or not—due process of law and equal protection. As Bickel argues, *Dred Scott* teaches that "[a] relationship between government and the governed that turns on citizenship can always be dissolved or denied [because] citizenship is a legal construct, an abstraction, a theory."[64] It is far more difficult to deny that a human being is a "person."

Third, the fact that the Constitution denies aliens the right to vote makes it that much more essential that the basic rights reflected in the Bill of Rights be extended to aliens in our midst. As a group that is subject to government regulation but denied a vote, aliens are without a meaningful voice in the political bargains struck by our representative system. Members of Congress have little reason to concern themselves with the rights and interests of those who cannot vote. . . .

The extension of basic constitutional rights to noncitizens must be qualified in at least three significant respects, however. First, immigrants are subject to the immigration power, which the Court has historically treated with substantial deference as a "plenary power." As a result, "Congress regularly makes rules that would be unacceptable if applied to citizens."[65] At the most basic level, immigrants can be expelled from the country, often for very minor infractions. Citizens, by contrast, cannot be banished and cannot have their citizenship taken away. . . .

Second, the extension of basic constitutional rights to aliens is complicated by territorial concerns. The Court has historically treated aliens within our jurisdiction very differently from those outside our border. As the Court noted last term, "it is well established that certain constitutional protections available to persons inside the United States are unavailable to aliens outside of our geographic borders. But once an alien enters the country, the legal circumstance changes, for the Due Process Clause applies to all 'persons' within the United States. . . ."[66]

. . . Finally, the Court has always treated the rights of "enemy aliens" as categorically different from the rights of citizens, and indeed of all other aliens. The Court has upheld the constitutionality of the Enemy Alien Act, which authorizes the President in a declared war to detain, deport, or otherwise restrict the freedom of any citizen 14 years of age or older of the country with which we are at war.[67] . . .

The constitutional arguments made in this section should impel us to respect immigrants' speech, associational, and due process rights as fully as our own even in those settings where infringing aliens' rights might advance our security. Most constitutional rights, as restrictions on the exercise of sovereign authority, potentially impede government efforts to make the nation more secure. That is an inevitable cost of a limited government. At the same time, most constitutional rights have not been interpreted as absolutes, but as presumptive prohibitions rebuttable by compelling showings of need and narrow tailoring. Thus, for example, the First Amendment right of free speech reflects a presumption of protection that is overridden where speech is intended and likely to incite imminent lawless action.[68] My claim is not that such categorical balancing is inappropriate, but that we must not cheat on the balance by drawing the line differently with respect to aliens and citizens. Aliens' speech may be punished, but only if it meets the *Brandenburg* standard. Aliens' liberty may be deprived, but only pursuant to the same procedural safeguards we demand for citizens. Thus, while the definition of most constitutional rights contains an implicit consequentialist balance, the balance should be struck equally for all—even if it might be convenient or effective to strike it differently for some. . . .

VI. CONCLUSION

Security is indisputably at a premium in the wake of the attacks of September 11. There may well be a justification for sacrificing some of our liberties if the sacrifice will make us more secure. But many of the measures we have undertaken after September 11 follow a disturbing historical pattern, in which we, the citizenry, sacrifice not our freedoms, but the freedoms of noncitizens, a minority group with no vote, in the interest of preserving citizens' security.

The post-September 11 response constitutes a reprise of some of the worst mistakes of our past. Once again, we are treating people as suspicious not for their conduct, but based on their racial, ethnic, or political identity. Once again, we are using the immigration power as a pretext for criminal law enforcement, and have undertaken a mass detention campaign directed at immigrants without probable cause that any of them are tied to the specific threats that we face. And once again, we have authorized the government to bypass procedures designed to distinguish the guilty from the innocent, holding secret hearings and authorizing executive detentions that challenge the most basic notions of fairness.

As politically tempting as the trade-off of immigrants' liberties for our security may appear, we should not make it. As a matter of principle, the rights that we have selectively denied to immigrants are not reserved for citizens. The rights of political freedom, due process, and equal protection belong to every person subject to United States legal obligations, irrespective of citizenship. As a pragmatic matter, reliance on double standards reduces the legitimacy of our struggle, and that legitimacy may be our most valuable asset, both at home and abroad. To paraphrase John Ashcroft himself: "To those who pit Americans against immigrants and citizens against non-citizens . . . my message is this: Your tactics only aid terrorism." And as a matter of self-interest, what we do to aliens today may well pave the way for what will be done to citizens tomorrow. In the end, however, it is principle that should drive us: the justice of our response should be judged by how we treat those who have no voice in the political process. Thus far, we have performed predictably, but not well.

NOTES

* Professor, Georgetown University Law Center. I benefitted from comments of many colleagues in connection with presentations of this paper at workshops and forums at Amherst College, Georgetown University Law Center, Howard Law School, University of Pittsburgh Law School, Stanford Law School, the Supreme Court Historical Society, Wayne State University, Wellesley College, and the University of Washington. Matthew Kilby and Jihee Suh provided invaluable research assistance.

1. *Senate Judiciary Committee Hearing on Anti-Terrorism Policy*, 106th Cong. (Dec. 6, 2001) (testimony of Attorney General John Ashcroft).

2. See *Senate Judiciary Committee Hearing on Anti-Terrorism Policy, supra* note 1.

3. See *Abrams v. United States*, 250 U.S. 616 (1919); *Debs v. United States*, 249 U.S. 211 (1919); *Frohwerk v. United States*, 249 U.S. 204 (1919); *Schenck v. United States*, 249 U.S. 47 (1919).

4. See, *e.g., Korematsu v. United States*, 323 U.S. 214, 236 (1944).

5. See, *e.g., Dennis v. United States*, 341 U.S. 494 (1951); Michal R. Belknap, *Cold War Political Justice: The Smith Act, the Communist Party, and American Civil Liberties* (1977); Victor S. Navasky, *Naming Names* (1983); Arthur J. Sabin, *In Calmer Times: The Supreme Court and Red Monday* (1999).

6. *Cf.* T.R. Reid, Britons Know Price of Averting Terrorism at Home, *Wash. Post*, Sept. 29, 2001 at A16 (maintaining that measures curtailing civil liberties in struggle against the Irish Republican Army did not lead to further security and that only the agreement to negotiate led to reduced violence). The Israelis have imposed guilt by association, collective punishment, summary execution of suspected terrorists, and torture of detainees, yet it would be difficult to claim that these measures have reduced terrorism. *See U.S. State Dep't, Country Report on Human Rights, 2001: Israel and the Occupied Territories*, available at http://www.state.gov/g/drl/rls/hrrpt/2001/nea/8262.htm (Mar. 4, 2002); *Amnesty International, Israeli Military Action is Collective Punishment*, http://www.amnesty-usa.org/news/2002/israel04122002.html (Apr. 12, 2002).

7. *Whitney v. California*, 274 U.S. 357, 375 (1927) (Brandeis, J., concurring).

8. *Kennedy v. Mendoza-Martinez*, 372 U.S. 144, 160 (1963).

9. As Chief Justice Rehnquist has written:

> It is not simply "liberty" but *civil* liberty of which we speak. The word "civil," in turn is derived from the Latin word *civis*, which means "citizen." A citizen is a person owing allegiance to some organized government, and not a person in an idealized "state of nature" free from any governmental restraint.
>
> William H. Rehnquist, *All the Laws But One: Civil Liberties in Wartime* 222 (1998) (emphasis in original).

10. See David E. Sanger, A Nation Challenged: The Treatment; Prisoners Straddle an Ideological Chasm, *N.Y. Times*, Jan. 27, 2002, at A16; Katharine Q. Seelye & David E. Sanger, Bush Reconsiders Stand on Treating Captives of War, *N.Y. Times*, Jan. 29, 2002, at A1; Katharine Q. Seelye, Criticized, U.S. Brings Visitors to Prison Camp, *N.Y. Times*, Jan. 26, 2002, at A8.

11. See generally *Institute for Energy and Environmental Research and Lawyers' Committee for Nuclear Policy, The Rule of Power or the Rule of Law?: An Assessment of U.S. Policies and Actions Regarding Security-Related Treaties* (2002), available at http://www.ieer.org/reports/treaties/fullrpt.pdf (criticizing U.S. pattern of rejecting or disregarding international treaties); Anthony Lewis, Captives And the Law, *N.Y. Times*, Jan. 26, 2002, at A15 (maintaining that "the prisoner issue touches a profound resentment abroad at what many see as an American tendency to lecture others about international standards while refusing to comply with those it urges"); The Guantanamo Story, *Wash. Post*, Jan. 25, 2002, at A24 (arguing that Administration response to criticism of treatment of detainees at Guantanamo "suggested that the Bush administration would respect international law only so far as it chose to").

12. Rowan Scarborough, Powell Wants Detainees to be Declared POWs; Memo Shows Difference with White House, *Wash. Times*, Jan. 26, 2002, at A1 (reporting an internal White House memorandum in which White House Counsel Alberto Gonzales noted Powell's request that Taliban and Al Qaeda detainees be declared prisoners of war).

13. Elisabeth Bumiller & Steven Lee Myers, Senior Administration Officials Defend Military Tribunals for Terrorist Suspects, *N.Y. Times*, Nov. 15, 2001, at B6.

14. Detention, Treatment, and Trial of Certain Non-Citizens in the War Against Terrorism, *66 Fed. Reg.* 57833 (Nov. 13, 2001).

15. Todd S. Purdum, A Nation Challenged: The Attorney General; Ashcroft's About-Face on the Detainees, *N.Y. Times*, Nov. 28, 2001, at B7.

16. David Firestone & Christopher Drew, A Nation Challenged: The Cases; Al Queda Link Seen in Only a Handful of 1,200 Detainees, *N.Y. Times*, Nov. 29, 2001, at A1.

17. Neil A. Lewis & Don Van Natta, Jr., A Nation Challenged: The Investigation; Ashcroft Offers Accounting of 641 Charged or Held, *N.Y. Times*, Nov. 28, 2001, at A1.

18. Amnesty International, *Amnesty International's Concerns Regarding Post September 11 Detentions in the USA*, (March 14, 2002), available at http://www.amnesty-usa.org/usacri-sis/9.11.detentions2.rtf; Christopher Drew & Judith Miller, A Nation Challenged: The Detainees; Though Not Linked to Terrorism, Many Detainees Cannot Go Home, *N.Y. Times*, Feb. 18, 2002, at A1.

19. *County of Riverside v. McLaughlin*, 500 U.S. 44 (1991) (holding that the Fourth Amendment presumptively requires probable cause hearing within 48 hours of arrest); *United States v. Salerno*, 481 U.S. 739 (1987) (upholding pre-trial preventive detention of criminal defendants who pose a danger or a flight risk under Bail Reform Act).

20. 18 U.S.C.S. 3161(b) (2002) (requiring that charges be filed within thirty days of an arrest); 18 U.S.C.S. 3161(c)(1) (2002) (requiring that trial must commence within seventy days of filing charges).

21. Uniting and Strengthening America by Providing Appropriate Tools Required to Intercept and Obstruct

Terrorism (USA PATRIOT Act) Act of 2001, Pub. L. No. 107-56, 115 Stat. 272 (2001) [hereinafter USA PATRIOT Act].

22. *NAACP v. Claiborne Hardware Co.*, 458 U.S. 886, 932 (1982) (citations omitted).

23. See generally David Cole, Hanging with the Wrong Crowd: Of Gangs, Terrorists, and the Right of Association, 1999 *Sup. Ct. Rev.* 203 (1999).

24. Immigration Act, 8 U.S.C. 1227(a)(4)(B) (2000); Id.at 1182(a)(3)(B)(iii).

25. Immigration Act, 8 U.S.C. 1182(a)(3)(B)(iii) (2000).

26. USA PATRIOT Act, *supra* note 21, at 411. The Act defines as a deportable offense the solicitation of members or funds for, or the provision of material support to, any group designated as terrorist. There is no defense available, not even for those who can show that their support had no connection to furthering terrorism. The government is free to designate any organization that uses or threatens to use violence as terrorist. In addition, the law makes aliens who support even nondesignated groups deportable if the group has engaged in or threatened violence, unless the alien can prove that he neither knew nor reasonably should have known that his support would further the group's terrorist activities.

27. USA PATRIOT Act, supra note 21 at 411.

28. *Brandenburg v. Ohio*, 395 U.S. 444, 447(1969).

29. See, *e.g., Kleindienst v. Mandel*, 408 U.S. 753 (1972) (assuming without deciding that alien outside the United States does not have First Amendment right to object to his exclusion); *United States ex rel. Knauff v. Shaughnessy*, 338 U.S. 537 (1950) (holding that aliens outside the United States do not have a right to enter protected by the Constitution).

30. See, *e.g., Kleindienst*, 408 U.S. at 775 (Marshall, J., dissenting) (recognizing that exclusion of alien for his political associations and views infringes on the rights of U.S. citizens to exchange ideas with him); *Abourezk v. Reagan*, 785 F.2d 1043 (D.C. Cir. 1986) (same), *aff'd per curiam*, 484 U.S. 1 (1987); Steven R. Shapiro, Ideological Exclusions: Closing the Border to Political Dissidents, 100 *Harv. L. Rev.* 930 (1987).

31. See Immigration and Nationality Act of 1990, 8 U.S.C. 1182(a)(3)(C) (repealing INA 212(a)(27) and (28) (1952), which excluded anarchists; members of the Communist party; aliens who advocated Communism or violent overthrow of the U.S. government; and aliens who wrote or published, or even knowingly had in their possession, material advocating such activities).

32. *O'Rourke v. Warden*, 539 F. Supp. 1131, 1135 (S.D.N.Y. 1982) ("The BIA . . . has construed [8 U.S.C. 1252(a)] to provide that the determination to release an alien pending deportation proceedings is 'not a discretionary form of relief' but rather 'an alien should be detained or required to post a bond, only if he is a threat to national security or is a poor bail risk.'") (quoting In re O'Rourke, A22 607 396, Decision

and Order of the BIA, August 13, 1980, at 3); *see also In re Drysdale*, 20 I. & N. Dec. 815, 817 (BIA 1994) ("Once it is determined that an alien does not present a danger to the community or any bail risk, then no bond should be required."); *In re De La Cruz*, 20 I. & N. Dec. 346, 349 (BIA 1991) (same); *Matter of Patel*, 15 I. & N. Dec. 666 (BIA 1976) (same).

33. USA PATRIOT Act, supra note 51 at 412(a)(3) (amending 8 U.S.C. 1226A(a) (2001)).

34. 8 U.S.C. 1182(a)(3)(B)(i)(V) (2001).

35. See 8 U.S.C. 1227(a)(4)(B) (2001); 8 U.S.C. 1182(a)(3)(B)(iv)(IV), (VI) (2001).

36. 8 U.S.C.S. 1182(a)(3)(B)(iii)(V)(b) (Law. Co-op. 2002).

37. USA PATRIOT Act, supra note 21, at 218 (amending 50 U.S.C. 1804(a)(7)(B) and 1823(a)(7)(B) (2001)).

38. Gallup Poll, Do You Approve or Disapprove of the Use of "Racial Profiling" by Police? (Dec. 9, 1999), available at WESTLAW, USGALLUP.120999 R6 009.

39. See generally *David Harris, Profiles in Injustice: Why Racial Profiling Cannot Work* (2002).

40. Sam Howe Verhovek, A Nation Challenged: Civil Liberties; Americans Give in to Race Profiling, *N.Y. Times*, Sept. 23, 2001, at A1. A *Detroit News* poll of Michigan residents found that while "70 percent generally opposed racial profiling, 70 percent also agreed that 'authorities should take extra precautions in screening people of Arab descent when flying.'" Gregg Krupa, Most in State Support Screening of Arabs, *Detroit News*, Feb. 28, 2002, at A1.

41. Stuart Taylor, Jr., The Case for Using Racial Profiling at Airports, 33 *Nat'l J.* 38, (2001). Before September 11, Taylor wrote that:

> Racial profiling by police should be held to be unconstitutional . . . even where there is a statistically valid basis for believing that it will help catch more drug dealers or illegal immigrants. . . . The negative impact of such profiling is far reaching . . . it subjects thousands of innocent people to the kind of inconvenience and humiliation most of us associate with police states; and it makes law enforcement more difficult by fomenting fear and distrust among potential witnesses and jurors. These costs far outweigh any law enforcement benefits.
>
> Stuart Taylor, Jr., Cabbies, Cops, Pizza Deliveries, and Racial Profiling, 32 *Nat'l J.* 1891, (2000).

42. Fox Butterfield, A Nation Challenged: The Interviews; Police are Split on Questioning of Mideast Men, *N.Y. Times*, Nov. 22, 2001, at A1; Laurie Goodstein, A Nation Challenged: Civil Rights; American Sikhs Contend They Have Become a Focus of Profiling at Airports, *N.Y. Times*, Nov. 10, 2001, at B6; Neil A. Lewis, A Nation Challenged: Immigration Control; I.N.S. to Focus on Muslims Who Evade Deportation, *N.Y. Times*, Jan. 9, 2002, at A12; Edward Walsh, Abusive Behavior, or Racial Profiling?; Airline, Attorneys Dispute Incident, *Wash. Post*, Jan. 4, 2002, at A25.

43. Naftali Bendavid, Bush OK's Terror Tribunals; U.S. Seeks 5,000 Foreign Nationals for Questioning in Investigation, *Chi. Trib.*, Nov. 14, 2001, at 1.

44. Butterfield, *supra* note 42.

45. Dan Eggen & Cheryl W. Thompson, U.S. Seeks Thousands of Fugitive Deportees; Middle Eastern Men Are Focus of Search, *Wash. Post*, Jan. 8, 2002, at A1.

46. *Miller v. Johnson*, 515 U.S. 900, 904 (1995).

47. *Craig v. Boren*, 429 U.S. 190, 201-04 (1976).

48. Warren Hoge, A Nation Challenged: The Convert; Shoe-Bomb Suspect Fell in With Extremists, *N.Y. Times*, Dec. 27, 2001, at B6.

49. *Cf.* Malcolm Gladwell, Safety in the Skies; How Far Can Airline Security Go?, *New Yorker*, Oct. 1, 2001, at 50 (arguing that it is cognitively impossible to remain alert in reviewing metal detectors at airports because the fact that the vast majority of luggage will pose no threat inevitably causes security personnel to let their guard down).

50. *See* Detention, Treatment, and Trial of Certain Non-Citizens in the War Against Terrorism, 66 *Fed. Reg.* 57833 (Nov. 13, 2001).

51. *See generally* Ronald Dworkin, The Trouble with the Tribunals, *N.Y. Rev. of Books*, Apr. 25, 2002, at 10.

52. *Kwong Hai Chew v. Colding*, 344 U.S. 590, 596 n.5 (1953) (construing immigration regulation permitting exclusion of aliens on secret evidence not to apply to a returning permanent resident alien because of the substantial constitutional concerns that such an application would present).

53. *Yick Wo v. Hopkins*, 118 U.S. 356, 369 (1886).

54. *Zadvydas v. Davis*, 533 U.S. 678, 121 S. Ct. 2491, 2500 (2001); *see also Mathews v. Diaz*, 426 U.S. 67, 77 (1976) (holding that due process applies to all aliens in the United States, even those whose presence is "unlawful, involuntary, or transitory").

55. *Almeida-Sanchez v. United States*, 413 U.S. 266 (1973). *See also Bridges v. Wixon*, 326 U.S. 135, 161 (1945) (Murphy. J., concurring) (arguing that aliens are protected by the First, Fifth, and Fourteenth Amendments); *Wong Wing v. United States*, 163 U.S. 228 (1896) (holding that aliens charged with crimes are protected by the Fifth, Sixth, and Fourteenth Amendments); *Fong Yue Ting v. United States*, 149 U.S. 698. 724 (1893) (observing that aliens are entitled to all "the safeguards of the Constitution, and to the protection of the laws, in regard to their rights of person of property, and to their civil and criminal responsibility"); *Nishimura Ekiu v. United States*, 142 U.S. 651, 660 (1892) (noting that aliens have a constitutional right to invoke habeas corpus). Chief Justice Rehnquist suggested some limitation on the rights of some aliens in the United States in his plurality opinion in *United States v. Verdugo-Urquidez*, 494 U.S. 259, 271 (1990), in which he suggested that an alien who had been involuntarily brought into this country for criminal prosecution was not part of "the people" eligible to invoke the Fourth Amendment. However, he was unable to garner a majority for that view, and Justice Kennedy, whose vote was necessary to the majority in that case, expressly rejected Rehnquist's suggestion that the Fourth Amendment did not extend to all persons present in the United States. 494 U.S. at 276-77 (Kennedy, J., concurring). Kennedy rested instead on the fact that the search took place beyond our borders, a factor also relied upon by Rehnquist. *Id.* at 278.

56. *See generally* Suzanna Sherry, The Founders' Unwritten Constitution, 54 *U. Chi. L. Rev.* 1127 (1987). The debate that accompanied the enactment and ultimate demise of the Alien and Sedition Acts suggests that there was in fact substantial disagreement about the status of aliens' rights in the early years of the republic, at least in a time of crisis. In debating the Alien Act, critics, mostly Republicans, pointed to the broad language of the Bill of Rights and the legal obligations we imposed on all persons residing within our territory as support for the notion that aliens were entitled to the protection of the Bill of Rights. Others, mostly Federalists, maintained that the Constitution was a more limited document that protected only "we the people." See Gerald L. Neuman, Strangers to the Constitution: Immigrants, Borders, and Fundamental Law 52-63 (1996). But as with the Sedition Act, so with the Alien Act, those espousing the more inclusive, rights-protective views ultimately prevailed. Cf. *N.Y. Times Co. v. Sullivan*, 376 U.S. 254, 273-76 (1964) (relying on history of repudiation of Sedition Act as evidence for importance of protecting political dissent under First Amendment).

57. The preamble to the Universal Declaration of Human Rights states: "Whereas recognition of the inherent dignity and of the equal and inalienable rights of all members of the human family is the foundation of freedom, justice and peace in the world. . . ." G.A. Res. 217A(III), U.N. GAOR, 3d. Sess., Supp. No. 13, at 71, U.N. Doc. A/810 (1948).

58. *Palko v. Connecticut*, 302 U.S. 319, 325 (1937).

59. Alexander M. Bickel, *The Morality of Consent* 33-54 (1975).

60. 60 U.S. (19 How.) 393 (1856).

61. *Id.* at 403.

62. *Id.* at 404–405. The Court eerily echoed this statement almost 100 years later when it held that an alien seeking admission to the country, and in detention on Ellis Island, could assert no constitutional objection to the fact that she was being excluded on the basis of secret evidence that she had no opportunity to confront because "whatever the procedure authorized by Congress is, it is due process as far as an alien denied entry is concerned." *United States ex rel. Knauff v. Shaugnessy*, 338 U.S. 537, 544 (1950).

63. Civil Rights Act of 1866, Ch. 31, 1, 14 Stat. 27.

64. Bickel, *supra* note 59, at 53.

65. *Mathews v. Diaz*, 426 U.S. 67, 80 (1976).

66. *Zadvydas*, 121 S. Ct. at 2500.

67. *Ludecke v. Watkins*, 335 U.S. 160 (1948). See 50 U.S.C.
21-24 (2002).

68. *Brandenburg v. Ohio*, 395 U.S. 444 (1969).

69. See Senate Judiciary Committee Hearing on Anti-
Terrorism Policy, *supra* note 1.

Questions for Analysis

1. Identify the use of slippery slope reasoning in Cole's arguments that we should not sacrifice liberty in the name of security. Is this reasoning persuasive in today's post-9/11 world?

2. Identify the consequentialist or utilitarian reasoning used by the U.S. government to justify increased restrictions on noncitizens, especially in the USA Patriot Act.

3. Cole relies extensively on appeals to basic human rights, a Kantian approach to ethical reasoning. What are the bases for believing these human rights exist? How are these rights the same and how are they different for citizens and nonci-tizens? Is this approach to the issues persuasive in overcoming the consequentialist appeal to security?

4. Cole also sometimes appeals to consequentialist reasoning in supporting his positions. Is this effective in addressing our very real interest in security today?

CASE PRESENTATION

Preemptive War

President George W. Bush has articulated a new strat-egy of "preemptive war," a marked change from the previous U.S. policy of deterrence to war and the use of force only in self-defense. *The National Security Strategy of the United States of America*, issued by President Bush on September 17, 2002, explains pre-emptive war as a way to "Prevent Our Enemies from Threatening Us, Our Allies, and Our Friends with Weapons of Mass Destruction":

> The nature of the Cold War threat required the United States—with our allies and friends—to emphasize deterrence of the enemy's use of force, producing a grim strategy of mutual assured destruction. With the collapse of the Soviet Union and the end of the Cold War, our security environment has undergone profound transformation. . . .

But new deadly challenges have emerged from rogue states and terrorists. None of these contemporary threats rival the sheer destructive power that was arrayed against us by the Soviet Union. However, the nature and motivations of these new adversaries, their determination to obtain destructive powers hitherto available only to the world's strongest states, and the greater likelihood that they will use weapons of mass destruction against us, make today's security environment more complex and dangerous.

In the 1990s we witnessed the emergence of a small number of rogue states that, while different in important ways, share a number of attributes. These states:

- brutalize their own people and squander their national resources for the personal gain of the rulers;

- display no regard for international law, threaten their neighbors, and callously violate international treaties to which they are party;

- are determined to acquire weapons of mass destruction, along with other advanced military technology, to be used as threats or offensively to achieve the aggressive designs of these regimes;

- sponsor terrorism around the globe; and

- reject basic human values and hate the United States and everything for which it stands.

At the time of the Gulf War, we acquired irrefutable proof that Iraq's designs were not limited to the chemical weapons it had used against Iran and its own people, but also extended to the acquisition of nuclear weapons and biological agents. In the past decade North Korea has become the world's principal purveyor of ballistic missiles, and has tested increasingly capable missiles while developing its own WMD arsenal. Other rogue regimes seek nuclear, biological, and chemical weapons as well. These states' pursuit of, and global trade in, such weapons has become a looming threat to all nations.

We must be prepared to stop rogue states and their terrorist clients before they are able to threaten or use weapons of mass destruction against the United States and our allies and friends. Our response must take full advantage of strengthened alliances, the establishment of new partnerships with former adversaries, innovation in the use of military forces, modern technologies, including the development of an effective missile defense system, and increased emphasis on intelligence collection and analysis. . . .

It has taken almost a decade for us to comprehend the true nature of this new threat. Given the goals of rogue states and terrorists, the United States can no longer solely rely on a reactive posture as we have in the past. The inability to deter a potential attacker, the immediacy of today's threats, and the magnitude of potential harm that could be caused by our adversaries' choice of weapons, do not permit that option. We cannot let our enemies strike first.

In the Cold War, especially following the Cuban missile crisis, we faced a generally status quo, risk-averse adversary. Deterrence was an effective defense. But deterrence based only upon the threat of retaliation is less likely to work against leaders of rogue states more willing to take risks, gambling with the lives of their people, and the wealth of their nations.

- In the Cold War, weapons of mass destruction were considered weapons of last resort whose use risked the destruction of those who used them. Today, our enemies see weapons of mass destruction as weapons of choice. For rogue states these weapons are tools of intimidation and military aggression against their neighbors. These weapons may also allow these states to attempt to blackmail the United States and our allies to prevent us from deterring or repelling the aggressive behavior of rogue states. Such states also see these weapons as their best means of overcoming the conventional superiority of the United States.

- Traditional concepts of deterrence will not work against a terrorist enemy whose avowed tactics are wanton destruction and the targeting of innocents; whose so-called soldiers seek martyrdom in death and whose most potent protection is statelessness. The overlap between states that sponsor terror and those that pursue WMD compels us to action.

For centuries, international law recognized that nations need not suffer an attack before they can lawfully take action to defend themselves against forces that present an imminent danger of attack. Legal scholars and international jurists often conditioned the legitimacy of preemption on the existence of an imminent threat—most often a visible mobilization of armies, navies, and air forces preparing to attack.

We must adapt the concept of imminent threat to the capabilities and objectives of today's adversaries. Rogue states and terrorists do not seek to attack us using conventional means. They know such attacks would fail. Instead, they rely on acts of terror and, potentially, the use of weapons of mass destruction—weapons that can be easily concealed, delivered covertly, and used without warning.

The targets of these attacks are our military forces and our civilian population, in direct violation of one of the principal norms of the law of warfare. As was demonstrated by the losses on September 11, 2001, mass civilian casualties is the specific objective of terrorists and these losses would be exponentially more severe if terrorists acquired and used weapons of mass destruction.

The United States has long maintained the option of preemptive actions to counter a sufficient threat to our national security. The greater the threat, the greater is the risk of inaction—and the more compelling the case for taking anticipatory action to defend ourselves, even if uncertainty remains as to the time and place of the enemy's attack. To forestall or prevent such hostile acts by our adversaries, the United States will, if necessary, act preemptively.

The United States will not use force in all cases to preempt emerging threats, nor should nations use preemption as a pretext for aggression. Yet in an age where the enemies of civilization openly and actively seek the world's most destructive technologies, the United States cannot remain idle while dangers gather. We will always proceed deliberately, weighing the consequences of our actions. To support preemptive options, we will:

- build better, more integrated intelligence capabilities to provide timely, accurate

information on threats, wherever they may emerge;

- coordinate closely with allies to form a common assessment of the most dangerous threats; and

- continue to transform our military forces to ensure our ability to conduct rapid and precise operations to achieve decisive results.

The purpose of our actions will always be to eliminate a specific threat to the United States or our allies and friends. The reasons for our actions will be clear, the force measured, and the cause just.

Questions for Analysis

1. President Bush states that preemptive war will be used only for a cause that is "just." How does he understand "just cause" from his statements here? Do his tests for when he would initiate preemptive war meet the traditional standards for just war?

2. Does his justification for preemptive war meet the tests for just war in David Luban's analysis based on human rights?

3. Can you think of other circumstances in our nation's history when a preemptive war would have been justified but was not initiated?

4. Are there circumstances in the world today in which preemptive war would be justified under the president's rationale? What arguments could be raised against engaging in such war?

CASE PRESENTATION
Driving While Veiled

In March 2002, an ultraorthodox Muslim woman, Sultaana Lakiana Myke Freeman, filed suit in Florida, claiming that the state's requirement that her photograph for her driver's license must be taken without her veil violated her "religious belief that her religion requires her to wear her veil in front of strangers and unrelated males." She argued that the state's revocation and cancellation of her driver's license because of her refusal to have her photograph taken without a veil violated her "religious freedom, freedom of speech, due process, equal protection and right to privacy."

After a trial in May 2003, a Florida court rejected her claim that the photographic requirement was an undue burden on the exercise of her religion:" . . . the

State apparently has a practice of accommodating Muslim women holding similar beliefs on veiling. A DHSMV [Department of Highway Safety and Motor Vehicles] manager testified that in several instances, upon appointment, DHSMV employees have escorted women to a private room, with only a female license examiner present. No males were allowed, and the room had no windows through which anyone could see. The State argued that the 'momentary' lifting of the veil in order to complete the digitalized image or photo, done in 'private circumstances' as described, does not constitute a substantial burden on Plaintiff's right to free exercise of religion. The State asserted that Plaintiff would be free to place the photo license in her pocket and never show it to anyone, except perhaps to law enforcement officers in specific situations. The Court agrees, and finds that given Plaintiff's own testimony plus the State's willingness to accommodate Plaintiff to the degree stated, the momentary raising of her veil for the purpose of the ID photo does not constitute a 'substantial burden' on her right to exercise her religion."

The court agreed with the argument of the state of Florida ". . . that when religious practices collide with public safety, public safety must prevail. . . . The State called an expert witness who has been employed in law enforcement for almost 40 years and is currently a consultant to DHSMV on security matters. He stated that a facial image is 'absolutely essential' to law enforcement officers, because without it, officers conducting traffic stops are at risk during the extra time needed to check identities to 'make sure that's the person standing in front of them.' He emphasized that it is crucial to both criminal and intelligence investigators to be able to identify possible suspects (and victims of crimes or accidents) as quickly as possible, and that this ability has a significant impact on public safety."

The court also rejected her argument ". . . that photo IDs are largely flawed and can easily be thwarted by people who change their hair, cover their foreheads and ears, wear large glasses, shave their heads, grow their beards, or alter their appearance by other means, including contact lenses and plastic surgery. She stressed that some people have aged years since their license photo was taken and for that reason alone look different from the image on the license. Plaintiff also claimed that religious hairstyles and headwear are permitted for persons of other faiths, and suggested that she is being singled out because she is Muslim." The state responded, ". . . some facial features do not change, despite changes in the individual's style or age, and that photographic images of drivers evidencing some differences are still of greater value than an image with facial features completely blocked by a mask or a veil."

The Court acknowledged ". . . that today it is a different world than it was 20–25 years ago. It would be foolish not to recognize that there are new threats to public safety, including both foreign and domestic terrorism, and increased potential for 'widespread abuse' that did not exist . . ." before. But, the Court insisted, "Plaintiff is not being singled out because she is Muslim. This Court would rule the same way for anyone—Christian, Jew, Buddhist, Atheist—who wished to have his or her driver's license identification photo taken while wearing anything—ski mask, costume mask, religious veil, hood—which cloaks all facial features except the eyes. Plaintiff's veiling practices must be subordinated to society's need to identify people as quickly as possible in situations in which safety and security of others could be at risk."

Questions for Analysis

1. The judge rejected an argument by the state of Florida that most Muslim women do not wear veils and that she was part of a very small minority. Would you agree that this should be irrelevant in this case? If the vast majority of women in Florida wanted to wear veils when obtaining their driver's licenses, do you think the state of Florida would change its position on the issues here?

2. Before 9/11, Illinois, and later Florida, had issued her a driver's license showing her wearing the veil. Only after 9/11 did the state of Florida send her a notice that if she did not agree to have her photograph taken without the veil, her license would be revoked. Does this sequence of events suggest that Florida was singling her out for discriminatory treatment because of terrorist fears? If Florida's concern was "public safety" and effective law enforcement, why wasn't it concerned before 9/11?

3. In her arguments to the court, plaintiff noted a precedent, a 1984 decision, *Quaring v. Peterson*, in which a Pentecostal Christian woman refused to have her picture taken for a Nebraska driver's license because she believed that it would constitute making a graven image. The court found that denying the woman her license did not serve a compelling state interest. How, if at all, is this case different, and should the Florida court have followed the same reasoning?

4. Can you think of other religious or cultural forms of dress that might interfere with the full facial photograph required by Florida? Should those be allowed?

5. Using the reasoning of this Florida decision, should she also be required to provide a full facial photograph, without her veil, if she applies for a passport? An employee ID for a job? A photo ID for medical insurance coverage? If she flies on an airplane and airport security needs to compare her photo ID with her actual face, should she have to comply before boarding the airplane? How can her religious beliefs be balanced against these other societal interests in security?

CASE PRESENTATION
Fear of Flying

On the evening of September 11, 2001, Secretary of Transportation Norman Y. Mineta issued a statement that "In a democracy, there is always a balance between freedom and security. Our transportation systems, reflecting the values of our society, have always operated in an open and accessible manner. And, they will again." Two months later, Congress established the Transportation Security Administration (TSA) to take over all security at the nation's airports. While many members of the flying public seem to think professionalism and security have improved at the airports, others complain of what they perceive to be silly random searches of elderly grandmothers and very young children with plastic toy guns. The TSA continually announces new security problems, including ballpoint pens that hide sharp weapons and bombs made of plastic materials that are difficult to detect. Newspaper reports tell of continuing security breaches with potentially lethal weapons somehow brought past security checks onto the planes.

Despite continuing security breaches, Mineta insisted that airport screeners should not use any kind of racial profiling in identifying persons for special searches, including persons who might "appear to be of Arab, Middle Eastern or south Asian descent and/or Muslim." Mineta himself was one of the 120,000 Americans interned by the U.S. government during World War II, and he has been adamant in his public statements that this nation should not ever again practice such discrimination against anyone solely because of nationality, ancestry, or appearance. Critics of airport security complain that limited resources should be focused on the persons most likely to be 9/11 hijackers and point out that all nineteen were men of Middle Eastern descent.

Questions for Analysis

1. If you were designing an appropriate security system for the nation's airports, how would you focus limited resources to make it most likely that you would catch persons who planned terrorist attacks on airports and airplanes? Would you single out any particular type of person for special searches to protect the flying public? On what basis would you justify these special searches? Can your security plan be criticized for engaging in such fallacies as hasty generalization or faulty analogy? What criticisms could be raised of your security plan?

2. No terrorist attacks have occurred in the United States using airplanes since 9/11. Air travel has increased after dropping off dramatically right after 9/11. Fear of flying because of concerns over terrorism has steadily declined. Do these consequences show that the current airport security system is the best approach for the nation? Are the inconveniences to ordinary citizens and the element of risk with continued security breaches outweighed by the respect for human

rights in the current approach that rejects singling out men of Middle Eastern descent during security searches at airports?

3. Some of Mineta's critics charged that his personal experiences during World War II made him unable to render objective decisions on airport security after 9/11. Is this an example of an *ad hominem* argument? Is this a justifiable criticism of Mineta's approach to airport security?

CASE PRESENTATION
Racial Profiling before and after 9/11

Before 9/11, extensive publicity about racial profiling in the "war on drugs" that focused on persons of African American and Latino descent aroused public criticism and outcry. After 9/11, many who had previously criticized this practice seemed to change positions to support some profiling, especially to identify potential terrorists in our midst.

When John Ashcroft, now the attorney general, was a senator from Missouri, he made this statement at hearings on racial profiling in the U.S. Senate in 1999:

Racial profiling is the use of race either as the sole predictor or one element in a group of predictors of potential illegal or criminal activity that justify traffic stops or border searches or airport detentions. It is a subject of growing public debate, particularly in recent months.

It is appropriate for this subcommittee to hold a hearing on this subject because it has clear constitutional implications. Our Constitution's 14th Amendment guarantees all persons the equal protection of the law, and the Supreme Court has made clear that any consideration of race by government officials, except in the narrowest of circumstances, is inconsistent with the 14th Amendment's guarantee of equal protection.

As applied to today's inquiry, while it is undoubtedly permissible to use a particular criminal suspect's race as an identifier, using race broadly as a profiler in lieu of individualized suspicion is, I believe, an unconstitutional practice. In other words, if I am mugged by a Caucasian male 6 foot 7 and 230 pounds, the police consider that, and they are entitled to and should consider that suspect's race in looking for the man who mugged me. What they cannot constitutionally do, in my judgment, is to start pulling over all caucasians in the future because they believe that they commit a disproportionate number of muggings.

Today, we will hear testimony about various serious allegations that traffic stops and other detentions happen on the basis of race, though there are differing points of view about the prevalence of the practice. Some will provide evidence that the practice is very prevalent and others that it is the result of random misdeeds in the law enforcement community.

We will also hear about the proposed legislation, the Traffic Stops Statistics Study Act, which is designed to try and find out exactly the extent or how large the problem is. That legislation is sponsored in the Senate by the ranking member of this subcommittee, my friend Senator Feingold, and Senator Lautenberg, who I am pleased is on our first panel today, and by Congressman Conyers in the House. We do need to find out how big the issue is, and I think the concepts included in the Traffic Stops Statistics Study Act represent a good start. I have some suggestions on how I think it could be improved. In particular, I would respectfully suggest that the statute make clear that the Attorney General's study of State and local law enforcement traffic stop data would be made from data collected voluntarily by those departments. It is my understanding that it is the intent of the bill, but I think the legislation would be well served to make that explicit by way of clarification.

Second, there are a few areas where I think that the data collected by the Attorney General should be expanded in order to get as full a picture as possible of what is happening on our highways and streets. In addition to the current provision that the Attorney General collect data about the traffic infraction alleged to have been committed that led to the stop, the Attorney General should consider any other factors supporting the officer's decision to make a traffic stop.

In addition, I think that it would be useful for the Attorney General to consider factors such as the race of the officer making the stop, the racial composition of the area in which the stop was made, and any other factors that will give us as full a picture as possible as to how officers are conducting traffic stops.

Finally, I think it would be beneficial to explain that nothing in this bill changes any burdens of proof for parties in litigation. It is my hope that Senator Feingold and the other Senate cosponsors will consider these suggestions because I think that with these changes, I could have the opportunity to completely support the measure. In any event, regardless of the prevalence of racial profiling, the mere fact that these allegations exist troubles me greatly. It troubles me not only for the constitutional implications that it raises, but also for the extraordinarily destructive effect that such allegations would have on the confidence of people in Government. A necessary component of our system of Government is public trust. No system of government, of the people, by the people, and for the people can long endure if some of the people have no confidence in the fairness of that government. So long as whole groups of our citizens believe that there is a two-tiered system of treatment by Government officials arbitrarily divided by race, they won't have confidence in that system. They will understandably conclude that if Government is improperly

motivated by race in some circumstances, it might be improperly motivated by race in all circumstances.

This is particularly true if that perception is held of law enforcement, the very Government agency entrusted with protecting citizens from injustice. Such an erosion of trust would not only undermine the ability of law enforcement officers to do their jobs, it would undermine any efforts that we in Government make to try and improve the lives of all Americans through Government.

With this in mind, the purpose of this hearing today is threefold: first, to raise public awareness of the issue regarding racial profiling; second, to discuss what we might do legislatively to understand more fully the extent of that problem; and, third, and most importantly, to try to restore some of the lost confidence and trust of some Americans by demonstrating that Government can work to correct any abuses that are even its own.[1]

---

1. "Racial Profiling within Law Enforcement Agencies," Hearing before the Subcommittee on the Constitution, Federalism, and Property Rights of the Committee on the Judiciary, United States Senate, S. Hrg. 106-996, 106th Cong., 2d sess., March 30, 2000.

Questions for Analysis

1. Before 9/11, would you have agreed with then-Senator Ashcroft on the injustice of racial profiling? Have your views changed because of 9/11? If they have, what considerations justify changing your views?

2. According to David Cole's discussion of ethnic profiling, the Department of Justice (now headed by Attorney General John Ashcroft) singled out for questioning some 5,000 young immigrants from mostly Arab nations two months after 9/11. Is this practice consistent with the statement against racial profiling Ashcroft made in 1999? Can this practice be justified consistently with our legal and ethical rights?

3. Given that all of the 9/11 hijackers were men of Middle Eastern descent, are we justified in concluding that all men of Middle Eastern descent are likely terrorists? As there are no recorded instances of terrorists who were grandmothers of Scandinavian descent, are we justified in concluding that men of Middle Eastern descent are more likely to be terrorists than grandmothers of Scandinavian descent? What informal fallacies are at issue in drawing these conclusions?

4. Does racial profiling today instill more or less trust in the government?

9

Welfare and
Social Justice

Although the U.S. presidential campaign of 1992 was waged over many issues, perhaps the most memorable campaign promise came from the eventual winner, Democrat Bill Clinton, who pledged to "end welfare as we know it." By "welfare," he meant Aid to Families with Dependent Children (AFDC), a program of assistance for low-income, single parents that dates back to Franklin Roosevelt's New Deal of the 1930s. And by ending "welfare as we know it," Clinton meant changing the program rather than abolishing it. Two particular changes were key to his plan: (1) to provide job training for welfare recipients and (2) to set a two-year limit on the time they could spend on welfare. If at the end of two years the welfare recipient could not find a job in the private sector, she would have to accept a community service job from the government or be left to her own devices.

Clinton's proposal marked a sharp turnaround from the legacy of Lyndon Johnson's Great Society of the 1960s. Not only did Johnson greatly expand AFDC, but he also instituted a number of other anti-poverty programs, including Medicaid, food stamps,

Head Start, and a variety of housing programs for the poor. The reasons for the turn-around are many, but they can be quickly summarized: For a small but significant por-tion of welfare recipients, AFDC did not seem to be working as intended.

From its inception, AFDC was always intended as a temporary helping hand to single mothers and their children. In Roosevelt's time, that meant widows and orphans in the vast majority of cases. Over the years, however, it came to mean an increasing number of women whose husbands had left them, and then, more recently, a startling rise in the number of mothers who had never been married. Many of these unwed mothers were teenaged, poor, and undereducated, and some con-tinued to have children out of wedlock. The result in such cases came to be known as welfare dependence. Rather than serving as a temporary helping hand for these young single mothers, AFDC became a way of life.

That was the problem Clinton's proposal was meant to solve. His goal, then, was not to end welfare but to end welfare dependence. And on August 22, 1996, Clinton signed into law a bill that did abolish AFDC, replacing it with a program called Temporary Assistance for Needy Families (TANF). For the first time in six decades, the federal government would no longer guarantee welfare payments to needy families. Instead, it would supply block grants (lump-sum payments) to the states and allow them considerable freedom in setting welfare policy. The new law also placed restrictions on length of benefits, setting a five-year limit per family and requiring recipients to find work within two years. These are maximum limits. States are free to require recipients to find work in a shorter time, and they are also free to limit duration on welfare to fewer years.

Much controversy surrounds the new law. While most attention goes to crit-ics who charge that the law is too harsh, other critics charge that the law does not go far enough. Some have called for the abolition of other anti-poverty programs. What these critics object to is a whole class of programs known as *transfer payments*.

TRANSFER PAYMENTS

AFDC was one of many federal programs that relied on transfer payments to help the needy. A **transfer payment**, as the term implies, involves the transfer of wealth from one segment of the population to another through taxation and dispersal. In the case of AFDC, the transfer payment came in the form of cash benefits. Other cash benefits included earned income tax credits, which provided generous tax refunds to the working poor, and Supplemental Security Income. But in other cases, benefits came in the form of such services as medical care (for instance, Medicaid and community health centers), low-rent public housing, food (from programs like food stamps and the School Lunch Program), job training, and edu-cation (Head Start and Pell grants, for instance).

TANF continues to provide many cash benefits, while also requiring participa-tion in Work First programs and limiting participation to no more than five years. Comparisons with previous cash outlays under AFDC are difficult, as much of the TANF funding is provided in block grants to the states, with considerable discretion on how they use the funds. Funds are typically provided for childcare expenses, education costs, job training, transportation, housing vouchers, and food stamps. Medicaid, however, is not available to all families in TANF, but only to those who would have been eligible under the old AFDC eligibility rules. In some cases, subsidies are provided to employers who hire persons in the TANF program. The federal government also provided $100 million in bonus grants to five states with the largest decrease in the percentage of births to unwed mothers from 1995 to 1998. Bonuses also have been paid to the states with the best improvement in such measures as job entry, job retention, and earnings gains by participants in TANF.[1]

In a report to Congress in 2001, the Congressional Research Service reported that families on welfare had plunged 50 percent since TANF was enacted in 1996 but also noted that this was assisted by the strong economy in those years. In June 2000, 2.208 million families were participating in TANF, down 2.9 million (57 percent) from the record-high level in AFDC in 1994, when 5.084 million families received benefits. The number of people receiving food stamps also declined dramatically from 28 million in 1994, the peak year, to 17 million in 2000, a 39 percent drop. The percentage of women with children in the work force has also increased from 62 percent in 1994 to 75 percent in 1999, a 21 percent increase.

In extensive congressional hearings on the renewal of TANF, many positive results were reported, along with some concerns.[2] Many people have now used their entire lifetime benefits of five years provided under TANF, and critics worry that they will slip into extreme poverty without government help, especially in a period with declining employment opportunities. According to the U.S. Department of Commerce, the nation's official poverty rate rose from 11.7 percent in 2001 (32.9 million people) to 12.1 percent in 2002 (34.6 million people).[3] The Census Bureau defined poverty in 2002, for one adult and one child, as $12,400 per year, and for one adult and two children as $14,494. Critics of TANF note that, despite its success in moving people off welfare, it has not succeeded in bringing people out of poverty. In all but a few states, the rate of unwed births has increased since the passage of TANF, not decreased. It also appears that many of the people remaining in TANF have serious health problems, including mental health problems, and are unable to work at any job.

The original TANF was set to expire on September 30, 2002, but Congress could not agree on revisions, so it simply extended the existing legislation. As of fall 2003, Congress still had not resolved disagreements, such as whether to increase the work requirement to forty hours per week, from the previous thirty hours, and the amount of support to provide for childcare to working mothers in the program.

DOES WELFARE WORK?

Franklin Roosevelt's New Deal was a response to the Great Depression, which at its depth saw as much as a third of the nation's labor force unemployed. Lyndon Johnson's Great Society, on the other hand, came during a period of national prosperity. It was inspired in part by a particular book, Michael Harrington's *The Other America*. Harrington's central thesis was that certain segments of the U.S. population are so

1.   Vee Burke, "IB93034: Welfare Reform: An Issue Overview," Congressional Research Service, March 15, 2001.

2.   Hearing on Welfare Reform, Subcommittee on Human Resources of the Committee on Ways and Means, House of Representatives, 107th Cong., 1st Sess., March 15, 2001.

3.   "Poverty, Income See Slight Changes; Child Poverty Rate Unchanged, Census Bureau Reports," *U.S Department of Commerce News*, September 26, 2003.

economically depressed that they constitute pockets of poverty that remain unaffected by economic growth in the country as a whole. The economy expands, new jobs are created, but people trapped in these pockets of poverty remain unemployed and poor. If they are to be lifted out of poverty, the government must help them through specific programs.

In the 1980s, another influential book came along with a conflicting message. That book was Charles Murray's *Losing Ground,* which argued that anti-poverty programs like the Great Society's actually encourage poverty rather than fight it. Part of his argument was statistical. Although the Great Society showed initial success in reducing poverty, the progress soon stopped. As benefits increased in the 1970s, the book argued, so did the number of people whose income placed them below the poverty line. The number of births to unwed mothers also rose during that time, as did the number of households headed by single women. Most disturbingly, the largest rise in single-woman households was among the poor.

Of course, such statistics lend themselves to a variety of interpretations. Why blame welfare programs for the rise in poverty and single-female households? Murray's answer is this: In certain circumstances, it is *rational* for a young, pregnant woman to keep her child and go on welfare. Suppose she is undereducated and comes from a poor family that wants her out of the house. Suppose further that she wants to leave the house as much as her family wants her out. If she aborts her pregnancy or gives the child up for adoption, she will have to support herself with a minimum-wage job. But if she keeps the child and goes on AFDC, she also gets her own apartment in addition to many other benefits. What about marrying the baby's father? That option is not always available, of course, but even when it is, she may be economically better off remaining single and accepting welfare. In either case, accepting welfare is the rational choice.

Murray's book proved to be highly controversial. For one thing, critics charge, it assumes that women bear out-of-wedlock children for economic benefit when many other factors, psychological and social, may be at work. Critics also argue that it plays down other causes of poverty, from racism to changes in the American economy, and that it also plays down the enormous good welfare accomplishes for the many women who use it as a temporary helping hand while they prepare to support themselves and their children in the workplace. In addition, many critics dispute Murray's analysis of the statistics.

Equally controversial is Murray's concluding "thought experiment," which portrays an optimistic picture of a future in which federal welfare programs have been totally eliminated. Still, the book focused attention on important questions that never quite go away: What do we want from welfare programs? Who should benefit from them? Why have welfare at all? Does welfare advance the cause of justice or hinder it?

WHY HAVE WELFARE?

Through most of U.S. history, the question of welfare rarely, if ever, arose. Help for the needy was expected to come from such private sources as charities, churches, and families. The turning point was the Great Depression, and two of the most important reasons advanced were compassion and social stability. With the economy unable to produce enough jobs, a great number of willing and able workers found themselves unemployed through no fault of their own, and private sources could not provide sufficient aid. To many Americans, the situation was intolerable. Something had to be done, both to help the victims of the Depression and to prevent unprecedented social upheaval. The only place to look, they felt, was the federal government.

Despite the widely shared sense of emergency, Roosevelt's New Deal legislation produced considerable debate. With its regulations on industry and banking as well as its social welfare programs, it greatly expanded the role of government. Critics charged that individual rights were being violated, property rights in particular, and that the New Deal amounted to "creeping socialism." (In fact, many New Deal programs had long been advocated by the American Socialist Party.) Helping people at the expense of individual rights, these critics argued, was unjust. New Deal proponents, on the other hand, argued that failing to provide the needed measures was unjust.

As with many issues in this book, the competing views turn on differing conceptions of justice. In the case of welfare and other transfer payments, it is a matter of economic justice, also called **distributive justice**. How should the wealth of society be distributed?

DISTRIBUTIVE JUSTICE

In Part 1, we looked at various principles of social justice, many of which bear on the question of distributive justice and welfare. In this section and those that follow, we will see how.

The Entitlement Conception of Justice

When discussing individual rights in Part 1, we noted the influence of the English philosopher John Locke on the U.S. Founding Fathers. According to Locke, we are born with the natural rights to life, liberty, and property, which we are free to exercise as long as we do not interfere with the natural rights of others. We are also born with the natural right to protect those three rights. In joining together to create a government, we transfer certain powers to society as a whole. That is, the government acts as our agent in exercising those powers. Because we cannot transfer to the government any powers that are not rightfully ours, the role of government is severely limited. We can transfer powers of protection—police and judicial powers, most notably—but not the power to interfere with the individual property rights of others.

How does this bear on welfare and distributive justice? According to Robert Nozick, whom we also considered in Part 1, the answer is simple: Welfare is beyond the rightful powers of government. Since no one has a natural right to force others to give to charity, we cannot transfer that power to society as a whole. However well intentioned, transfer payments are no different from ordinary theft. To demand on threat of imprisonment that individuals pay taxes to support such programs is equivalent to holding a gun to their heads and demanding that they give to our favorite charities.

On this view, then, government should not be in the business of distributing wealth at all. Wealth is not, as Nozick puts it, "manna from heaven." It does not magically appear from the sky, belonging to no one. Instead, society's wealth already belongs to particular individuals who came by it either honestly or dishonestly, through either the legitimate exercise of their natural rights or the violation of the natural rights of others. If they came by it dishonestly, they should be punished and their ill-gotten gains returned to the rightful owners. Otherwise, it is rightfully theirs. They alone are *entitled* to it, and no one, including the government, has the right to take it away from them without their consent. Thus, Nozick calls his view the **entitlement** conception of justice.

Justice as Fairness

We also looked at the views of John Rawls in Part 1. Rawls rejects the notion of natural rights. To him, social justice is a matter of fairness, in which case the just distribution of wealth is the fairest distribution. How do we decide on the fairest distribution?

Rawls's answer goes like this: Societies operate according to certain fundamental rules, and it is up to the members of society to set those rules. One such fundamental rule governs the distribution of wealth. If the rule is to be fair, it must give no member of society unfair advantage over any other members. And we can guarantee that outcome by requiring that the rule be acceptable to all members of society without knowing how the rule will work out for them. That is, they will know how wealth will be distributed among different segments of the population but not which segment they will belong to. In that case, they must be willing to accept the rule no matter what segment they will belong to.

Would an entitlement rule like Nozick's pass that test? Rawls says no because it allows for unacceptably large gaps between rich and poor. We would not know whether we will have the high-paying jobs that will make us wealthy or the low-paying jobs that will leave us unable to support our families. Nor would we know whether we will find ourselves impoverished due to a sudden loss of work or some other catastrophe. As long as we don't know where we will end up, we will demand a rule that allows every member of society a sufficient share of the wealth.

One way to accomplish this goal (Rawls's preferred way) is through transfer payments. Those nearer to the top will be taxed to supplement the incomes of the poor.

EQUALITY, NEED, AND MERIT

If we accept the justice of transfer payments, we still have to determine how generous to make the payments and under what circumstances to pay them out. That is, we will need to select a *principle* of distribution. The three most commonly cited are the principles of equality, need, and merit.

Equality

According to the **equality principle** of distribution, everyone in society ought to end up with an equal share of the wealth. Why choose this principle? Because, proponents say, when it comes to sharing the wealth, all humans deserve to be treated equally. The fact that someone is better looking than the norm (or a better athlete or musician), or lucky enough to be born into a wealthy family (or marry into one), does not make that person more deserving of wealth than others less fortunate. In that case, taxes and transfer payments should be set at rates that guarantee an equal distribution of wealth for all.

Whatever initial appeal this principle may have, at least one problem is readily apparent for those who advocate it. An equal distribution of wealth can lead to significant inequalities among individual lives. Consider healthcare, for example. To achieve real equality between a healthy person and a person with kidney failure, say, the second will need far greater benefits than the first to cover the cost of dialysis. The same consideration also applies to many other areas of life, such as education. It costs far more to educate a child with serious learning disabilities than a child without them. That's why many transfers come in the form of services rather than cash benefits, to accommodate the differing needs of different individuals. It is also why people who lean toward equal distribution usually adopt a different but related principle as well—the principle of need.

Need

According to the principle of need, everyone has an equal right to have his or her economic needs satisfied, and wealth should therefore be distributed according to the economic needs of society's members. Advocates of this principle often combine it with the principle of equality. *Basic* needs like food, housing, education, and medical care are to be taken care of according to individual need, and the remaining wealth is to be distributed equally. Other advocates demand only that everyone's basic needs be met without asking for further redistribution. In both cases, the justification of the principle of need is the same. When it comes to basic needs, everyone deserves to be treated equally. No one's basic needs should go unmet.

Opponents of both principles—need and equality—cite a variety of objections. First, of course, there are Nozick's moral arguments that government should not be in the business of redistributing wealth at all. Other objections are more practical. Rawls, for example, argues that certain inequalities ought to be allowed because they are to everyone's advantage, even those at the bottom. If we are to have an adequate supply of surgeons, for example, we must compensate them for their years spent in medical school. Many critics also argue that distribution according to need and equality discourages hard work. Why put in extra hours if we will earn no extra compensation? Indeed, why work at all if the government will take care of our basic needs and guarantee us an income equal to the income of those who do work? And even if the government guarantees our basic needs only, won't many people see that as sufficient reason not to work?

What's missing, these objectors say, is recognition of individual *merit*. Those who deserve more wealth than others—those who have earned it—should have it.

Merit

The appeal of merit as a principle of distributing wealth is more than merely practical. To many people, it is a matter of simple justice. Why should Mary, who works to support herself and her family, pay taxes on her hard-earned income so that John, a total stranger who refuses to work at all, can enjoy a standard of living equal to her own? To ask this question is to distinguish between the deserving poor and the undeserving poor, between those who can't work and those who simply won't work, between those who work hard at low wages and those who choose to freeload. To people who make this distinction, the deserving poor should be helped by transfer payments but not the undeserving poor.

Although it may be difficult to sort out the deserving poor from the undeserving poor in particular cases, at least the underlying principle seems quite clear: Freeloaders don't merit our help. But many advocates of the merit principle want to extend it to cover all members of society. In that case, matters grow far less clear. The question now becomes: How are we to rank individual merit? To see how hard it is to answer this question, ask yourself who are the most meritorious among us. Those who work the hardest? Put in the most hours every week? Shoulder the heaviest responsibility? Those who perform the most difficult tasks? The least desirable tasks? The tasks most needed by society? Or is it the best educated? The most skilled? Or those who fill the most seats at a football stadium for a concert? Or create the greatest number of jobs? Depending on how we answer these questions, the most meritorious can be a laborer, a traveling salesperson, an airline mechanic, a school bus driver, a sanitation worker, the nation's president, the founders of such enterprises as Microsoft and McDonald's, a college professor, or U2's Bono.

As matters stand in the United States, we generally let economic forces sort out such questions. The law of supply and demand is supposed to set prices and wages throughout the economy, and those who command the highest pay on the open market are said to merit it. But even if we allow that the best ballplayers, for example, make the most money in their respective sports, we might still ask if they deserve on their merits to be paid a hundred times more money than the best elementary schoolteachers. We might also ask if a nonworking mother married to a millionaire merits a standard of living considerably higher than a nonworking mother on TANF.

The answer to both questions, many would argue, is no. But if the market doesn't always reward merit, we are faced with still another question: Can society do a better job of determining the relative merits of its members? On the answer to this question, there is no clear agreement.

LIBERTARIANISM, WELFARE LIBERALISM, AND SOCIALISM

Robert Nozick's view of economic justice is often called **libertarianism** because it seeks to maximize individual liberty. In general, the libertarian view is that all forms of coercion—except to prevent harm to life, liberty, and property—are wrong, whether they come from other individuals or from the government. Because we need a police force to protect life, liberty, and property, we may be coerced into paying taxes to support one. Because transfer payments are a matter of charity, not protection, we may not be coerced into paying taxes to support them.

John Rawls's view is often called *welfare liberalism* or **welfare capitalism**. Like Nozick, Rawls recognizes many property rights—the right to own a business, the right to hire and fire workers, and the right to make economic decisions according to market forces. In other words, he supports a *capitalist* economy. But he also supports transfer payments to rectify what he considers the economic injustices of capitalism.

One way of expressing the differences between the two positions goes like this: Are we to think of the wealth in society as merely the sum of individual wealth or as society's wealth as well. Nozick gives the former answer because of his belief in natural rights. Rawls gives the latter answer because of his belief that all members of society cooperate in the creation of that wealth. Why? Because what makes it possible for individuals to earn the wealth they do are the mutually agreed upon fundamental rules of society.

There is another possible reason for giving the same answer as Rawls. This reason comes from proponents of **socialism**. Socialists ask us to consider who creates the wealth in any society. Their answer is the workers, those who turn raw materials into commodities that are sold for profit. Then they ask us to consider who, in a capitalist society, gets rich off those profits. Their answer to this question is the owners, the top executives, the bankers, the landlords, and so forth—those who don't create any wealth. The real producers of wealth, in other words, don't own the wealth they produce. They receive only a small portion of it in the form of wages. Nor do they even own a guaranteed stake in their own jobs. After investing as many as twenty years or more of their lives to create enormous wealth for others, they can be laid off or fired by the bosses they made rich.

The socialist way of achieving economic justice is to replace a capitalist economy with a socialist economy. The change involves two major steps. First, the means of production are transferred from private ownership to public ownership. Factories, mines, and other productive property will be owned by society as a whole, not by private individuals. Second, the major economic decisions—the setting of prices, wages, employment levels, and production levels—become a matter of public policy instead of being set by market forces. In a perfect socialist economy, the policy will have three crucial features: Everyone's basic needs are taken care of, everyone is guaranteed a job, and everyone receives equal pay. Welfare in such an economy becomes unnecessary.

Why adopt such sweeping measures? First, proponents argue, socialism provides true economic justice and full social equality. Second, it maximizes freedom for everyone, not just the rich. The right to liberty, they claim, like the rights to life and property, is meaningless to people who can't afford a decent standard of living. Third, socialism extends democracy from the political realm to the economic realm. Not only does everyone have an equal say in how political decisions are made, but everyone has an equal say in how major economic decisions are made as well. Fourth, it replaces the indignity of welfare with the dignity of work.

Socialism's critics raise a number of objections, many of which we have already discussed. The objections include the libertarian arguments based on liberty and natural rights, plus the moral and practical objections to the need and equality principles of distribution. Another important criticism concerns the relative merits of planned economies and market economies. Planned economies, critics say, do not work as well as market economies. As evidence, they point to the failures of Eastern Europe's planned economies, which are now being converted to market economies. They also point to the many socialist parties in Western Europe that have shifted policies in favor of a market-oriented approach.

ARGUMENTS FOR WELFARE

1. *You can't let people starve.*

POINT: "You just can't let people starve; it's as simple as that. And you can't leave them homeless, either, or make them go without adequate healthcare and clothing.

Food, housing, healthcare, and clothing are the very basics of human existence. Without them, the promise of life, liberty, and the pursuit of happiness is empty."

COUNTERPOINT: "Of course our basic needs are important, but that's not the real issue. The real issue is: Who's responsible for making sure that their needs are met? And the answer is obvious. We're all responsible for ourselves. It's up to every one of us to see that our basic needs are met. If you're out of work, get yourself a job—any job. If you can't afford children, don't have them. And most important, if you're young, stay in school."

   2.   *Society is responsible for helping the unfortunate.*

POINT: "You make it sound as though it's the fault of the poor that they're poor, as though they all deserve their poverty. Maybe that's true in some cases, but look around you. If you do, you'll see people struggling to get by on inadequate incomes, people thrown out of work through no fault of their own, and people struck by disabling injuries and illnesses. And you'll also see people who never had a fair chance to begin with because they grew up in hopeless poverty or because they went to schools that couldn't give them a decent education. These unfortunates were let down by society, and it's up to all of us to give them a helping hand."

COUNTERPOINT: "Look, I'm not in favor of cutting off all kinds of help to every person who needs it. I'm not saying we should do away with unemployment compensation for people who are laid off. And I'm not saying we should cut off Social Security disability payments, either. Those programs are insurance, not welfare, and the only thing I'm talking about is welfare. If *you* want to help those 'unfortunates' who 'grew up in hopeless poverty,' go right ahead. That's what private charities are for. But don't force everyone else to help them out, especially when we see how many other people there are who grew up in poverty and turned out to be productive members of society."

   3.   *Ending welfare will hurt innocent children.*

POINT: "One thing you're forgetting is the children of the poor. When you talk about cutting off welfare, you're talking about cutting off TANF, and the main recipients of TANF are innocent children. You can't blame them for their predicament, can you?"

COUNTERPOINT: "Of course not, but the answer to that problem is to stop encouraging kids to have kids, and that's exactly what TANF does—encourage kids to have kids. Have a kid, you get a place to live and a steady income. Have another one, you get a raise. I know it sounds harsh, but the only way to turn the situation around is to send poor single teenagers a message—if you have children out of wedlock, you're on your own. As for the illegitimate children already with us, there's plenty we can do. The mothers' families can take care of them, they can be put up for adoption, and private charities can give them a helping hand."

   4.   *Poverty breeds other social problems.*

POINT: "Poverty is everybody's problem, not just the poor's. Where you find poverty, you find crime. Where you find poverty, you find contagious diseases. You also find drug use, fear, despair, and a terrible waste of human resources. Poverty is ruining our great cities, and the problems associated with it—street gangs, for instance—are spreading into small towns throughout the country. It's in everyone's interest to eradicate poverty."

COUNTERPOINT: "I couldn't agree with you more. It's your next step I disagree with, that welfare is the solution to all those problems. With decades of evidence staring us in the face, anyone can see that it isn't."

ARGUMENTS AGAINST WELFARE

1. *Welfare is unjust.*

POINT: "The first thing to point out about welfare is that it's a violation of individual freedom and individual rights, pure and simple. What's mine is mine, and no one has the right to take it away from me. Don't get me wrong. I'm not in favor of selfishness. I think everyone should give to charity. I certainly do. But like everyone else, I have the right to give to the charities of my own choosing. I even have the right not to give at all if I don't want to. Selfishness may be immoral, but so are a lot of other things, like cheating at tennis. It's not government's job to outlaw either one of them. Government's job is to protect my rights, not to interfere with them."

COUNTERPOINT: "Don't we also have the right to live in dignity? The right to a decent standard of living? And don't those rights count at least as much as your property rights? Besides, where do these property rights come from? Where is it written that you're entitled to *everything* you make? After all, where would you be without the cooperation of society as a whole—without our public roads and airports, for instance, or our legal systems at the federal, state, and municipal levels, or our federal banking system? Society contributes in any number of ways. Asking you to help people who haven't benefited as much as you have isn't asking too much."

2. *Welfare is bad social policy.*

POINT: "How much does welfare really help? There was a time when young single women didn't get pregnant, and in the rare cases that they did, they either married the father or put the baby up for adoption and went on with their lives. They finished school or they found jobs. Now they're getting pregnant in record numbers, and instead of choosing marriage or adoption, they have the baby and go on welfare. Not only that, but they stay on welfare and continue to have babies. In the old days, illegitimate births were rare, and the women who had them could salvage their lives. Now, with all the welfare benefits available, illegitimate children are all too common, and unwed mothers end up dependent on welfare."

COUNTERPOINT: "I won't deny that welfare dependence is a problem, but you have to look at the larger picture. First of all, most welfare recipients don't end up dependent on welfare. Second, you can't blame welfare alone for the rise in out-of-wedlock births. Do you really think teenage girls have future welfare benefits on their minds when they engage in sex? Do you really think the only reason they keep their children is the money? There are a lot of factors that contribute to teenage sex, from abuse in the home and the need for love to a lack of parental supervision and a general decline in values. And just as many factors contribute to a single woman's decision to keep the child if she becomes pregnant, including the same need for love and attention, the need for a feeling of self-worth, and all the satisfactions of motherhood. The way to fight welfare dependence is through welfare *reform,* not abolition. We have to make it easier to get off."

3. *Welfare removes stigmas that uphold important values.*

POINT: "We both agree that it's better to work than receive welfare. We also agree that illegitimacy is a serious problem among the young and poor. But one of the biggest flaws of welfare is that it makes being a single mother on welfare an acceptable lifestyle. There used to be a stigma attached to having illegitimate children. Pregnant teenagers were sent to homes for unwed mothers and kept out of sight. There was a stigma attached to taking handouts too. People were expected to earn their own way. That's a large part of what human dignity was about, and what it should still be about. But now those stigmas are gone. We tell kids that getting pregnant when they're still in school is nothing to be ashamed of, that it's fine to set up house at taxpayer expense. Maybe they're not thinking about welfare when they become pregnant, but you can't deny that welfare produces enough role models for them in poor neighborhoods."

COUNTERPOINT: "Do you really want to make these young girls ashamed of themselves? To make them outcasts? I'd say they have enough problems already. Besides, abolishing welfare won't bring back any stigmas, especially to single motherhood. Let's face it. Single motherhood is a fact of life throughout society."

4. *Welfare rewards fraud and freeloading.*

POINT: "What about fraud and freeloading? It's bad enough that the rest of us have to work to support the people you call unfortunate victims, but even you have to admit that a lot of cheating goes on. Will welfare reform stop people from hiding their incomes to keep the welfare checks coming in? Will it purge the welfare rolls of every freeloader who has no excuse not to be working? Will it guarantee that those of us who work for a living won't be supporting drug habits?"

COUNTERPOINT: "No, probably not. You'll find abuses in every government program. But that's no excuse to penalize honest welfare recipients, especially the children."

What Libertarianism Is

John Hospers

In the following essay, John Hospers both defines and defends the libertarian view. Central to libertarianism, he says, is the doctrine that by right every individual is in charge of his or her own life. We all have the right to live as we choose, as long as we don't infringe on the rights of others to live as they choose. In particular, we have the rights to life, liberty, and

From John Hospers, "What Libertarianism Is," in *The Libertarian Alternative*, ed. Tibor R. Machan. © 1974 by Tibor R. Machan. Reprinted by permission of Nelson-Hall, Inc., Publishers.

property, and each of these rights serves as a "no trespassing" sign against interference by governments as well as other individuals. The only proper role of government is to protect those rights.

In discussing the right to property, Hospers calls it the most misunderstood and unappreciated of all rights and the right most violated by governments. It is not, he says, the right to take property but the right to obtain it without coercion. When people claim other property rights, such as the right to welfare or the right to housing at others' expense, they are claiming rights that don't exist.

The political philosophy that is called libertarianism (from the Latin *libertas,* liberty) is the doctrine that every person is the owner of his own life, and that no one is the owner of anyone else's life; and that consequently every human being has the right to act in accordance with his own choices, unless those actions infringe on the equal liberty of other human beings to act in accordance with their choices.

There are several other ways of stating the same libertarian thesis:

1. *No one is anyone else's master, and no one is anyone else's slave.* Since I am the one to decide how my life is to be conducted, just as you decide about yours, I have no right (even if I had the power) to make you my slave and be your master, nor have you the right to become the master by enslaving me. Slavery is *forced* servitude, and since no one owns the life of anyone else, no one has the right to enslave another. Political theories past and present have traditionally been concerned with who should be the master (usually the king, the dictator, or government bureaucracy) and who should be the slaves, and what the extent of the slavery should be. Libertarianism holds that no one has the right to use force to enslave the life of another, or any portion or aspect of that life.

2. *Other men's lives are not yours to dispose of.* I enjoy seeing operas; but operas are expensive to produce. Opera-lovers often say, "The state (or the city, etc.) should subsidize opera, so that we can all see it. Also it would be for people's betterment, cultural benefit, etc." But what they are advocating is nothing more or less than legalized plunder. They can't pay for the productions themselves, and yet they want to see opera, which involves a large number of people and their labor; so what they are saying in effect is, "Get the money through legalized force. Take a little bit more out of every worker's paycheck every week to pay for the operas we want

to see." But I have no right to take by force from the workers' pockets to pay for what I want.

Perhaps it would be better if he *did* go to see opera—then I should try to convince him to go voluntarily. But to take the money from him forcibly, because in my opinion it would be good for *him,* is still seizure of his earnings, which is plunder.

Besides, if I have the right to force him to help pay for my pet projects, hasn't he equally the right to force me to help pay for his? Perhaps he in turn wants the government to subsidize rock-and-roll, or his new car, or a house in the country? If I have the right to milk him, why hasn't he the right to milk me? If I can be a moral cannibal, why can't he too?

We should beware of the inventors of utopias. They would remake the world according to their vision—with the lives and fruits of the labor of other human beings. Is it someone's utopian vision that others should build pyramids to beautify the landscape? Very well, then other men should provide the labor; and if he is in a position of political power, and he can't get men to do it voluntarily, then he must *compel* them to "cooperate"—i.e., he must enslave them.

A hundred men might gain great pleasure from beating up or killing just one insignificant human being; but other men's lives are not theirs to dispose of. "In order to achieve the worthy goals of the next five-year-plan, we must forcibly collectivize the peasants . . ." but other men's lives are not theirs to dispose of. Do you want to occupy, rent-free, the mansion that another man has worked for twenty years to buy? But other men's lives are not yours to dispose of. Do you want operas so badly that everyone is forced to work harder to pay for their subsidization through taxes? But other men's lives are not yours to dispose of. Do you want to have free medical care at the expense of other people, whether they wish to provide it or not? But this would require them to work longer for you whether they want to or not, and other men's lives are not yours to dispose of.

> The freedom to engage in any type of enterprise, to produce, to own and control property, to buy and sell on the free market, is derived from the rights to life, liberty, and property . . . which are stated in the Declaration of Independence . . . [but] when a government guarantees a "right" to an education or parity on farm products or a guaranteed annual income, it is staking a claim on the property of one group of citizens for the sake of another group. In short, it is violating one of the fundamental rights it was instituted to protect.[1]

3. *No human being should be a nonvoluntary mortgage on the life of another.* I cannot claim your life, your work, or the products of your effort as mine. The fruit of one man's labor should not be fair game for every freeloader who comes along and demands it as his own. The orchard that has been carefully grown, nurtured, and harvested by its owner should not be ripe for the plucking for any bypasser who has a yen for the ripe fruit. The wealth that some men have produced should not be fair game for looting by government, to be used for whatever purposes its representatives determine, no matter what their motives in so doing may be. The theft of your money by a robber is not justified by the fact that he used it to help his injured mother.

It will already be evident that libertarian doctrine is embedded in a view of the rights of man. Each human being has the right to live his life as he chooses, compatibly with the equal right of all other human beings to live their lives as they choose.

All man's rights are implicit in the above statement. Each man has the right to life: any attempt by others to take it away from him, or even to injure him, violates this right, through the use of coercion against him. Each man has the right to liberty: to conduct his life in accordance with the alternatives open to him without coercive action by others. And every man has the right to property: to work to sustain his life (and the lives of whichever others he chooses to sustain, such as his family) and to retain the fruits of his labor.

People often defend the rights of life and liberty but denigrate property rights, and yet the right to property is as basic as the other two, indeed, without property rights no other rights are possible. Depriving you of property is depriving you of the means by which you live.

> . . . All that which an individual possesses by right (including his life and property) are morally his to use, dispose of and even destroy, as he sees fit. If I own my life, then it follows that I am free to associate with whom I please and not to associate with whom I please. If I own my knowledge and services it follows that I may ask any compensation I wish for providing them for another, or I may abstain from providing them at all, if I so choose. If I own my house, it follows that I may decorate it as I please and live in it with whom I please. If I control my own business, it follows that I may charge what I please for my products or services, hire whom I please and not hire whom I please. All that which I own in fact, I may dispose of as I choose to in reality. For anyone to attempt to limit my freedom to do so is to violate my rights.
>
> Where do my rights end? Where yours begin. I may do anything I wish with my own life, liberty and property without your consent; but I may do nothing with your life, liberty and property without your consent. If we recognize the principle of man's rights, it follows that the individual is sovereign of the domain of his own life and property, and is sovereign of no other domain. To attempt to interfere forcibly with another's use, disposal or destruction of his own property is to initiate force against him and to violate his rights.

I have no right to decide how you should spend your time or your money. I can make that decision for myself, but not for you, my neighbor. I may deplore your choice of life-style, and I may talk with you about it provided you are willing to listen to me. But I have no right to use force to change it. Nor have I the right to decide how you should spend the money you have earned. I may appeal to you to give it to the Red Cross, and you may prefer to go to prizefights. But that is your decision, and however much I may chafe about it I do not have the right to interfere forcibly with it, for example by robbing you in order to use the money in accordance with *my* choices. (If I have the right to rob you, have you also the right to rob me?)

When I claim a right, I carve out a niche, as it were, in my life, saying in effect, "This activity I must be able to perform without interference from others. For you and everyone else, this is off limits." And so I put up a "no trespassing" sign, which marks off the area of my right. Each individual's right is his "no trespassing" sign in relation to me and others. I may not encroach upon his domain any more than he upon mine, without my consent. Every right entails a duty, true—but the duty is only that of *forbearance*—that is, of *refraining* from violating the other person's right. If you have a right to life, I have no right to take your life; if you have a right to the products of your labor (property), I have no right to take it from you without your consent. The non-violation of these rights will not guarantee you protection against natural catastrophes such as floods and earthquakes, but it will protect you against the aggressive activities of *other men*. And rights, after all, have to do with one's relations to other human beings, not with one's relations to physical nature.

Nor were these rights created by government; governments—some governments, obviously not all—*recognize* and *protect* the rights that individuals already have. Governments regularly forbid homicide and theft; and, at a more advanced stage, protect individuals against such things as libel and breach of contract.

> It cannot be by chance that they thus agree. They agree because the alleged creating of rights [by government] was nothing else than giving formal sanction and better definition to those assertions of claims and recognitions of claims which naturally originate from the individual desires of men who have to live in presence of one another.
>
> ...Those who hold that life is valuable, hold, by implication, that men ought not to be prevented from carrying on life-sustaining activities.... Clearly the conception of "natural rights" originates in recognition of the truth that if life is justifiable, there must be a justification for the performance of acts essential to its preservation; and, therefore, a justification of those liberties and claims which make such acts possible.

> ...To recognize and enforce the rights of individuals, is at the same time to recognize and enforce the conditions to a normal social life.[2]

The *right to property* is the most misunderstood and unappreciated of human rights, and it is one most constantly violated by governments. "Property" of course does not mean only real estate; it includes anything you can call your own—your clothing, your car, your jewelry, your books and papers.

The right of property is not the right to just *take* it from others, for this would interfere with *their* property rights. It is rather the right to work for it, to obtain non-coercively, the money or services which you can present in voluntary exchange.

The right to property is consistently underplayed by intellectuals today, sometimes even frowned upon, as if we should feel guilty for upholding such a right in view of all the poverty in the world. But the right to property is absolutely basic. It is your hedge against the future. It is your assurance that what you have worked to earn will still be there, and be yours, when you wish or need to use it, especially when you are too old to work any longer....

Indeed, only if property rights are respected is there any point to planning for the future and working to achieve one's goals. *Property rights are what makes long-range planning possible*—the kind of planning which is a distinctively human endeavor, as opposed to the day-by-day activity of the lion who hunts, who depends on the supply of game tomorrow but has no real insurance against starvation in a day or a week. Without the right to property, the right to life itself amounts to little: how can you sustain your life if you cannot plan ahead? and how can you plan ahead if the fruits of your labor can at any moment be confiscated by government? ...

"But why have *individual* property rights? Why not have lands and houses owned by everybody together?" Yes, this involves no violation of individual rights, as long as everybody consents to this arrangement and no one is forced to join it. The parties to it may enjoy the communal living enough (at least for a time) to overcome certain inevitable problems: that some will work and some not, that some will achieve more in an hour than others can do in a day, and still they will all get the same income. The few who do the most will in the end consider themselves "workhorses" who do the work of two or three or twelve, while the others will be "freeloaders" on the efforts of these few. But as long as they can get out of the arrangement if they no longer like it, no violation of rights is involved. They got in voluntarily, and they can get out voluntarily; no one has used force.

"But why not say that everybody owns everything? That we *all* own everything there is?"

To some this may have a pleasant ring—but let us try to analyze what it means. If everybody owns everything, then everyone has an equal right to go everywhere, do what he pleases, take what he likes, destroy if he wishes, grow crops or burn them, trample them under, and so on. Consider what it would be like in practice. Suppose you have saved money to buy a house for yourself and your family. Now suppose that the principle, "everybody owns everything," becomes adopted. Well then, why shouldn't every itinerant hippie just come in and take over, sleeping in your beds and eating in your kitchen and not bothering to replace the food supply or clean up the mess? After all, it belongs to all of us, doesn't it? So we have just as much right to it as you, the buyer, have. What happens if we *all* want to sleep in the bedroom and there's not room for all of us? Is it the strongest who wins?

What would be the result? Since no one would be responsible for anything, the property would soon be destroyed, the food used up, the facilities nonfunctional. Beginning as a house that *one* family could use, it would end up as a house that *no one* could use. And if the principle continued to be adopted, no one would build houses any more—or anything else. What for? They would only be occupied and used by others, without remuneration. . . .

GOVERNMENT

Government is the most dangerous institution known to man. Throughout history it has violated the rights of men more than any individual or group of individuals could do: it has killed people, enslaved them, sent them to forced labor and concentration camps, and regularly robbed and pillaged them of the fruits of their expended labor. Unlike individual criminals, government has the power to arrest and try; unlike individual criminals, it can surround and encompass a person totally, dominating every aspect of one's life, so that one has no recourse from it but

to leave the country (and in totalitarian nations even that is prohibited). Government throughout history has a much sorrier record than any individual, even that of a ruthless mass murderer. The signs we see on bumper stickers are chillingly accurate: "Beware: the Government is Armed and Dangerous."

The only proper role of government, according to libertarians, is that of the protector of the citizen against aggression by other individuals. The government, of course, should never initiate aggression; its proper role is as the embodiment of the *retaliatory* use of force against anyone who initiates its use.

If each individual had constantly to defend himself against possible aggressors, he would have to spend a considerable portion of his life in target practice, karate exercises, and other means of self-defenses, and even so he would probably be helpless against groups of individuals who might try to kill, maim, or rob him. He would have little time for cultivating those qualities which are essential to civilized life, nor would improvements in science, medicine, and the arts be likely to occur. The function of government is to take this responsibility off his shoulders: the government undertakes to defend him against aggressors and to punish them if they attack him. When the government is effective in doing this, it enables the citizen to go about his business unmolested and without constant fear for his life. To do this, of course, government must have physical power—the police, to protect the citizen from aggression within its borders, and the armed forces, to protect him from aggressors outside. Beyond that, the government should not intrude upon his life, either to run his business, or adjust his daily activities, or prescribe his personal moral code.

Government, then, undertakes to be the individual's protector; but historically governments have gone far beyond this function. Since they already have the physical power, they have not hesitated to use it for purposes far beyond that which was entrusted to them in the first place. Undertaking initially to protect its citizens against aggression, it has often itself become an aggressor—a far greater aggressor, indeed, than the criminals against whom it was supposed to protect its citizens. Governments have done what no private citizens can do: arrest and imprison individuals without a trial and send them to slave labor camps. Government must have power in order to be effective—and yet the very means by which alone it can be effective make it vulnerable to the abuse of power, leading to managing the lives of individuals and even inflicting terror upon them.

What then should be the function of government? In a word, the *protection of human rights*.

1. *The right to life:* libertarians support all such legislation as will protect human beings against the use of force by others, for example, laws against killing, attempted killing, maiming, beating, and all kinds of physical violence.

2. *The right to liberty:* there should be no laws compromising in any way freedom of speech, of the press, and of peaceable assembly. There should be no censorship of ideas, books, films, or of anything else by government.

3. *The right to property:* libertarians support legislation that protects the property rights of individuals against confiscation, nationalization, eminent domain, robbery, trespass, fraud and misrepresentation, patent and copyright, libel and slander.

Someone has violently assaulted you. Should he be legally liable? Of course. He has violated one of your rights. He has knowingly injured you, and since he has initiated aggression against you he should be made to expiate.

Someone has negligently left his bicycle on the sidewalk where you trip over it in the dark and injure yourself. He didn't do it intentionally; he didn't mean you any harm. Should he be legally liable? Of course; he has, however unwittingly, injured you, and since the injury is caused by him and you are the victim, he should pay.

Someone across the street is unemployed. Should you be taxed extra to pay for his expenses? Not at all. You have not injured him, you are not responsible for the fact that he is unemployed (unless you are a senator or bureaucrat who agitated for further curtailing of business, which legislation passed, with the result that your neighbor was laid off by the curtailed business). You may voluntarily wish to help him out, or better still, try to get him a job to put him on his feet again; but since you have initiated no aggressive act against him, and neither purposely nor accidentally injured him in any way, you should not be legally penalized for the fact of his unemployment. (Actually, it is just such penalties that increase unemployment.)

One man, A, works hard for years and finally earns a high salary as a professional man. A second man, B, prefers not to work at all, and to spend wastefully what money he has (through inheritance), so that after a year or two he has nothing left. At the end of this time he has a long siege of illness and lots of medical bills to pay. He demands that the bills be paid by the government—that is, by the taxpayers of the land, including Mr. A.

But of course B has no such right. He chose to lead his life in a certain way—that was his voluntary decision. One consequence of that choice is that he must depend on charity in case of later need. Mr. A chose not to live that way. (And if everyone lived like Mr. B, on whom would he depend in case of later need?) Each has a right to live in the way he pleases, but each must live with the consequences of his own decision (which, as always, fall primarily on himself). He cannot, in time of need, claim A's beneficence as his right. . . .

Laws may be classified into three types: (1) laws protecting individuals against themselves, such as laws against fornication and other sexual behavior, alcohol, and drugs; (2) laws protecting individuals against aggressions by other individuals, such as laws against murder, robbery, and fraud; (3) laws requiring people to help one another; for example, all laws which rob Peter to pay Paul, such as welfare.

Libertarians reject the first class of laws totally. Behavior which harms no one else is strictly the individual's own affair. Thus, there should be no laws against becoming intoxicated, since whether or not to become intoxicated is the individual's own decision; but there should be laws against driving while intoxicated, since the drunken driver is a threat to every other motorist on the highway (drunken driving falls into type 2). Similarly, there should be no laws against drugs (except the prohibition of sale of drugs to minors) as long as the taking of these drugs poses no threat to anyone else. Drug addiction is a psychological problem to which no present solution exists. Most of the social harm caused by addicts, other than to themselves, is the result of thefts which they perform in order to continue their habit—and then the *legal* crime is the theft, not the addiction. The actual cost of heroin is about ten cents a shot; if it were legalized, the enormous traffic in illegal sale and purchase of it would stop, as well as the accompanying proselytization to get new addicts (to make more money for the pusher) and the thefts performed by addicts who often require eighty dollars a day just to keep up the habit. Addiction would not stop, but the crimes would: it is estimated that 75 percent of the burglaries in New York City today are performed by addicts, and all these crimes could be wiped out at one stroke through the legalization of drugs. (Only when the taking of drugs could be shown to constitute a threat to *others,* should it be prohibited by law. It is only laws protecting people against *themselves* that libertarians oppose.)

Laws should be limited to the second class only: aggression by individuals against other individuals. These are laws whose function is to protect human beings against encroachment by others; and this, as we have seen, is (according to libertarianism) the sole function of government.

Libertarians also reject the third class of laws totally: no one should be forced by law to help others, not even to tell them the time of day if requested, and certainly not to give them a portion of one's weekly paycheck. Governments, in the guise of humanitarianism, have given to some by taking from others (charging a "handling fee" in the process, which, because of the government's waste and inefficiency, sometimes is several hundred percent). And in so doing they have decreased incentive, violated the rights of individuals, and lowered the standard of living of almost everyone.

All such laws constitute what libertarians call *moral cannibalism.* A cannibal in the physical sense is a person who lives off the flesh of other human beings. A *moral* cannibal is one who believes he has a right to live off the "spirit" of other human beings—who believes that he has a moral claim on the productive capacity, time, and effort expended by others.

It has become fashionable to claim virtually everything that one needs or desires as one's *right.* Thus, many people claim that they have a right to a job, the right to free medical care, to free food and clothing, to a decent home, and so on. Now if one asks, apart from any specific context, whether it would be desirable if everyone had these things, one might well say yes. But there is a gimmick attached to each of them: *At whose expense?* Jobs, medical care,

education, and so on, don't grow on trees. These are goods and services *produced only by men.* Who, then, is to provide them, and under what conditions?

If you have a right to a job, who is to supply it? Must an employer supply it even if he doesn't want to hire you? What if you are unemployable, or incurably lazy? (If you say "the government must supply it," does that mean that a job must be created for you which no employer needs done, and that you must be kept in it regardless of how much or little you work?) If the employer is forced to supply it at his expense even if he doesn't need you, then isn't *he* being enslaved to that extent? What ever happened to *his* right to conduct his life and his affairs in accordance with his choices?

If you have a right to free medical care, then, since medical care doesn't exist in nature as wild apples do, some people will have to supply it to you for free: that is, they will have to spend their time and money and energy taking care of you whether they want to or not. What ever happened to *their* right to conduct their lives as they see fit? Or do you have a right to violate theirs? Can there be a right to violate rights?

All those who demand this or that as a "free service" are consciously or unconsciously evading the fact that there is in reality no such thing as free services. All man-made goods and services are the result of human expenditure of time and effort. There is no such thing as "something for nothing" in this world. If you demand something free, you are demanding that other men give their time and effort to you without compensation. If they voluntarily choose to do this, there is no problem; but if you demand that they be *forced* to do it, you are interfering with their right not to do it if they so choose. "Swimming in this pool ought to be free!" says the indignant passerby. What he means is that others should build a pool, others should provide the materials, and still others should run it and keep it in functioning order, so that *he* can use it without fee. But what right has he to the expenditure of *their* time and effort? To expect something "for free" is to expect it *to be paid for by others* whether they choose to or not.

Many questions, particularly about economic matters, will be generated by the libertarian account of human rights and the role of government. Should government have no role in assisting the needy, in providing social security, in legislating minimum wages, in fixing prices and putting a ceiling on rents, in curbing monopolies, in erecting tariffs, in guaranteeing jobs, in managing the money supply? To these and all similar questions the libertarian answers with an unequivocal no.

"But then you'd let people go hungry," comes the rejoinder. This, the libertarian insists, is precisely what would not happen; with the restrictions removed, the economy would flourish as never before. With the controls taken off business, existing enterprises would expand and new ones would spring into existence satisfying more and more consumer needs; millions more people would be gainfully employed instead of subsisting on welfare, and all kinds of research and production, released from the stranglehold of

government, would proliferate, fulfilling man's needs and desires as never before. It has always been so whenever government has permitted men to be free traders on a free market. But *why* this is so, and how the free market is the best solution to all problems relating to the material aspect of man's life, is another and far longer story. It is told in detail in chapters 3 to 9 of my book, *Libertarianism*.

NOTES

1. William W. Bayes, "What Is Property?" *The Freeman,* July 1970, p. 348.

2. Herbert Spencer, *The Man vs. the State* (1884; reprinted., Caldwell, Id.: Caxton Printers, 1940), p. 191.

Questions for Analysis

1. Hospers says that no one has the right "to enslave the life of another, or any portion or aspect of that life." Libertarians argue that the portion of their lives they spend working to earn the taxes they pay to support welfare payments amounts to a term of enslavement. Do you agree?

2. According to Hospers, property rights make all other rights possible. Why? Do you agree? If so, do property rights have to be as strong as Hospers insists to preserve our other rights?

3. Hospers says our right to property, like our rights to life and liberty, was not created by governments. Where does it come from, then?

4. Why does Hospers think that the right to property is a right to individual ownership? Why does he reject the idea that land belongs to everybody?

5. Hospers calls government "the most dangerous institution known to man." Why? Is he right?

6. How could an advocate of welfare argue against Hospers?

The Right to Eat and the Duty to Work

Trudy Govier

In the following essay, philosopher Trudy Govier examines three positions on welfare rights for the needy. The first is the libertarian position, which she calls the individualist view. The second, which she calls the permissive view, holds that everyone by legal right should have his or her basic needs satisfied, regardless of behavior. The third, which she calls the puritan

From Trudy Govier, "The Right to Eat and the Duty to Work," in *Philosophy of the Social Sciences,* vol. 5, pp. 363–375. © 1975 by Sage Publications, Inc. Reprinted by permission of Sage Publications, Inc.

view, holds that the legal right to welfare benefits should be conditional on the individual's willingness to work.

    After surveying these three positions, Govier evaluates them. First, she asks which has the most desirable social consequences. (This question she calls the teleological appraisal.) Second, she asks which best serves social justice. In both cases, she concludes, the permissive view is the best of the three.

Although the topic of welfare is not one with which philosophers have often concerned themselves, it is a topic which gives rise to many complex and fascinating questions—some in the area of political philosophy, some in the area of ethics, and some of a more practical kind. The variety of issues related to the subject of welfare makes it particularly necessary to be clear just which issue one is examining in a discussion of welfare. In a recent book on the subject, Nicholas Rescher asks:

> In what respects and to what extent is society, working through the instrumentality of the state, responsible for the welfare of its members? What demands for the promotion of his welfare can an individual reasonably make upon his society? These are questions to which no answer can be given in terms of some *a priori* approach with reference to universal ultimates. Whatever answer can appropriately be given will depend, in the final analysis, on what the society decides it should be.[1]

Rescher raises this question only to avoid it. His response to his own question is that a society has all and only those responsibilities for its members that it thinks it has. Although this claim is trivially true as regards legal responsibilities, it is inadequate from a moral perspective. If one imagines the case of an affluent society which leaves the blind, the disabled, and the needy to die of starvation, the incompleteness of Rescher's account becomes obvious. In this imagined case one is naturally led to raise the question as to whether those in power ought to supply those in need with the necessities of life. Though the needy have no legal right to welfare benefits of any kind, one might very well say that they ought to have such a right. It is this claim which I propose to discuss here.[2]

    I shall approach this issue by examining three positions which may be adopted in response to it. These are:

1. *The Individualist Position:* Even in an affluent society, one ought not to have any legal right to state-supplied welfare benefits.

2. *The Permissive Position:* In a society with sufficient resources, one ought to have an unconditional legal right to receive state-supplied welfare benefits. (That is, one's right to receive such benefits ought not to depend on one's behaviour; it should be guaranteed.)

3. *The Puritan Position:* In a society with sufficient resources one ought to have a legal right to state-supplied welfare benefits; this right ought to be conditional, however, on one's willingness to work.

But before we examine these positions, some preliminary clarification must be attempted. . . .

    Welfare systems are state-supported systems which supply benefits, usually in the form of cash income, to those who are in need. Welfare systems thus exist in the sort of social context where there is some private ownership of property. If no one owned anything individually (except possibly his own body), and all goods were considered to be the joint property of everyone, then this type of welfare system could not exist. A state might take on the responsibility for the welfare of its citizens, but it could not meet this responsibility by distributing a level of cash income which such citizens would spend to purchase the goods essential for life. The welfare systems which exist in the western world do exist against the background of extensive private ownership of property. It is in this context that I propose to discuss moral questions about having a right to welfare benefits. By setting out my questions in this way, I do not intend to endorse the institution of private property, but only to discuss questions which many people find real and difficult in the context of the social organization which they actually do experience. The present analysis of welfare is intended to apply to societies which (*a*) have the institution of private property, if not for means of production, at least for some basic good; and (*b*) possess sufficient resources so that it is at least possible for every member of the society to be supplied with the necessities of life.

1 The Individualist View

It might be maintained that a person in need has no legitimate moral claim on those around him and that the hypothetical inattentive society which left its blind citizens to beg or starve cannot rightly be censured for doing so. This view, which is dramatically at odds with most of contemporary social thinking, lives on in the writings of Ayn Rand and her followers.[3] The Individualist sets a high value on uncoerced personal choice. He sees each person as a responsible agent who is able to make his own decisions and to plan his own life. He insists that with the freedom to make decisions goes responsibility for the consequences of those decisions. A person has every right, for example, to spend ten years of his life studying Sanskrit—but if, as a result of this choice, he is unemployable, he ought not to expect others to labour on his behalf. No one has a proper claim on the labour of another, or on the income ensuing from that labour, unless he can repay the labourer in a way acceptable to that labourer himself. Government welfare schemes provide benefits from funds gained largely by taxing earned income. One cannot "opt out" of such schemes. To the Individualist, this means that a person is forced to work part of his time for others.

Suppose that a man works forty hours and earns two hundred dollars. Under modern-day taxation, it may well be that he can spend only two-thirds of that money as he chooses. The rest is taken by government and goes to support programmes which the working individual may not himself endorse. The beneficiaries of such programmes—those beneficiaries who do not work themselves—are as though they have slaves working for them. Backed by the force which government authorities can command, they are able to exist on the earnings of others. Those who support them do not do so voluntarily, out of charity; they do so on government command.

> Someone across the street is unemployed. Should you be taxed extra to pay for his expenses? Not at all. You have not injured him, you are not responsible for the fact that he is unemployed (unless you are a senator or bureaucrat who agitated for further curtailing of business which legislation passed, with the result that your neighbour was laid off by the curtailed business). You may voluntarily wish to help him out, or better still, try to get him a job to put him on his feet again; but since you have initiated no aggressive act against him, and neither purposefully nor accidentally injured him in any way, you should not be legally penalized for the fact of his unemployment.[4]

The Individualist need not lack concern for those in need. He may give generously to charity; he might give more generously still, if his whole income were his to use, as he would like it to be. He may also believe that, as a matter of empirical fact, existing government programmes do not actually help the poor. They support a cumbersome bureaucracy and they use financial resources which, if untaxed, might be used by those with initiative to pursue job-creating endeavours. The thrust of the Individualist's position is that each person owns his own body and his own labour; thus each person is taken to have a virtually unconditional right to the income which that labour can earn him in a free market place.[5] For anyone to pre-empt part of a worker's earnings without that worker's voluntary consent is tantamount to robbery. And the fact that the government is the intermediary through which this deed is committed does not change its moral status one iota.

On an Individualist's view, those in need should be cared for by charities or through other schemes to which contributions are voluntary. Many people may wish to insure themselves against unforeseen calamities and they should be free to do so. But there is no justification for nonoptional government schemes financed by taxpayers' money. . . .

2 The Permissive View

Directly contrary to the Individualist view of welfare is what I have termed the Permissive view. According to this view, in a society which has sufficient resources so that everyone could be supplied with the necessities of life, every individual ought to be given the legal right to social security, and this right ought not to be conditional in any way upon an individual's behavior. *Ex hypothesi* the society which we are discussing has sufficient goods to provide everyone with food, clothing, shelter and other necessities. Someone who does without these basic goods is scarcely living at all, and a society which takes no steps to change this state of affairs implies by its inaction that the life of such a person is without value. It does not execute him; but it may allow him to die. It does not put him in prison; but it may leave him with a life of lower quality than that of some prison inmates. A society which can rectify these circumstances and does not can justly be accused of imposing upon the needy either death or lifelong deprivation. And those characteristics which make a person needy—whether they be illness, old age, insanity, feeblemindedness, inability to find paid work, or even poor moral character—are insufficient to make him deserve the fate to which an inactive society would in effect condemn him. One would not be executed for inability or failure to find paid work; neither should one be allowed to die for this misfortune or failing.

A person who cannot or does not find his own means of social security does not thereby forfeit his status as a human being. If other human beings, with physical, mental and moral qualities different from his, are regarded as having the right to life and to the means of life, then so too should he be regarded. A society which does not accept the responsibility for supplying such a person with the basic necessities of life is, in effect, endorsing a difference between its members which is without moral justification. . . .

The adoption of a Permissive view of welfare would have significant practical implications. If there were a legal right, unconditional upon behaviour, to a specified level of state-supplied benefits, then state investigation of the prospective welfare recipient could be kept to a minimum. Why he is in need, whether he can work, whether he is willing to work, and what he does while receiving welfare benefits are on this view quite irrelevant to his right to receive those benefits. A welfare recipient is a person who claims from his society that to which he is legally entitled under a morally based welfare scheme. The fact that he makes this claim licenses no special state or societal interference with his behaviour. If the Permissive view of welfare were widely believed, then there would be no social stigma attached to being on welfare. There is such a stigma,

and many long-term welfare recipients are considerably demoralized by their dependent status.[6] These facts suggest that the Permissive view of welfare is not widely held in our society.

3 The Puritan View

This view of welfare rather naturally emerges when we consider that no one can have a right to something without someone else's, or some group of other persons', having responsibilities correlative to this right. In the case in which the right in question is a legal right to social security, the correlative responsibilities may be rather extensive. They have been deemed responsibilities of "the state." The state will require resources and funds to meet these responsibilities, and these do not emerge from the sky miraculously, or zip into existence as a consequence of virtually effortless acts of will. They are taken by the state from its citizens, often in the form of taxation on earned income. The funds given to the welfare recipient and many of the goods which he purchases with these funds are produced by other members of society, many of whom give a considerable portion of their time and their energy to this end. If a state has the moral responsibility to ensure the social security of its citizens then all the citizens of that state have the responsibility to provide state agencies with the means to carry out their duties. This responsibility, in our present contingent circumstances, seems to generate an obligation to *work*.

A person who works helps to produce the goods which all use in daily living and, when paid, contributes through taxation to government endeavours. The person who does not work, even though able to work, does not make his contribution to social efforts towards obtaining the means of life. He is not entitled to a share of the goods produced by others if he chooses not to take part in their labours. Unless he can show that there is a moral justification for his not making the sacrifice of time and energy which others make, he has no legitimate claim to welfare benefits. If he is disabled or unable to obtain work, he cannot work; hence he has no need to justify his failure to work. But if he does choose not to work, he would have to justify his choice by saying "others should sacrifice their time and energy for me; I have no need to sacrifice time and energy for them." This principle, a version of what Rawls refers to as a free-rider's principle, simply will not stand up to criticism.[7] To deliberately avoid working and benefit from the labours of others is morally indefensible.

Within a welfare system erected on these principles, the right to welfare is conditional upon one's satisfactorily accounting for his failure to obtain the necessities of life by his own efforts. Someone who is severely disabled mentally or physically, or who for some other reason cannot work, is morally entitled to receive welfare benefits. Someone who chooses not to work is not. The Puritan view of welfare is a kind of compromise between the Individualist view and the Permissive view. . . .

The Puritan view of welfare, based as it is on the inter-relation between welfare and work, provides a rationale for two connected principles which those establishing welfare schemes in Canada and in the United States seem to endorse. First of all, those on welfare should never receive a higher income than the working poor. Secondly, a welfare scheme should, in some way or other, incorporate incentives to work. These principles, which presuppose that it is better to work than not to work, emerge rather naturally from the contingency which is at the basis of the Puritan view: the goods essential for social security are products of the labour of some members of society. If we wish to have a continued supply of such goods, we must encourage those who work to produce them. . . .

APPRAISAL OF POLICIES: SOCIAL CONSEQUENCES AND SOCIAL JUSTICE

In approaching the appraisal of prospective welfare policies under these two aspects I am, of course, making some assumptions about the moral appraisal of suggested social policies. Although these cannot possibly be justified here, it may be helpful to articulate them, at least in a rough way.

Appraisal of social policies is in part teleological. To the extent that a policy, P, increases the total human welfare more than does an alternative policy, P', P is a better social policy than P'. Or, if P leaves the total human welfare as it is, while P' diminishes it, then to that extent, P is a better social policy than P'. Even this skeletal formulation of the teleological aspect of appraisal reveals why appraisal cannot be entirely teleological. We consider

total consequences—effect upon the total of "human well-being" in a society. But this total is a summation of consequences on different individuals. It includes no judgements as to how far we allow one individual's well-being to decrease while another's increases, under the same policy. Judgements relating to the latter problems are judgements about social justice.

In appraising social policies we have to weigh up considerations of total well-being against considerations of justice. Just how this is to be done, precisely, I would not pretend to know. However, the absence of precise methods does not mean that we should relinquish attempts at appraisal: some problems are already with us, and thought which is necessarily tentative and imprecise is still preferable to no thought at all.

1 Consequences of Welfare Schemes

First, let us consider the consequences of the non-scheme advocated by the Individualist. He would have us abolish all non-optional government programmes which have as their goal the improvement of anyone's personal welfare. This rejection extends to health schemes, pension plans and education, as well as to welfare and unemployment insurance. So following the Individualist would lead to very sweeping changes.

The Individualist will claim (as do Hospers and Ayn Rand) that on the whole his non-scheme will bring beneficial consequences. He will admit, as he must, that there are people who would suffer tremendously if welfare and other social security programmes were simply terminated. Some would even die as a result. We cannot assume that spontaneously developing charities would cover every case of dire need. Nevertheless the Individualist wants to point to benefits which would accrue to businessmen and to working people and their families if taxation were drastically cut. It is his claim that consumption would rise, hence production would rise, job opportunities would be extended, and there would be an economic boom, if people could only spend all their earned income as they wished. This boom would benefit both rich and poor.

There are significant omissions which are necessary in order to render the Individualist's optimism plausible. Either workers and businessmen would have insurance of various kinds, or they would be insecure in their prosperity. If they did have insurance to cover health problems, old age and possible job loss, then they would pay for it; hence they would not be spending their whole earned income on consumer goods. Those who run the insurance schemes could, of course, put this money back into the economy—but government schemes already do this. The economic boom under Individualism would not be as loud as originally expected. Furthermore the goal of increased consumption-increased productivity must be questioned from an ecological viewpoint: many necessary materials are available only in limited quantities.

Finally, a word about charity. It is not to be expected that those who are at the mercy of charities will benefit from this state, either materially or psychologically. Those who prosper will be able to choose between giving a great deal to charity and suffering from the very real insecurity and guilt which would accompany the existence of starvation and grim poverty outside their padlocked doors. It is to be hoped that they would opt for the first alternative. But, if they did, this might be every bit as expensive for them as government-supported benefit schemes are now. If they did not give generously to charity, violence might result. However one looks at it, the consequences of Individualism are unlikely to be good.

Welfare schemes operating in Canada today are almost without exception based upon the principles of the Puritan view. To see the consequences of that type of welfare scheme we have only to look at the results of our own welfare programmes. Taxation to support such schemes is high, though not so intolerably so as to have led to widescale resentment among taxpayers. Canadian welfare programmes are attended by complicated and often cumbersome bureaucracy, some of which results from the interlocking of municipal, provincial and federal governments in the administration and financing of welfare programmes. The cost of the programmes is no doubt increased by this bureaucracy; not all the tax money directed to welfare programmes goes to those in need. Puritan welfare schemes do not result in social catastrophe or in significant business stagnation—this much we know, because we already

live with such schemes. Their adverse consequences, if any, are felt primarily not by society generally nor by businessmen and the working segment of the public, but rather by recipients of welfare.

Both the Special Senate Committee Report on Poverty and the Real Poverty Report criticize our present system of welfare for its demoralization of recipients, who often must deal with several levels of government and are vulnerable to arbitrary interference on the part of administering officials. Welfare officials have the power to check on welfare recipients and cut off or limit their benefits under a large number of circumstances. The dangers to welfare recipients in terms of anxiety, threats to privacy and loss of dignity are obvious. According to the Senate Report, the single aspect shared by all Canada's welfare systems is "a record of failure and insufficiency, of bureaucratic rigidities that often result in the degradation, humiliation and alienation of recipients."[8] The writers of this report cite many instances of humiliation, leaving the impression that these are too easily found to be "incidental aberrations."[9] Concern that a welfare recipient either be unable to work or be willing to work (if unemployed) can easily turn into concern about how he spends the income supplied him, what his plans for the future are, where he lives, how many children he has. And the rationale underlying the Puritan scheme makes the degradation of welfare recipients a natural consequence of welfare institutions. Work is valued and only he who works is thought to contribute to society. Welfare recipients are regarded as parasites and spongers—so when they are treated as such, this is only what we should have expected. Being on welfare in a society which thinks and acts in this fashion can be psychologically debilitating. Welfare recipients who are demoralized by their downgraded status and relative lack of personal freedom can be expected to be made less capable of self-sufficiency. To the extent that this is so, welfare systems erected on Puritan principles may defeat their own purposes.

In fairness, it must be noted here that bureaucratic checks and controls are not a feature only of Puritan welfare systems. To a limited extent, Permissive systems would have to incorporate them too. Within those systems, welfare benefits would be given only to those whose income was inadequate to meet basic needs. However, there would be no checks on "willingness to work," and there would be no need for welfare workers to evaluate the merits of the daily activities of recipients. If a Permissive guaranteed income system were administered through income tax returns, everyone receiving the basic income and those not needing it paying it back in taxes, then the special status of welfare recipients would fade. They would no longer be singled out as a special group within the population. It is to be expected that living solely on government-supplied benefits would be psychologically easier in that type of situation.

Thus it can be argued that for the recipients of welfare, a Permissive scheme has more advantages than a Puritan one. This is not a very surprising conclusion. The Puritan scheme is relatively disadvantageous to recipients, and Puritans would acknowledge this point; they will argue that the overall consequences of Permissive schemes are negative in that these schemes benefit some at too great a cost to others. (Remember, we are not yet concerned with the *justice* of welfare policies, but solely with their consequences as regards *total* human well-being within the society in question.) The concern which most people have regarding the Permissive scheme relates to its costs and its dangers to the "work ethic." It is commonly thought that people work only because they have to work to survive in a tolerable style. If a guaranteed income scheme were adopted by the government, this incentive to work would disappear. No one would be faced with the choice between a nasty and boring job and starvation. Who would do the nasty and boring jobs then? Many of them are not eliminable and they have to be done somehow, by someone. Puritans fear that a great many people—even some with relatively pleasant jobs—might simply cease to work if they could receive non-stigmatized government money to live on. If this were to happen, the Permissive society would simply grind to a halt.

In addressing these anxieties about the consequences of Permissive welfare schemes, we must recall that welfare benefits are set to ensure only that those who do not work have a bearable existence, with an income sufficient for basic needs, and that they have this income regardless of why they fail to work. Welfare benefits will not finance luxury living for a family of five! If jobs are adequately paid so that workers receive more than the minimum welfare income in an earned salary, then there will still be a financial incentive to take jobs. What guaranteed income schemes will do is to raise the salary floor. This change will benefit the many non-unionized workers in service and clerical occupations.

Furthermore it is unlikely that people work solely due to (i) the desire for money and the things it can buy and (ii) belief in the Puritan work ethic. There are many other reasons for working, some of which would persist in a society which had adopted a Permissive welfare system. Most people are happier when their time is structured in some way, when they are active outside their own homes, when they feel themselves part of an endeavour whose purposes transcend their particular egoistic ones. Women often choose to work outside the home for these reasons as much as for financial ones. With these and other factors operating I cannot see that the adoption of a Permissive welfare scheme would be followed by a level of slothfulness which would jeopardize human well-being.

Another worry about the Permissive scheme concerns cost. It is difficult to comment on this in a general way, since it would vary so much from case to case. Of Canada at the present it has been said that a guaranteed income scheme administered through income tax would cost less than social security payments administered through the present bureaucracies. It is thought that this saving would result from a drastic cut in administrative costs. The matter of the work ethic is also relevant to the question of costs. Within a Puritan framework it is very important to have a high level of employment and there is a tendency to resist any reorganization which results in there being fewer jobs available. Some of these proposed reorganizations would save money; strictly speaking we should count the cost of keeping jobs which are objectively unnecessary as part of the cost of Puritanism regarding welfare.

In summary, we can appraise Individualism, Puritanism and Permissivism with respect to their anticipated consequences, as follows: Individualism is unacceptable; Puritanism is tolerable, but has some undesirable consequences for welfare recipients; Permissivism appears to be the winner. Worries about bad effects which Permissive welfare schemes might have due to high costs and (alleged) reduced work-incentives appear to be without solid basis.

2 Social Justice under
Proposed Welfare Schemes

We must now try to consider the merits of
Individualism, Puritanism and Permissivism with
regard to their impact on the distribution of the
goods necessary for well-being. [Robert] Nozick
has argued against the whole conception of a distributive justice on the grounds that it presupposes
that goods are like manna from heaven: we simply
get them and then have a problem—to whom to
give them. According to Nozick we know where
things come from and we do not have the problem of to whom to give them. There is not really a
problem of distributive justice, for there is no central distributor giving out manna from heaven! It
is necessary to counter Nozick on this point since
his reaction to the (purported) problems of distributive justice would undercut much of what follows.[10]

There is a level at which Nozick's point is obviously valid. If A discovers a cure for cancer, then it
is A and not B or C who is responsible for this discovery. On Nozick's view this is taken to imply
that A should reap any monetary profits which are
forthcoming; other people will benefit from the
cure itself. Now although it cannot be doubted
that A is a bright and hardworking person, neither
can it be denied that A and his circumstances are the
product of many co-operative endeavours: schools
and laboratories, for instance. Because this is so, I
find Nozick's claim that "we know where things
come from" unconvincing at a deeper level. Since
achievements like A's presuppose extensive social cooperation, it is morally permissible to regard even
the monetary profits accruing from them as share-
able by the "owner" and society at large.

Laws support existing income levels in many
ways. Governments specify taxation so as to further
determine net income. Property ownership is a legal
matter. In all these ways people's incomes and possibilities for obtaining income are affected by deliberate state action. It is always possible to raise questions
about the moral desirability of actual conventional
arrangements. Should university professors earn less
than lawyers? More than waitresses? Why? Why not?
Anyone who gives an account of distributive justice is trying to specify principles which will make
it possible to answer questions such as these, and
nothing in Nozick's argument suffices to show that
the questions are meaningless or unimportant.

Any human distribution of anything is unjust
insofar as differences exist for no good reason. If
goods did come like manna from heaven and the
Central Distributor gave A ten times more than B,
we should want to know why. The skewed distribution might be deemed a just one if A's needs
were objectively ten times greater than B's, or if B
refused to accept more than his small portion of
goods. But if no reason at all could be given for it,
or if only an irrelevant reason could be given (e.g.,
A is blue-eyed and B is not), then it is an unjust distribution. All the views we have expounded concerning welfare permit differences in income level.
Some philosophers would say that such differences
are never just, although they may be necessary, for
historical or utilitarian reasons. Whether or not this
is so, it is admittedly very difficult to say just what
would constitute a good reason for giving A a
higher income than B. Level of need, degree of
responsibility, amount of training, unpleasantness
of work—all these have been proposed and all have
some plausibility. We do not need to tackle all this
larger problem in order to consider justice under
proposed welfare systems. For we can deal here
solely with the question of whether everyone
should receive a floor level of income; decisions
on this matter are independent of decisions on
overall equality or principles of variation among
incomes above the floor. The Permissivist contends
that all should receive at least the floor income;
the Individualist and the Puritan deny this. All
would claim justice for their side.

The Individualist attempts to justify extreme
variations in income, with some people below the
level where they can fulfill their basic needs, with
reference to the fact of people's actual accomplishments. This approach to the question is open
to the same objections as those which have already
been raised against Nozick's non-manna-from-
heaven argument, and I shall not repeat them here.
Let us move on to the Puritan account. It is because
goods emerge from human efforts that the Puritan
advances his view of welfare. He stresses the unfairness of a system which would permit some people
to take advantage of others. A Permissive welfare
system would do this, as it makes no attempt to
distinguish between those who choose not to work
and those who cannot work. No one should be
able to take advantage of another under the auspices

of a government institution. The Puritan scheme seeks to eliminate this possibility, and for that reason, Puritans would allege, it is a more just scheme than the Permissive one.

Permissivists can best reply to this contention by acknowledging that any instance of free-riding would be an instance where those working were done an injustice, but by showing that any justice which the Puritan preserves by eliminating freeriding is outweighed by *injustice* perpetrated elsewhere. Consider the children of the Puritan's freeriders. They will suffer greatly for the "sins" of their parents. Within the institution of the family, the Puritan cannot suitably hurt the guilty without cruelly depriving the innocent. There is a sense, too, in which Puritanism does injustice to the many people on welfare who are not freeriders. It perpetuates the opinion that they are non-contributors to society and this doctrine, which is over-simplified if not downright false, has a harmful effect upon welfare recipients.

Social justice is not simply a matter of the distribution of goods, or the income with which goods are to be purchased. It is also a matter of the protection of rights. Western societies claim to give their citizens equal rights in political and legal contexts; they also claim to endorse the larger conception of a right to life. Now it is possible to interpret these rights in a limited and formalistic way, so that the duties correlative to them are minimal. On the limited, or negative, interpretation, to say that A has a right to life is simply to say that others have a duty not to interfere with A's attempts to keep himself alive. This interpretation of the right to life is compatible with Individualism as well as with Puritanism. But it is an inadequate interpretation of the right to life and of other rights. A right to vote is meaningless if one is starving and unable to get to the polls; a right to equality before the law is meaningless if one cannot afford to hire a lawyer. And so on.

Even a Permissive welfare scheme will go only a very small way towards protecting people's rights. It will amount to a meaningful acknowledgment of a right to life, by ensuring income adequate to purchase food, clothing and shelter—at the very least. These minimum necessities are presupposed by all other rights a society may endorse in that their possession is a precondition of being able to exercise these other rights. Because it protects the

rights of all within a society better than do Puritanism and Individualism, the Permissive view can rightly claim superiority over the others with regard to justice.

NOTES

1. Nicholas Rescher, *Welfare: Social Issues in Philosophical Perspective*, p. 114.

2. One might wish to discuss moral questions concerning welfare in the context of natural rights doctrines. Indeed, Article 22 of the United Nations Declaration of Human Rights states, "Everyone, as a member of society, has the right to social security and is entitled, through national effort and international cooperation and in accordance with the organization and resources of each State, to the economic, social and cultural rights indispensable for his dignity and the free development of his personality." I make no attempt to defend the right to welfare as a natural right. Granting that rights imply responsibilities or duties that "ought" implies "can," it would only be intelligible to regard the right to social security as a natural right if all states were able to ensure the minimum well-being of their citizens. This is not the case. And a natural right is one which is by definition supposed to belong to all human beings simply in virtue of their status as human beings. The analysis given here in the Permissive view is compatible with the claim that all human beings have a *prima facie* natural right to social security. It is not, however, compatible with the claim that all human beings have a natural right to social security if this right is regarded as one which is so absolute as to be inviolable under any and all conditions.

3. See, for example, Ayn Rand's *Atlas Shrugged, The Virtue of Selfishness,* and *Capitalism: The Unknown Ideal.*

4. John Hospers, *Libertarianism: A Political Philosophy for Tomorrow,* p. 67.

5. I say virtually unconditional, because an Individualist such as John Hospers sees a legitimate moral role for government in preventing the use of force by some citizens against others. Since this is the case, I presume that he would also regard as legitimate such taxation as was necessary to support this function. Presumably that taxation would be seen as consented to by all, on the grounds that all "really want" government protection.

6. Ian Adams, William Cameron, Brian Hill, and Peter Penz, *The Real Poverty Report,* pp. 167–187.

7. See *A Theory of Justice,* pp. 124, 136. Rawls defines the free-rider as one who relies on the principle "everyone is to act justly except for myself, if I choose not to," and says that his position is a version of egoism which is eliminated as a morally acceptable principle by formal constraints. This conclusion regarding the tenability of egoism is one which I accept and which is taken for granted in the present context.

8. *Senate Report on Poverty*, p. 73.

9. The Hamilton Public Welfare Department takes automobile license plates from recipients, making them available again only to those whose needs meet with the Department's approval. (*Real Poverty Report*, p. 186.) *The Globe and Mail* for 12 January 1974 reported that welfare recipients in the city of Toronto are to be subjected to computerized budgeting. In the summer of 1973, the two young daughters of an Alabama man on welfare were sterilized against their own wishes and without their parents' informed consent. (See *Time,* 23 July 1973.)

10. Robert Nozick, "Distributive Justice," *Philosophy and Public Affairs,* Fall 1973.

Questions for Analysis

1. What practical advantages does the permissive view have over the puritan view according to Govier? What practical advantages does it have over the individualist view? Do you agree?

2. How does Govier respond to the charge that the permissive view discourages people from working? How convincing is her response?

3. One problem with welfare programs based on the puritan view, Govier says, is that it demoralizes welfare recipients. How does it demoralize them? How could a proponent of the puritan view respond?

4. How does Govier criticize Nozick's entitlement conception of justice? How could Nozick respond? How could Hospers respond?

5. Govier admits that the permissive view allows free-riders to sponge off others. She also admits that free-riders create an injustice to people who work to support themselves and their families. Why does she consider the permissive view to be more just than the puritan view anyway?

6. In today's United States, there are increasing calls to move closer to the individualist position and the puritan position. Why? According to Govier's discussion, the calls are misguided. Are they, or does Govier's discussion neglect important issues in the welfare debate?

Radical Egalitarianism

Kai Nielsen

In this selection from the last chapter of *Equality and Liberty,* Kai Nielsen defends a position he calls *radical* **egalitarianism**, which combines the principle of need and the equality principle but also recognizes limited entitlements. In a society that can afford to do so, Nielsen argues, everyone's needs should be satisfied. Then, after providing for common social and economic goods—and without violating individual entitlements—society should distribute the remaining wealth equally. He calls this view radical egalitarianism because it insists on equality of *condition* for all, not just equality of opportunity.

After setting out his position, Nielsen defends it against the charge that too much equality interferes with individual liberty. He claims we have rights to fair terms of cooperation as well as rights to noninterference. That is, we have a right not to be dominated or exploited by others. Maximizing that right, he says, results in the greatest liberty for all, even if it means limiting some rights of noninterference. He also defends his position against two other criticisms: (1) that egalitarianism penalizes the talented and (2) that no one has the authority to force egalitarianism on those who object to it. Against the first, he says money is not the only way to reward talent. Against the second, he appeals to moral authority. Anyone who considers the matter impartially, he says, and genuinely cares for humankind and is not "ideologically mystified," will see the merits of egalitarianism—at least in the abstract.

I

I have talked of equality as a right and of equality as a goal. And I have taken, as the principal thing, to be able to state what goal we are seeking when we say equality is a goal. When we are in a position actually to achieve that goal, then that same equality becomes a right. The goal we are seeking is an equality of basic condition for everyone. Let me say a bit what this is: everyone, as far as possible, should have equal life prospects, short of genetic engineering and the like and the rooting out of any form of the family and the undermining of our basic freedoms. There should, where this is possible, be an equality of access to equal resources over each person's life as a whole, though this should be qualified by people's varying needs. Where psychiatrists are in short supply only people who are in need of psychiatric help should have equal access to such help. This equal access to resources should be such that it stands as a barrier to their being the sort of differences between people that allow some to be in a position to control and to exploit others; such equal access to resources should also stand as a barrier to one adult person having power over other adult persons that does not rest on the revocable consent on the part of the persons over whom he comes to have power. Where, because of some remaining scarcity in a society of considerable productive abundance, we cannot reasonably distribute resources equally, we should first, where considerations of desert are not at issue, distribute according to stringency of need, second according to the strength of unmanipulated preferences and third, and finally, by lottery. We should, in trying to attain equality of condition, aim at a condition of autonomy (the fuller and the more rational the better) for everyone and at a condition where everyone alike, to the fullest extent possible, has his or her needs and wants satisfied. The limitations on the satisfaction of people's wants should be only

where that satisfaction is incompatible with everyone getting the same treatment. Where we have conflicting wants, such as where two persons want to marry the same person, the fair thing to do will vary with the circumstances. In the marriage case, freedom of choice is obviously the fair thing. But generally, what should be aimed at is having everyone have their wants satisfied as far as possible. To achieve equality of condition would be, as well, to achieve a condition where the necessary burdens of the society are equally shared, where to do so is reasonable, and where each person has an equal voice in deciding what these burdens shall be. Moreover, everyone, as much as possible, should be in a position—and should be equally in that position—to control his own life. The goals of egalitarianism are to achieve such equalities. . . .

II

Robert Nozick asks "How do we decide how much equality is enough?"[1] In the preceding section we gestured in the direction of an answer. I should now like to be somewhat more explicit. Too much equality, as we have been at pains to point out, would be to treat everyone identically, completely ignoring their differing needs. Various forms of "barracks equality" approximating that would also be too much. Too little equality would be to limit equality of condition, as did the old egalitarianism, to achieving equal legal and political rights, equal civil liberties, to equality of opportunity and to a redistribution of gross disparities in wealth sufficient to keep social peace, the rationale for the latter being that such gross inequalities if allowed to stand would threaten social stability. This Hobbesist stance indicates that the old egalitarianism proceeds in a very pragmatic manner. Against the old egalitarianism I would argue that we must at least aim at an equality of whole life prospects, where that is not read simply as the right to compete for scarce positions of advantage, but where there is to be brought into being the kind of equality of condition that would provide everyone equally, as far as possible, with the resources and the social conditions to satisfy their needs as fully as possible compatible with everyone else doing likewise. (Note that between people these needs will be partly the same but will still often be importantly different as well.) Ideally, as a kind of ideal limit for a society of wondrous abundance, a radical egalitarianism would go beyond that to a similar thing for wants. We should, that is, provide all people equally, as far as possible, with the resources and social conditions to satisfy their wants, as fully as possible compatible with everyone else doing likewise. (I recognize that there is a slide between wants and needs. As the wealth of a society increases and its structure changes, things that started out as wants tend to become needs, e.g., someone in the Falkland Islands might merely reasonably want an auto while someone in Los Angeles might not only want it but need it as well. But this does not collapse the distinction between wants and needs. There are things in any society people need, if they are to survive at all in anything like a commodious condition, whether they want them or not, e.g., they need food, shelter, security, companionship and the like. An egalitarian starts with basic needs, or at least with what are taken in the cultural environment in which a given person lives to be basic needs, and moves out to other needs and finally to wants as the productive power of the society increases.)

I qualified my above formulations with "as far as possible" and with "as fully as possible compatible with everyone else doing likewise." These are essential qualifications. Where, as in societies that we know, there are scarcities, even rather minimal scarcities, not everyone can have the resources or at least all the resources necessary to have their needs satisfied. Here we must first ensure that, again as far as possible, their basic needs are all satisfied and then we move on to other needs and finally to wants. But sometimes, to understate it, even in very affluent societies, everyone's needs cannot be met, or at least they cannot be equally met. In such circumstances we have to make some hard choices. I am thinking of a situation where there are not enough dialysis machines to go around so that everyone who needs one can have one. What then

should we do? The thing to aim at, to try as far as possible to approximate, if only as a heuristic ideal, is the full and equal meeting of needs and wants of everyone. It is when we have that much equality that we have enough equality. But, of course, "ought implies can," and where we can't achieve it we can't achieve it. But where we reasonably can, we ought to do it. It is something that fairness requires.

The "reasonably can" is also an essential modification: we need situations of sufficient abundance so that we do not, in going for such an equality of condition, simply spread the misery around or spread very Spartan conditions around. Before we can rightly aim for the equality of condition I mentioned, we must first have the productive capacity and resource conditions to support the institutional means that would make possible the equal satisfaction of basic needs and the equal satisfaction of other needs and wants as well. . . .

In talking about how much equality is enough, I have so far talked of the benefits that equality is meant to provide. But egalitarians also speak of an equal sharing of the necessary burdens of the society as well. Fairness requires a sharing of the burdens, and for a radical egalitarian this comes to an equal sharing of the burdens where people are equally capable of sharing them. Translated into the concrete this does *not* mean that a child or an old man or a pregnant woman are to be required to work in the mines or that they are required to collect garbage, but it would involve something like requiring every able-bodied person, say from nineteen to twenty, to take his or her turn at a fair portion of the necessary unpleasant jobs in the world. In that way we all, where we are able to do it, would share equally in these burdens—in doing the things that none of us want to do but that we, if we are at all reasonable, recognize the necessity of having done. (There are all kinds of variations and complications concerning this—what do we do with the youthful wonder at the violin? But, that notwithstanding, the general idea is clear enough.) And, where we think this is reasonably feasible, it squares with our considered judgments about fairness.

I have given you, in effect appealing to my considered judgments but considered judgments I do not think are at all eccentric, a picture of what I would take to be enough equality, too little equality and not enough equality. But how can we know that my proportions are right? I do not think we can avoid or should indeed try to avoid an appeal to considered judgments here. But working with them there are some arguments we can appeal to get them in wide reflective equilibrium. Suppose we go back to the formal principle of justice, namely that we must treat like cases alike. Because it does not tell us *what* are like cases, we cannot derive substantive criteria from it. But it may, indirectly, be of some help here. We all, if we are not utterly zany, want a life in which our needs are satisfied and in which we can live as we wish and do what we want to do. Though we differ in many ways, in our abilities, capacities for pleasure, determination to keep on with a job, we do not differ about wanting our needs satisfied or being able to live as we wish. Thus, *ceterus paribus* [other things being equal], where questions of desert, entitlement and the like do not enter, it is only fair that all of us should have our needs equally considered and that we should, again *ceterus paribus,* all be able to do as we wish in a way that is compatible with others doing likewise. From the formal principle of justice and a few key facts about us, we can get to the claim that *ceterus paribus* we should go for this much equality. But this is the core content of a radical egalitarianism.

However, how do we know that *ceterus is paribus* here? What about our entitlements and deserts? Suppose I have built my house with my own hands, from materials I have purchased and on land that I have purchased and that I have lived in it for years and have carefully cared for it. The house is mine and I am entitled to keep it even if by dividing the house into two apartments greater and more equal satisfaction of need would obtain for everyone. Justice requires that such an entitlement be respected here. (Again, there is an implicit *ceterus paribus* clause. In extreme situations, say after a war with housing in extremely short supply, that entitlement could be rightly overridden.)

There is a response on the egalitarian's part.... One of the things that people in fact need, or at least reflectively firmly want, is to have such entitlements respected. Where they are routinely overridden to satisfy other needs or wants, we would *not* in fact have a society in which the needs of everyone are being maximally met. To the reply, but what if more needs for everyone were met by ignoring or overriding such entitlements, the radical egalitarian should respond that that is, given the way

we are, a thoroughly hypothetical situation and that theories of morality cannot be expected to give guidance for all logically possible worlds but only for worlds which are reasonably like what our actual world is or plausibly could come to be....

There are without doubt genuine entitlements and a theory of justice must take them seriously, but they are not absolute. If the need is great enough we can see the merit in overriding them, just as in law as well as morality the right of eminent domain is recognized. Finally, while I have talked of entitlements here, parallel arguments will go through for desert.

III

I want now to relate this articulation of what equality comes to my radically egalitarian principles of justice. My articulation of justice is a certain spelling out of the slogan proclaimed by Marx "From each according to his ability, to each according to his needs." The egalitarian conception of society argues for the desirability of bringing into existence a world, once the springs of social wealth flow freely, in which everyone's needs are as fully satisfied as possible and in which everyone gives according to his ability. Which means, among other things, that everyone, according to his ability, shares the burdens of society. There is an equal giving and equal responsibility here according to ability. It is here, with respect to giving according to ability and with respect to receiving according to need, that a complex equality of result, equality of condition, is being advocated by the radical egalitarian. What it comes to is this: each of us, where each is to count for one and none to count for more than one, is to give according to ability and receive according to need.

My radical egalitarian principles of justice, as we have seen, read as follows:

(1) Each person is to have an equal right to the most extensive total system of equal basic liberties and opportunities (including equal opportunities for meaningful work, for self-determination and political and economic participation) compatible with a similar treatment of all. (This principle gives expression to a commitment to attain and/or sustain equal moral autonomy and equal self-respect.)

(2) After provisions are made for common social (community) values, for capital overhead to preserve the society's productive capacity, allowances made for differing unmanipulated needs and preferences, and due weight is given to the just entitlements of individuals, the income and wealth (the common stock of means) is to be so divided that each person will have a right to an equal share. The necessary burdens requisite to enhance human well-being are also to be equally shared, subject, of course, to limitations by differing abilities and differing situations. (Here I refer to different natural environments and the like and not to class position and the like.)

Here we are talking about equality as a right rather than about equality as a goal as has previously been the subject matter of equality in this chapter. These principles of egalitarianism spell out rights people have and duties they have under *conditions of very considerable productive abundance.* We have a right to certain basic liberties and opportunities and we have, subject to certain limitations spelled out in the second principle, a right to an equal share of the income and wealth in the world. We also have a duty, again subject to the qualifications mentioned in the principle, to do our equal share in shouldering the burdens necessary to protect us from ills and to enhance our well-being.

What is the relation between these rights and the ideal of equality of condition discussed earlier? That is a goal for which we can struggle now to bring about conditions which will some day make its achievement possible, while these rights only become rights when the goal is actually achievable. We have no such rights in slave, feudal or capitalist societies or such duties in those societies. In that important way they are not natural rights for they depend on certain social conditions and certain social structures (socialist ones) to be realizable. What we can say is that it is always desirable that socio-economic conditions come into being which would make it possible to achieve the goal of equality of condition so that these rights and duties I speak of could obtain. But that is a far cry from saying we have such rights and duties now.

It is a corollary of this, if these radical egalitarian principles of justice are correct, that capitalist societies (even capitalist welfare state societies such as Sweden) and statist societies such as the Soviet Union or the People's Republic of China cannot be just societies or at least they must be societies, structured as they are, which are defective in justice. (This is not to say that some of these societies are not juster than others. . . .) But none of these statist or capitalist societies can satisfy these radical egalitarian principles of justice, for equal liberty, equal opportunity, equal wealth or equal sharing of burdens are not at all possible in societies having their social structure. So we do not have such rights now but we can take it as a goal that we bring such a society into being with a commitment to an equality of condition in which we would have these rights and duties. Here we require first the massive development of productive power.

The connection between equality as a goal and equality as a right spelled out in these principles of justice is this. The equality of condition appealed to in equality as a goal would, if it were actually to obtain, have to contain the rights and duties enunciated in those principles. There could be no equal life prospects between all people or anything approximating an equal satisfaction of needs if there were not in place something like the system of equal basic liberties referred to in the first principle. Furthermore, without the rough equality of wealth referred to in the second principle, there would be disparities in power and self-direction in society which would render impossible an equality of life prospects or the social conditions required for an equal satisfaction of needs. And plainly, without a roughly equal sharing of burdens, there cannot be a situation where everyone has equal life prospects or has the chance equally to satisfy his needs. The principles of radical egalitarian justice are implicated in its conception of an ideally adequate equality of condition. . . .

[IV]

It has been repeatedly argued that equality undermines liberty. Some would say that a society in which principles like my radical egalitarian principles were adopted, or even the liberal egalitarian principles of Rawls or Dworkin were adopted, would not be a free society. My arguments have been just the reverse.

I have argued that it is only in an egalitarian society that full and extensive liberty is possible.

Perhaps the egalitarian and the anti-egalitarian are arguing at cross purposes? What we need to recognize, it has been argued, is that we have two kinds of rights both of which are important to freedom but to rather different freedoms and which are freedoms which not infrequently conflict.[2] We have rights to *fair terms of cooperation* but we also have rights to *non-interference*. If a right of either kind is overridden our freedom is diminished. The reason why it might be thought that the egalitarian and the anti-egalitarian may be arguing at cross purposes is that the egalitarian is pointing to the fact that rights to fair terms of cooperation and their associated liberties require equality while the anti-egalitarian is pointing to the fact that rights to non-interference and their associated liberties conflict with equality. They focus on different liberties.

What I have said above may not be crystal clear, so let me explain. People have a right to fair terms of cooperation. In political terms this comes to the equal right of all to effective participation in government and, in more broadly social terms, and for a society of economic wealth, it means people having a right to a roughly equal distribution of the benefits and burdens of the basic social arrangements that affect their lives and for them to stand in such relations to each other such that no one has the power to dominate the life of another. By contrast, rights to non-interference come to the equal right of all to be left alone by the government and more broadly to live in a society in which people have a right peacefully to pursue their interests without interference.

The conflict between equality and liberty comes down to, very essentially, the conflicts we get in modern societies between rights to fair terms of cooperation and rights to non-interference. As Joseph Schumpeter saw and J. S. Mill before him, one could have a thoroughly democratic society (at least in conventional terms) in which rights to noninterference might still be extensively violated. A central anti-egalitarian claim is that we cannot have an egalitarian society in which the very precious liberties that go with the rights to non-interference would not be violated.

Socialism and egalitarianism plainly protect rights to fair terms of cooperation. Without the social (collective) ownership and control of the means of production, involving with this, in the initial stages of socialism at least, a workers' state, economic power will be concentrated in the hands of a few who will in turn, as a result, dominate effective participation in government. Some rightwing libertarians blind themselves to that reality, but it is about as evident as can be. Only an utter turning away from the facts of social life could lead to any doubts about this at all. But then this means that in a workers' state, if some people have capitalistic impulses, that they would have their rights peacefully to pursue their own interests interfered with. They might wish to invest, retain and bequeath in economic domains. In a workers' state these capitalist acts in many circumstances would have to be forbidden, but that would be a violation of an individual's right to non-interference and the fact, if it was a fact, that we by democratic vote, even with vast majorities, had made such capitalist acts illegal would still not make any difference because individuals' rights to non-interference would still be violated....

The proper response to this, as should be apparent from what I have argued throughout, is that to live in any society at all, capitalist, socialist or whatever, is to live in a world in which there will be some restriction or other on our rights peacefully to pursue our interests without interference. I can't lecture in Albanian or even in French in a standard philosophy class at the University of Calgary, I can't jog naked on most beaches, borrow a book from your library without your permission, fish in your trout pond without your permission, take your dog for a walk without your say so and the like. At least some of these things have been thought to be things which I might peacefully pursue in my own interests. Stopping me from doing them is plainly interfering with my peaceful pursuit of my own interests. And indeed it is an infringement on liberty, an interference with my doing what I may want to do.

However, for at least many of these activities, and particularly the ones having to do with property, even right-wing libertarians think that such interference is perfectly justified. But, justified or not, they still plainly constitute a restriction on our individual freedom. However, what we must also recognize is that there will always be some such restrictions on freedom in any society whatsoever, just in virtue of the fact that a normless society, without the restrictions that having norms imply, is a contradiction in terms.[3] Many restrictions are hardly felt as restrictions, as in the attitudes of many people toward seat-belt legislation, but they are, all the same, plainly restrictions in our liberty. It is just that they are thought to be unproblematically justified.

To the question would a socialism with a radical egalitarianism restrict some liberties, including some liberties rooted in rights to non-interference, the answer is that it indeed would; but so would laissez-faire capitalism, aristocratic conceptions of justice, liberal conceptions or any social formations at all, with their associated conceptions of justice. The relevant question is which of these restrictions are justified.

The restrictions on liberty proffered by radical egalitarianism and socialism, I have argued, are justified for they, of the various alternatives, give us both the most extensive and the most abundant system of liberty possible in modern conditions with their thorough protection of the right to fair terms of cooperation. Radical egalitarianism will also, and this is central for us, protect our civil liberties and these liberties are, of course, our most basic liberties. These are the liberties which are the most vital for us to protect. What it will not do is to protect our unrestricted liberties to invest, retain and bequeath in the economic realm and it will not protect our unrestricted freedom to buy and sell. There is, however, no good reason to think that these restrictions are restrictions of anything like a basic liberty. Moreover, we are justified in restricting our freedom to buy and sell if such restrictions strengthen, rather than weaken, our total system of liberty. This is in this way justified, for only by such market restrictions can the rights of the vast majority of people to effective participation in government and an equal role in the control of their social lives be protected. I say this because if we let the market run free in this way, power will pass into the hands of a few who will control the lives of the many and determine the fundamental design of the society. The actual liberties that are curtailed in a radically egalitarian social order are inessential liberties whose restriction in contemporary circumstances enhances human well-being and indeed makes for a firmer entrenchment of basic liberties and for their greater extension globally. That is to say, we here restrict some liberty in order to attain more liberty and a more equally distributed pattern of liberty. More people will be able to do what they want and have a greater control over their own lives than in a capitalist world order with its at least implicit inegalitarian commitments.

However, some might say I still have not faced the most central objection to radical egalitarianism, namely its statism. (I would prefer to say its putative statism.) The picture is this. The egalitarian state must be in the redistribution business. It has to make, or make sure there is made, an equal relative contribution to the welfare of every citizen. But this in effect means that the socialist state or, for that matter, the welfare state, will be deeply interventionist in our personal lives. It will be in the business, as one right-winger emotively put it, of cutting one person down to size in order to bring about that person's equality with another person who was in a previously disadvantageous position.[4] That is said to be morally objectionable and it would indeed be deeply morally objectionable in many circumstances. But it isn't in the circumstances in which the radical egalitarian presses for redistribution. (I am not speaking of what might be mere equalizing upwards.) The circumstances are these: Capitalist A gets his productive property confiscated so that he could no longer dominate and control the lives of proletarians B, C, D, E, F, and G. But what is wrong with it where this "cutting down to size"— in reality the confiscation of productive property or the taxation of the capitalist—involves no violation of A's civil liberties or the harming of his actual well-being (health, ability to work, to cultivate the arts, to have fruitful personal relations, to live in comfort and the like) and where B, C, D, E, F, and G will have their freedom and their well-being thoroughly enhanced if such confiscation or taxation occurs? Far from being morally objectionable, it is precisely the sort of state of affairs that people ought to favor. It certainly protects more liberties and more significant liberties than it undermines.

There is another familiar anti-egalitarian argument designed to establish the liberty-undermining qualities of egalitarianism. It is an argument we have touched upon in discussing meritocracy. It turns on the fact that in any society there will be both talents and handicaps. Where they exist, what do we want to do about maintaining equal distribution? Egalitarians, radical or otherwise, certainly do not want to penalize people for talent. That being so, then surely people should be allowed to retain the benefits of superior talent. But this in some circumstances will lead to significant inequalities in resources and in the meeting of needs. To sustain equality there will have to be an ongoing redistribution in the direction of the less talented and less fortunate. But this redistribution from the more to the less talented does plainly penalize the talented for their talent. That, it will be said, is something which is both unfair and an undermining of liberty.

The following, it has been argued, makes the above evident enough.[5] If people have talents they will tend to want to use them. And if they use them they are very likely to come out ahead. Must not egalitarians say they ought not to be able to come out ahead no matter how well they use their talents and no matter how considerable these talents are? But that is intolerably restrictive and unfair.

The answer to the above anti-egalitarian argument is implicit in a number of things I have already said. But here let me confront this familiar argument directly. Part of the answer comes out in probing some of the ambiguities of "coming out ahead." Note, incidentally, that (1) not all reflective, morally sensitive people will be so concerned with that, and (2) that being very concerned with that is a mentality that capitalism inculcates. Be that as it may, to turn to the ambiguities, note that some take "coming out ahead" principally to mean "being paid well for the use of those talents" where "being paid well" is being paid sufficiently well so that it creates inequalities sufficient to disturb the preferred egalitarian patterns. (Without that, being paid well would give one no relative advantage.) But, as we have seen, "coming out ahead" need not take that form at all. Talents can be recognized and acknowledged in many ways. First, in just the respect and admiration of a fine employment of talents that would naturally come from people seeing them so displayed where these people were not twisted by envy; second, by having, because of these talents, interesting and secure work that their talents fit them for and they merit in virtue of those talents. Moreover, having more money is not going to matter much—for familiar marginal utility reasons—where what in capitalist societies would be called the welfare floors are already very high, this being made feasible by the great productive wealth of the society. Recall that in such a society of abundance everyone will be well off and secure. In such a society people are not going to be very concerned about

being a little better off than someone else. The talented are in no way, in such a situation, robbed to help the untalented and handicapped or penalized for their talents. They are only prevented from amassing wealth (most particularly productive wealth), which would enable them to dominate the untalented and the handicapped and to control the social life of the world of which they are both a part. . . .

Some anti-egalitarians would say, shifting now to another argument, that egalitarianism undermines liberty because it is in effect *authoritarian*.[6] It assumes someone, the government or an egalitarian secular mandarin, has the right to divvy up resources in such a way as maximally and equally to answer to the needs of everyone alike. But by whose *authority* are such actions taken? Egalitarians, the argument goes, just assume that someone has the authority to do this but no one has any such authority. *Perhaps* there would be such an authority if everyone had *unanimously* agreed that resources are to be divided up equally or even (though this is less likely) if they had all agreed to settle such fundamental moral issues by majority vote or a two-thirds majority vote or something of the sort. But it is perfectly evident that none of these agreements obtain in the real world or are even in the offing. There is no such consensus among our contemporaries. Moreover, it is simply not true, that as a matter of fact, everyone has an equal concern for everybody's interests. In no literal sense is it true that even in a single society every person in that society matters, and matters equally, to every other person in the society. Moreover, it is absurd to think that anything like that obtains, could obtain, or even should obtain, if it could. We typically care much more about our family, friends and close associates than we do about total strangers and it is both natural and appropriate that this should be so. But, the argument goes, to give egalitarianism the requisite moral authority, there would have to be something like this kind of consensus. But there plainly isn't and (more arguably) should not be. Moreover, we can't, even if we had such a majoritarian consensus, rely on the majority, for such fundamental issues are not vote issues. We cannot rightly railroad a dissenting minority.

I think that the moral authority for abstract egalitarianism, for the belief that the interests of everyone matter and matter equally, comes from its being the case that it is *required by the moral point of view*.[7] What I am predicting is that a person who has a good understanding of what morality is, has a good knowledge of the facts, is not ideologically mystified, takes an impartial point of view, and has an attitude of impartial caring, would, if not conceptually confused, come to accept the abstract egalitarian thesis. I see no way of arguing someone into such an egalitarianism who does not have that attitude of impartial caring, who does not in this general way have a love of humankind.[8] A hardhearted Hobbesist is not reachable here. But given that a person has that love of humankind—that impartial and impersonal caring—together with the other qualities mentioned above, then, I predict, that that person would be an egalitarian at least to the extent of accepting the abstract egalitarian thesis. What I am claiming is that if these conditions were to obtain (if they ceased to be just counterfactuals), then there would be a consensus among moral agents about accepting the abstract egalitarian thesis.

Whether that consensus would be extendible to my specific formulations of radical egalitarian principles of justice would depend on how cogent my arguments are for them. . . .

NOTES

1. See the debate between Robert Nozick, Daniel Bell and James Tobin, "If Inequality Is Inevitable What Can Be Done About It?" *The New York Times,* January 3, 1982, p. E5. The exchange between Bell and Nozick reveals the differences between the old egalitarianism and right-wing libertarianism. It is not only that the right and left clash but sometimes right clashes with right.

2. Richard W. Miller, "Marx and Morality," in *Marxism,* eds. J. R. Pennock and J. W. Chapman, *Nomos* 26 (New York: New York University Press, 1983), pp. 9–11.

3. This has been argued from both the liberal center and the left. Ralf Dahrendorf, *Essays in the Theory of Society* (Stanford, Cal.: Stanford University Press, 1968), pp. 151–78; and G. A. Cohen, "Capitalism, Freedom and the Proletariat" in *The Idea of Freedom: Essays in Honour of Isaiah Berlin,* ed. Alan Ryan (Oxford: Oxford University Press, 1979).

4. The graphic language should be duly noted. Jan Narveson, "On Dworkinian Equality," *Social Philosophy and Policy* 1, no. 1 (Autumn 1983): 4.

5. Ibid., pp. 1–24.

6. Jan Narveson, "Reply to Dworkin," *Social Philosophy and Policy* 1, no. 1 (Autumn 1983): 42–44.

7. Some will argue that there is no such thing as a moral point of view. My differences with him about the question of whether the amoralist can be argued into morality not withstanding. I think Kurt Baier, in a series of articles written subsequent to his *The Moral Point of View,* has clearly shown that there is something reasonably determinate that can, without ethnocentrism, be called "the moral point of view."

8. Richard Norman has impressively argued that this is an essential background assumption of the moral point of view. Richard Norman, "Critical Notice of Rodger Beehler's *Moral Life,"* *Canadian Journal of Philosophy* 11, no. 1 (March 1981): 157–83.

Questions for Analysis

1. According to Nielsen, justice requires more than equality of opportunity. It also requires equality of "whole life prospects." What does he mean by that? Do you agree?

2. Nielsen is a socialist as well as a radical egalitarian. That is, he believes the means of production should be owned by society as a whole. Could radical egalitarianism be achieved without socialism? Why does Nielsen believe it can't?

3. Is Nielsen's egalitarianism too radical? Why or why not?

4. Nielsen gives only one example of a just entitlement, ownership of a house the owner built himself and lived in for years. What other entitlements do you think he would recognize? Are they enough?

5. Do you agree that radical egalitarianism maximizes liberty? Why or why not?

6. According to Nielsen, confiscating productive property involves no violation of civil liberties. How would a libertarian respond? Who do you think is right?

Choosing a Future

Charles Murray

In this selection from the final chapter of *Losing Ground,* social scientist Charles Murray engages in what he calls a **thought experiment**. What would happen, he asks, if all federal transfer payments to the poor were abolished? His answer is that society would reap large benefits, from a reduction in births to unwed teenagers to an increase in the ability of the hard-core unemployed to find work. What would happen to individuals now on welfare? Some would find jobs, some would receive help from family, local services, or private charities, and some, he admits, would "fall between the cracks." But those who would, he suggests, would be responsible for their own failures.

In defending this outcome, Murray argues that it rewards merit and increases self-respect. He also argues that it is more compassionate than our current system of transfer payments. Still, he does not call for an immediate end to welfare, which he considers politically impossible. Instead, he recommends a gradual course of radical reforms, though he doesn't say what they should be.

In the last two chapters I suggested that the kinds of help we want to provide are more limited than we commonly suppose and that, even when we want to help, the conditions under which a national program can do so without causing more harm than good are more tightly constrained than we suppose. My arguments might seem tailor-made to relieve us of responsibility for persons in need. But I believe just the contrary: that the moral imperative to do something to correct the situation of poor people and especially the minority poor is at least as powerful now as when Lyndon Johnson took office. I have for the most part used the data to make a case that the reforms flowing from the new wisdom of the 1960s were a blunder on purely pragmatic grounds. But another theme of the discussion has been that what we did was wrong on moral grounds, however admirable our intentions may have been.

It was wrong to take from the most industrious, most responsible poor—take safety, education, justice, status—so that we could cater to the least industrious, least responsible poor. It was wrong to impose rules that made it rational for adolescents to behave in ways that destroyed their futures. The changes we made were not just policy errors, not just inexpedient, but unjust. The injustice of the

policies was compounded by the almost complete immunity of the elite from the price they demanded of the poor. . . .

[I]f the behaviors of members of the underclass are founded on a rational appreciation of the rules of the game, and as long as the rules encourage dysfunctional values and behaviors, the future cannot look bright. Behaviors that work will tend to persist until they stop working. The rules will have to be changed. . . .

A PROPOSAL FOR PUBLIC WELFARE

I begin with the proposition that it is within our resources to do enormous good for some people quickly. We have available to us a program that would convert a large proportion of the younger generation of hardcore unemployed into steady workers making a living wage. The same program would drastically reduce births to single teenage girls. It would reverse the trendline in the breakup of poor families. It would measurably increase the upward socioeconomic mobility of poor families. These improvements would affect some millions of persons.

All these are results that have eluded the efforts of the social programs installed since 1965, yet, from everything we know, there is no real question about whether they would occur under the program I propose. A wide variety of persuasive evidence from our own culture and around the

From pp. 219–220 and 227–236 from *Losing Ground: American Social Policy, 1950–1980* by Charles Murray. Copyright © 1984 by Charles Murray. Reprinted by permission of Basic Books, a division of HarperCollins Publishers, Inc.

world, from experimental data and longitudinal studies, from theory and practice, suggests that the program would achieve such results.

The proposed program, our final and most ambitious thought experiment, consists of scrapping the entire federal welfare and income-support structure for working-aged persons, including AFDC, Medicaid, Food Stamps, Unemployment Insurance, Worker's Compensation, subsidized housing, disability insurance, and the rest. It would leave the working-aged person with no recourse whatsoever except the job market, family members, friends, and public or private locally funded services. It is the Alexandrian solution: cut the knot, for there is no way to untie it.

It is difficult to examine such a proposal dispassionately. Those who dislike paying for welfare are for it without thinking. Others reflexively imagine bread lines and people starving in the streets. But as a means of gaining fresh perspective on the problem of effective reform, let us consider what this hypothetical society might look like.

A large majority of the population is unaffected. A surprising number of the huge American middle and working classes go from birth to grave without using any social welfare benefits until they receive their first Social Security check. Another portion of the population is technically affected, but the change in income is so small or so sporadic that it makes no difference in quality of life. A third group comprises persons who have to make new arrangements and behave in different ways. Sons and daughters who fail to find work continue to live with their parents or relatives or friends. Teenaged mothers have to rely on support from their parents or the father of the child and perhaps work as well. People laid off from work have to use their own savings or borrow from others to make do until the next job is found. All these changes involve great disruption in expectations and accustomed roles.

Along with the disruptions go other changes in behavior. Some parents do not want their young adult children continuing to live off their income, and become quite insistent about their children learning skills and getting jobs. This attitude is most prevalent among single mothers who have to depend most critically on the earning power of their offspring.

Parents tend to become upset at the prospect of a daughter's bringing home a baby that must be entirely supported on an already inadequate income. Some become so upset that they spend considerable parental energy avoiding such an eventuality. Potential fathers of such babies find themselves under more pressure not to cause such a problem, or to help with its solution if it occurs.

Adolescents who were not job-ready find they are job-ready after all. It turns out that they can work for low wages and accept the discipline of the workplace if the alternative is grim enough. After a few years, many—not all, but many—find that they have acquired salable skills, or that they are at the right place at the right time, or otherwise find that the original entry-level job has gradually been transformed into a secure job paying a decent wage. A few—not a lot, but a few—find that the process leads to affluence.

Perhaps the most rightful, deserved benefit goes to the much larger population of low-income families who have been doing things right all along and have been punished for it: the young man who has taken responsibility for his wife and child even though his friends with the same choice have called him a fool; the single mother who has worked full time and forfeited her right to welfare for very little extra money; the parents who have set an example for their children even as the rules of the game have taught their children that the example is outmoded. For these millions of people, the instantaneous result is that no one makes fun of them any longer. The longer-term result will be that they regain the status that is properly theirs. They will not only be the bedrock upon which the community is founded (which they always have been), they will be recognized as such. The process whereby they regain their position is not magical, but a matter of logic. When it becomes highly dysfunctional for a person to be dependent, status will accrue to being independent, and in fairly short order. Noneconomic rewards will once again reinforce the economic rewards of being a good parent and provider.

The prospective advantages are real and extremely plausible. In fact, if a government program of the traditional sort (one that would "do" something rather than simply get out of the way) could *as plausibly* promise these advantages, its passage would be a foregone conclusion. Congress, yearning for programs that are not retreads of failures, would be prepared to spend billions. Negative side-effects (as long as they were the traditionally acceptable negative side-effects) would be brushed aside as trivial in return for the benefits. For let me be quite clear: I am not suggesting that we dismantle income support for the working-aged to balance the budget or punish welfare cheats. I am hypothesizing, with the advantage of powerful collateral evidence, that the lives of large numbers of poor people would be radically changed for the better.

There is, however, a fourth segment of the population yet to be considered, those who are pauperized by the withdrawal of government supports and unable to make alternate arrangements: the teenaged mother who has no one to turn to; the incapacitated or the inept who are thrown out of the house; those to whom economic conditions have brought long periods in which there is no work to be had; those with illnesses not covered by insurance. What of these situations?

The first resort is the network of local services. Poor communities in our hypothetical society are still dotted with storefront health clinics, emergency relief agencies, employment services, legal services. They depend for support on local taxes or local philanthropy, and the local taxpayers and philanthropists tend to scrutinize them rather closely. But, by the same token, they also receive considerably more resources than they formerly did. The dismantling of the federal services has poured tens of billions of dollars back into the private economy. Some of that money no doubt has been spent on Mercedes and summer homes on the Cape. But some has been spent on capital investments that generate new jobs. And some has been spent on increased local services to the poor, voluntarily or as decreed by the municipality. In many cities, the coverage provided by this network of agencies is more generous, more humane, more wisely distributed, and more effective in its results than the services formerly subsidized by the federal government.

But we must expect that a large number of people will fall between the cracks. How might we go about trying to retain the advantages of a zero-level welfare system and still address the residual needs?

As we think about the nature of the population still in need, it becomes apparent that their basic problem in the vast majority of the cases is the lack of a job, and this problem is temporary. What they need is something to tide them over while finding a new place in the economy. So our first step is to re-install the Unemployment Insurance program in more or less its previous form. Properly administered, unemployment insurance makes sense. Even if it is restored with all the defects of current practice, the negative effects of Unemployment Insurance alone are relatively minor. Our objective is not to wipe out chicanery or to construct a theoretically unblemished system, but to meet legitimate human needs without doing more harm than good. Unemployment Insurance is one of the least harmful ways of contributing to such ends. Thus the system has been amended to take care of the victims of short-term swings in the economy.

Who is left? We are now down to the hardest of the hard core of the welfare-dependent. They have no jobs. They have been unable to find jobs (or have not tried to find jobs) for a longer period of time than the unemployment benefits cover. They have no families who will help. They have no friends who will help. For some reason, they cannot get help from local services or private charities except for the soup kitchen and a bed in the Salvation Army hall.

What will be the size of this population? We have never tried a zero-level federal welfare system under conditions of late-twentieth-century national wealth, so we cannot do more than speculate. But we may speculate. Let us ask of whom the population might consist and how they might fare.

For any category of "needy" we may name, we find ourselves driven to one of two lines of thought. Either the person is in a category that is going to be at the top of the list of services that localities vote for themselves, and at the top of the list of private services, or the person is in a category where help really is not all that essential or desirable. The burden of the conclusion is not that every single person will be taken care of, but that the extent of resources to deal with needs is likely to be very great—not based on wishful thinking, but on extrapolations from reality.

To illustrate, let us consider the plight of the stereotypical welfare mother—never married, no skills, small children, no steady help from a man.

It is safe to say that, now as in the 1950s, there is no one who has less sympathy from the white middle class, which is to be the source of most of the money for the private and local services we envision. Yet this same white middle class is a soft touch for people trying to make it on their own, and a soft touch for "deserving" needy mothers—AFDC was one of the most widely popular of the New Deal welfare measures, intended as it was for widows with small children. Thus we may envision two quite different scenarios.

In one scenario, the woman is presenting the local or private service with this proposition: "Help me find a job and day-care for my children, and I will take care of the rest." In effect, she puts herself into the same category as the widow and the deserted wife—identifies herself as one of the most obviously deserving of the deserving poor. Welfare mothers who want to get into the labor force are likely to find a wide range of help. In the other scenario, she asks for an outright and indefinite cash grant—in effect, a private or local version of AFDC—so that she can stay with the children and not hold a job. In the latter case, it is very easy to imagine situations in which she will not be able to find a local service or a private philanthropy to provide the help she seeks. The question we must now ask is: What's so bad about that? If children were always better off being with their mother all day and if, by the act of giving birth, a mother acquired the inalienable right to be with the child, then her situation would be unjust to her and injurious to her children. Neither assertion can be defended, however—especially not in the 1980s, when more mothers of all classes work away from the home than ever before, and even more especially not in view of the empirical record for the children growing up under the current welfare system. Why should the mother be exempted by the system from the pressures that must affect everyone else's decision to work?

As we survey these prospects, important questions remain unresolved. The first of these is why, if federal social transfers are treacherous, should locally mandated transfers be less so? Why should a municipality be permitted to legislate its own AFDC or Food Stamp program if their results are so inherently bad?

Part of the answer lies in conceptions of freedom. I have deliberately avoided raising them—the discussion is about how to help the disadvantaged, not about how to help the advantaged cut their taxes, to which arguments for personal freedom somehow always get diverted. Nonetheless, the point is valid: Local or even state systems leave much more room than a federal system for everyone, donors and recipients alike, to exercise freedom of choice about the kind of system they live under. Laws are more easily made and changed, and people who find them unacceptable have much more latitude in going somewhere more to their liking.

But the freedom of choice argument, while legitimate, is not necessary. We may put the advantages of local systems in terms of the Law of Imperfect Selection. A federal system must inherently employ very crude, inaccurate rules for deciding who gets what kind of help, and the results are as I outlined them in chapter 16. At the opposite extreme—a neighbor helping a neighbor, a family member helping another family member—the law loses its validity nearly altogether. Very fine-grained judgments based on personal knowledge are being made about specific people and changing situations. In neighborhoods and small cities, the procedures can still bring much individualized information to bear on decisions. Even systems in large cities and states can do much better than a national system; a decaying industrial city in the Northeast and a booming sunbelt city of the same size can and probably should adopt much different rules about who gets what and how much.

A final and equally powerful argument for not impeding local systems is diversity. We know much more in the 1980s than we knew in the 1960s about what does not work. We have a lot to learn about what *does* work. Localities have been a rich source of experiments. Marva Collins in Chicago gives us an example of how a school can bring inner-city students up to national norms. Sister Falaka Fattah in Philadelphia shows us how homeless youths can be rescued from the streets. There are numberless such lessons waiting to be learned from the diversity of local efforts. By all means, let a hundred flowers bloom, and if the federal government can play a useful role in lending a hand and spreading the word of successes, so much the better.

The ultimate unresolved question about our proposal to abolish income maintenance for the working-aged is how many people will fall through the cracks. In whatever detail we try to foresee the consequences, the objection may always be raised: We cannot be *sure* that everyone will be taken care of in the degree to which we would wish. But this observation by no means settles the question. If one may point in objection to the child now fed by Food Stamps who would go hungry, one may also point with satisfaction to the child who would have an entirely different and better future. Hungry children should be fed; there is no argument about that. It is no less urgent that children be allowed to grow up in a system free of the forces that encourage them to remain poor and dependent. If a strategy reasonably promises to remove those forces, after so many attempts to "help the poor" have failed, it is worth thinking about.

But that rationale is too vague. Let me step outside the persona I have employed and put the issue in terms of one last intensely personal hypothetical example. Let us suppose that you, a parent, could know that tomorrow your own child would be made an orphan. You have a choice. You may put your child with an extremely poor family, so poor that your child will be badly clothed and will indeed sometimes be hungry. But you also know that the parents have worked hard all their lives, will make sure your child goes to school and studies, and will teach your child that independence is a primary value. Or you may put your child with a family with parents who have never worked, who will be incapable of overseeing your child's education— but who have plenty of food and good clothes, provided by others. If the choice about where one would put one's own child is as clear to you as it is to me, on what grounds does one justify support of a system that, indirectly but without doubt, makes the other choice for other children? The answer that "What we really want is a world where that choice is not forced upon us" is no answer. We have tried to have it that way. We failed. Everything we know about why we failed tells us that more of the same will not make the dilemma go away.

THE IDEAL OF OPPORTUNITY

Billions for equal opportunity, not one cent for equal outcome—such is the slogan to inscribe on the banner of whatever cause my proposals constitute. Their common theme is to make it possible to get as far as one can go on one's merit, hardly a new ideal in American thought.

The ideal itself has never lapsed. What did lapse was the recognition that practical merit exists. Some people are better than others. They deserve more of society's rewards, of which money is only one small part. A principal function of social policy is to make sure they have the opportunity to reap those rewards. Government cannot identify the worthy, but it can protect a society in which the worthy can identify themselves.

I am proposing triage of a sort, triage by self-selection. In triage on the battlefield, the doctor makes the decision—this one gets treatment, that one waits, the other one is made comfortable while waiting to die. In our social triage, the decision is left up to the patient. The patient always has the right to say "I can do X" and get a chance to prove it. Society always has the right to hold him to that pledge. The patient always has the right to fail. Society always has the right to let him.

There is in this stance no lack of compassion but a presumption of respect. People—all people, black or white, rich or poor—may be unequally responsible for what has happened to them in the past, but all are equally responsible for what they do next. . . . [I]n our idealized society a person can fail repeatedly and always be qualified for another chance—to try again, to try something easier, to try something different. The options are always open. Opportunity is endless. There is no punishment for failure, only a total absence of rewards. Society—or our idealized society—should be preoccupied with making sure that achievement is rewarded.

There is no shortage of people to be rewarded. Go into any inner-city school and you will find students of extraordinary talent, kept from knowing how good they are by rules we imposed in the name of fairness. Go into any poor community, and you will find people of extraordinary imagination and perseverance, energy and pride, making tortured accommodations to the strange world we created in the name of generosity. The success stories of past generations of poor in this country are waiting to be repeated.

There is no shortage of institutions to provide the rewards. Our schools know how to educate students who want to be educated. Our industries know how to find productive people and reward them. Our police know how to protect people who are ready to cooperate in their own protection. Our system of justice knows how to protect the rights of individuals who know what their rights are. Our philanthropic institutions know how to multiply the effectiveness of people who are already trying to help themselves. In short, American society is very good at reinforcing the investment of an individual in himself. For the affluent and for the middle-class, these mechanisms continue to work about as well as they ever have, and we enjoy their benefits. Not so for the poor. American government, in its recent social policy, has been ineffectual in trying to stage-manage their decision to invest, and it has been unintentionally punitive toward those who would make the decision on their own. It is time to get out of their way.

ESCAPISM

It is entertaining to indulge in speculations about solutions, but they remain only speculations. Congress will not abolish income-maintenance for the working-aged. . . . More generally, it is hard to imagine any significant reform of social policy in the near future. When one thinks of abolishing income maintenance, for example, one must recall that ours is a system that, faced with the bankruptcy of Social Security in the early 1980s, went into paroxysms of anxiety at the prospect of delaying the cost-of-living increase for six months.

But the cautiousness of the system is not in itself worrisome. Reforms should be undertaken carefully and slowly, and often not at all. What should worry us instead is a peculiar escapism that

has gripped the consideration of social policy. It seems that those who legislate and administer and write about social policy can tolerate any increase in actual suffering as long as the system in place does not explicitly permit it. It is better, by the logic we have been living with, that we try to take care of 100 percent of the problem and make matters worse than that we solve 75 percent of the problem with a solution that does not try to do anything about the rest.

Escapism is a natural response. Most of us want to help. It makes us feel bad to think of neglected children and rat-infested slums, and we are happy to pay for the thought that people who are good at taking care of such things are out there. If the numbers of neglected children and numbers of rats seem to be going up instead of down, it is understandable that we choose to focus on how much we put into the effort instead of what comes out. The tax checks we write buy us, for relatively little money and no effort at all, a quieted conscience. The more we pay, the more certain we can be that we have done our part, and it is essential that we feel that way regardless of what we accomplish. A solution that would have us pay less *and* acknowledge that some would go unhelped is unacceptable.

To this extent, the barrier to radical reform of social policy is not the pain it would cause the intended beneficiaries of the present system, but the pain it would cause the donors. The real contest about the direction of social policy is not between people who want to cut budgets and people who want to help. When reforms finally do occur, they will happen not because stingy people have won, but because generous people have stopped kidding themselves.

Questions for Analysis

1. Is Murray's picture of a future without welfare overly optimistic? How many people would "fall between the cracks"? Do you agree that they would be responsible for their failures?

2. When discussing single mothers, Murray denies that a woman has an "inalienable right" to be with her child. Do you agree? Should a woman who cannot support her children be forced to turn them over to a state-run orphanage, as some welfare opponents in Congress have advocated?

3. Do you agree with Murray's preference for local welfare programs over federal welfare programs? Will local governments find themselves overburdened if federal welfare programs are eliminated?

4. Murray asks us to imagine our own orphaned children in two different settings. In one, they are poorly clothed and fed but their adoptive parents are hard-working. In the other, their needs are amply met but they live in a welfare family. Which would you prefer? Why?

5. Murray writes, "Government cannot identify the worthy, but it can protect a society in which the worthy can identify themselves." Would a society without federal welfare programs be such a society?

6. According to Murray, compassion, not stinginess, should lead us to make radical changes in welfare policy. Do you agree?

7. Would justice be served by the elimination of federal welfare programs?

CASE PRESENTATION
Marta Green

Marta Green was nineteen years old when she and her husband left Honduras for the United States. By her mid-twenties, broke and with little in the way of job skills, she was a divorced mother with two daughters and on welfare. In *Living on the Edge: The Realities of Welfare in America,*[1] she described to author Mark Robert Rank the impact of the divorce:

> To me my divorce and the breaking up of my house was a crisis. I had everything. Everything I needed, you know, like electrical knives. That probably doesn't sound like much to you. But I did have all my utensils in the kitchen. And then, I come to an empty place, like we came here. We didn't have a frying pan. We didn't have a plate, a cup, or anything.
>
> When you get married you get everything in the bridal shower. And in the wedding you get stuff. And then little by little, before the kids come, you get things that you need, so you're all set up. But when we moved here, I had to buy the bed for my kids because we were sleeping on the floor. That's money from the same grant, from welfare. But I could not buy

that bed with the money left in one month. I had to save three-and-a-half months before I got the bed. And then there's things like the bed sheets and pillow cases. This is a crisis to me. It is. And then you come into the kitchen, and the kids want pancakes, and you don't have a frying pan (pp. 41–42).

Asked by Rank about her activities with her children, she answered:

> In the winter we don't go anywhere. Because it's very hard without a car. I always had a car until last winter. It was very hard. Because we had to wait there sometimes twenty minutes for the bus. And with the kids and the very cold days, it's very hard. I only took them out last winter once, besides the Saturday afternoons that we go to church.
>
> One Sunday, they had some free tickets to go to the circus. And I only had to buy my ticket. They both had theirs free. The circus was at seven. And it was done by ten. And we were waiting for the bus until eleven thirty that Sunday night. In the middle of the winter. And then finally we started walkin' home. We walked all the way home. We made it home by twelve thirty. They were tired and almost frozen. And then I thought, this is it, no more.

---

1. From *Living on the Edge,* by Mark Robert Rank. © 1994 by Columbia University Press. Reprinted by permission of the publisher.

So we really don't go very much anywhere (pp. 53–54).

Equally frustrating for Green is her inability to afford many things her daughters ask for, including the status symbols other parents can afford:

> Like the kids at school, they wear Nike tennis shoes. Name-brand tennis shoes. And then I go and buy them a five-dollar pair of tennis shoes. And they say, "Mom, no. We want the Nike shoes because my girlfriend, Emily, has them." And I say, "No, because for thirteen dollars I can buy shoes for both of you." And they get angry and they don't understand. But I try to talk to them. They are very good kids. They get upset for a little while and sometimes they cry, but after they get over it, I just talk to them and say, "Listen, this is the situation that we are going through. But we'll get over this. And in a couple of years, Mommy's going to buy you some nicer stuff. But right now we have to take it like it is" (p. 69).

When Rank asked her if she thought she would ever want more children, she answered:

> No. No. I don't think that I *ever* want to have another child. I think that will stop me from doing things that I want to do. And it won't be fair to me. It won't be fair for the new child. And it won't be fair at all for the two that I have (p. 77).

In Rank's study of Wisconsin welfare recipients from 1981 to 1986, 4 percent of the sample reported that welfare initially made them lazy and continued to make them lazy. Another 14 percent reported that they stopped feeling lazy as their sense of pride led them to seek work. Still another 8 percent reported that welfare made them feel trapped and depressed. Marta Green belongs to the 16 percent reporting that welfare makes them work harder. As she told Rank:

> It's not makin' me lazy. It's makin' me more ambitious than I was before. Because when I was livin' with my husband, I had my house and food and my part-time job. I had everything I wanted for my life. Now I am here. And I go to school in the morning. Then I come home and do something around the house. And then I look at this place empty and I say, "Welfare, is this what you're going to give me all my life?" And I do not want it. I want to get over this. It's not making me lazy. Because I do not like it. I like to be able to be free (*chooses words very carefully*) (p. 136).

Asked about her hopes, she told him:

> And the hope that I have is . . . (*sigh*) after I start workin'; I'll pay the state back somehow. I keep track of everythin' I get from them. And I already know how much I received last year from them. And this year. And if my taxes are not enough, I put in something if I am able to, to the Red Cross, Salvation Army. And this is the hope that I have. To know that I do not owe anythin'. That if ever someone ask me, "Did you ever receive welfare?" I say, "Yes. But I paid back. It was a loan that I got." That's my hope, pretty much (p. 99).

Questions for Analysis

1. What are the most common stereotypes of a welfare mother? Does Marta Green fit them?

2. Does Marta Green seem destined for welfare dependence? Why or why not?

3. Is Marta Green one of the women who would fall through the cracks in Murray's "thought experiment"?

4. Does Marta Green's story change your opinion one way or the other about welfare? If so, how?

CASE PRESENTATION
The Poorest Place in America

"The town has no public parks or swimming pools, no movie theaters, no shopping malls, not even a McDonald's or a Wal-Mart. In fact, business in Lake Providence, Louisiana, is so bad that even the pawnshop has shut down."

So begins Jack E. White's profile of "The Poorest Place in America," which appeared in the August 15, 1994, issue of *Time*. Among the other depressing facts pointed out in the article are the following:

1. According to the 1990 census, one Census Block Number within the city, which contains three-quarters of the city's population, had the lowest median annual household income in the country, only $6,536.

2. According to a 1992 study by the Children's Defense Fund, the parish in which Lake Providence is located had the country's highest rate of children under eighteen years old living in poverty. The rate was 70.1 percent.

The article also highlights the lack of year-round work in Lake Providence, noting that jobs are "scarce, low paying and seasonal," often "back-breaking work in the nearby cotton fields," and that hundreds of families in the town of 5,500 people live on meager welfare payments most of the year. How meager? For a single mother of one, the monthly payment is $123. For a single mother of four, it amounts to only $370.

Most Lake Providence residents who can escape, the article says, do escape. Those who cannot escape have set their hopes on an application to become part of a federal empowerment zone. An empowerment zone is an area eligible for a variety of programs meant to spur economic development, including tax incentives to attract employers and jobs, federal job-training subsidies, and other grants from Washington. In the case of Lake Providence, the hopes are to attract a factory, to open a federal-loan office serving small businesses throughout the country, and to become a tourist destination. How successful the town will be remains in doubt.

Questions for Analysis

1. Lake Providence seems a perfect example of Michael Harrington's pockets of poverty. What's the best way to deal with its problems?

2. Does Charles Murray's "thought experiment" pay sufficient attention to people like Lake Providence's poor? If not, what could Murray say about them?

3. Critics of empowerment zones say that tax breaks are not enough to bring employers to areas like Lake Providence. Employers also require a reliable work force, good schools, and a decent quality of life. Do you agree? If so, what alternatives are there for the people of Lake Providence?

4. What would Kai Nielsen say about Lake Providence? What would his solution be?

5. The total cost of proposed tax breaks and grants in the application is $100 million. Can you think of a better way of using the money to help the people of Lake Providence?

CASE PRESENTATION
Welfare as We've Begun to Know It

The 1996 welfare reform law replaced Aid to Families with Dependent Children with a program known as Temporary Assistance to Needy Families (TANF), which gives states considerable freedom in limiting benefits, cutting them off completely, and requiring recipients to work for their benefits. Many have taken advantage of this freedom.

For instance, while the law sets a lifetime limit of sixty months on benefits, many states have set even stricter limits. Some limit benefits to a specific number of months over a set period of consecutive months. In four states (Arizona, Florida, Louisiana, and Massachusetts), the limit is twenty-four months of benefits over sixty consecutive months. In Nebraska, it's twenty-four over forty-eight consecutive months; in Oregon, twenty-four over eighty-four consecutive months. Other states limit consecutive months of benefits. In four states (Illinois, Nevada, South Carolina, and Virginia), the limit is twenty-four consecutive months. In Tennessee, the limit is eighteen. Four states limit total lifetime benefits to fewer than sixty months—Connecticut to twenty-one, Delaware to forty-eight, and New Mexico and Utah to thirty-six. One state, Texas, reduces benefits every twelfth month up to the thirty-sixth month on welfare, while two others, Arizona and Indiana, reduce them after the twenty-fourth. (Not all of these limits are exceptionless. Indiana, for instance, allows an extra month of benefits for every six months of work, up to twenty-four months of extra benefits. Tennessee allows an extra six months in counties with high unemployment rates. Connecticut allows six-month extensions for victims of family violence.)

In addition to these restrictions, seventeen states deny additional benefits for a child born to a family on TANF, and two provide only partial additional benefits. Two others, Oklahoma and South Carolina, provide additional benefits only in the form of a voucher, and Maryland provides the additional benefit only to a third party.

TANF also places work requirements on recipients, who are required to seek jobs or join a work program after either twenty-four months of benefits or when the state determines that they are ready to work, whichever comes first. Here, also, the states are free to set stricter requirements, and thirty-two of them have reduced the number of months to within six. Nine require work or a job search immediately after application for benefits. Wisconsin has replaced welfare with workfare, requiring TANF families to work thirty hours a week. In thirty-five states, recipients who do not comply can lose their full cash benefits; in seven of the states, the loss of benefits can last a lifetime. (Again, there are exceptions. Twenty-four states exempt parents of children younger than one-year-old, and all states allow health exemptions.)

Questions for Analysis

1. How would Trudy Govier and Charles Murray evaluate the changes in welfare policy?
2. Critics of the new welfare system call it an attack on the poor. Supporters call it a means of ending welfare dependence. Which side, if either, do you agree with?
3. How strict should the limits on TANF benefits be? How strict the work requirements?
4. In terms of social justice, is TANF an improvement over AFDC, a setback, or neither better nor worse? How would John Hospers and Kai Nielsen answer this question?

CASE PRESENTATION
The Women of Project Match[1]

Roslyn Hale is the thirty-year-old mother of a four-year-old son, both of them living on welfare. She had been on welfare once before but left it to take a job as a hotel maid. After being fired because of a fight with her supervisor, she began working the overnight shift at a convenience store. She left that job after a drunk from a nearby bar threatened her with a knife. Then she took a job at another convenience store, only to be laid off because of slowing business.

1. The information comes from Jason DeParle's front-page article in *The New York Times*, "Welfare Mothers Find Jobs Easy to Get but Hard to Hold," October 24, 1994.

Alesia Watts, twenty-six, also left welfare to take a job. Hers was a telemarketing job at $5.25 an hour with no health insurance. She quit and returned to welfare after her daughter injured her foot, but she was unhappy with her job in any case. She felt sexually harassed by some of the men she called, resented the close watch by her supervisor, and considered her two bathroom breaks every five hours insufficient. Unlike Roslyn Hale, she is now back at work, this time at a race track concession. The pay is better, the job comes with health insurance, and she enjoys the work.

Vanessa Williams was less fortunate. After she left welfare, she lost a succession of jobs because of bad experiences with boyfriends. One boyfriend threw drug parties in their house when he was supposed to be babysitting, and another, after severely beating her, came to her workplace and threatened further beatings. Now, at the age of thirty-four, she is back on welfare.

All three women have been through the doors of Project Match, an employment program in the inner city of Chicago that tracks the successes and failures of the women it helps to get off welfare. They are among the increasing number of women known as welfare cyclers. According to one estimate—by LaDonna A. Pavetti of Washington's Urban Institute—about 40 percent of the women who go on welfare can be considered cyclers, which she defines as women who spend a total of twenty-four months on welfare scattered over a sixty-month period.

What causes welfare cycling? Researchers from Northwestern University who studied Project Match cite a variety of factors, including the lack of health insurance and childcare, the lack of social skills required to keep a job, resentment of supervisors, and habitual lateness. Toby Herr, the project's director, points to the frequency of Vanessa Williams's problem—resentful boyfriends. Alesia Watts, who seems to have broken the cycle, has this to say: "You have to like where you're working at. And like the money. And have the benefits. And get a babysitter. Then there's no reason for you to go on welfare."

Questions for Analysis

1. Would ending welfare payments after two years help the women of Project Match? Would abolishing all federal transfer payments to the poor help?

2. Suppose that women who left welfare for low-paying jobs were provided with health insurance, childcare, and wage subsidies. Would that reduce welfare cycling?

3. According to project director Toby Herr, cases like Vanessa Williams's show that welfare reform cannot work until the employment rates for women are improved. Do you agree?

4. Do the women of Project Match deserve sympathy, or are they to blame for their situations?

10

Discrimination

On December 10, 1970, the Equal Employment Opportunity Commission (EEOC) petitioned the Federal Communications Commission not to back a request by American Telephone and Telegraph (AT&T) for a rate increase on the grounds that AT&T was engaging in pervasive, systemwide, and blatantly unlawful discrimination against women, blacks, Spanish-surnamed Americans, and other minorities. After nearly two years of negotiation with the EEOC, AT&T finally reached an agreement with the government on December 28, 1972, whereby it agreed, among other things, not to discriminate in the future and to set up goals and timetables for hiring women and minorities into all non-management job classifications where they were underrepresented. For its part, the EEOC agreed to drop all outstanding equal-employment actions against AT&T.

Three years later, on December 8, 1975, AT&T was sued by Dan McAleer, an AT&T service representative. McAleer claimed he had lost out on a promotion to a less qualified female employee as a result of AT&T's implementation of its agreement with the EEOC. McAleer had worked for AT&T for five years and had scored thirty-four of thirty-five on the company's performance rating. Sharon

Hullery, the woman who beat McAleer for the promotion, had worked at AT&T for less than five years and had scored thirty points.

On June 9, 1976, the U.S. District Court in Washington, D.C., ruled that AT&T owed McAleer monetary compensation but not the promotion. AT&T owed McAleer the money, said the court, because he was an innocent victim of an agreement intended to remedy the company's wrongdoing. But the court didn't think AT&T owed McAleer the promotion because, in the court's view, that might help perpetuate and prolong the effects of the discrimination that the AT&T–EEOC agreement was designed to eliminate.

On January 18, 1979, the agreement between AT&T and the EEOC expired. AT&T had reached 99.7 percent of the female-hiring goals it had set up in 1973.

In recent years, laws have been passed and programs formulated to ensure fair and equal treatment of all people in employment practices. Nevertheless, unequal practices still exist. To help remedy these, the federal government in the early 1970s instituted an affirmative-action program.

Before affirmative action, many institutions already followed nondiscriminatory as well as merit-hiring employment practices to equalize employment opportunities. In proposing affirmative action, the government recognized the worth of such endeavors, but said that it did not think they were enough. *Affirmative action, therefore, refers to positive measures beyond neutral nondiscriminatory and merit-hiring employment practices.* It is an aggressive program intended to identify and remedy unfair discrimination practiced against many people who are qualified for jobs. Although most of our discussion focuses on discrimination in employment, closely analogous arguments apply in debates over admission to competitive colleges and universities, especially when racial minorities or women have been admitted historically in much smaller number than their presence in the applicant pool or the general population.

Among the most controversial versions of affirmative action are preferential- and quota-hiring systems. *Preferential hiring* is an employment practice designed to give special consideration to people from groups that traditionally have been victimized by racism, sexism, or other forms of discrimination. *Quota hiring* was sometimes ordered by the courts for a specific organization that had expressly refused to hire certain groups, until some appropriate balance could be achieved. For example, companies and unions were required to provide apprentice and reapprentice training to hire, promote, and train minorities and women in specified numerical ratios, in specified job categories, until specified remedial goals were achieved. But in other situations, a less rigid "goal" is established to assess whether hiring has indeed been nondiscriminatory over a period of time. For example, if a company has hired 20 percent women for a certain type of job over a number of years, but the labor pool of persons qualified and available to work in that job was 50 percent women, then this disparity raises a presumption that discrimination against women occurred in the hiring. Although not a "quota," this use of statistical analysis has also sometimes been called "quota hiring," though supporters object that this is a misleading label for the use of statistics to analyze discrimination.

But critics charge that at least in some instances, implementing affirmative-action guidelines has led to *reverse discrimination—that is, the unfair treatment of a majority member (usually a white male).* Presumably, this was the basis for McAleer's complaint.

Was he treated unfairly? Was AT&T's action moral? Would it have been fairer had the employees names been thrown into a hat from which one was drawn? Obviously, such preferential programs raise questions of social justice.

Affirmative action also has meanings other than "preferential hiring." In its mildest form, it means simply an aggressive program of recruitment of candidates to ensure that qualified women and racial minorities are appropriately represented in the applicant pool. In a somewhat stronger form, it involves a conclusion that traditional hiring criteria have masked hidden biases against certain groups, requiring a modification of those criteria to more appropriately match the actual qualifications needed for the position in a way as free of bias as possible. Ferreting out qualifications that might seem on the surface to be appropriate distinguishing criteria is a long process upon which this version of affirmative action has focused.

Undoubtedly, some will wonder: Why not focus directly on the morality of sexism? By *sexism*, we mean the unfair treatment of a person exclusively on the basis of sex. Perhaps we should focus on it, but consider that in all our discussions so far, we have made reasonable cases for at least two sides of an issue. True, perhaps one side was more flawed than another, but in all cases, reasonable people could disagree. But the fact is that few seriously argue any more that sexism, as defined, is moral. So if we focused on sexism, we would be inviting a most lopsided discussion. This would be unfortunate in the light of so many aspects of sexism that genuinely deserve moral debate. One of these aspects involves such proposed remedies as preferential treatment.

Another reason for not considering sexism exclusively is that this chapter naturally raises questions of social justice. Many discussions of social justice founder because they remain abstract, content to theorize while scrupulously avoiding practice. For example, it is easy and safe to argue that a government must remedy racial injustice. It is far more controversial to argue that a government must implement forced busing to do so. The same applies to sexism. Most would agree that the government has an obligation to correct the social injustice of sexism, but how?

It is one thing to recognize, deplore, and want to correct any injustice. It is entirely another thing to remedy the injustice fairly. Sadly, too many discussions of social justice ignore means entirely, often offering the defense that the means vary from situation to situation. This is undoubtedly true, but the debate flying around so many social justice questions today concerns proposed means. We should learn to examine every situation's means and also the common but agonizing predicament of applauding the intention and even the probable consequences of an action, but deploring the action itself. For many people, preferential treatment is just such a problem.

Although we focus on issues of race and sex discrimination in this chapter, it is worth noting the emergence in recent years of very similar issues for people with disablities, especially in the workplace. The Americans with Disabilities Act of 1990 requires that employers and educational institutions make "reasonable accommodation" so that individuals with disablities can compete to the best of their abilities in employment and education. While everyone would agree that we should not discriminate *against* people with disablities simply because of a disability, the controversy emerges over what some consider favoritism or special treatment of individuals with disablities. In a 2001 decision, the U.S. Supreme Court held that the PGA tour must allow disabled golfer Casey Martin to use a golf cart in professional tournaments, even though the other players must all walk the course. The PGA had argued that his request would "fundamentally alter the nature" of the game, but this was rejected by the Court. By considering whether this is fair to other players, we confront many of the same issues concerning justice in society that we face with discrimination by race and sex. Is society obligated to do whatever it takes to create a truly "level playing field" for everyone? Do these programs give unfair advantages to some groups but not others? Or is society obligated only to make sure we do not discriminate *against* people based on race, sex, or disability, but otherwise let people fend for themselves?

DISCRIMINATION: ITS NATURE AND FORMS

To discriminate in employment is to make an adverse decision against employees based on their membership in a certain class.[1] Included in the preceding definition of discrimination in employment are three basic elements: (1) The decision is against employees solely because of their membership in a certain group. (2) The decision is based on the assumption that the group is in some way inferior to some other group and thus deserving of unequal treatment. (3) The decision in some way harms those it's aimed at. Since, traditionally, most of the discrimination in the American workplace has been aimed at women and minorities such as blacks and Hispanics, the following discussion focuses on these groups.

On-the-job discrimination can be intentional or unintentional, practiced by a single individual or individuals in a company or by the institution itself. *Intentional* here means knowingly or consciously; *unintentional* means unthinkingly or not consciously. *Institution* refers to the business, company, corporation, profession, or even the system within which the discrimination operates. These distinctions provide a basis for identifying four forms of discrimination: (1) intentional individual, (2) unintentional individual, (3) intentional institutional, and (4) unintentional institutional.

1. *Intentional individual* discrimination is an isolated act of discrimination *knowingly* performed by some individual out of personal prejudice. Example: A male personnel director routinely passes over females for supervisory jobs because he believes and knowingly acts on the belief that "lady bosses mean trouble."

2. *Unintentional individual* discrimination is an isolated act of discrimination performed by some individual who *unthinkingly* or *unconsciously* adopts traditional practices and stereotypes. Example: If the male in the preceding case acted without being aware of the bias underlying his decisions, his action would fall into this category.

3. *Intentional institutional* discrimination is an act of discrimination that is part of the reactive behavior of a company or profession which knowingly discriminates out of the personal prejudices of its members. Example: The male personnel director passes over women for supervisory jobs because "the boys in the company don't like to take orders from females."

---

1. Manuel G. Velasquez, *Business Ethics: Concepts and Cases* (Englewood Cliffs, N.J.: Prentice-Hall, 1982), p. 266.

4. *Unintentional institutional* discrimination is an act of discrimination that is part of the routine behavior of a company or profession that has unknowingly incorporated sexually or racially prejudicial practices into its operating procedures. Example: An engineering firm routinely avoids hiring women because of the stereotypical assumption that women don't make good engineers or that its clients won't do business with women.

In recent years, discussions of discrimination have focused on institutional forms, with special emphasis on the unintentional institutional. In fact, it's been this kind of discrimination that some believe only affirmative-action programs can root out. Others consider programs like this inherently unjust or counterproductive. They say that workplace discrimination can be corrected through strict enforcement of anti-discrimination law without resorting to preferential-treatment programs. The force of these positions depends in part on whether the body of anti-discriminatory legislation that has developed over the past twenty years has, in fact, tended to reduce discrimination in the workplace. If it has, then it would lend weight to the anti-affirmative-action positions. If it hasn't, then the proaffirmative-action position would be strengthened. So before inspecting the two positions, let's briefly examine the relative positions of whites and minorities and of males and females in the American workplace to see if they say anything about ongoing discrimination.

EVIDENCE OF DISCRIMINATION

Determining the presence of discrimination isn't easy because many factors could possibly account for the relative positions of various groups in the work world. But generally speaking, there are reasonable grounds for thinking that an institution is practicing discrimination (intentional or unintentional) when (1) statistics indicate that members of a group are being treated unequally in comparison with other groups, and (2) endemic attitudes, and formal and informal practices and policies, seem to account for the skewed statistics.

Statistical Evidence

Compelling statistical evidence points to the fact that a disproportionate number of women and minority members hold the less desirable jobs and get paid less than their white male counterparts. For example, at all occupational levels, women make less money than men—even for the same work—despite legislation forbidding discrimination on the basis of sex. According to Census Bureau statistics from 1999 (see table), women working full time earned only 75.1 percent as much as full-time male workers. Moreover, the disparity cut across all occupational categories from salaried administrators and officials (the highest paid) to farming, forestry, and fishing (the lowest paid). In the former category, the median income for men in 1998 was $55,664, while the median for women was $36,389; in the latter, the respective median incomes were $18,855 and $15,865. Even though much of the gap between men and women reflects differences among older workers, the 1999 average yearly earnings for female full-time workers under thirty years old remained lower than the average for men under thirty at every education level. For instance, the average income for male high school graduates between twenty-five and twenty-nine was $25,559 compared to $20,669 for women; among college graduates with only a bachelor's degree, the respective figures were $40,098 and $35,295; among those with a master's degree, $54,777 and $42,834.

Similar disparities show up between non-Hispanic white males and black and Hispanic males. The 1999 median income for full-time workers over twenty-five of the first group was $41,555 compared to $30,926 for their black counterparts and $25,242 for their Hispanic counterparts. Once again, the disparities applied to all educational levels. Among high school graduates, for example, the respective figures were $34,839, $27,408, and $25,291; among college graduates with only a bachelor's degree, $51,884, $40,805, and $41,467; among those with a master's degree, $61,904, $52,308, and $50,410.[2] These and other statistics indicate that women and minorities are still not treated as equals of white men.

Additional Evidence

Although some would disagree, the statistics alone don't establish discrimination, for one could always argue that other factors account for these disparities. But there are indications of widespread attitudes and formal and informal institutional practices and policies which, taken collectively, point to discrimination as the cause of these statistical differences.

One such indication is the number of job requirements that are not related to job performance but discriminate against minorities and women. Standardized intelligence tests, for example, are thought by many people to be culturally biased against blacks. Yet in many cases, standardized intelligence tests are required, and applicants scoring the highest are given the available jobs, even though lower scores do not correlate with poor job performance. Similarly, weight requirements often rule out women from jobs involving physical work even though they have the physical ability to perform well.

Then there's the commonplace practice in many trades and industries of filling positions by word-of-mouth recruitment policies. In jobs dominated by white males, the word of a job vacancy tends to reach other white males. And even when others do learn of the vacancy, they may not be in any position to be hired to fill it. The problem is particularly acute at the executive level, where many women and minorities hit "an invisible ceiling" beyond which they have difficulty rising. Part of the problem, many claim, is the existence of private white male clubs, where important business contacts are made and developed. Another, they claim, is the resistance of people at the level to those who are "not like us."

Taken together, the statistics, personal and institutional attitudes, assumptions, and practices provide powerful evidence of intractable discrimination against women and minorities in the American workplace. Recognizing the existence of such discrimination and believing that, for a variety of reasons, it's wrong, we have as a nation passed laws expressly forbidding discrimination in recruitment, screening, promotion, compensation, and firing practices. In short, specific laws have been enacted to ensure equal

---

2. These figures come from the Census Bureau's Web site at Historical Income Tables—People, table P-48, and Money Income in the United States: 1999, tables 9 and 10.

U.S. Census Bureau
Selected Characteristics of People—Total Money Income in 1999 of
People 15 Years Old and Over by Work Experience in 1999 and Sex

[Numbers in thousands. People 15 years old and over as of March of the following year.]

Characteristic	Total	With Income							
		Total	$1 to $4,999 or loss	$5,000 to $9,999	$10,000 to $14,999	$15,000 to $24,999	$25,000 to $34,999	$35,000 to $49,999	$50,000 to $74,999
Male									
Full-Time, Year-Round Worker									
All males	57,530	57,519	698	1,009	3,217	9,944	10,712	12,457	10,914
Race and Hispanic Origin									
White	49,150	49,149	605	825	2,553	7,946	8,985	10,826	9,668
Non-Hispanic White	42,993	42,981	522	589	1,628	5,888	7,799	9,911	9,138
Black	5,642	5,642	64	135	445	1,509	1,225	1,110	769
Hispanic origin[1]	6,476	6,476	85	250	963	2,156	1,242	968	567
Age									
Under 65 years	56,245	56,234	664	994	3,177	9,760	10,505	12,247	10,714
15 to 24 years	4,463	4,457	73	337	937	1,760	844	365	105
25 to 34 years	14,139	14,136	149	218	88	3,097	3,285	3,482	2,090
35 to 44 years	17,603	17,603	189	189	738	2,521	3,273	4,119	3,879
45 to 54 years	13,816	13,813	150	149	473	1,601	2,079	3,047	3,303
55 to 64 years	6,224	6,224	102	100	240	782	1,023	1,233	1,336
65 years and over	1,285	1,285	35	15	41	184	207	210	200
65 to 74 years	1,063	1,063	24	15	31	137	177	174	173
75 years and over	222	222	11	–	9	48	30	36	27
Educational Attainment									
Total, 25 years and over	53,068	53,062	625	671	2,280	8,185	9,867	12,092	10,089
Less than 9th grade	1,993	1,993	41	112	361	795	349	221	79
9th to 12th grade (no diploma)	3,298	3,295	81	97	447	1,018	841	524	216
High school graduate (includes equivalency)	16,592	16,589	231	234	840	3,475	3,986	4,235	2,640
Some college, no degree	9,684	9,684	109	118	288	1,463	1,986	2,682	1,967
Associate degree	4,359	4,359	44	34	98	561	819	1,215	1,090
Bachelor's degree or more	17,142	17,142	118	77	247	873	1,886	3,213	4,816
Bachelor's degree	11,142	11,142	72	58	188	700	1,458	2,432	3,238
Master's degree	3,725	2,735	20	13	38	134	322	556	1,138
Professional degree	1,267	1,267	16	6	11	16	57	116	200
Doctorate degree	1,008	1,008	10	–	9	23	50	109	240
Female									
Full-time, Year-Round Worker									
All females	40,421	40,421	633	1,391	4,059	11,049	9,433	7,656	4,185
Race and Hispanic Origin									
White	32,557	32,557	513	1,034	3,119	8,760	7,584	6,321	3,495
Non-Hispanic White	28,985	28,985	428	807	2,334	7,572	6,957	5,897	3,327
Black	5,899	5,899	86	279	743	1,810	1,434	964	423
Hispanic origin[1]	3,770	3,770	87	234	817	1,273	652	451	184
Age									
Under 65 years	39,734	39,734	626	1,352	4,012	10,876	9,288	7,526	4,084
15 to 24 years	3,330	3,330	84	361	703	1,388	531	209	37
25 to 34 years	9,791	9,791	117	300	997	2,913	2,551	1,788	722
35 to 44 years	11,875	11,875	179	298	1,157	3,003	2,796	2,449	1,337
45 to 54 years	10,380	10,380	153	247	835	2,408	2,455	2,212	1,429
55 to 64 years	4,358	4,358	94	145	320	1,164	954	867	559
65 years and over	687	687	6	39	47	173	144	131	102
65 to 74 years	554	554	6	39	25	141	122	108	82
75 years and over	134	134	–	6	22	33	22	23	20
Educational Attainment									
Total, 25 years and over	37,091	37,091	549	1,030	3,355	9,661	8,901	7,447	4,149
Less than 9th grade	886	886	22	107	310	310	70	43	11
9th to 12th grade (no diploma)	1,883	1,883	68	152	492	752	277	111	22
High school graduate (includes equivalency)	11,824	11,824	191	444	1,512	4,356	3,105	1,609	490
Some college, no degree	7,453	7,453	106	166	554	2,107	2,082	1,465	659
Associate degree	3,804	3,804	68	64	258	896	1,055	971	363
Bachelor's degree or more	11,242	11,242	93	97	230	1,231	2,312	3,249	2,604
Bachelor's degree	7,607	7,607	67	75	183	1,036	1,851	2,184	1,501
Master's degree	2,818	2,818	8	22	32	149	406	879	902
Professional degree	470	470	11	–	7	28	38	103	103
Doctorate degree	346	346	7	–	8	18	17	83	98

[1]Hispanics may be of any race.

Characteristic	With Income				
	$75,000 and over	Median income		Mean income	
		Value (dollars)	Standard error (dollars)	Value (dollars)	Standard error (dollars)
Male					
Full-Time, Year-Round Worker					
All males	8,569	37,574	247	50,438	398
Race and Hispanic Origin					
White.	7,740	39,331	332	52,040	448
Non-Hispanic White.	7,507	41,406	152	55,216	477
Black.	385	30,297	364	36,387	663
Hispanic origin[1]	246	23,342	519	29,982	687
Age					
Under 65 years	8,175	37,430	193	49,911	393
15 to 24 years	36	19,515	336	21,433	293
25 to 34 years	1,026	32,599	368	40,048	586
35 to 44 years	2,695	40,916	242	52,019	674
45 to 54 years	3,010	46,228	437	60,922	923
55 to 64 years	1,407	44,264	968	62,307	1,564
65 years and over	393	45,781	1,790	73,462	4,616
65 to 74 years	332	46,933	2,235	74,648	5,370
75 years and over	61	40,622	3,156	67,776	7,212
Educational Attainment					
Total, 25 years and over.	8,533	40,333	144	52,873	427
Less than 9th grade	35	20,429	444	24,237	709
9th to 12th grade (no diploma).	70	25,035	535	28,069	556
High school graduate (includes equivalency)	947	33,184	388	38,566	402
Some college, no degree.	1,070	39,221	581	47,082	822
Associate degree.	498	41,638	459	48,346	1,105
Bachelor's degree or more	5,912	60,201	439	79,239	1,058
Bachelor's degree	2,996	52,985	722	68,101	1,028
Master's degree.	1,504	66,243	690	81,866	2,178
Professional degree	845	100,000	37,836	140,591	6,813
Doctorate degree.	567	81,687	3,953	115,509	6,172
Female					
Full-time, Year-Round Worker					
All females	2,015	27,370	121	33,303	236
Race and Hispanic Origin					
White	170	28,023	229	34,005	275
Non-Hispanic White.	1,663	29,369	221	35,194	285
Black.	162	25,142	311	28,894	487
Hispanic origin[1]	71	20,052	414	24,475	645
Age					
Under 65 years	1,970	27,337	122	33,232	238
15 to 24 years	17	17,851	340	19,599	338
25 to 34 years	402	26,670	228	31,137	359
35 to 44 years	655	29,155	418	34,673	475
45 to 54 years	640	30,848	244	36,706	437
55 to 64 years	256	28,764	716	36,154	1,055
65 years and over	45	30,013	11,294	27,415	2,051
65 to 74 years	36	30,297	1,452	37,565	2,332
75 years and over	8	28,191	3,880	36,793	4,233
Educational Attainment	1,998	28,844	216	34,533	253
Total, 25 years and over.					
Less than 9th grade	4	15,098	492	17,647	634
9th to 12th grade (no diploma).	9	17,015	29	20,683	1,610
High school graduate (includes equivalency)	117	23,061	279	25,741	291
Some college, no degree.	313	27,757	269	32,653	433
Associate degree.	128	30,919	318	33,788	572
Bachelor's degree or more	1,426	41,747	275	48,930	579
Bachelor's degree	711	27,993	614	43,950	670
Master's degree.	420	48,097	862	54,354	923
Professional degree	180	59,904	4,479	77,478	4,395
Doctorate degree.	115	60,079	3,130	75,494	5,053

opportunity in employment. The aim of these policies is to prevent further discrimination, and they probably have prevented egregious instances of discrimination. But the evidence indicates that they have not had the effect of providing equal opportunity to women and minorities as groups. Furthermore, anti-discrimination laws do not address the present-day effects of past discrimination. They ignore, for example, the fact that because of past discrimination women and minorities in general lack the skills of white males and are disproportionately underrepresented in more prestigious and better paying jobs. To remedy the effects of past discrimination and seeing no other way to counteract apparently visceral racism and sexism, many people today call for specific affirmative-action programs.

AFFIRMATIVE ACTION: PREFERENTIAL TREATMENT?

As amended by the Equal Employment Opportunity Act of 1972, the Civil Rights Act of 1964 requires businesses that have substantial dealings with the federal government to undertake affirmative-action programs. *Affirmative-action programs are plans designed to correct imbalances in employment that exist directly as a result of past discrimination.* Even though these acts do not technically require companies to undertake affirmative-action programs, courts responded to acts of job discrimination by ordering the offending firms to implement such programs to combat the effects of past discrimination. In effect, then, all business institutions must adopt affirmative-action programs either in theory or in fact. They must be able to prove that they have not been practicing institutional sexism or racism, and if they cannot prove this, they must undertake programs to ensure against racism or sexism.

What do affirmative-action programs involve? The EEOC lists general guidelines as steps to affirmative action. Under these steps, firms must issue a written equal-employment policy and an affirmative-action commitment. They must appoint a top official with responsibility and authority to direct and implement their program and to publicize their policy and affirmative-action commitment. In addition, firms must survey current female and minority employment by department and job classification. Where underrepresentation of these groups is evident, firms must develop goals and timetables to improve in each area of underrepresentation. They then must develop specific programs to achieve these goals, establish an internal audit system to monitor them, and evaluate progress in each aspect of the program. Finally, companies must develop supportive in-house and community programs to combat discrimination.

In implementing such programs, some companies have adopted a policy of preferential treatment for women and minorities. *Preferential treatment refers to the practice of giving individuals favored consideration in hiring or promotions for other than job-related reasons* (such as the person is female or black). Those espousing preferential treatment argue that such a policy is the only way to remedy traditional sexism and racism or at least that it is the most expeditious and fairest way to do it. In some instances, preferential treatment for women and minorities takes the form of a quota system—that is, *an employment policy of representing women and minorities in the firm in direct proportion to their numbers in society or in the community at large.* Thus, a firm operating in a community which has a 20 percent black population might try to ensure that 20 percent of its work force be black.[3]

To unravel some of the complex moral issues affirmative-action programs can raise, let's look at a specific instance of preferential hiring. Suppose an equally qualified man and woman are applying for a job. The employer, conscious of affirmative-action guidelines and realizing that the company has historically discriminated against women in its employment policies, adopts a preferential hiring system. Since males are already disproportionately well represented and females underrepresented, the preferential system gives the female applicant a decided advantage. As a result, the employer hires the female. Is this action moral? Are affirmative-action programs that operate in the preferential way moral?

Many people argue that affirmative-action programs are inherently discriminatory and therefore unjust. In this context, *discriminatory* should be understood to refer to policies that favor individuals on non-job-related grounds (for example, on the basis of sex, color, or ethnic heritage). It has been argued that preferential hiring is unjust because it involves giving preferential treatment to women and minorities over equally qualified white males, a practice that is clearly discriminatory, albeit in reverse.

Some in favor of affirmative action, however, attempt to rebut this objection by appealing to principles of *compensatory justice. Since women and minorities clearly continue to be victimized directly and indirectly by traditional discrimination in the workplace, they are entitled to some compensation.* This is one basis for preferential treatment. The soundness of this contention seems to rely on at least two factors: (1) that affirmative-action programs involving preferential treatment will in fact provide adequate compensation and (2) that they will provide compensation more fairly than any other alternative.[4] Since the justice and the morality of affirmative-action programs depend to a large degree on these assumptions, we should examine them.

The question that comes to mind in regard to the first assumption is: adequate compensation for whom? The answer seems obvious: for women and minorities. But does this mean *individual* women and minority-group members or women and minorities taken *collectively?* University of Tampa Professor Herman J. Saatkamp, Jr., has demonstrated that this question, far from being merely a technical one, bears directly on the morality of affirmative-action programs and how they are implemented.[5]

Saatkamp points out that the question of the conflict between individual and collective merit typifies the debate between government agencies and business over employment policies. On the one hand, business is ordinarily concerned with the

---

3. Some institutions simply reserve a number of places for women and minority members. The University of California at Davis, for example, had such a policy in its medical school when it denied Alan Bakke admission. Bakke appealed to the Supreme Court, which—in a 5 to 4 decision in 1978—ordered that he be admitted to the medical school and struck down the set-aside quota for racial minorities that Davis had in place at the time. However, the Court also said the university may take race into account in their admissions as long as they did not establish rigid quotas for any particular group.

4. Albert W. Flores, "Reverse Discrimination: Towards a Just Society," in *Business & Professional Ethics,* a quarterly newsletter/report (Troy, N.Y.: Center for the Study of the Human Dimensions of Science & Technology, Rensselaer Polytechnic Institute, Jan. 1978), p. 4.

5. Flores, "Reverse Discrimination," pp. 5–6.

individual merit and deserts of its employees. On the other hand, government agencies primarily focus on the relative status of groups within the population at large. To put the conflict in perspective, employment policies based solely on individual merit would try to ensure that only those individuals who could prove they deserved compensation would benefit and only those proved to be the source of discrimination would suffer. Of course, such a focus places an almost unbearable burden on the resources of an individual to provide sufficient, precise data to document employment discrimination, which is commonly acknowledged to exist at times in subtle, perhaps even imperceptible, forms at various organizational levels. Indeed, social policies recognize this difficulty by focusing on discrimination on an aggregate level. Individuals, then, need not prove they themselves were discriminated against but only that they are members of groups that have traditionally suffered because of discrimination.

Taking the collective approach to remedying job discrimination is not without its own disadvantages.

1. Policies based on collective merit tend to pit one social group against another. White males face off against all nonwhite males; women find themselves jockeying with other disadvantaged groups for priority employment status; black females can end up competing with Hispanic males for preferential treatment. This factionalizing aspect of policies based on collective merit can prove detrimental to society.

2. Policies based on collective merit victimize some individuals. The individual white male who loses out on a job because of preferential treatment given a woman or a minority-group member is penalized.

3. In some cases, the women and minority members selected under preferential treatment are in fact less deserving of compensation than those women and minorities who are not selected. In short, those most in need may not benefit at all when preference by group membership is divorced from individual need.

4. Some members of majority groups may be just as deserving or more deserving of compensation than some women or members of minority groups. Many white males, for example, are more seriously limited in seeking employment than some women and minority-group members are.

5. Policies based on collective merit can be prohibitively expensive for business. To enforce such programs, businesses must hire people to collect data, process forms, deal with government agencies, and handle legal procedures. From business's viewpoint, this additional time, energy, and expense could have been channeled into more commercially productive directions.

In sum, those who argue that affirmative-action programs will provide adequate compensation for the victims of discrimination must grapple with the problems of determining the focus of the compensation: on the individual or on the group. While both focuses have merit, neither is without disadvantages. Furthermore, it seems neither approach can be implemented without first resolving a complex chain of moral concerns.

But even if we assume that affirmative-action programs will provide adequate compensation, it is still difficult to demonstrate the validity of the second assumption of those who endorse affirmative action by appealing to principles of compensatory justice: that such programs will provide compensation more fairly than any other alternative. By nature, affirmative-action programs provide compensation at the expense of the white males' right to fair and equal employment treatment. In other words, affirmative-action programs in the form of preferential treatment undermine the fundamental principle of just employment practice: that a person should be hired or promoted only on job-related grounds. Apparently, then, it is an awesome undertaking to defend the proposition that affirmative action will provide compensation more fairly than any other alternative when such a proposition makes a non-job-related factor (membership in a group) a relevant employment criterion.

Although it would appear that reverse discrimination may not be justified on grounds of compensation, we should not conclude that it cannot be justified. In fact, some people contend that a more careful examination of the principles of justice suggests an alternative defense. As we have mentioned, those who argue against affirmative-action programs do so because such programs allegedly involve unequal treatment and are therefore unjust. The clear assumption here is that whatever involves unequal treatment is in and of itself unjust. But as Professor Albert W. Flores points out, while justice would demand that equals receive equal treatment, it is likewise true that unequals should receive treatment appropriate to their differences. Hence, he concludes that "unfair or differential treatment may be required by the principles of justice."[6] In other words, unequal treatment is unfair in the absence of any characteristic difference between applicants which, from the viewpoint of justice, would constitute relevant differences. Following this line of reasoning, we must wonder whether being a female or a minority member would constitute a "relevant difference" that would justify unequal treatment.

To illustrate, let's ask how one could justify giving preferential consideration to a female job applicant over an equally qualified white male. Flores contends that while sex may be irrelevant to the job, it may be a relevant consideration as to who should be selected. In effect, he distinguishes between criteria relevant to a job and those relevant to candidate selection. He clearly bases this distinction on a concept of business's social responsibilities. As has been amply demonstrated elsewhere, business does not exist in a commercial vacuum. It is part of a social system and, as such, has obligations that relate to the welfare and integrity of society at large. Thus, Flores argues that when a firm must decide between two equally qualified applicants, say a white male and a female, it is altogether justified in introducing as a selection criterion some concept of social justice, which in this case takes cognizance of a fair distribution of society's resources amid scarcities among competing groups. From the viewpoint of justice, business may be correct in hiring the qualified female or minority member. Notice, however, that this contention is based primarily not on principles of compensatory justice but on a careful examination of the nature of justice.

The moral issues that affirmative-action programs raise in regard to justice are profound and complex. In this brief overview, we have been able to raise only a few, but these demonstrate that the morality of preferential treatment through affirmative action cuts to our basic assumptions about the nature of human beings and the principles of justice. Any moral resolution of the problem of discrimination in the workplace will not only reflect these assumptions but must justify them.

---

6. Flores, "Reverse Discrimination," p. 4.

ARGUMENTS AGAINST AFFIRMATIVE ACTION

1. *All discrimination on the basis of race and sex is inherently unfair.*

POINT: "All human beings deserve equal treatment. No one should be denied a job because of sex or skin color. It's a simple matter of fairness that all people of good will should be able to agree on. Isn't that what the civil rights movement was originally all about? Isn't that what the feminist movement was originally all about? To discriminate against anyone on the basis of race or sex, white males included, is inherently unfair."

COUNTERPOINT: "You can't equate affirmative action with racism and sexism. The purpose of racism and sexism is to deny equal opportunity. The purpose of affirmative action is to provide it, first by ensuring that employers don't discriminate against groups that have traditionally suffered from discrimination and, second, by compensating these groups for past discrimination. Certainly, a color-blind society is the ideal, but affirmative action is necessary in today's society if we're going to achieve it someday."

2. *Affirmative action leads to resentment and social tensions.*

POINT: "Whatever the purpose of affirmative action, the result is racial tension and increased sexism. A lot of white males justifiably feel cheated by affirmative action. Denied jobs and promotions they're qualified for because they're white males, they naturally come to resent women and minorities. Just look at the rise of racial tensions in our cities. Or look at the prevalence of racism and sexism in recent popular music and comedy acts. Affirmative action isn't bringing us to a color-blind society but to an increasingly polarized one."

COUNTERPOINT: "You could say the same thing about the original civil rights and feminist movements. Remember the name calling and rock throwing when blacks first tried to integrate public schools, buses, and lunch counters? Or all the bra-burning women's libber jokes when women began demanding equal pay for equal work? What the resentment and tensions show is pervasive racism and sexism, not the wrongness of affirmative action."

3. *Affirmative action stigmatizes minorities and women.*

POINT: "It's not only white males who suffer from affirmative action. Minorities and women who rise to the top on their own merits also suffer. Instead of being respected for their accomplishments, they're objects of suspicion. There will always be people who believe women and minorities got where they are through preferential treatment. Not only that, but affirmative action can actually harm their careers. Given the choice between a doctor who got into medical school on his or her own merits and one who may have got in through an affirmative-action system, which would you pick? That's the stigma of affirmative action, and talented minorities and women will always have to live with it."

COUNTERPOINT: "The stigma you talk about is nothing but prejudice. Whether hired through affirmative action or not, whether admitted into medical school through affirmative action or not, people still have to prove themselves afterward. After all, the idea behind affirmative action isn't to give women and minorities a leg up through their entire careers but to give them an opportunity to prove themselves on a level playing field. And anyone who accomplishes that deserves as much respect as anyone else."

4. *Affirmative action wastes the best human resources.*

POINT: "The real idea behind affirmative action is to make sure that the best people for the job don't get it. Places in professional schools are taken from superior students who happen to be white males. More qualified applicants who happen to be white males are denied important jobs in business and industry. No society can afford to waste its best resources like that, especially in a world as competitive as ours has become."

COUNTERPOINT: "You could just as easily say that no society can afford to waste over half its human resources by denying them the opportunity to prove themselves in areas traditionally closed to them. Remember, affirmative-action guidelines aren't designed to result in the hiring of unqualified applicants. They're designed to help less qualified applicants whose relative lack of qualifications are the product of institutional racism and sexism. By giving them that help, we give them the opportunity to overcome impediments in their background and improve their qualifications. Though there are unfortunate abuses in affirmative-action programs, in the end we still have a much larger pool of qualified workers to choose from."

ARGUMENTS FOR AFFIRMATIVE ACTION

1. *Justice requires that we compensate for the results of past discrimination.*

POINT: "No one can deny the United States's history of racism and sexism. If the effects of that history were behind us, affirmative action would be unnecessary. But they're not behind us. Walk into any inner city neighborhood and try to tell me the children playing in the streets have the same opportunities as their white suburban counterparts. If we really believe in justice and equal opportunity, we have to compensate for the effects of our history."

COUNTERPOINT: "Compensatory justice is certainly a noble ideal, but there are two serious flaws in your argument. First, compensatory justice for one group brings harm to another, and when the harmed group isn't responsible for the plight of the others, you're punishing the innocent for the sins of their ancestors. To tell a young white male to forget about his share of the American Dream because of what happened before he was born is no kind of justice at all. Second, not all women and minorities suffer from the effects of past discrimination, whereas many white males have led truly disadvantaged lives. Take a middle-class black man or white woman who went to good schools and was always encouraged to aspire to great success. Why is that person entitled to preferential treatment over a white male from the most depressed area of Appalachia or a severely distressed manufacturing community?"

2. *Affirmative action is the only way to overcome current racism and sexism.*

POINT: "Despite the passage of numerous civil rights laws, bias in the workplace is still with us. Women remain subject to sexual harassment. Racial and sexual stereotypes continue to take their toll. You don't even need statistics to know how bad it is. You can hear it in casual conversation and you can see it in a seemingly never-ending stream of lawsuits won by women and minorities who were denied promotions. Employers can always find a way to justify hiring or promoting a white male over a black or a woman. The only way to overcome such discrimination is through affirmative-action guidelines."

COUNTERPOINT: "The fact that women and minorities are winning their discrimination suits shows that we don't need affirmative action. The Civil Rights Act and the Equal Employment Opportunity Act give them all the legal teeth they need to fight bias, on the job or anywhere else. The just way to fight discrimination is to take the discriminators to court, not to institutionalize affirmative action."

3.   *Women and minorities need role models in all walks of life.*

POINT: "One of the most unfortunate effects of past discrimination is the lack of role models for young women and minorities. Before Sandra Day O'Connor, how many young women could aspire to be an associate justice of the U.S. Supreme Court? Before Colin Powell, how many young black men could aspire to be secretary of state? We need women and minority physics professors, architects, welders, electricians, bank presidents, and anything else you can think of to let *all* young people know that all possibilities are open to them if they have the talent and perseverance."

COUNTERPOINT: "Certainly, role models are important, but unfair discrimination against white males is too high a price to pay, especially when adequate enforcement of anti-discrimination legislation will provide them anyway. After all, Colin Powell wasn't selected for his position *because* of his race. Nor were many other talented blacks in many other kinds of work. Nor were many talented women selected for their positions because of their gender. Furthermore, many of them got where they are without any role models at all. As important as role models may be, they can't replace encouragement from parents and teachers, and they can't replace hard work."

4.   *It's just not true that all decisions in employment and education are made on the basis of pure objective merit, even leaving aside affirmative-action programs.*

POINT: "It's hypocritical to say that if it were not for affirmative action, everyone would have a fair chance to compete based strictly on merit. Many decisions are made on factors that have little to do with so-called objective merit. Many universities give preference to the children of alumni, even if they don't meet normal admissions standards. Universities seek a wide range of abilities and talents, whether athletes or musicians or artists, even if they don't meet the narrowly defined standards of grade point and SAT scores. Many corporations are notorious for hiring relatives and cronies for jobs for which those persons are less qualified. As long as we allow these other forms of unfair discrimination, we shouldn't complain about giving a break to underrepresented minorities and women."

COUNTERPOINT: "Perhaps we should insist that those other forms of discrimination be abolished too. But even if they are allowed to continue, race and gender go to core constitutional values, while those other factors don't. If you own a business, there's nothing wrong with showing favoritism to your relatives. And universities rely on their alumni for financial contributions, so why not reward them by showing a little favoritism to admissions for their children?"

The Justification of Reverse Discrimination

Tom L. Beauchamp

In this essay, professor of philosophy Tom L. Beauchamp assumes that affirmative action is reverse discrimination and that it can be morally justified. Though he concedes that reverse discrimination can create injustices, he defends the practice on two grounds. First, the eradication of pervasive discrimination in hiring and promotion requires enforced goals and quotas. Second, goals and quotas serve corporate interests as well as the public interest.

In defending his claim that discrimination in the workplace is pervasive, Beauchamp appeals to a wide range of statistical evidence. He then argues that nondiscriminatory hiring and promotion practices can be meaningfully enforced only with specified goals and timetables.

During the past two decades, government and corporate policies aimed at hiring women and racial minorities by setting numerical goals have been sharply criticized on grounds that they discriminate in reverse, often against more qualified white males. My objective in this paper is to defend such policies. I agree with those critics who maintain that some policies have created situations of injustice. However, I do not agree with the presumption that when policies with numerical goals create *injustices* they are necessarily *unjustified*. Equal opportunity is but one principle of justice, and justice is but one demand of ethics. We need also to take account of principles of just compensation (compensatory justice) and the public interest (utility).

A policy can create or perpetuate injustices, such as violations of principles of equal opportunity, and yet be justified by other reasons. It would, for example, be an injustice in one respect for a bank to fire one of two branch managers with identical professional credentials while retaining the other; yet the financial condition of the bank or compensation owed the retained person might provide compelling reasons that justify the action. An established seniority system might justifiably be used to decide such a matter; indeed, a devoted employee with long service might be retained in preference to a younger person with better credentials and higher productivity. In some circumstances, when implementing schemes of hiring, promoting, and firing, equal opportunity and the blinded

evaluations of persons will have to yield on the scales of justice to the weight of other principles.

I shall use this general line of argument in defense of numerical targets, goals, quotas, and timetables. I contend that goals and even quotas are congenial to management, not hostile to business, as academic and government agency officials generally seem to presume. I also believe that business's long-range interest and the public interest are best served by preferential hiring, advancement, and layoff policies.

TWO POLAR POSITIONS

The U.S. Supreme Court and numerous scholars in ethics and legal theory have struggled with these problems of principle and balance in combating discrimination, at least since President Lyndon Johnson's 1965 executive order that announced a toughened federal initiative by requiring specific goals and timetables for equal employment opportunity. This struggle has led to two primary competing schools of thought on the justifiability of preferential programs.

The first school locates justice in the claim that we are all entitled to an equal opportunity and to constitutional guarantees of equal protection in a color-blind, nonsexist society. An entitlement of this sort is an entitlement that only individuals possess. Civil rights laws therefore should offer protection not to aggregate groups but only to specific individuals who have been demonstrably victimized by racial, sexual, religious, or other forms of discrimination. Hiring goals, timetables, and quotas violate these laws as well as our moral sense of justice, because they create new victims of discrimination. The U.S. Department of Justice has spearheaded this view in recent years, but it has found adherents in many quarters as well.

The second school believes that mandated goals and enforced hiring measures are essential to ensure fairness in hiring and to achieve meaningful results in the attempt to eradicate discrimination. This group believes it is too onerous to require the actual identification of individual victims of discrimination—an assignment that is generally impossible because of secrecy (and sometimes even unintentional discrimination). Even the victims may not know they are victims. As the editors of the *New York Times* put it, finding actual victims as the means of ending discrimination would be the "project of a century and [would] leave most victims of discrimination with only empty legal rights. [Many] are still victims of the myths of racial superiority that once infused the law itself." The *Times* joined the Supreme Court in calling for the "adequate remedy" of "race-conscious relief" in the form of goals and timetables to the extent necessary to achieve the end of a nondiscriminatory society.[1] The second group thus tends to see the first group as construing "equal opportunity" and "civil rights" so narrowly that those affected by discrimination can receive no practical aid in overcoming the phenomenon of prejudice. That is, the noble ideal of equal opportunity is viewed as but a theoretical postulate that has no practical application in the real world under the first group's policies.

These two groups are perhaps not as far apart as they appear at first glance. Edwin Meese, Attorney General during the Reagan administration and the most publicly visible proponent of the first viewpoint in recent memory, dismissed the seemingly enormous gulf between his views and those of the U.S. Supreme Court—which has endorsed the second viewpoint—by saying that the Court *accepted* his views that racial preferences are wrong and merely "carved out various exceptions to that general rule, even while affirming the rule itself." There is something to be said for Meese's bold statement (although I think not quite what he intended): The second group need not disagree with the first group if legal enforcement were adequate to identify discriminatory treatment and to protect its victims. If we lived in such a society, then the second group

could easily agree that the first group's policies are preferable for that society.

But there are two reasons why no member of the second group will agree to this solution at the present time. First, there is the unresolved issue of whether those in contemporary society who have been advantaged by *past* discrimination deserve their advantages, and thus whether classes such as blacks and women deserve some of those advantages. This thorny issue is surpassed in importance, however, by the second reason, which is whether *present,* ongoing discrimination can be successfully, comprehensively, and fairly combatted by identifying and prosecuting the violators. I do not believe that the form of enforcement so essential to the first group's position is possible. But I do believe that the enforcement of goals and quotas is both possible and necessary. Two reasons now to be discussed lead me to the conclusion that the second position is preferable to the first.

THE DATA ON DISCRIMINATION

My argument rests on the hypothesis that invidious discrimination that affects hiring and promotion is present in our society—not everywhere, of course, but pervasively. Such a claim requires empirical evidence; and like almost any broad generalization, the evidence is not entirely conclusive. However, I believe the claim can be adequately substantiated, as some representative samples of available data indicate.

Statistical imbalances in hiring and admission and promotion are often discounted because so many variables can be hypothesized to explain why, for nondiscriminatory reasons, an imbalance exists. We can all think of plausible nondiscriminatory reasons why almost half of the graduate students in the United States are women but the tenured Arts and Sciences graduate faculties often hover around 5 to 10 percent women—and in some of the most prestigious schools, even lower. Occasionally we are able to discover firm evidence supporting the claim that such skewed statistics are not random but are the result of discrimination. Quantities of such discriminatory findings, in turn, raise questions about the real reasons for suspicious statistics in those cases where we have not been able to determine these reasons.

An impressive body of statistics constituting prima facie evidence of discrimination has been assembled in recent years indicating that women with identical credentials are promoted at almost exactly one-half the rate of their male counterparts; that 69 percent or more of the white-collar positions in the United States are presently held by women, but only 10 percent or so of the management positions are held by women (and again their pay is significantly lower); that 87 percent of all professionals in the private business sector are Orientals, but they comprise only 1.3 percent of management; that in the population as a whole in the United States 3 out of 7 employees hold white-collar positions, but only 1 of 7 blacks holds such a position (and these positions are clustered in professions that have the fewest jobs to offer in top-paying positions); and that numerous major U.S. corporations have settled discrimination suits out of court for hundreds of millions of dollars.[2]

Such statistics are far from decisive indicators of discrimination. But further evidence concerning the reasons for the statistics can sometimes be discovered to prove a discriminatory influence.[3] Other facts support the general conclusion that racist and sexist biases have a powerful influence in the marketplace. For example, from 1965 to 1975 the number of blacks in college doubled, but from 1975 to 1985 it leveled off without increase. The number of blacks making more than $25,000 in constant-dollar salary also doubled from 1965 to 1975, but dropped from 1975 to 1985.[4] There is a ready reason for both statistics. Both the Crier Partnership and the Urban League produced separate studies completed in 1985 that show striking disparities in the employment levels of college-trained blacks and whites in the job market in Washington, D.C.— one of the best markets for blacks. Both studies found that college-trained blacks find far more frustration in landing a position and that discrimination is a major underlying factor.[5]

Another example of prevailing biases in marketplace transactions is found in real estate rentals and sales. In a 1985 statement, Lucius McKelvey, president of a large Cleveland real estate firm, publicly proclaimed what numerous real estate agents had already privately reported: "You'd be surprised at the number of professional people, white-collar people, who ask us to discriminate—it's discouraging." Surveys have shown that blacks face an 85 percent probability of encountering discrimination in rental housing and almost 50 percent in buying a house.[6]

These studies and dozens that replicate their findings indicate that we live in a discriminatory society whose laws will make little difference in practice unless the laws are tough and are gauged to change the practices and underlying attitudes. The law cannot wait for evidence of abuse confined to demonstrable individual victims without permitting the continuation of present injustices.

PROBLEMS OF PROOF AND INTENTION

The central problems of proof and enforcement in individual cases can best be captured by taking a particular case that illustrates the difficulty in determining whether discrimination—especially intentional discrimination—is occurring.

In December 1974 a decision was reached by the Commission against Discrimination of the Executive Department of the State of Massachusetts regarding a case at Smith College; the two complainants were women who were denied tenure and dismissed by the English Department.[7] The women claimed sex discrimination and based their case on the following: (1) Women at the full professor level in the college declined from 54 percent in 1958 to 21 percent in 1972, and in the English Department from 57 percent in 1960 to 11 percent in 1972. These statistics compare unfavorably at all levels with data from Mt. Holyoke, a comparable institution (since both have an all-female student body and are located in western Massachusetts). (2) Thirteen of the department's fifteen associate and full professorships at Smith belonged to men. (3) The two tenured women had obtained tenure under "distinctly peculiar experiences," including a stipulation that one be only part-time and that the other not be promoted when given tenure. (4) The department's faculty members conceded that tenure standards were applied subjectively, were vague, and lacked the kind of precision that would avoid discriminatory application. (5) The women denied tenure were at no time given advance warning that their work was deficient. Rather, they were given favorable evaluations of their teaching and were encouraged to believe that they would receive tenure. (6) Some of the stated reasons for the dismissals were later demonstrated to be rationalizations, and one letter from a senior member to the tenure and promotion committee contradicted his own appraisal of teaching ability filed with the department. (7) The court accepted expert testimony that any deficiencies in the women candidates were also found in male candidates promoted and given tenure in the same period and that the women's positive credentials were at least as good as the men's.[8]

The commissioner's opinion found that "the Complainants properly used statistics to demonstrate that the Respondents' practices operate with a discriminatory effect." Citing *Parham v. Southwestern Bell Telephone Co.,* the commissioner argued that "in such cases extreme statistics may establish discrimination as a matter of law, without additional supportive evidence." But in this case the commissioner found abundant additional evidence in the form of the "historical absence of women," "word-of-mouth recruitment policies" that operate discriminatorily, and a number of "subtle and not so subtle, societal patterns" existing at Smith.[9] On December 30, 1974, the commissioner ordered the two women reinstated with tenure and ordered the department to submit an affirmative action program within sixty days.

There is little in the way of clinching proof that the members of the English Department held discriminatory attitudes. Yet so consistent a pattern of *apparently* discriminatory results must be regarded, according to this decision, as de facto discrimination. The commissioner's ruling and other laws explicitly state that "intent or lack thereof is of no consequence." If a procedure constitutes discriminatory treatment, then the parties discriminated against must be recompensed. If irresistible statistics and other sociological evidence of "social exclusion" and "subtle societal patterns" provide compelling evidence that quotas, goals, or strong court-backed measures are necessary to overcome the discriminatory pattern (as the Respondents' testimony in the case indicates),[10] I find this fact sufficient to justify the measures.

In early 1985 the U.S. Supreme Court came down with perhaps its clearest example of this general point in the case of *Alexander v. Choate*. The Court held unanimously—against the U.S. Justice Department and the state of Tennessee—that states may be held guilty of discriminating against the handicapped because such discrimination is "most often the product not of invidious animus, but rather of thoughtlessness and indifference—of benign neglect." The Court rightly held that discrimination would be "difficult if not impossible to ban if only *intentional* acts of discrimination qualified as discrimination."[11]

PROBLEMS OF ENFORCEMENT

The protective camouflage surrounding discriminatory attitudes makes enforcement difficult in both the particular case and in the general case of monitoring nondiscriminatory guidelines. This problem is lessened by having specific goals and quotas, which are easier to meet and to enforce. In this section I want to present two cases that show how difficult—indeed meaningless—enforcement can be in the absence of specified goals and tough-minded control.

The January 1975 Report of the United States Commission on Civil Rights contains a section of "compliance reviews" of various universities.[12] The commissioners reviewed four major campuses in the United States: Harvard, University of Michigan, University of Washington, and Berkeley. They concluded that there has been a pattern of inadequate compliance reviews, inordinate delays, and inexcusable failures to take enforcement action where there were clear violations of the executive order regulations.[13]

Consider the example of the "case history of compliance contracts" at the University of California at Berkeley. When the Office for Civil Rights (OCR) of HHS determined to investigate Berkeley (April 1971), after several complaints, including a class action sex discrimination complaint, the university refused to permit access to its personnel files and refused to permit the interviewing of faculty members without an administrator present. Both refusals are, as the report points out, "direct violations of the Executive order's equal opportunity clause," under which Berkeley held contracts. A year and a half later, after negotiations and more complaints, the university was instructed to develop a written affirmative action plan to correct "documented deficiencies" of "pervasive discrimination." The plan was to include target goals and timetables wherever job underutilization had been identified.[14]

In January 1973 the university submitted a draft affirmative action plan that was judged "totally unacceptable." Throughout 1973 Berkeley received "extensive technical assistance" from the government to aid it in developing a better plan. No such plan emerged, and OCR at the end of the year began to question "the university's commitment to comply with the executive order." The university submitted other unacceptable plans, and finally in March 1974 a conciliation document was reached. However, the document was vague and the university and OCR continued for years to be in disagreement on the meaning of key provisions.

Berkeley is an instructive case study, because it was at the time among the most concerned institutions in the United States over issues of race and civil rights. If it and the other three universities studied by the Commission on Civil Rights have troubled histories in installing and monitoring antidiscrimination laws, one can imagine the problems found elsewhere. Consider, as a revealing example of far more egregious resistance, what is perhaps the most important Supreme Court case on the issues of quotas and reverse discrimination: the case of *Local 28 v. Equal Employment Opportunity Commission,* generally known as *Sheet Metal Workers.*[15] Although this case was decided in 1986, the discriminatory actions of Local 28 of the Sheet Metal Workers International had been in and out of court since 1963. The record, says the Supreme Court, was one of complete "foot-dragging resistance" to the idea of hiring from minority groups into the apprenticeship training programs that supply workers for construction in the New York City metropolitan area. In 1964 the New York Commission for Human Rights investigated the union and concluded that it excluded nonwhites through an impenetrable barrier of hiring by discriminatory selection. The state Supreme Court concurred and issued a "cease and desist" order. The union ignored it. Eventually, in a 1975 trial, the U.S. District Court found a record "replete with instances of bad faith" and ordered a "remedial racial goal" of 29 percent nonwhite membership (based on the percentage of nonwhites in the local labor pool). Another court then found that the union had "consistently and egregiously violated"

the law of the land (Title 7, in particular). In 1982 and 1983 court fines and civil contempt proceedings were issued. In 1981, virtually nothing had been done to modify the discriminatory hiring practices after twenty-two years of struggle.

The Supreme Court held that one need not produce "identified victims" of discrimination and that goals such as the 29 percent quota are justified when "an employer or a labor union has been engaged in persistent or egregious discrimination, or where necessary to dissipate the lingering effects of pervasive discrimination." I find the latter clause particularly suitable. Goals and quotas are needed where there are lingering effects of pervasive preference for particular groups (e.g. white male graduates of certain schools) or discriminatory attitudes that control hiring. Otherwise, goals and quotas are not needed, and no one should invoke them. But if these problems are not restricted to a few isolated cases involving Sheet Metal Workers Unions or Departments of English, then it makes sense to see goals and quotas as a basic tool for eradicating discriminatory practices.

The Supreme Court points out that the present laws in the United States were enacted by Congress to prevent "pervasive and systematic discrimination in employment." No one should expect that practices like those of the Sheet Metal Workers can easily be removed by exhortations or by finding "identified victims." The stronger the resistance, the tougher the rules must be.

I might add, however, that the Supreme Court has not said, nor have I, that there cannot be a case of reverse discrimination in which a white male has unjustifiably been excluded for consideration from employment and has a right to compensation. Certainly *unwarranted* discrimination in reverse is no better than unwarranted discrimination in forward speed. But the following should also be considered: There is an important distinction between real reverse discrimination and merely apparent reverse discrimination. Sometimes persons who appear to be displacing better applicants will be hired or admitted—on a quota basis, for example, but the appearance may be the result of discriminatory perceptions of the person's qualifications. In this case there will appear to be reverse discrimination, and this impression will be reinforced by knowledge that quotas were used.

However, the allegation of reverse discrimination will be mistaken. On other occasions there will be genuine reverse discrimination, and on many occasions it will be impossible to determine whether this consequence occurs.

I have argued that real and not merely apparent reverse discrimination is justified. But it is justified only as a means to the end of ensuring nondiscriminatory treatment of all persons. If the use of goals and quotas functioned as a vindictive tool (and, let us suppose, the end of nondiscrimination had already been achieved), then no reverse discriminatory effects would be justified.

WHY CORPORATIONS SHOULD WELCOME GOALS AND QUOTAS

Little has been said thus far about the relevance of these arguments to employment in business, largely because we have been concentrating on public policy affecting all institutions. In conclusion, I turn to corporate policy, which I believe would be aided by the use of goals and targets in the late 1980s and early 1990s. Here I shall discuss only policies voluntarily adopted by corporations—that is, voluntary programs using target goals and quotas. These programs stand in contrast to agency-ordered objectives featured in some previous examples.

Because of this shift to voluntary programs, my argument may seem a trivial addition to the problems mentioned above; a corporation can either accept or reject a program at its discretion. However, the issue of voluntary goals and quotas is far from trivial, for two reasons. First, the Justice Department has sought in recent years to ban voluntary corporate programs using goals and quotas, on grounds that these policies result in reverse discrimination. Many corporations and municipalities have resisted these government moves, and some have flatly refused to ease their affirmative action goals. Second, I believe that the active good will of corporations will prove to be more important than any other development (with the possible exception of activity in the U.S. Supreme Court) in ending discrimination and prejudice in the American workplace; and the workplace more than any other environment will serve as the melting pot of American society.

I offer four reasons why it is in the interest of responsible businesses to use aggressive plans involving goals and quotas. The judgment that such plans are fair and justified—as I have argued previously—could be appended as a reason, but it is not the type of reason needed in the present context.

(1) First, to the extent that a corporation either discriminates or fails to look at the full range of qualified persons in the market, to that extent it will eventually wind up with a larger percentage of second-best employees. Corporations continue to report that they find fewer qualified workers for available positions than they formerly did, and that they have profited from rules of nonracial, nonsexist hiring.[16] Hal Johnson, a senior vice-president at Travelers Companies, projects that, "In 1990 more of the work force is going to be minorities—Hispanics, blacks—and women. The companies that started building bridges back in the 1970s will be all right. Those that didn't won't."[17] The free market has its own way of eroding color and sexual barriers in the search for the best talent. No one would argue, for example, that baseball has poorer talent for dropping its color barrier. To find that talent in its best form, bridges had to be built that extended far into, for example, the population of Puerto Rico. Businesses will be analogously improved if they extend their boundaries and provide the proper training programs. Bill McEwen of Monsanto Corporation and spokesperson for the National Association of Manufacturers notes that this extension not only will happen but has been happening at NAM companies for twenty years:

> We have been utilizing affirmative action plans for over 20 years. We were brought into it kicking and screaming. But over the past 20 years we've learned that there's a reservoir of talent out there, of minorities and women that we hadn't been using before. We found that it works.[18]

Some corporations have found it difficult to find and keep these talented persons and therefore have developed incentives and special benefits, such as job-sharing, home work, flextime, extended maternity leave, and day-care centers in order to keep them. These companies include Gannett, General Foods, General Motors, IBM, Lotus Development, Mellon Bank, Mutual Life, Peat Marwick Mitchell, and Procter & Gamble.[19]

(2) A second reason is that pulling the foundations from beneath affirmative action hiring would open old sores, especially for municipalities and corporations who over a period of years have developed target goals and quotas either through a consent-decree process with courts or direct negotiations with representatives of minority groups such as PUSH and the NAACP. These plans—which now cover over 20 million Americans employed by federal contractors alone—have been agonizingly difficult to develop in some cases and would be disintegrated by the principle that goals and timetables are impermissible. Removal might also stigmatize a business by signalling to minority groups a return to older patterns of discrimination.[20]

(3) Third, the risk of reverse discrimination suits would be minimized, not maximized, by the use of goals and quotas. This paradox has been explained by Peter Robertson of Organizational Resource Counselors:

> In a recent survey of chief executive officers by the management consulting firm for which I work, 95 percent indicated that they will use numbers as a management tool to measure corporate progress whether the government requires them or not. However, once the government requirements are gone, there would be a risk of so-called "reverse discrimination" suits alleging that employers have gone too far with affirmative action.[21]

Thus, government programs and court decisions that *allow* voluntary goals and quotas actually protect good-faith employers rather than undermining them. As Robertson points out, the president of the National Association of Manufacturers, Alexander Trowbridge, has been making exactly that point to affiliate manufacturers. It has also been reported that many corporations enthusiastically greeted the 1986 and 1987 pro-affirmative-action decisions in the U.S. Supreme Court, because they feared that if the Justice Department's argument had been victorious, then employers would have been exposed to reverse discrimination suits by white males because of the plans corporations already had in effect.[22]

(4) Finally, the editors of *Business Week* have offered the following general reason in favor of voluntary and negotiated goals and quotas: "Over the years business and regulators have worked out rules and procedures for affirmative action, including numerical yardsticks for sizing up progress, that both sides understand. It has worked and should be left alone."[23] The reason why it has worked is intrinsic to a businesslike approach to problems: Managers set goals and timetables for almost everything they hope to achieve—from profits to salary bonuses. From a manager's point of view, setting goals and timetables is simply a basic way of measuring progress. One survey of 200 major American corporations found that over 75 percent already use "voluntary internal numerical objectives to assess [equal employment opportunity] performance."[24] A side benefit of the use of such numerical objectives is to create a ready defense of one's practices for government investigators, unions, or minority group representatives who inquire into the company's historical record. Many corporations have also promoted their record through public reports and recruiting brochures. Such reports and brochures have been developed, for example, by Schering-Plough, Philip Morris, Exxon, AT&T, IBM, Westinghouse, and Chemical Bank.[25]

CONCLUSION

Early in this paper I acknowledged that all racial and sexual discrimination, including reverse discrimination, is prima facie immoral, because a basic principle of justice creates a duty to abstain from such treatment of persons. But no absolute duty is created come what may. The thesis I have defended is that considerations of compensatory justice, equal opportunity, and utility are *conjointly* of sufficient weight to neutralize and overcome the quite proper presumption of immorality in the case of some policies productive of reverse discrimination.

My conclusion is premised on balancing several moral principles as well as on empirical judgments about the actual state of discrimination in American society. With some basic changes, the presumption might turn in a different direction, and thus my claims are contingent on the social circumstances. Moreover, I agree with critics of the position I have defended that the introduction of preferential treatment on a large scale might in some measure produce economic advantages to some who do not deserve them, protracted court battles, jockeying for favored position by other minorities, congressional lobbying by power groups, a lowering of admission and work standards in vital institutions, reduced social and economic efficiency, increased racial hostility, and continued suspicion that well-placed women and minority group members received their positions purely on the basis of quotas. Conjointly these reasons constitute a strong case against policies that use numerical goals and quotas in hiring, promotion, firing, and layoffs. However, this powerful case is not strong enough to overcome the even more powerful case against it.

NOTES

1. "Their Right to Remedy, Affirmed," *New York Times*, July 3, 1986, p. A30.

2. See the date and comments in the following sources: Kenneth M. Davidson, Ruth B. Ginsburg, and Herman H. Kay, eds., *Sex-Based Discrimination: Text, Cases and Materials* (Minneapolis: West Publishing Company, 1974), esp. Ch. 3. Hereafter *Sex-Based Discrimination;* Irene Pave, "A Woman's Place is at GE, Federal Express, P&G . . . ," *Business Week*, June 23, 1986, pp. 75–76; Winifred Yu, "Asian Americans Charge Prejudice Slows Climb to Management Rank," *Wall Street Journal*, September 11, 1985, p. 35.

3. From *Discrimination Against Women: Congressional Hearings on Equal Rights in Education and Employment,* ed. Catherine R. Stimpson (New York: R. R. Bowker, 1973), 505–506.

4. See Juan Williams, "The Vast Gap Between Black and White Visions of Reality" and "Blacks Don't See It the Way Whites Do," *Washington Post*, March 31, 1985, pp. K1, K4.

5. As reported by Rudolf A. Pyatt, Jr., "Significant Job Studies," *Washington Post*, April 30, 1985, pp. D1–D2.

6. See "Business Bulletin," *Wall Street Journal*, February 28, 1985, p. 1.

7. *Maurianne Adams and Mary Schroeder v. Smith College,* Massachusetts Commission Against Discrimination, Nos. 72-S-53, 72-S-54 (December 30, 1974). Hereafter *The Smith College Case.*

8. 433 F.2d 421, 426 (8 cir. 1970).

9. *The Smith College Case,* pp. 23, 26.

10. *Ibid.,* pp. 26–27.

11. As reported by and quoted in Al Kamen, "Justices Attack Inadvertent Bias," *Washington Post*, January 10, 1985, p. A4.

12. *The Federal Civil Rights Enforcement Effort—1974,* 2: p. 276.

13. *Ibid.,* p. 281.

14. *Ibid.,* all the following text references are from pp. 281–286.

15. *Local 28 v. Equal Employment Opportunity Commission,* U.S. 84-1656. All the following quotations are from this case.

16. See Pave, "A Woman's Place," p. 76.

17. As quoted in Walter Kiechel, "Living with Human Resources," *Fortune*, August 18, 1986, p. 100.

18. As quoted in Peter Perl, "Rulings Provide Hiring Direction: Employers Welcome Move," *Washington Post*, July 3, 1986, pp. A1, A11.

19. See Alex Taylor, "Why Women Managers are Bailing Out," *Fortune*, August 18, 1986, pp. 16–23 (cover story).

20. See Mary Thornton, "Justice Dept. Stance on Hiring Goals Resisted," *Washington Post*, May 25, 1985, p. A2; Linda Williams, "Minorities Find Pacts with Corporations Are Hard to Come By and Enforce," *Wall Street Journal*, August 23, 1985, p. 13; and Perl, "Rulings Provide Hiring Direction," pp. A1, A11.

21. Peter C. Robertson. "Why Bosses Like to Be Told to Hire Minorities," *Washington Post*, November 10, 1985, pp. D1–D2.

22. Perl, "Rulings Provide Hiring Direction," p. I; Al Kamen, "Justice Dept. Surrenders in War on Hiring Goals," *Washington Post*, March 28, 1987, p. A4.

23. Editorial, "Don't Scuttle Affirmative Action," *Business Week*, April 5, 1985, p. 174.

24. Robertson, "Why Bosses Like to Be Told," p. 2.

25. *Ibid.*

Questions for Analysis

1. According to Beauchamp, policies that create *injustices* are not necessarily *unjustified.* How does he support the claim? How does he apply it to reverse discrimination?

2. What statistical evidence does Beauchamp cite in support of his claim that current job discrimination is pervasive? How convincing is it?

3. Opponents of reverse discrimination argue that protection should be offered only to individuals who have suffered from discrimination, not to groups. Why does Beauchamp consider such a policy unworkable?

4. On what grounds does Beauchamp argue that reverse discrimination is required for the elimination of job discrimination?

5. Why does Beauchamp think that quotas and timetables are consistent with a businesslike approach to problems?

6. What problems does Beauchamp think businesses would face if goals and quotas were no longer allowed by law?

7. In the conclusion of his essay, Beauchamp presents the case against reverse discrimination and admits that it is a powerful one. Nevertheless, he concludes that the case in favor of reverse discrimination is even more powerful? Do you agree? Why or why not?

A Defense of Programs of Preferential Treatment

Richard Wasserstrom

In this essay, philosophy professor Richard Wasserstrom provides a limited defense of preferential hiring by attacking two of the opposition's major arguments. First, opponents of preferential treatment often charge proponents with "intellectual inconsistency." They argue that those now supporting preferential treatment opposed it in the past. But Wasserstrom feels that social realities in respect to the distribution of resources and opportunities make present preferential-treatment programs enormously different from those of the past.

The second argument commonly raised is that preferential-treatment programs, by introducing sex and race, compromise what really should matter: individual qualifications. Wasserstrom counters this charge on both an operational and a theoretical level. He feels that to be decisive, this argument must appeal not to efficiency but to desert: Those who are most qualified deserve to receive the benefits. But Wasserstrom sees no necessary connection between qualifications and desert.

Many justifications of programs of preferential treatment depend upon the claim that in one respect or another such programs have good consequences or that they are effective means by which to bring about some desirable end, e.g., an integrated, equalitarian society. I mean by "programs of preferential treatment" to refer to programs such as those at issue in the *Bakke* case—programs which set aside a certain number of places (for example, in a law school) as to which members of minority groups (for example, persons who are non–white or female) who possess certain minimum qualifications (in terms of grades and test scores) may be preferred for admission to those places over some members of the majority group who possess higher qualifications (in terms of grades and test scores).

Many criticisms of programs of preferential treatment claim that such programs, even if effective, are unjustifiable because they are in some important sense unfair or unjust. In this paper I present a limited defense of such programs by showing that two of the chief arguments offered for the unfairness or injustice of these programs do not work in the way or to the degree supposed by critics of these programs.

The first argument is this. Opponents of preferential treatment programs sometimes assert that proponents of these programs are guilty of intellectual inconsistency, if not racism or sexism. For, as is readily acknowledged, at times past employers,

From Richard Wasserstrom, "A Defense of Programs of Preferential Treatment," *Phi Kappa Phi Journal*, vol. 58 (Winter 1978); originally Part II of "Racism, Sexism, and Preferential Treatment: An Approach to the Topics," *U.C.L.A. Law Review*, vol. 24 (1977): 581. Reprinted by permission of the author.

universities, and many other social institutions did have racial or sexual quotas (when they did not practice overt racial or sexual exclusion), and many of those who were most concerned to bring about the eradication of those racial quotas are now untroubled by the new programs which reinstitute them. And this, it is claimed, is inconsistent. If it was wrong to take race or sex into account when blacks and women were the objects of racial and sexual policies and practices of exclusion, then it is wrong to take race or sex into account when the objects of the policies have their race or sex reversed. Simple considerations of intellectual consistency—of what it means to give racism or sexism as a reason for condemning these social policies and practices—require that what was a good reason then is still a good reason now.

The problem with this argument is that despite appearances, there is no inconsistency involved in holding both views. Even if contemporary preferential treatment programs which contain quotas are wrong, they are not wrong for the reasons that made quotas against blacks and women pernicious. The reason why is that the social realities do make an enormous difference. The fundamental evil of programs that discriminated against blacks or women was that these programs were a part of a larger social universe which systematically maintained a network of institutions which unjustifiably concentrated power, authority, and goods in the hands of white male individuals, and which systematically consigned blacks and women to subordinate positions in the society.

Whatever may be wrong with today's affirmative action programs and quota systems, it should be clear that the evil, if any, is just not the same. Racial and sexual minorities do not constitute the dominant social group. Nor is the conception of who is a fully developed member of the moral and social community one of an individual who is either female or black. Quotas which prefer women or blacks do not add to an already relatively overabundant supply of resources and opportunities at the disposal of members of these groups in the way in which the quotas of the past did maintain and augment the overabundant supply of resources and opportunities already available to white males.

The same point can be made in a somewhat different way. Sometimes people say that what was wrong, for example, with the system of racial discrimination in the South was that it took an irrelevant characteristic, namely race, and used it systematically to allocate social benefits and burdens of various sorts. The defect was the irrelevance of the characteristic used—race—for that meant that individuals ended up being treated in a manner that was arbitrary and capricious.

I do not think that was the central flaw at all. Take, for instance, the most hideous of the practices, human slavery. The primary thing that was wrong with the institution was not that the particular individuals who were assigned the place of slaves were assigned there arbitrarily because the assignment was made in virtue of an irrelevant characteristic, their race. Rather, it seems to me that the primary thing that was and is wrong with slavery is the practice itself—the fact of some individuals being able to own other individuals and all that goes with that practice. It would not matter by what criterion individuals were assigned; human slavery would still be wrong. And the same can be said for most if not all of the other discrete practices and institutions which comprised the system of racial discrimination even after human slavery was abolished. The practices were unjustifiable—they were oppressive—and they would have been so no matter how the assignment of victims had been made. What made it worse, still, was that the institutions and the supporting ideology all interlocked to create a system of human oppression whose effects on those living under it were as devastating as they were unjustifiable.

Again, if there is anything wrong with the programs of preferential treatment that have begun to flourish within the past ten years, it should be evident that the social realities in respect to the distribution of resources and opportunities make the difference. Apart from everything else, there is simply no way in which all of these programs taken together could plausibly be viewed as capable of relegating white males to the kind of genuinely oppressive status characteristically bestowed upon women and blacks by the dominant social institutions and ideology.

The second objection is that preferential treatment programs are wrong because they take race or sex into account rather than the only thing that does matter—that is, an individual's qualification. What all such programs have in common and what makes them all objectionable, so this argument goes, is that they ignore the persons who are more qualified by bestowing a preference on those who are less qualified in virtue of their being black or female.

There are, I think, a number of things wrong with this objection based on qualifications, and not the least of them is that we do not live in a society in which there is even the serious pretense of a qualification requirement for many jobs of substantial power and authority. Would anyone claim, for example, that the persons who comprise the judiciary are there because they are the most qualified lawyers or the most qualified persons to be judges? Would anyone claim that Henry Ford II is the head of the Ford Motor Company because he is the most qualified person for the job? Part of what is wrong with even talking about qualifications and merit is that the argument derives some of its force from the erroneous notion that we would have a meritocracy were it not for programs of preferential treatment. In fact, the higher one goes in terms of prestige, power and the like, the less qualifications seem ever to be decisive. It is only for certain jobs and certain places that qualifications are used to do more than establish the possession of certain minimum competencies.

But difficulties such as these to one side, there are theoretical difficulties as well which cut much more deeply into the argument about qualifications. To begin with, it is important to see that there is a serious inconsistency present if the person who favors "pure qualifications" does so on the ground that the most qualified ought to be selected because this promotes maximum efficiency. Let us suppose that the argument is that if we have the most qualified performing the relevant tasks we will get those tasks done in the most economical and efficient manner. There is nothing wrong in principle with arguments based upon the good consequences that will flow from maintaining a social practice in a certain way. But it is inconsistent for the opponent of preferential treatment to attach much weight to qualifications on this ground, because it was an analogous appeal to the good consequences that the opponent of preferential treatment thought was wrong in the first place. That is to say, if the chief thing to be said in favor of strict qualifications and preferring the most qualified is that it is the most efficient way of getting things done, then we are right back to an assessment of the different consequences that will flow from different programs, and we are far removed from the

considerations of justice or fairness that were thought to weigh so heavily against these programs.

It is important to note, too, that qualifications—at least in the educational context—are often not connected at all closely with any plausible conception of social effectiveness. To admit the most qualified students to law school, for example—given the way qualifications are now determined—is primarily to admit those who have the greatest chance of scoring the highest grades at law school. This says little about efficiency except perhaps that these students are the easiest for the faculty to teach. However, since we know so little about what constitutes being a good, or even successful lawyer, and even less about the correlation between being a very good law student and being a very good lawyer, we can hardly claim very confidently that the legal system will operate more efficiently if we admit only the most qualified students to law school.

To be at all decisive, the argument for qualifications must be that those who are the most qualified deserve to receive the benefits (the job, the place in law school, etc.) because they are the most qualified. The introduction of the concept of desert now makes it an objection as to justice or fairness of the sort promised by the original criticism of the programs. But now the problem is that there is no reason to think that there is any strong sense of "desert" in which it is correct that the most qualified deserve anything.

Let us consider more closely one case, that of preferential treatment in respect to admission to college or graduate school. There is a logical gap in the inference from the claim that a person is most qualified to perform a task, e.g., to be a good student, to the conclusion that he or she deserves to be admitted as a student. Of course, those who deserve to be admitted should be admitted. But why do the most qualified deserve anything? There is simply no necessary connection between academic merit (in the sense of being most qualified) and deserving to be a member of a student body. Suppose, for instance, that there is only one tennis court in the community. Is it clear that the two best tennis players ought to be the ones permitted to use it? Why not those who were there first? Or those who will enjoy playing the most? Or those who are the worst and, therefore, need the greatest opportunity to practice? Or those who have the chance to play least frequently?

We might, of course, have a rule that says that the best tennis players get to use the court before the others. Under such a rule the best players would deserve the court more than the poorer ones. But that is just to push the inquiry back one stage. Is there any reason to think that we ought to have a rule giving good tennis players such a preference? Indeed, the arguments that might be given for or against such a rule are many and varied. And few if any of the arguments that might support the rule would depend upon a connection between ability and desert.

Someone might reply, however, that the most able students deserve to be admitted to the university because all of their earlier schooling was a kind of competition, with university admission being the prize awarded to the winners. They deserve to be admitted because that is what the rule of the competition provides. In addition, it might be argued, it would be unfair now to exclude them in favor of others, given the reasonable expectations they developed about the way in which their industry and performance would be rewarded. Minority-admission programs, which inevitably prefer some who are less qualified over some who are more qualified, all possess this flaw.

There are several problems with this argument. The most substantial of them is that it is an empirically implausible picture of our social world. Most of what are regarded as the decisive characteristics for higher education have a great deal to do with things over which the individual has neither control nor responsibility: such things as home environment, socioeconomic class of parents, and, of course, the quality of the primary and secondary schools attended. Since individuals do not deserve having had any of these things vis-à-vis other individuals, they do not, for the most part, deserve their qualifications. And since they do not deserve their abilities they do not in any strong sense deserve to be admitted because of their abilities.

To be sure, if there has been a rule which connects, say, performance at high school with admission to college, then there is a weak sense in which those who do well at high school deserve, for that reason alone, to be admitted to college. In addition, if persons have built up or relied upon their reasonable expectations concerning performance and admission, they have a claim to be admitted on this ground

as well. But it is certainly not obvious that these claims of desert are any stronger or more compelling than the competing claims based upon the needs of or advantages to women or blacks from programs of preferential treatment. And as I have indicated, all rule-based claims of desert are very weak unless and until the rule which creates the claim is itself shown to be a justified one. Unless one has a strong preference for the status quo, and unless one can defend that preference, the practice within a system of allocating places in a certain way does not go very far at all in showing that this is the right or the just way to allocate those places in the future.

A proponent of programs of preferential treatment is not at all committed to the view that qualifications ought to be wholly irrelevant. He or she can agree that, given the existing structure of any institution, there is probably some minimal set of qualifications without which one cannot participate meaningfully within the institution. In addition, it can be granted that the qualifications of those involved will affect the way the institution works and the way it affects others in the society. And the consequences will vary depending upon the particular institution. But all of this only establishes that qualifications, in this sense, are relevant, not that they are decisive. This is wholly consistent with the claim that race or sex should today also be relevant when it comes to matters such as admission to college or law school. And that is all that any preferential treatment program—even one with the kind of quota used in the *Bakke* case—has ever tried to do.

I have not attempted to establish that programs of preferential treatment are right and desirable. There are empirical issues concerning the consequences of these programs that I have not discussed, and certainly not settled. Nor, for that matter, have I considered the argument that justice may permit, if not require, these programs as a way to provide compensation or reparation for injuries suffered in the recent as well as distant past, or as a way to remove benefits that are undeservedly enjoyed by those of the dominant group. What I have tried to do is show that it is wrong to think that programs of preferential treatment are objectionable in the centrally important sense in which many past and present discriminatory features of our society have been and are racist and sexist. The social realities as to power and opportunity do make a fundamental difference. It is also wrong to think that programs of preferential treatment could, therefore, plausibly rest both on the view that such programs are not unfair to white males (except in the weak, rule-dependent sense described above) and on the view that it is unfair to continue the present set of unjust—often racist and sexist—institutions that comprise the social reality. And the case for these programs could rest as well on the proposition that, given the distribution of power and influence in the United States today, such programs may reasonably be viewed as potentially valuable, effective by which to achieve means admirable and significant social ideals of equality and integration.

Questions for Analysis

1. What does it mean to claim that proponents of preferential treatment are guilty of "intellectual inconsistency"? Do you think that Wasserstrom convincingly refutes this charge?

2. What moral principle (or principles) underlies Wasserstrom's objection to slavery?

3. How does Wasserstrom respond to the charge that preferential-treatment programs compromise the only thing that really matters: individual qualifications?

4. Describe the inconsistency present for the person who favors "pure qualifications" on grounds of maximum efficiency.

5. Do you agree that there is no necessary connection between qualifications and desert?

6. Do you think Wasserstrom's tennis analogy is a sound one?

7. Would it be accurate to say that Wasserstrom unequivocally supports preferential-treatment programs? Explain.

Reverse Discrimination and Compensatory Justice
William T. Blackstone

In this essay, philosophy professor William T. Blackstone is concerned with a single question: Is reverse discrimination ever justified on grounds of repairing past wrongs done to women and minorities? Blackstone thinks not. In his view, reverse discrimination cannot be so justified either morally or legally.

Blackstone builds his case primarily on a utilitarian foundation. He believes that more harm than good would result from a systematic policy of reverse discrimination. (Curiously, as he points out, reverse discrimination often is justified on an appeal to utility.) Since reverse discrimination is not justified on utilitarian or justice-regarding grounds, Blackstone concludes that compensation through reverse discrimination is not justifiable. Indeed, he argues that affirmative-action programs, despite how they have sometimes been implemented, not only oppose reverse discrimination but forbid it.

Is reverse discrimination justified as a policy of compensation or of preferential treatment for women and racial minorities? That is, given the fact that women and racial minorities have been invidiously discriminated against in the past on the basis of the irrelevant characteristics of race and sex—are we now justified in discriminating in their favor on the basis of the same characteristics? This is a central ethical and legal question today and it is one which

From *Social Theory and Practice*, vol. 3, no. 3 (Spring 1975). Reprinted with permission of the publisher and Mrs. Jean T. Blackstone.

is quite unresolved. Philosophers, jurists, legal scholars, and the man-in-the-street line up on both sides of this issue. These differences are plainly reflected (in the Supreme Court's majority opinion and Justice Douglas's dissent) in *DeFunis v. Odegaard*.[1] . . .

I will argue that reverse discrimination is improper on both moral and constitutional grounds, though I focus more on moral grounds. However, I do this with considerable ambivalence, even "existential guilt." Several reasons lie behind that ambivalence. First, there are moral and constitutional arguments on both sides. The ethical waters are very muddy and I simply argue that the balance of the arguments are against a policy of reverse discrimination.[2] My ambivalence is further due not only to the fact that traditional racism is still a much larger problem than that of reverse discrimination but also because I am sympathetic to the *goals* of those who strongly believe that reverse discrimination as a policy is the means to overcome the debilitating effects of past injustice. Compensation and remedy are most definitely required both by the facts and by our value commitments. But I do not think that reverse discrimination is the proper means of remedy or compensation. . . .

I

Let us now turn to the possibility of a utilitarian justification of reverse discrimination and to the possible conflict of justice-regarding reasons and those of social utility on this issue. The category of morally relevant reasons is broader, in my opinion, than reasons related to the norm of justice. It is broader than those related to the norm of utility. Also it seems to me that the norms of justice and utility are not reducible one to the other. We cannot argue these points of ethical theory here. But, if these assumptions are correct, then it is at least possible to morally justify injustice or invidious discrimination in some contexts. A case would have to be made that such injustice, though regrettable, will produce the best consequences for society and that this fact is an overriding or weightier moral reason than the temporary injustice. Some arguments for reverse discrimination have taken this line. Professor Thomas Nagel argues that such discrimination is justifiable as long as it is "clearly contributing to the eradication of great social evils."[3] . . .

Another example of what I would call a utilitarian argument for reverse discrimination was recently set forth by Congressman Andrew Young of Georgia. Speaking specifically of reverse discrimination in the context of education, he stated: "While that may give minorities a little edge in some instances, and you may run into the danger of what we now commonly call reverse discrimination, I think the educational system needs this. Society needs this as much as the people we are trying to help . . . a society working toward affirmative action and inclusiveness is going to be a stronger and more relevant society than one that accepts the limited concepts of objectivity. . . . I would admit that it is perhaps an individual injustice. But it might be necessary in order to overcome an historic group injustice or series of group injustices."[4] Congressman Young's basic justifying grounds for reverse discrimination, which he recognizes as individual injustice, are the results which he thinks it will produce: a stronger and more relevant education system and society, and one which is more just overall. His argument may involve pitting some justice-regarding reasons (the right of women and racial minorities to be compensated for past injustices) against others (the right of the majority to the uniform application of the same standards of merit to all). But a major thrust of his argument also seems to be utilitarian.

Just as there are justice-regarding arguments on both sides of the issue of reverse discrimination, so also there are utilitarian arguments on both sides. In a nutshell, the utilitarian argument in favor runs like this: Our society contains large groups of persons who suffer from past institutionalized injustice. As a result, the possibilities of social discord and disorder are high indeed. If short-term reverse discrimination were to be effective in overcoming the effects of past institutionalized injustice and if this policy could alleviate the causes of disorder and bring a higher quality of life to millions of persons, then society as a whole would benefit.

There are moments in which I am nearly convinced by this argument, but the conclusion that such a policy would have negative utility on the whole wins out. For although reverse discrimination might appear to have the effect of getting more persons who have been disadvantaged by past inequities into the mainstream quicker, that is, into jobs, schools, and practices from which they have been excluded, the cost would be invidious discrimination against majority group members of society. I do not think that majority members of society would find this acceptable, i.e., the disadvantaging of themselves for past inequities which they did not control and for which they are not responsible. If such policies were put into effect by government, I would predict wholesale rejection or noncooperation, the result of which would be negative not only for those who have suffered past inequities but also for the justice-regarding institutions of society. Claims and counter-claims would obviously be raised by other ethnic or racial minorities—by Chinese, Chicanos, American Indians, Puerto Ricans—and by orphans, illegitimate children, ghetto residents, and so on. Literally thousands of types or groups could, on similar grounds as blacks or women, claim that reverse discrimination is justified on their behalf. What would happen if government attempted policies of reverse discrimination for all such groups? It would mean the arbitrary exclusion or discrimination against all others relative to a given purpose and a given group. Such a policy would itself create an injustice for which those newly excluded persons could then, themselves, properly claim the need for reverse discrimination to offset the injustice to them. The circle is plainly a vicious one. Such policies are simply self-destructive. In place of the ideal of equality and distributive justice based on relevant criteria, we would be left with the special pleading of self-interested power groups, groups who gear criteria for the distribution of goods, services, and opportunities to their special needs and situations, primarily. Such policies would be those of special privilege, not the appeal to objective criteria which apply to all.[5] They would lead to social chaos, not social justice.

Furthermore, in cases in which reverse discrimination results in a lowering of quality, the consequences for society, indeed for minority victims of injustice for which reverse discrimination is designed to help, may be quite bad. It is no easy matter to calculate this, but the recent report sponsored by the Carnegie Commission on Higher Education points to such deleterious consequences.[6] If the quality of instruction in higher education, for example, is lowered through a policy of primary attention to race or sex as opposed to ability and training, everyone—including victims of past injustice—suffers. Even if such policies are clearly seen as temporary

with quite definite deadlines for termination, I am skeptical about their utilitarian value. . . .

II

The inappropriateness of reverse discrimination, both on utilitarian and justice-regarding grounds, in no way means that compensation for past injustices is inappropriate. It does not mean that those who have suffered past injustices and who have been disadvantaged by them are not entitled to compensation or that they have no moral right to remedy. It may be difficult in different contexts to translate that moral right to remedy into practice or into legislation. When has a disadvantaged person or group been compensated enough? What sort of allocation of resources will compensate without creating additional inequities or deleterious consequences? There is no easy answer to these questions. Decisions must be made in particular contexts. Furthermore, it may be the case that the effects of past injustices are so severe (poverty, malnutrition, and the denial of educational opportunities) that genuine compensation—the balancing of the scales—is impossible. The effects of malnutrition or the lack of education are often nonreversible (and would be so even under a policy of reverse discrimination). This is one of the tragedies of injustice. But if reverse discrimination is inappropriate as a means of compensation and if (as I have argued) it is unjust to make persons who are not responsible for the suffering and disadvantaging of others to suffer for those past injuries, then other means must be employed unless overriding moral considerations of another type (utilitarian) can be clearly demonstrated. That compensation must take a form which is consistent with our constitutional principles and with reasonable principles of justice. Now it seems to me that the Federal Government's Equal Opportunity and Affirmative Action programs are consistent with these principles, that they are not only not committed to reverse discrimination but rather absolutely forbid it.[7] However, it also seems to me that some officials authorized or required to implement these compensatory efforts have resorted to reverse discrimination and hence have violated the basic principles of justice embodied in these programs. I now want to argue both of these points: first, that these federal programs reject reverse discrimination in their basic principles; secondly, that some implementers of these programs have violated their own principles.

Obviously our country has not always been committed constitutionally to equality. We need no review of our social and political heritage to document this. But with the Fourteenth Amendment, equality as a principle was given constitutional status. Subsequently, social, political, and legal practices changed radically and they will continue to do so. The Fourteenth Amendment declares that states are forbidden to deny any person life, liberty, or property without due process of law or to deny to any person the equal protection of the laws. In my opinion the principles of the Equal Opportunity and Affirmative Action Programs reflect faithfully this constitutional commitment. I am more familiar with those programs as reflected in universities. In this context they require that employers "recruit, hire, train, and promote persons in all job classifications without regard to race, color, religion, sex or national origin, except where sex is a bona fide occupational qualification."[8] They state explicitly that "goals may not be rigid and inflexible quotas which must be met, but must be targets reasonably attainable by means of good faith effort."[9] They require the active recruitment of women and racial minorities where they are "underutilized," this being defined as a context in which there are "fewer minorities or women in a particular job classification than would reasonably be expected by their availability."[10] This is sometimes difficult to determine; but some relevant facts do exist and hence the meaning of a "good faith" effort is not entirely fluid. In any event the Affirmative Action Program in universities requires that "goals, timetables and affirmative action commitment, must be designed to correct any identifiable deficiencies," with separate goals and timetables for minorities and women.[11] It recognizes that there has been blatant discrimination against women and racial minorities in universities and elsewhere, and it assumes that there are "identifiable deficiencies." But it does not require that blacks be employed because they are black or women employed because they are women; that is, it does not require reverse discrimination with rigid quotas to correct the past. It requires a good faith effort in the present based on data on the availability of qualified women and racial minorities in various disciplines and other relevant facts. (Similar requirements hold, of course, for non-

academic employment at colleges and universities.) It does not mandate the hiring of the unqualified or a lowering of standards; it mandates only equality of opportunity for all which, given the history of discrimination against women and racial minorities, requires affirmative action in recruitment.

Now if this affirmative action in recruitment, which is not only consistent with but required by our commitment to equality and social justice, is translated into rigid quotas and reverse discrimination by those who implement equal opportunity and affirmative action programs in the effort to get results immediately—and there is no doubt in my mind that this has occurred—then such action violates the principles of these programs.

This violation—this inconsistency of principle and practice—occurs, it seems to me, when employers hire with *priority emphasis* on race, sex, or minority-group status. This move effectively eliminates others from the competition. It is like pretending that everyone is in the game from the beginning while all the while certain persons are systematically excluded. This is exactly what happened recently when a judge declared that a certain quota or number of women were to be employed by a given agency regardless of their qualifications for the job,[12] when some public school officials fired a white coach in order to hire a black one,[13] when a DeFunis is excluded from law school on racial grounds, and when colleges or universities announce that normal academic openings will give preference to female candidates or those from racial minorities.

If reverse discrimination is prohibited by our constitutional and ethical commitments, what means of remedy and compensation are available? Obviously, those means which are consistent with those commitments. Our commitments assure the right to remedy to those who have been treated unjustly, but our government has not done enough to bring this right to meaningful fruition in practice. Sound progress has been made in recent years, especially since the Equal Employment Opportunity Act of 1972 and the establishment of the Equal Employment Opportunities Commission. This Act and other laws have extended anti-discrimination protection to over 60% of the population.[14] The Commission is now authorized to enforce anti-discrimination orders in court and, according to one report, it has negotiated out-of-court settlements which brought 44,000 minority workers over 46 million dollars in back pay.[15] Undoubtedly this merely scratches the surface. But now the framework exists for translating the right to remedy into practice, not just for sloughing off race and sex as irrelevant criteria of differential treatment but other irrelevant criteria as well—age, religion, the size of hips (I am thinking of airline stewardesses), the length of nose, and so on.

Adequate remedy to overcome the sins of the past, not to speak of the present, would require the expenditure of vast sums for compensatory programs for those disadvantaged by past injustice in order to assure equal access. Such programs should be racially and sexually neutral, benefiting the disadvantaged of *whatever sex or race*. Such neutral compensatory programs would have a high proportion of blacks and other minorities as recipients, for they as members of these groups suffer more from the injustices of the past. But the basis of the compensation would be that fact, not sex or race. Neutral compensatory policies have definite theoretical and practical advantages in contrast to policies of reverse discrimination: Theoretical advantages, in that they are consistent with our basic constitutional and ethical commitments whereas reverse discrimination is not; practical advantages, in that their consistency, indeed their requirement by our constitutional and ethical commitments, means that they can marshal united support in overcoming inequalities whereas reverse discrimination, in my opinion, can not.

NOTES

1. 94 S. Ct. 1704 (1974).

2. I hasten to add a qualification—more ambivalence!—resulting from discussion with Tom Beauchamp of Georgetown University. In cases of extreme recalcitrance to equal employment by certain institutions or businesses some quota requirements (reverse discrimination) may be justified. I regard this as distinct from a general policy of reverse discrimination.

3. "Equal Treatment and Compensatory Discrimination," *Philosophy and Public Affairs,* 2 (Summer 1974).

4. *Atlanta Journal and Constitution,* Sept. 22, 1974, p. 20-A.

5. For similar arguments see Lisa Newton, "Reverse Discrimination as Unjustified," *Ethics,* 83 (1973).

6. Richard A. Lester, *Antibias Regulation of Universities* (New York, 1974); discussed in *Newsweek,* July 15, 1974, p. 78.

7. See The Civil Rights Act of 1964, especially Title VII (which created the Equal Employment Opportunity Commission), amended by The Equal Employment Opportunity Act of 1972, found in *ABC's of The Equal Employment Opportunity Act,* prepared by the Editorial Staff of The Bureau of National Affairs, Inc., 1972. Affirmative Action Programs came into existence with Executive Order 11246. Requirements for affirmative action are found in the rules and regulations I21-CFR Part 60-2, Order #4 (Affirmative Action Programs) generally known as Executive Order #4 and Revised Order #4 41-CFT 60-2 B. For discussion see Paul Brownstein, "Affirmative Action Programs," in *Equal Employment Opportunities Compliance,* Practising Law Institute, New York City (1972), pp. 73–111.

8. See Brownstein, "Affirmative Action Programs" and, for example, *The University of Georgia Affirmative Action Plan,* Athens, Ga., 1973–74, viii, pp. 133, 67.

9. Brownstein and *The University of Georgia Affirmative Action Plan,* Athens, Ga., 1973-74, p. 71.

10. *Ibid.,* p. 69.

11. *Ibid.,* p. 71.

12. See the *Atlanta Journal and Constitution,* June 9, 1974, p. 26-D.

13. See *Atlanta Constitution,* June 7, 1974, p. 13-B.

14. *Newsweek,* June 17, 1974, p. 75.

15. *Ibid.,* p. 75.

Questions for Analysis

1. Why does Blackstone argue his case with a certain amount of "existential guilt"?

2. State the utilitarian argument for reverse discrimination.

3. Would it be accurate to say that Blackstone rejects utility as a legitimate standard for determining the morality of reverse discrimination?

4. Consider this proposition: "Blackstone is opposed to compensating those who have suffered past injustices." Is this statement true or false? Explain.

5. What are some of the problems that compensation raises?

6.   Some people would claim that it is wrong to hold people today responsible for the wrongs of their ancestors and that it is equally as wrong to compensate people today for the wrongs their ancestors may have experienced. Do you agree? Explain your answers by appeal to some concept of justice.

7.   What reasons does Blackstone offer for saying that affirmative-action programs actually forbid reverse discrimination? Do you think his argument is persuasive? What objections to his interpretations might you raise?

8.   Granted that reverse discrimination is prohibited by our constitution and ethical commitments, what means of redress are available? Do you agree that a vigorous and unflinching implementation of these means will satisfy the obligation to eradicate discrimination?

Reverse Discrimination as Unjustified

Lisa Newton

Professor of philosophy Lisa Newton delivered a version of the following essay at a meeting of the Society for Women in Philosophy in 1972. She argues that reverse discrimination cannot be justified by an appeal to the ideal of equality. Indeed, according to Newton, reverse discrimination does not advance but actually undermines equality because it violates the concept of equal justice under law for all citizens.

Specifically, Newton attacks the defense for reverse discrimination on grounds of equality. She contends that no violation of justice can be justified by an appeal to the ideal of equality, for the idea of equality is logically dependent on the notion of justice.

In addition to this theoretical objection to reverse discrimination, Newton opposes it because she believes it raises insoluble problems. Among them are determining what groups have been sufficiently discriminated against in the past to deserve preferred treatment in the present and determining the degree of reverse discrimination that will be compensatory. Newton concludes that reverse discrimination destroys justice, law, equality, and citizenship itself.

I have heard it argued that "simple justice" requires that we favor women and blacks in employment and educational opportunities, since women and blacks were "unjustly" excluded from such opportunities for so many years in the not so distant past. It is a strange argument, an example of a possible implication of a true proposition advanced to dispute the proposition itself, like an octopus absentmindedly slicing off his head with a stray tentacle. A fatal confusion underlies this argument, a confusion fundamentally relevant to our understanding of the notion of the rule of law.

Two senses of justice and equality are involved in this confusion. The root notion of justice, progenitor of the other, is the one that Aristotle (*Nicomachean Ethics* 5.6; *Politics* 1.2; 3. 1) assumes to be the foundation and proper virtue of the political association. It is the conclusion which free men establish among themselves when they "share a common life in order that their association bring them self-sufficiency"—the regulation of their relationship by law, and the establishment, by law, of equality before the law. Rule of law is the name and pattern of this justice; its equality stands against the inequalities—of wealth, talent, etc.—otherwise obtaining among its participants, who by virtue of that equality are called "citizens." It is an achievement—complete, or, more frequently, partial—of

From Lisa H. Newton, "Reverse Discrimination as Unjustified," *Ethics* 83 (1973): 308–12. Copyright © 1973 by The University of Chicago Press. Reprinted by permission of the publisher and the author.

certain people in certain concrete situations. It is fragile and easily disrupted by powerful individuals who discover that the blind equality of rule of law is inconvenient for their interests. Despite its obvious instability, Aristotle assumed that the establishment of justice in this sense, the creation of citizenship, was a permanent possibility for men and that the resultant association of citizens was the natural home of the species. At levels below the political association, this rule-governed equality is easily found; it is exemplified by any group of children agreeing together to play a game. At the level of the political association, the attainment of this justice is more difficult, simply because the stakes are so much higher for each participant. The equality of citizenship is not something that happens of its own accord, and without the expenditure of a fair amount of effort it will collapse into the rule of a powerful few over an apathetic many. But at least it has been achieved, at some times in some places; it is always worth trying to achieve, and eminently worth trying to maintain, wherever and to whatever degree it has been brought into being.

Aristotle's parochialism is notorious; he really did not imagine that persons other than Greeks could associate freely in justice, and the only form of association he had in mind was the Greek *polis*. With the decline of the *polis* and the shift in the center of political thought, his notion of justice underwent a sea change. To be exact, it ceased to represent a political type and became a moral ideal: the ideal of equality as we know it. This ideal demands that all men be included in citizenship—that one Law govern all equally, that all men regard all other men as fellow citizens, with the same guarantees, rights, and protections. Briefly, it demands that the circle of citizenship achieved by any group be extended to include the entire human race. Properly understood, its effect on our associations can be excellent: It congratulates us on our achievement of rule of law as a process of government but refuses to let us remain complacent until we have expanded the associations to include others within the ambit of the rules, as often and as far as possible. While one man is a slave, none of us may feel truly free. We are constantly prodded by this ideal to look for possible unjustifiable discrimination, for inequalities not absolutely required for the functioning of the society and advantageous to all. And after twenty centuries of pressure, not at

all constant, from this ideal, it might be said that some progress has been made. To take the cases in point for this problem, we are now prepared to assert, as Aristotle would never have been, the equality of sexes and of persons of different colors. The ambit of American citizenship, once restricted to white males of property, has been extended to include all adult free men, then all adult males including ex-slaves, then all women. The process of acquisition of full citizenship was for these groups a sporadic trail of half-measures, even now not complete; the steps on the road to full equality are marked by legislation and judicial decisions which are only recently concluded and still often not enforced. But the fact that we can now discuss the possibility of favoring such groups in hiring shows that over the area that concerns us, at least, full equality is presupposed as a basis for discussion. To that extent, they are full citizens, fully protected by the law of the land.

It is important for my argument that the moral ideal of equality be recognized as logically distinct from the condition (or virtue) of justice in the political sense. Justice in this sense exists *among* a citizenry, irrespective of the number of the populace included in that citizenry. Further, the moral ideal is parasitic upon the political virtue, for "equality" is unspecified—it means nothing until we are told in what respect that equality is to be realized. In a political context, "equality" is specified as "equal rights"—equal access to the public realm, public goods and offices, equal treatment under the law—in brief, the equality of citizenship. If citizenship is not a possibility, political equality is unintelligible. The ideal emerges as a generalization of the real condition and refers back to that condition for its content.

Now, if justice (Aristotle's justice in the political sense) is equal treatment under law for all citizens, what is injustice? Clearly, injustice is the violation of that equality, discrimination for or against a group of citizens, favoring them with special immunities and privileges or depriving them of those guaranteed to the others. When the southern employer refuses to hire blacks in white-collar jobs, when Wall Street will only hire women as secretaries with new titles, when Mississippi high schools routinely flunk all the black boys above ninth grade, we have examples of injustice, and we work to restore the equality of the public realm by ensuring that equal opportunity will be provided in such cases in the future. But of course, when the employers and the schools *favor* women and blacks, the same injustice is done. Just as the previous discrimination did, this reverse discrimination violates the public equality which defines citizenship and destroys the rule of law for the areas in which these favors are granted. To the extent that we adopt a program of discrimination, reverse or otherwise, justice in the political sense is destroyed, and none of us, specifically affected or not, is a citizen, a bearer of rights—we are all petitioners for favors. And to the same extent, the ideal of equality is undermined, for it has content only where justice obtains, and by destroying justice we render the ideal meaningless. It is, then, an ironic paradox, if not a contradiction in terms, to assert that the ideal of equality justifies the violation of justice; it is as if one should argue, with William Buckley, that an ideal of humanity can justify the destruction of the human race.

Logically, the conclusion is simple enough: All discrimination is wrong prima facie because it violates justice, and that goes for reverse discrimination too. No violation of justice among the citizens may be justified (may overcome the prima facie objection) by appeal to the ideal of equality, for that ideal is logically dependent upon the notion of justice. Reverse discrimination, then, which attempts no other justification than an appeal to equality, is wrong. But let us try to make the conclusion more plausible by suggesting some of the implications of the suggested practice of reverse discrimination in employment and education. My argument will be that the problems raised there are insoluble, not only in practice but in principle.

We may argue, if we like, about what "discrimination" consists of. Do I discriminate against blacks if I admit none to my school when none of the black applicants are qualified by the tests I always give? How far must I go to root out cultural bias from my application forms and tests before I can say that I have not discriminated against those of different cultures? Can I assume that women are not strong enough to be roughnecks on my oil rigs, or must I test them individually? But this controversy, the most popular and well-argued aspect of the issue, is not as fatal as two others which cannot be avoided: If we are regarding the blacks as a "minority" victimized by discrimination, what is a "minority"? And for any group—blacks, women, whatever— that has been discriminated against, what amount

of reverse discrimination wipes out the initial discrimination? Let us grant as true that women and blacks were discriminated against, even where laws forbade such discrimination, and grant for the sake of argument that a history of discrimination must be wiped out by reverse discrimination. What follows?

First, are there other groups which have been, discriminated against? For they should have the same right of restitution. What about American Indians, Chicanos, Appalachian Mountain whites, Puerto Ricans, Jews, Cajuns, and Orientals? And if these are to be included, the principle according to which we specify a "minority" is simply the criterion of "ethnic (sub) group," and we're stuck with every hyphenated American in the lower middle class clamoring for special privileges for *his* group—and with equal justification. For be it noted, when we run down the Harvard roster, we find not only a scarcity of blacks (in comparison with the proportion in the population) but an even more striking scarcity of those second-, third-, and fourth-generation ethnics who make up the loudest voice of Middle America. Shouldn't they demand *their* share? And eventually, the WASPs will have to form their own lobby; for they too are a minority. The point is simply this: There is no "majority" in America who will not mind giving up just a bit of their rights to make room for a favored minority. There are only other minorities, each of which is discriminated against by the favoring. The initial injustice is then repeated dozens of times, and if each minority is granted the same right of restitution as the others, an entire area of rule governance is dissolved into a pushing and shoving match between self-interested groups. Each works to catch the public eye and political popularity by whatever means of advertising and power politics lend themselves to the effort, to capitalize as much as possible on temporary popularity until the restless mob picks another group to feel sorry for. Hardly an edifying spectacle, and in the long run no one can benefit: The pie is no larger—it just that instead of setting up and enforcing rules for getting a piece, we've turned the contest into a free-for-all, requiring much more effort for no larger a reward. It would be in the interests of all the participants to reestablish an objective rule to govern the process, carefully enforced and the same for all.

Second, supposing that we do manage to agree in general that women and blacks (and all the others) have some right of restitution, some right to a privileged place in the structure of opportunities for a while, how will we know when that while is up? How much privilege is enough? When will the guilt be gone, the price paid, the balance restored? What recompense is right for centuries of exclusion? What criterion tells us when we are done? Our experience with the Civil Rights movement shows us that agreement on these terms cannot be presupposed: A process that appears to some to be going at a mad gallop into a black takeover appears to the rest of us to be at a standstill. Should a practice of reverse discrimination be adopted, we may safely predict that just as some of us begin to see "a satisfactory start toward righting the balance," others of us will see that we "have already gone too far in the other direction" and will suggest that the discrimination ought to be reversed again. And such disagreement is inevitable, for the point is that we could not *possibly* have any criteria for evaluating the kind of recompense we have in mind. The context presumed by any discussion of restitution is the context of the rule of law: Law sets the rights of men and simultaneously sets the method for remedying the violation of those rights. You may exact suffering from others and/or damage payments for yourself if and only if the others have violated your rights; the suffering you have endured is not sufficient reason for them to suffer. And remedial rights exist only where there is law: Primary

human rights are useful guides to legislation but cannot stand as reasons for awarding remedies for injuries sustained. But then, the context presupposed by any discussion of restitution is the context of preexistent full citizenship. No remedial rights could exist for the excluded; neither in law nor in logic does there exist a right to *sue* for a standing to sue.

From these two considerations, then, the difficulties with reverse discrimination become evident. Restitution for a disadvantaged group whose rights under the law have been violated is possible by legal means, but restitution for a disadvantaged group whose grievance is that there was no law to protect them simply is not. First, outside of the area of justice defined by the law, no sense can be made of "the group's rights," for no law recognizes that group or the individuals in it, qua members, as bearers of rights (hence *any* group can constitute itself as a disadvantaged minority in some sense and demand similar restitution). Second, outside of the area of protection of law, no sense can be made of the violation of rights (hence the amount of the recompense cannot be decided by any objective criterion). For both reasons, the practice of reverse discrimination undermines the foundation of the very ideal in whose name it is advocated; it destroys justice, law, equality, and citizenship itself, and replaces them with power struggles and popularity contests.

Questions for Analysis

1. What is the "fatal confusion" underlying the argument that "simple justice" requires preferential treatment?

2. Can you describe how justice under Aristotle moved from a "political type" to a "moral ideal"?

3. Why is it important for Newton's argument that she distinguish the moral ideal of equality from the condition of justice in the political sense?

4. Central to Newton's argument is her definition of justice and her assumptions about the relationship between justice and equality. Do you agree with her?

5. Do you think Rawls would agree with Newton's analysis? Explain.

6. Would you agree that in part Newton objects to reverse discrimination on utilitarian grounds? Explain.

7. Do you agree that the problems Newton says surround reverse discrimination really are "insoluble"?

CASE PRESENTATION
Brian Weber

From its beginning in 1958, the Kaiser Aluminum plant in Grammercy, Louisiana, had very few black workers. By 1965, Kaiser had hired only 4.7 percent blacks, although 39 percent of the local work force were black. As of 1970, none of Kaiser's fifty professional employees was black; of 132 supervisors, one was black; of 146 skille craft workers, none was black. In the fifteen years between 1958 and 1973, Kaiser had allowed several whites with no prior craft experience to transfer into skilled craft positions, whereas blacks were required to have at least five years' prior craft experience before being permitted to transfer. But getting this experience was difficult, since blacks were largely excluded from craft unions. As a result, only 2 percent of Grammercy's skilled craft workers were black.

A federal review in 1975 found things at Grammercy basically unchanged. Only 2.2 percent of its 290 craft workers and 7 percent of its professional employees were black. No blacks were among its eleven draftsmen. Although the percentage of blacks in Grammercy's overall work force had increased to 13.3, the local labor force remained constant at 39 percent black. Only the lowest paying category of workers, so-called unskilled workers, included a large proportion of blacks, 35.5 percent, a proportion brought about by Kaiser's implementing a 1968 policy of hiring one black unskilled worker for every white unskilled worker.

As an upshot of these racial disparities in the allocation of jobs, federal agencies started pressuring Kaiser to employ more blacks in its betterpaying skilled craft position. At the same time, the United Steelworkers Union was pressuring Kaiser to institute programs for training its own workers in the crafts, instead of hiring all craft workers from outside the company. In response to both pressures, Kaiser set up a training program intended to qualify its own white and black workers for agreed-to craft positions. Under the program, Kaiser would pay for the training of its own workers who would be selected for the program on the basis of seniority. One-half of the training slots would be set aside for blacks until the percentage of black skilled craft workers at Grammercy approximated the percentage of blacks in the local labor force. Openings in the programs would be filled by alternating between the most senior qualified white employee and the most senior qualified black employee.

Thirteen workers—seven blacks and six whites—were selected during the first year of the program. Brian Weber, a young, white, semiskilled worker at Grammercy, was not among those selected, although he'd applied. Upon investigation, Weber discovered that he in fact had several months' more seniority than two of the blacks who had been admitted into the training program. Indeed, forty-three other white workers who had applied for the program and had been rejected had even more seniority than Weber. The conclusion was unmistakable: Junior black employees were receiving training in preference to more senior white employees. Weber didn't think this was fair, especially since none of the blacks admitted to the program had themselves been discriminated against by Kaiser during their prior employment.

Weber decided to sue Kaiser. The case was eventually heard by the U.S. Supreme Court, which ruled that Kaiser's affirmative-action program didn't violate the Civil Rights Act of 1964.

Questions for Analysis

1. Do you think Kaiser's preferential treatment program was fair? Explain in terms of ethical principles and concepts of justice.

2. Do you think Weber was treated unfairly, as he claimed? Defend your response on the basis of the moral principles you think are involved.

3. Companies frequently use seniority as the sole or primary basis of promotions or, as in Kaiser's case, for admission into training programs. Do you think this is fair? (Seniority generally refers to longevity on a job or with a company.)

CASE PRESENTATION
Piscataway v. Taxman

They had both taught business classes at Piscataway High School since 1980. In fact, they had been hired on the same day. But it was now April 1989, and the New Jersey township's school board faced budget cuts. One of the teachers would lose her job, and each received a letter of warning that she might be laid off. One month later, Sharon Taxman learned that she was the unfortunate one. Debra Williams would continue teaching.

When making its decision, the board concluded that both teachers were equally qualified, though Williams had a master's degree and Taxman only a bachelor's. And since they had been hired the same day, seniority could not settle the issue. One difference did stand out, however, and it proved decisive. Williams is black, Taxman white. To preserve racial diversity on the faculty, they chose to keep Williams.

Taxman promptly filed a complaint with the Equal Employment Opportunity Commission. Two years later, the U.S. Department of Justice sued the school board, claiming that Taxman was the victim of illegal racial discrimination. Taxman joined the suit, seeking reinstatement and back pay. Before her case came to trial, the school board rehired her. Still, she continued her suit to recover the back pay, and in September 1993, a U.S. District Court Judge in Newark awarded her $144,000. The school board appealed; again it lost. In its opinion, the U.S. Court of Appeals for the Third Circuit ruled that the board had violated the Civil Rights Act of 1964. Diversity alone could never justify making a personnel decision on the basis of race,

the court said. Race-based personnel decisions can only be justified by past discrimination. When the U.S. Supreme Court agreed to hear the case, expectations of a landmark affirmative-action ruling were high.

Meanwhile, the Department of Justice made two turnarounds. George Bush had been president when the department first brought suit. By September 1994, Bill Clinton was in the White House, and the department now argued that racial diversity *can* be considered in voluntary affirmative-action plans. But three years later, fearing that the Supreme Court would uphold the appellate ruling and thereby set a national precedent severely restricting affirmative action, the Clinton administration asked the Court not to hear the case.

Part of the administration's fear concerned the composition of the Court, which had not ruled in favor of an affirmative-action plan during the preceding decade. But another part concerned the case itself, which it did not consider typical of most affirmative-action cases. Here was an instance of a woman laid off solely because of her race, not of an individual who missed out on gaining a job because of an affirmative-action program.

Other affirmative-action proponents were equally concerned, and just months before the Supreme Court was to hear the case, a coalition of civil rights groups agreed to raise $308,500 to help the school board settle the suit. According to the terms of the settlement, announced in November 1997, Taxman would receive $433,500 in back pay, damages, and legal fees.

Questions for Analysis

1. Do you agree that this case is not a typical affirmative-action case? Why or why not?

2. As a general rule, should employers be allowed to consider the racial diversity of their staffs when making personnel decisions? What about the particular case of school boards, which often seek minority teachers to provide role models for minority students?

3. If not on the basis of racial diversity, how should the school board have made its decision? By the flip of a coin? What moral directions do the principles of Chapter 1 provide?

4. Should the school board have settled the suit, or should it have given the Supreme court a chance to rule on it?

CASE PRESENTATION
Proposition 209

Over the years, California voters have passed many controversial ballot initiatives that proved to be bellwethers for the rest of the nation. Among the most controversial is Proposition 209, an amendment to the state constitution that appeared on the 1996 ballot and passed by a margin of 54 percent to 45 percent. According to that measure, "The state shall not discriminate against, or grant preferential treatment to, any individual or group on the basis of race, sex, color, ethnicity, or national origin in the operation of public employment, public education, or public contracting."

These words may seem innocuous at first. In fact, they are modeled on the Civil Rights Act of 1964. But they sparked a lawsuit in federal court seeking to have the amendment declared unconstitutional. The problem, the plaintiffs argued, is that the measure puts an end to all state-sponsored affirmative-action programs, and in doing so, it places an unconstitutional hardship on minorities and women. A district court judge agreed and blocked the law with a preliminary injunction, but the Ninth Circuit Court of Appeals overruled him, and the law went into effect in August 1997. Still, the legal battle did not end until November 3 of that year, when the U.S. Supreme Court unanimously declined to hear the plaintiffs' challenge to the law.

California Governor Pete Wilson hailed the ruling. The *Los Angeles Times* quoted him as saying, "It is time for those who have resisted Prop. 209 to acknowledge that equal rights under law, not special preferences, is the law of the land. A measure that eliminates any form of discrimination based on race and gender violates no one's constitutional rights." The paper also quoted Mark Rosenbaum of the American Civil Liberties Union, the plaintiffs' chief attorney, who called the measure "mean-spirited and unjust" and "1990s-style discrimination against minorities and women, more insidious than any state-wide measure since the era of Southern resistance to *Brown v. Board of Education*."

But the story doesn't quite end there. Two years later, Wilson's successor to the California governorship, Gray Davis, announced a new admissions policy designed to limit the effects of Proposition 209. Under the new policy, all California students in the top 4 percent of their high school graduating class would be guaranteed admission into the University of California system, though not to the campus of their choice. How this policy change will play out remains to be seen, but the results in its first years have been mixed. While minority enrollment in the flagship campuses at Berkeley and Los Angeles have dwindled, they remain as strong or have grown even stronger at many other campuses in the system.

Questions for Analysis

1. Opponents of Proposition 209 charge that it targets minorities and women. Does it?

2. Proponents of Proposition 209 hail the Supreme Court decision as a major step toward a color-blind society. Do you agree?

3. According to one perspective, affirmative action leads to greater racial discord. According to another, measures like Proposition 209 do. Which view do you think is right?

4. Some observers call the change in admissions policy by Governor Davis a resounding success because of the high rates of minority enrollments at many UC campuses. Others criticize it as a form of apartheid because it confines most blacks and Hispanics to second-tier campuses. Which side do you agree with and why?

5. Voters in several other states have begun movements to repeal affirmative-action laws. Is this activity a sign that affirmative action is on the way out? Should it be on the way out?

CASE PRESENTATION

Grutter v. Bollinger: **Taking Race into Account**

In June 2003, the U.S. Supreme Court announced the *Grutter v. Bollinger* decision, reaffirming a controversial element of the 1978 *Bakke* decision. In *Bakke*, the Court had said that universities may not set aside a rigid quota of places in its entering class limited to particular racial minorities but that they may "take race into account." They reasoned that diversity in college classrooms was a legitimate goal in college admissions. Just as colleges seek a diversity of athletes, musicians, artists, scholars, and scientists, so too can they legitimately pursue cultural and racial diversity in their classes of students.

The *Grutter* case challenged the policy for admission to the highly competitive University of Michigan Law School. Admissions were based on a student's academic abilities along with an assessment of a range of talents, experiences, and potential. Among the factors considered were each student's contribution to the diversity of the law school. While not limited to racial diversity, the Law School said that it was committed to including a "critical mass" of underrepresented minorities, especially African American, Hispanic, and Native American students. The majority decision, written by Justice Sandra Day O'Conner, said in part:

> . . . Today, we hold that the Law School has a compelling interest in attaining a diverse student body. The Law School's educational judgment that such diversity is essential to its educational mission is one to which we defer. . . . Our scrutiny of the interest asserted by the Law School is no less strict for taking into account complex educational judgments in an area that lies primarily within the expertise of the university. Our holding today is in keeping with our tradition of giving a degree of deference to a university's academic decisions, within constitutionally prescribed limits. . . .
>
> We have long recognized that, given the important purpose of public education and the expansive freedoms of speech and thought associated with the university environment, universities occupy a special niche in our constitutional tradition. . . . Our conclusion that the Law School has a compelling interest in a diverse student body is informed by our view that attaining a diverse student body is at the heart of the Law School's proper institutional mission, and that "good faith" on the part of a university is

"presumed" absent "a showing to the contrary."

> As part of its goal of "assembling a class that is both exceptionally academically qualified and broadly diverse," the Law School seeks to "enroll a 'critical mass' of minority students." . . . The Law School's interest is not simply "to assure within its student body some specified percentage of a particular group merely because of its race or ethnic origin." . . . That would amount to outright racial balancing, which is patently unconstitutional. . . . Rather, the Law School's concept of critical mass is defined by reference to the educational benefits that diversity is designed to produce. . . .
>
> These benefits are not theoretical but real, as major American businesses have made clear that the skills needed in today's increasingly global marketplace can only be developed through exposure to widely diverse people, cultures, ideas, and viewpoints. . . . What is more, high-ranking retired officers and civilian leaders of the United States military assert that, "[b]ased on [their] decades of experience," a "highly qualified, racially diverse officer corps . . . is essential to the military's ability to fulfill its principle mission to provide national security." . . . The primary sources for the Nation's officer corps are the service academies and the Reserve Officers Training Corps (ROTC), the latter comprising students already admitted to participating colleges and universities. . . . At present, "the military cannot achieve an officer corps that is both highly qualified and racially diverse unless the service academies and the ROTC used limited race-conscious recruiting and admissions policies." . . . To fulfill its mission, the military "must be selective in admissions for training and education for the officer corps, and it must train and educate a highly qualified, racially diverse officer corps in a racially diverse setting." . . . We agree that "[i]t requires only a small step from this analysis to conclude that our country's other most selective institutions must remain both diverse and selective."
>
> We have repeatedly acknowledged the overriding importance of preparing students for work and citizenship, describing education as pivotal to "sustaining our political and cultural heritage" with a fundamental role in maintaining the fabric of society. . . . Effective participation by

members of all racial and ethnic groups in the civic life of our Nation is essential if the dream of one Nation, indivisible, is to be realized.

Moreover, universities, and in particular, law schools, represent the training ground for a large number of our Nation's leaders. . . . Individuals with law degrees occupy roughly half the state governorships, more than half the seats in the United States Senate, and more than a third of the seats in the United States House of Representatives. . . . The pattern is even more striking when it comes to highly selective law schools. A handful of these schools accounts for 25 of the 100 United States Senators, 74 United States Courts of Appeals judges, and nearly 200 of the more than 600 United States District Court judges. . . .

In order to cultivate a set of leaders with legitimacy in the eyes of the citizenry, it is necessary that the path to leadership be visibly open to talented and qualified individuals of every race and ethnicity. All members of our heterogeneous society must have confidence in the openness and integrity of the educational institutions that provide this training. As we have recognized, law schools "cannot be effective in isolation from the individuals and institutions with which the law interacts." . . . Access to legal education (and thus the legal profession) must be inclusive of talented and qualified individuals of every race and ethnicity, so that all members of our heterogeneous society may participate in the educational institutions that provide the training and education necessary to succeed in America. . . .

Questions for Analysis

1. Critics of the *Bakke* decision had hoped that the Court in *Grutter* would overturn the principle that it was constitutional for colleges and universities to take race into account in admission decisions, especially after a quarter of a century of continued efforts to improve opportunities for racial minorities in this country. Has the time come for a truly color-blind society in which admission decisions based solely on scholarly measures will result in a diverse student body without having to consider race during the admission process? Will such a time ever come?

2. Identify the use of consequentialist reasoning in the excerpt here. Is this persuasive? What consideration is given to the reasoning of human rights in this decision? Does the Court reason appropriately in defending its decision? Do you believe there are additional considerations that should be taken into account?

3. Can the arguments about the importance of law schools as a training ground for the nation's leaders be extended to all levels of education? Are there alternative ways of meeting that societal goal that would not involve taking race into account in law school admissions?

4. Some critics of this decision have claimed that admitting students not as well qualified academically as most entering students actually backfires because as they do not make law review or graduate at the top of the class, as they might at a less prestigious institution where their academic work would be more comparable to the other students. Is this a persuasive argument against the Michigan admissions program?

5. In California, public law schools are prohibited under Proposition 209 from taking race into account, despite this Supreme Court decision. Instead, those law schools now emphasize a variety of additional factors in their admissions, such as overcoming adversity in completing college and preparing for law school. Does this approach achieve appropriate diversity in ways that do not unfairly disadvantage white applicants?

11

Animal Rights

In 1975, Australian philosopher Peter Singer published his landmark book, *Animal Liberation*. The title of the first chapter, like the title of the book itself, clearly announced the author's basic moral message: "All Animals Are Equal." Succeeding chapters documented another message: All animals are not treated equally.

The dividing line is drawn between human and nonhuman animals. While our shared morality protects *human* animals from innumerable kinds of treatment we find intolerable, it is far less protective of *nonhuman* animals. Here is some of the information that readers of Singer's book learned:

1. Psychologist Martin Seligman performed a series of experiments involving dogs and a contraption known as the shuttle box. A shuttle box is a box with two compartments. One has electrified floors, allowing the experimenter to administer shocks to its occupant. The other, separated from the first by a barrier, does not. The experiments concerned two groups of dogs. The "naive" group (dogs with no prior training) reacted to the electric shocks by howling, running about, and defecating and urinating until they managed to escape to the other compartment. The trained group (dogs who had been given inescapable electric shocks before being put in the box) reacted differently. After some initial running, howling, and so forth, they simply gave up. That is, they lay in the box and passively accepted

the shocks. Moreover, repeated trials brought out another difference. The naive group learned to escape more quickly. The trained group learned not to make any attempt to escape.

2. The U.S. Food and Drug Administration tests new cosmetics by dripping concentrated solutions of the products into the eyes of rabbits and then measuring the amount of damage, which may include total loss of vision. To keep the squealing rabbits from clawing at and shutting their eyes and thereby removing the drops, researchers often immobilize the rabbits and clamp their eyes open.

3. Chickens raised for food on "factory" farms are packed so tightly into long windowless sheds that by the end of their short lives each chicken has as little as a half square foot of space. The crowding is so stressful to them that they take to pecking one another's feathers and even eating one another. Farmers often solve the problem by painfully removing the chickens' beaks.

4. Veal calves are raised in stalls so narrow that they cannot even turn around. The purpose of confining the calves is to keep them from grazing (grass makes the color of veal meat less appealing to veal eaters) and developing muscles (which make the meat tough). The purpose of confining them in stalls so narrow is to prevent them from licking their own urine to satisfy their natural craving for iron. (Because the meat of anemic calves has a more appealing color to veal eaters, their diet is kept low in iron.)

It is difficult to read detailed accounts of these and other experiments and farm procedures without feeling great sympathy for the animals involved. To be sure, scientists and farmers have what they take to be good reasons for doing such things. Seligman's experiments provided a new understanding of human depression and led to new therapies for treating it. FDA tests help to ensure that new products are safe for human consumers. Factory farm practices allow for efficient food production. Standard treatment of veal calves results in the kind of meat humans desire.

But are these reasons good enough? Can they morally justify such cruel treatment of nonhuman animals? Aren't the human interests served by such treatment (a new line of makeup or an "appealing" color of meat) downright trivial compared to the nonhuman interests denied by it? Aren't those of us who support such treatment by eating veal and buying cosmetics guilty of **speciesism**—the view that all human animals have greater moral worth than nonhuman animals? And isn't that just as bad as racism or sexism?

WHAT DO WE OWE
NONHUMAN ANIMALS?

Singer's point is simple. Nonhuman animals, like human animals, can experience both pleasure and pain. And that is a morally important fact. If it is wrong to cause human suffering to achieve a good that does not outweigh that suffering, Singer argues, it is wrong to cause nonhuman suffering to achieve such a good. Given the variety of nutritious and tasty vegetarian recipes available, the suffering caused by factory farms is not justified by the human desire for meat. Given the availability of canvas shoes and leather substitutes for belts and such, human demand for leather is not worth the suffering it brings to nonhuman animals.

Historically, the weight of Western opinion has not been on Singer's side. Both our religious and philosophical traditions have been inhospitable to the notion that we have moral obligations to other animals. Let's take a brief look at both.

The Judeo-Christian Tradition

Beginning with the creation story of Genesis, Judeo-Christian thought has told us that other animals were put here for our purposes. According to that story, we are to "fill the earth and subdue it; and have dominion over the fish of the sea and over the birds of the air and over every living thing that moves upon the earth." And later in Genesis, after the flood, we are told, "Every moving thing that lives shall be food for you; and as I gave you the green plants, I give you everything."

Of course, not all Jewish and Christian thought has viewed animals as merely there for our use. St. Francis of Assisi, for example, who once preached to sparrows, is as well known for his love of animals as for founding the Franciscan order. Still, these biblical injunctions have been supported by centuries of Christian theology. Humans are created in the image of God; other animals are not. Humans have immortal souls; other animals do not. Humans belong to both the spiritual and the material worlds; other animals belong only to the material. Given these differences, plus the influence of Christian thought on Western culture, no one should be surprised by our treatment of nonhuman animals.

The Philosophical Tradition

Secular philosophers have, in the main, given nonhuman animals no greater consideration. Writing at a time when such scientists as Galileo were ushering in the era of modern science, the great French philosopher René Descartes (1596–1650) argued that nonhuman animals are no better than biological robots, incapable of feeling any sensations, even pain. The nonphysical mind is the seat of sensation, he argued, and only creatures capable of reason have nonphysical minds. Since nonhuman animals cannot reason, they are simply physical creatures. Therefore, they cannot feel pain.

Immanuel Kant had other reasons for excluding nonhuman animals from moral consideration. As we saw in Part 1, Kant put respect for *persons* at the center of morality; we are not to treat other *persons* merely as a means to our own ends. Although Kant did not deny that animals can suffer, he did deny that they are persons. To be a person, he said, is to be an autonomous being, one that has the capacity to act for reasons and to reason about its reasons. And that capacity does not belong to nonhuman animals. They are, then, beyond the pale of morality. (Kant did recommend that we be nice to animals, though—not out of moral obligation, of course, but for another reason. If we treat animals cruelly, he felt, we run the risk of developing insensitive characters.)

Another strain in moral philosophy—**social contract theory**—is equally exclusive of nonhuman animals. According to this view, morality is the product of an informal agreement among the members of society. Each of us agrees to follow certain rules on the condition that others do the same. The purpose of the agreement is to ensure that all of us act in dependable ways, providing the mutual trust necessary for social cooperation. An important aspect of social contract theory is that this informal agreement is the source of all moral obligation. We have moral obligations to others who have entered into the agreement with us. We have no such obligations to those who are not part of the agreement. Nonhuman animals, who are incapable of entering into contracts, are not part of the agreement. Therefore, we have no moral obligations to them.

In traditional Western views, then, we owe nonhuman animals nothing. We have no moral obligations to them. We may have moral obligations *concerning* them, but those obligations are *to* other people. We ought not, for example, poison somebody else's pet for the same reason that we ought not destroy somebody else's sofa. The pet and the sofa are another person's property, and our obligations to that person forbid us to destroy his or her property. The pet itself is due no more moral consideration than the sofa—none.

Much has happened since Singer published his landmark book, and Singer himself recently noted some improvements.[1] Sales of fur clothing have never regained the levels of the 1980s when animal rights activists first targeted them. An animal rights group called People for the Ethical Treatment of Animals (PETA) was formed in response to his revelations and now has 750,000 members. Animal rights groups have been formed in many countries, especially Europe. The original Animal Welfare Act was passed in 1966, and the act has been strengthened repeatedly through various amendments. The U.S. Department of Agriculture has issued extensive regulations protecting the interest of animals used in federally funded research to ensure humane treatment and recognition of pain experienced by animals. According to Singer, the number of animals killed in shelters as strays has been reduced by more than half in the last thirty years. But he laments that factory farming of animals has increased dramatically and slaughterhouse practices remain needlessly cruel to those animals. Most people now seem to recognize that animals can suffer pain, which has led to some improvements in their treatment. But even so, animals do not receive the full moral consideration that Singer urged long ago.

ANIMAL RIGHTS

The basis of Singer's moral appeal is the principle of utility: Since we morally ought to maximize happiness and minimize suffering, and since nonhuman animals are just as capable of happiness and suffering as human animals, our calculations ought to include them as well. Against our own pleasure in eating veal, we ought to balance the suffering of veal calves. Against the benefits of research on animals, we ought to balance the suffering of laboratory animals. Their pain should matter just as much as ours.

Other animal advocates make a different moral appeal. As they see it, the principle of utility does not guarantee fit treatment of nonhuman animals. Suppose, for example, that the elimination of factory farms would create such havoc in our economy that utility is maximized by keeping them. Would that justify keeping them? If our answer is yes, we should ask ourselves an analogous question: Suppose we could maximize utility by reintroducing slavery. Would that justify doing so? Presumably, our answer to that question is no. Humans have certain rights that we morally cannot violate, regardless of utility. If we do not feel the same about at least some animals, aren't we guilty of speciesism?

---

1. Peter Singer, "Animal Liberation at 30," *The New york Review of Books*, May 15, 2003.

Thus, philosophers like Tom Regan focus their attention on animal rights. He argues that just as respect for persons requires that we not treat other humans in certain ways, regardless of utility, so should respect for at least some nonhuman animals require that we not treat them in certain ways, regardless of utility.

Which animals? At the very least, those that, like us, are experiencing subjects of their own lives. By that phrase, Regan means the following: conscious creatures that are aware of their environment, that have desires, feelings, emotions, memories, beliefs, preferences, goals, and a sense of their own identity and future. Although we cannot be sure precisely where we can draw the line between animals that meet these criteria and animals that do not, we can be sure of one thing, he says. Adult mammals do. And because they do, their lives, like ours, have inherent value—value independent of any use they may be to us. In that case, we ought not use them merely as a means to our own ends.

WHAT'S WRONG WITH SPECIESISM?

Most of us are, undeniably, speciesists. But what, you may be wondering, is wrong with that? Most of us agree that pointless cruelty to animals should not be tolerated, but that is a far cry from agreeing that animals are our moral equals. Why should they be? Shouldn't human beings matter more than other animals?

The Conventional View Defended

Certainly, speciesism doesn't *seem* to be as bad as racism or sexism. To deny full moral equality to other people on the basis of skin color is totally arbitrary, since skin color is of no moral importance whatever. We are all capable of the same aspirations, we desire to be treated with dignity and respect, we participate in social arrangements believing that we deserve from others what they believe they deserve from us, we can develop the same virtues and talents—we can, in short, belong to the same moral community regardless of race. To exclude someone from that community because of race is unjustifiable.

The same remarks hold for gender, of course. But for species? Can pigs and cows make the same moral claims on us as other people? Can we really say that the differences between rabbits and humans are as trivial, morally speaking, as the differences between blacks and whites, women and men? The common-sense answer to these questions is, of course, no. The conventional view is that morality is our own—humankind's—institution, developed and maintained and improved for our own purposes, for our own individual and social good. To the extent that the good of other animals contributes to our own good, it should be of concern to us. Because our pets play unique and rewarding roles in our lives, we should treat them as more than mere things. Because sympathy, compassion, and kindness contribute in crucial ways to the human good, we should not accept needless cruelty to nonhuman animals. But we have no obligation to promote the good of nonhuman animals at humankind's own expense. To do that would be to undercut the whole purpose of morality.

In other words, the conventional view says this: The difference between human and nonhuman animals is not merely a matter of species, while the difference between black and white is merely a matter of race, and the difference between women and men is merely a matter of gender. If there were another species that resembled us in morally relevant ways—the highly evolved apes of the *Planet of the Apes* film series, for example, or people from Mars—then we would welcome them into our moral community. That is, we don't discriminate against rabbits on the basis of species. We exclude them from our moral community because of crucial moral distinctions. So it is unfair to call us "speciesists," since the term implies otherwise. Like "racism" and "sexism," it implies that our distinctions cannot be morally justified.

This conventional view reflects, of course, the influence of Kant and the social contract view of morality. Like Kant, it draws the line at persons, although not necessarily human persons. And like the social contract view, it emphasizes a moral community of fully participating members, again not necessarily human. Moreover, as conventional views always do, it strikes us as eminently reasonable, even if we have never heard of Kant or social contract theory.

The Conventional View Criticized

However reasonable the conventional view may seem, animal rights advocates attack it on two fronts. First, they claim, we do not apply the conventional view consistently. Humans who are not fully persons are protected by our morality; humans who cannot fully participate in our moral community are granted moral rights. We do not test new cosmetics on people who are severely retarded. We do not run cruel psychological experiments on infants. We do not conduct medical experiments on irreversibly comatose humans. Why not? Because they are human. Why do we test cosmetics on rabbits, experiment on dogs, raise veal calves for food? Because they are not human. And that, animal rights activists say, *is* discrimination purely on the basis of species.

Second, even if the conventional view were applied consistently, they claim, it would still be inadequate. Granted, difference of species is not the only difference between normal adult humans and farm animals, but the differences stressed by the conventional view are not morally crucial ones. What is so morally important about the fact that steers cannot enter into our social contract? Why should it matter so much that pigs can't have all the aspirations that humans have or that sheep can't develop the same virtues and talents? What the conventional view boils down to, they say, is this: Only moral *agents* can have rights.

What are moral agents? Creatures that have two closely related abilities. The first is the ability to take on moral duties toward others, to understand that they have obligations toward others that they ought to fulfill. The second is the ability to make moral claims against others, to understand that they have moral rights that others can violate. But why, critics of the conventional view ask, should those abilities be crucial?

For Singer, we saw earlier, the really crucial point is the ability to feel pleasure and pain. Calves, chickens, and rabbits can suffer, they have a real interest in avoiding suffering, and that interest matters. The fact that they are not human or persons does not make that interest any less real, nor should it make that interest matter any less.

For Regan, the crucial point is inherent value. Whatever has inherent value deserves respect, and whatever deserves respect should not be used as a mere thing. Any creature that is a subject of its own life passes that crucial test, regardless of its inability to be a moral agent. Such a creature is still a moral *patient*. It may not have any duties toward us, but we have duties toward it. It may not be able to respect our rights, but we ought to respect its rights.

The Conventional View Reconsidered

The foregoing criticisms show that the acceptability of our treatment of other animals turns on two points. The first is consistency. Do we apply the conventional view consistently? And if not, can we justify our inconsistency? The second strikes at the heart of the conventional view. Does it draw a morally defensible line between human and nonhuman animals? And if so, is there an even better place to draw the line between creatures with rights (or as Singer would put it, creatures whose interests matter as much as our own) and creatures without rights (or creatures whose interests do not matter as much as our own)?

Regarding the first point, defenders of current treatment of other animals can say this: If we do apply the conventional view inconsistently, we do so in a *principled* way. Moral agents—persons—stand at the center of our morality. They are the primary holders of moral rights. We grant rights to human infants because they will *become* moral agents and so deserve our respect. We grant rights to humans in comas because they *were* moral agents and so also deserve our respect. We grant rights to people who are severely retarded because they are so much like some other holders of rights that it seems almost incoherent not to. In other words, we welcome these noncentral humans into our moral community because of the important similarities they bear to the rest of us. Not only that. They are also our parents, our children, and our brothers and sisters. Their good is deeply connected to our good.

As for the second point, defenders of current practices can do little more than repeat the reasons for drawing the line where we now do and then throw the question back to their critics: Why is Singer's dividing line or Regan's any better than the one we now draw? The fact that nonhuman animals can suffer should certainly have some moral weight, but why should it lead us to put them on an equal footing with full members of our moral community? The fact that some of them are experiencing subjects of their own lives should also have some moral weight, but why should it have as much weight as other facts about ourselves?

Whether these answers are acceptable depends on two further questions. First, are at least some nonhuman animals so much like some humans that it seems almost incoherent to deny them rights? Second, assuming that morality did arise to advance the human good, should we now say that the time has come to recognize that other goods are of equal value? Critics of our treatment of other animals answer yes to both questions. Defenders answer no.

ARGUMENTS FOR EQUAL TREATMENT OF ANIMALS

1. *Human beings hold no special place in nature.*

POINT: "What's so special about humans, anyway? From Mother Nature's point of view, *all* animals are equal. We all evolved from the same beginnings, we're all made of the same stuff, and we all belong to the same biosphere. The world wasn't made for any one species. It's here for all of us. And it's nothing but pure arrogance for humans to think that *we're* the pinnacle of creation, that we have the right to treat the rest of the animal kingdom any way we want. It's time we recognize that we're part of nature, not lords over it, and we ought to act accordingly."

COUNTERPOINT:　"Of course, we're part of nature. But what does that prove? Tigers, eagles, and other predators are also part of nature. What can be more natural than eating other animals? Besides, why stop at animals? Plants are part of nature too. So are rocks, rivers, and dirt. From Mother Nature's point of view, they must matter just as much as animals. Should we treat them equally too? Finally, why should we even care about Mother Nature's point of view (whatever *that* might be)? We have our own point of view—the human point of view—and if that point of view is no better than any other, it's no worse either. It's ours, and we're entitled to live our lives according to it."

2.　*All pain is equally bad.*

POINT:　"We all know that pain is bad. We begin to think morally when we recognize that somebody else's pain is just as bad as our own pain and that we shouldn't cause unnecessary pain to others. Well, an animal's pain is just as bad as a human being's pain; it hurts every bit as much as ours, and animals try just as hard to avoid it as we do. So the moral thing is to recognize that. We have to admit that all pain is equally bad, and we have to stop causing unnecessary pain to animals. We don't need to do cruel research on animals, so we should stop it. We don't need to eat meat, so we should become vegetarians. We should treat all animals, human and nonhuman, equally."

COUNTERPOINT:　"Sure, pain is bad. And I'm willing to admit that animal pain is bad too. I'm even willing to admit that we shouldn't cause unnecessary pain to animals. But a lot of pain that you call unnecessary isn't. What makes something necessary, after all, is that we need it to serve our interests. We have an interest in medical and other kinds of scientific research, and even if we don't always have to experiment on live subjects to serve that interest, sometimes we do. And even if we don't absolutely have to eat meat, most of us certainly like to, and that makes meat eating a real human interest. What you're missing is this: Even if all pain is bad, that doesn't mean that nonhuman interests count as much as human interests."

3.　*Trivial human interests don't count as much as important animal interests.*

POINT:　"Now you're missing the point. Maybe some animal pain really is necessary to serve important human interests. But how important are the interests you mentioned? Take eating meat. That's downright trivial. It's not needed for health, and vegetarian meals can taste every bit as good. And what about eye makeup? You can't call that an important interest. I'll concede that some research isn't trivial, but you have to concede that a whole lot of it is. And even when we're dealing with important research interests, there are a lot of ways of finding out what we want to know without torturing animals. The only reason we go on as we do is because we're too lazy or thoughtless to change."

COUNTERPOINT: "Whether an interest is trivial or not depends on how much it matters to us, and what you call trivial matters a whole lot to a whole lot of people. Look at what a big deal most of us make about going out for a steak dinner. We get all dressed up and spend a fortune. To some people, it's more than just nontrivial—it's the highlight of their week. Besides, what does it matter even if we say that such interests *are* trivial? If humans matter more to us than nonhumans, why shouldn't even trivial human interests matter more to us than any animal interest?"

4. *The interests of at least some animals count as much as ours.*

POINT: "Let's talk about what makes an interest important. What makes one of *your* interests important to *you* is that it matters to you. And that makes it important to *me* too. Since I want you to respect the interests that matter to me, simple golden-rule reasoning tells me to do likewise. Well, there are at least some animals who care about their own interests as much as we care about ours. The animals I have in mind are the ones that are aware of themselves and their futures, and have memories and beliefs and preferences, just like us. Their interests matter to them, and that makes their interests important to them. And that should make their interests important to us too."

COUNTERPOINT: "What you're saying is that the golden rule applies to monkeys and pigs. But an important part of the golden rule is reciprocity. If we're going to count on others to treat us in certain ways, then we ought to treat them the same. And that makes no sense when those others are monkeys and pigs. They can't reciprocate. All we can expect of them is that they'll act like monkeys and pigs. We certainly can't expect them to apply the golden rule to us. If you want to apply it to them, if it makes you feel better to do it, fine. But you can't tell me we have a moral *obligation* to do it."

ARGUMENTS AGAINST
EQUAL TREATMENT OF ANIMALS

1. *Equal treatment would have disastrous consequences.*

POINT: "Have you thought of the consequences of your position? Suppose we did treat other animals as equals. What would that do to ranchers, farmers, workers at meat packaging plants, butchers, fishermen, and all the other people whose livelihoods would disappear? And think what that would mean for the economy as a whole. What you're talking about is the closing of vast markets and the dislocation of millions of people. You're also talking about giving up important research and who knows what else. Whatever good would come to nonhuman animals, the consequences for humans would be disastrous. And that can't be right."

COUNTERPOINT: "Slaveholders could have used—and did use—the same arguments against abolitionists before the Civil War. Don't forget, the economies of many states depended on slavery then even more than the economies of many states depend on meat today. And the answer to the arguments is the same now as it was then. If something's wrong, it's wrong, and we have no right to base our economies on enslavement or slaughter. Besides, the dislocations will be temporary. The South did rise again, and so will we."

   2.   *You can't compare other species to minorities and women.*

   POINT: "All this talk of animal liberation, animal rights, and speciesism is an insult to women and minorities. How can you equate sheep and women, cows and blacks? How can you compare raising animals for food to denying our fellow human beings the attainment of their most fundamental aspirations? Farm animals can't feel humiliated. They can't feel robbed of their dignity. They can't feel the outrage that humans feel when denied recognition of their worth. They can't know what it's like to be treated like a thing instead of a person. They have no idea what it means to be a person, to have rights, to be treated fairly."

   COUNTERPOINT: "My point isn't to compare animals *just* to women and minorities, but to *all* humans—and that includes white men. It's not to insult anybody either. Nobody wants to demean humans. I just want to give nonhumans the respect they deserve. And all that stuff about a sense of dignity and the rest is irrelevant. All it shows is that some things that matter to us don't matter to them. But other things do. Avoiding pain, for instance. And freedom. And to many of them, their lives. Animals want to roam free, have enough space to do what comes natural to them, and lead pain-free lives. Their aspirations may not be precisely the same as ours, but they're equally real."

   3.   *Giving animals rights would lead to absurd interference with nature.*

   POINT: "Humans aren't the only animals that eat other animals, you know. What about wolves, eagles, tigers, and other predators? If we grant rights to their prey, then we'll have to protect animals from each other, not least from ourselves. After all, if we don't have the right to violate another animal's rights, neither does a wolf. But if we do protect the prey, what happens to the predator? What, for that matter, happens to all of nature? If you follow your position to its logical conclusion, the results are absurd."

   COUNTERPOINT: "The kind of interference that worries you is *not* a logical consequence of my position. What you're forgetting is that tigers and wolves aren't moral *agents*. They don't have any obligations to other animals, so there's nothing immoral about their preying on other animals. Humans are moral agents, though, so there is something immoral about our preying on other animals."

   4.   *Putting our own species first is the natural thing to do.*

   POINT: "It's only natural that we care more about other humans than we care about nonhumans. After all, being members of the same species is an important relationship, like being members of the same family. We care more about our parents than we do about strangers, so why shouldn't we care more about our fellow humans than we do about sheep? And just take a look at the rest of the animal kingdom. A lot of animals cooperate with members of their own species but not with other animals, and in some cases, animals will even lay down their lives for other members of their species. As the old saying goes, birds of a feather flock together. Why should humans be any different?"

COUNTERPOINT: "Humans are different. We can rise above our natural inclinations. That's what civilization and culture are all about. It's why we have laws
and morality. And since you're so fond of old sayings, it's why a tiger can't change
its stripes but a human can. We know the difference between right and wrong, and
the point of teaching that difference is to get people to put a check on some of their
natural inclinations. Selfishness is just as natural as altruism, you know—maybe
even more natural—but I don't hear you saying that we shouldn't try to curb our
selfishness. So even if speciesism is natural, if it's wrong we should stamp it out."

All Animals Are Equal . . . or Why Supporters of Liberation for Blacks and Women Should Support Animal Liberation Too

Peter Singer

In this selection from the first chapter of *Animal Liberation,* Peter Singer, now a professor of
philosophy at Princeton Unversity, compares speciesism to sexism and racism, and he argues
that the same considerations that make sexism and racism morally unjustifiable make
speciesism morally unjustifiable. He bases his argument on the *principle of equal consideration,* according to which the pain that nonhuman animals feel is of equal moral importance
to the pain that humans feel.

While supporting the principle of equal consideration, Singer stresses that it does not
always require equal treatment of all animals, since the same treatment can cause unequal
amounts of suffering to different animals. He also points out that the principle does not
require us to say that all lives are equal. Often, a human life is morally more important than
the life of a nonhuman animal. Sometimes, though, it is not. When forced to choose
between a human and nonhuman animal's life, we should base our decision on the mental
capacities of the individuals involved, not on species.

"Animal Liberation" may sound more like a parody
of other liberation movements than a serious objective. The idea of "The Rights of Animals" actually
was once used to parody the case for women's
rights. When Mary Wollstonecraft, a forerunner of
today's feminists, published her *Vindication of the
Rights of Women* in 1792, her views were widely
regarded as absurd, and before long an anonymous
publication appeared entitled *A Vindication of the
Rights of Brutes.* The author of this satirical work
(now known to have been Thomas Taylor, a distinguished Cambridge philosopher) tried to refute
Mary Wollstonecraft's arguments by showing that
they could be carried one stage further. If the argument for equality was sound when applied to
women, why should it not be applied to dogs, cats,

and horses? The reasoning seemed to hold for these
"brutes" too; yet to hold that brutes had rights was
manifestly absurd; therefore the reasoning by which
this conclusion had been reached must be unsound,
and if unsound when applied to brutes, it must also
be unsound when applied to women, since the
very same arguments had been used in each case.

In order to explain the basis of the case for the
equality of animals, it will be helpful to start with
an examination of the case for the equality of
women. Let us assume that we wish to defend the
case for women's rights against the attack by Thomas
Taylor. How should we reply?

One way in which we might reply is by saying
that the case for equality between men and women
cannot validly be extended to nonhuman animals.
Women have a right to vote, for instance, because
they are just as capable of making rational decisions about the future as men are; dogs, on the

From Peter Singer, *Animal Liberation* (New York: New York Review,
1975), pp. 1–23. Reprinted with permission of the author.

other hand, are incapable of understanding the significance of voting, so they cannot have the right to vote. There are many other obvious ways in which men and women resemble each other closely, while humans and animals differ greatly. So, it might be said, men and women are similar beings and should have similar rights, while humans and nonhumans are different and should not have equal rights.

The reasoning behind this reply to Taylor's analogy is correct up to a point, but it does not go far enough. There *are* important differences between humans and other animals, and these differences must give rise to *some* differences in the rights that each have. Recognizing this obvious fact, however, is no barrier to the case for extending the basic principle of equality to nonhuman animals. The differences that exist between men and women are equally undeniable, and the supporters of Women's Liberation are aware that these differences may give rise to different rights. Many feminists hold that women have the right to an abortion on request. It does not follow that since these same feminists are campaigning for equality between men and women they must support the right of men to have abortions too. Since a man cannot have an abortion, it is meaningless to talk of his right to have one. Since a dog can't vote, it is meaningless to talk of its right to vote. There is no reason why either Women's Liberation or Animal Liberation should get involved in such nonsense. The extension of the basic principle of equality from one group to another does not imply that we must treat both groups in exactly the same way, or grant exactly the same rights to both groups. Whether we should do so will depend on the nature of the members of the two groups. The basic principle of equality does not require equal or identical *treatment;* it requires equal *consideration.* Equal consideration for different beings may lead to different treatment and different rights.

So there is a different way of replying to Taylor's attempt to parody the case for women's rights, a way that does not deny the obvious differences between humans and nonhumans but goes more deeply into the question of equality and concludes by finding nothing absurd in the idea that the basic principle of equality applies to so-called "brutes." At this point such a conclusion may appear odd; but if we examine more deeply the basis on which our

opposition to discrimination on grounds of race or sex ultimately rests, we will see that we would be on shaky ground if we were to demand equality for blacks, women, and other groups of oppressed humans while denying equal consideration to nonhumans. To make this clear we need to see, first, exactly why racism and sexism are wrong.

When we say that all human beings, whatever their race, creed, or sex, are equal, what is it that we are asserting? Those who wish to defend hierarchical, inegalitarian societies have often pointed out that by whatever test we choose it simply is not true that all humans are equal. Like it or not we must face the fact that humans come in different shapes and sizes; they come with different moral capacities, different intellectual abilities, different amounts of benevolent feeling and sensitivity to the needs of others, different abilities to communicate effectively, and different capacities to experience pleasure and pain. In short, if the demand for equality were based on the actual equality of all human beings, we would have to stop demanding equality.

Still, one might cling to the view that the demand for equality among human beings is based on the actual equality of the different races and sexes. Although, it may be said, humans differ as individuals there are no differences between the races and sexes *as such.* From the mere fact that a person is black or a woman we cannot infer anything about that person's intellectual or moral capacities. This, it may be said, is why racism and sexism are wrong. The white racist claims that whites are superior to blacks, but this is false—although there are differences among individuals, some blacks are superior to some whites in all of the capacities and abilities that could conceivably be relevant. The opponent of sexism would say the same: a person's sex is no guide to his or her abilities, and this is why it is unjustifiable to discriminate on the basis of sex.

The existence of individual variations that cut across the lines of race or sex, however, provides us with no defense at all against a more sophisticated opponent of equality, one who proposes that, say, the interests of all those with IQ scores below 100 be given less consideration than the interests of those with ratings over 100. Perhaps those scoring below the mark would, in this society, be made the slaves of those scoring higher. Would a hierarchical society of this sort really be so much better than one based on race or sex? I think not. But if we tie the moral principle of equality to the factual equality of the different races or sexes, taken as a whole, our opposition to racism and sexism does not provide us with any basis for objecting to this kind of inegalitarianism.

There is a second important reason why we ought not to base our opposition to racism and sexism on any kind of actual equality, even the limited kind that asserts that variations in capacities and abilities are spread evenly between the different races and sexes: we can have no absolute guarantee that these capacities and abilities really are distributed evenly, without regard to race or sex, among human beings. So far as actual abilities are concerned there do seem to be certain measurable differences between both races and sexes. These differences do not, of course, appear in each case, but only when averages are taken. More important still, we do not yet know how much of these differences is really due to the different genetic endowments of the different races and sexes, and how much is due to poor schools, poor housing, and other factors that are the result of past and continuing discrimination. Perhaps all of the important differences will eventually prove to be environmental rather than genetic. Anyone opposed to racism and sexism will certainly hope that this will be so, for it will make the task of ending discrimination a lot easier; nevertheless it would be dangerous to rest the case against racism and sexism on the belief that all significant differences are environmental in origin. The opponent of, say, racism who takes this line will be unable to avoid conceding that *if* differences in ability do after all prove to have some genetic connection with race, racism would in some way be defensible.

Fortunately there is no need to pin the case for equality to one particular outcome of a scientific investigation. The appropriate response to those who claim to have found evidence of genetically based differences in ability between the races or sexes is not to stick to the belief that the genetic explanation must be wrong, whatever evidence to the contrary may turn up: instead we should make it quite clear that the claim to equality does not depend on intelligence, moral capacity, physical strength, or similar matters of fact. Equality is a moral idea, not an assertion of fact. There is no

logically compelling reason for assuming that a factual difference in ability between two people justifies any difference in the amount of consideration we give to their needs and interests. *The principle of the equality of human beings is not a description of an alleged actual equality among humans: it is a prescription of how we should treat humans.*

Jeremy Bentham, the founder of the reforming utilitarian school of moral philosophy, incorporated the essential basis of moral equality into his system of ethics by means of the formula: "Each to count for one and none for more than one." In other words, the interests of every being affected by an action are to be taken into account and given the same weight as the like interests of any other being. A later utilitarian, Henry Sidgwick, put the point in this way: "The good of any one individual is of no more importance, from the point of view (if I may say so) of the Universe, than the good of any other." More recently the leading figures in contemporary moral philosophy have shown a great deal of agreement in specifying as a fundamental presupposition of their moral theories some similar requirement which operates so as to give everyone's interests equal consideration—although these writers generally cannot agree on how this requirement is best formulated.[1]

It is an implication of this principle of equality that our concern for others and our readiness to consider their interests ought not to depend on what they are like or on what abilities they may possess. Precisely what this concern or consideration requires us to do may vary according to the characteristics of those affected by what we do: concern for the well-being of a child growing up in America would require that we teach him to read; concern for the well-being of a pig may require no more than that we leave him alone with other pigs in a place where there is adequate food and room to run freely. But the basic element—the taking into account of the interests of the being, whatever those interests may be—must, according to the principle of equality, be extended to all beings, black or white, masculine or feminine, human or nonhuman.

Thomas Jefferson, who was responsible for writing the principle of the equality of men into the American Declaration of Independence, saw this point. It led him to oppose slavery even though he was unable to free himself fully from his slave-holding background. He wrote in a letter to the author of a book that emphasized the notable intellectual achievements of Negroes in order to refute the then common view that they had limited intellectual capacities:

> Be assured that no person living wishes more sincerely than I do, to see a complete refutation of the doubts I have myself entertained and expressed on the grade of understanding allotted to them by nature, and to find that they are on a par with ourselves . . . but whatever be their degree of talent it is no measure of their rights. Because Sir Isaac Newton was superior to others in understanding, he was not therefore lord of the property or person of others.[2]

Similarly when in the 1850s the call for women's rights was raised in the United States a remarkable black feminist named Sojourner Truth made the same point in more robust terms at a feminist convention:

> . . . they talk about this thing in the head; what do they call it? ["Intellect," whispered someone near by.] That's it. What's that got to do with women's rights or Negroes' rights? If my cup won't hold but a pint and yours holds a quart, wouldn't you be mean not to let me have my little half-measure full?[3]

It is on this basis that the case against racism and the case against sexism must both ultimately rest; and it is in accordance with this principle that the attitude that we may call "speciesism," by analogy with racism, must also be condemned. Speciesism—the word is not an attractive one, but I can think of no better term—is a prejudice or attitude of bias toward the interests of members of one's own species and against those of members of other species. It should be obvious that the fundamental objections to racism and sexism made by Thomas Jefferson and Sojourner Truth apply equally to speciesism. If possessing a higher degree of intelligence does not entitle one human to use another for his own ends, how can it entitle humans to exploit nonhumans for the same purpose?[4]

Many philosophers and other writers have proposed the principle of equal consideration of interests, in some form or other, as a basic moral principle; but not many of them have recognized

that this principle applies to members of other species as well as to our own. Jeremy Bentham was one of the few who did realize this. In a forward-looking passage written at a time when black slaves had been freed by the French but in the British dominions were still being treated in the way we now treat animals, Bentham wrote:

> The day *may* come when the rest of the animal creation may acquire those rights which never could have been withholden from them but by the hand of tyranny. The French have already discovered that the blackness of the skin is no reason why a human being should be abandoned without redress to the caprice of a tormentor. It may one day come to be recognized that the number of the legs, the villosity of the skin, or the termination of the *os sacrum* are reasons equally insufficient for abandoning a sensitive being to the same fate. What else is it that should trace the insuperable line? Is it the faculty of reason, or perhaps the faculty of discourse? But a full-grown horse or dog is beyond comparison a more rational, as well as a more conversable animal, than an infant of a day or a week or even a month, old. But suppose they were otherwise, what would it avail? The question is not, Can they *reason?* nor Can they *talk?* but, *Can they suffer?*[5]

In this passage Bentham points to the capacity for suffering as the vital characteristic that gives a being the right to equal consideration. The capacity for suffering—or more strictly, for suffering and/or enjoyment or happiness—is not just another characteristic like the capacity for language or higher mathematics. Bentham is not saying that those who try to mark "the insuperable line" that determines whether the interests of a being should be considered happen to have chosen the wrong characteristic. By saying that we must consider the interests of all beings with the capacity for suffering or enjoyment Bentham does not arbitrarily exclude from consideration any interests at all—as those who draw the line with reference to the possession of reason or language do. The capacity for suffering and enjoyment is *a prerequisite for having interests at all*, a condition that must be satisfied before we can speak of interests in a meaningful way. It would be nonsense to say that it was not in the interests of a stone to be kicked along the road by a schoolboy. A stone does not have interests because it cannot suffer. Nothing that we can do to it could possibly make any difference to its welfare. A mouse, on the other hand, does have an interest in not being kicked along the road, because it will suffer if it is.

If a being suffers there can be no moral justification for refusing to take that suffering into consideration. No matter what the nature of the being, the principle of equality requires that its suffering be counted equally with the like suffering—insofar as rough comparisons can be made—of any other being. If a being is not capable of suffering, or of experiencing enjoyment or happiness, there is nothing to be taken into account. So the limit of sentience (using the term as a convenient if not strictly accurate shorthand for the capacity to suffer and/or experience enjoyment) is the only defensible boundary of concern for the interests of others. To mark this boundary by some other characteristic like intelligence or rationality would be to mark it in an arbitrary manner. Why not choose some other characteristic, like skin color?

The racist violates the principle of equality by giving greater weight to the interests of members of his own race when there is a clash between their interests and the interests of those of another race. The sexist violates the principle of equality by favoring the interests of his own sex. Similarly the speciesist allows the interests of his own species to override the greater interests of members of other species. The pattern is identical in each case.

Most human beings are speciesists. The following chapters show that ordinary human beings—not a few exceptionally cruel or heartless humans, but the overwhelming majority of humans—take an active part in, acquiesce in, and allow their taxes to pay for practices that require the sacrifice of the most important interests of members of other species in order to promote the most trivial interests of our own species.

There is, however, one general defense of the practices to be described in the next two chapters that needs to be disposed of before we discuss the practices themselves. It is a defense which, if true, would allow us to do anything at all to nonhumans for the slightest reason, or for no reason at all, without incurring any justifiable reproach. This defense claims that we are never guilty of neglecting the interests of other animals for one breathtakingly simple reason: they have no interests. Nonhuman animals have no interests, according to this view, because they are not capable of suffering. By this is not meant merely that they are not capable of suffering in all the ways that humans are—for instance, that a calf is not capable of suffering from the knowledge that it will be killed in six months time. That modest claim is, no doubt, true; but it does not clear humans of the charge of speciesism, since it allows that animals may suffer in other ways—for instance, by being given electric shocks, or being kept in small, cramped cages. The defense I am about to discuss is the much more sweeping, although correspondingly less plausible, claim that animals are incapable of suffering in any way at all; that they are, in fact, unconscious automata, possessing neither thoughts nor feelings nor a mental life of any kind.

Although, as we shall see in a later chapter, the view that animals are automata was proposed by the seventeenth-century French philosopher René Descartes, to most people, then and now, it is obvious that if, for example, we stick a sharp knife into the stomach of an unanesthetized dog, the dog will feel pain. That this is so is assumed by the laws in most civilized countries which prohibit wanton cruelty to animals. Readers whose common sense tells them that animals do suffer may prefer to skip the remainder of this section, moving straight on to page 466, since the pages in between do nothing but refute a position which they do not hold. Implausible as it is, though, for the sake of completeness this skeptical position must be discussed.

Do animals other than humans feel pain? How do we know? Well, how do we know if anyone, human or nonhuman, feels pain? We know that we ourselves can feel pain. We know this from the direct experiences of pain that we have when, for instance, somebody presses a lighted cigarette against the back of our hand. But how do we know that anyone else feels pain? We cannot directly experience anyone else's pain, whether that "anyone" is our best friend or a stray dog. Pain is a state of consciousness, a "mental event," and as such it can never be observed. Behavior like writhing, screaming, or drawing one's hand away from the lighted cigarette is not pain itself; nor are the recordings a neurologist might make of activity within the brain observations of pain itself. Pain is something that we feel, and we can only infer that others are feeling it from various external indications.

In theory, we *could* always be mistaken when we assume that other human beings feel pain. It is conceivable that our best friend is really a very cleverly constructed robot, controlled by a brilliant scientist so as to give all the signs of feeling pain, but really no more sensitive than any other machine. We can never know, with absolute certainty, that this is not the case. But while this might present a puzzle for philosophers, none of us has the slightest real doubt that our best friends feel pain just as we do. This is an inference, but a perfectly reasonable one, based on observations of their behavior in situations in which we would feel pain, and on the fact that we have every reason to assume that our friends are beings like us, with nervous systems like ours that can be assumed to function as ours do, and to produce similar feelings in similar circumstances.

If it is justifiable to assume that other humans feel pain as we do, is there any reason why a similar inference should be unjustifiable in the case of other animals?

Nearly all the external signs which lead us to infer pain in other humans can be seen in other species, especially the species most closely related to us—other species of mammals, and birds. Behavioral signs—writhing, facial contortions, moaning, yelping or other forms of calling, attempts to avoid the source of pain, appearance of fear at the prospect of its repetition, and so on—are present. In addition, we know that these animals have nervous systems very like ours, which respond physiologically as ours do when the animal is in circumstances in which we would feel pain: an initial rise of blood pressure, dilated pupils, perspiration, an increased pulse rate, and, if the stimulus continues, a fall in blood pressure. Although humans have a more developed cerebral cortex than other animals, this part of the brain is concerned with thinking functions rather than with basic impulses, emotions, and feelings. These impulses, emotions, and feelings are located in the diencephalon, which is well developed in many other species of animals, especially mammals and birds.[6]

We also know that the nervous systems of other animals were not artificially constructed to mimic the pain behavior of humans, as a robot might be artificially constructed. The nervous systems of animals evolved as our own did, and in fact the evolutionary history of humans and other animals, especially mammals, did not diverge until the central features of our nervous systems were already in existence. A capacity to feel pain obviously enhances a species' prospects of survival, since it causes members of the species to avoid sources of injury. It is surely unreasonable to suppose that nervous systems which are virtually identical physiologically have a common origin and a common evolutionary function, and result in similar forms of behavior in similar circumstances should actually operate in an entirely different manner on the level of subjective feelings.

It has long been accepted as sound policy in science to search for the simplest possible explanation of whatever it is we are trying to explain. Occasionally it has been claimed that it is for this reason "unscientific" to explain the behavior of animals by theories that refer to the animal's conscious feelings, desires, and so on—the idea being that if the behavior in question can be explained without invoking consciousness or feelings, that will be the simpler theory. Yet we can now see that such explanations, when placed in the overall context of the behavior of both human and nonhuman animals, are actually far more complex than their rivals. For we know from our own experience that explanations of our own behavior that did not refer to consciousness and the feeling of pain would be incomplete; and it is simpler to assume that the similar behavior of animals with similar nervous systems is to be explained in the same way than to try to invent some other explanation for the behavior of nonhuman animals as well as an explanation for the divergence between humans and nonhumans in this respect.

The overwhelming majority of scientists who have addressed themselves to this question agree. Lord Brain, one of the most eminent neurologists of our time, has said:

> I personally can see no reason for conceding mind to my fellow men and denying it to animals. . . . I at least cannot doubt that the interests and activities of animals are correlated with awareness and feeling in the same way as my own, and which may be, for aught I know, just as vivid.[7]

While the author of a recent book on pain writes:

> Every particle of factual evidence supports the contention that the higher mammalian vertebrates experience pain sensations at least as acute as our own. To say that they feel less because they are lower animals is an absurdity; it can easily be shown that many of their senses are far more acute than ours—visual acuity in certain birds, hearing in most wild animals, and touch in others; these animals depend more than we do today on the sharpest possible awareness of a hostile environment. Apart from the complexity of the cerebral cortex (which does not directly perceive pain) their nervous systems are almost identical to ours and their reactions to pain remarkably similar, though lacking (so far as we know) the philosophical and moral overtones. The emotional element is all too evident, mainly in the form of fear and anger.[8]

In Britain, three separate expert government committees on matters relating to animals have accepted the conclusion that animals feel pain. After noting the obvious behavioral evidence for this view, the Committee on Cruelty to Wild Animals said:

> . . . we believe that the physiological, and more particularly the anatomical, evidence fully justifies and reinforces the common sense belief that animals feel pain.

And after discussing the evolutionary value of pain they concluded that pain is "of clear-cut biological usefulness" and this is "a third type of evidence that animals feel pain." They then went on to consider forms of suffering other than mere physical pain, and added that they were "satisfied that animals do suffer from acute fear and terror." In 1965, reports by British government committees on experiments on animals, and on the welfare of animals under intensive farming methods, agreed with this view, concluding that animals are capable of suffering both from straightforward physical injuries and from fear, anxiety, stress, and so on.[9]

That might well be thought enough to settle the matter; but there is one more objection that needs to be considered. There is, after all, one behavioral sign that humans have when in pain which nonhumans do not have. This is a developed language. Other animals may communicate with each other, but not, it seems, in the complicated way we do. Some philosophers, including Descartes, have thought it important that while humans can tell each other about their experience of pain in great detail, other animals cannot. (Interestingly, this once neat dividing line between humans and other species has now been threatened by the discovery that chimpanzees can be taught a language.)[10] But as Bentham pointed out long ago, the ability to use language is not relevant to the question of how a being ought to be treated—unless that ability can be linked to the capacity to suffer, so that the absence of a language casts doubt on the existence of this capacity.

This link may be attempted in two ways. First, there is a hazy line of philosophical thought, stemming perhaps from some doctrines associated with the influential philosopher Ludwig Wittgenstein, which maintains that we cannot meaningfully attribute states of consciousness to beings without language. This position seems to me very implausible. Language may be necessary for abstract thought, at some level anyway; but states like pain are more primitive, and have nothing to do with language.

The second and more easily understood way of linking language and the existence of pain is to say that the best evidence that we can have that another creature is in pain is when he tells us that he is. This is a distinct line of argument, for it is not being denied that a non-language-user conceivably *could* suffer, but only that we could ever have sufficient reason to believe that he is suffering. Still, this line of argument fails too. As Jane Goodall has pointed out in her study of chimpanzees, *In the Shadow of Man,* when it comes to the expressions of feelings and emotions language is less important than in other areas. We tend to fall back on nonlinguistic modes of communication such as a cheering pat on the back, an exuberant embrace, a clasp of the hands, and so on. The basic signals we use to convey pain, fear, anger, love, joy, surprise, sexual arousal, and many other emotional states are not specific to our own species.[11]

Charles Darwin made an extensive study of this subject, and the book he wrote about it, *The Expression of the Emotions in Man and Animals,* notes countless nonlinguistic modes of expression. The statement "I am in pain" may be one piece of evidence for the conclusion that the speaker is in pain, but it is not the only possible evidence, and since people sometimes tell lies, not even the best possible evidence.

Even if there were stronger grounds for refusing to attribute pain to those who do not have a language, the consequences of this refusal might lead us to reject the conclusion. Human infants and young children are unable to use language. Are we to deny that a year-old child can suffer? If not, language cannot be crucial. Of course, most parents understand the responses of their children better than they understand the responses of other animals; but this is just a fact about the relatively greater knowledge that we have of our own species, and the greater contact we have with infants, as compared to animals. Those who have studied the behavior of other animals, and those who have pet animals, soon learn to understand their responses as well as we understand those of an infant, and sometimes better. Jane Goodall's account of the chimpanzees she watched is one instance of this, but the same can be said of those who have observed species less closely related to our own. Two among many possible examples are Konrad Lorenz's observations of geese and jackdaws, and N. Tinberger's extensive studies of herring gulls.[12] Just as we can understand infant human behavior in the light of adult human behavior, so we can understand the behavior of other species in the light of our own behavior—and sometimes we can understand our own behavior better in the light of the behavior of other species.

So to conclude: there are no good reasons, scientific or philosophical, for denying that animals feel pain. If we do not doubt that other humans feel pain we should not doubt that other animals do so too.

Animals can feel pain. As we saw earlier, there can be no moral justification for regarding the pain (or pleasure) that animals feel as less important than the same amount of pain (or pleasure) felt by humans. But what exactly does this mean, in practical terms? To prevent misunderstanding I shall spell out what I mean a little more fully.

If I give a horse a hard slap across its rump with my open hand, the horse may start, but it presumably feels little pain. Its skin is thick enough to protect it against a mere slap. If I slap a baby in the same way, however, the baby will cry and presumably does feel pain, for its skin is more sensitive. So it is worse to slap a baby than a horse, if both slaps are administered with equal force. But there must be some kind of blow—I don't know exactly what it would be, but perhaps a blow with a heavy stick—that would cause the horse as much pain as we cause a baby by slapping it with our hand. That is what I mean by "the same amount of pain" and if we consider it wrong to inflict that much pain on a baby for no good reason then we must, unless we are speciesists, consider it equally wrong to inflict the same amount of pain on a horse for no good reason.

There are other differences between humans and animals that cause other complications. Normal adult human beings have mental capacities which will, in certain circumstances, lead them to suffer more than animals would in the same circumstances. If, for instance, we decided to perform extremely painful or lethal scientific experiments on normal adult humans, kidnapped at random from public parks for this purpose, every adult who entered a park would become fearful that he would be kidnapped. The resultant terror would be a form of suffering additional to the pain of the experiment. The same experiments performed on nonhuman animals would cause less suffering since the animals would not have the anticipatory dread of being kidnapped and experimented upon. This does not mean, of course, that it would be right to perform the experiment on animals, but only that there is a reason, which is *not* speciesist, for preferring to use animals rather than normal adult humans, if the experiment is to be done at all. It should be noted, however, that this same argument gives us a reason for preferring to use human infants—orphans perhaps—or retarded humans for experiments, rather than adults, since infants and retarded humans would also have no idea of what was going to happen to them. So far as this argument is concerned nonhuman animals and infants and retarded humans are in the same category; and if we use this argument to justify experiments on nonhuman animals we have to ask ourselves whether we are also prepared to allow experiments on human infants and retarded adults; and if we make a distinction between animals and these humans, on what basis can we do it, other than a barefaced—and morally indefensible—preference for members of our own species?

There are many areas in which the superior mental powers of normal adult humans make a difference: anticipation, more detailed memory, greater knowledge of what is happening, and so on. Yet these differences do not all point to greater suffering on the part of the normal human being. Sometimes an animal may suffer more because of his more limited understanding. If, for instance, we are taking prisoners in wartime we can explain to them that while they must submit to capture, search, and confinement they will not otherwise be harmed and will be set free at the conclusion of hostilities. If we capture a wild animal, however, we cannot explain that we are not threatening its life. A wild animal cannot distinguish an attempt to overpower and confine from an attempt to kill; the one causes as much terror as the other.

It may be objected that comparisons of the sufferings of different species are impossible to make, and that for this reason when the interests of animals and humans clash the principle of equality gives no guidance. It is probably true that comparisons of suffering between members of different species cannot be made precisely, but precision is not essential. Even if we were to prevent the infliction of suffering on animals only when it is quite certain that the interests of humans will not be affected to anything like the extent that animals are affected, we would be forced to make radical changes in our treatment of animals that would involve our diet, the farming methods we use, experimental procedures in many fields of science, our approach to wildlife and to hunting, trapping and the wearing of furs, and areas of entertainment like circuses, rodeos, and zoos. As a result, a vast amount of suffering would be avoided.

So far I have said a lot about the infliction of suffering on animals, but nothing about killing them. This omission has been deliberate. The application of the principle of equality to the infliction of suffering is, in theory at least, fairly straightforward. Pain and suffering are bad and should be prevented or minimized, irrespective of the race, sex, or species of the being that suffers. How bad a pain is depends on how intense it is and how long it lasts, but pains of the same intensity and duration are equally bad, whether felt by humans or animals.

The wrongness of killing a being is more complicated. I have kept, and shall continue to keep, the question of killing in the background because in the present state of human tyranny over other species

the more simple, straightforward principle of equal consideration of pain or pleasure is a sufficient basis for identifying and protesting against all the major abuses of animals that humans practice. Nevertheless, it is necessary to say something about killing.

Just as most humans are speciesists in their readiness to cause pain to animals when they would not cause a similar pain to humans for the same reason, so most humans are speciesists in their readiness to kill other animals when they would not kill humans. We need to proceed more cautiously here, however, because people hold widely differing views about when it is legitimate to kill humans, as the continuing debates over abortion and euthanasia attest. Nor have moral philosophers been able to agree on exactly what it is that makes it wrong to kill humans, and under what circumstances killing a human being may be justifiable.

Let us consider first the view that it is always wrong to take an innocent human life. We may call this the "sanctity of life" view. People who take this view oppose abortion and euthanasia. They do not usually, however, oppose the killing of nonhumans— so perhaps it would be more accurate to describe this view as the "sanctity of *human* life" view.

The belief that human life, and only human life, is sacrosanct is a form of speciesism. To see this, consider the following example.

Assume that, as sometimes happens, an infant has been born with massive and irreparable brain damage. The damage is so severe that the infant can never be any more than a "human vegetable," unable to talk, recognize other people, act independently of others, or develop a sense of self-awareness. The parents of the infant, realizing that they cannot hope for any improvement in their child's condition and being in any case unwilling to spend, or ask the state to spend, the thousands of dollars that would be needed annually for proper care of the infant, ask the doctor to kill the infant painlessly.

Should the doctor do what the parents ask? Legally, he should not, and in this respect the law reflects the sanctity of life view. The life of every human being is sacred. Yet people who would say this about the infant do not object to the killing of nonhuman animals. How can they justify their different judgments? Adult chimpanzees, dogs, pigs, and many other species far surpass the brain-damaged infant in their ability to relate to others, act independently, be self-aware, and any other capacity that could reasonably be said to give value to life. With the most intensive care possible, there are retarded infants who can never achieve the intelligence level of a dog. Nor can we appeal to the concern of the infant's parents, since they themselves, in this imaginary example (and in some actual cases), do not want the infant kept alive.

The only thing that distinguishes the infant from the animal, in the eyes of those who claim it has a "right to life," is that it is, biologically, a member of the species Homo sapiens, whereas chimpanzees, dogs, and pigs are not. But to use *this* difference as the basis for granting a right to life to the infant and not to the other animals is, of course, pure speciesism.[*] It is exactly the kind of arbitrary difference that the most crude and overt kind of racist uses in attempting to justify racial discrimination.

This does not mean that to avoid speciesism we must hold that it is as wrong to kill a dog as it is to kill a normal human being. The only position that is irredeemably speciesist is the one that tries to make the boundary of the right to life run exactly parallel to the boundary of our own species. Those who hold the sanctity of life view do this because while distinguishing sharply between humans and other animals they allow no distinctions to be made within our own species, objecting to the killing of the severely retarded and the hopelessly senile as strongly as they object to the killing of normal adults.

To avoid speciesism we must allow that beings which are similar in all relevant respects have a similar right to life—and mere membership in our own biological species cannot be a morally relevant criterion for this right. Within these limits we could

still hold that, for instance, it is worse to kill a normal adult human, with a capacity for self-awareness, and the ability to plan for the future and have meaningful relations with others, than it is to kill a mouse, which presumably does not share all of these characteristics; or we might appeal to the close family and other personal ties which humans have but mice do not have to the same degree; or we might think that it is the consequences for other humans, who will be put in fear of their own lives, that makes the crucial difference; or we might think it is some combination of these factors, or other factors altogether.

Whatever criteria we choose, however, we will have to admit that they do not follow precisely the boundary of our own species. We may legitimately hold that there are some features of certain beings which make their lives more valuable than those of other beings; but there will surely be some non-human animals whose lives, by any standards, are more valuable than the lives of some humans. A chimpanzee, dog, or pig, for instance, will have a higher degree of self-awareness and a greater capacity for meaningful relations with others than a severely retarded infant or someone in a state of advanced senility. So if we base the right to life on these characteristics we must grant these animals a right to life as good as, or better than, such retarded or senile humans.

Now this argument cuts both ways. It could be taken as showing that chimpanzees, dogs, and pigs, along with some other species, have a right to life and we commit a grave moral offense whenever we kill them, even when they are old and suffering and our intention is to put them out of their misery. Alternatively one could take the argument as showing that the severely retarded and hopelessly senile have no right to life and may be killed for quite trivial reasons, as we now kill animals.

Since the focus of this book is on ethical questions concerning animals and not on the morality of euthanasia I shall not attempt to settle this issue finally. I think it is reasonably clear, though, that while both of the positions just described avoid speciesism, neither is entirely satisfactory. What we need is some middle position which would avoid speciesism but would not make the lives of the retarded and senile as cheap as the lives of pigs and dogs now are, nor make the lives of pigs and dogs so

[*]I am here putting aside religious views, for example the doctrine that all and only humans have immortal souls, or are made in the image of God. Historically these views have been very important, and no doubt are partly responsible for the idea that human life has a special sanctity. Logically, however, these religious views are unsatisfactory, since a reasoned explanation of why it should be that all humans and no nonhumans have immortal souls is not offered. This belief too, therefore, comes under suspicion as a form of speciesism. In any case, defenders of the "sanctity of life" view are generally reluctant to base their position on purely religious doctrines, since these doctrines are no longer as widely accepted as they once were.

sacrosanct that we think it wrong to put them out of hopeless misery. What we must do is bring nonhuman animals within our sphere of moral concern and cease to treat their lives as expendable for whatever trivial purposes we may have. At the same time, once we realize that the fact that a being is a member of our own species is not in itself enough to make it always wrong to kill that being, we may come to reconsider our policy of preserving human lives at all costs, even when there is no prospect of a meaningful life or of existence without terrible pain.

I conclude, then, that a rejection of speciesism does not imply that all lives are of equal worth. While self-awareness, intelligence, the capacity for meaningful relations with others, and so on are not relevant to the question of inflicting pain—since pain is pain, whatever other capacities, beyond the capacity to feel pain, the being may have—these capacities may be relevant to the question of taking life. It is not arbitrary to hold that the life of a self-aware being, capable of abstract thought, of planning for the future, of complex acts of communication, and so on, is more valuable than the life of a being without these capacities. To see the difference between the issues of inflicting pain and taking life, consider how we would choose within our own species. If we had to choose to save the life of a normal human or a mentally defective human, we would probably choose to save the life of the normal human; but if we had to choose between preventing pain in the normal human or the mental defective—imagine that both have received painful but superficial injuries, and we only have enough painkiller for one of them—it is not nearly so clear how we ought to choose. The same is true when we consider other species. The evil of pain is, in itself, unaffected by the other characteristics of the being that feels the pain; the value of life is affected by these other characteristics.

Normally this will mean that if we have to choose between the life of a human being and the life of another animal we should choose to save the life of the human; but there may be special cases in which the reverse holds true, because the human being in question does not have the capacities of a normal human being. So this view is not speciesist, although it may appear to be at first glance. The preference, in normal cases, for saving a human life over the life of an animal when a choice *has* to be made is a preference based on the characteristics that normal humans have, and not on the mere fact that they are members of our own species. This is why when we consider members of our own species who lack the characteristics of normal humans we can no longer say that their lives are always to be preferred to those of other animals. This issue comes up in a practical way in the following chapter. In general, though, the question of when it is wrong to kill (painlessly) an animal is one to which we need give no precise answer. As long as we remember that we should give the same respect to the lives of animals as we give to the lives of those humans at a similar mental level, we shall not go far wrong.

In any case, the conclusions that are argued for in this book flow from the principle of minimizing suffering alone. The idea that it is also wrong to kill animals painlessly gives some of these conclusions additional support which is welcome, but strictly unnecessary. Interestingly enough, this is true even of the conclusion that we ought to become vegetarians, a conclusion which in the popular mind is generally based on some kind of absolute prohibition on killing.

NOTES

1. For Bentham's moral philosophy, see his *Introduction to the Principles of Morals and Legislation,* and for Sidgwick's see *The Methods of Ethics* (the passage quoted is from the seventh edition, p. 382). As examples of leading contemporary moral philosophers who incorporate a requirement of equal consideration of interests, see R. M. Hare, *Freedom and Reason* (New York: Oxford University Press, 1963) and John Rawls, *A Theory of Justice* (Cambridge: Harvard University Press, Belknap Press, 1972). For a brief account of the essential agreement on this issue between these and other positions, see R. M. Hare, "Rules of War and Moral Reasoning," *Philosophy and Public Affairs,* vol. 1, no. 2 (1972).

2. Letter to Henri Gregoire, February 25, 1809.

3. Reminiscences by Francis D. Gage, from Susan B. Anthony, *The History of Woman Suffrage,* vol. 1; the passage is to be found in the extract in Leslie Tanner, ed., *Voices from Women's Liberation* (New York: Signet, 1970).

4. I owe the term "speciesism" to Richard Ryder.

5. *Introduction to the Principles of Morals and Legislation,* chapter 17.

6. Lord Brain, "Presidential Address" in C. A. Keele and R. Smith, eds., *The Assessment of Pain in Men and Animals* (London: Universities Federation for Animal Welfare, 1962).

7. Ibid., p. 11.

8. Richard Serjeant, *The Spectrum of Pain* (London: Hart-Davis, 1969), p. 72.

9. See the reports of the committee on Cruelty to Wild Animals (Command Paper 8266, 1951), paragraphs 36–42; the Departmental Committee on Experiments on Animals (Command Paper 2641, 1965), paragraphs 179–182; and the Technical Committee to Enquire into the Welfare of Animals Kept under Intensive Livestock Husbandry Systems (Command Paper 2836, 1965), paragraphs 26–28 (London: Her Majesty's Stationery Office).

10. One chimpanzee, Washoe, has been taught the sign language used by deaf people, and acquired a vocabulary of 350 signs. Another, Lana, communicates in structured sentences by pushing buttons on a special machine. For a brief account of Washoe's abilities, see Jane van Lawick-Goodall, *In the Shadow of Man* (Boston: Houghton Mifflin, 1971), pp. 252–254; and for Lana, see *Newsweek*, 7 January 1974, and *New York Times*, 4 December 1974.

11. *In the Shadow of Man*, p. 225; Michael Peters makes a similar point in "Nature and Culture," in Stanley and Roslind Godlovitch and John Harris, eds., *Animals, Men and Morals* (New York: Taplinger Publishing Co., 1972).

12. Konrad Lorenz, *King Solomon's Ring* (New York: T.Y. Crowell, 1952); N. Tinbergen, *The Herring Gull's World*, rev. ed. (New York: Basic Books, 1974).

Questions for Analysis

1. What does Singer mean by his claim that the principle of human equality is not a description of actual equality but a prescription of how we should treat humans?

2. On what grounds does Singer equate speciesism with sexism and racism?

3. What reasons have been advanced in favor of the view that animals cannot suffer? How does Singer rebut them?

4. Singer notes certain differences between human and nonhuman capacities and the complications that follow from them. What are these differences, and what kinds of complications follow from them?

5. To reject speciesism, Singer says, is not to say that all lives are of equal worth. Why not?

6. Normally, Singer says, we should choose a human over a nonhuman life if forced to choose between them. Why? Under what circumstances should we choose the nonhuman one?

7. In what way is Singer's principle of equal consideration related to the principle of utility?

The Case for Animal Rights

Tom Regan

In this essay, Tom Regan, now a professor emeritus of philosophy at North Carolina State University, offers an alternative approach to Peter Singer's. Like Singer, he opposes speciesism. Unlike Singer, he does not offer a utilitarian moral theory. He argues that the focus of our moral concern should not be to minimize suffering and maximize pleasure but to avoid treating individual animals (human and nonhuman alike) in certain ways regardless of the consequences.

All animals that are the experiencing subjects of their own lives, he says, have inherent value. They, like humans, deserve what we called in Part 1 Kantian respect. They are not to

From "The Case for Animal Rights," in *In Defense of Animals* edited by Peter Singer (1985), pp. 13–26. Reprinted by permission of Peter Singer and Tom Regan.

be treated as mere things, even if we can maximize happiness by doing so. What makes eating meat or experimenting on animals wrong, then, is not that the human benefit does not outweigh the animal suffering, but that such practices deny the inherent value of the animals involved.

In defending his position, Regan criticizes *contractarian* views of morality, which deny that nonhuman animals can have rights. He also disagrees with Singer's view that some lives of creatures with the right to life are more valuable than others. All lives that have inherent value, he says, are equal.

I regard myself as an advocate of animal rights — as a part of the animal rights movement. That movement, as I conceive it, is committed to a number of goals, including:

> the total abolition of the use of animals in science;
>
> the total dissolution of commercial animal agriculture;
>
> the total elimination of commercial and sport hunting and trapping.

There are, I know, people who profess to believe in animal rights but do not avow these goals. Factory farming, they say, is wrong—it violates animals' rights—but traditional animal agriculture is all right. Toxicity tests of cosmetics on animals violates their rights, but important medical research—cancer research, for example—does not. The clubbing of baby seals is abhorrent, but not the harvesting of adult seals. I used to think I understood this reasoning. Not any more. You don't change unjust institutions by tidying them up.

What's wrong—fundamentally wrong—with the way animals are treated isn't the details that vary from case to case. It's the whole system. The forlornness of the veal calf is pathetic, heart wrenching; the pulsing pain of the chimp with electrodes planted deep in her brain is repulsive; the slow, tortuous death of the raccoon caught in the leg-hold trap is agonizing. But what is wrong isn't the pain, isn't the suffering, isn't the deprivation. These compound what's wrong. Sometimes—often—they make it much, much worse. But they are not the fundamental wrong.

The fundamental wrong is the system that allows us to view animals as *our resources*, here for *us*—to be eaten, or surgically manipulated, or exploited for sport or money. Once we accept this view of ani-

mals as our resources—the rest is as predictable as it is regrettable. Why worry about their loneliness, their pain, their death? Since animals exist for us, to benefit us in one way or another, what harms them really doesn't matter—or matters only if it starts to bother us, makes us feel a trifle uneasy when we eat our veal escalope, for example. So, yes, let us get veal calves out of solitary confinement, give them more space, a little straw, a few companions. But let us keep our veal escalope.

But a little straw, more space and a few companions won't eliminate—won't even touch—the basic wrong that attaches to our viewing and treating these animals as our resources. A veal calf killed to be eaten after living in close confinement is viewed and treated in this way: but so, too, is another who is raised (as they say) "more humanely." To right the wrong of our treatment of farm animals requires more than making rearing methods "more humane"; it requires the total dissolution of commercial animal agriculture.

How we do this, whether we do it or, as in the case of animals in science, whether and how we abolish their use—these are to a large extent political questions. People must change their beliefs before they change their habits. Enough people, especially those elected to public office, must believe in change—must want it—before we will have laws that protect the rights of animals. This process of change is very complicated, very demanding, very exhausting, calling for the efforts of many hands in education, publicity, political organization and activity, down to the licking of envelopes and stamps. As a trained and practising philosopher, the sort of contribution I can make is limited but, I like to think, important. The currency of philosophy is ideas—their meaning and rational foundation—not the nuts and bolts of the legislative process, say, or the mechanics of community organization. That's what

I have been exploring over the past ten years or so in my essays and talks and, most recently, in my book, *The Case for Animal Rights*. I believe the major conclusions I reach in the book are true because they are supported by the weight of the best arguments. I believe the idea of animal rights has reason, not just emotion, on its side.

In the space I have at my disposal here I can only sketch, in the barest outline, some of the main features of the book. Its main themes—and we should not be surprised by this—involve asking and answering deep, foundational moral questions about what morality is, how it should be understood and what is the best moral theory, all considered. I hope I can convey something of the shape I think this theory takes. The attempt to do this will be (to use a word a friendly critic once used to describe my work) cerebral, perhaps too cerebral. But this is misleading. My feelings about how animals are sometimes treated run just as deep and just as strong as those of my more volatile compatriots. Philosophers do—to use the jargon of the day— have a right side to their brains. If it's the left side we contribute (or mainly should), that's because what talents we have reside there.

How to proceed? We begin by asking how the moral status of animals has been understood by thinkers who deny that animals have rights. Then we test the mettle of their ideas by seeing how well they stand up under the heat of fair criticism. If we start our thinking in this way, we soon find that some people believe that we have no duties directly to animals, that we owe nothing to them, that we can do nothing that wrongs them. Rather, we can do wrong acts that involve animals, and so we have duties regarding them, though none to them. Such views may be called indirect duty views. By way of illustration: suppose your neighbour kicks your dog. Then your neighbour has done something wrong. But not to your dog. The wrong that has been done is a wrong to you. After all, it is wrong to upset people, and your neighbour's kicking your dog upsets you. So you are the one who is wronged, not your dog. Or again: by kicking your dog your neighbour damages your property. And since it is wrong to damage another person's property, your neighbour has done something wrong—to you, of course, not to your dog. Your neighbour no more wrongs your dog than your car would be wronged if the windshield were smashed. Your neighbour's duties involving your dog are indirect duties to you. More generally, all of our duties regarding animals are indirect duties to one another—to humanity.

How could someone try to justify such a view? Someone might say that your dog doesn't feel anything and so isn't hurt by your neighbour's kick, doesn't care about the pain since none is felt, is as unaware of anything as is your windshield. Someone might say this, but no rational person will, since, among other considerations, such a view will commit anyone who holds it to the position that no human being feels pain either—that human beings also don't care about what happens to them. A second possibility is that though both humans and your dog are hurt when kicked, it is only human pain that matters. But, again, no rational person can believe this. Pain is pain wherever it occurs. If your neighbour's causing you pain is wrong because of the pain that is caused, we cannot rationally ignore or dismiss the moral relevance of the pain that your dog feels.

Philosophers who hold indirect duty views— and many still do—have come to understand that they must avoid the two defects just noted: that is, both the view that animals don't feel anything as well as the idea that only human pain can be morally relevant. Among such thinkers the sort of view now favoured is one or other form of what is called *contractarianism*.

Here, very crudely, is the root idea: morality consists of a set of rules that individuals voluntarily agree to abide by, as we do when we sign a contract (hence the name contractarianism). Those who understand and accept the terms of the contract are covered directly; they have rights created and recognized by, and protected in, the contract. And these contractors can also have protection spelled out for others who, though they lack the ability to understand morality and so cannot sign the contract themselves, are loved or cherished by those who can. Thus young children, for example, are unable to sign contracts and lack rights. But they are protected by the contract none the less because of the sentimental interests of others, most notably their parents. So we have, then, duties involving these children, duties regarding them, but no duties to them. Our duties in their case are indirect duties to other human beings, usually their parents.

As for animals, since they cannot understand contracts, they obviously cannot sign; and since they cannot sign, they have no rights. Like children, however, some animals are the objects of the sentimental interest of others. You, for example, love your dog or cat. So those animals that enough people care about (companion animals, whales, baby seals, the American bald eagle), though they lack rights themselves, will be protected because of the sentimental interests of people. I have, then, according to contractarianism, no duty directly to your dog or any other animal, not even the duty not to cause them pain or suffering; my duty not to hurt them is a duty I have to those people who care about what happens to them. As for other animals, where no or little sentimental interest is present—in the case of farm animals, for example, or laboratory rats—what duties we have grow weaker and weaker, perhaps to vanishing point. The pain and death they endure, though real, are not wrong if no one cares about them.

When it comes to the moral status of animals, contractarianism could be a hard view to refute if it were an adequate theoretical approach to the moral status of human beings. It is not adequate in this latter respect, however, which makes the question of its adequacy in the former case, regarding animals, utterly moot. For consider: morality, according to the (crude) contractarian position before us, consists of rules that people agree to abide by. What people? Well, enough to make a difference— enough, that is, *collectively* to have the power to enforce the rules that are drawn up in the contract. That is very well and good for the signatories but not so good for anyone who is not asked to sign. And there is nothing in contractarianism of the sort we are discussing that guarantees or requires that everyone will have a chance to participate equally in framing the rules of morality. The result is that this approach to ethics could sanction the most blatant forms of social, economic, moral and political injustice, ranging from a repressive caste system to systematic racial or sexual discrimination. Might, according to this theory, does make right. Let those who are the victims of injustice suffer as they will. It matters not so long as no one else—no contractor, or too few of them—cares about it. Such a theory takes one's moral breath away . . . as if, for example, there would be nothing

wrong with apartheid in South Africa if few white South Africans were upset by it. A theory with so little to recommend it at the level of the ethics of our treatment of our fellow humans cannot have anything more to recommend it when it comes to the ethics of how we treat our fellow animals.

The version of contractarianism just examined is, as I have noted, a crude variety, and in fairness to those of a contractarian persuasion it must be noted that much more refined, subtle and ingenious varieties are possible. For example, John Rawls, in his *A Theory of Justice,* sets forth a version of contractarianism that forces contractors to ignore the accidental features of being a human being—for example, whether one is white or black, male or female, a genius or of modest intellect. Only by ignoring such features, Rawls believes, can we ensure that the principles of justice that contractors would agree upon are not based on bias or prejudice. Despite the improvement a view such as Rawls's represents over the cruder forms of contractarianism, it remains deficient: it systematically denies that we have direct duties to those human beings who do not have a sense of justice—young children, for instance, and many mentally retarded humans. And yet it seems reasonably certain that, were we to torture a young child or a retarded elder, we would be doing something that wronged him or her, not something that would be wrong if (and only if) other humans with a sense of justice were upset. And since this is true in the case of these humans, we cannot rationally deny the same in the case of animals.

Indirect duty views, then, including the best among them, fail to command our rational assent. Whatever ethical theory we should accept rationally, therefore, it must at least recognize that we have some duties directly to animals, just as we have some duties directly to each other. The next two theories I'll sketch attempt to meet this requirement.

The first I call the cruelty–kindness view. Simply stated, this says that we have a direct duty to be kind to animals and a direct duty not to be cruel to them. Despite the familiar, reassuring ring of these ideas, I do not believe that this view offers an adequate theory. To make this clearer, consider kindness. A kind person acts from a certain kind of motive—compassion or concern, for example. And that is a virtue. But there is no guarantee that a kind act is a right act. If I am a generous racist, for example, I will be inclined to act kindly towards members of my own race, favouring their interests above those of others. My kindness would be real and, so far as it goes, good. But I trust it is too obvious to require argument that my kind acts may not be above moral reproach—may, in fact, be positively wrong because rooted in injustice. So kindness, notwithstanding its status as a virtue to be encouraged, simply will not carry the weight of a theory of right action.

Cruelty fares no better. People or their acts are cruel if they display either a lack of sympathy for or, worse, the presence of enjoyment in another's suffering. Cruelty in all its guises is a bad thing, a tragic human failing. But just as a person's being motivated by kindness does not guarantee that he or she does what is right, so the absence of cruelty does not ensure that he or she avoids doing what is wrong. Many people who perform abortions, for example, are not cruel, sadistic people. But that fact alone does not settle the terribly difficult question of the morality of abortion. The case is no different when we examine the ethics of our treatment of animals. So, yes, let us be for kindness and against cruelty. But let us not suppose that being for the one and against the other answers questions about moral right and wrong.

Some people think that the theory we are looking for is utilitarianism. A utilitarian accepts two moral principles. The first is that of equality: everyone's interests count, and similar interests must be counted as having similar weight or importance. White or black, American or Iranian, human or animal—everyone's pain or frustration matters, and matters just as much as the equivalent pain or frustration of anyone else. The second principle a utilitarian accepts is that of utility: do the act that will bring about the best balance between satisfaction and frustration for everyone affected by the outcome.

As a utilitarian, then, here is how I am to approach the task of deciding what I morally ought to do: I must ask who will be affected if I choose to do one thing rather than another, how much each individual will be affected, and where the best results are most likely to lie—which option, in other words, is most likely to bring about the best results, the best balance between satisfaction and frustration. That option, whatever it may be, is the one I ought to choose. That is where my moral duty lies.

The great appeal of utilitarianism rests with its uncompromising *egalitarianism*: everyone's interests count and count as much as the like interests of everyone else. The kind of odious discrimination that some forms of contractarianism can justify—discrimination based on race or sex, for example—seems disallowed in principle by utilitarianism, as is speciesism, systematic discrimination based on species membership.

The equality we find in utilitarianism, however, is not the sort an advocate of animal or human rights should have in mind. Utilitarianism has no room for the equal moral rights of different individuals because it has no room for their equal inherent value or worth. What has value for the utilitarian is the satisfaction of an individual's interests, not the individual whose interests they are. A universe in which you satisfy your desire for water, food and warmth is, other things being equal, better than a universe in which these desires are frustrated. And the same is true in the case of an animal with similar desires. But neither you nor the animal has any value in your own right. Only your feelings do.

Here is an analogy to help make the philosophical point clearer: a cup contains different liquids, sometimes sweet, sometimes bitter, sometimes a mix of the two. What has value are the liquids: the sweeter the better, the bitterer the worse. The cup, the container, has no value. It is what goes into it, not what they go into, that has value. For the utilitarian you and I are like the cup; we have no value as individuals and thus no equal value. What has value is what goes into us, what we serve as receptacles for; our feelings of satisfaction have positive value, our feelings of frustration negative value.

Serious problems arise for utilitarianism when we remind ourselves that it enjoins us to bring about the best consequences. What does this mean? It doesn't mean the best consequences for me alone, or for my family or friends, or any other person taken individually. No, what we must do is, roughly, as follows: we must add up (somehow!) the separate satisfactions and frustrations of everyone likely to be affected by our choice, the satisfactions in one column, the frustrations in the other. We must total each column for each of the options before us.

That is what it means to say the theory is aggregative. And then we must choose that option which is most likely to bring about the best balance of totaled satisfactions over totaled frustrations. Whatever act would lead to this outcome is the one we ought morally to perform—it is where our moral duty lies. And that act quite clearly might not be the same one that would bring about the best results for me personally, or for my family or friends, or for a lab animal. The best aggregated consequences for everyone concerned are not necessarily the best for each individual.

That utilitarianism is an aggregative theory—different individuals' satisfactions or frustrations are added, or summed, or totaled—is the key objection to this theory. My Aunt Bea is old, inactive, a cranky, sour person, though not physically ill. She prefers to go on living. She is also rather rich. I could make a fortune if I could get my hands on her money, money she intends to give me in any event, after she dies, but which she refuses to give me now. In order to avoid a huge tax bite, I plan to donate a handsome sum of my profits to a local children's hospital. Many, many children will benefit from my generosity, and much joy will be brought to their parents, relatives and friends. If I don't get the money rather soon, all these ambitions will come to naught. The once-in-a-lifetime opportunity to make a real killing will be gone. Why, then, not kill my Aunt Bea? Of course I *might* get caught. But I'm no fool and, besides, her doctor can be counted on to cooperate (he has an eye for the same investment and I happen to know a good deal about his shady past). The deed can be done . . . professionally, shall we say. There is *very* little chance of getting caught. And as for my conscience being guilt-ridden, I am a resourceful sort of fellow and will take more than sufficient comfort—as I lie on the beach at Acapulco—in contemplating the joy and health I have brought to so many others.

Suppose Aunt Bea is killed and the rest of the story comes out as told. Would I have done anything wrong? Anything immoral? One would have thought that I had. Not according to utilitarianism. Since what I have done has brought about the best balance between totaled satisfaction and frustration for all those affected by the outcome, my action is not wrong. Indeed, in killing Aunt Bea the physician and I did what duty required.

This same kind of argument can be repeated in all sorts of cases, illustrating, time after time, how the utilitarian's position leads to results that impartial people find morally callous. It is wrong to kill my Aunt Bea in the name of bringing about the best results for others. A good end does not justify an evil means. Any adequate moral theory will have to explain why this is so. Utilitarianism fails in this respect and so cannot be the theory we seek.

What to do? Where to begin anew? The place to begin, I think, is with the utilitarian's view of the value of the individual—or, rather, lack of value. In its place, suppose we consider that you and I, for example, do have value as individuals—what we'll call *inherent value*. To say we have such value is to say that we are something more than, something different from, mere receptacles. Moreover, to ensure that we do not pave the way for such injustices as slavery or sexual discrimination, we must believe that all who have inherent value have it equally, regardless of their sex, race, religion, birthplace and so on. Similarly to be discarded as irrelevant are one's talents or skills, intelligence and wealth, personality or pathology, whether one is loved and admired or despised and loathed. The genius and the retarded child, the prince and the pauper, the brain surgeon and the fruit vendor, Mother Teresa and the most unscrupulous used-car salesman—all have inherent value, all possess it equally, and all have an equal right to be treated with respect, to be treated in ways that do not reduce them to the status of things, as if they existed as resources for others. My value as an individual is independent of my usefulness to you. Yours is not dependent on your usefulness to me. For either of us to treat the other in ways that fail to show respect for the other's independent value is to act immorally, to violate the individual's rights.

Some of the rational virtues of this view—what I call the rights view—should be evident. Unlike (crude) contractarianism, for example, the rights view in *principle* denies the moral tolerability of any and all forms of racial, sexual or social discrimination; and unlike utilitarianism, this view *in principle* denies that we can justify good results by using evil means that violate an individual's rights—denies, for example, that it could be moral to kill my Aunt Bea to harvest beneficial consequences for others. That would be to sanction the disrespectful treatment of the individual in the name of the social good, something the rights view will not—categorically will not—ever allow.

The rights view, I believe, is rationally the most satisfactory moral theory. It surpasses all other theories in the degree to which it illuminates and explains the foundation of our duties to one another—the domain of human morality. On this score it has the best reasons, the best arguments, on its side. Of course, if it were possible to show that only human beings are included within its scope, then a person like myself, who believes in animal rights, would be obliged to look elsewhere.

But attempts to limit its scope to humans only can be shown to be rationally defective. Animals, it is true, lack many of the abilities humans possess. They can't read, do higher mathematics, build a bookcase or make *baba ghanoush*. Neither can many human beings, however, and yet we don't (and shouldn't) say that they (these humans) therefore have less inherent value, less of a right to be treated with respect, than do others. It is the *similarities* between those human beings who most clearly, most non-controversially have such value (the people reading this, for example), not our differences, that matter most. And the really crucial, the basic similarity is simply this: we are each of us the experiencing subject of a life, a conscious creature having an individual welfare that has importance to us whatever our usefulness to others. We want and prefer things, believe and feel things, recall and expect things. And all these dimensions of our life, including our pleasure and pain, our enjoyment and suffering, our satisfaction and frustration, our continued existence or our untimely death—all make a difference to the quality of our life as lived, as experienced, by us as individuals. As the same is true of those animals that concern us (the ones that are eaten and trapped, for example), they too must be viewed as the experiencing subjects of a life, with inherent value of their own.

Some there are who resist the idea that animals have inherent value. "Only humans have such value," they profess. How might this narrow view be defended? Shall we say that only humans have the requisite intelligence, or autonomy, or reason? But there are many, many humans who fail to meet these standards and yet are reasonably viewed as having value above and beyond their usefulness to others. Shall we claim that only humans belong to the right species, the species *Homo sapiens?* But this is blatant speciesism. Will it be said, then, that all and only—humans have immortal souls? Then our opponents have their work cut out for them. I am myself not ill-disposed to the proposition that there are immortal souls. Personally, I profoundly hope I have one. But I would not want to rest my position on a controversial ethical issue on the even more controversial question about who or what has an immortal soul. That is to dig one's hole deeper, not to climb out. Rationally, it is better to resolve moral issues without making more controversial assumptions than are needed. The question of who has inherent value is such a question, one that is resolved more rationally without the introduction of the idea of immortal souls than by its use.

Well, perhaps some will say that animals have some inherent value, only less than we have. Once again, however, attempts to defend this view can be shown to lack rational justification. What could be the basis of our having more inherent value than animals? Their lack of reason, or autonomy, or intellect? Only if we are willing to make the same judgment in the case of humans who are similarly deficient. But it is not true that such humans—the retarded child, for example, or the mentally deranged—have less inherent value than you or I. Neither, then, can we rationally sustain the view that animals like them in being the experiencing subjects of a life have less inherent value. All who have inherent value have it *equally,* whether they be human animals or not.

Inherent value, then, belongs equally to those who are the experiencing subjects of a life. Whether it belongs to others—to rocks and rivers, trees and glaciers, for example—we do not know and may never know. But neither do we need to know, if we are to make the case for animal rights. We do not need to know, for example, how many people are eligible to vote in the next presidential election before we can know whether I am. Similarly, we do not need to know how many individuals have inherent value before we can know that some do. When it comes to the case for animal rights, then, what we need to know is whether the animals that, in our culture, are routinely eaten, hunted and used in our laboratories, for example, are like us in being subjects of a life. And we do know this. We do know that many—literally, billions and billions—of these animals are the subjects of a life in the sense explained and so have inherent value if we do. And since, in order to arrive at the best theory of our duties to one another, we must recognize our equal inherent value as individuals, reason—not sentiment, not emotion—reason compels us to recognize the equal inherent value of these animals and, with this, their equal right to be treated with respect.

That, *very* roughly, is the shape and feel of the case for animal rights. Most of the details of the supporting argument are missing. They are to be found in the book to which I alluded earlier. Here, the details go begging, and I must, in closing, limit myself to four final points.

The first is how the theory that underlies the case for animal rights shows that the animal rights movement is a part of, not antagonistic to, the human rights movement. The theory that rationally grounds the rights of animals also grounds the rights of humans. Thus those involved in the animal rights movement are partners in the struggle to secure respect for human rights—the rights of women, for example, or minorities, or workers. The animal rights movement is cut from the same moral cloth as these.

Second, having set out the broad outlines of the rights view, I can now say why its implications for farming and science, among other fields, are both clear and uncompromising. In the case of the use of animals in science, the rights view is categorically abolitionist. Lab animals are not our tasters; we are not their kings. Because these animals are treated routinely, systematically as if their value were reducible to their usefulness to others, they are routinely, systematically treated with a lack of respect, and thus are their rights routinely, systematically violated. This is just as true when they are used in trivial, duplicative, unnecessary or unwise research as it is when they are used in studies that hold out real promise of human benefits. We can't justify harming or killing a human being (my Aunt Bea, for example) just for these sorts of reason. Neither can we do so even in the case of so lowly a creature as a laboratory rat. It is not just refinement or reduction that is called for, not just larger, cleaner cages, not just more generous use of anaesthetic or the elimination of multiple surgery, not just tidying up the system. It is complete replacement. The best we can do when it comes to using animals in science

is—not to use them. That is where our duty lies, according to the rights view.

As for commercial animal agriculture, the rights view takes a similar abolitionist position. The fundamental moral wrong here is not that animals are kept in stressful close confinement or in isolation, or that their pain and suffering, their needs and preferences are ignored or discounted. All these *are* wrong, of course, but they are not the fundamental wrong. They are symptoms and effects of the deeper, systematic wrong that allows these animals to be viewed and treated as lacking independent value, as resources for us—as, indeed, a renewable resource. Giving farm animals more space, more natural environments, more companions does not right the fundamental wrong, any more than giving lab animals more anaesthesia or bigger, cleaner cages would right the fundamental wrong in their case. Nothing less than the total dissolution of commercial animal agriculture will do this, just as, for similar reasons I won't develop at length here, morality requires nothing less than the total elimination of hunting and trapping for commercial and sporting ends. The rights view's implications, then, as I have said, are clear and uncompromising.

My last two points are about philosophy, my profession. It is, most obviously, no substitute for political action. The words I have written here and in other places by themselves don't change a thing. It is what we do with the thoughts that the words express—our acts, our deeds—that changes things. All that philosophy can do, and all I have attempted, is to offer a vision of what our deeds should aim at. And the why. But not the how.

Finally, I am reminded of my thoughtful critic, the one I mentioned earlier, who chastised me for being too cerebral. Well, cerebral I have been: indirect duty views, utilitarianism, contractarianism—hardly the stuff deep passions are made of. I am also reminded, however, of the image another friend once set before me—the image of the ballerina as expressive of disciplined passion. Long hours of sweat and toil, of loneliness and practice, of doubt and fatigue: those are the discipline of her craft. But the passion is there too, the fierce drive to excel, to speak through her body, to do it right, to pierce our minds. That is the image of philosophy I would leave with you, not "too cerebral" but *disciplined passion*. Of the discipline enough has been seen. As for the passion: there are times, and these not infrequent, when tears come to my eyes when I see, or read, or hear of the wretched plight of animals in the hands of humans. Their pain, their suffering, their loneliness, their innocence, their death. Anger. Rage. Pity. Sorrow. Disgust. The whole creation groans under the weight of the evil we humans visit upon these mute, powerless creatures. It is our hearts, not just our heads, that call for an end to it all, that demand of us that we overcome, for them, the habits and forces behind their systematic oppression. All great movements, it is written, go through three stages: ridicule, discussion, adoption. It is the realization of this third stage, adoption, that requires both our passion and our discipline, our hearts and our heads. The fate of animals is in our hands. God grant we are equal to the task.

Questions for Analysis

1. What is the difference between direct and indirect duties? Why does Regan reject the view that we can have only indirect duties to nonhuman animals?

2. On what grounds does Regan reject contractarian views of moral obligations?

3. What is the cruelty–kindness view of morality? Why does Regan find it inadequate?

4. What does Regan find appealing about utilitarian thinking? What does he find objectionable about it?

5. What does Regan mean by inherent value? What traits must a creature possess to have it?

6. What objections to the view that some animals have inherent value does Regan consider? How does he rebut them?

7. What practical differences can you see between Regan's view and Singer's?

Do Animals Have Rights?

Tibor R. Machan

In the following selection, Tibor R. Machan takes issue with both Peter Singer and Tom Regan. Animals have no rights, he says, and they need no liberation. His principle target, though, is Regan. According to Machan, there is a clear distinction between humans and other animals that forms the basis of human rights. Because humans are capable of moral choices, he says, we need the "moral space" to make those choices freely—a guarantee of noninterference. Our natural rights to life, liberty, and property provide that guarantee. Because other animals cannot make moral choices, they have no need of moral space and therefore have no natural rights. Machan also argues that our moral capacity makes us more important than other species, and this greater importance justifies our use of animals for our benefit.

But Machan does not argue that we can use animals in any way we please. To have no regard for animals, he says, is "a defect of character." Machan, professor emeritus of philosophy at Auburn University, is now a fellow at the Hoover Institution and teaches at Chapman University.

From Tibor R. Machan, "Do Animals Have Rights?" *Public Affairs Quarterly,* vol. 5, no. 2.
Copyright 1991 *Public Affairs Quarterly.* Reprinted by permission of the publisher.

Although the idea that animals have rights goes back to the 18th century, at least, it has only recently become something of a *cause celebre* among numerous serious and well-placed intellectuals, including moral and political philosophers. Although Jeremy Bentham seems to have suggested legislation requiring humane treatment of animals, he didn't defend animal rights, per se—not surprisingly, since Bentham himself had not been impressed with the more basic (Lockean) doctrine of natural rights—calling them "nonsense upon stilts." John Locke's idea of individual rights has had enormous influence and even where it is not respected, it is ultimately invoked as some kind of model for what it would take for something to have rights.

In recent years the doctrine of animals rights has found champions in important circles where the general doctrine of rights is itself well respected. For example, Professor Tom Regan, in his important book *The Case for Animal Rights* (UC Press, 1983), finds the idea of natural rights intellectually congenial but then extends this idea to cover animals near humans on the evolutionary scale. The tradition from within which Regan works is clearly Lockean, only he does not agree that human nature is distinctive enough, in relevant respects, to restrict the scope of natural rights to human beings alone.

Following a different tradition, namely, utilitarianism, the idea of animal liberation has emerged. And this idea comes to roughly the same thing, practically speaking. Only the argument is different because for utilitarians what is important is not that someone or something must have a specific sphere of dominion but that they be well off in their lives. So long as the bulk of the relevant creatures enjoy a reasonably high living standard, the moral and political objectives for us will have been met. But if this goal is neglected, moral and political steps are required to improve on the situation. Animal liberation is such a step.

This essay will maintain that animals have no rights and need no liberation. I will argue that to think they do is a category mistake—it is, to be blunt, to unjustifiably anthropomorphize animals, to treat them as if they were what they are not, namely, human beings. Rights and liberty are political concepts applicable to human beings because human beings are moral agents, in need of what Harvard philosopher Robert Nozick calls "moral

space," that is, a definite sphere of moral jurisdiction where their authority to act is respected and protected so it is they, not intruders, who govern themselves and either succeed or fail in their moral tasks.

Oddly, it is clearly admitted by most animal rights or liberation theorists that only human beings are moral agents—for example, they never urge animals to behave morally (by, e.g., standing up for their rights, by leading a political revolution). No animal rights theorist proposes that animals be tried for crimes and blamed for moral wrongs.

If it is true that the moral nature of human beings gives rise to the conception of basic rights and liberties, then by this alone animal rights and liberation theorists have made an admission fatal to their case.

Before getting under way I want to note that rights and liberty are certainly not the whole of moral concern to us. There are innumerable other moral issues one can raise, including about the way human beings relate to animals. In particular, there is the question how should people treat animals. Should they be hunted even when this does not serve any vital human purpose? Should they be utilized in hurtful—indeed, evidently agonizing—fashion even for trivial human purposes? Should their pain and suffering be ignored in the process of being made use of for admittedly vital human purposes?

It is clear that once one has answered the question of whether animals have rights (or ought to be liberated from human beings) in the negative, one has by no means disposed of these other issues. In this essay I will be dealing mostly with the issue of animal rights and liberation. Yet I will also touch briefly on the other moral issues just raised. I will indicate why they may all be answered in the negative without it being the case that animals have rights or should be liberated—i.e., without raising any serious political issues.

WHY MIGHT ANIMALS HAVE RIGHTS?

To have a right amounts to having those around one who have the choice to abstain from intruding on one within a given sphere of jurisdiction. If I have the right to the use of our community swimming pool, no one may prevent me from making the decision as to whether I do or do not use the pool. Someone's having a right is a kind of freedom from the unavoidable interference of moral agents, beings who are capable of choosing whether they will interfere or not interfere with the rights holder.

When a right is considered natural, the freedom involved in having this right is supposed to be justified by reference to the kind of being one is, one's nature as a certain kind of entity. The idea of natural rights was formulated in connection with the issue of the proper relationship between human beings, especially citizens and governments. The idea goes back many centuries. . . .

The major political thinker with an influential doctrine of natural rights was John Locke. In his *Second Treatise on Government* he argued that each human being is responsible to follow the Law of Nature, the source of morality. But to do so, each also requires a sphere of personal authority, which is identified by the principle of the natural right to property—including one's person and estate. In other words, to be a morally responsible being in the company of other persons one needs what Robert Nozick has called "moral space," i.e., a sphere of sovereignty or personal jurisdiction so that one can engage in self-government—for better or for worse. . . .

Since Locke's time the doctrine of natural rights has undergone a turbulent intellectual history, falling into disrepute at the hands of empiricism and positivism but gaining a revival at the hands of some influential political philosophers of the second half of the twentieth century.

Ironically, at a time in recent intellectual history when natural rights theory had not been enjoying much support, the idea that animals might also have rights came under increasing discussion. Most notable among those who proposed such a notion was Thomas Taylor, whose anonymous work, *Vindication of the Rights of Brutes,* was published in 1792 but discussed animal rights only in the context of demeaning human rights. More positive (though brief) was the contribution of Jeremy Bentham, who in his *An Introduction to The Principles of Morals and Legislation* (1789), argued that those animals that can suffer are owed moral consideration, even if those that molest us or those we may make good use of may be killed—but not "tormented."

In the latter part of the 19th century an entire work was devoted to the idea by Henry S. Salt, entitled *Animals' Rights*.[1] And in our time numerous philosophers and social commentators have made the attempt to demonstrate that if we are able to ascribe basic rights to life, liberty and property to human beings, we can do the same for many of the higher animals. In essentials their arguments can be broken down into two parts. First, they subscribe to Darwin's thesis that no difference of kind, only a difference of degree, can be found between other animals and human beings.[2] Second, even if there were a difference in kind between other animals—especially mammals—and human beings, since they both can be shown to have interests (e.g., the avoidance of pain or suffering), for certain moral and legal purposes the difference does not matter, only the similarity does. In connection with both of these arguments the central conclusion is that if human beings can be said to have certain basic rights—e.g., to life, liberty or consideration for their capacity to suffer—then so do (higher) animals.[3]

Now I do not wish to give the impression that no diversity exists among those who defend animal rights. Some do so from the viewpoint of natural rights, treating animal rights as basic limiting principles which may not be ignored except when it would also make sense to disregard the rights of human beings. Even on this matter are there serious differences among defenders of animal rights—some do not allow any special regard for human beings,[4] some hold that when it comes to a choice between a person and a dog, it is ordinarily the person who should be given protection.[5] But others choose to defend animal rights on utilitarian grounds—to the extent that it amounts to furthering overall pleasure or happiness in the world, animals must be given equal consideration to what human beings receive. Thus only if there really is demonstrable contribution to the overall pleasure or happiness on earth, may an animal capable of experiencing pleasure or happiness be sacrificed for the sake of some human purpose. Barring such demonstrable contribution, animals and humans enjoy equal rights.[6]

At times the argument for animal rights begins with the rather mild point that "reason requires that other animals are as much within the scope of moral concern as are men" but then moves on to the more radical claim that therefore "we must view our entire history as well as all aspects of our daily lives from a new perspective."[7]

Of course, people have generally invoked some moral considerations as they treated animals—I can recall living on a farm in Hungary when I was 11 and getting all kinds of lectures about how I ought to treat the animals, receiving severe rebuke when I mistreated a cat and lots of praise when I took the favorite cow grazing every day and established a close bond with it over time. Hardly anyone can have escaped one or another moral lecture from parents or neighbors concerning the treatment of pets, household animals, or birds. When a young boy once tried out an air gun by shooting a pigeon sitting on a telephone wire before the apartment house in which he lived, I recall that there was no end of rebuke in response to his wanton callousness. Yet none of those who engaged in the moralizing ever entertained the need to "view our entire history as well as all aspects of our daily lives from a new perspective." Rather they seemed to have understood that reckless disregard for the life or well being of animals shows a defect of character, lack of sensitivity, callousness—realizing, at the same time, that numerous human purposes justify our killing and using animals in the various ways most of us do use them.

And this really is the crux of the matter. But why? Why is it more reasonable to think of animals as available for our sensible use rather than owed the kind of respect and consideration we ought to extend to other human beings? It is one thing to have this as a common sense conviction, it is another to know it as a sound viewpoint, in terms of which we may confidently conduct ourselves.

WHY WE MAY USE ANIMALS

While I will return to the arguments for animal rights, let me first place on record the case for the use of animals for human purposes. Without this case reasonably well established, it will not be possible to critically assess the case for animal rights. After all, this is a comparative matter—which viewpoint makes better sense, which is, in other words, more likely to be true?

One reason for the propriety of our use of animals is that we are more important or valuable than other animals and some of our projects may require animals for them to be successful. Notice that this is different from saying that human beings are

"uniquely important," a position avidly ridiculed by Stephen R. L. Clark, who claims that "there seems no decent ground in reason or revelation to suppose that man is uniquely important or significant."[8] If man were uniquely important, that would mean that one could not assign any value to plants or non-human animals apart from their relationship to human beings. That is not the position I am defending. I argue that there is a scale of importance in nature, and among all the various kinds of being, human beings are the most important—even while it is true that some members of the human species may indeed prove themselves to be the most vile and worthless, as well.

How do we establish that we are more important or valuable? By considering whether the idea of lesser or greater importance or value in the nature of things makes clear sense and applying it to an understanding of whether human beings or other animals are more important. If it turns out that ranking things in nature as more or less important makes sense, and if we qualify as more important than other animals, there is at least the beginning of a reason why we may make use of other animals for our purposes.

That there are things of different degree of value in nature is admitted by animal rights advocates, so there is no great need here to argue about that. When they insist that we treat animals differently from the way we treat, say, rocks or iron ore—so that while we may not use the former as we choose, we may use the latter—they testify, at least by implication, that animals are more important than, say, iron ore. Certainly they invoke some measure of importance or value and place animals higher in line with this measure than they place other aspects of nature. They happen, also, to deny that human beings rank higher than animals, or at least they do not admit that human beings' higher ranking warrants their using animals for their purposes. But that is a distinct issue which we can consider later.

Quite independently of the implicit acknowledgment by animal rights advocates of the hierarchy of nature, there simply is evidence through the natural world of the existence of beings of greater complexity and of higher value. For example, while it makes no sense to evaluate as good or bad such things as planets or rocks or pebbles—except as they may relate to human purposes—when it comes to plants and animals the process of evaluation commences very naturally indeed. We can speak of better or worse trees, oaks, redwoods, or zebras, foxes or chimps. While at this point we confine our evaluation to the condition or behavior of such beings without any intimation of their responsibility for being better or worse, when we start discussing human beings our evaluation takes on a moral component. Indeed, none are more ready to testify to this than animal rights advocates who, after all, do not demand any change of behavior on the part of non-human animals and yet insist that human beings conform to certain moral edicts as a matter of their own choice. This means that even animal rights advocates admit outright that to the best of our knowledge it is with human beings that the idea of moral goodness and moral responsibility enters the universe.

Clearly this shows a hierarchical structure in nature: some things do not invite evaluations at all—it is a matter of no significance or of indifference whether they are or are not or what they are or how they behave. Some things invite evaluation but without implying any moral standing with reference to whether they do well or badly. And some things—namely, human beings—invite moral evaluation. The level of importance or value may be noted to move from the inanimate to the animate world, culminating, as far as we now know, with human life. Normal human life involves moral tasks, and that is why we are more important than other beings in nature—we are subject to moral appraisal, it is a matter of our doing whether we succeed or fail in our lives.

Now when it comes to our moral task, namely, to succeed as human beings, we are dependent upon reaching sensible conclusions about what we should do. We can fail to do this and too often do so. But we can also succeed. The process that leads to our success involves learning, among other things, what it is that nature avails us with to achieve our highly varied tasks in life. Clearly among these highly varied tasks could be some that make judicious use of animals—for example, to find out whether some medicine is safe for human use, we might wish to use animals. To do this is the rational thing for us to do, so as to make the best use of nature for our success in living our lives. That does not mean there need be no guidelines involved in how we might make

use of animals—any more than there need be no guidelines involved in how we use anything else.

WHY INDIVIDUAL HUMAN RIGHTS?

Where do individual *human* rights come into this picture? The rights being talked of in connection with human beings have as their source, as we have noted earlier, the human capacity to make moral choices. We have the right to life, liberty and property—as well as more specialized rights connected with politics, the press, religion—because we have as our central task in life to act morally. And in order to be able to do this throughout the scope of our lives, we require a reasonably clear sphere of personal jurisdiction—a dominion where we are sovereign and can either succeed or fail to live well, to do right, to act properly.

If we did not have rights, we would not have such a sphere of personal jurisdiction and there would be no clear idea as to whether we are acting in our own behalf or those of other persons. No one could be blamed or praised for we would not know clearly enough whether what the person is doing is in his or her authority to do or in someone else's. This is precisely the problem that arises in communal living and, especially, in totalitarian countries where everything is under forced collective governance. The reason moral distinctions are still possible to make under such circumstances is that in fact—as distinct from law—there is always some sphere of personal jurisdiction wherein people may exhibit courage, prudence, justice, honesty, and other virtues. But where collectivism has been successfully enforced, there is no individual responsibility at play and people's morality and immorality is submerged within the group.

Indeed the main reason for governments has for some time been recognized to be nothing other than that our individual human rights should be protected. In the past—and in many places even today—it was thought that government (or the State) has some kind of leadership role in human communities. This belief followed the view that human beings differ amongst themselves radically, some being lower, some higher class, some possessing divine rights, others lacking them, some having a personal communion with God, others lacking this special advantage.

With such views in place, it made clear enough sense to argue that government should have a patriarchal role in human communities—the view against which John Locke forcefully argued his theory of natural individual human rights.[9]

WHERE IS THERE ROOM FOR ANIMAL RIGHTS?

We have seen that the most sensible and influential doctrine of human rights rests on the fact that human beings are indeed members of a discernibly different species—the members of which have a moral life to aspire to and must have principles upheld for them in communities that make their aspiration possible. Now there is plainly no valid intellectual place for rights in the non-human world, the world in which moral responsibility is for all practical purposes absent. Some would want to argue that some measure of morality can be found within the world of at least higher animals—e.g., dogs. For example, Rollin holds that "In actual fact, some animals even seem to exhibit behavior that bespeaks something like moral agency or moral agreement."[10] His argument for this is rather anecdotal but it is worth considering:

> Canids, including the domesticated dog, do not attack another when the vanquished bares its throat, showing a sign of submission. Animals typically do not prey upon members of their own species. Elephants and porpoises will and do feed injured members of their species. Porpoises will help humans, even at risk to themselves. Some animals will adopt orphaned young of other species. (Such cross-species "morality" would certainly not be explainable by simple appeal to mechanical evolution, since there is no advantage whatever to one's own species.) Dogs will act 'guilty' when they break a rule such as one against stealing food from a table and will, for the most part, learn not to take it.[11]

Animal rights advocates such as Rollin maintain that it is impossible to clearly distinguish between human and non-human animals, including on the grounds of the former's characteristic as a moral agent. Yet what they do to defend this point is to invoke borderline cases, imaginary hypothesis, and anecdotes.

In contrast, in his book *The Difference of Man and the Difference It Makes*, Mortimer Adler undertakes the painstaking task of showing that even with the full acknowledgment of the merits of Darwinian and, especially, post-Darwinian evolutionary theory, there is ample reason to uphold the doctrine of species-distinction—a distinction, incidentally, that is actually presupposed within Darwin's own work.[12] Adler shows that although the theistic doctrine of radical species differences is incompatible with current evolutionary theory, the more naturalistic view that species are superficially (but non-negligibly) different is indeed necessary to it. The fact of occasional borderline cases is simply irrelevant—what is crucial is that the generalization is true that human beings are basically different from other animals—by virtue of "a crucial threshold in a continuum of degrees." As Adler explains:

> . . . distinct species are genetically isolated populations between which interbreeding is impossible, arising (except in the case of polyploidy) from varieties between which interbreeding was not impossible, but between which it was prevented. Modern theorists, with more assurance than Darwin could manage, treat distinct species as natural kinds, not as man-made class distinctions.[13]

Adler adds that "Without the critical insight provided by the distinction between superficial and radical differences in kind, biologists [as well as animal rights advocates, one should add] might be tempted to follow Darwin in thinking that all differences in kind must be apparent, not real."[14]

Since Locke's admittedly incomplete—sometimes even confusing—theory had gained respect and, especially, practical import (e.g., in British and American political history), it became clear enough that the only justification for the exercise of state power—namely the force of the law—is that the rights of individuals are being or have been violated. But as with all successful doctrines, Locke's idea became corrupted by innumerable efforts to concoct rights that government must protect, rights that were actually disguised special interest objectives—values that some people, perhaps quite legitimately, wanted very badly to have secured for them.

While it is no doubt true that many animal rights advocates sincerely believe that they have found a justification for the actual existence of animal rights, it is equally likely that if the Lockean doctrine of rights had not become so influential, they would now be putting their point differently—in a way, namely, that would secure for them what they, as a special interest group, want: the protection of animals they have such love and sympathy for.

CLOSING REFLECTIONS

As with most issues on the minds of many intelligent people as well as innumerable crackpots, a discussion of whether there are animal rights and how we ought to treat animals cannot be concluded with dogmatic certainty one way or the other. Even though those who defend animal rights are certain almost beyond a shadow of doubt, all I can claim is to being certain beyond a reasonable doubt. Animals are not the sort of beings with basic rights to life, liberty and property, whereas human beings, in the main, are just such beings. Yet we know that animals can feel pain and can enjoy themselves and this must give us pause when we consider using them for our legitimate purposes. We ought to be humane, we ought to kill them and rear them and train them and hunt them in a fashion consistent with such care about them as sentient beings.

In a review of Tom Regan's provocative book already mentioned, *The Case for Animal Rights,* John Hospers makes the following observations that I believe put the matter into the best light we can shed on our topic:

> As one reads page after page of Regan's book, one has the growing impression that his thesis is in an important way "going against nature." It is a fact of nature that living things have to live on other living things in order to stay alive themselves. It is a fact of nature that carnivores must consume, not plants (which they can't digest), but other sentient beings capable of intense pain and suffering, and that they can survive in no other way. It is a fact of nature that animal reproduction is such that far more creatures are born or hatched than can possibly survive. It is a fact of nature that most creatures die slow lingering tortuous deaths, and that few animals in the wild ever reach old age. It is a fact of nature that we cannot take one step in the

woods without killing thousands of tiny organisms whose lives we thereby extinguish. This has been the order of nature for millions of years before man came on the scene, and has indeed been the means by which any animal species has survived to the present day; to fight it is like trying to fight an atomic bomb with a dartgun. . . . This is the world as it is, nature in the raw, unlike the animals in Disney cartoons.[15]

Of course, one might then ask, why should human beings make any attempt to behave differently among themselves, why bother with morality at all?

The fact is that with human nature a problem arose in nature that had not been there before—basic choices had to be confronted, which other animals do not have to confront. The question "How should I live?" faces each human being. And that is what makes it unavoidable for human beings to dwell on moral issues as well as to see other human beings as having the same problem to solve, the same question to dwell on. For this reason we are very different from other animals—we also do terrible, horrible, awful things to each other as well as to nature, but we can also do much, much better and achieve incredible feats nothing else in nature can come close to.

Indeed, then, the moral life is the exclusive province of human beings, so far as we can tell for now. Other—lower(!)—animals simply cannot be accorded the kind of treatment that such a moral life demands, namely, respect for and protection of basic rights.

NOTES

1. Henry S. Salt, *Animals' Rights* (London: George Bell & Sons, Ltd., 1892; Clark Summit, PA: Society for Animals Rights, Inc., 1980). This is perhaps *the* major philosophical effort to defend animals rights prior to Tom Regan's treatise on the same topic.

2. Charles Darwin, *The Descent of Man,* Chpts. 3 and 4. Reprinted in Tom Regan and Peter Singer, eds., *Animal Rights and Human Obligations* (Englewood Cliffs, NJ: Prentice-Hall, 1976), pp. 72–81.

3. On these points both the deontologically oriented Tom Regan and the utilitarian Peter Singer tend to agree, although they differ considerably in their arguments.

4. Peter Singer holds that "we would be on shaky grounds if we were to demand equality for blacks, women, and other groups of oppressed humans while denying equal considera-

tion to nonhumans." "All Animals Are Equal," *op. cit.,* Regan & Singer, *Animal Rights,* p. 150.

5. Tom Regan contends that "[it] is not to say that practices that involve taking the lives of animals cannot possibly be justified . . . in order to seriously consider approving such a practice [it] would [have to] prevent, reduce, or eliminate a much greater amount of evil . . . there is no other way to bring about these consequences . . . and . . . we have very good reason to believe that these consequences will obtain." "Do Animals Have a Right to Life?" *Op. cit.,* Regan & Singer, *Animal Rights,* pp. 205–4.

6. This is the gist of Singer's thesis.

7. Bernard E. Rollin, *Animal Rights and Human Morality* (Buffalo, NY: Prometheus Books, 1981), p. 4.

8. Stephen R. L. Clark, *The Moral Status of Animals* (Oxford, England: Clarendon Press, 1977), p. 13.

9. John Locke, *Two Treatises.*

10. Rollin, *Animal Rights,* p. 14.

11. *Ibid.*

12. See a discussion of this in Mortimer Adler, *The Difference of Man and the Difference It Makes* (New York: World Publishing Co., 1968), pp. 73ff.

13. *Ibid.*

14. *Ibid.,* p. 75.

15. John Hospers, "Review of The Case for Animal Rights," *Reason Papers,* No. 10, p. 123.

Questions for Analysis

1. Why does Machan think humans are more important than animals? Do his reasons stand up to Singer's and Regan's arguments? Why or why not?

2. According to Regan, rights rest on being the subject of a life. According to Machan, they rest on the capacity to make moral choices. Can the issue be decided? If so, how?

3. Machan's basic claim rests on John Locke's theory of natural rights. Many philosophers have argued that there are no natural rights. Does his argument fall apart if they are correct?

4. According to Kant, we have no moral obligations to animals, but we should treat them kindly to avoid developing insensitive characters. How, if it all, does Machan's view differ?

5. Toward the end of his essay, Machan says that Locke's idea of natural rights has been "corrupted." How? Do you agree? If Machan is right, does that make animal rights advocates a "special interest group" as he charges?

6. In a passage that Machan quotes with approval, John Hospers criticizes the animal rights movement for "going against nature." Why? Do you agree?

Speciesism and the Idea of Equality

Bonnie Steinbock

This essay by Bonnie Steinbock, a professor of philosophy at SUNY Albany and a fellow of the Hastings Center, is a defense of our common practice of putting human interests ahead of the interests of other animals. Although Singer is right in claiming that nonhuman pain deserves some moral consideration, she says, he is wrong in claiming that there are no morally important differences between humans and other animals. Among the important

From *Philosophy,* vol. 53, no. 204 (April 1978), pp. 247–256. © 1978 Cambridge University Press. Reprinted by permission of Cambridge University Press.

differences are the human capacities to be held morally responsible for their actions, to reciprocate in ways that nonhuman animals can't, and to desire self-respect.

Against Singer's charge that we treat humans who don't have these capacities better than nonhuman animals, she argues as follows: To extend special care to others out of sympathy is not morally wrong, even if we don't extend it to all. It is not, for example, wrong to go beyond obligations to members of our own race, as long as we do not fail in our obligations to members of other races. Similarly, it is not wrong to give special care to severely retarded humans out of sympathy for them, even though we don't do the same for nonhuman animals.

Most of us believe that we are entitled to treat members of other species in ways which would be considered wrong if inflicted on members of our own species. We kill them for food, keep them confined, use them in painful experiments. The moral philosopher has to ask what relevant difference justifies this difference in treatment. A look at this question will lead us to re-examine the distinctions which we have assumed make a moral difference.

It has been suggested by Peter Singer[1] that our current attitudes are "speciesist," a word intended to make one think of "racist" or "sexist." The idea is that membership in a species is in itself not relevant to moral treatment, and that much of our behaviour and attitudes towards nonhuman animals is based simply on this irrelevant fact.

There is, however, an important difference between racism or sexism and "speciesism." We do not subject animals to different moral treatment simply because they have fur and feathers, but because they are in fact different from human beings in ways that could be morally relevant. It is false that women are incapable of being benefited by education, and therefore that claim cannot serve to justify preventing them from attending school. But this is not false of cows and dogs, even chimpanzees. Intelligence is thought to be a morally relevant capacity because of its relation to the capacity for moral responsibility.

What is Singer's response? He agrees that nonhuman animals lack certain capacities that human animals possess, and that this may justify different *treatment*. But it does not justify giving less consideration to their needs and interests. According to Singer, the moral mistake which the racist or sexist makes is not essentially the factual error of thinking that blacks or women are inferior to white men. For even if there were no factual error, even

if it were true that blacks and women are less intelligent and responsible than whites and men, this would not justify giving less consideration to their needs and interests. It is important to note that the term "speciesism" is in one way like, and in another way unlike, the terms "racism" and "sexism." What the term "speciesism" has in common with these terms is the reference to focusing on a characteristic which is, in itself, irrelevant to moral treatment. And it is worth reminding us of this. But Singer's real aim is to bring us to a new understanding of the idea of equality. The question is, on what do claims to equality rest? The demand for *human* equality is a demand that the interests of all human beings be considered equally, unless there is a moral justification for not doing so. But why should the interests of all human beings be considered equally? In order to answer this question, we have to give some sense to the phrase, "All men (human beings) are created equal." Human beings are manifestly not equal, differing greatly in intelligence, virtue and capacities. In virtue of what can the claim to equality be made?

It is Singer's contention that claims to equality do not rest on factual equality. Not only do human beings differ in their capacities, but it might even turn out that intelligence, the capacity for virtue, etc., are not distributed evenly among the races and sexes:

> The appropriate response to those who claim to have found evidence of genetically based differences in ability between the races or sexes is not to stick to the belief that the genetic explanation must be wrong, whatever evidence to the contrary may turn up; instead we should make it quite clear that the claim to equality does not depend on intelligence, moral capacity, physical strength, or similar matters of fact. Equality is a moral ideal, not a simple assertion

of fact. There is no logically compelling reason for assuming that a factual difference in ability between two people justifies any difference in the amount of consideration we give to satisfying their needs and interests. The principle of equality of human beings is not a description of an alleged actual equality among humans: it is a prescription of how we should treat humans.[2]

Insofar as the subject is human equality, Singer's view is supported by other philosophers. Bernard Williams, for example, is concerned to show that demands for equality cannot rest on factual equality among people, for no such equality exists.[3] The only respect in which all men are equal, according to Williams, is that they are all equally men. This seems to be a platitude, but Williams denies that it is trivial. Membership in the species *homo sapiens* in itself has no special moral significance, but rather the fact that all men are human serves as a *reminder* that being human involves the possession of characteristics that are morally relevant. But on what characteristics does Williams focus? Aside from the desire for self-respect (which I will discuss later), Williams is not concerned with uniquely human capacities. Rather, he focuses on the capacity to feel pain and the capacity to feel affection. It is in virtue of these capacities, it seems, that the idea of equality is to be justified.

Apparently Richard Wasserstrom has the same idea as he sets out the racist's "logical and moral mistakes" in "Rights, Human Rights and Racial Discrimination."[4] The racist fails to acknowledge that the black person is as capable of suffering as the white person. According to Wasserstrom, the reason why a person is said to have a right not to be made to suffer acute physical pain is that we all do in fact value freedom from such pain. Therefore, if anyone has a right to be free from suffering acute physical pain, *everyone* has this right, for there is no possible basis of discrimination. Wasserstrom says, "For, if all persons do have equal capacities of these sorts and if the existence of these capacities is the reason for ascribing these rights to anyone, then all persons ought to have the right to claim equality of treatment in respect to the possession and exercise of these rights."[5] The basis of equality, for Wasserstrom as for Williams, lies not in some uniquely human capacity, but rather in the fact that all human beings are alike in their capacity to suffer.

Writers on equality have focused on this capacity, I think, because it functions as some sort of lowest common denominator, so that whatever the other capacities of a human being, he is entitled to equal consideration because, like everyone else, he is capable of suffering.

If the capacity to suffer is the reason for ascribing a right to freedom from acute pain, or a right to well being, then it certainly looks as though these rights must be extended to animals as well. This is the conclusion Singer arrives at. The demand for human equality rests on the equal capacity of all human beings to suffer and to enjoy well being. But if this is the basis of the demand for equality, then this demand must include all beings which have an equal capacity to suffer and enjoy well being. That is why Singer places at the basis of the demand for equality, not intelligence or reason, but sentience. And equality will mean, not equality of treatment, but "equal consideration of interests." The equal consideration of interests will often mean quite different treatment, depending on the nature of the entity being considered. (It would be as absurd to talk of a dog's right to vote, Singer says, as to talk of a man's right to have an abortion.)

It might be thought that the issue of equality depends on a discussion of rights. According to this line of thought, animals do not merit equal consideration of interests because, unlike human beings, they do not, or cannot, have rights. But I am not going to discuss rights, important as the issue is. The fact that an entity does not have rights does not necessarily imply that its interests are going to count for less than the interests of entities which are right-bearers. According to the view of rights held by H. L. A. Hart and S. I. Benn, infants do not have rights, nor do the mentally defective, nor do the insane, in so far as they all lack certain minimal conceptual capabilities for having rights.[6] Yet it certainly does not seem that either Hart or Benn would agree that *therefore* their interests are to be counted for less, or that it is morally permissible to treat them in ways in which it would not be permissible to treat right-bearers. It seems to mean only that we must give different sorts of reasons for our obligations to take into consideration the interests of those who do not have rights.

We have reasons concerning the treatment of other people which are clearly independent of the notion of rights. We would say that it is wrong to punch someone because doing that infringes his rights. But we could also say that it is wrong because doing that hurts him, and that is, ordinarily, enough of a reason not to do it. Now this particular reason extends not only to human beings, but to all sentient creatures. One has a *prima facie* reason not to pull the cat's tail (whether or not the cat has rights) because it hurts the cat. And this is the only thing, normally, which is relevant in this case. The fact that the cat is not a "rational being," that it is not capable of moral responsibility, that it cannot make free choices or shape its life—all of these differences from us have nothing to do with the justifiability of pulling its tail. Does this show that rationality and the rest of it are irrelevant to moral treatment?

I hope to show that this is not the case. But first I want to point out that the issue is not one of cruelty to animals. We all agree that cruelty is wrong, whether perpetrated on a moral or nonmoral, rational or nonrational agent. Cruelty is defined as the infliction of unnecessary pain or suffering. What is to count as necessary or unnecessary is determined, in part, by the nature of the end pursued. Torturing an animal is cruel, because although the pain is logically necessary for the action to be torture, the end (deriving enjoyment from seeing the animal suffer) is monstrous. Allowing animals to suffer from neglect or for the sake of large profits may also be thought to be unnecessary and therefore cruel. But there may be some ends, which are very good (such as the advancement of medical knowledge), which can be accomplished by subjecting animals to pain in experiments. Although most people would agree that the pain inflicted on animals used in medical research ought to be kept to a minimum, they would consider pain that cannot be eliminated "necessary" and therefore not cruel. It would probably not be so regarded if the subjects were nonvoluntary human beings. Necessity, then, is defined in terms of human benefit, but this is just what is being called into question. The topic of cruelty to animals, while important from a practical viewpoint, because much of our present treatment of animals involves the infliction of suffering for no good reason, is not very interesting philosophically. What is philosophically interesting is whether we are justified in having different standards of necessity for human suffering and for animal suffering.

Singer says, quite rightly I think, "If a being suffers, there can be no moral justification for refusing to take that suffering into consideration."[7] But he thinks that the principle of equality requires that, no matter what the nature of the being, its suffering be counted equally with the like suffering of any other being. In other words sentience does not simply provide us with reasons for acting; it is the *only* relevant consideration for equal consideration of interests. It is this view that I wish to challenge.

I want to challenge it partly because it has such counter-intuitive results. It means, for example, that feeding starving children before feeding starving dogs is just like a Catholic charity's feeding hungry Catholics before feeding hungry non-Catholics. It is simply a matter of taking care of one's own, something which is usually morally permissible. But whereas we would admire the Catholic agency which did not discriminate, but fed all children, first come, first served, we would feel quite differently about someone who had this policy for dogs and children. Nor is this, it seems to me, simply a matter of sentimental preference for our own species. I might feel much more love for my dog than for a strange child—and yet I might feel morally obliged to feed the child before I fed my dog. If I gave in to the feelings of love and fed my dog and let the child go hungry I would probably feel guilty. This is not to say that we can simply rely on such feelings. Huck Finn felt guilty at helping Jim escape, which he viewed as stealing from a woman who had never done him any harm. But while the existence of such feelings does not settle the morality of an issue, it is not clear to me that they can be explained away. In any event, their existence can serve as a motivation for trying to find a rational justification for considering human interests above non-human ones.

However, it does seem to me that this *requires* a justification. Until now, common sense (and academic philosophy) have seen no such need. Benn says, "No one claims equal consideration for all mammals—human beings count, mice do not, though it would not be easy to say *why* not. . . . Although we hesitate to inflict unnecessary pain on sentient creatures, such as mice or dogs, we are quite sure that we do not need to show good reasons for putting human interests before theirs."[8]

I think we do have to justify counting our interests more heavily than those of animals. But how? Singer is right, I think, to point out that it will not do to refer vaguely to the greater value of human life, to human worth and dignity:

> Faced with a situation in which they see a need for some basis for the moral gulf that is commonly thought to separate humans and animals, but can find no concrete difference that will do this without undermining the equality of humans, philosophers tend to waffle. They resort to high-sounding phrases like 'the intrinsic dignity of the human individual.' They talk of 'the intrinsic worth of all men' as if men had some worth that other beings do not have or they say that human beings, and only human beings, are 'ends in themselves,' while 'everything other than a person can only have value for a person'. . . . Why should we not attribute 'intrinsic dignity' or 'intrinsic worth' to ourselves? Why should we not say that we are the only things in the universe that have intrinsic value? Our fellow human beings are unlikely to reject the accolades we so generously bestow upon them, and those to whom we deny the honour are unable to object.[9]

Singer is right to be skeptical of terms like "intrinsic dignity" and "intrinsic worth." These phrases are no substitute for a moral argument. But they may point to one. In trying to understand what is meant by these phrases, we may find a difference or differences between human beings and non-human animals that will justify different treatment while not undermining claims for human equality. While we are not compelled to discriminate among people because of different capacities, if we can find a significant difference in capacities between human and non-human animals, this could serve to justify regarding human interests as primary. It is not arbitrary or smug, I think, to maintain that human beings have a different moral status from members of other species because of certain capacities which are characteristic of being human. We may not all be equal in these capacities, but all human beings possess them to some measure, and nonhuman animals do not. For example, human beings are normally held to be responsible for what they do. In

recognizing that someone is responsible for his or her actions, you accord that person a respect which is reserved for those possessed of moral autonomy, or capable of achieving such autonomy. Secondly, human beings can be expected to reciprocate in a way that non-human animals cannot. Non-human animals cannot be motivated by altruistic or moral reasons; they cannot treat you fairly or unfairly. This does not rule out the possibility of an animal being motivated by sympathy or pity. It does rule out altruistic motivation in the sense of motivation due to the recognition that the needs and interests of others provide one with certain reasons for acting.[10] Human beings are capable of altruistic motivation in this sense. We are sometimes motivated simply by the recognition that someone else is in pain, and that pain is a bad thing, no matter who suffers it. It is this sort of reason that I claim cannot motivate an animal or any entity not possessed of fairly abstract concepts. (If some non-human animals do possess the requisite concepts—perhaps chimpanzees who have learned a language—they might well be capable of altruistic motivation.) This means that our moral dealings with animals are necessarily much more limited than our dealings with other human beings. If rats invade our houses, carrying disease and biting our children, we cannot reason with them, hoping to persuade them of the injustice they do us. We can only attempt to get rid of them. And it is this that makes it reasonable for us to accord them a separate and not equal moral status, even though their capacity to suffer provides us with some reason to kill them painlessly, if this can be done without too much sacrifice of human interests. Thirdly, as Williams points out, there is the "desire for self-respect": "a certain human desire to be identified with what one is doing, to be able to realize purposes of one's own, and not to be the instrument of another's will unless one has willingly accepted such a role."[11] Some animals may have some form of this desire, and to the extent that they do, we ought to consider their interest in freedom and self-determination. (Such considerations might affect our attitudes toward zoos and circuses.) But the desire for self-respect *per se* requires the intellectual capacities of human beings, and this desire provides us with special reasons not to treat human beings in certain ways. It is an affront to the dignity of a human being to be a slave (even if a well-treated one); this cannot be true for a horse or a cow. To point this out is of course only to say that the justification for the treatment of an entity will depend on the sort of entity in question. In our treatment of other entities, we must consider the desire for autonomy, dignity and respect, but only where such a desire exists. Recognition of different desires and interests will often require different treatment, a point Singer himself makes.

But is the issue simply one of different desires and interests justifying and requiring different treatment? I would like to make a stronger claim, namely, that certain capacities, which seem to be unique to human beings, entitle their possessors to a privileged position in the moral community. Both rats and human beings dislike pain, and so we have a *prima facie* reason not to inflict pain on either. But if we can free human beings from crippling diseases, pain and death through experimentation which involves making animals suffer, and if this is the only way to achieve such results, then I think that such experimentation is justified because human lives are more valuable than animal lives. And this is because of certain capacities and abilities that normal human beings have which animals apparently do not, and which human beings cannot exercise if they are devastated by pain or disease.

My point is not that the lack of the sorts of capacities I have been discussing gives us a justification for treating animals just as we like, but rather that it is these differences between human beings and nonhuman animals which provide a rational basis for different moral treatment and consideration. Singer focuses on sentience alone as the basis of equality, but we can justify the belief that human beings have a moral worth that nonhuman animals do not, in virtue of specific capacities, and without resorting to "high-sounding phrases."

Singer thinks that intelligence, the capacity for moral responsibility, for virtue, etc., are irrelevant to equality, because we would not accept a hierarchy based on intelligence any more than one based on race. We do not think that those with greater capacities ought to have their interests weighed more heavily than those with lesser capacities, and this, he thinks, shows that differences in such capacities are irrelevant to equality. But it does not show this at all. Kevin Donaghy argues (rightly, I think) that what entitles us human beings to a privileged

position in the moral community is a certain minimal level of intelligence, which is a prerequisite for morally relevant capacities.[12] The fact that we would reject a hierarchical society based on degree of intelligence does not show that a minimal level of intelligence cannot be used as a cut-off point, justifying giving greater consideration to the interests of those entities which meet this standard.

Interestingly enough, Singer concedes the rationality of valuing the lives of normal human beings over the lives of nonhuman animals.[13] We are not required to value equally the life of a normal human being and the life of an animal, he thinks, but only their suffering. But I doubt that the value of an entity's life can be separated from the value of its suffering in this way. If we value the lives of human beings more than the lives of animals, this is because we value certain capacities that human beings have and animals do not. But freedom from suffering is, in general, a minimal condition for exercising these capacities, for living a fully human life. So, valuing human life more involves regarding human interests as counting for more. That is why we regard human suffering as more deplorable than comparable animal suffering.

But there is one point of Singer's which I have not yet met. Some human beings (if only a very few) are less intelligent than some nonhuman animals. Some have less capacity for moral choice and responsibility. What status in the moral community are these members of our species to occupy? Are their interests to be considered equally with ours? Is experimenting on them permissible where such experiments are painful or injurious, but somehow necessary for human well being? If it is certain of our capacities which entitle us to a privileged position, it looks as if those lacking those capacities are not entitled to a privileged position. To think it is justifiable to experiment on an adult chimpanzee but not on a severely mentally incapacitated human being seems to be focusing on membership in a species where that has no moral relevance. (It is being "speciesist" in a perfectly reasonable use of the word.) How are we to meet this challenge?

Donaghy is untroubled by this objection. He says that it is fully in accord with his intuitions, that he regards the killing of a normally intelligent human being as far more serious than the killing of a person so severely limited that he lacked the intellectual capacities of an adult pig. But this parry really misses the point. The question is whether Donaghy thinks that the killing of a human being so severely limited that he lacked the intellectual capacities of an adult pig would be less serious than the killing of that pig. If superior intelligence is what justifies privileged status in the moral community, then the pig who is smarter than a human being ought to have superior moral status. And I doubt that this is fully in accord with Donaghy's intuitions.

I doubt that anyone will be able to come up with a concrete and morally relevant difference that would justify, say, using a chimpanzee in an experiment rather than a human being with less capacity for reasoning, moral responsibility, etc. Should we then experiment on the severely retarded? Utilitarian considerations aside (the difficulty of comparing intelligence between species, for example), we feel a special obligation to care for the handicapped members of our own species, who cannot survive in this world without such care. Non-human animals manage very well, despite their "lower intelligence" and lesser capacities; most of them do not require special care from us. This does not, of course, justify experimenting on them. However, to subject to experimentation those people who depend on us seems even worse than subjecting members of other species to it. In addition, when we consider the severely retarded, we think, "That could be me." It makes sense to think that one might have been born retarded, but not to think that one might have been born a monkey. And so, although one can imagine oneself in the monkey's place, one feels a closer identification with the severely retarded human being. Here we are getting away from such things as "morally relevant differences" and are talking about something much more difficult to articulate, namely, the role of feeling and sentiment in moral thinking. We would be *horrified* by the use of the retarded in medical research. But what are we to make of this horror? Has it moral significance or is it "mere" sentiment, of no more import than the sentiment of whites against blacks? It is terribly difficult to know how to evaluate such feelings.[14] I am not going to say more about this, because I think that the treatment of severely incapacitated human beings does not pose an insurmountable objection to the privileged status principle. I am willing to admit that my horror at the thought of experiments being performed on severely mentally incapacitated human beings in

cases in which I would find it justifiable and preferable to perform the same experiments on non-human animals (capable of similar suffering) may not be a moral emotion. But it is certainly not wrong of us to extend special care to members of our own species, motivated by feelings of sympathy, protectiveness, etc. If this is speciesism, it is stripped of its tone of moral condemnation. It is not racist to provide special care to members of your own race; it is racist to fall below your moral obligation to a person because of his or her race. I have been arguing that we are morally obliged to consider the interests of all sentient creatures, but not to consider those interests equally with human interests. Nevertheless, even this recognition will mean some radical changes in our attitude toward and treatment of other species.[15]

NOTES

1. Peter Singer, *Animal Liberation* (A New York Review Book, 1975).

2. Singer, 5.

3. Bernard Williams, "The Idea of Equality," *Philosophy, Politics and Society* (Second Series), Laslett and Runciman (eds.) (Blackwell, 1962), 110–131, reprinted in *Moral Concepts,* Feinberg (ed.) (Oxford, 1970), 153–171.

4. Richard Wasserstrom, "Rights, Human Rights, and Racial Discrimination," *Journal of Philosophy* 61, No. 20 (1964), reprinted in *Human Rights,* A. I. Melden (ed.) (Wadsworth, 1970), 96–110.

5. Ibid., 106.

6. H. L. A. Hart, "Are There Any Natural Rights?," *Philosophical Review* 64 (1955), and S. I. Benn, "Abortion, Infanticide, and Respect for Persons," *The Problem of Abortion,* Feinberg (ed.) (Wadsworth, 1973), 92–104.

7. Singer, 9.

8. Benn, "Equality, Moral and Social," *The Encyclopedia of Philosophy* 3, 40.

9. Singer, 266–267.

10. This conception of altruistic motivation comes from Thomas Nagel's *The Possibility of Altruism* (Oxford, 1970).

11. Williams, op. cit., 157.

12. Kevin Donaghy, "Singer on Speciesism," *Philosophic Exchange* (Summer 1974).

13. Singer, 22.

14. We run into the same problem when discussing abortion. Of what significance are our feelings toward the unborn when discussing its status? Is it relevant or irrelevant that it looks like a human being?

15. I would like to acknowledge the help of, and offer thanks to, Professor Richard Arneson of the University of California, San Diego; Professor Sidney Gendin of Eastern Michigan University; and Professor Peter Singer of Monash University, all of whom read and commented on earlier drafts of this paper.

Questions for Analysis

1. In the beginning of the essay, Steinbock writes, "We do not subject animals to different moral treatment simply because they have fur and feathers, but because they are in fact different from human beings in ways that could be morally relevant." What ways does she mean? Are they morally relevant?

2. On what points does Steinbock agree with Singer?

3. Steinbock says that the issue between her and Singer is not cruelty to animals. Why not?

4. According to Steinbock, the view that the capacity to feel pain is the only relevant consideration for equal consideration leads to counterintuitive results. What results does she mean? Do they run counter to your intuitions?

5. How does Steinbock answer Singer's charge that unequal treatment of animals and severely retarded humans is speciesist? How would Singer respond?

6. Does Steinbock provide a compelling refutation of Singer? Do her arguments have any force against Regan?

CASE PRESENTATION
Putting Her to Sleep

In their first home, the cat had always used the litter box. Now, after a couple of days in their new home, they noticed the smell of cat urine on the landing of the stairs. They scrubbed the carpet and sprayed it with disinfectant, but soon afterward, the urine smell returned.

They tried covering the spot that the cat had chosen as its new urinating site, but she picked another place two steps down. They bought child barriers for the top and bottom of the stairs, but she had little trouble negotiating them. They tried yelling at her, rubbing her nose in the spot, and even whacking her with rolled-up newspaper as they would a dog, but nothing worked.

They'd have to give the cat away.

It was a painful realization. They'd had her for six years, ever since she turned up at their door as a forlorn kitten who, from the looks of her, had lost at least one fight. And though they'd often joked about how silly it was that two intelligent adults could grow so fond of a creature as dumb as a cat, they were

indeed fond of her and knew that they would miss her. What they did not yet know, however, was that none of their acquaintances would take her.

That left them with two options—keep the cat and live with the urine smell, which was beginning to penetrate into the wood beneath the carpet, or take her to the SPCA, which would keep her in a cage for a week or so and then, they didn't doubt, destroy her. She was a beautiful animal, but people looking to "adopt" a pet are not looking for a six-year-old cat, however beautiful. Although they considered the first option intolerable, they put off taking the second for one week, then another, hoping that the cat would return to using her litter box.

Finally, tears streaming down his face, he took her to the SPCA. The woman who accepted the cat told him what she must have told countless children. "She's so beautiful, maybe I'll take her home myself."

He was feeling childlike enough to pretend to believe her, but the tears did not stop.

Questions for Analysis

1. Some animal rights activists think that owning house pets is a form of slavery. Does anything about this incident suggest that they might have a point?

2. Pet owners love their pets, but they often declaw them, spay them, or neuter them. What would Singer say about such ordinary practices? Regan?

3. Dogs and cats, like other animals, like to roam free. If a cat is always kept indoors, or a dog is confined to a small apartment and allowed outside only at the end of a leash, is it being treated immorally?

4. Did the couple miss any options? Should they have talked to a veterinarian about possible medical causes of the problem? Consulted an animal behaviorist? Taken the cat into the country and set it free?

5. Did the cat's interest in staying alive outweigh the couple's interest in protecting their floor or getting rid of the urine smell? What would Singer say?

6. Did the couple, despite loving the cat, treat her as a mere thing? What would Regan say?

CASE PRESENTATION
Animal Liberators

On May 24, 1984, five members of the Animal Liberation Front (ALF) raided the University of Pennsylvania's Experimental Head Injury Lab, located in the subbasement of the Anatomy-Chemistry Building. Although the purpose of most ALF raids is to liberate laboratory animals, this raid was different. This time, the goal was to "liberate" videotapes of the experiments being conducted in the lab, experiments that included using a hydraulic jack to compress the heads of monkeys. They found what they came for, and along the way, they ransacked the lab—destroying equipment and removing files.

What the videotapes showed was gruesome. There were images of pistons piercing the heads of baboons and of unanesthetized primates crawling in pain from operating tables. There were also images that showed clear violations of standard research procedures, such as operations performed without surgical masks while workers were smoking cigarettes.

A great controversy followed the release of the tapes. Dr. Thomas Gennarelli, head of the lab, defended his research and decried the raid. All animals were anesthetized and felt no pain, he insisted, and the raid had seriously set back important medical research. The university also defended Dr.

Gennarelli's research, as did the National Institutes of Health (NIH), which, despite protests from People for the Ethical Treatment of Animals, gave the lab a new grant of $500,000.

The raiders, in an interview that appeared in the November 1986 issue of *Omni* ("Inhuman Bondage" by Robert Well), likened the research to the cruel medical experiments that Nazi Dr. Josef Mengele conducted on humans. (Indeed, one of the raiders was himself a survivor of a Nazi concentration camp.)

As the controversy continued, protesters demonstrated at the Penn campus, and animal rights activists staged a sit-in at the NIH until Secretary of Health and Human Services Margaret Heckler ordered a halt to all federal funding of the Head Injury Lab. That was July 18, 1985. Four months later, Penn agreed to pay a $4,000 fine for violating the Animal Welfare Act. The university also agreed to improve its use of pain-relieving drugs, its care of injured animals, and its training of research workers who handle laboratory animals.

And the raiders? Despite a grand jury investigation, no indictments were handed down. ALF members, invoking their Fifth Amendment rights, refused to testify against themselves.

Questions for Analysis

1. Is the comparison between Drs. Gennarelli and Mengele justified?

2. Dr. Gennarelli and the NIH obviously believed that his research would bring significant medical benefit. If his research workers had not violated standard research procedures, would that benefit have justified it?

3. Suppose that ALF and Tom Regan are right about such experiments violating animals' rights. Does that justify ALF's tactics?

4. Which is the more important moral issue—the research itself or the violations of the Animal Welfare Act? Why?

5. If similar research was done on mice, would your reaction to it be any different?

CASE PRESENTATION
Religious Sacrifice

Of the many Cubans who have come to southern Florida in recent decades, some 70,000 practice the religion of Santería. Santería is a distinctively Afro-Cuban religion. It combines the Roman Catholicism of Cuba's Spanish settlers and the traditional Yoruba religion of West Africa, which came to the Caribbean island on the slave ships. Among Santería's traditional Yoruba rituals is animal sacrifice. Turtles, pigeons, chickens, goats, and sheep are slaughtered to appease the Santería gods, after which they are usually eaten by adherents in attendance.

Like other cities in southern Florida, Hialeah has its share of Cuban immigrants. In 1987, the Church of Lukumi Babalu Aye announced its plans to build a Santería church and community center in Hialeah.

The city responded with a series of ordinances banning the ritual sacrifice of animals, with one of the ordinances defining the outlawed practice this way: To perform a ritual animal sacrifice is to "unnecessarily kill, torment, torture or mutilate an animal in a public or private ritual or ceremony not for the primary purpose of food consumption."

The church went to court, charging that the ordinances violated the religious freedom of its members. Hialeah defended the ordinances as a public health measure. In a unanimous decision announced in June of 1993, the U.S. Supreme Court ruled in favor of the church. Santería's adherents were jubilant, but opponents of cruelty to animals worried about the fate of animal cruelty laws throughout the country.

Questions for Analysis

1. The Court saw the case as a matter of religious freedom, not as a matter of cruelty to animals. Hialeah claimed to see the case as a matter of public health rather than a matter of cruelty to animals. How do you think Singer and Regan would feel about that?

2. In an earlier case, Native Americans who use peyote in religious rituals sought exemption from drug laws that ban peyote's use. The Court ruled against them because the drug laws were not designed to interfere with religion. But the Hialeah ordinances were so designed, according to the Court, because they singled out only one reason for killing animals. Should Hialeah have broadened them to include other reasons? If so, how?

3. Should animal sacrifices be permitted? How would Singer and Regan answer?

4. If you agree that at least some animals have rights, how would you balance them against human rights to practice religion?

CASE PRESENTATION
A Himalayan Snow Leopard of One's Own[1]

Most of us rarely get to see an animal that belongs to an endangered species, and when we do, it's likely to be in a public zoo. For those of us who can afford it, however, the country's Fish and Wildlife Service allows us to own such animals—as long as they were bred in captivity and as long as we register them under the Captive Bred Wildlife Registration Program.

Gary and Kari Johnson, for example, keep eight Indian elephants on their south California property. In suburban Boston, Albert H. Porge keeps his Himalayan snow leopard in his backyard. And Miki Sparzak keeps her White Rothschild's myna inside her Baltimore house. In all, some 850 people have registered animals under the program, including 125 big cats such as Porge's snow leopard. The purpose of the program is to help protect endangered species, and Fish and Wildlife believes that some species have been moved from the endangered list to the threatened list at least in part because of the program's success.

Still, the program has its critics. One source of criticism concerns breeding. Some animals registered in the program are given no opportunity to breed. Others are bred unwisely, with owners mating closely related animals and perpetuating genetic defects. In other cases, different subspecies are interbred, resulting in offspring not found in the wild. Critics also point to another problem. Sometimes breeding is *too* successful, and owners end up killing unwanted offspring. Then there's the matter of how the animals are treated. The Johnsons' elephants, for example, are put to work to earn their keep, appearing in movies and magazines and at promotional events for a fee of $2,000 a day.

Finally, some critics charge that the concept behind the program is wrong headed because there is a fundamental difference between animals in captivity and animals in the wild. As Lucy R. Kaplan, staff attorney for PETA (People for the Ethical Treatment of Animals), put it, "It is possible for a species to be extinct and there still to be living specimens with the same genetic makeup."

---

1. The information comes from the June 25, 1992, edition of *The New York Times*.

Questions for Analysis

1. Is the Captive Bred Wildlife Registration program in the interest of the owned animals? Is it in the interest of the species? Which interest is more important?

2. Many animals bred in captivity cannot survive in the wild. What should be done with them? What would Regan and Singer say?

3. Are there important differences between allowing zoos to own members of endangered species and allowing private individuals to own them? If so, what are they?

4. Should Fish and Wildlife tighten regulations on the program, leave it as is, or abolish it?

5. Do you agree with Kaplan's criticism of the program? Why or why not?

12

Environmental Ethics

Environmental Problems
The Moral Issue
Why Environmental Ethics?
Arguments for an Environmental Ethic
Arguments against an Environmental Ethic
Aldo Leopold, "The Land Ethic"
Paul W. Taylor, "The Ethics of Respect for Nature"
William F. Baxter, "People or Penguins"
J. Baird Callicott, "An Ecocentric Environmental Ethic"
CASE PRESENTATION, "A Metaphor for the Energy Debate"
CASE PRESENTATION, "The Spotted Owl"
CASE PRESENTATION, "Environmental Resistance: The
Chipko Movement and the Earth Liberation Front"
CASE PRESENTATION, "The Wildlands Project"

In April 1990, the United States celebrated the twentieth anniversary of Earth Day, which is often considered the beginning of the modern environmental movement. On that day, April 22, 1970, millions of Americans across the country gathered together to listen to speeches, join in song, and demonstrate their concern for the future of the planet.

Since then, the federal government and state and local governments have enacted various pieces of legislation to protect the environment, including laws governing auto emissions, toxic waste disposal, and recycling. And even casual followers of the news have grown familiar with such practices as the filing of environmental impact statements.

By April 1990, it seemed that almost everyone was claiming to be an environmentalist. It grew difficult to find a politician who ran for office on an antienvironment platform, for example, and major corporations were announcing a variety of moves designed to protect the environment. StarKist, Chicken of the Sea, and Bumblebee announced that they would stop selling tuna that was caught with dolphins. Shell Oil announced that it had changed the formula of its premium gasoline to reduce harmful emissions by 10 percent. Conoco announced that it would build double-hull oil tankers to avoid massive oil spills like the *Exxon Valdez* spill in Alaskan waters in March 1989. Many others announced that they would sell their products in recyclable or biodegradable packaging. Environmentalism now seems to be both good politics and good business. As Conoco chief executive Constantine Nicandros was widely quoted as saying. "We're all environmentalists. We have to be."

ENVIRONMENTAL PROBLEMS

Despite the recent expressions of concern for the environment, environmental problems continue to abound and, in many cases, worsen. Species are dying out on a daily basis; air quality is worsening in many cities; the earth's protective ozone layer is thinning; we are creating increasing amounts of trash with no place to put it; and, many scientists argue, emissions of carbon dioxide and methane gases are turning the earth's atmosphere into a greenhouse. Although such problems receive considerable attention in the media, it is worthwhile to take a brief look at them.

Ozone Depletion

Extending from approximately seven to thirty miles above the earth, the layer of the earth's atmosphere known as the stratosphere is an area of little temperature change above the earth's rain clouds. An important component of the stratosphere is ozone, which acts as a shield against the sun's ultraviolet rays. Without this shield, or even with a thinner shield, we would see a significant increase in skin cancer and diseases of the immune system. We would also see considerable damage to food crops and phytoplankton—marine plants that are a vital link in our oceans' food chain.

In June 1974, scientists Mario Molina and Sherry Rowland presented a theory in the British scientific journal *Nature*. Chlorofluorocarbons (CFCs), commonly used as a refrigerant and in aerosol sprays and Styrofoam containers, were drifting into the stratosphere, where the sun's ultraviolet rays were breaking the compounds apart and the resultant chlorine molecules were destroying ozone molecules. In 1975, scientists confirmed that CFCs were reaching the stratosphere. The next year, scientists confirmed that a chain reaction between CFCs and ozone was occurring. Since then, scientists have found continued evidence of ozone depletion, including a massive ozone hole above Antarctica. In 2003, the National Aeronautics and Space Administration reported that the hole is now 10.9 million square miles, slightly larger than North America.

Although CFCs were banned in 1997 under an international agreement called the Montreal Protocol, they are very long-lived in the environment. NASA predicts that it will take fifty years for the Antarctica ozone hole to disappear. But the World Meteorological Organization and United Nations Environmental Programme reported in 2002 that ozone-depleting compounds in the lower atmosphere have been declining slowly since their peak in 1994. EPA scientists report that every 1 percent drop in the ozone layer results in a 5 percent increase in skin cancer.

Development of CFC alternatives has been very expensive, but the consequences to human health have been recognized as more important than these economic costs of product development, an example of consequentialist ethical reasoning.

Global Warming

Although life on the planet depends on the sun for the radiation of heat, it does not depend only on the sun. In fact, radiation from the sun raises the average temperature of the earth to only 0° Fahrenheit, far lower than the actual average temperature, which is about 60° Fahrenheit. For the rest, we depend on the greenhouse effect. The earth's surface absorbs the sun's heat and then radiates it back into the atmosphere, which contains gases like carbon dioxide and methane that capture the heat—just as the glass panes of a greenhouse capture heat.

Throughout the earth's history, average temperatures have changed as the atmosphere has changed, growing warmer with an increase in greenhouse gases—most notably carbon dioxide—and cooler with a decrease. The modern industrial world, chiefly through increased use of fossil fuels and through deforestation, has seen a sharp increase of greenhouse gases. Using computer models, scientists have predicted an increase in the earth's temperatures of from three to nine degrees by the middle of the twenty-first century. An increase that large would lead to severe inland droughts, resultant food shortages, coastal flooding, mass extinctions of species, and increased pollution in overheated cities.

Although most scientists agree on the dangers of global warming, the solutions are the subject of much debate. The Kyoto Protocol, an international proposal for emission reductions, was rejected by the U.S. Senate in 1997. The treaty imposed restrictions the Senate thought were unfairly burdensome on the most industrialized nations, including the United States, while allowing less well-developed nations to continue dangerous emissions. President George W. Bush has repeatedly rejected the Kyoto Protocol and insists that developing nations must also agree to emissions reductions. In 2003, a bipartisan delegation in Congress introduced the Climate Stewardship Act, which would require activities by American companies to reduce global warming, but without the most stringent rules of the Kyoto Protocol. Much of the current debate centers on consequentialist arguments, such as the economic cost to industry and the possible loss of jobs resulting from the proposed measures to reduce global warming.

Acid Rain

Like the threat of global warming, the problem of acid rain is somewhat controversial. Most scientists believe that acid rain is caused primarily by pollutants from the burning of fossil fuels—carbon dioxide, sulfur dioxide, and nitrogen oxides. These pollutants, which can be carried thousands of miles by the wind, mix with other chemicals in the atmosphere to form corrosive and poisonous compounds that are washed back to earth by rainfall.

The effects of acid rain are believed to be wide ranging. They include damage to rivers and lakes, ground water, soil, forests, and buildings. But because there have been relatively few studies on the subject, the extent of damage due to acid rain is difficult to gauge.

Still, twenty-one countries agreed to reduce sulfur dioxide emissions 30 percent below 1980 levels by 1993. The U.S. Congress established the Acid Rain Program under the Clean Air Act in 1990, with the goal of reducing the main chemical component of acid rain. According to the U.S. Environmental Protection Agency, acid rain deposits have been reduced by 25 percent in the Northeast and Mid-Atlantic regions of the country, the areas which have the greatest problems.

Trash

From September 1986 to October 1988, a ship called *The Pelicano* traveled the world searching for a place to unload its cargo, 14,000 tons of toxic incinerator ash loaded in Philadelphia. Although Haiti allowed the ship to unload a small amount of the ash on one of its beaches, no other country was willing to accept the rest, at least not publicly. The ship's captain claimed that one country did accept the rest, but because he refused to identify it, suspicions persisted that the ash was illegally dumped at sea.

The sight of a shipload of trash wandering the world in search of a home is uncommon. But the problem of what to do with the trash of a society that throws away 16 billion disposable diapers and 2 billion disposable razors annually, yet recycles only 10 percent of its trash, is a serious one. The most common solution to the trash problem is sanitary landfills, where 80 percent of the country's solid waste ends up. But this solution is far from ideal. First, since much of our trash is non-biodegradable plastic, we are quickly running out of space. Second, landfills pose risks to surface and ground water. For combustible waste, the chief alternative is incineration, which has its own problems. The ash must be treated and then disposed of, and the gases released during incineration contribute to air pollution.

Extinction of Species

One of the culprits in global warming, we noted earlier, is deforestation. Through photosynthesis, green plants take in carbon dioxide and emit oxygen; therefore, the loss of our forests means an increase in greenhouse gases. Another result of deforestation is the extinction of species. The problem is particularly acute in the Amazon region, where developing South American countries are destroying acres of tropical rain forest every day. According to a 1990 report prepared by the World Resources Institute and the United Nations, Brazil alone is losing between 12.5 and 22.5 million acres a year, while a total of nine countries, including Brazil, are losing over 29 million acres a year.

Though the problem of species extinction is most acute in the Amazon, development of land by humans throughout the world is causing the loss of species at a rate estimated to be as high as one a day.

The threat of extinction is most highly publicized in cases like the tiger, blue whale, giant panda, and other animal species that humans have a particularly high regard for. But the loss of many other species—plant species as well as animal species, many of which are still unidentified—should also concern us. Species in tropical rain forests, for instance, are valuable in the development of cancer drugs and antibiotics. They also give us valuable genetic information that contributes to the raising of domestic animals and the growing of food crops.

Despite these legitimate concerns, the problem of deforestation and extinction continues to worsen.

THE MORAL ISSUE

A loss of the ozone layer and significant global warming would be disastrous for human beings. And it is because of our shared sense of impending disaster that most people now claim to be environmentalists.

In other cases of environmental damage, however, the issue is not serious danger to human life but diminishing quality of human life. We view nature as a valuable resource for recreation as well as economic development. We want to be able to fish and swim in our rivers and lakes, for instance, or camp and hike in our forests. We want to save species of concern to us, like the blue whale and tiger. We want to save the magnificent views in our national parks.

All such concerns are **anthropocentric** at heart; that is, they center on human well-being. We should care about the environment because it is *our* environment. We should care about the survival of various plant and animal species because they matter to *us*.

But other things matter to us as well. We want a strong economy that will produce the goods, jobs, and tax revenues we desire. We like our cars and the highways we drive them on. We like air-conditioning. We like to hold down the costs of producing consumer goods in order to hold down prices. We like the convenience of plastics, electric appliances, and disposable razors and pens.

So when acting both as individuals and as a society, we weigh our concern for the environment against these other concerns. The result is often a compromise, such as auto emission controls that are not as strong as they otherwise might be. Because of these compromises, the most committed environmentalists have begun arguing for radical changes in our moral and legal reasoning, changes that give nature a special place in our thinking. Two proposed changes have received the most attention. Both have one thing in common. They are nonanthropocentric.

The Land Ethic

In his much discussed book, *A Sand County Almanac*, environmentalist Aldo Leopold proposed what he called the land ethic. According to Leopold's land ethic, humans are to begin thinking of themselves as part of a wider community, the biotic community, which includes not only all living things but also all members of the ecological system, including water, soil, and air. To think of ourselves in that way is to reject the view that we are masters of nature and that nature is there to be exploited by us. It is to think of ourselves as members of a team, living and working harmoniously with our teammates. It is also to recognize that the crucial moral question is not what benefits individual human beings or the human community as a whole, but what benefits the biotic community as a whole.

According to Leopold, "A thing is right when it tends to preserve the integrity, stability, and beauty of the biotic community. It is wrong when it tends otherwise."

Two things are notable about this point of view. First, of course, it is nonanthropocentric. But equally important, it is not individualistic. What is to be considered as morally fundamental is not the good of individual members of the biotic community but the good of the community itself. Thus, the land ethic is often considered to be a **holistic ethic**; that is, we have duties not just to individuals but to the whole—in this case, the biotic community.

The source of the land ethic, Leopold tells us, is ecology, the science of the interrelationships among organisms and their environment. Given a full understanding of the interdependence of plant and animal life, soil, air, and water, we should come to think of the biotic community as a vast collective organism, with its own morally important interests.

Environmental Individualism

Other forms of environmental ethics tend to be **biocentric** but nonholistic. They stress duties to individual members of the biotic community but not to the community itself. According to this view, the good of individual plants, animals, and streams—not just the good of individual humans—must be taken into account in moral and legal reasoning.

In the moral realm, this involves balancing the interests of nonhuman members of the environment against human interests. Chopping down a tree, for instance, would become a morally significant act independent of damage to its owner. In the legal realm, it involves giving trees, lakes, and animals standing in the courts. To give them standing would be to make them interested parties in lawsuits and allow lawyers to bring suit on their behalf, not just on behalf of humans who are affected by their treatment. As matters now stand, the interests of nature are irrelevant in legal matters, unless human interests are also affected.

Holism and Individualism Compared

Although both views promote the interests of plants, animals, water, air, and soil as independent goods, their practical payoffs may be far different. To see how, we can consider the problem of endangered species.

According to the holistic point of view, a threat to an entire species is more significant than the sum total of the threats to the individual members of the species because what is morally most important is the species' contribution to the biotic community. Because species diversity contributes to ecological stability, the loss of a member of an endangered species counts more than the loss of a member of a nonendangered one. According to the nonholistic point of view, on the other hand, a threat to a species is not in itself more significant than the sum total of the threats to individual members. All other things being equal, the loss of a member of a nonendangered species is morally equivalent to the loss of a member of an endangered one.

Holists and individualists may differ on other points as well. The holistic view contains no grounds to reject hunting, for instance, unless it damages the environment. There is nothing *inherently* immoral about hunting, and when hunting contributes to the well-being of the biotic community, it is morally good. The individualistic view, however, naturally leans toward an anti-hunting position. The life of an individual deer is not to be sacrificed for the sake of the whole.

In his book *Animal Rights* (see Chapter 11), Tom Regan, a critic of the holistic view, likens the land ethic to fascism, a political movement in which the good of individuals is superseded by the good of the state. Indeed, he says, it seems consistent with the land ethic to destroy the city of Cleveland to save endangered wild grasses because the city contributes less to the well-being of the biotic community than the grasslands do.

Against the charge of environmental fascism, J. Baird Callicott argues that the land ethic need not replace our duties to our fellow humans but need only be joined to it. Far from calling for the destruction of humans to save endangered species, he says, it calls only for the inclusion of the biotic community in our moral lives. Just as our recognition that we live in a global human community leads us to make some—but not excessive—sacrifices for people outside our own families, local communities, and nations, so should our recognition that we live in a biotic community lead us to make some—but not excessive—sacrifices to protect nature.

WHY ENVIRONMENTAL ETHICS?

That greater efforts to protect our environment are required is not controversial among people who have given the matter serious thought. That we need to change our ethical views in a radical way—that we need a distinctively environmental ethics—is a highly controversial view.

Why, then, do environmentalists call for a radical change in our ethical thinking? The impetus toward environmental ethics has two sources. The first, as we saw, is the belief that anthropocentric ethics and law are inadequate to deal with the vast array of environmental problems that face us. The second is the belief that nature, wilderness areas, and nonhuman life have their own inherent value and therefore deserve moral consideration.

Anthropocentric Ethics

Is traditional anthropocentric thinking inadequate? Certainly, we have not done an adequate job in protecting the environment so far, but the fault may be short-sightedness or ignorance rather than anthropocentrism. The problem may be that not enough of us have been aware of the damage we are doing to our environment or that we have not taken into sufficient account how the damage will harm us in the long run.

Proponents of this view deny that we need a land ethic or legal standing for trees. What we need instead, they say, are better cost-benefit analyses of decisions that affect the environment. We need to make sure that these analyses take adequate account of the harm to human interests that environmental damage can cause. In considering what limit to place on auto emissions, for example, we should take into account not only the added costs to automakers and consumers but also the costs in human disease and death from pollutants and greenhouse gases.

Critics of this approach argue that cost-benefit analyses in such cases are inadequate. The basic problem, they claim, is that cost-benefit analyses calculate only *economic* costs and benefits. But certain goods cannot be given an economic value. How much is a human life worth, for instance? How much is a beautiful view worth? How much is it worth to be able to swim or fish in a river?

Furthermore, even if we could assign economic value to such goods, is it possible to identify all the relevant costs and benefits? And even if we could identify them, why should economic costs and benefits be the only deciding factors?

Respect for Nature

A key point of environmental ethics is that nature itself or individual natural objects have their own interests and goods, which are omitted from cost-benefit analyses. We should value nature not because of its value to us but because of its inherent value.

According to this view, even if we minimize human costs and maximize human benefits, we do not act morally if we significantly harm nature. To some extent, arguments over this point can parallel animal rights disputes discussed in Chapter 11. Various arguments for or against animal rights can be used as arguments for or against rights or standing for streams, species, trees, and so forth. But for many environmentalists, the issue is different. We don't have to grant nature *rights* to ensure adequate moral treatment. We only have to treat it in accordance with an attitude of proper *respect*.

Many people normally manifest respect for nature in a variety of ways. Backpackers in wilderness areas often leave nothing behind. If they do so to let future hikers enjoy the wilderness as they did, they manifest respect for their fellow hikers. If they do so because they want to leave the wilderness as they found it regardless of future hikers, they manifest respect for nature. The goal of environmental ethics is to incorporate this kind of respect into all human decisions that affect the environment.

ARGUMENTS FOR AN ENVIRONMENTAL ETHIC

1. *Nature isn't here just for human purposes.*

POINT: "When too many humans look at nature, all they see is something to be exploited. They look at forests and they see timber. They look at rivers and oceans and they see places to dump their waste. As far as they're concerned, nature is there for us, period. What they can use they take, and what they can't use they're willing to sacrifice because it's of no importance to them. But nature was here long before we were, with its own majesty and its own integrity. We're just a part of it, not its master, and we have no right to upset that integrity. To think of ourselves as nature's master is nothing but hubris."

COUNTERPOINT: "Of course we're part of nature. And like everything else in nature, we use what's useful to us. The problem isn't our tendency to look on nature as something that's there to be used by us—nothing could be more natural than that—but our tendency to use it unwisely. As long as we keep our own long-term interests clearly in mind, as long as we remember that we need trees for oxygen as well as timber, for instance, and that species of no direct use to us now can be important to us in ways we don't recognize yet, we and nature will be fine."

2. *Human good is not the only good.*

POINT: "You make it sound as though human good is the only good that counts for anything. But what about the good of a species, a forest, a river, or a lake? Or even a single redwood tree? What right do we have to cut down something that's been alive for thousands of years just to make a picnic table? After all, human interests aren't the only interests. Why must our interests always come first?"

COUNTERPOINT: "To hear you tell it, someone might think a redwood tree actually cares what happens to it. But a tree has no interest in its own survival. It can't have an interest in anything. Don't get me wrong. I'm not saying we should destroy entire redwood forests just to make picnic tables. No one's saying that. I'm just as impressed by the beauty of a redwood forest as you are, and I'm just as concerned about saving that beauty for my children and grandchildren. But it's preposterous to say that our concerns don't matter more than a tree's."

3. *The biotic community is like a human community.*

POINT: "The first principle of any community is cooperation. We have to cooperate with our family members, we have to cooperate with our fellow workers, and we have to cooperate with our fellow citizens. Not only do we have to cooperate with one another, but we also have to treat one another with respect. The same holds for the biotic community as well. Ecology has taught us that each part of an ecosystem is a member of a community, with all members working together to maintain the good of the whole. It's time that humans recognized that we're also part of the biotic community. It's time for us to work together with our fellow members and show them the respect they deserve."

COUNTERPOINT: "This notion of a biotic community is nothing but a metaphor at best. Do predators cooperate with their prey? Do members of different species resolve their differences the way people of varying interests do? Are insects and the soil members of the same team the way a pitcher and catcher are? What we've learned from ecology is certainly important, and we ignore its lessons at our own risk. But we gain nothing by sentimentalizing nature to the extent that we work against our own interests."

4. *It's time we gave something back to nature.*

POINT: "Humans have been taking from nature for centuries without giving anything back. We've destroyed entire species, turned forests into wasteland, ruined water and air, turned soil infertile, and scarred land to get at the resources beneath it. We've even turned the once magnificent Yosemite Valley into a crowded tourist resort, traffic congestion and all. We owe nature, and though we can't replace all we've taken, we can stop inflicting senseless damage and give something back."

COUNTERPOINT: "Certainly, we should stop inflicting senseless damage. But what counts as senseless and what counts as damage? Take your own example, Yosemite Valley. Why should it be reserved for backpackers only? Why shouldn't there be motels and restaurants for people who want to enjoy its beauty in comfort? What good is protecting nature if people don't have the opportunity to enjoy it?"

ARGUMENTS AGAINST
AN ENVIRONMENTAL ETHIC

1. *People count more than trees.*

POINT: "What environmental ethicists fail to see is that the environment matters because it's *our* environment—our water, our air, our forests. No one denies that we have to protect the environment to protect ourselves and advance our own interests. But you want to go further than that. You want to protect the environment *against* our own interests. You want to sacrifice logging jobs, wreck entire economies, to protect owls. You want to deny us badly needed power plants to protect fish. And that's just crazy. Any way you look at it, people matter more than trees, owls, and fish."

COUNTERPOINT: "As of matter of fact, people don't matter more than trees, owls, and fish any way you look at it. To nature, all species are equal. That doesn't mean human interests *never* come first, of course, but it does mean they don't *always* come first. Job losses are unfortunate, but economies and individuals rebound. And as for your badly needed power plants, Americans rely too much on electricity as it is. Giving up some of our electric appliances is a small enough sacrifice, not only to protect an entire species but also to protect the environment as a whole."

2. *Environmental ethics is elitist.*

POINT: "The 'small' sacrifices you call for aren't all that small to most people. When a mining, manufacturing, or logging region dies, the human costs are enormous, whether the region eventually bounces back or not. And many of them don't. Even added costs to consumer goods can be a major burden for many people. The problem with environmental ethics is that it's elitist. The well-off can easily afford the costs of putting nature on an equal footing with humans, but the rest of us can't."

COUNTERPOINT: "Nature is everyone's home, and there's nothing elitist about trying to save our home. I realize that the costs of environmentalism fall heavier on some people than others, but the answer isn't to reject environmental ethics. The answer is to adopt social policies that will compensate them for their loss—retraining, public investment, tax breaks, and other measures to help them out. If we all share the burden, it can be a small one for each of us."

3. *Environmental ethics is unnecessary.*

POINT: "Everyone not motivated by selfishness and greed agrees that we have to protect the environment. We all want clean air and water for ourselves and future generations, and we all want to leave future generations a livable planet. By educating people about the importance of the environment to human life and health, by educating them about the kinds of damage we inflict on the environment and how that damage threatens us all, we can solve all our environmental problems. Focusing our moral attention on our fellow humans is enough. Focusing on trees and soil is unnecessary."

COUNTERPOINT: "Whether environmental ethics is unnecessary is an open question at best. After all, we certainly haven't compiled a very good record without it. But equally important, we have to ask ourselves, 'Necessary for what?' If all we care about is a *survivable* planet, maybe environmental ethics is unnecessary. But if we care about a planet with wilderness areas and a great diversity of plant and animal life, a planet that bears some resemblance to the planet we started with, a planet that preserves the majesty of nature, environmental ethics is essential."

The Land Ethic

Aldo Leopold

In the following selection from *A Sand County Almanac,* naturalist Aldo Leopold (1887–1948) introduces the land ethic. Beginning with an evolutionary view of ethics, he argues that a new stage of ethical development is required, a stage that deals with our relationship to the land. Central to his argument is his concept of the **biotic community**, the community of all living things, including soil and water. As members of the biotic community, which he also calls the land, we have obligations to preserve its integrity, stability, and beauty, just as we have obligations to the human community.

In defending his position, Leopold criticizes alternative views, most notably conservation systems based on economic value. Many species and ecological systems without economic value, he writes, provide valuable contributions to the biotic community.

Leopold, often called the father of wildlife ecology, grew up in Iowa on bluffs overlooking the Mississippi River. Educated at Yale, he served for many years in the U.S. Forest Service and was later a professor of game management at the University of Wisconsin.

When god-like Odysseus returned from the wars in Troy, he hanged all on one rope a dozen slave-girls of his household whom he suspected of misbehavior during his absence.

This hanging involved no question of propriety. The girls were property. The disposal of property was then, as now, a matter of expediency, not of right and wrong.

Concepts of right and wrong were not lacking from Odysseus' Greece: witness the fidelity of his wife through the long years before at last his black-prowed galleys clove the wine-dark seas for home. The ethical structure of that day covered wives, but had not yet been extended to human chattels. During the three thousand years which have since elapsed, ethical criteria have been extended to many fields of conduct, with corresponding shrinkages in those judged by expediency only.

THE ETHICAL SEQUENCE

This extension of ethics, so far studied only by philosophers, is actually a process in ecological evolution. Its sequences may be described in ecological as well as in philosophical terms. An ethic, ecologically, is a limitation on freedom of action in the struggle for existence. An ethic, philosophically, is a differentiation of social from anti-social conduct. These are two definitions of one thing. The thing has its origin in the tendency of interdependent individuals or groups to evolve modes

of cooperation. The ecologist calls these symbioses. Politics and economics are advanced symbioses in which the original free-for-all competition has been replaced, in part, by cooperative mechanisms with an ethical content.

The complexity of cooperative mechanisms has increased with population density, and with the efficiency of tools. It was simpler, for example, to define the anti-social uses of sticks and stones in the days of the mastodons than of bullets and billboards in the age of motors.

The first ethics dealt with the relation between individuals; the Mosaic Decalogue is an example. Later accretions dealt with the relation between the individual and society. The Golden Rule tries to integrate the individual to society; democracy to integrate social organization to the individual.

There is as yet no ethic dealing with man's relation to land and to the animals and plants which grow upon it. Land, like Odysseus' slavegirls, is still property. The land-relation is still strictly economic, entailing privileges but not obligations.

The extension of ethics to this third element in human environment is, if I read the evidence correctly, an evolutionary possibility and an ecological necessity. It is the third step in a sequence. The first two have already been taken. Individual thinkers since the days of Ezekiel and Isaiah have asserted that the despoliation of land is not only inexpedient but wrong. Society, however, has not yet affirmed their belief. I regard the present conservation movement as the embryo of such an affirmation.

An ethic may be regarded as a mode of guidance for meeting ecological situations so new or intricate, or involving such deferred reactions, that the path of social expediency is not discernible to the average individual. Animal instincts are modes of guidance for the individual in meeting such situations. Ethics are possibly a kind of community instinct in-the-making.

THE COMMUNITY CONCEPT

All ethics so far evolved rest upon a single premise: that the individual is a member of a community of interdependent parts. His instincts prompt him to compete for his place in the community, but his ethics prompt him also to cooperate (perhaps in order that there may be a place to compete for).

The land ethic simply enlarges the boundaries of the community to include soils, waters, plants, and animals, or collectively: the land.

This sounds simple: do we not already sing our love for and obligation to the land of the free and the home of the brave? Yes, but just what and whom do we love? Certainly not the soil, which we are sending helter-skelter downriver. Certainly not the waters, which we assume have no function except to turn turbines, float barges, and carry off sewage. Certainly not the plants, of which we exterminate whole communities without batting an eye. Certainly not the animals, of which we have already extirpated many of the largest and most beautiful species. A land ethic of course cannot prevent the alteration, management, and use of these "resources," but it does affirm their right to continued existence, and, at least in spots, their continued existence in a natural state.

In short, a land ethic changes the role of *Homo sapiens* from conqueror of the land-community to plain member and citizen of it. It implies respect for his fellow-members, and also respect for the community as such.

In human history, we have learned (I hope) that the conqueror role is eventually self-defeating. Why? Because it is implicit in such a role that the conqueror knows, *ex cathedra,* just what makes the community clock tick, and just what and who is valuable, and what and who is worthless, in community life. It always turns out that he knows neither, and this is why his conquests eventually defeat themselves.

In the biotic community, a parallel situation exists. Abraham knew exactly what the land was for: it was to drip milk and honey into Abraham's mouth. At the present moment, the assurance with which we regard this assumption is inverse to the degree of our education.

The ordinary citizen today assumes that science knows what makes the community clock tick; the scientist is equally sure that he does not. He knows that the biotic mechanism is so complex that its workings may never be fully understood.

That man is, in fact, only a member of a biotic team is shown by an ecological interpretation of history. Many historical events, hitherto explained solely in terms of human enterprise, were actually biotic interactions between people and land. The characteristics of the land determined the facts quite as potently as the characteristics of the men who lived on it.

Consider, for example, the settlement of the Mississippi valley. In the years following the Revolution, three groups were contending for its control: the native Indian, the French and English traders, and the American settlers. Historians wonder what would have happened if the English at Detroit had thrown a little more weight into the Indian side of those tipsy scales which decided the outcome of the colonial migration into the canelands of Kentucky. It is time now to ponder the fact that the cane-lands, when subjected to the particular mixture of forces represented by the cow, plow, fire, and axe of the pioneer, became bluegrass. What if the plant succession inherent in this dark and bloody ground had, under the impact of these forces, given us some worthless sedge, shrub, or weed? Would Boone and Kenton have held out? Would there have been any overflow into Ohio, Indiana, Illinois, and Missouri? Any Louisiana Purchase? Any transcontinental union of new states? Any Civil War?

Kentucky was one sentence in the drama of history. We are commonly told what the human actors in this drama tried to do, but we are seldom told that their success, or the lack of it, hung in large degree on the reaction of particular soils to the impact of the particular forces exerted by their occupancy. In the case of Kentucky, we do not even know where the bluegrass came from—whether it is a native species, or a stowaway from Europe.

Contrast the cane-lands with what hindsight tells us about the Southwest, where the pioneers were equally brave, resourceful, and persevering. The impact of occupancy here brought no bluegrass, or other plant fitted to withstand the bumps and buffetings of hard use. This region, when grazed by livestock, reverted through a series of more and more worthless grasses, shrubs, and weeds to a condition of unstable equilibrium. Each recession of plant types bred erosion; each increment to erosion bred a further recession of plants. The result today is a progressive and mutual deterioration, not only of plants and soils, but of the animal community subsisting thereon. The early settlers did not expect this: on the cienegas of New Mexico some even cut ditches to hasten it. So subtle has been its progress that few residents of the region are aware of it. It is quite invisible to the tourist who finds this wrecked landscape colorful and charming (as indeed it is, but it bears scant resemblance to what it was in 1848).

This same landscape was "developed" once before, but with quite different results. The Pueblo Indians settled the Southwest in pre-Columbian times, but they happened not to be equipped with range livestock. Their civilization expired, but not because their land expired.

In India, regions devoid of any sod-forming grass have been settled, apparently without wrecking the land, by the simple expedient of carrying the grass to the cow, rather than vice versa. (Was this the result of some deep wisdom, or was it just good luck? I do not know.)

In short, the plant succession steered the course of history; the pioneer simply demonstrated, for good or ill, what successions inhered in the land. Is history taught in this spirit? It will be, once the concept of land as a community really penetrates our intellectual life.

THE ECOLOGICAL CONSCIENCE

Conservation is a state of harmony between men and land. Despite nearly a century of propaganda, conservation still proceeds at a snail's pace; progress still consists largely of letterhead pieties and convention oratory. On the back forty we still slip two steps backward for each forward stride.

The usual answer to this dilemma is "more conservation education." No one will debate this, but is it certain that only the *volume* of education needs stepping up? Is something lacking in the *content* as well?

It is difficult to give a fair summary of its content in brief form, but, as I understand it, the con-

tent is substantially this: obey the law, vote right, join some organizations, and practice what conservation is profitable on your own land; the government will do the rest.

Is not this formula too easy to accomplish anything worthwhile? It defines no right or wrong, assigns no obligation, calls for no sacrifice, implies no change in the current philosophy of values. In respect of land-use, it urges only enlightened self-interest. Just how far will such education take us? An example will perhaps yield a partial answer.

By 1930 it had become clear to all except the ecologically blind that southwestern Wisconsin's top-soil was slipping seaward. In 1933 the farmers were told that if they would adopt certain remedial practices for five years, the public would donate CCC labor to install them, plus the necessary machinery and materials. The offer was widely accepted, but the practices were widely forgotten when the five-year contract period was up. The farmers continued only those practices that yielded an immediate and visible economic gain for themselves.

This led to the idea that maybe farmers would learn more quickly if they themselves wrote the rules. Accordingly the Wisconsin Legislature in 1937 passed the Soil Conservation District Law. This said to farmers, in effect: *We, the public, will furnish you free technical service and loan you specialized machinery, if you will write your own rules for land-use. Each county may write its own rules, and these will have the force of law.* Nearly all the counties promptly organized to accept the proffered help, but after a decade of operation, *no county has yet written a single rule.* There has been visible progress in such practices as strip-cropping, pasture renovation, and soil liming, but none in fencing woodlots against grazing, and none in excluding plow and cow from steep slopes. The farmers, in short, have selected those remedial practices which were profitable anyhow, and ignored those which were profitable to the community, but not clearly profitable to themselves.

When one asks why no rules have been written, one is told that the community is not yet ready to support them; education must precede rules. But the education actually in progress makes no mention of obligations to land over and above those dictated by self-interest. The net result is that we have more education but less soil, fewer healthy woods, and as many floods as in 1937.

The puzzling aspect of such situations is that the existence of obligations over and above self-interest is taken for granted in such rural community enterprises as the betterment of roads, schools, churches, and baseball teams. Their existence is not taken for granted, nor as yet seriously discussed, in bettering the behavior of the water that falls on the land, or in the preserving of the beauty or diversity of the farm landscape. Land-use ethics are still governed wholly by economic self-interest, just as social ethics were a century ago.

To sum up: we asked the farmer to do what he conveniently could to save his soil, and he has done just that, and only that. The farmer who clears the woods off a 75 per cent slope, turns his cows into the clearing, and dumps its rainfall, rocks, and soil into the community creek, is still (if otherwise decent) a respected member of society. If he puts lime on his fields and plants his crops on contour, he is still entitled to all the privileges and emoluments of his Soil Conservation District. The District is a beautiful piece of social machinery, but it is coughing along on two cylinders because we have been too timid, and too anxious for quick success, to tell the farmer the true magnitude of his obligations. Obligations have no meaning without conscience, and the problem we face is the extension of the social conscience from people to land.

No important change in ethics was ever accomplished without an internal change in our intellectual emphasis, loyalties, affections, and convictions. The proof that conservation has not yet touched these foundations of conduct lies in the fact that philosophy and religion have not yet heard of it. In our attempt to make conservation easy, we have made it trivial.

SUBSTITUTES FOR A LAND ETHIC

When the logic of history hungers for bread and we hand out a stone, we are at pains to explain how much the stone resembles bread. I now describe some of the stones which serve in lieu of a land ethic.

One basic weakness in a conservation system based wholly on economic motives is that most members of the land community have no economic value. Wildflowers and songbirds are examples. Of the 22,000 higher plants and animals native to Wisconsin, it is doubtful whether more than 5 per cent can be sold, fed, eaten, or otherwise put to economic use. Yet these creatures are members of the biotic community, and if (as I believe) its stability depends on its integrity, they are entitled to continuance.

When one of these non-economic categories is threatened, and if we happen to love it, we invent subterfuges to give it economic importance. At the beginning of the century songbirds were supposed to be disappearing. Ornithologists jumped to the rescue with some distinctly shaky evidence to the effect that insects would eat us up if birds failed to control them. The evidence had to be economic in order to be valid.

It is painful to read these circumlocutions today. We have no land ethic yet, but we have at least drawn nearer the point of admitting that birds should continue as a matter of biotic right, regardless of the presence or absence of economic advantage to us.

A parallel situation exists in respect of predatory mammals, raptorial birds, and fish-eating birds. Time was when biologists somewhat overworked the evidence that these creatures preserve the health of game by killing weaklings, or that they control rodents for the farmer, or that they prey only on "worthless" species. Here again, the evidence had to be economic in order to be valid. It is only in recent years that we hear the more honest argument that predators are members of the community, and that no special interest has the right to exterminate them for the sake of a benefit, real or fancied, to itself. Unfortunately this enlightened view is still in the talk stage. In the field the extermination of predators goes merrily on: witness the impending erasure of the timber wolf by fiat of Congress, the Conservation Bureaus, and many state legislatures.

Some species of trees have been "read out of the party" by economics-minded foresters because they grow too slowly, or have too low a sale value to pay as timber crops: white cedar, tamarack, cypress, beech, and hemlock are examples. In Europe, where forestry is ecologically more advanced, the non-commercial tree species are recognized as members of the native forest community, to be preserved as such, within reason. Moreover some (like beech) have been found to have a valuable function in building up soil fertility. The interdependence of the forest and its constituent tree species, ground flora, and fauna is taken for granted.

Lack of economic value is sometimes a character not only of species or groups, but of entire biotic communities: marshes, bogs, dunes, and "deserts" are examples. Our formula in such cases is to relegate their conservation to government as refuges, monuments, or parks. The difficulty is that these communities are usually interspersed with more valuable private lands; the government cannot possibly own or control such scattered parcels. The net effect is that we have relegated some of them to ultimate extinction over large areas. If the private owner were ecologically minded, he would be proud to be the custodian of a reasonable proportion of such areas, which add diversity and beauty to his farm and to his community.

In some instances, the assumed lack of profit in these "waste" areas has proved to be wrong, but only after most of them had been done away with. The present scramble to reflood muskrat marshes is a case in point.

There is a clear tendency in American conservation to relegate to government all necessary jobs that private landowners fail to perform. Government ownership, operation, subsidy, or regulation is now widely prevalent in forestry, range management, soil and watershed management, park and wilderness conservation, fisheries management, and migratory bird management, with more to come. Most of this growth in governmental conservation is proper and logical, some of it is inevitable. That I imply no disapproval of it is implicit in the fact that I have spent most of my life working for it. Nevertheless the question arises: What is the ultimate magnitude of the enterprise? Will the tax base carry its eventual ramifications? At what point will governmental conservation, like the mastodon, become handicapped by its own dimensions? The answer, if there is any, seems to be in a land ethic, or some other force which assigns more obligation to the private landowner.

Industrial landowners and users, especially lumbermen and stockmen, are inclined to wail long and loudly about the extension of government ownership and regulation to land, but (with notable exceptions) they show little disposition to develop the only visible alternative: the voluntary practice of conservation on their own lands.

When the private landowner is asked to perform some unprofitable act for the good of the community, he today assents only with outstretched palm. If the act costs him cash this is fair and proper, but when it costs only forethought, openmindedness, or time, the issue is at least debatable. The overwhelming growth of land-use subsidies in recent years must be ascribed, in large part, to the government's own agencies for conservation education: the land bureaus, the agricultural colleges, and the extension services. As far as I can detect, no ethical obligation toward land is taught in these institutions.

To sum up: a system of conservation based solely on economic self-interest is hopelessly lopsided. It tends to ignore, and thus eventually to eliminate, many elements in the land community that lack commercial value, but that are (as far as we know) essential to its healthy functioning. It assumes, falsely, I think, that the economic parts of the biotic clock will function without the uneconomic parts. It tends to relegate to government many functions eventually too large, too complex, or too widely dispersed to be performed by government.

An ethical obligation on the part of the private owner is the only visible remedy for these situations.

THE LAND PYRAMID

An ethic to supplement and guide the economic relation to land presupposes the existence of some mental image of land as a biotic mechanism. We can be ethical only in relation to something we can see, feel, understand, love, or otherwise have faith in.

The image commonly employed in conservation education is "the balance of nature." For reasons too lengthy to detail here, this figure of speech fails to describe accurately what little we know about the land mechanism. A much truer image is the one employed in ecology: the biotic pyramid. I shall first sketch the pyramid as a symbol of land, and later develop some of its implications in terms of land-use.

Plants absorb energy from the sun. This energy flows through a circuit called the biota, which may be represented by a pyramid consisting of layers.

The bottom layer is the soil. A plant layer rests on the soil, an insect layer on the plants, a bird and rodent layer on the insects, and so on up through various animal groups to the apex layer, which consists of the larger carnivores.

The species of a layer are alike not in where they came from, or in what they look like, but rather in what they eat. Each successive layer depends on those below it for food and often for other services, and each in turn furnishes food and services to those above. Proceeding upward, each successive layer decreases in numerical abundance. Thus, for every carnivore there are hundreds of his prey, thousands of their prey, millions of insects, uncountable plants. The pyramidal form of the system reflects this numerical progression from apex to base. Man shares an intermediate layer with the bears, raccoons, and squirrels which eat both meat and vegetables.

The lines of dependency for food and other services are called food chains. Thus soil-oak-deer-Indian is a chain that has now been largely converted to soil-corn-cow-farmer. Each species, including ourselves, is a link in many chains. The deer eats a hundred plants other than oak, and the cow a hundred plants other than corn. Both, then, are links in a hundred chains. The pyramid is a tangle of chains so complex as to seem disorderly, yet the stability of the system proves it to be a highly organized structure. Its functioning depends on the cooperation and competition of its diverse parts.

In the beginning, the pyramid of life was low and squat; the food chains short and simple. Evolution has added layer after layer, link after link. Man is one of thousands of accretions to the height and complexity of the pyramid. Science has given us many doubts, but it has given us at least one certainty: the trend of evolution is to elaborate and diversify the biota.

Land, then, is not merely soil; it is a fountain of energy flowing through a circuit of soils, plants, and animals. Food chains are the living channels which conduct energy upward; death and decay return it to the soil. The circuit is not closed; some energy is dissipated in decay, some is added by absorption from the air, some is stored in soils, peats, and long-lived forests; but it is a sustained circuit, like a slowly augmented revolving fund of life. There is always a net loss by downhill wash, but this is normally small

and offset by the decay of rocks. It is deposited in the ocean and, in the course of geological time, raised to form new lands and new pyramids.

The velocity and character of the upward flow of energy depend on the complex structure of the plant and animal community, much as the upward flow of sap in a tree depends on its complex cellular organization. Without this complexity, normal circulation would presumably not occur. Structure means the characteristic numbers, as well as the characteristic kinds and functions, of the component species. This interdependence between the complex structure of the land and its smooth functioning as an energy unit is one of its basic attributes.

When a change occurs in one part of the circuit, many other parts must adjust themselves to it. Change does not necessarily obstruct or divert the flow of energy: evolution is a long series of self-induced changes, the net result of which has been to elaborate the flow mechanism and to lengthen the circuit. Evolutionary changes, however, are usually slow and local. Man's invention of tools has enabled him to make changes of unprecedented violence, rapidity, and scope.

One change is in the composition of floras and faunas. The larger predators are lopped off the apex of the pyramid; food chains, for the first time in history, become shorter rather than longer. Domesticated species from other lands are substituted for wild ones, and wild ones are moved to new habitats. In this worldwide pooling of faunas and floras, some species get out of bounds as pests and diseases, others are extinguished. Such effects are seldom intended or foreseen; they represent unpredicted and often untraceable readjustments in the structure. Agricultural science is largely a race between the emergence of new pests and the emergence of new techniques for their control.

Another change touches the flow of energy through plants and animals and its return to the soil. Fertility is the ability of soil to receive, store, and release energy. Agriculture, by overdrafts on the soil, or by too radical a substitution of domestic for native species in the superstructure, may derange the channels of flow or deplete storage. Soils depleted of their storage, or of the organic matter which anchors it, wash away faster than they form. This is erosion.

Waters, like soil, are part of the energy circuit. Industry, by polluting waters or obstructing them with dams, may exclude the plants and animals necessary to keep energy in circulation.

Transportation brings about another basic change: the plants or animals grown in one region are now consumed and returned to the soil in another. Transportation taps the energy stored in rocks, and in the air, and uses it elsewhere; thus we fertilize the garden with nitrogen gleaned by the guano birds from the fishes of seas on the other side of the Equator. Thus the formerly localized and self-contained circuits are pooled on a worldwide scale.

The process of altering the pyramid for human occupation releases stored energy, and this often gives rise, during the pioneering period, to a deceptive exuberance of plant and animal life, both wild and tame. These releases of biotic capital tend to becloud or postpone the penalties of violence.

This thumbnail sketch of land as an energy circuit conveys three basic ideas:

1. That land is not merely soil.
2. That the native plants and animals kept the energy circuit open; others may or may not.
3. That man-made changes are of a different order than evolutionary changes, and have effects more comprehensive than is intended or foreseen.

These ideas, collectively, raise two basic issues: Can the land adjust itself to the new order? Can the desired alterations be accomplished with less violence?

Biotas seem to differ in their capacity to sustain violent conversion. Western Europe, for example, carries a far different pyramid than Caesar found there. Some large animals are lost; swampy forests have become meadows or plowland; many new plants and animals are introduced, some of which escape as pests; the remaining natives are greatly changed in distribution and abundance. Yet the soil is still there and, with the help of imported nutrients, still fertile; the waters flow normally; the new structure seems to function and to persist. There is no visible stoppage or derangement of the circuit.

Western Europe, then, has a resistant biota. Its inner processes are tough, elastic, resistant to strain. No matter how violent the alterations, the pyramid, so far, has developed some new *modus vivendi* which preserves its habitability for man, and for most of the other natives.

Japan seems to present another instance of radical conversion without disorganization.

Most other civilized regions, and some as yet barely touched by civilization, display various stages of disorganization, varying from initial symptoms to advanced wastage. In Asia Minor and North Africa diagnosis is confused by climatic changes, which may have been either the cause or the effect of advanced wastage. In the United States the degree of disorganization varies locally; it is worst in the Southwest, the Ozarks, and parts of the South, and least in New England and the Northwest. Better land-uses may still arrest it in the less advanced regions. In parts of Mexico, South America, South Africa, and Australia a violent and accelerating wastage is in progress, but I cannot assess the prospects.

This almost worldwide display of disorganization in the land seems to be similar to disease in an animal, except that it never culminates in complete disorganization or death. The land recovers, but at some reduced level of complexity, and with a reduced carrying capacity for people, plants, and animals. Many biotas currently regarded as "lands of opportunity" are in fact already subsisting on exploitative agriculture, i.e. they have already exceeded their sustained carrying capacity. Most of South America is overpopulated in this sense.

In arid regions we attempt to offset the process of wastage by reclamation, but it is only too evident that the prospective longevity of reclamation projects is often short. In our own West, the best of them may not last a century.

The combined evidence of history and ecology seems to support one general deduction: the less violent the man-made changes, the greater the probability of successful readjustment in the pyramid. Violence, in turn, varies with human population density; a dense population requires a more violent conversion. In this respect, North America has a better chance for permanence than Europe, if she can contrive to limit her density.

This deduction runs counter to our current philosophy, which assumes that because a small increase in density enriched human life, that an indefinite increase will enrich it indefinitely. Ecology knows of no density relationship that holds for indefinitely wide limits. All gains from density are subject to a law of diminishing returns.

Whatever may be the equation for men and land, it is improbable that we as yet know all its terms. Recent discoveries in mineral and vitamin nutrition reveal unsuspected dependencies in the up-circuit: incredibly minute quantities of certain substances determine the value of soils to plants, of plants to animals. What of the down-circuit? What of the vanishing species, the preservation of which we now regard as an esthetic luxury? They helped build the soil; in what unsuspected ways may they be essential to its maintenance? Professor Weaver proposes that we use prairie flowers to refloccu- late the wasting soils of the dust bowl; who knows for what purpose cranes and condors, otters and grizzlies may some day be used?

LAND HEALTH AND THE A–B CLEAVAGE

A land ethic, then, reflects the existence of an eco- logical conscience, and this in turn reflects a con- viction of individual responsibility for the health of the land. Health is the capacity of the land for self- renewal. Conservation is our effort to understand and preserve this capacity.

Conservationists are notorious for their dis- sentions. Superficially these seem to add up to mere confusion, but a more careful scrutiny reveals a sin- gle plane of cleavage common to many specialized fields. In each field one group (A) regards the land as soil, and its function as commodity production; another group (B) regards the land as a biota, and its function as something broader. How much broader is admittedly in a state of doubt and confusion.

In my own field, forestry, group A is quite con- tent to grow trees like cabbages, with cellulose as the basic forest commodity. It feels no inhibition against violence; its ideology is agronomic. Group B, on the other hand, sees forestry as fundamentally dif- ferent from agronomy because it employs natural species, and manages a natural environment rather than creating an artificial one. Group B prefers nat- ural reproduction on principle. It worries on biotic as well as economic grounds about the loss of species like chestnut, and the threatened loss of the white pines. It worries about a whole series of sec- ondary forest functions: wildlife, recreation, water-

sheds, wilderness areas. To my mind, Group B feels the stirrings of an ecological conscience.

In the wildlife field, a parallel cleavage exists. For Group A the basis commodities are sport and meat; the yardsticks of production are ciphers of take in pheasants and trout. Artificial propagation is accept- able as a permanent as well as a temporary recourse—if its unit costs permit. Group B, on the other hand, worries about a whole series of biotic side-issues. What is the cost in predators of pro- ducing a game crop? Should we have further recourse to exotics? How can management restore the shrinking species, like prairie grouse, already hopeless as shootable game? How can management restore the threatened rarities, like trumpeter swan and whooping crane? Can management principles be extended to wildflowers? Here again it is clear to me that we have the same A–B cleavage as in forestry.

In the larger field of agriculture I am less compe- tent to speak, but there seem to be somewhat par- allel cleavages. Scientific agriculture was actively developing before ecology was born, hence a slower penetration of ecological concepts might be expected. Moreover the farmer, by the very nature of his techniques, must modify the biota more rad- ically than the forester or the wildlife manager. Nevertheless, there are many discontents in agri- culture which seem to add up to a new vision of "*biotic farming.*"

Perhaps the most important of these is the new evidence that poundage or tonnage is no measure of the food-value of farm crops; the products of fertile soil may be qualitatively as well as quantita- tively superior. We can bolster poundage from de- pleted soils by pouring on imported fertility, but we are not necessarily bolstering food-value. The possible ultimate ramifications of this idea are so immense that I must leave their exposition to abler pens.

The discontent that labels itself "organic farm- ing," while bearing some of the earmarks of a cult, is nevertheless biotic in its direction, particularly in its insistence on the importance of soil flora and fauna.

The ecological fundamentals of agriculture are just as poorly known to the public as in other fields of land-use. For example, few educated people real- ize that the marvelous advances in technique made during recent decades are improvements in the pump, rather than the well. Acre for acre, they have barely sufficed to offset the sinking level of fertility.

In all of these cleavages, we see repeated the same basic paradoxes: man the conqueror *versus* man the biotic citizen; science the sharpener of his sword *versus* science the searchlight on his universe; land the slave and servant *versus* land the collective organism. Robinson's injunction to Tristram may well be applied, at this juncture, to *Homo sapiens* as a species in geological time:

> Whether you will or not
> You are a King, Tristram, for you are one
> Of the time-tested few that leave the world,
> When they are gone, not the same place it was.
> Mark what you leave.

THE OUTLOOK

It is inconceivable to me that an ethical relation to land can exist without love, respect, and admiration for land, and a high regard for its value. By value, I of course mean something far broader than mere economic value; I mean value in the philosophical sense.

Perhaps the most serious obstacle impeding the evolution of a land ethic is the fact that our educational and economic system is headed away from, rather than toward, an intense consciousness of land. Your true modern is separated from the land by many middlemen, and by innumerable physical gadgets. He has no vital relation to it; to him it is the space between cities on which crops grow. Turn him loose for a day on the land, and if the spot does not happen to be a golf links or a "scenic" area, he is bored stiff. If crops could be raised by hydroponics instead of farming, it would suit him very well. Synthetic substitutes for wood, leather, wool, and other natural land products suit him better than the originals. In short, land is something he has "outgrown."

Almost equally serious as an obstacle to a land ethic is the attitude of the farmer for whom the land is still an adversary, or a taskmaster that keeps him in slavery. Theoretically, the mechanization of farming ought to cut the farmer's chains, but whether it really does is debatable.

One of the requisites for an ecological comprehension of land is an understanding of ecology, and this is by no means co-extensive with "education"; in fact, much higher education seems deliberately to avoid ecological concepts. An understanding of ecology does not necessarily originate in courses bearing ecological labels; it is quite as likely to be labeled geography, botany, agronomy, history, or economics. This is as it should be, but whatever the label, ecological training is scarce.

The case for a land ethic would appear hopeless but for the minority which is in obvious revolt against these "modern" trends.

The "key-log" which must be moved to release the evolutionary process for an ethic is simply this: quit thinking about decent land-use as solely an economic problem. Examine each question in terms of what is ethically and esthetically right, as well as what is economically expedient. A thing is right when it tends to preserve the integrity, stability, and beauty of the biotic community. It is wrong when it tends otherwise.

It of course goes without saying that economic feasibility limits the tether of what can or cannot be done for land. It always has and it always will. The fallacy the economic determinists have tied around our collective neck, and which we now need to cast off, is the belief that economics determines *all* land-use. This is simply not true. An innumerable host of actions and attitudes, comprising perhaps the bulk of all land relations, is determined by the land-users' tastes and predilections, rather than by his purse. The bulk of all land relations hinges on investments of time, forethought, skill, and faith rather than on investments of cash. As a land-user thinketh, so is he.

I have purposely presented the land ethic as a product of social evolution because nothing so important as an ethic is ever "written." Only the most superficial student of history supposes that Moses "wrote" the Decalogue; it evolved in the minds of a thinking community, and Moses wrote a tentative summary of it for a "seminar." I say tentative because evolution never stops.

The evolution of a land ethic is an intellectual as well as emotional process. Conservation is paved with good intentions which prove to be futile, or even dangerous, because they are devoid of critical understanding either of the land, or of economic land-use. I think it is a truism that as the ethical frontier advances from the individual to the community, its intellectual content increases.

The mechanism of operation is the same for any ethic: social approbation for right actions: social disapproval for wrong actions.

By and large, our present problem is one of attitudes and implements. We are remodeling the Alhambra with a steam-shovel, and we are proud of our yardage. We shall hardly relinquish the shovel, which after all has many good points, but we are in need of gentler and more objective criteria for its successful use.

Questions for Analysis

1. According to Leopold, humanity is "only a member of a biotic team." What does he mean by that claim? What leads him to make it?

2. What does Leopold mean by the *ecological conscience?* Why do we need one? How do we develop it?

3. Leopold distinguishes economic value and ecological value. What examples does he give of each? How do they differ from each other?

4. According to Leopold, "man-made changes [in the land] are of a different order than evolutionary changes." Why? What marks the difference? How should the difference affect our behavior?

5. Do you agree with Leopold that "a thing is right when it tends to preserve the integrity, stability, and beauty of the biotic community" and "wrong when it tends otherwise"?

The Ethics of Respect for Nature

Paul W. Taylor

The following essay by Paul W. Taylor, professor emeritus of philosophy, Brooklyn College, presents an alternative theory of environmental ethics to Aldo Leopold's land ethic. Though nonanthropocentric and sensitive to ecological issues, it is individualistic rather than holistic. According to Taylor, the principal moral concern of environmental ethics is individual organisms, not the biotic community. Ecological relationships provide us with important knowledge that help us in our dealings with individual organisms, he says, but they do not provide us with moral norms.

In developing his view of respect for nature, Taylor emphasizes that the respect he means is an ultimate attitude, one that is not derived from some other moral norm but is fundamental, like Kantian respect for persons. We should adopt that attitude, he says, because of a recognition that all living things, not just humans, have inherent worth.

I. HUMAN-CENTERED AND LIFE-CENTERED SYSTEMS OF ENVIRONMENTAL ETHICS

In this paper I show how the taking of a certain ultimate moral attitude toward nature, which I call

From *Environmental Ethics,* vol. 3 (Fall 1981), pp. 197–218. Reprinted by permission of the author.

"respect for nature," has a central place in the foundations of a life-centered system of environmental ethics. . . .

In designating the theory to be set forth as life-centered, I intend to contrast it with all anthropocentric views. According to the latter, human actions affecting the natural environment and its nonhuman inhabitants are right (or wrong) by either of two criteria: they have consequences which are favorable (or unfavorable) to human well-being, or they are consistent (or inconsistent) with the system of norms that protect and implement human rights. From this human-centered standpoint it is to humans and only to humans that all duties are ultimately owed. We may have responsibilities *with regard to* the natural ecosystems and biotic communities of our planet, but these responsibilities are in every case based on the contingent fact that our treatment of those ecosystems and communities of life can further the realization of human values and/or human rights. We have no obligation to promote or protect the good of nonhuman living things, independently of this contingent fact.

A life-centered system of environmental ethics is opposed to human-centered ones precisely on this point. From the perspective of a life-centered theory, we have prima facie moral obligations that are owed to wild plants and animals themselves as members of the Earth's biotic community. We are morally bound (other things being equal) to protect or promote their good for *their* sake. Our duties to respect the integrity of natural ecosystems, to preserve endangered species, and to avoid environmental pollution stem from the fact that these are ways in which we can help make it possible for wild species populations to achieve and maintain a healthy existence in a natural state. Such obligations are due those living things out of recognition of their inherent worth. They are entirely additional to and independent of the obligations we owe to our fellow humans. Although many of the actions that fulfill one set of obligations will also fulfill the other, two different grounds of obligation are involved. Their well-being, as well as human well-being, is something to be realized *as an end in itself*.

If we were to accept a life-centered theory of environmental ethics, a profound reordering of our moral universe would take place. We would begin to look at the whole of the Earth's biosphere in a new light. Our duties with respect to the "world" of nature would be seen as making prima facie claims upon us to be balanced against our duties with respect to the "world" of human civilization. We could no longer simply take the human point of view and consider the effects of our actions exclusively from the perspective of our own good.

II. THE GOOD OF A BEING AND THE CONCEPT OF INHERENT WORTH

. . . Two concepts are essential to the taking of a moral attitude of the sort in question. A being which does not "have" these concepts, that is, which is unable to grasp their meaning and conditions of applicability, cannot be said to have the attitude as part of its moral outlook. These concepts are, first, that of the good (well-being, welfare) of a living thing, and second, the idea of an entity possessing inherent worth. I examine each concept in turn.

1. Every organism, species population, and community of life has a good of its own which moral agents can intentionally further or damage by their actions. To say that an entity has a good of its own is simply to say that, without reference to any other entity, it can be benefited or harmed. One can act in its overall interest or contrary to its overall interest, and environmental conditions can be good for it (advantageous to it) or bad for it (disadvantageous to it). What is good for an entity is what "does it good" in the sense of enhancing or preserving its life and well-being. What is bad for an entity is something that is detrimental to its life and well-being.[1]

We can think of the good of an individual nonhuman organism as consisting in the full development of its biological powers. Its good is realized to the extent that it is strong and healthy. It possesses whatever capacities it needs for successfully coping with its environment and so preserving its existence throughout the various stages of the normal life cycle of its species. The good of a population or community of such individuals consists in the population or community maintaining itself from generation to generation as a coherent system of genetically and ecologically related organisms whose average good is at an optimum level for the given environment. (Here *average good* means that the degree of realization of the good of *individual organisms* in the population or community is, on average, greater than would be the case under any other ecologically functioning order of interrelations among those species populations in the given ecosystem.)

The idea of a being having a good of its own, as I understand it, does not entail that the being must have interests or take an interest in what affects its life for better or for worse. We can act in a being's interest or contrary to its interest without its being interested in what we are doing to it in the sense of wanting or not wanting us to do it. It may, indeed, be wholly unaware that favorable and unfavorable events are taking place in its life. I take it that trees, for example, have no knowledge or desires or feelings. Yet it is undoubtedly the case that trees can be harmed or benefited by our actions. We can crush their roots by running a bulldozer too close to them. We can see to it that they get adequate nourishment and moisture by fertilizing and watering the soil around them. Thus we can help or hinder them in the realization of their good. It is the good of trees themselves that is thereby affected. We can similarly act so as to further the good of an entire tree population of a certain species (say, all the redwood trees in a California valley) or the good of a whole community of plant life in a given wilderness area, just as we can do harm to such a population or community. . . .

2. The second concept essential to the moral attitude of respect for nature is the idea of inherent worth. We take that attitude toward wild living things (individuals, species populations, or whole biotic communities) when and only when we regard them as entities possessing inherent worth. . . .

What does it mean to regard an entity that has a good of its own as possessing inherent worth? Two general principles are involved: the principle of moral consideration and the principle of intrinsic value.

According to the principle of moral consideration, wild living things are deserving of the concern and consideration of all moral agents simply in virtue of their being members of the Earth's community of life. From the moral point of view their good must be taken into account whenever it is affected for better or worse by the conduct of rational agents. This holds no matter what species the creature belongs to. The good of each is to be accorded some value and so acknowledged as having some weight in the deliberations of all rational agents. Of course, it may be necessary for such agents to act in ways contrary to the good of this or that particular organism or group of organisms in order to further the good of others, including the good of humans. But the principle of moral con-

sideration prescribes that, with respect to each being an entity having its own good, every individual is deserving of consideration.

The principle of intrinsic value states that, regardless of what kind of entity it is in other respects, if it is a member of the Earth's community of life, the realization of its good is something *intrinsically* valuable. This means that its good is prima facie worthy of being preserved or promoted as an end in itself and for the sake of the entity whose good it is. Insofar as we regard any organism, species population, or life community as an entity having inherent worth, we believe that it must never be treated as if it were a mere object or thing whose entire value lies in being instrumental to the good of some other entity. The well-being of each is judged to have value in and of itself.

Combining these two principles, we can now define what it means for a living thing or group of living things to possess inherent worth. To say that it possesses inherent worth is to say that its good is deserving of the concern and consideration of all moral agents, and that the realization of its good has intrinsic value, to be pursued as an end in itself and for the sake of the entity whose good it is. . . .

III. THE ATTITUDE OF RESPECT FOR NATURE

Why should moral agents regard wild living things in the natural world as possessing inherent worth? To answer this question we must first take into account the fact that, when rational, autonomous agents subscribe to the principles of moral consideration and intrinsic value and so conceive of wild living things as having that kind of worth, such agents are *adopting a certain ultimate moral attitude toward the natural world.* This is the attitude I call "respect for nature." It parallels the attitude of respect for persons in human ethics. When we adopt the attitude of respect for persons as the proper (fitting, appropriate) attitude to take toward all persons as persons, we consider the fulfillment of the basic interests of each individual to have intrinsic value. We thereby make a moral commitment to live a certain kind of life in relation to other persons. We place ourselves under the direction of a system of standards and rules that we consider validly binding on all moral agents as such.[2]

Similarly, when we adopt the attitude of respect for nature as an ultimate moral attitude we make a commitment to live by certain normative principles. These principles constitute the rules of conduct and standards of character that are to govern our treatment of the natural world. This is, first, an *ultimate* commitment because it is not derived from any higher norm. The attitude of respect for nature is not grounded on some other, more general, or more fundamental attitude. It sets the total framework for our responsibilities toward the natural world. It can be justified, as I show below, but its justification cannot consist in referring to a more general attitude or a more basic normative principle.

Second, the commitment is a *moral* one because it is understood to be a disinterested matter of principle. It is this feature that distinguishes the attitude of respect for nature from the set of feelings and dispositions that comprise the love of nature. The latter stems from one's personal interest in and response to the natural world. Like the affectionate feelings we have toward certain individual human beings, one's love of nature is nothing more than the particular way one feels about the natural environment and its wild inhabitants. And just as our love for an individual person differs from our respect for all persons as such (whether we happen to love them or not), so love of nature differs from respect for nature. Respect for nature is an attitude we believe all moral agents ought to have simply as moral agents, regardless of whether or not they also love nature. Indeed, we have not truly taken the attitude of respect for nature ourselves unless we believe this. . . .

Although the attitude of respect for nature is in this sense a disinterested and universalizable attitude, anyone who does adopt it has certain steady, more or less permanent dispositions. These dispositions, which are themselves to be considered disinterested and universalizable, comprise three interlocking sets: dispositions to seek certain ends, dispositions to carry on one's practical reasoning and deliberation in a certain way, and dispositions to have certain feelings. We may accordingly analyze the attitude of respect for nature into the following components. (a) The disposition to aim at, and to take steps to bring about, as final and disinterested ends, the promoting and protecting of the good of organisms, species populations, and life communities in natural ecosystems. (These ends are "final" in

not being pursued as means to further ends. They are "disinterested" in being independent of the self-interest of the agent.) (b) The disposition to consider actions that tend to realize those ends to be prima facie obligatory *because* they have that tendency. (c) The disposition to experience positive and negative feelings toward states of affairs in the world *because* they are favorable or unfavorable to the good of organisms, species populations, and life communities in natural ecosystems.

IV. THE JUSTIFIABILITY OF THE ATTITUDE OF RESPECT FOR NATURE

I return to the question posed earlier, which has not yet been answered: why *should* moral agents regard wild living things as possessing inherent worth? . . .

We must keep in mind that inherent worth is not some mysterious sort of objective property belonging to living things that can be discovered by empirical observation or scientific investigation. To ascribe inherent worth to an entity is not to describe it by citing some feature discernible by sense perception or inferable by inductive reasoning. Nor is there a logically necessary connection between the concept of a being having a good of its own and the concept of inherent worth. We do not contradict ourselves by asserting that an entity that has a good of its own lacks inherent worth. In order to show that such an entity "has" inherent worth we must give good reasons for ascribing that kind of value to it (placing that kind of value upon it, conceiving of it to be valuable in that way). Although it is humans (persons, valuers) who must do the valuing, for the ethics of respect for nature, the value so ascribed is not a human value. That is to say, it is not a value derived from considerations regarding human well-being or human rights. It is a value that is ascribed to non-human animals and plants themselves, independently of their relationship to what humans judge to be conducive to their own good.

Whatever reasons, then, justify our taking the attitude of respect for nature as defined above are also reasons that show why we *should* regard the living things of the natural world as possessing inherent worth. We saw earlier that, since the attitude is an ultimate one, it cannot be derived from a more fundamental attitude nor shown to be a special case of a more general one. On what sort of grounds, then, can it be established?

The attitude we take toward living things in the natural world depends on the way we look at them, on what kind of beings we conceive them to be, and on how we understand the relations we bear to them. Underlying and supporting our attitude is a certain *belief system* that constitutes a particular world view or outlook on nature and the place of human life in it. To give good reasons for adopting the attitude of respect for nature, then, we must first articulate the belief system which underlies and supports that attitude. If it appears that the belief system is internally coherent and well-ordered, and if, as far as we can now tell, it is consistent with all known scientific truths relevant to our knowledge of the object of the attitude (which in this case includes the whole set of the Earth's natural ecosystems and their communities of life), then there remains the task of indicating why scientifically informed and rational thinkers with a developed capacity of reality awareness can find it acceptable as a way of conceiving of the natural world and our place in it. To the extent we can do this we provide at least a reasonable argument for accepting the belief system and the ultimate moral attitude it supports.

I do not hold that such a belief system can be *proven* to be true, either inductively or deductively. As we shall see, not all of its components can be stated in the form of empirically verifiable propositions. Nor is its internal order governed by purely logical relationships. But the system as a whole, I contend, constitutes a coherent, unified, and rationally acceptable "picture" or "map" of a total world. By examining each of its main components and seeing how they fit together, we obtain a scientifically informed and well-ordered conception of nature and the place of humans in it.

This belief system underlying the attitude of respect for nature I call (for want of a better name) "the biocentric outlook on nature." . . . It might best be described as a philosophical world view, to distinguish it from a scientific theory or explanatory system. However, one of its major tenets is the great lesson we have learned from the science of ecology: the interdependence of all living things in an organ-

ically unified order whose balance and stability are necessary conditions for the realization of the good of its constituent biotic communities.

Before turning to an account of the main components of the biocentric outlook, it is convenient here to set forth the overall structure of my theory of environmental ethics as it has now emerged. The ethics of respect for nature is made up of three basic elements: a belief system, an ultimate moral attitude, and a set of rules of duty and standards of character. These elements are connected with each other in the following manner. The belief system provides a certain outlook on nature which supports and makes intelligible an autonomous agent's adopting, as an ultimate moral attitude, the attitude of respect for nature. It supports and makes intelligible the attitude in the sense that, when an autonomous agent understands its moral relations to the natural world in terms of this outlook, it recognizes the attitude of respect to be the only *suitable* or *fitting* attitude to take toward all wild forms of life in the Earth's biosphere. Living things are now viewed as *the appropriate objects of the attitude of respect* and are accordingly regarded as entities possessing inherent worth. One then places intrinsic value on the promotion and protection of their good. As a consequence of this, one makes a moral commitment to abide by a set of rules of duty and to fulfill (as far as one can by one's own efforts) certain standards of good character. Given one's adoption of the attitude of respect, one makes that moral commitment because one considers those rules and standards to be validly binding on all moral agents. They are seen as embodying forms of conduct and character structures in which the attitude of respect for nature is manifested.

This three-part complex which internally orders the ethics of respect for nature is symmetrical with a theory of human ethics grounded on respect for persons. Such a theory includes, first, a conception of oneself and others as persons, that is, as centers of autonomous choice. Second, there is the attitude of respect for persons as persons. When this is adopted as an ultimate moral attitude it involves the disposition to treat every person as having inherent worth or "human dignity." Every human being, just in virtue of her or his humanity, is understood to be worthy of moral consideration, and intrinsic value is placed on the autonomy and well-being of each. This is what Kant meant by conceiving of persons as ends in themselves. Third, there is an ethical system of duties which are acknowledged to be owed by everyone to everyone. These duties are forms of conduct in which public recognition is given to each individual's inherent worth as a person. . . .

V. THE BIOCENTRIC OUTLOOK ON NATURE

The biocentric outlook on nature has four main components. (1) Humans are thought of as members of the Earth's community of life, holding that membership on the same terms as apply to all the nonhuman members. (2) The Earth's natural ecosystems as a totality are seen as a complex web of interconnected elements, with the sound biological functioning of each being dependent on the sound biological functioning of the others. (This is the component referred to above as the great lesson that the science of ecology has taught us.) (3) Each individual organism is conceived of as a teleological center of life, pursuing its own good in its own way. (4) Whether we are concerned with standards of merit or with the concept of inherent worth, the claim that humans by their very nature are superior to other species is a groundless claim and, in the light of elements (1), (2), and (3) above, must be rejected as nothing more than an irrational bias in our own favor.

The conjunction of these four ideas constitutes the biocentric outlook on nature. In the remainder of this paper I give a brief account of the first three components, followed by a more detailed analysis of the fourth. I then conclude by indicating how this outlook provides a way of justifying the attitude of respect for nature.

VI. HUMANS AS MEMBERS OF THE EARTH'S COMMUNITY OF LIFE

We share with other species a common relationship to the Earth. In accepting the biocentric outlook we take the fact of our being an animal species to be a fundamental feature of our existence. We consider it an essential aspect of "the human condition." We do not deny the differences between ourselves and other species, but we keep in the forefront of our consciousness the fact that in relation to our planet's natural ecosystems we are but one species population among many. Thus we acknowledge our origin in the very same evolutionary process that gave rise to all other species and we recognize ourselves to be confronted with similar environmental challenges to those that confront them. The laws of genetics, of natural selection, and of adaptation apply equally to all of us as biological creatures. In this light we consider ourselves as one with them, not set apart from them. We, as well as they, must face certain basic conditions of existence that impose requirements on us for our survival and well-being. Each animal and plant is like us in having a good of its own. Although our human good (what is of true value in human life, including the exercise of individual autonomy in choosing our own particular value systems) is not like the good of a nonhuman animal or plant, it can no more be realized than their good can without the biological necessities for survival and physical health.

When we look at ourselves from the evolutionary point of view, we see that not only are we very recent arrivals on Earth, but that our emergence as a new species on the planet was originally an event of no particular importance to the entire scheme of things. The Earth was teeming with life long before we appeared. Putting the point metaphorically, we are relative newcomers, entering a home that has been the residence of others for hundreds of millions of years, a home that must now be shared by all of us together.

The comparative brevity of human life on Earth may be vividly depicted by imagining the geological time scale in spatial terms. Suppose we start with algae, which have been around for at least 600 million years. (The earliest protozoa actually predated this by several *billion* years.) If the time that algae have been here were represented by the length of a football field (300 feet), then the period during which sharks have been swimming in the world's oceans and spiders have been spinning their webs would occupy three quarters of the length of the field; reptiles would show up at about the center of the field; mammals would cover the last third of the field; hominids (mammals of the family *Hominidae*) the last two feet; and the species *Homo sapiens* the last six inches.

Whether this newcomer is able to survive as long as other species remains to be seen. But there is surely something presumptuous about the way humans look down on the "lower" animals, especially those that have become extinct. We consider the dinosaurs, for example, to be biological failures, though they existed on our planet for 65 million years. One writer has made the point with beautiful simplicity:

> We sometimes speak of the dinosaurs as failures; there will be time enough for that judgment when we have lasted even for one tenth as long. . . .[3]

The possibility of the extinction of the human species, a possibility which starkly confronts us in the contemporary world, makes us aware of another respect in which we should not consider ourselves privileged beings in relation to other species. This is the fact that the well-being of humans is dependent upon the ecological soundness and health of many plant and animal communities, while their soundness and health does not in the least depend upon human well-being. Indeed, from their standpoint the very existence of humans is quite unnecessary. Every last man, woman, and child could disappear from the face of the Earth without any significant detrimental consequence for the good of wild animals and plants. On the contrary, many of them would be greatly benefited. The destruction of their habitats by human "developments" would cease. The poisoning and polluting of their environment would come to an end. The Earth's land, air, and water would no longer be subject to the degradation they are now undergoing as the result of large-scale technology and uncontrolled population growth. Life communities in natural ecosystems would gradually return to their former healthy state. Tropical forests, for example, would again be able to make their full contribution to a life-sustaining atmosphere for the whole planet. The rivers, lakes, and oceans of the world would (perhaps) eventually become clean again. Spilled oil, plastic trash, and even radioactive waste might finally, after many centuries, cease doing their terrible work. Ecosystems would return to their proper balance, suffering only the disruptions of natural events such as volcanic eruptions and glaciation. From these the community of life could recover, as it has so often done in the past. But the ecological disasters now perpetrated on it by humans—disasters from which it might never recover—these it would no longer have to endure.

If, then, the total, final, absolute extermination of our species (by our own hands?) should take place and if we should not carry all the others with us into oblivion, not only would the Earth's community of life continue to exist, but in all probability its well-being would be enhanced. Our presence, in short, is not needed. If we were to take the standpoint of the community and give voice to its true interest, the ending of our six-inch epoch would most likely be greeted with a hearty "Good riddance!"

VII. THE NATURAL WORLD AS AN ORGANIC SYSTEM

To accept the biocentric outlook and regard ourselves and our place in the world from its perspective is to see the whole natural order of the Earth's biosphere as a complex but unified web of interconnected organisms, objects, and events. The ecological relationships between any community of living things and their environment form an organic whole of functionally interdependent parts. Each ecosystem is a small universe itself in which the interactions of its various species populations comprise an intricately woven network of cause–effect relations. Such dynamic but at the same time relatively stable structures as food chains, predator–prey relations, and plant succession in a forest are self-regulating, energy-recycling mechanisms that preserve the equilibrium of the whole.

As far as the well-being of wild animals and plants is concerned, this ecological equilibrium must not be destroyed. The same holds true of the well-being of humans. When one views the realm of nature from the perspective of the biocentric outlook, one never forgets that in the long run the integrity of the entire biosphere of our planet is essential to the realization of the good of its constituent communities of life, both human and nonhuman.

Although the importance of this idea cannot be overemphasized, it is by now so familiar and so widely acknowledged that I shall not further elaborate on it here. However, I do wish to point out that this "holistic" view of the Earth's ecological systems does not itself constitute a moral norm. It is a factual aspect of biological reality, to be understood as a set of causal connections in ordinary empirical terms. Its significance for humans is the same as its significance for nonhumans, namely, in setting basic conditions for the realization of the good of living things. Its ethical implications for our treatment of the natural environment lie entirely in the fact that our *knowledge* of these causal connections is an essential *means* to fulfilling the aims we set for ourselves in adopting the attitude of respect for nature. In addition, its theoretical implications for the ethics of respect for nature lie in the fact that it (along with the other elements of the biocentric outlook) makes the adopting of that attitude a rational and intelligible thing to do.

VIII. INDIVIDUAL ORGANISMS AS TELEOLOGICAL CENTERS OF LIFE

As our knowledge of living things increases, as we come to a deeper understanding of their life cycles, their interactions with other organisms, and the manifold ways in which they adjust to the environment, we become more fully aware of how each of them is carrying out its biological functions according to the laws of its species-specific nature. But besides this, our increasing knowledge and understanding also develop in us a sharpened awareness of the uniqueness of each individual organism. Scientists who have made careful studies of particular plants and animals, whether in the field or in laboratories, have often acquired a knowledge of their subjects as identifiable individuals. Close observation over extended periods of time has led them to an appreciation of the unique "personalities" of their subjects. Sometimes a scientist may come to take a special interest in a particular animal or plant, all the while remaining strictly objective in the gathering and recording of data. Nonscientists may likewise experience this development of interest when, as amateur naturalists, they make accurate observations over sustained periods of close acquaintance with an individual organism. As one becomes more and more familiar with the organism and its behavior, one becomes fully sensitive to the particular way it is living out its life cycle. One may become fascinated by it and even experience some involvement with its good and bad fortunes (that is, with the occurrence of

environmental conditions favorable or unfavorable to the realization of its good). The organism comes to mean something to one as a unique, irreplaceable individual. The final culmination of this process is the achievement of a genuine understanding of its point of view and, with that understanding, an ability to "take" that point of view. *Conceiving of it as a center of life, one is able to look at the world from its perspective.*

This development from objective knowledge to the recognition of individuality, and from the recognition of individuality to full awareness of an organism's standpoint, is a process of heightening our consciousness of what it means to be an individual living thing. We grasp the particularity of the organism as a teleological center of life, striving to preserve itself and to realize its own good in its own unique way,

It is to be noted that we need not be falsely anthropomorphizing when we conceive of individual plants and animals in this manner. Understanding them as teleological centers of life does not necessitate "reading into" them human characteristics. We need not, for example, consider them to have consciousness. Some of them may be aware of the world around them and others may not. Nor need we deny that different kinds and levels of awareness are exemplified when consciousness in some form is present. But conscious or not, all are equally teleological centers of life in the sense that each is a unified system of goal-oriented activities directed toward their preservation and well-being.

When considered from an ethical point of view, a teleological center of life is an entity whose "world" can be viewed from the perspective of *its* life. In looking at the world from that perspective we recognize objects and events occurring in its life as being beneficent, maleficent, or indifferent. The first are occurrences which increase its powers to preserve its existence and realize its good. The second decrease or destroy those powers. The third have neither of these effects on the entity. With regard to our human role as moral agents, we can conceive of a teleological center of life as a being whose standpoint we can take in making judgments about what events in the world are good or evil, desirable or undesirable. In making those judgments it is what promotes or protects the being's own good, not what benefits moral agents themselves, that sets the standard of evaluation. Such judgments can be made about anything that happens to the entity which is favorable or unfavorable in relation to its good. As was pointed out earlier, the entity itself need not have any (conscious) interest in what is happening to it for such judgments to be meaningful and true.

It is precisely judgments of this sort that we are disposed to make when we take the attitude of respect for nature. In adopting that attitude those judgments are given weight as reasons for action in our practical deliberation. They become morally relevant facts in the guidance of our conduct.

IX. THE DENIAL OF HUMAN SUPERIORITY

This fourth component of the biocentric outlook on nature is the single most important idea in establishing the justifiability of the attitude of respect for nature. Its central role is due to the special relationship it bears to the first three components of the outlook. This relationship will be brought out after the concept of human superiority is examined and analyzed.[4]

In what sense are humans alleged to be superior to other animals? We are different from them in having certain capacities that they lack. But why should these capacities be a mark of superiority? From what point of view are they judged to be signs of superiority and what sense of superiority is meant? After all, various nonhuman species have capacities that humans lack. There is the speed of a cheetah, the vision of an eagle, the agility of a monkey. Why should not these be taken as signs of *their* superiority over humans?

One answer that comes immediately to mind is that these capacities are not as *valuable* as the human capacities that are claimed to make us superior. Such uniquely human characteristics as rational thought, aesthetic creativity, autonomy and self-determination, and moral freedom, it might be held, have a higher value than the capacities found in other species. Yet we must ask: valuable to whom, and on what grounds?

The human characteristics mentioned are all valuable to humans. They are essential to the preservation and enrichment of our civilization and culture. Clearly it is from the human standpoint that they are being judged to be desirable and good. It is not difficult here to recognize a begging of the question. Humans are claiming human superiority from a strictly human point of view, that is, from a point of view in which the good of humans is taken as the standard of judgment. All we need to do is to look at the capacities of nonhuman animals (or plants, for that matter) from the standpoint of *their* good to find a contrary judgment of superiority. The speed of the cheetah, for example, is a sign of its superiority to humans when considered from the standpoint of the good of its species. If it were as slow a runner as a human, it would not be able to survive. And so for all the other abilities of nonhumans which further their good but which are lacking in humans. In each case the claim to human superiority would be rejected from a nonhuman standpoint.

. . . There is, however, another way of understanding the idea of human superiority. According to this interpretation, humans are superior to nonhumans not as regards their merits but as regards their inherent worth. Thus the claim of human superiority is to be understood as asserting that all humans, simply in virtue of their humanity, have *a greater inherent worth* than other living things.

The inherent worth of an entity does not depend on its merits.[5] To consider something as possessing inherent worth, we have seen, is to place intrinsic value on the realization of its good. This is done regardless of whatever particular merits it might have or might lack, as judged by a set of grading or ranking standards. In human affairs, we are all familiar with the principle that one's worth as a person does not vary with one's merits or lack of merits. The same can hold true of animals and plants. To regard such entities as possessing inherent worth entails disregarding their merits and deficiencies, whether they are being judged from a human standpoint or from the standpoint of their own species.

The idea of one entity having more merit than another, and so being superior to it in merit, makes perfectly good sense. Merit is a grading or ranking concept, and judgments of comparative merit are based on the different degrees to which things satisfy a given standard. But what can it mean to talk about one thing being superior to another in inherent worth? In order to get at what is being asserted in such a claim it is helpful first to look at the social origin of the concept of degrees of inherent worth.

The idea that humans can possess different degrees of inherent worth originated in societies having rigid class structures. Before the rise of modern democracies with their egalitarian outlook, one's membership in a hereditary class determined one's social status. People in the upper classes were looked up to, while those in the lower classes were looked down upon. In such a society one's social superiors and social inferiors were clearly defined and easily recognized.

Two aspects of these class-structured societies are especially relevant to the idea of degrees of inherent worth. First, those born into the upper classes were deemed more worthy of respect than those born into the lower orders. Second, the superior worth of upper class people had nothing to do with their merits nor did the inferior worth of those in the lower classes rest on their lack of merits. One's superiority or inferiority entirely derived from a social position one was born into. The modern concept of a meritocracy simply did not apply. One could not advance into a higher class by any sort of moral or nonmoral achievement. Similarly, an aristocrat held his title and all the privileges that went with it just because he was the eldest son of a titled nobleman. Unlike the bestowing of knighthood in contemporary Great Britain, one did not earn membership in the nobility by meritorious conduct.

We who live in modern democracies no longer believe in such hereditary social distinctions. Indeed, we would wholeheartedly condemn them on moral grounds as being fundamentally unjust. We have come to think of class systems as a paradigm of social injustice, it being a central principle of the democratic way of life that among humans there are no superiors and no inferiors. . . . That idea is incompatible with our notion of human equality based on the doctrine that all humans, simply in virtue of their humanity, have the same inherent worth. (The belief in universal human rights is one form that this egalitarianism takes.)

The vast majority of people in modern democracies, however, do not maintain an egalitarian outlook when it comes to comparing human beings with other living things. Most people consider our own species to be superior to all other species and this superiority is understood to be a matter of inherent worth, not merit. There may exist thoroughly vicious and depraved humans who lack all merit. Yet because they are human they are thought to belong to a higher class of entities than any plant or animal. That one is born into the species *Homo sapiens* entitles one to have lordship over those who are one's inferiors, namely, those born into other species. The parallel with hereditary social classes is very close. Implicit in this view is a hierarchical conception of nature according to which an organism has a position of superiority or inferiority in the Earth's community of life simply on the basis of its genetic background. The "lower" orders of life are looked down upon and it is considered perfectly proper that they serve the interests of those belonging to the highest order, namely humans. The intrinsic value we place on the well-being of our fellow humans reflects our recognition of their rightful position as our equals. No such intrinsic value is to be placed on the good of other animals, unless we choose to do so out of fondness or affection for them. But their well-being imposes no moral requirement on us. In this respect there is an absolute difference in moral status between ourselves and them.

This is the structure of concepts and beliefs that people are committed to insofar as they regard humans to be superior in inherent worth to all other species. . . . This structure of concepts and beliefs is completely groundless. If we accept the first three components of the biocentric outlook and from that perspective look at the major philosophical traditions which have supported that structure, we find it to be at bottom nothing more than the expression of an irrational bias in our own favor.

. . . That [it] is nothing more than a deep-seated prejudice is brought home to us when we look at our relation to other species in the light of the first three elements of the biocentric outlook. Those elements taken conjointly give us a certain overall view of the natural world and of the place of humans in it. When we take this view we come to understand other living things, their environmental conditions, and their ecological relationships in such a way as to awake in us a deep sense of our kinship with them as fellow members of the Earth's community of life. Humans and nonhumans alike are viewed together as integral parts of one unified whole in which all living things are functionally interrelated. Finally, when our awareness focuses on the individual lives of plants and animals, each is seen to share with us the characteristic of being a teleological center of life striving to realize its own good in its own unique way.

...Rejecting the notion of human superiority entails its positive counterpart: the doctrine of species impartiality. One who accepts that doctrine regards all living things as possessing inherent worth—the *same* inherent worth, since no one species has been shown to be either "higher" or "lower" than any other. Now we saw earlier that, insofar as one thinks of a living thing as possessing inherent worth, one considers it to be the appropriate object of the attitude of respect and believes that attitude to be the only fitting or suitable one for all moral agents to take toward it. . . .

X. MORAL RIGHTS AND THE MATTER OF COMPETING CLAIMS

I have not asserted anywhere in the foregoing account that animals or plants have moral rights. This omission was deliberate. I do not think that the reference class of the concept, bearer of moral rights, should be extended to include nonhuman living things. My reasons for taking this position, however, go beyond the scope of this paper. I believe I have been able to accomplish many of the same ends which those who ascribe rights to animals or plants wish to accomplish. There is no reason, moreover, why plants and animals, including whole species populations and life communities, cannot be accorded *legal* rights under my theory. To grant them legal protection could be interpreted as giving them legal entitlement to be protected, and this, in fact, would be a means by which a society that subscribed to the ethics of respect for nature could give public recognition to their inherent worth.

There remains the problem of competing claims, even when wild plants and animals are not thought of as bearers of moral rights. If we accept the bio-centric outlook and accordingly adopt the attitude of respect for nature as our ultimate moral attitude, how do we resolve conflicts that arise from our respect for persons in the domain of human ethics and our respect for nature in the domain of environmental ethics? This is a question that cannot adequately be dealt with here. My main purpose in this paper has been to try to establish a base point from which we can start working toward a solution to the problem. I have shown why we cannot just begin with an initial presumption in favor of the interests of our own species. It is after all within our power as moral beings to place limits on human population and technology with the deliberate intention of sharing the Earth's bounty with other species. That such sharing is an ideal difficult to realize even in an approximate way does not take away its claim to our deepest moral commitment.

NOTES

1. The conceptual links between an entity *having* a good, something being good *for* it, and events doing good to it are examined by G. H. Von Wright in *The Varieties of Goodness* (New York: Humanities Press, 1963), chaps. 3 and 5.

2. I have analyzed the nature of this commitment of human ethics in "On Taking the Moral Point of View," *Midwest Studies in Philosophy,* vol. 3, *Studies in Ethical Theory* (1978), pp. 35–61.

3. Stephen R. L. Clark, *The Moral Status of Animals* (Oxford: Clarendon Press, 1977), p. 112.

4. My criticisms of the dogma of human superiority gain independent support from a carefully reasoned essay by R. and V. Routley showing the many logical weaknesses in arguments for human-centered theories of environmental ethics. R. and V. Routley, "Against the Inevitability of Human Chauvinism," in K. E. Goodpaster and K. M. Sayre, eds., *Ethics and Problems of the 21st Century* (Notre Dame: University of Notre Dame Press, 1979), pp. 36–59.

5. For this way of distinguishing between merit and inherent worth, I am indebted to Gregory Vlastos, "Justice and Equality," in R. Brandt, ed., *Social Justice* (Englewood Cliffs, N.J.: Prentice-Hall, 1962), pp. 31–72.

Questions for Analysis

1. According to Taylor, every "organism, species population, and community of life has a good of its own." What does he mean by that claim? What importance does it have for environmental ethics?

2. Taylor says that inherent worth is not an objective property. He also says that the attitude of ultimate respect for nature is supported by a belief system that cannot be proven true. Why, then, should we adopt that attitude?

3. In discussing individual organisms as teleological centers of life, Taylor says that we can look at the world from a plant's point of view without engaging in "false anthropomorphizing." What does he mean by that? How is it possible?

4. Much of Taylor's argument against human superiority rests on the claim that inherent worth does not admit of degrees. Do you agree? Why or why not?

5. Though Taylor does not advocate giving nonhuman organisms moral rights, he does advocate giving them *legal* rights. What might his justification be for denying one but granting the other?

6. Is Taylor's individualistic view preferable to Leopold's holistic view?

People or Penguins

William F. Baxter

The following selection by William F. Baxter (1929–1998) presents an anthropocentric view of environmental issues. In contrast to Taylor, Baxter argues that Kantian respect should not be extended to nonhuman organisms. In contrast to Leopold, he argues that an economic approach to environmental issues is the correct one. Thus, he favors a cost-benefit analysis of environmental impact, where the economic costs and benefits involved are applicable to humans only. Baxter was a professor of law at Stanford University.

I start with the modest proposition that, in dealing with pollution, or indeed with any problem, it is helpful to know what one is attempting to accomplish. Agreement on how and whether to pursue a particular objective, such as pollution control, is not possible unless some more general objective has been identified and stated with reasonable precision. We talk loosely of having clean air and clean water, of preserving our wilderness areas, and so forth. But none of these is a sufficiently general objective: each is more accurately viewed as a means rather than as an end.

With regard to clean air, for example, one may ask, "how clean?" and "what does clean mean?" It is even reasonable to ask, "why have clean air?" Each of these questions is an implicit demand that

a more general community goal be stated—a goal sufficiently general in its scope and enjoying sufficiently general assent among the community of actors that such "why" questions no longer seem admissible with respect to that goal.

If, for example, one states as a goal the proposition that "every person should be free to do whatever he wishes in contexts where his actions do not interfere with the interests of other human beings," the speaker is unlikely to be met with a response of "why." The goal may be criticized as uncertain in its implications or difficult to implement, but it is so basic a tenet of our civilization—it reflects a cultural value so broadly shared, at least in the abstract—that the question "why" is seen as impertinent or imponderable or both.

I do not mean to suggest that everyone would agree with the "spheres of freedom" objective just stated. Still less do I mean to suggest that a society could subscribe to four or five such general objectives that would be adequate in their coverage to serve as testing criteria by which all other dis-agreements might be measured. One difficulty in the attempt to construct such a list is that each new goal added will conflict, in certain applications, with each prior goal listed; and thus each goal serves as a limited qualification on prior goals.

Without any expectation of obtaining unani-mous consent to them, let me set forth four goals that I generally use as ultimate testing criteria in attempting to frame solutions to problems of human organization. My position regarding pollution stems from these four criteria. If the criteria appeal to you and any part of what appears hereafter does not, our disagreement will have a helpful focus: which of us is correct, analytically, in supposing that his position on pollution would better serve these general goals. If the criteria do not seem acceptable to you, then it is to be expected that our more particular judgments will differ, and the task will then be yours to identify the basic set of criteria upon which your particular judgments rest.

My criteria are as follows:

1. The spheres of freedom criterion stated above.

2. Waste is a bad thing. The dominant feature of human existence is scarcity—our available resources, our aggregate labors, and our skill in employing both have always been, and will continue for some time to be, inadequate to yield to every man all the tangible and intangible satisfactions he would like to have. Hence, none of those resources, or labors, or skills, should be wasted—that is, employed so as to yield less than they might yield in human satisfactions.

3. Every human being should be regarded as an end rather than as a means to be used for the betterment of another. Each should be afforded dignity and regarded as having an absolute claim to an evenhanded application of such rules as the community may adopt for its governance.

4. Both the incentive and the opportunity to improve his share of satisfactions should be preserved to every individual. Preservation of incentive is dictated by the "no-waste" criterion and enjoins against the continuous,

totally egalitarian redistribution of satisfac-tions, or wealth; but subject to that constraint, everyone should receive, by continuous redistribution if necessary, some minimal share of aggregate wealth so as to avoid a level of privation from which the opportunity to improve his situation becomes illusory.

The relationship of these highly general goals to the more specific environmental issues at hand may not be readily apparent, and I am not yet ready to demonstrate their pervasive implications. But let me give one indication of their implica-tions. Recently scientists have informed us that use of DDT in food production is causing damage to the penguin population. For the present pur-poses let us accept that assertion as an indisputable scientific fact. The scientific fact is often asserted as if the correct implication—that we must stop agri-cultural use of DDT—followed from the mere statement of the fact of penguin damage. But plainly it does not follow if my criteria are employed.

My criteria are oriented to people, not pen-guins. Damage to penguins, or sugar pines, or geo-logical marvels is, without more, simply irrelevant. One must go further, by my criteria, and say: Penguins are important because people enjoy see-ing them walk about rocks; and furthermore, the well-being of people would be less impaired by halting use of DDT than by giving up penguins. In short, my observations about environmental prob-lems will be people-oriented, as are my criteria. I have no interest in preserving penguins for their own sake.

It may be said by way of objection to this posi-tion, that it is very selfish of people to act as if each person represented one unit of importance and nothing else was of any importance. It is undeni-ably selfish. Nevertheless I think it is the only ten-able starting place for analysis for several reasons. First, no other position corresponds to the way most people really think and act—i.e., corresponds to reality.

Second, this attitude does not portend any mas-sive destruction of nonhuman flora and fauna, for people depend on them in many obvious ways, and they will be preserved because and to the degree that humans do depend on them.

Third, what is good for humans is, in many respects, good for penguins and pine trees—clean air for example. So that humans are, in these respects, surrogates for plant and animal life.

Fourth, I do not know how we could administer any other system. Our decisions are either private or collective. Insofar as Mr. Jones is free to act privately, he may give such preferences as he wishes to other forms of life: he may feed birds in winter and do with less himself, and he may even decline to resist an advancing polar bear on the ground that the bear's appetite is more important than those portions of himself that the bear may choose to eat. In short my basic premise does not rule out private altruism to competing life-forms. It does rule out, however, Mr. Jones' inclination to feed Mr. Smith to the bear, however hungry the bear, however despicable Mr. Smith.

Insofar as we act collectively, on the other hand, only humans can be afforded an opportunity to participate in the collective decisions. Penguins cannot vote now and are unlikely subjects for the franchise—pine trees more unlikely still. Again each individual is free to cast his vote so as to benefit sugar pines if that is his inclination. But many of the more extreme assertions that one hears from some conservationists amount to tacit assertions that they are specially appointed representatives of sugar pines, and hence that their preferences should be weighted more heavily than the preferences of other humans who do not enjoy equal rapport with "nature." The simplistic assertion that agricultural use of DDT must stop at once because it is harmful to penguins is of that type.

Fifth, if polar bears or pine trees or penguins, like men, are to be regarded as ends rather than means, if they are to count in our calculus of social organization, someone must tell me how much each one counts, and someone must tell me how these life-forms are to be permitted to express their preferences, for I do not know either answer. If the answer is that certain people are to hold their proxies, then I want to know how those proxy-holders are to be selected: self-appointment does not seem workable to me.

Sixth, and by way of summary of all the foregoing, let me point out that the set of environmental issues under discussion—although they raise very complex technical questions of how to achieve any objective—ultimately raise a normative question: what *ought* we to do. Questions of *ought* are unique to the human mind and world—they are meaningless as applied to a nonhuman situation.

I reject the proposition that we *ought* to respect the "balance of nature" or to "preserve the environment" unless the reason for doing so, express or implied, is the benefit of man.

I reject the idea that there is a "right" or "morally correct" state of nature to which we should return. The word "nature" has no normative connotation. Was it "right" or "wrong" for the earth's crust to heave in contortion and create mountains and seas? Was it "right" for the first amphibian to crawl up out of the primordial ooze? Was it "wrong" for plants to reproduce themselves and alter the atmospheric composition in favor of oxygen? For animals to alter the atmosphere in favor of carbon dioxide both by breathing oxygen and eating plants? No answers can be given to these questions because they are meaningless questions.

All this may seem obvious to the point of being tedious, but much of the present controversy over environment and pollution rests on tacit normative assumptions about just such nonnormative phenomena: that it is "wrong" to impair penguins with DDT, but not to slaughter cattle for prime rib roasts. That it is wrong to kill stands of sugar pines with industrial fumes, but not to cut sugar pines and build housing for the poor. Every man is entitled to his own preferred definition of Walden Pond, but there is no definition that has any moral superiority over another, except by reference to the selfish needs of the human race.

From the fact that there is no normative definition of the natural state, it follows that there is no normative definition of clean air or pure water—hence no definition of polluted air—or of pollution—except by reference to the needs of man. The "right" composition of the atmosphere is one which has some dust in it and some lead in it and some hydrogen sulfide in it—just those amounts that attend a sensibly organized society thoughtfully and knowledgeably pursuing the greatest possible satisfaction for its human members.

The first and most fundamental step toward solution of our environmental problems is a clear recognition that our objective is not pure air or water but rather some optimal state of pollution. That step immediately suggests the question:

How do we define and attain the level of pollution that will yield the maximum possible amount of human satisfaction?

Low levels of pollution contribute to human satisfaction but so do food and shelter and education and music. To attain ever lower levels of pollution, we must pay the cost of having less of these other things. I contrast that view of the cost of pollution control with the more popular statement that pollution control will "cost" very large numbers of dollars. The popular statement is true in some senses, false in others; sorting out the true and false senses is of some importance. The first step in that sorting process is to achieve a clear understanding of the difference between dollars and resources. Resources are the wealth of our nation; dollars are merely claim checks upon those resources. Resources are of vital importance; dollars are comparatively trivial.

Four categories of resources are sufficient for our purposes: At any given time a nation, or a planet if you prefer, has a stock of labor, of technological skill, of capital goods, and of natural resources (such as mineral deposits, timber, water, land, etc.). These resources can be used in various combinations to yield goods and services of all kinds—in some limited quantity. The quantity will be larger if they are combined efficiently, smaller if combined inefficiently. But in either event the resource stock is limited, the goods and services that they can be made to yield are limited; even the most efficient use of them will yield less than our population, in the aggregate, would like to have.

If one considers building a new dam, it is appropriate to say that it will be costly in the sense that it will require x hours of labor, y tons of steel and concrete, and z amount of capital goods. If these resources are devoted to the dam, then they cannot be used to build hospitals, fishing rods, schools, or electric can openers. That is the meaningful sense in which the dam is costly.

Quite apart from the very important question of how wisely we can combine our resources to produce goods and services, is the very different question of how they get distributed—who gets how many goods? Dollars constitute the claim checks which are distributed among people and which control their share of national output. Dollars are nearly valueless pieces of paper except to the extent that they do represent claim checks to some fraction of the output of goods and services. Viewed as claim checks, all the dollars outstanding during any period of time are worth, in the aggregate, the goods and services that are available to be claimed with them during that period—neither more nor less.

It is far easier to increase the supply of dollars than to increase the production of goods and services—printing dollars is easy. But printing more dollars doesn't help because each dollar then simply becomes a claim to fewer goods, i.e., becomes worth less.

The point is this: many people fall into error upon hearing the statement that the decision to build a dam, or to clean up a river, will cost $X million. It is regrettably easy to say: "It's only money. This is a wealthy country, and we have lots of money." But you cannot build a dam or clean a river with $X million—unless you also have a match, you can't even make a fire. One builds a dam or cleans a river by diverting labor and steel and trucks and factories from making one kind of goods to making another. The cost in dollars is merely a shorthand way of describing the extent of the diversion necessary. If we build a dam for $X million, then we must recognize that we will have $X million less housing and food and medical care and electric can openers as a result.

Similarly, the costs of controlling pollution are best expressed in terms of the other goods we will have to give up to do the job. This is not to say the job should not be done. Badly as we need more housing, more medical care, and more can openers, and more symphony orchestras, we could do with somewhat less of them, in my judgment at least, in exchange for somewhat cleaner air and rivers. But that is the nature of the tradeoff, and analysis of the problem is advanced if that unpleasant reality is kept in mind. Once the trade-off relationship is clearly perceived, it is possible to state in a very general way what the optimal level of pollution is. I would state it as follows:

People enjoy watching penguins. They enjoy relatively clean air and smog-free vistas. Their health is improved by relatively clean water and air. Each of these benefits is a type of good or service. As a society we would be well advised to give up one washing machine if the resources that would have gone into that washing machine can yield greater human satisfaction when diverted into pollution control. We should give up one hospital if the resources thereby freed would yield more human satisfaction when devoted to elimination of noise in our cities. And so on, trade-off by trade-off, we should divert our productive capacities from the production of existing goods and services to the production of a cleaner, quieter, more pastoral nation up to—and no further than—the point at which we value more highly the next washing machine or hospital that we would have to do without than we value the next unit of environmental improvement that the diverted resources would create.

Now this proposition seems to me unassailable but so general and abstract as to be unhelpful—at least unadministerable in the form stated. It assumes we can measure in some way the incremental units of human satisfaction yielded by very different types of goods. The proposition must remain a pious abstraction until I can explain how this measurement process can occur. In subsequent chapters I will attempt to show that we can do this—in some contexts with great precision and in other contexts only by rough approximation. But I insist that the proposition stated describes the result for which we should be striving—and again, that it is always useful to know what your target is even if your weapons are too crude to score a bull's eye.

Questions for Analysis

1. According to Baxter, there is no right or wrong level of pollution independent of human needs. How does he support his claim? How would Taylor and Leopold respond?

2. Baxter argues that "the costs of controlling pollution are best expressed in terms of the other goods we will have to give up to do the job." What kinds of other goods does he include?

3. In viewing environmental decisions as trade-offs between environmental goals and other goods, Baxter argues that we should divert our resources to improve the environment until we value the next improvement less than "the next washing machine or hospital that we would have to do without." If the value we assign to each is based on adequate information, would this approach make for a sound environmental policy?

4. Baxter admits that there are serious difficulties in assigning economic values to all human satisfactions. Do those difficulties damage his argument?

An Ecocentric Environmental Ethic

J. Baird Callicott

The following selection is excerpted from J. Baird Callicott's longer essay, "The Search for an Environmental Ethic." In earlier sections, Callicott criticizes traditional ethical views for their inability to deal adequately with environmental problems. For the same reason, he also criticizes the "extensionist" ethics of philosophers like Peter Singer and Tom Regan (see Chapter 11), who argue that nonhuman animals deserve the same moral consideration that humans deserve.

From "The Search for an Environmental Ethic," in *Matters of Life and Death*, edited by Tom Regan. Copyright © 1980, 1986 by Random House, Inc. Reprinted by permission of McGraw-Hill Companies, Inc.

Callicott's **ecocentric** ethic is based on Aldo Leopold's land ethic. The principal concern of this selection is to defend Leopold's environmental holism against two charges—that it leads to unacceptable treatment of individuals and that it requires excessive sacrifice by humans. He concludes with a sketch of modern life in a world consistent with his views. Callicott is a professor of philosophy at the University of North Texas.

The stress upon the value of the biotic community is the distinguishing characteristic of the land ethic and its cardinal strength as an *adequate* environmental ethic. The land ethic directs us to take the welfare of nature—the diversity, stability, and integrity of the biotic community or, to mix metaphors, the health of the land organism—to be the standard of the moral quality, the rightness or wrongness, of our actions. Practically, this means that we should assess the "environmental impact" of any proposed project, whether it be a personal, corporate, or public undertaking, and choose that course of action which will enhance the diversity, integrity, beauty, and stability of the biotic community, the health and well-being of the land organism. Quite obviously, then, environmental problems, from billboards and strip-development to radioactive-waste generation and species extirpation, are directly addressed by the land ethic. It is specifically tailored to be an *adequate* environmental ethic.

THE DANGERS OF AN UNTEMPERED HOLISTIC ENVIRONMENTAL ETHIC

But, as with so many things, the cardinal strength of the land ethic is also its cardinal weakness. What are the moral (to say nothing of the economic) costs of the land ethic? Most seriously, it would seem to imply a draconian policy toward the human population, since almost all ecologists and environmentalists agree that, from the perspective of the integrity, diversity, and stability of the biotic community, there are simply too many people and too few redwoods, white pines, wolves, bears, tigers, elephants, whales, and so on. Philosopher William Aiken has recoiled in horror from the land ethic, since in his view it would imply that "massive human diebacks would be good. It is our species' duty to eliminate 90 percent of our numbers."[1] It would also seem to imply a merciless attitude toward nonhuman individual members of the biotic community. Sentient members of overabundant species, like rabbits and deer, may be (as actually presently they are) routinely culled, for the sake of the ecosystems of which they are a part, by hunting or other methods of liquidation. Such considerations have led philosopher Edward Johnson to complain that "we should not let the land ethic distract us from the concrete problems about the treatment of animals which have been the constant motive behind the animal liberation movement."[2] From the perspective of both humanism and its humane extension, the land ethic appears nightmarish in its own peculiar way. It seems more properly the "ethic" of a termitarium or beehive than of anything analogous to a human community. It appears richly to deserve Tom Regan's epithet "environmental fascism."

THE RELATION OF THE LAND ETHIC TO PRIOR ACCRETIONS

Despite Leopold's narrative drift away from attention to *members* of the biotic community to the *community per se* and despite some of Leopold's more radical exponents who have confrontationally stressed the holistic dimension of the land ethic, its theoretical foundations yield a subtler, richer, far more complex system of morals than simple environmental holism. The land ethic is the latest step in an evolutionary sequence, according to its own theoretical foundations. Each succeeding step in social–moral evolution—from the savage clan to the family of man—does not cancel or invalidate the earlier stages. Rather, each succeeding stage is layered over the earlier ones, which remain operative.

A graphic image of the evolution of ethics has been suggested by extensionist Peter Singer. Singer suggests we imagine the evolutionary development of ethics to be an "expanding circle."[3] According to this image, as the charmed circle of moral considerability expands to take in more and more beings, its previous boundaries disappear. Singer thus feels compelled by the logic of his

own theory to give as much weight to the interests of a person (or, for that matter, a sentient animal) halfway around the world as to the interests
of his own children! "I ought to give as much
weight to the interests of people in Chad or
Cambodia as I do to the interests of my family or
neighbors; and this means that if people in those
countries are suffering from famine and my money
can help, I ought to give and go on giving until the
sacrifices that I and my family are making begin to
match the benefits the recipients obtain from my
gifts."[4] When he chooses to give preference to his
own or his children's interests, he has, according to
his own account, morally failed. This is because
the basic moral logic of traditional Western humanism and its extensions rests moral considerability on
a criterion that is supposed to be both morally
relevant and *equally* present in the members of the
class of morally considerable beings. Hence, all
who equally qualify are *equally* considerable. The
circle expands as the criterion for moral considerability is changed in accordance with critical
discussion of it.

A similar but crucially different image of the
evolution of ethics has been suggested by Richard
Sylvan and Val Plumwood. According to them,

> What emerges is a picture of types of moral
> obligation as associated with a nest of rings or
> annular boundary classes. . . . In some cases
> there is no sharp division between the rings.
> But there is no single uniform privileged class
> of items [i.e., rational beings, sentient beings,
> living beings], no one base class, to which all
> and only moral principles directly apply.[5]

The evolutionary development of ethics is less
well represented by means of Singer's image of an
expanding circle, a single ballooning circumference,
within which moral principles *apply equally to all*
than by means of the image of annular tree rings in
which social structures and their correlative ethics
are nested in a graded, differential system. That I
am now a member of the global human community,
and hence have correlative moral obligations to all
mankind does not mean that I am no longer a member of my own family and citizen of my local community and of my country or that I am relieved of
the peculiar and special limitations on freedom of
action attendant upon these relationships.

THE PLACE OF HUMAN BEINGS IN THE LAND ETHIC

Therefore, just as the existence of a global human
community with its humanitarian ethic does not
submerge and override smaller, more primitive
human communities and their moral codes, neither does the newly discovered existence of a global
biotic community and its land ethic submerge and
override the global human community and its
humanitarian ethic. To seriously propose, then, that
to preserve the integrity, beauty, and stability of the
biotic community we ought summarily to eliminate
90 percent of the current human population is as
morally skewed as Singer's apparent belief that he
ought to spend 90 percent of his income relieving
the hunger of people in Chad and Cambodia and,
in consequence, to reduce himself and his own
family to a meager, ragged subsistence.

However, just as it is not unreasonable for one
to suppose that he or she has *some* obligation and
should make *some* sacrifice for the "wretched of the
earth," so it is not unreasonable to suppose that the
human community should assume *some* obligation
and make *some* sacrifice for the beleaguered and
abused biotic community. To agree that the human
population should not, in gross and wanton violation of our humanitarian moral code, be immediately reduced by deliberate acts of war or by equally
barbaric means does not imply that the human population should not be scaled down, as time goes on,
by means and methods that are conscionable from
a humanitarian point of view. How obligations across
the outermost rings of our nested sociomoral matrix
may be weighed and compared is admittedly uncertain—just as uncertain as how one should weigh
and compare one's duty, say, to one's family against
one's duty to one's country. In the remainder of this
essay, I shall go on to discuss some general considerations applying to this problem.

INTRA- AND INTERSPECIES RELATIONSHIPS IN THE LAND ETHIC

Although I have, for purposes of illustration, stressed
the differences between the evolved layers of *human*
society and thus the differences in their correlative
ethics, these differences pale in comparison with

the difference between any and all *human communities,* on the one hand, and the *biotic community,* on the other. While an Ihalmiute village in the remote wilds of the Arctic and the United States of America are both literally societies, the biotic community is a "society" only by analogy. Its form or structure is, in some respects, *like* and, in other respects, *very unlike* that of a human community or society. . . .

Let us recall, once again, that energy is the "currency" of the "economy" of nature, the "coin" of the realm in the biotic community, and further, that energy is transferred by means of what ecologists euphemistically call phagic or trophic relations (more bluntly, by one thing *eating* another). The extensionist approach to an environmental ethic is utterly incapable of countenancing intrinsic value or moral considerability for wholes. Moreover, for the community per se and its various subsystems and populations, it cannot take into account the fundamental moral differences between intraspecies and interspecies "social" relationships. Extensionists contemplating the "expanding circle" thus think that since it is wrong to kill and eat a human being, a fellow member of the human community, it must also be wrong to kill and eat a fellow member of the expanded moral community. Hence, first-phase extensionists (animal liberationists/rightists) insist that human beings have a moral obligation to become vegetarians. Second-phase extensionists, life-principle extensionists (or plant liberationists), wonder if it is permissible for people to eat at all.

The land ethic requires neither vegetarianism, at least not for the same reasons, nor certainly self-starvation as moral imperatives (although a vegetarian diet might for other reasons, reasons I shall explain [below], contribute to the integrity, stability, and beauty of the biotic community). To argue that since it is wrong to kill and eat a human being, it is wrong to kill and eat, say, a rabbit or deer, is, from the evolutionary ethical sequence here recommended, analogous to arguing that since it is wrong for one not to give one's personal attention and affection to one's own children, it is wrong not to give equal personal attention and affection to all children. In neither instance do the precepts of the ethic reflect or nurture the structure of the community that is correlative to it.

So, if the land ethic does not translate the precepts of the humanitarian or humanistic ethic, *simpliciter,*

through the next step in the sequence, what provision does the land ethic make for nonhuman members of the biotic community *individually?* Leopold is quite clear about what the land ethic requires vis-à-vis the ecosystem or biotic community as a whole—the preservation of its diversity, integrity, and stability. But what about individual plants and animals?

THE PLACE OF INDIVIDUAL NONHUMANS IN THE LAND ETHIC

Richard Sylvan and Val Plumwood have developed the view that Leopold briefly suggests, namely, that an ecosystemic ethic primarily provides not rights but *respect* for individual nonhuman members of the biotic community. Although the concept of respect is singular and simple, its practical implications are varied and complex. These thinkers further suggest that American Indian environmental attitudes and values provide a well-developed, rich exemplar of *respectful* participation in the economy of nature, a participation that permits human beings morally to eat and otherwise consumptively to utilize their fellow citizens of the organic society:

> The view that the land, animals, and the natural world should be treated with *respect* was a common one in many hunting–gathering societies . . . Respect adds a moral dimension to relations with the natural world . . . The conventional wisdom of Western society tends to offer a false dichotomy of use versus respectful non-use . . . of using animals, for example, in the ways characteristic of large-scale mass-production farming . . . *or* on the other hand of not making use of animals at all . . . What is left out of this choice is the alternative the Indians . . . recognized . . . of limited and respectful use. . . .[6]

A great deal of controversy has surrounded the hypothesis of an American Indian land ethic. Recent studies, empirically based upon actual cultural materials, have shown beyond reasonable doubt that at least some American Indian cultures did in fact have an ecosystemic or environmental ethic *and* that such an ethic maps conceptually upon the Leopold land ethic.[7] In other words, some American Indian cultures—among them, for example, the Ojibwa of the western Great Lakes—represented the plants and animals of their environment as engaged in *social* and *economic* intercourse with one another and with human beings. And such a social picture of human–environment interaction gave rise to correlative moral attitudes and behavioral restraints. The Ojibwa cultural narratives (myths, stories, and tales), which served as the primary vehicles of enculturation or education, repeatedly stress that animals, plants, and even rocks and rivers (natural entities that Western culture regards as inanimate) are *persons* engaged in reciprocal, mutually beneficial exchange with human beings. A cardinal precept embellished again and again in these narratives is that nonhuman natural entities, both individually and as species, must be treated with respect and restraint. The Ojibwa were primarily a hunting-gathering people, which perforce involved them in killing animals as well as plants for food, clothing, and shelter. But they nevertheless represented the animals and plants of their biotic community as *voluntarily* participating in a mannerized economic exchange with people who, for their part, gave tokens of gratitude and reimbursement and offered guest friendship.

For example, in one such Ojibwa story called "The Woman Who Married a Beaver," we find a particularly succinct statement of this portrait of the human–animal relationship. Here is an excerpt from the story:

> Now and then by a person would they be visited; then they would go to where the person lived, whereupon the person would slay the beavers, yet they really did not kill them; back home would they come again . . . in the same way as people are when visiting one another, so were the beavers in their mental attitude toward people. . . . They were very fond of the tobacco that was given them by the people; at times they were also given clothing by the people.
>
> When finally the woman returned to her own (human) kin, she was wont to say, "Never speak you ill of a beaver . . . ! Just the same as the feelings of one who is disliked, so is the feeling of the beaver. And he who never speaks ill of a beaver is very much loved by it; in the same way as people often love one another, so is one held in the mind of the beaver; particularly lucky then is one at killing beavers."[8]

MODERN LIFE IN ACCORDANCE WITH AN ECOSYSTEMIC ENVIRONMENTAL ETHIC

Of course, most people today do not live by hunting and gathering. Nevertheless, the general ideal provided by American Indian cultures of respectful, restrained, mutually beneficial human use of the environment is certainly applicable in today's context. An ecosystemic environmental ethic does not prohibit human use of the environment; it requires, rather, that that use be subject to two ethical limitations. The first is holistic, the second individualistic.

The first requires that human use of the environment, as nearly as possible, should enhance the diversity, integrity, stability, and beauty of the biotic community. Biologist René Dubos has argued that Western Europe was, prior to the industrial revolution, biologically richer *as a result* of human settlement and cultivation.[9] The creation and cultivation of small fields, hedgerows, and forest edges measurably (objectively and quantitatively) enhanced the diversity and integrity and certainly the beauty of the preindustrial European landscape. Ethnobotanist Gary Nabhan has recently drawn a similar picture of the Papago inhabitation of the Sonoran desert.[10] Human occupation and use of the environment from the perspective of the quality of the environment as a whole does not *have* to be destructive. On the contrary, it can be, as both hunter–gatherers and yeoman farmers have proved, mutually beneficial.

The second, individualistic ethical limitation on human use of the environment requires that trees cut for shelter or to make fields, animals slain for food or for fur, and so on should be thoughtfully selected, skillfully and humanely dispatched, and carefully used so as to neither waste nor degrade them. The *individual* plant, animal, or even rock or river consumed or transformed by human use deserves to be used respectfully.

Surely we can envision an eminently livable, modern, systemic, *civilized* technological society well adapted to and at peace and in harmony with its organic environment. Human technological civilization can live not merely in peaceful coexistence but in benevolent symbiosis with nature. Is our current *mechanical* technological civilization the only one imaginable? Aren't there alternative technologies? Isn't it possible to envision, for example, a human civilization based upon nonpolluting solar energy for domestic use, manufacturing, and transportation and small-scale, soil-conserving organic agriculture? There would be fewer material *things* and more *services, information,* and opportunity for aesthetic and recreational *activities;* fewer people and more bears; fewer parking lots and more wilderness. I think it is possible. It is a vision shared with individual variations by designer Ian McHarg, biologist René Dubos, poets Wendell Berry and Gary Snyder, and philosophers Holmes Rolston and William Aiken, to mention only a few.

In the meantime, while such an adaptive organic civilization gradually evolves out of our present grotesque mechanical civilization, the most important injunction of ecosystemic ethics remains the one stressed by Leopold—subject, of course, to the humanitarian, humane, arid life-respecting qualifications that, as I have just argued, are theoretically consistent with it. We should strive to preserve the diversity, stability, and integrity of the biotic community.

Before ending, it is appropriate to ask what the implications of an ecocentric ethic would be for our daily lives. After all, one value of this ethic, no less than any other, is that it gives meaning to choices that otherwise remain unconscious or arbitrary. If as I have claimed, an ecocentric ethic is the most practicable environmental ethic, how does it actually inform our real-life choices?

Integrating an ecocentric ethic into our lives would provide new criteria for choices we make everyday in virtually every arena of our lives. Some of these choices are obvious; others, less so.

Most obviously, because a vegetarian diet, more directly and efficiently than a meat-centered diet, conducts solar energy into human bodies, the practice of vegetarianism could not only help reduce human hunger and animal suffering, it would free more land and solar energy for the restoration of natural communities.[11] (Note that eating wild game, respectfully, lawfully, and humanely harvested, would be an exception to the vegetarian implications of ecocentric ethics. Only grain-fed, domestic livestock should in general be avoided.)

Above all, one should try to avoid fast-food beef (McDonald's, Hardee's, and the like) made mostly from the imported carcasses of cattle, not only

because consuming such food contributes to the political and economic causes of hunger in the countries from which it is exported, but also because it is produced on lands once covered by rain forests.[12] Hence, the consumption of such foods not only implicates one (in all probability) in the destructive politics of world hunger and the disrespectful use of animals, it implicates one (almost certainly) in the extinction of endemic species (those specifically adapted to particular rain-forest habitats).

But what we eat is only the most obvious link between our daily choices and the integrity of the biotic community of which we are part. In a multitude of other roles, our choices either contribute to its regeneration or its continued ruin. As *consumers,* do we weigh our purchases according to the environmental consequences of their production? As *students,* do we utilize our learning time to hone our knowledge and sensibilities so as to more effectively live an ecocentric ethic? As *citizens,* of both a nation and a community, do we elect leaders whose policies ignore the need for environmental protection and reparation? As *workers,* do we choose to be employed by corporations whose activities degrade the environment? As *parents and individuals whose opinions necessarily influence others,* do we work to impart to others an understanding of the importance of an ecocentric ethic? As *decisionmakers over resources*—from real estate to other large or small assets—do we assume responsibility for their use? Or do we simply turn a blind eye, allowing others to use them for environmentally destructive ends?

Asking ourselves such questions, we discover that the implications of an ecocentric ethic cannot be reduced to one or even several major life choices. Rather, the contribution of an ecocentric ethic is to be found in the myriad of mundane, even banal decisions we make everyday. A grounding in an ecocentric ethic would thus shape the entire unfolding of one's life.

The second most serious moral issue of our times—second only to our individual and collective responsibility to prevent thermonuclear holocaust—is our responsibility to preserve the biological diversity of the earth. Later, when an appropriately humble, sane, ecocentric civilization comes into being, as I believe it will, its government and citizens will set about rehabilitating this bruised and tattered planet. For their work, they must have as great a library of genetic material as it is possible for us to save. Hence, it must be our immediate goal to prevent further destruction of the biosphere, to save what species we can, and to preserve the biotic diversity and beauty that remains.

NOTES

1. William Aiken, "Ethical Issues in Agriculture," in Tom Regan, ed., *Earthbound: New Introductory Essays in Environmental Ethics*. (New York: Random House, 1984), p. 269.

2. Edward Johnson, "Animal Liberation vs. the Land Ethic," *Environmental Ethics* 3 (1981): 271.

3. Peter Singer, *The Expanding Circle: Ethics and Sociobiology.* (New York: Farrar, Straus & Giroux, 1982).

4. Ibid., p. 153.

5. Richard Routley and Val Routley, "Human Chauvinism and Environmental Ethics," p. 107.

6. Ibid., pp. 178–179.

7. Cf. Thomas W. Overholt and J. Baird Callicott, *Clothed-in-Fur and Other Tales: An Introduction to an Ojibwa World View.* (Washington, D.C.: University Press of America, 1982), and J. Baird Callicott, "American Indian and Western European Attitudes Toward Nature: An Overview," *Environmental Ethics* 4 (1982): 293–318.

8. Ibid., pp. 74–75.

9. Cf. René Dubos, "Franciscan Conservation and Benedictine Stewardship," in David and Eileen Spring, eds., *Ecology and Religion in History.* (New York: Harper & Row, 1974), pp. 114–136.

10. Gary Nabhan, *The Desert Smells Like Rain.* San Francisco: Northpoint, 1982.

11. Frances Moore Lappé, *Diet for a Small Planet* (New York: Ballantine Books, 1982).

12. Frances Moore Lappé and Joseph Collins, *Food First: Beyond the Myth of Scarcity* (New York: Ballantine Books, 1979).

Questions for Analysis

1. What does Callicott mean when he says that the land ethic doesn't replace traditional ethics but is joined to it?

2. Callicott says that the land ethic does not require vegetarianism for traditional reasons but may require that we not eat certain kinds of meat for other reasons. What other reasons does he have in mind? What kinds of meat should we avoid eating?

3. What lesson does Callicott want us to learn from the Ojibwa story, "The Woman Who Married a Beaver"?

4. Does Callicott's ecocentric ethic avoid the "nightmarish" aspect that some people see in Leopold's land ethic? Why or why not?

CASE PRESENTATION

A Metaphor for the Energy Debate

In the worst oil spill in U.S. history, the *Exxon Valdez* tanker spilled 11 million gallons of crude oil into Alaska's Prince William Sound. The March 24, 1989, spill affected more than 1,000 miles of shoreline, including three national wildlife refuges, and left many thousands of animals dead, including an estimated 100,000 birds and 1,000 sea otters.

At the time of the spill, the oil industry had been hoping that the federal government would open the coastal plain of Alaska's Arctic National Wildlife Refuge to drilling. Two hundred and fifty miles north of the Arctic Circle, this tundra area is inhabited by caribou and musk oxen. Since only a few hundred Eskimos also live there, its 19 million acres are practically untouched by humans. The coastal plain area of the preserve, which covers 1.5 million acres, may also be home to the largest untapped oil reserve in the country. A five-year study by the Department of the Interior had reported in 1987 that the plain presented "the best single opportunity to increase significantly domestic oil production." But after the massive public outrage sparked by the *Exxon Valdez* spill, opening the plain to drilling was politically unthinkable.

A year and a half later, the unthinkable suddenly became thinkable when Iraq invaded Kuwait and the flow of oil from the two Persian Gulf countries was halted. Public attention quickly focused on U.S. dependence on foreign oil, and with the renewed attention came a renewal of the drilling debate. In the words of Alaska's Governor Steve Cowper, who noted that Alaska was both the country's wilderness and major source of energy, "This is a metaphor for the energy debate."

That debate, and the refuge's centrality to it, continues to this day, reaching another peak in the year 2000. After years of decline, energy prices suddenly soared to near record levels, and the Clinton administration, bowing to public pressure, released oil from the strategic oil reserve in an effort to lower fuel prices. Once again, concern grew over U.S. dependence on foreign oil, and the question of drilling in

the refuge became a major issue in that year's presidential election campaign. George W. Bush, the eventual winner of the election in a very close race, campaigned in favor of drilling. Gale Norton, his selection to head the Department of the Interior, had also voiced support for it.

To those who favor drilling, the plain is a frozen desert with significant potential to strengthen national security and improve the economy of the northern part of the state. To those who oppose drilling, the plain is a magnificent wilderness that must be protected from aesthetic and ecological damage. And while drilling proponents point to the Department of the Interior's conclusion that development of the plain would have no significant environmental impact, opponents continue to challenge the report in the courts.

Questions for Analysis

1. Many people consider reliance on foreign oil a threat to national security. Options for reducing U.S. reliance include energy conservation, alternative fuels, and increased domestic drilling. Should drilling be allowed in areas currently protected by federal law?

2. Oil companies and the Department of the Interior claim that drilling in the coastal plain will not harm the environment. The environmentalists dispute the claim but also argue that aesthetic damage will occur in any case. How much weight should aesthetics be given when balanced against energy needs and economic concerns?

3. The Arctic National Wildlife Refuge is isolated, generally considered less attractive than many other protected areas, and rarely visited by outsiders. Do those factors improve the case of drilling proponents, or are they irrelevant to the dispute?

4. Debate also surrounds the issue of new drilling off the coasts of California and Florida. Given our dependence on foreign oil, should offshore drilling be increased in those areas?

CASE PRESENTATION
The Spotted Owl

On June 22, 1990, the U.S. Fish and Wildlife Service declared the northern spotted owl a threatened species. Under the Endangered Species Act of 1973, the declaration made it illegal to harm the owl or its habitat, the Pacific Northwest forests.

Though environmentalists hailed the declaration, other groups, most notably the timber industry, objected. The Pacific Northwest forests are home to giant cedars, Douglas firs, and redwood trees, and the

timber industry constituted a large portion of the economies of Washington, Oregon, and northern California. Of the seventeen national forests involved, the timber industry cleared 70,000 acres annually. Under a plan proposed by federal biologists, 4 million acres were to be added to the 1.5 million acres already off limits to logging.

Like many such disputes, this one pitted environmental concerns against economic ones. On the one side was not only the future of the spotted owls—which were down to 3,000 mating pairs—but the future of the forests, which had already lost 90 percent of their ancient trees. On the other side was the future of the area's economy. According to government estimates, 28,000 jobs would be lost over a ten-year period. According to industry officials' estimates, the number could be as high as 50,000.

Four days later, the Bush administration, which initially said it would not interfere with plans to protect the owl's habitat, reversed itself. Instead of going ahead with the original plans, it decided to delay protection of the forests while it set up a commission to study ways of balancing the interests of the logging industry and the owls. It also decided to seek changes in the Endangered Species Act to make it easier to permit some species to diminish in order to avoid severe economic consequences. As the law stood at the time (and still does), such permission could be given only by a committee of federal agency heads, informally known as the "God Committee." Because of the difficulties involved in convening a meeting of the committee and the time involved in coming to a decision, the procedure is rarely used.

Neither side was pleased by the administration's plan to delay a solution to the problem. Environmentalists claimed that the administration was declaring war on the Endangered Species Act, while the timber industry argued that the delay would aggravate the region's economic uncertainty. Then, in 1991, a federal judge in Seattle ordered an end to the logging, ruling that the Bush administration was in violation of federal laws. Judge William Dryer also ordered the government to devise an environmental plan for the region. Until an acceptable plan was presented to him, the ban on logging would remain.

The issue wasn't settled until December 1994, when the same judge gave final approval to a plan proposed fifteen months earlier by the newly inaugurated Clinton administration. Under that plan, which the administration hailed as a way to protect the region's economy as well as its natural habitats, logging resumed at a reduced level. The plan also included restoration projects for damaged forests and streams in addition to other forms of economic aid to the region. Once again, neither side was satisfied, especially the timber industry, which vowed to continue its battle over the Endangered Species Act in Congress.

Questions for Analysis

1. To what extent should economic impact be considered when seeking a plan to protect an endangered species or a forest area?

2. Since most of the timber harvested in the seventeen northwestern forests is exported to other countries, closing an additional 4 million acres to foresting will not affect lumber supplies or building costs in the United States. Is that a relevant factor in deciding whether to close off the acres to logging?

3. Environmental groups had been trying to save the Pacific Northwest forests long before the spotted owl was declared a threatened species. What economic costs should we be willing to allow to protect our forests, even when diminishing them does not affect a threatened species?

4. Should it be easier or more difficult to allow a species to become extinct in order to prevent severe economic harm?

CASE PRESENTATION

Environmental Resistance: The Chipko Movement and the Earth Liberation Front

The term *tree hugger* has long been used as a term of derision by anti-conservationists. But to many ecofeminist activists—women who see feminism and envi-ronmentalism as closely connected fronts of the same struggle—a group of literal tree huggers in India has served as a source of both inspiration and tactics.

The Chipko (hugging) movement, as it is known, began in 1973 in the Indian village of Gopeshwar. The occasion was the arrival of a group of loggers to chop down 300 ash trees for a sporting goods company. Here is how ecofeminist Pamela Philipose describes what happened next:

> [The villagers] walked in a procession, beating drums and singing traditional songs. They had decided to hug the trees that the laborers, hired by the company, were to axe. The agents of the sports company had to retreat in the face of the unexpected onslaught.[1]

Although women were enthusiastic participants in this first Chipko demonstration, they acted along with equally enthusiastic male villagers. But later demonstrations were carried out by women alone. Philipose discusses one 1980 incident in which the women of another village acted in defiance of the all-male village council, which had agreed to let the Horticultural Department chop down an oak forest in exchange for various civic improvements.

> . . . the women in the village decided they would protect the oak forest at any cost. The men were so incensed by this that they warned the women they would be killed if they defied the council's decision. Undeterred, a large

number of women went ahead, held a Chipko demonstration, and saved the forest.[2]

From Chipko demonstrations, the women moved on to more conventional political activities, including membership in village councils and the creation of committees to save their forests. Thus, tree hugging provided a catalyst for enhancing the participation of women in the civic affairs of India.

Tree hugging, of course, is a very gentle form of environmental resistance. Far less gentle in its tactics is the Earth Liberation Front, an American ecoterrorist group that has claimed responsibility for a number of arson fires in the American West. The group's most notorious attack came in October 1998, when it set a series of seven fires at the top of Colorado's Vail Mountain, home to the one of the world's most popular ski resorts. The reported damage to buildings and chairlifts was $12 million.

Vail Resorts had just begun clearing trees for a controversial 885-acre expansion when the group attacked. The planned expansion had sparked opposition from many environmentalists and neighboring residents because of a government program to reintroduce the lynx to the Colorado Rockies. The expansion site overlooks a national forest area designated as a habitat for the cats, and opponents feared that its development would endanger the success of the reintroduction. The Earth Liberation Front agreed. An e-mail message claiming responsibility for the fires said, "Putting profits ahead of Colorado's wildlife will not be tolerated."

---

1. "Women Act: Women and Environmental Protection in India," *Radical Environmentalism,* Peter C. List, ed. (Belmont, CA: Wadsworth, 1992), p. 215.

2. *Ibid.*, p. 216.

Questions for Analysis

1. Among the civic improvements promised by the Horticultural Department were a paved road, a hospital, a school, and electricity for the village. Under those circumstances, should the women have prevented the felling of the forest? More generally, how should we decide when environmental civil disobedience is justified?

2. Many ecofeminists see the Chipko movement as the interweaving of struggles against four kinds of domination—of women, the environment, people of color, and Third World nations. All four, they say, are different aspects of the struggle against the dominating power of Western white males. Do you agree?

3. Many ecofeminists argue that women, whether because of biology or their assigned roles in male-dominated societies, have a closer connection to nature than men. Do you agree?

4. Reintroducing lynx to the Colorado Rockies has proven more difficult than expected. Few cats have managed to survive. Given the difficulty, should Vail Resorts have been permitted to interfere with their habitat?

5. Can you think of circumstances that would justify an act of ecoterrorism like the Earth Liberation Front's?

CASE PRESENTATION
The Wildlands Project[1]

What will it take to preserve the biodiversity of North America? What must we do to prevent further loss of species on the continent? How much land must we set aside to protect existing species?

One startling answer comes from the Wildlands Project, which was presented at the seventh annual meeting of the Society for Conservation Biology on June 11, 1993: Roughly one-fourth of the continent must be returned to wilderness ("core reserves"), and roughly another fourth must be set aside for "buffer zones" and "corridors," where human activity would be severely restricted.

According to the project's architects, the vast wilderness areas are needed for two reasons. First, many species, the big carnivores especially, require large home ranges. (A single grizzly bear, for instance, requires seventy-six square kilometers (about forty-eight square miles) of roadless land.) Second, the wilderness areas must be large enough to maintain as many members of such species as are needed to guarantee their survival.

The purpose of the buffer zones is to prevent edges, sudden transformations from wilderness to human-use areas, which present multiple dangers to species on the wilderness side. Each buffer zone will permit gradations of human activity. The area closest to the core reserve will allow relatively harmless activities like hiking. Moving outward, other buffer areas will allow limited logging and low-density housing. The corridors will link neighboring core reserves, providing safe passage for species with small populations in each and thereby increasing their chances of survival.

To get an idea of how radical the project is, consider that only 4.7 percent of U.S. land is now wilderness and that the project's architects estimate that it would take about 200 years to implement. The costs would be enormous, of course. Not only would countless miles of roads have to be torn up, but large numbers of humans would have to be relocated as well. The project's Florida plan, for example, turns half of Miami into a core reserve and the other half into a buffer zone. It also turns half of Orlando into a corridor.

Then again, the project's fundamental idea—ending the fragmentation of wildlife preserves into small areas that are isolated from one another—is not at all radical. In fact, government agencies have already begun to think seriously about it. To take just one example, the Fish and Wildlife Service plans to create a network of large preserves in Montana and Idaho to protect the grizzly bear.

---

1. The information comes from "The High Cost of Biodiversity," by Charles C. Mann and Mark L. Plummer, in *Science* 260 (June 25, 1993), 1868–1871.

Questions for Analysis

1. Is a plan like the Wildlands Project politically or economically feasible?

2. Does it make sense to implement the project in sparsely populated states like Idaho and to try scaled-back versions in densely populated states like Florida?

3. One assumption of the project is that humans and other species cannot live together compatibly. That's why so much land must be set aside for other species. Do you agree? Does biodiversity really require such a drastic plan?

4. What would life in North America be like if the project were implemented? How many changes do you think implementation would bring?

5. Is the goal of saving existing species important enough to justify implementing the project?

Afterword

More than one cynic has claimed that logical arguments are nothing but rationalizations of our prejudices. And there is, unfortunately, some truth to that claim, at least when it comes to people who spout reason but refuse to listen to reason. But when we are truly open to the arguments of others, the claim clearly misses, especially when we allow ourselves to be convinced by compelling arguments and consequently change our minds.

Now that your course in applied ethics is finished, it might be wise to ask yourself a few questions about it. Did the arguments you came across, either in class or in this book, cause you to reevaluate your positions on some topics? Did any one of them cause you to soften a given position? Cause you to change your mind completely? If you can answer yes to any or all of these questions, the course has served you well, regardless of your grade. If you cannot, you might want to ask yourself another question. Why can't you? And if your quick answer is that you were right all along, you might want to search for a not-so-quick one.

That's one point worth making at the end of your course. Another concerns all the topics you didn't cover, including some in this book (no single-semester course can cover them all) and those not in this book. (For reasons of space and format, we could not include every possible issue in applied ethics.) The latter include questions about "political correctness," say, and about sexual harassment, and the extent of our obligations to starving peoples throughout the world; also about healthcare, scientific experimentation, genetic engineering; all that, plus the many issues we can't anticipate but which are sure to arise over the years. Like the issues you did cover, each of them is difficult, involving complex matters of fact, morality, and often law. We hope your experiences in this course have prepared you to deal with them in a thorough, dispassionate way and maybe to reevaluate your views on some of them.

Finally, we hope the course has been a real eye-opener for you. Even if you changed your mind about nothing, we hope you at least were struck by the complexities of the issues you studied, the many ingenious approaches to them you encountered, and the reasonableness of your opponents' positions.

Glossary

abolitionist   Someone who advocates doing away with a particular practice, such as the death penalty.

active euthanasia   The act of painlessly putting to death persons suffering from incurable conditions or diseases.

ad hominem **argument**   An **argument** that relies on attacking the opponent rather than the opponent's argument. When the attack is irrelevant to whether we should accept the opponent's argument, it is considered a **fallacy.**

anthropocentric   Centering on human beings, or regarding human beings as central to any larger group. In ethics, it means centering on human welfare or regarding the environment as important only as it affects human welfare.

argument   A collection of statements containing a conclusion and supporting statements (also called *evidence, reasons, grounds,* or *premises*) whose purpose is to show that the conclusion is true or likely to be true.

argument by analogy   An **argument** that concludes that two different things are alike in some ways because they are alike in some other ways. When such an argument fails to make its case, it is considered both a **faulty analogy** and a **fallacy.**

assisted suicide   Suicide by a patient, with assistance from a physician, usually by prescribing a lethal dose of drugs.

autonomy   Independence, particularly from the control of outside forces. In philosophy, it refers to the capacity to act on our choices, where these choices are the product of our own goals, desires, and reasoning powers. To have this capacity is to be an autonomous being.

biocentric   Centering on the *biosphere,* or the earth's ecological system. In ethics, it means regarding the health of the ecological system as central rather than the welfare of humans.

biotic community   In the philosophy of Aldo Leopold and his followers, a community made up of all members of the ecological system, including water, soil, and air as well as living things.

capitalism   An economic system in which the means of production are in private hands and economic decisions are made by private individuals in response to market forces.

casuistic   Determining what is right and wrong by appeal to principles in ethics.

categorical imperative   In the philosophy of Kant, a command that applies to all rational beings independent of their desires; a command they ought to follow whether they want to or not.

causal generalization   The conclusion that one thing causes another because of observations that the first has been followed by the other.

certiorari   Agreement by an appeals court to review the decision of a lower court.

charity, principle of   Understanding the arguments of opponents in the most reasonable or plausible way possible to give them a fair hearing.

civil union   A formal partnership between two people with some, but not necessarily all, of the rights of a married couple, as recognized by a governmental authority.

clone   An exact genetic copy of a cell, plant, or animal.

consequentialist   Ethical reasoning that looks to the consequences of alternative actions to determine which is right.

contractarianism   An ethical theory based on appeal to a social contract entered into voluntarily.

counterexample   An example that shows a generalization to be false or a rule of reasoning to be invalid.

cultural relativism   In ethics, the view that moral truths are not absolutely true but are relative to a particular society, that whether an act is right or wrong depends on the moral norms of society and not on an absolute standard.

deductive argument   An **argument** that claims to follow **truth-preserving** rules.

deductive logic   The area of logic that deals with **deductive arguments.**

deterrence   The preventing or discouraging of an act, often by fear or doubt.

difference principle   In the philosophy of John Rawls, the principle that determines what kinds of inequalities can exist in a just society.

distributive justice   The area of justice that deals with how society's wealth should be distributed among its members.

ecocentric   Centering on the ecological health of the environment. See **biocentric.**

egalitarianism   The belief in equal rights for all people, including political, economic, and social rights.

entitlement   A right or a claim to something.

equality principle   In the philosophy of John Rawls, the principle that every person has a right to the greatest basic freedom compatible with equal freedom for all.

equivocation   Implicitly relying on two or more meanings of the same word. When an **argument** relies on the premise to reach a conclusion, it is a **fallacy.**

ethical relativism   The view that moral truths are not absolutely true but true relative to some particular standards.

eudaimonia   Happiness, or total well-being.

euthanasia   Literally, "good death." The term is usually applied to the act of ending the life of someone suffering from a fatal or incurable disease or, most commonly in the case of nonhuman animals, ending a life painlessly.

ex parte   Done for one party only, in the absence of the other party in a legal proceeding.

ex post facto **law**   A law passed after the fact; a retroactive law.

fallacy   An unreliable way of reasoning that does not provide good reason for accepting an **argument**'s conclusion.

faulty analogy   An **argument by analogy** that fails to make its case.

formal fallacy   A rule of reasoning that appears to be **truth preserving** but isn't.

germ cell   A sperm or an egg.

greatest happiness principle   See **principle of utility.**

hegemony   Predominance, or predominant influence, of one state over others.

holistic ethics   Ethical views that focus on duties to some particular whole, such as the **biotic community** or the state.

hypothetical imperative   In the philosophy of Kant, a command we have reason to follow only if it serves a desire of ours.

idealist   Someone who has high ideals, even if unrealistic and visionary; a philosophical theory that ideas are more real than external objects of perception.

in camera   In private; in the chambers of the judge in a legal proceeding.

individual relativism   In ethics, the view that moral truths are not absolute but relative to individuals, that whether an act is right or wrong depends on the convictions of the person performing it and not on an absolute standard.

inductive argument   An **argument** in which the supporting statements, or evidence, aim to show that it is reasonable to accept that the conclusion is true.

informal fallacy   A common but unreliable reasoning strategy that generally relies on hidden **premises** that are false, irrelevant, or otherwise suspect.

involuntary euthanasia   Termination of a life when decision is made by someone else, and the patient has never made preferences known to anyone.

jus ad bellum   The justice of war; the law on the use of force.

jus cogens   Overriding principles of general international law.

jus in bello   The law or justice within a war, regardless of the justifiability of the war itself.

libertarianism   In political thought, the view that all forms of coercion—except to prevent harm to life, liberty, and property—are wrong, whether they come from individuals or from the government.

living will   A document executed by a competent adult directing physicians not to use artificial or extraordinary measures to prolong the person's life.

maxim   In the philosophy of Kant, a general principle of behavior; for example, whenever someone hurts me, I will hurt him back.

moral agent   A being capable of making moral claims and accepting moral duties.

moral intuition   A moral conviction arrived at after careful consideration of the relevant facts.

natural law   Any law of nature, as opposed to a state law or federal law. In ethics, moral laws that are embedded in nature as scientific laws are.

natural rights   Rights that all persons are born with. Rights that all persons have by virtue of being persons.

nonvoluntary euthanasia   Ending the life of a person suffering a fatal or incurable disease, in which the decision is made by someone other than the patient.

ontological   Relating to the theory and nature of being and existence.

ontology   The theory and nature of being and existence.

passive euthanasia   Any act of allowing a patient to die.

paternalism   The practice of treating others as a father would. In political thought, government policies that limit individual rights to protect individuals from harming themselves.

person   In ethics, either an **autonomous** being or a being who is a full-fledged member of the moral community.

pluralism   The existence of many independent centers of power within a society.

practical imperative   In Kant's philosophy, respect for persons as ends, never as means.

premise   A supporting statement in an **argument**. A statement that aims to show that the conclusion is true or likely to be true.

***prima facie* duty or obligation**   An obligation that may or may not be binding at a given time depending on whether some other obligation takes precedence at that time.

principle of utility   The moral principle that we should produce the greatest balance of happiness over unhappiness, giving equal consideration to the happiness and unhappiness of everyone who will be affected by our actions.

Procrustes' bed   In Greek mythology, cutting off one's feet to fit the size of the bed; in reasoning, altering important facts to meet an arbitrary or inappropriate standard or rule.

question-begging argument   A form of **fallacy** in which you assume as a **premise** what you want to prove.

realism   A political theory favoring pragmatism and literal truth; a philosophical position that universal principles are more real than sensory objects.

red herring   A form of **fallacy** in which an irrelevant issue is introduced to distract attention from the issue at hand.

respect for persons   The moral principle that we should never use another person merely as a means to our own ends.

retentionist   Someone who advocates keeping in place a particular practice, such as the death penalty.

retribution   Punishment for wrongdoing.

sexual libertarianism   The view that sex is morally no different from any other activity, that there are no special moral rules that apply only to sexual behavior.

Si vis pacem, para bellum   If you wish for peace, prepare for war.

sine qua non   Without which not; something essential or indispensable.

slippery slope argument   Assuming that an action will lead to an unwanted outcome as a result of many small steps that will inevitably follow. If the assumption is not sufficiently justified, it is a **fallacy.**

social contract theory   Ethical or political thought that views morality or the state as the product of an agreement (a social contract) among individuals.

socialism   An economic system in which the means of production are collectively owned and the major economic decisions are made by society rather than private individuals.

somatic cell   Any cell that is not a **germ cell.**

sound deductive argument   An argument that is valid *and* in which all premises are true.

speciesism   The position that it is ethically justifiable to give preference to members of the species *Homo sapiens* over other animal species.

stare decisis   The tradition in English common law of following the precedent of previous decisions.

straw man   A form of **fallacy** in which the opponent's position is distorted.

teleological Pertaining to design or ultimate purpose.

thought experiment A mental exercise in which someone imagines a set of circumstances to try to discover what would follow from it. In ethics, the purpose is usually to test moral principles or rules.

transfer payment A payment that involves the transfer of wealth from one segment of the population to another—for example, welfare payments.

truth-preserving rule A valid rule of **deductive logic;** a rule of reasoning that guarantees that the conclusion is true if the **premises** are true.

utilitarianism The moral philosophy that considers the **principle of utility** to be the one basic moral principle.

valid deductive argument An **argument** that follows **truth-preserving rules** only.

veil of ignorance In the philosophy of John Rawls, a condition for deciding if the basic structures of society are just. To decide from behind a veil of ignorance is to decide without knowing how any one individual will be affected by these structures.

virtue A habit, tendency, or disposition that helps us to achieve our goals.

voluntary euthanasia Ending the life of someone who is a competent adult patient requesting or giving informed consent to a particular course of medical treatment or nontreatment.

welfare capitalism An economic system that follows most tenets of **capitalism** but also includes **transfer payments.**

warranted argument An **inductive argument** in which the supporting statements, or evidence, show that it is reasonable to accept the conclusion.

APPENDIX A

How to Write a Philosophy Paper

Philosophy professors assign several types of writing assignments to assist you in understanding the material and developing your analytical and writing skills. You should always be certain you understand the instructions and what your professor is looking for. Here are some of the most popular kinds of writing assignments in introductory classes and suggestions for what to include.

Article summaries or abstracts   You might be assigned to write a brief summary or abstract of an article in the textbook. The goal is to focus on the most important aspects of the material from a philosophical perspective, including:

1.   What is the main claim or thesis of the article? What position is the author trying to convince you of?

2.   What are the main arguments offered in favor of this thesis? Restate these as succinctly and precisely as possible.

3.   Does the author identify possible objections to the arguments? Are there responses or answers to those objections?

Journals   Some professors ask you to keep a written journal during the course and turn in your entries periodically during the semester. Typically, the goal is to reflect on theoretical material from classwork and consider examples of those issues you see in your daily life. For example, if you are studying euthanasia and read about a local person with terminal cancer who has requested assisted suicide, consider what factors would be helpful in determining whether or not it would be ethical in that situation and what you would do if someone in your own family made that request.

Hypothetical problems or puzzle cases   Writing an analysis of a hypothetical problem, perhaps something like the case studies in this text, is a good way to test your understanding of philosophical principles by applying them to specific factual situations. Be sure you provide a comprehensive analysis in two respects:

1.   Consider all the details in the hypothetical problem. Small changes in the facts can have major ramifications for the justifiability of your conclusions. Hypothetical

problems include these details for a reason, namely, to see whether you can recognize their significance in your analysis.

2. Use the range of material you are studying in class and bring it to bear on the problem. Different theoretical ideas and principles can address and help you resolve the puzzle. Don't limit yourself to just one theory or idea in analyzing a complex hypothetical problem.

Term papers   You might be assigned to pick a thesis or claim you want to defend and write a paper supporting that claim. Some important elements in this type of paper are:

1. Pick a precise thesis that reasonable people could debate philosophically, not just a general area of interest that does not frame a dialogue or disagreement. A good thesis might be: "Capital punishment is immoral in all circumstances." A general area of interest that would be difficult to focus in a paper might be: "Capital punishment is a form of punishment allowed under our Constitution."

2. Clearly identify specific arguments in support of the position you are defending. Use good reasoning principles in your arguments and avoid the common fallacies presented in Chapter 2.

3. To further bolster your arguments, anticipate objections someone might make to your position and explain how you would answer them. Identify tough objections, not wishy-washy "straw men" that are easy to shoot down.

4. Use the ideas of philosophers and other writers as a starting point for your paper but not for the ending point. Don't simply summarize other people's ideas, but use those ideas as a way to frame your own arguments. In all cases, though, you must give credit to other writers when you use their ideas, whether you use direct quotations or close paraphrases or distinctive ideas. But you should try to move beyond those ideas to make your own contribution to the philosophical dialogue on the issue, however modest you might think it is.

APPENDIX B

Plagiarism: What It Is, Why It's Wrong, and How to Avoid It

What it is   Plagiarism is stealing the words and ideas of another person and passing them off as your own.

Why it's wrong   One of the most important goals of a college education is to learn to think independently and to express your own ideas, whether orally or in writing. If you steal someone else's words and ideas and pretend they are yours, you have violated this basic purpose and undercut the core of your own education. Everyone understands that if you stole a painting someone else had created and turned it in to your art class, claiming you had painted this work yourself, it would be dishonest. Stealing the intellectual property of someone else, whether they are words or ideas, is just as wrong and just as dishonest.

Plagiarism is one of the most serious transgressions any student can commit in pursuit of an education, and college professors take it very seriously. At most schools, plagiarism can result in such severe consequences as failing an entire course and even being suspended or expelled from school.

How to avoid it   Using the words and ideas of another person is fine—but only if that person is credited. Indeed, much of your college work includes learning how to conduct research into other people's work, and this is both allowable and to be encouraged. But it is essential that you credit those words and ideas properly so they are not misrepresented as your own. Using the citation forms appropriate for your discipline meets the simple goal of providing credit to those other persons whose work you are using.

If you use the exact words of someone else, you *must* put those words in quotation marks and include the source. If you use a close paraphrase of someone else's words, you do not put the words in quotation marks, but you must still include the source, as you have closely approximated their words. If you use a distinctive and unique idea from one source, you should also give credit to the source. If you are in doubt, give credit. There is no shame in giving credit to a source. Outstanding researchers never hesitate to give credit where credit is due. The shame—and possibly the offense of plagiarism—is in failing to give credit.

Good habits in conducting research for your class assignments will help you avoid inadvertently using the words of someone else as your own. If you take notes on notecards, make sure you put all exact quotes into quotation marks with the source, so you will remember later that those words were written by someone else. If you jot down ideas for a rough draft after looking at your notes, make sure you immediately put quotation marks around the words from those sources, so you don't later inadvertently submit those words as your own.

Plagiarism is much easier for faculty members to detect today than it was before the advent of the World Wide Web. Many will take a distinctive phrase from your paper and put it in quotation marks into a search engine, such as Google.com; within seconds, your professor can identify the source of suspicious quotes from the vast material on the Web. As easy as it is for students to steal material from the Web, it's just as easy for faculty members to identify the source and uncontrovertible evidence that you plagiarized. The consequences for students can be dire.

Thousands of college and universities now use "originality checkers," such as Turnitin.org, in which papers can be submitted for checking against a huge database of other material—not just material on the Web but also papers from "paper mills" and papers submitted by other students around the country, including your own campus. If you are in a class using one of these checkers, you might ask if you can check your own papers for originality, just to be safe.

APPENDIX C

How to Do Research and Citation on the Web

Research on the Web Conducting research on any subject imaginable has never been easier, thanks to the World Wide Web—nor has it been more difficult! The ease with which anyone can post material on the Web and the ease with which you can find it with search engines make the task of determining what material is reliable and worth considering enormously difficult.

In a typical college or university library, the librarians sift through the vast amounts of material available in the world and make selections that they believe will be most useful for students and faculty on your campus. That does not mean they believe everything they select is "true" or the "best" source on a topic, but that it has some credibility or value that makes it worth considering for educational and research purposes. On the Web, you must learn to be your own librarian in sifting through the material available and determining what is worth using in your work.

Many major university libraries have helpful guides for how to evaluate the quality and usefulness of the research material you find on the World Wide Web. For example,

University of California, Berkeley:
http://www.lib.berkeley.edu/TeachingLib/Guides/Internet/Evaluate.html
Johns Hopkins University:
http://www.library.jhu.edu/elp/useit/evaluate/

Here are few points to keep in mind:

Consider the source of the material: A personal Web page with information on a topic of interest might be fun to read, but you are not likely to know if it is reliable or valid. A Web site from a major organization that has established credentials in a certain area will be more worthy of your serious attention—whether a university or a research institute or a government agency or a national public service or advocacy organization.

Check the dates of the Web page: Most include a date for "last updated" on their page. The Web has become notorious for out-of-date material that has been posted for years and forgotten about. If it's out of date or does not appear to be regularly updated and maintained, proceed with special caution.

Watch out for parodies and spoofs: For almost any famous organization you can think of—from the White House to *The New York Times*—somebody has probably posted a Web site with a very similar URL ("Uniform Resource Locator" or "Web address"). Even experienced users can be misled by these, so watch for telltale signs.

Citation on the Web The basic principles of citation of sources are the same on the Web as they are for print materials. First, your readers should be told enough to locate the material you used as your source. Second, the citation should give full and appropriate credit to the author of the work.

For the Web, the most important citation is the complete URL, which begins with http:// . . . But you should also give the same credit you would for a print source, if it exists, including the author's name, the title of the work (or "page"), and the date if one is given for when the page was posted. You should also include the "date accessed" because material at that URL can change over time. Some instructors might want you to keep a printout of the material on the day you referenced it.

Many excellent style guides are on the Web. One of the best is available from the University of California, Berkeley: http://www.lib.berkeley.edu/TeachingLib/Guides/Internet/Style.html.

Index